THE SECRET HISTORY OF THE
IRAQ WAR

Also by Yossef Bodansky

*The High Cost of Peace: How Washington's Middle East Policy
Left America Vulnerable to Terrorism*

Bin Laden: The Man Who Declared War on America

Islamic Anti-Semitism as a Political Instrument

Some Call It Peace: Waiting for the War in the Balkans

*Offensive in the Balkans: Potential for a Wider War as a Result of Foreign
Intervention in Bosnia-Herzegovina*

Terror: The Inside Story of the Terrorist Conspiracy in America

Target America and the West: Terrorism Today

THE SECRET HISTORY OF THE
IRAQ WAR
YOSSEF BODANSKY

10 ReganBooks
Celebrating Ten Bestselling Years
An Imprint of HarperCollins*Publishers*

A hardcover edition of this book was published in 2004 by ReganBooks, an imprint of HarperCollins Publishers

First paperback edition published 2005.

Designed by Erin Benach

The Library of Congress has cataloged the hardcover edition as follows:

Bodansky, Yossef.
    The secret history of the Iraq war / Yossef Bodansky.—1st ed.
        p. cm.
    Includes bibliographical references (p.) and index.
    ISBN 0-06-073679-8
    1. Iraq War, 2003. I. Title.

DS79.76.B633 2004
956.7044'3—dc22   2004042115

0-06-073680-1 (pbk.)

05   06   07   08   09   WBC/QW   10   9   8   7   6   5   4   3   2   1

CONTENTS

INTRODUCTION

Had it not been for the bravery, commitment, professionalism, and resilience of America's fighting forces, the United States would have suffered an embarrassing debacle in its war against Saddam Hussein's regime. His Iraq was a developing country emaciated by a previous destructive war, a decade of debilitating sanctions, and popular discontent. This kind of war, which found a uniquely mighty superpower embroiled in the Middle Eastern quicksand, need not have happened.

There is no doubt that America had a viable, urgent imperative to go to war against Iraq when it did. The primary reason was the ongoing cooperation between Saddam Hussein's intelligence services and Osama bin Laden's terrorists, which began in earnest in the early 1990s when the jihadist forces in Somalia, under the command of Ayman al-Zawahiri, received extensive military assistance from the Iraqis via Sudan. That alliance was solidified in 1998–99, as Saddam and bin Laden realized that they needed each other's resources in order to confront the United States. Moreover, Iraq (working in conjunction with Yasser Arafat) had resolved to throw the Middle East into chaos—a move that threatened to imperil the vital interests of America and its allies. The war Saddam Hussein contemplated, which included the use of weapons of mass destruction, would have caused inestimable damage to the global economy by disrupting energy supplies from the Persian Gulf.

In the fall of 2002 Iraq crossed an unacceptable threshold, supplying operational weapons of mass destruction (WMD) to bin Laden's terrorists. These developments were confirmed to the Western intelligence services after several terrorists—graduates of WMD training programs—were captured in Israel, Chechnya, Turkey, and France, along with documents related to their activities. On the basis of pure threat analysis, the United

States should have gone to war against Iraq, as well as its partners Syria and Iran, in fall 2002. By then there was already unambiguous evidence indicating the urgency of defusing the imminent danger posed by Iraq and its primary allies in the growing terrorist conspiracy.

As mighty as it is, however, America does not exist in a vacuum. Not without reason, the Bush administration elected to first attempt to build wider support for an American-led war, an undertaking that pushed the opening of hostilities to spring 2003.

The quintessence of American government emerges when the nation goes to war. Americans elect their presidents, senators, and congressmen believing that they have sound judgment and, far more important, vision—that is, ability to chart the country's course, make tough decisions on behalf of the people, and lead the country at times of need and challenge. Americans do not elect their leaders believing that they know everything, nor do they expect them to. For that knowledge, the leaders are served by a comprehensive and well-funded system of experts that includes the intelligence community and senior officials in the National Security Council, the Defense Department, and the Department of State. The essence of policy formulation is the practical, real-life melding of vision with the facts on the ground. It is only natural that the elected leaders would prefer that national policy follow their vision as closely as possible; but most leaders are sufficiently experienced to know the limits of power, and thus closely study the world situation on the basis of material provided by the experts and institutions before making their decisions.

In official Washington, the policy formulation and decision-making processes usually fail when the delicate balance between leaders and professionals is distorted—when the intelligence community and other institutions fail the political leadership by providing inaccurate information and poor analysis, or when the leaders ignore that expert advice. In the case of the war in Iraq, the professional establishment failed the White House. When put into practice, the administration's policy fell short of expectations. The preparations for and conduct of the war were marred by endemic and profound intelligence failures and unprecedented politicization of the military planning and actual fighting. American forces reached Baghdad in nineteen days, overcoming a tenacious enemy, horrific weather, and dubious instructions. A full year later, however, Iraq is still far from being pacified, and a guerrilla war is rapidly escalating—metamorphosing in the process from a Baathist reaction to the U.S. invasion to an anti-American jihad conducted by a coalition of nationalists and Islamists.

The errors that have plagued the U.S. war in Iraq can be traced directly to long-term institutional problems within the intelligence community and defense establishment. These problems are the aggregate outcome of forty-five years of warranted fixation with the Soviet Union, followed by eight years of systemic emaciation and abuse of the intelligence agencies by the Clinton administration. The gravity of these endemic problems was made clear on September 11, 2001. Although the new administration immediately committed to an uncompromising war against international terrorism and its sponsoring states, no administration has the ability to instantaneously reverse decades-old institutional shortcomings in intelligence collection and analysis. However, much more could have been done since 2001 to improve American capabilities, better preparing troops for the challenges of the war on terrorism that is likely to continue for years to come.

Rather than focusing on beating back postwar recriminations, the administration should now be soberly analyzing the war in Iraq so that the mistakes made in all phases of the crisis and conflict are not repeated in the future. This is an essential and urgent task, as the United States is only at the beginning of a lengthy and arduous war. Former CIA director Jim Woolsey has correctly identified the war on terrorism as World War IV (the Cold War being World War III), saying: "This fourth world war, I think, will last considerably longer than either World Wars I or II did for us. . . . As we move toward a new Middle East, over the years and, I think, over the decades to come . . . we will make a lot of people very nervous." It is only logical to assume that America's myriad enemies will make every effort to escalate the war in their own favor—unleashing terrorism, subversion, and insurgency wherever they can. Throughout, America must project a message of resolve to the ruling elites of the Muslim world. "We want you to realize that now, for the fourth time in one hundred years, this country is on the march," Woolsey has declared, addressing his remarks directly to the terrorists and dictators of the world. "And we are on the side of those whom you most fear—your own people."

It is imperative that we strive to comprehend the intricacies of the war in Iraq—the achievements and the shortcomings—so that we learn appropriate lessons, correct endemic problems, and improve contingency plans and intelligence collection. America's soldiers deserve no less.

American military operations in Iraq did not unfold as planned. Their successful outcome is largely the result of the battlefield performance of the American fighting forces rather than the quality of the war plans and intelligence these troops acted upon. This is not an abstract issue: the American leadership's profound misunderstanding of the situation in Iraq led them to adopt overly optimistic notions about such crucial issues as the fighting capabilities of the Iraqi military, popular hostility to American forces, and the ease of establishing a new Iraqi government in post-Saddam Baghdad. This level of ignorance is inexplicable considering that American intelligence agencies have monitored Iraq since the early 1970s, when the Soviet Union attempted to use the nation as a springboard for attacking Iran and the Persian Gulf. During the 1980s, the United States was intimately involved in supporting Saddam's Iraq in its war against Iran. And since 1990, when America went to war against Iraq to liberate Kuwait, Washington has remained obsessed with Saddam Hussein.

After Bush won the White House in 2000, the Arab world had no illusions about the new administration's determination to confront Saddam Hussein. These convictions were reinforced by reports of secret contacts between George Tenet and pro-U.S. Arab leaders early in Bush's term (followed by Colin Powell's first visit to the Middle East) in an effort to restore the anti-Iraq coalition assembled by the previous President Bush. In private conversations, however, Arab leaders were extremely reluctant to form a new coalition against Iraq despite tremendous U.S. pressure. The Middle East was marching to its own drum, these leaders warned Washington, and America must adjust its pace accordingly if it wanted the Arab world to cooperate. The administration's obsession with Iraq was out of sync with the realities of the region, these leaders stressed. These leaders' strong warnings should have convinced American intelligence agencies to study the situation more closely, but instead the administration committed itself to a series of maneuvers aimed at persuading or compelling Arab nations to cooperate with the United States and support its plans to attack Iraq.

In 2001, after the United States formally declared the war on terrorism, Saddam became convinced that Iraq would have to prepare for a guerrilla war in the event that the United States resolved to attack his regime. In early 2002, the Bush administration had excellent intelligence from numerous reliable human sources about the profound shift in Iraq's war policy. Among the most important sources was Lieutenant Colonel al-Dabbagh, who reported to London through Dr. Ayad Allawi, now a member of the Iraqi Governing Council. Al-Dabbagh (who has asked that his first name not be given in public) acquired the minutes of a December 2001 meeting of Iraq's top commanders that was chaired by Saddam himself; the meeting was devoted to formulating military strategy for the coming war with the United States. "The battle with America is inevitable," Saddam said, according to these minutes. "What is of paramount importance is how to sustain the continuation of war after [the American] occupation."

In early 2002, Saddam ordered that about a third of Iraq's arsenal, particularly weapons suitable for protracted guerrilla warfare, be hidden throughout Iraq in desolate spots marked only by encrypted GPS readings. The only people who knew the precise locations of these caches were Saddam, his son Qusay, and his private secretary, Abid Hamid Humud. "Saddam Hussein said that if any of these weapons were found by ordinary Iraqi people then the head of the military unit would be hanged immediately," al-Dabbagh told Con Coughlin of the London *Sunday Telegraph*.

Given this level of interest and exposure, it is staggering how thoroughly the U.S. intelligence community failed to comprehend Baghdad. Indeed, throughout the war, not only did the United States adhere to incorrect assessments of the situation in Iraq; its overconfidence in flawed intelligence actually resulted in the military's taking unwarranted risks.

The specific challenges of an occupation of Iraq were recognized by both American and outside experts and analysts from the very beginning of the offensive. In a March 24, 2003, report to the Kremlin, the GRU (Russia's military intelligence) described the unexpected predicament American forces were facing. "The U.S. made serious errors in their estimates of the Iraqi army's strength and combat readiness. U.S. military intelligence and the CIA failed to uncover the true potential of the Iraqi forces and, in essence, misinformed the top military and civilian leadership of the coalition member countries," the Russian experts concluded.

American experts outside the administration agreed that America's leadership—military and political—erred in its fundamental assessment of Iraq and the challenges American forces would face there. "Their assumptions were wrong," observed retired Gen. Barry M. McCaffrey, commander of the 24th Mechanized Division during the 1991 Gulf War. "There is a view [held by the administration] that the nature of warfare has fundamentally changed, that numbers don't count, that armor and artillery don't count. They went into battle with a plan that put a huge air and sea force into action with an unbalanced ground combat force." Indeed, the November 2003 after-action report of the 3rd Infantry Division identified serious problems with supplies and security that were a direct result of decisions by "higher headquarters" or other parts of the defense establishment. "The Division crossed [into Iraq] short the ammunition it had declared necessary to commit to combat," the report stated, and the situation only deteriorated during the war. "Most units literally spent 21 days in continuous combat operations without receiving a single repair part," the report noted. "The Army's current supply system failed before and during the operation," the report concluded.

As the war progressed in Iraq, battlefield commanders acknowledged that if the long-term war were going to succeed it must be "very different" from the initial fighting. Other senior officers observed that the war was hampered by what they called "an unexpected and confused start," a development widely attributed to the original war plans. "The war plan . . . had more gambles built into it than is usual for the U.S. military," officials told the *Washington Post* in April, "and it was designed to encourage military leaders from [Gen. Tommy] Franks down to take chances."

In the case of the march on Baghdad, the ensuing changes in the war plans were fundamental and profound, covering the entire scope of the invasion, from battlefield tactics to axes of advance. "You adjust the plan," an army general in Iraq told the *Washington Post* in March. "The initial strategy was to get to Baghdad as rapidly as you can, change the regime, bring in humanitarian aid and declare victory. Now it's going to take longer." To a great extent, the debilitating impact of U.S. airpower guided by Special Forces against Republican Guard divisions counterbalanced the shortages of ground forces and ammunition. Still, the effectiveness of these air strikes fell short of its full potential because both the Special Forces and the air crews were working with faulty and incomplete intelligence. American airpower was able to inflict extremely heavy casualties on select units, mainly two Republican Guard divisions, but was unable to prevent the Iraqis from deploying in accordance with their plans, albeit with significantly fewer men and weapons. Ultimately, if not for the excellence of the troops, the overstretched, exhausted, and numerically inferior U.S. forces would have succumbed to attrition and exhaustion at the gates of Baghdad.

It's not surprising that America's initial performance in World War IV was wanting. (This observation applies equally to the war in Afghanistan, where al-Qaeda and the Taliban are on the rebound, the Pashtun tribal population has become hostile to both the United States and the international forces, and the Karzai government lacks popular support and broad legitimacy.) As in its three previous major conflicts, the United States was caught woefully unprepared when hostilities commenced. In the past world wars, America suffered initial setbacks before it was able to learn the appropriate lessons, mobilize its vast resources, and ultimately triumph.

Only after making a thorough study of errors in the amphibious landings in Dieppe (1942) and Sicily (1943), for example, were American forces able to make their strategic breakthrough on the beaches of Normandy in 1944. This world war is no different.

At this writing, the war in Iraq is far from over. The conduct of the war to date has exposed Washington's failure to grasp the profound differences between the United States and the Arab and Muslim world. Put simply, America fought the war in English, in a region that marches to Arabic drums. The United States has repeatedly demonstrated the most basic misunderstanding of the Iraqi theater, the intricacies of the Iraqi population, and the role of Islam in shaping regional events and grassroots militancy. These blunders exceed the predictable failure to find Saddam's WMD, as American forces are still paying the price of Washington's profound misconceptions about the Iraqis' behavior—from the extent of military resistance, to the population's unwillingness to participate in the building of a new pro-U.S. Iraq, to the type and duration of the postwar insurrection.

The primary reason the United States went to war was the revival and rejuvenation of Iraq's WMD programs in recent years, which had progressed to the point that Hussein could credibly threaten the entire Middle East, unbalancing the region's strategic posture. The fact that Saddam Hussein had been a thorn in Washington's side for more than a decade—as well as a symbol of the Bush family's unfinished business—only added to the reasons to confront Iraq. Indeed, President Bush did not conceal the personal aspect of his enmity toward Saddam Hussein, repeatedly referring to him as "a guy that tried to kill my dad" (referring to the assassination attempt that occurred during the senior Bush's 1993 visit to Kuwait).

For the entire Muslim world, however, America's looming war with Iraq had far broader significance. To them, this was not a war to defend Saddam's regime, but rather a phase in the divine recurrence of Islam's historic struggle against the Mongol-Tartar invaders of the thirteenth century—a series of events starting with calamity and ending in the surge of jihad and an unprecedented spread of Islamic power. In 1258, Baghdad—the capital of the Caliphate and the center of Islam—was occupied and destroyed by Mongol-Tartar armies under Hulagu Khan, Genghis Khan's grandson. The Mongol-Tartar advance westward was blocked in 1260 by an inferior Islamic army in the battle of Ayn Jallout (in today's northern Israel). Significantly, the Islamic victory was achieved in a series of ambushes employing irregular warfare in the aftermath of a routing by the Mongol-Tartar army in conventional frontal battle. The subsequent decades of fighting led to the emergence of the jihadist ideology and its most important proponent, Ibn Taimiyah (1262–1327).

As the war with Iraq seemed inevitable and imminent, theologians and scholars from all branches of Islam began referring to the legacy of the tumultuous thirteenth century as the key to interpreting current events. In February 2003, Osama bin Laden stressed in a secret message the significance of "Ibn Taymiyyah's description of the situation today, written several hundred years ago," to assembling the doctrine for confronting America and the West. For Ahmad Al-Sayyid Taqiy-al-Din of Cairo's al-Azhar University (Islam's most important institute of higher learning), the dramatic turn of events between the sacking of Baghdad and the triumph in Ayn Jallout "kept for the Nation of Islam its existence and entity and restored its lost dignity." In an opinion published on March 1, he stressed that "now, seven and a half centuries later, the Tartars of globalization are confronting us. The armies of evil are standing on the doors of Baghdad demanding the same thing that Hulagu had demanded, after they have spread terror and destruction in Afghanistan and threatened to punish the world unless it supports their evil policy." Pakistani-Afghan scholar Husain Haqqani, in a February 12 article, took Islam's argument even further, stressing the relevance of the historic lessons to the prevailing percepts throughout the Muslim world:

> While Colin Powell probably has never thought about this episode
> in history, Saddam Hussein and Al-Qaeda have both referred to
> the 1258 sacking of Baghdad in recent statements. The allusion is
> significant for true believers and for those who seek to defy rather
> than coexist with and learn from unbelievers. For militant Islamists, the military defeat and humiliation at the hand of the
> Mongols marked the beginnings of a religious revival. In less than
> a century, the Mongol conquerors had converted to Islam and Islamic power, uprooted from the Arabian heartland, had been reestablished in Turkey and Northern India. Islamist movements are
> already arguing that the defeat of the Taliban in Afghanistan and
> the coming sacking of Baghdad should be seen as cataclysmic
> events that would purify Muslim souls and prepare them for an
> ideological battle with the West.

In April 2003, after U.S. forces entered Baghdad, much of the Muslim world lamented the fall of the city (and the looting that followed) as a revisiting of Hulagu's occupation; the comparison reaffirmed prevailing fears of America's grand designs and conspiracies against the entire Muslim world. An April 11 editorial in the Karachi *Ummat* stressed this theme: "The Hulagu Khan of the present era, after storming Afghanistan and Iraq, is advancing toward Syria and Iran telling them to learn a lesson from Iraq. But the biggest lesson of the second fall of Baghdad for the leaders of the Muslim world is that they make all-out military preparations vis-à-vis weapons and equipment as ordained by the Holy Koran and then make advancements. Only then can victory and success be expected." In his April 14 editorial in the London *Al-Quds al-Arabi*, chief editor Abdul Barri al-Atwan, one of the most influential and perceptive political commentators in the Arab world, expanded on the comparison. "The U.S. forces have not liberated Iraq; they have humiliated it, occupied it, torn it apart, and subjugated its sons. The United States is now preparing to subjugate the rest of the Arabs in the same way and by the same destructive operation; therefore, it will not meet with anything except resistance and hatred. . . . This means that the aggression will not stop at the borders of Iraq, exactly the same as when Hulagu occupied Baghdad, looted it, enslaved its inhabitants, and destroyed it as a springboard to occupy the entire region."

Sermons delivered on Friday, April 18, all over the Middle East dealt heavily with the Mongol precedent, framing the fall of Baghdad as a historic turning point leading to the ultimate defeat of the invaders and the surge of Islam. In a sermon in the Grand Mosque of Mecca, Sheikh Salih Muhammad al-Talib compared the fall of Baghdad to its occupation by Hulagu; but commenting on the mujahedin's defeat of the Mongols, he added, "The Mongol invaders eventually became Muslim rulers, fought under the Banner of Islam, and led its conquests." Sheikh Talib asked Allah to support the contemporary mujahedin in their efforts to unleash a comparable process. "O Lord, support the mujahedin for your sake everywhere and bring relief to Muslims on every land and under every sky. O Lord, support the oppressed Muslims in Palestine, Iraq, and all countries." In northern Lebanon, Sheikh Khaldun Uraymit stressed the same theme: "The American occupation of Iraq must mark the beginning of a popular revolution [in] the Arab homeland and the Islamic world to get rid of the political and economic hegemony and the direct and indirect occupation by the American Hulagu, who invaded the capital of *Harun al-Rashid* [Baghdad]," he declared.

Even the new Iraqi press, published in U.S.-controlled Baghdad, used the comparison, characterizing the war as a conspiracy aimed at gaining international support for American exploitation of Iraq. In his June 15 editorial in the *Sawt al-Taliah,* Yahya al-Najjar warned all Iraqis against the reincarnation of the Mongol threat: "Hulagu said he had come as a liberator, not as an occupier. It did not take long before he set Baghdad and its people on fire. . . . President Bush said he had come as a liberator, not as an occupier, and that he would turn Iraq into a Mecca for everybody. However, Operation Iraqi Freedom cost the Iraqis thousands of martyrs, wounded, missing, and handicapped, who were all innocent. Between Hulagu and Bush the best of Iraq's sons fell on the altar of freedom, which they did not win, and Iraq's wealth was stolen." Najjar further warned that the American threat to all Iraqis was even greater than that of the Mongols: "The U.S. aim is to facilitate the settling of old scores among tribesmen and political parties and movements, encourage acts of political assassination, and incite thieves and thugs to steal and break the law. It wants to convey this picture to the world to justify its custodianship and control of Iraq," he concluded.

While a majority of the American government and public considered the war in Iraq an effort to disarm Saddam Hussein, the entire Arab and Muslim world saw it differently. And today, while the United States is attempting to shape a postwar government in Baghdad, the Muslim world is preparing for a fateful jihad over the shape of the postwar world. In today's Arab world, the modern-day Mongols have already sacked Baghdad; the modern-day Ibn Taimiyah—Osama bin Laden—incites the masses to jihad; the warriors of the next Ayn Jallout are already staking their claim to that legacy, and their numbers are growing. The conflict to come will be a total war for all involved: a fateful clash of civilizations and religions for the future of the respective peoples. The ramifications of this clash already far exceed the confines of the battlefields of Iraq. Ultimately, they will have a decisive impact on the conduct of the war on terror, and on the lessons derived from it on all sides.

Even as the crisis in Iraq unfolds, there's much that can already be learned about aspects of the war as diverse as the role of intelligence, the presence of terrorist forces, the history of clandestine negotiations, and the success or failure of various covert operations. Only by undertaking a comprehensive review of these factors can the true inside story of the war be understood.

This book is an attempt to suggest the singular importance of the current phase of this ongoing war on terrorism, addressing issues beyond the confines of the Iraqi battlefield. Relying on unique primary source material, in *The Secret History of the Iraq War* I have tried to articulate how and why the Arab and Muslim world has embarked on its fateful confrontation with the U.S.-led West over the ultimate fate of Baghdad.

Addressing intelligence and military issues while American troops are still in harm's way is not an easy undertaking. Special efforts must be made to ensure that disclosed details do not risk their lives and endanger their missions. Similarly, any attempt to describe American intelligence data and capabilities always runs the risk of assisting its enemies. At this turning point in the broader war, however, it is essential that we take honest stock of events and reflect on the record to date. If we are to improve American performance in the future, it is imperative to take the debate into the public domain. In a democratic society, this is the only way to ensure that a wide variety of opinions and observations are generated. The war on terrorism is a war all Americans must share, and they have not only the sacred obligation to shed their blood in pursuit of the national interest, but the sacred right to have their opinions heard and counted.

Washington, D.C.
February 2004

1
EARLY STEPS—
THE LOSS OF DETERRENCE

There is a unique, and exceptionally well-defended upper-class compound in the al-Jazair neighborhood of Baghdad. It is a retirement community, but its residents are no ordinary senior citizens. They include retirees from Iraqi intelligence, former senior security officials, and a host of terrorists, most of them Arabs, who have cooperated with Baghdad over the years.

Since 2000, Sabri al-Banna—better known as Abu Nidal—had been one of the preeminent members of this community. Then, on the night of August 16, 2002, a few gunmen made their way through the well-protected gates and into a three-story house where they swiftly killed Abu Nidal and four of his aides. They then walked out without uttering a word. None of the guards or security personnel attempted to interfere with the assassination, because the assassins, like the guards themselves, worked for the Mukhabarat—Iraq's internal security and intelligence service.

Abu Nidal had been one of the world's most brutal terrorist leaders since rising to prominence in the 1960s. His people were involved not only in countless assassinations and bombings, but also in comprehensive support operations for diverse terrorist groups all over the world—from Latin America to Northern Ireland to Japan. He was the mastermind of some of the most lethal terrorist strikes in history, and his organization was responsible for the deaths of hundreds of civilians around the world.

Over the years, Abu Nidal closely cooperated with any number of intelligence services, including those of the Soviet Union, Romania, North Korea, Pakistan, Libya, Egypt, and Iraq. But in August 2002 the sixty-five-year-old murderer was old and infirm, bound to a wheelchair by heart disease and cancer. There seemed to be no logic to Baghdad's decision to assassinate Abu Nidal at the height of its crisis with America; at the very least, the assassination reminded friends and foes alike of the shelter and sponsorship the Iraqi government provided to the world's terrorist elite.

Like all aspects of the war in Iraq, the undercurrents surrounding the assassination are far more important than the action itself. And like many other facets of this crisis, they still leave more questions than answers. Quite simply, Saddam Hussein, who personally authorized the assassination of his longtime personal friend, had little reason for doing so. The act was merely an attempt to please two close allies, Hosni Mubarak and Yasser Arafat, who were desperate to ensure that American forces entering Baghdad would not be able to interrogate Abu Nidal.

Mubarak was anxious to conceal the fact that during the late 1990s Egyptian intelligence used Abu Nidal's name to run a series of covert assassinations and "black operations" against Egyptian al-Qaeda elements. Posing as Abu Nidal's terrorists, Egyptian intelligence operatives ruthlessly destroyed British and other intelligence networks standing in their way. They killed Egyptian Islamists Cairo knew to be spying for some of Egypt's closest allies and benefactors. At the same time, Egyptian intelligence was receiving comprehensive assistance from the CIA. Egypt had sworn that it was not involved in these black operations, since the United States considers them illegal and the CIA is not permitted to cooperate with any country performing them, even indirectly. Egypt also adamantly denied that Abu Nidal was being sheltered in Cairo at the time, although he was receiving medical care in return for his cooperation with Egyptian intelligence.

Arafat was desperate to conceal the long-term cooperation between his Fatah movement and Abu Nidal's Black June organization. Ion Pacepa, the former chief of Romanian intelligence, disclosed that in the late 1970s Hanni al-Hassan, one of Arafat's closest confidants, took over Abu Nidal's Black June organization on Arafat's behalf so that Arafat could "have the last word in setting terrorist priorities" while enhancing his own image as a moderate. Arafat was anxious to hide his terrorist connections and maintain the charade that he was a peacemaker. Desperate to distance himself and the Palestinian Authority from the specter of terrorism (and thus exempt himself from the American war on terror), Arafat could not afford to allow Abu Nidal to reveal their quarter-century of close cooperation, during which Arafat was actually the dominant partner.

But there was a darker facet to the Abu Nidal story. In the weeks prior to the assassination, Iraqi intelligence received warnings from the intelligence services of several Gulf States that Abu Nidal was trying to reach an agreement with Britain's Secret Intelligence Service (SIS), which the Arab world respects and dreads far more than the CIA. Unhappy with the medical treatment he was getting in Baghdad, Abu Nidal had offered to divulge secrets in exchange for superior medical treatment in England. When London was cool to the original offer, Abu Nidal professed that he could provide the latest information about Iraqi cooperation with international terrorism generally, and al-Qaeda in particular.

Iraqi intelligence was reluctant to accept these reports because it knew the ailing Abu Nidal had few aides left, and most of these were actually working for Iraqi intelligence. After extended consideration, Saddam and the Mukhabarat high command concluded that the warnings had actually been a crude disinformation effort by the CIA or the SIS—a sting aimed to manipulate Baghdad into exposing its growing cooperation with bin Laden, giving the administration an excuse to strike. The Iraqis, it turns out, were correct: the SIS was indeed trying to provoke the Iraqis into reckless actions, using its allies in the Gulf States as conduits for the flow of "chicken feed" to Baghdad.

The assassination destroyed all remaining hopes in Washington and London for extracting information from Abu Nidal. Baghdad further capitalized on the event by delivering a message to the Western intelligence services. On August 21, Mukhabarat chief Taher Habush appeared in a rare press conference, showing grainy pictures of a blasted and thoroughly bandaged body he claimed was Abu Nidal's. Habush admitted that the longtime terrorist had been hiding in Baghdad, but alarmed at his recent discovery by police, he had committed suicide rather than face Iraqi authorities.

On its own, the Abu Nidal assassination would have been a negligible episode, lost in the flurry of activity as the American invasion neared. After the fall of Baghdad, though, British intelligence investigators searching through the devastated Mukhabarat building stumbled on parts of a file pertaining to Abu Nidal. The key document in the file was an Iraqi analysis of a Russian document delivered to Saddam Hussein on behalf of Vladimir Putin in the summer of 2002. According to the Iraqi documents, the Russians warned Hussein that Abu Nidal had sent emissaries to the Gulf States to negotiate a deal with the CIA, planning to betray Saddam's secrets in return for American shelter and medical care.

It may have appeared that Russian intelligence had fallen victim to the British sting and decided to gain favor with Saddam by recycling the information the Gulf States were already feeding Baghdad, but that is not the case. In March 2003 the Mukhabarat conducted, with the help of Russian experts, a thorough cleanup and evacuation of its Baghdad headquarters, and in April, key archives were evacuated to Moscow via Damascus by Russian diplomats. Needless to say, special attention was paid to documents pertaining to Soviet and Russian cooperation with Iraq. The Russians handle these matters efficiently, and the likelihood of so sensitive a file being lost in the chaos is very slim. This leads to the lingering questions: Is the Iraqi document genuine—that is, did the Russians deliver such a warning? Or was the document manufactured to confuse? And in any case, why was it left behind to be found by a coalition intelligence service? What message were the Russians trying to tacitly deliver: A simple reminder to the West that Moscow was aware of the intricacies of Western intelligence activities in the region? A more subtle message that Russia's presence and interests in Iraq were not to be ignored? Or as British intelligence officials suggest, a reminder that ultimately, Russia and the leading Western powers have common interests and goals in this turbulent, vital region of the world?

Just such complex intelligence matters are at the core of the seemingly straightforward confrontation between the United States and Iraq.

In the summer of 2002, the Middle East was baking in an unprecedented heat wave, waiting anxiously for the inevitable eruption of a regional war. These expectations derived from the administration's growing interest in confronting Saddam Hussein, and its attempt to revitalize Israeli-Palestinian negotiations by disengaging from Yasser Arafat and his corrupt coterie. Although Washington regarded the confrontation with Iraq as an integral part of the war on terrorism declared after September 11, in the region the imminent American attack exacerbated troubling regional dynamics driven by the ascent of militant Islam.

The White House had by then concluded that it could not expect Arab support for the broader war on terrorism or the effort to destroy Saddam's regime. America would instead work with a small group of close allies rather than strive for wider coalitions and tacit endorsements. Indicative of this novel approach to the Middle East was the new policy toward Israeli-Palestinian fighting as elucidated in President Bush's speech on June 24, 2002. The United States urged the Palestinians to get rid of Arafat and establish democracy as preconditions for negotiating peace with Israel and establishing statehood. This new American vision for the Middle East confirmed the Arabs' worst fears and reinforced their long-standing conviction that only a cataclysmic regional war would be able to stifle the American campaign against terrorism and the quest for a democratically inclined Arab world at peace with a strong and secure Israel.

Meanwhile, the mere continuation of Israeli-Palestinian fighting and the growing defiance of Iraq, now back in the fold of the Arab League, had a profound impact on the region. Despite America's declared policy, and Israel's reputed military might, both Washington and Jerusalem proved incapable of drastically affecting the overall situation in the Middle East. In July, Maj. Gen. Amos Malka, just retired from the Israel Defense Forces as the chief of military intelligence, warned that the United States had lost "its deterrence capacity in the Middle East." The Arab hierarchy felt confident that it would be able survive the U.S. war on terrorism, and the fall of the Taliban had had no tangible impact on Arab governments, if only because of the continued flow of Arab "Afghans" back to the Middle East. Emboldened by these currents, the Syrians and Iranians launched a plan to proactively thwart the war on terrorism.

Compounding the situation, no Arab elite could ignore the threat posed by militant Islamists in their midst. Indeed, the region's key figures gravitated toward radical Islam because they recognized its rising popularity and resolve. For virtually all Arab leaders, confronting Islamists meant risking popular uprisings, terrorism, and potential coups; adopting an extreme anti-American posture was an easy way to placate the Islamists.

At the same time, convinced that an attack was imminent, Saddam boldly restated his defiance. In a major speech commemorating the 1968 Baath Revolution, Saddam railed against the United States, warning "all evil tyrants and oppressors of the world: You will never defeat me this time. Never! Even if you come together from all over the world, and invite all the devils as well, to stand by you." Iraq's revolutionary steadfastness was "armed with swords, bow and spear, carrying its shield or gun and cannon," he declared. Saddam prepared the Iraqis to endure suffering in the coming war but assured them of an ultimate victory just like that awaiting the Palestinians. "The Palestinian people are victorious thanks to the stance of every Palestinian man and woman and their generous sacrifices and their readiness to give more," he declared.

Saddam's speech effectively solidified support because he used Islamist terminology made immensely popular by bin Laden and the Palestinian Islamists in order to inspire confidence in Iraq's ultimate triumph. Abdul Barri al-Atwan, in an interview with al-Jazeera TV, stressed that "the Iraqi president spoke with the spirit of martyrdom, exactly like the

Palestinian martyrs before they carry out their attacks against Israeli targets, just like the martyr who appears on a videotape, whether he is from HizbAllah, al-Aqsa [Martyrs] Brigades, or Izz-al-Din al-Qassim Brigades [the military wing of HAMAS]." Atwan also singled out the language and metaphors used by Saddam: "In addition to the tone of self-confidence and defiance, the Iraqi president was speaking like Sheikh Saddam Hussein or Mujahid Sheikh Saddam Hussein and not like the Iraqi Baath Party leader," Atwan emphasized. "In fact he was just like Sheikh Osama bin Laden, the same Koranic verses, the same prayers, the same confidence in victory. This demonstrates a new phase in the Iraqi president's strategy." Saddam's Islamic fervor and military brinkmanship conspired to make him a populist hero.

Contributing to Saddam's new popular appeal, the Arab world dreaded the consequences that an American war against Iraq and the toppling of Saddam Hussein would hold for them. Mostly they were apprehensive that Saddam's defeat would lead to the dismemberment of Iraq, regardless of America's plans for the country, and that a myriad of Islamist terrorist and militant groups would rise to export their brands of Islamic revolution to the rest of the Arab world.

The Islamists relished this scenario. Abd-al-Fattah Fahmi, an Egyptian "Afghan" who had just returned from Afghanistan via Iran and Iraqi-Kurdistan, warned Egyptian officials that "a U.S. attack on Iraq would unite terrorist networks." He explained that the emergence of a post-Saddam westernized Iraq recognizing the rights and distinctions of the Shiite, Kurdish, and Sunni communities would empower the militant Islamists:

> The nationalist and ethnic organizations have fallen and—as I have seen for myself—a Kurd no longer trusts anybody but the Islamists. Thus, the Islamic currents will be able to move easily inside the Kurdish community, and they will definitely be provoked by the U.S. action. They will resist it in a more fierce and vicious manner, without caring about reactions, as is the case at present in the Saddam era. Meanwhile in the Shiite regions in the south, which have the reservoirs of Iraqi petroleum, they will most certainly fall into the bosom of Shiite Iran. A new HizbAllah will arise from them, in a manner similar to what happened in Lebanon. Iraq will be turned into a crocodile lake that tears off U.S. legs. As for the Sunnis in the north, they will come out from Saddam's repression and oppression to freedom and adhesion to the teachings

of their religion. Radical organizations will also emerge, and they will have no enemy in front of them worse than the United States that fights Islam, in their perception, and that has been subjecting the Iraqi people to bitter suffering for two decades. Iraq will become another Somalia where the snobbish American nose will be rubbed in the dust. It will be an international haven for global terrorism and a formidable incubator for internal terrorism. The solution from America's point of view would then be military presence, as in the case of Afghanistan.

Meanwhile, the United States worked urgently to consolidate a viable Iraqi opposition movement. First, Washington endorsed the creation in London of an umbrella group called the Iraqi National Forces Coalition (INFC), comprising thirteen groups, including democratic activists, Islamists, and nationalists as well as minority groups representing the Assyrians, Kurds, and Turkman. The new coalition had friction with the U.S.-funded Iraqi National Congress (INC), and Baghdad ridiculed the new exercise. Uday Saddam Hussein's newspaper *Babil* even published the coalition's first communiqué along with details of the event, suggesting that Saddam's spies were present.

Undaunted, a few days later the United States sponsored another London meeting—this time of some seventy Iraqi military defectors, most of them affiliated with the INC. The group was to form a military council of up to ten members who would "draft strategy for the overthrow of Saddam" with special emphasis put on devising ways "to recruit Iraqi commanders to join a coup against Saddam." Significantly, the conference organizers were Iraqi generals—Tawfiq Yassiri and Saad Ubeidi—who had been active in violently crushing the anti-Saddam insurgency of 1991. Later, Washington sponsored a major opposition meeting in London of two hundred civic, intellectual, and religious leaders as well as a few military defectors. Prince Hassan of Jordan and Sharif Ali bin-Hussein, the claimant to the Iraqi throne, were present. Again, military issues were widely discussed. Brig. Gen. Najib al-Sali, a former commander of a Republican Guards tank brigade, was highlighted as a key leader. He and other senior officers spread hints that they were involved in clandestine negotiations between Washington and dissident elements in the Iraqi armed forces.

The Arab world reacted with fury to the obvious American effort to topple the Iraqi regime. Egyptian journalist and expert on U.S. policy

Ayman El-Amir wrote in a July issue of the government's *Al-Ahram Weekly* that Washington was confronting Saddam solely for domestic political reasons: "Without the forced removal of Saddam Hussein, the battle will be judged a fiasco. And it is not a fiasco that President Bush can afford in his quest for a second Republican term."

As El-Amir saw it, although Washington justified the confrontation in the context of the war on terrorism, the United States was actually taking on the entire religion of Islam and its practitioners worldwide. Indeed, the United States was so hostile that even "religious education that elevates Jihad and death in the cause of Allah to the highest rank of martyrdom is regarded [by Washington] as a terrorism assembly line."

But raising the issue of terrorism, in El-Amir's eyes, was nothing but an excuse for a cynical policy: "The targeting of President Saddam Hussein is consistent with that strand of U.S. political thinking that legitimizes the ouster of political leaders who may pose a threat to Washington's perception of its national interests," he explained. "The U.S. is now embracing a change-of-leaders doctrine and in a relatively short time the justification will be as varied as harboring terrorism, suppressing political dissent, or endangering U.S. economic interests by, say, enforcing an oil embargo."

Ultimately, El-Amir warned, the thwarting of the U.S. conspiracy against Baghdad was a vital and urgent imperative of all Arab leaders because "should the ouster of President Saddam Hussein be as swift and surgical as the U.S. military would like it to be, [other Arab] leaders in the region and elsewhere may soon find themselves added to President Bush's laundry list." This point did not go unnoticed in Cairo, where President Mubarak was desperately working to establish his son Gamal as his heir. The recipient of billions of dollars in U.S. foreign and military aid (Egypt's yearly sum is second only to Israel's), Cairo was under mounting U.S. pressure to further democratize its regime, improve human rights, and establish a legal mechanism for succession. Mubarak understood that it was only a question of time before he would have to choose between Gamal's empowerment and implementing the American demands. Deeply committed to turning the presidency over to his son, Mubarak was also eager to preserve the flow of American funds for as long as he could, even though he and his inner circle were convinced that a major crisis with the United States over Egypt's future was inevitable.

In Saudi Arabia, King Fahd and his family were petrified at the prospect of America's replacing errant Arab leaders. Summer 2002 was already a troubling time for the Saudi leadership, as the health of King Fahd suddenly deteriorated, fueling a bitter succession struggle. Major cracks then emerged in the uppermost echelons of the House of al-Saud; that weakness was demonstrated in May in an attempt on Fahd's life in Jeddah. Roughly twelve Saudi Islamists—all of whom had returned from Afghanistan via Iran in January 2002—tried to break into Fahd's palace. After blowing up the main gate with a large, sophisticated bomb, they fought at the gate area with the king's bodyguards and numerous reinforcements from other palaces and installations. Ultimately, three attackers were killed and the rest melted away; one of the dead was identified as a bodyguard of a sheikh considered a key supporter of Crown Prince Abdallah. Immediately the House of al-Saud became rife with rumors that the attack was actually part of the succession struggle rather than an Islamist strike inspired by Osama bin Laden.

Shortly afterward, King Fahd and a large retinue left for Geneva, where he could find both medical treatment and safe refuge. In July, King Fahd was well enough to conduct a series of summit meetings concerning the dire ramifications of a U.S. attack on Iraq for both the Arab world and the House of al-Saud. First, Fahd hosted Egyptian President Hosni Mubarak and later United Arab Emirates Sheikh Zayed Bin Sultan Al Nayhan. Returning from Geneva, Mubarak informed Washington that Egypt would not support or provide assistance for any campaign against Saddam. Both Mubarak and Sheikh Zayed also warned King Fahd that Crown Prince Abdallah's influence was growing through his close relations with the administration.

King Fahd then decided to consult his Sudayri brothers (the Sudayri are the seven sons of Saudi Arabia's former king Abdul Aziz and his favorite wife, Hassa bint Ahmad al-Sudayri) about the next phase of the succession struggle. Two of the brothers—Prince Salman (the governor of Riyadh) and Prince Abdul-Rahman (deputy minister of defense)—arrived in Geneva in July to discuss the deteriorating situation in the country due to the rise of militant Islamists and the willingness of certain elements within the House of al-Saud to make deals with them. Prince Salman openly blamed Crown Prince Abdallah, alleging that his decision to permit the "Afghans" to return to Saudi Arabia was the main reason for the instability and, by extension, the attempt on King Fahd's life. The three decided to support the ascent of two other Sudayri brothers—Defense Minister Prince Sultan and Interior Minister Prince Nayif—at the expense of Crown Prince Abdallah, arguing that his policies were endangering the House of al-Saud's survival. Riyadh then adopted an increasingly militant anti-American posture in order to pacify the Islamists. Abdallah notified Washington of Riyadh's opposition to any move against Iraq and refusal to permit the use of Saudi territory, bases, and installations against Iraq or any other of its "Arab brethren."

At the same time, British experts warned Tony Blair that the House of al-Saud was "on the verge of collapse" because of building tension and Islamist fervor as reflected in the growing pace of riots and demonstrations denouncing Crown Prince Abdallah's pro-U.S. policies. The experts warned that extremists might soon seize power in Saudi Arabia if the anti-Abdallah protests continued to rock the kingdom. British intelligence reported that "opponents of Abdallah are believed to have sponsored a wave of attacks against Western targets" in order to implicate him in a crisis with the West. "There is now an undeclared war between the factions in the Saudi royal family," noted Saudi dissident Saad Al Fagih.

America's resolve to attack Iraq was not lost on either Baghdad or the region's other rogue regimes, primarily Syria and Iran. All clearly understood that Saddam Hussein's collapse might induce a ripple effect that would ultimately pave the way for their toppling as well; both Damascus and Tehran considered the emergence of a pro-U.S. Iraq extremely dangerous and resolved to thwart such a development, and although Tehran would not forgive the Iraqi invasion and debilitating war of the 1980s, Iran's leaders gave the pragmatic strategic interest top priority. In Damascus, the decision-making was dominated by the close personal friendship between Bashar al-Assad, his brother Maher, his brother-in-law Assaf Shawkat, and Saddam Hussein's sons Uday and Qusay—which dated back to the 1990s. This friendship led Syria to contribute directly to Iraq's war effort.

Syria's first move was to vastly expand military assistance to Iraq, establishing a network of fictitious and offshore companies—mostly registered in Western Europe and the Far East—to purchase military equipment for Iraq in Eastern Europe and the former Soviet Union. Syria, Yemen, and several African states provided false end-user certificates for these weapons. This was clearly an undertaking of Syria's preeminent leaders because these companies were primarily supervised by Firas Tlass—the son of Syrian Minister of Defense Mustafa Tlass. Firas was also instrumental in the gray-market sale of Iraqi oil smuggled to Syria in order to pay for weapon acquisitions. Significantly, the profits from all these deals were shared by Bashar, Maher, and Assaf Shawkat.

The main items on the Iraqi shopping list were ammunition and spare parts for tanks, artillery, and antiaircraft batteries, and engines for tanks and MiG fighters. Since most of these items were also used by the Syrian armed forces, Damascus took no great risk in purchasing them. But Baghdad was also seeking unique systems that Damascus had no reason to purchase for its own use. Most urgent were spare parts for and additional units of the Kolchuga early-warning radars that Iraq had acquired clandestinely from Ukraine. The Iraqis also asked for the long-range, laser-guided Kornet, the newest Russian antitank missile, and the Igla-S, a shoulder-fired antiaircraft missile. By early 2003, Syria was able to deliver about a thousand Kornets and a few hundred Igla-S systems to the Iraqis. All of these supplies were shipped to Syria's Mediterranean ports and then driven in heavy truck convoys across Syria to Iraq. However, in the few months leading to the outbreak of the war, the Iraqis stored large quantities of weapons and spare parts in Syrian facilities so that they would survive the anticipated U.S. bombing.

By summer 2002, Damascus had became the enthusiastic leader of the regional effort to confront the United States. "It appears that the Syrians have chosen to take a different path [from the rest of the Arab world]: they are busy cementing their ties with Washington's rivals," observed Syrian journalist Ibrahim Hamidi. Damascus demonstrated its commitment to radical anti-American causes through strategic military cooperation with Iraq, Iran, North Korea, and a host of terrorist organizations. Syria, in concert with Iraq and Iran, was convinced that once Washington realized that any invasion of Iraq would be tantamount to a war against three countries and would lead to attacks against Israel and friendly Arab states, it would be more reluctant to launch an invasion for fear of igniting a massive regional war and risking the survival of the House of al-Saud and allied royal families in the Gulf States. Syria also envisioned that the myriad terrorist groups sponsored by the three countries would be unleashed against regional governments and Western nations in response to an invasion. Adopting such an audacious policy called for serious deliberation, and Damascus became the seat of high-level consultations and coordination within the anti-American camp.

First to arrive was the head of the Iranian Judiciary Authority, Ayatollah Mahmud Hashemi Shahroudi. Shahroudi first discussed regional issues—particularly in regard to Iraq and Israel—with Bashar al-Assad and numerous Syrian leaders. After meeting Bashar, Shahroudi warned against foreign intervention in Iraq, explaining that "it is up to the Iraqi nation to decide on its own government system, and any foreign aggression on Iraq may entail irreparable and unpredictable consequences for the region."

Shahroudi then met with HizbAllah leader Sheikh Hassan Nasrallah to discuss the next phases in the jihad against Israel and the United States Shahroudi lauded "the achievements and victory of the resistance movement against the occupier Zionist regime" and anticipated that "HizbAllah's achievements would be a turning point in the success of the Muslim and Arab nations."

Bashar al-Assad considered Nasrallah "a strategic partner" and HizbAllah the primary instrument for changing the strategic posture in the Middle East. As a consequence of Shahroudi's meetings, Syria and Iran agreed to jointly explore new ways to exploit both HizbAllah and Palestinian terrorism in order to reverse the potential impact of a U.S. attack on Iraq. Ramadan Shalah, the head of Palestinian Islamic Jihad, traveled from Damascus to Tehran a few days later to further the discussions.

The next key figure to arrive in Damascus was Kim Yong-Nam, president of the North Korean Supreme People's Assembly Presidium—essentially the number two position in the North Korean hierarchy. Greeting Nam, Bashar stressed Syria's "efforts to forge closer ties . . . with Cuba, Sudan, Iraq, and Iran," in order to forge opposition to America's "policy of tyranny." Bashar and Kim also discussed the expansion of North Korean support for the Syrian ballistic missile and WMD industry. However, multilateral issues took precedence in Kim Yong-Nam's discussions in the Middle East. He first met Shahroudi to discuss North Korea's contribution of technology, engineers, and technicians for Iran's strategic weapons and nuclear programs. Kim committed Pyongyang to broadening its role in the development of the Shehab 4, 5, and 5B surface-to-surface missiles (SSMs), as well as accelerating mass production of the Shehab-3 ballistic missiles, which can reach Israel from the safety of fortified bases inside Iran. The North Koreans also agreed to expedite the delivery of rocket engines—which were thereafter delivered in six special flights of Il-76 transport aircraft—so that the first Iranian Shehab-3 batteries could quickly become operational.

Another of Kim Yong-Nam's key meetings was with an Iraqi delegation led by Vice President Izzat Ibrahim al-Durri. The Iraqi–North Korean bilateral discussions centered on the sale of strategic weapons, particularly ballistic missiles, to Iraq, and the Iraqis did not flinch at the extravagant prices and elaborate conditions demanded by Kim. Pyongyang agreed to quickly deliver twenty-two to twenty-five NoDong SSMs (with a range of 900 miles) and ten to twelve TaepoDong SSMs (with a range of 1,300 miles). The discussion explored two venues of supply: either by air via Uzbekistan, Belarus, Ukraine, or Bulgaria and then on to Syria; or by sea to Yemen and then via Egypt to Syria. Damascus committed to providing the necessary end-user certificates.

Most important were the multilateral discussions Kim Yong-Nam had with Bashar, Shahroudi, and Izzat. The four leaders coordinated the eruption of a crisis in the Far East if American pressure in the Middle East became unbearable. In these conversations, Kim reiterated Pyongyang's commitment to the strategic agreements and understandings with Tehran and Damascus that have been in place since the early 1990s. All agreed that since American victory in Iraq and the ascent of a pro-Western government in Baghdad constituted mortal threats to each of their regimes, drastic steps had to be taken to thwart the United States and its allies.

To some, North Korea's threats issued at the time of the invasion of Iraq were more than the accidentally timed posturing of a tin-pot dictator. In reality, Kim Jong Il was following the long-held strategies of his father, Kim Il Sung, in supporting the anti-American and proterrorist policies of Iran, Syrian, and more recently Iraq. However, even though several allied intelligence services—including those of Russia, Israel, and the United Kingdom—provided their American counterparts with extensive information about these grand designs, Washington elected to ignore the possibility of a regional or global conflagration when formulating its policy on Iraq.

Meanwhile, Baghdad reached out directly to Iran. In July, Qusay Saddam Hussein led a high-level military delegation to Tehran to plead for Iranian weapons. The Iraqis were particularly interested in the Shehab-3 intermediate-range missiles, and hoped also to recover up to a hundred combat aircraft, especially twenty-four Mirage F-1Es, that the Iranians had seized during their war in 1991. (Actually, only forty or so were able to fly.) Baghdad would pay any price for ballistic missiles, and was not only willing to purchase up to a hundred aging combat aircraft for half their original price, but offered to return them to Iran once they were no longer required to fight the United States. The startled Iranians did not refuse, but rather proposed that a panel chaired by Brig. Gen. Mohammed Baqir Zolqadr, deputy commander of the Islamic Revolutionary Guard Corps

(IRGC), examine ways to ensure that any weapons supplied by Tehran would not be used against it. Meanwhile, Qusay agreed to allow Iran to transport missiles, rockets, and other weapons through Iraqi territory and airspace to HizbAllah positions in Syria and Lebanon. Ultimately, Iran would supply Iraq with various munitions and spare parts but no ballistic missiles or combat aircraft.

The only note of caution about Iran, coming from a member of Qusay's delegation, reflected Baghdad's growing apprehension over Tehran's increasing support for the Shiite opposition against Saddam. In the aftermath of Qusay's visit, the leadership in Tehran deliberated the ramifications of the forthcoming U.S. invasion of Iraq and concluded that the best outcome for Iran would be for the United States to destroy the Baathist regime and for an Iran-sponsored Shiite-Islamist regime to rise from the ashes.

Tehran ordered the IRGC to launch a crash program to train a force of 500 intelligence and Special Forces operatives to infiltrate the Iraqi Shiite heartland in order to collect intelligence and organize and activate local leaders and activists in support of Iran's policies; 350 Iraqi Shiites long in Iran were tapped for the mission along with 150 Iranian Arabs from Khuzistan, all of them were veterans of the IRGC intelligence and Special Forces. The commander was an Iranian IRGC colonel, Hosni Merza Khalil. A special training facility was established at a camp in western Iran. Pretending to be members of the Iraq-based Badr Corps of Ayatollah Muhammad Baqir al-Hakim, the first operatives crossed into Iraq in the early fall. If Iraqi intelligence knew about the infiltration, Baghdad decided not to react, fearing that antagonizing Tehran would ruin the prospects for all-important shipments of weapons and supplies.

Meanwhile, Tehran decided to consult further with Damascus about their common position toward Iraq and the forthcoming war. In July, IRGC commander Yahya Rahim-Safavi was dispatched on a secret visit to Syria and Lebanon in order to review Syria's preparations for joining the war once the United States attacked Iraq or Saddam and, in reaction, Arafat decided to initiate a preemptive strike against Israel. Meeting with Bashar, Rahim-Safavi delivered a special message from Iranian spiritual leader Ayatollah Ali Khamenei urging close cooperation to reverse the consequences of a U.S. strike on Iraq and the dangers of "the possibility of installing a pro-U.S. regime in Iraq, like the Hamid Karzai regime in Afghanistan." Knowing that Washington was adamant about removing Saddam, Bashar and Rahim-Safavi recommended that Saddam "take measures according to which power would be transferred to one of his close associates while he

continues to run the show behind the scenes" and that "the most prominent candidate to succeed President Saddam Hussein could be his son
Qusay." Iran promised to supply Iraq with strategic weapons if Saddam accepted the Syrian-Iranian recommendations.

From Damascus, Rahim-Safavi traveled to the Bekaa Valley in
Lebanon where he met with senior commanders from HizbAllah and
HAMAS. He visited two training camps and conferred with the Iranian
staff about the operational capabilities of their charges. Rahim-Safavi then
traveled to the Ein al-Hilweh refugee camp and met with Sultan Abu-al-
Aynayn, the commander of the Fatah movement in Lebanon. They discussed Arafat's plans for the escalation of the intifada against Israel and
how Iran could contribute to the effort.

The declared policy and actions of both Tehran and Damascus reflected a new sense of urgency. On August 1, Iran's military chief, Hassan
Firuzabadi, put the Iranian armed forces on high alert and ordered a general mobilization of the IRGC. The same day, Bashar al-Assad delivered a
speech to his armed forces, ordering them to be at a high state of readiness
and vigilance and to be fully prepared to meet the forthcoming challenges.

Meanwhile, preparations in Washington were progressing expeditiously.
Midsummer required decisions about the imminence of the war and the
overall character of the key military operations. At the strategic and political levels, tensions grew between the leading proponents of an early war—
senior civilian political nominees led by Defense Secretary Donald H.
Rumsfeld—and the habitually cautious and prudent senior military officers, including members of the Joint Chiefs of Staff. While both President
Bush and Vice President Cheney were inclined to support the Rumsfeld
camp, they permitted the debate to mature inside the Pentagon, making
sure that all sides could air their opinions before a decision was made in
the Oval Office. Essentially, Rumsfeld's supporters argued that recent developments in the Middle East left no doubt about Saddam's aggressive behavior and the threat posed to Iraq's neighbors. The rejuvenation of Iraq's
WMD programs and sponsorship of terrorism meant that it was only a
question of time before Saddam Hussein initiated some sort of attack, and
therefore it was prudent to invade preemptively. By contrast, senior officers
argued that since Iraq posed no immediate threat to the United States, an
expanded policy of containment should be exhausted before going to war.

At the heart of this debate was a fierce disagreement on the validity of conflicting intelligence assessments on the state of Iraqi WMD programs and ballistic missile capabilities, as well as the strength and endurance of the Iraqi armed forces. Essentially, Washington was consumed by two separate, though at times related, debates over the issue of Iraq's WMD capabilities. The first took place within the intelligence community and was divided into two distinct issues. The first questioned the extent to which Iraq's history of WMD programs should be taken into account when analyzing and interpreting the latest intelligence. Some analysts argued that all incoming data should be examined against known patterns, while others insisted that all data should be studied at face value. The second disagreement pivoted on how to read the latest intelligence, given the great discrepancy between the UN inspectors' inability to find anything incriminating, the explicit and detailed reports by human sources, and the strong circumstantial evidence collected by various technical means (which unearthed evidence of the type presented by Secretary Powell at the UN in February 2003). These debates were conducted internally and behind closed doors, going unresolved throughout the summer, despite a constant flow of new intelligence.

The second specific debate was a very noisy one, overtly politicized, turning on the legitimacy of the administration's posture on Iraq. In this argument the proponents of going to war against Saddam made every effort to heighten the WMD threat Iraq presented, while opponents of the engagement, calling for political and economic containment, made every effort to downplay the threat. To strengthen their respective conclusions, both sides used self-serving fragmentary evidence, frequently out of context. As this conversation grew louder, both sides swamped the media with leaks of "intelligence data" that were usually skewed to support ideological positions at the expense of accuracy. Both public debate and policy formulation suffered tremendously from this dynamic.

Even the most ardent supporters of the containment policy acknowledged that any war with Iraq would end with a quick victory. There was no profound disagreement over the basic principles of the war plans the Joint Chiefs had studied since spring, which were based on a U.S. force of about 225,000 troops invading Iraq from the south, north, and west under an umbrella of massive air and cruise missile strikes. However, many senior officers argued that overconfidence in American capabilities was being demonstrated in addressing the challenges posed by Saddam's WMD, urban warfare in Baghdad, and the character and duration of the postvictory occupation of Iraq.

Significantly, not all the senior officers were opposed to the policies articulated by the Rumsfeld camp. Gen. Tommy Franks at U.S. Central Command (CENTCOM) devised a war plan to suit the requirements of the White House: at the core was a novel though risky concept called the "inside-out approach," according to which the swift seizure of Baghdad, as well as one or two key command centers and weapons depots, by a relatively small force would result in the quick collapse of the Iraqi regime. Militarily, the plan relied heavily on the unprecedented ability of the U.S. armed forces to strike over long distances while avoiding major obstacles such as cities or rivers. The planners argued that no country could withstand the sudden devastation U.S. airpower could deliver, followed by the shock of a deep land strike radiating outward. The primary objectives of the deep strike would be killing Saddam and his inner circle and preempting the possible use of biological, chemical, or nuclear weapons. By summer, CENTCOM planners had already narrowed the plan to troop deployments of about 250,000 in theater, estimating that 70,000 of them would participate in the invasion.

Although President Bush and senior members of his national security team had not yet been briefed on any formal war plan, key members of the Rumsfeld camp were enthusiastic about CENTCOM's ideas. In the first days of August, a wintertime war was being openly discussed in Washington as a given. In political circles, the cynics wondered whether the war would be launched before or after the November midterm elections. There was a flow of leaks from the White House and the Pentagon about the "magic war plan" CENTCOM had formulated.

CENTCOM's plan anticipated a swift and small war involving a minimum of troops operating from a myriad of bases throughout the region so that there would be no advance concentration or buildup capable of irritating the Gulf States. The actual invasion of Iraq would be carried out by a total of 30,000 to 40,000 ground troops advancing from three directions; the U.S. force would peak at 75,000 troops during the postwar consolidation and hunt for weapons of mass destruction. CENTCOM also expected allies to contribute to the U.S. war effort: the northern approach would be carried out by a column originating in Turkey and would include U.S.-controlled Kurds and Turkish forces. This column would seize all of Iraqi Kurdistan, particularly oil-rich Kirkuk and Mosul, sweep through Iraq's western desert, and establish Turkman and Kurdish entities. The western column would originate in Jordan and be composed mainly of helicopter and airborne forces. With extensive assistance from the Jordanian military, this column would swiftly seize key military facilities in central Iraq and advance on Baghdad. The southern approach would include a combination of ground forces coming out of Kuwait and Saudi Arabia and an assortment of Special Forces teams surging from Kuwait, Egypt, Eritrea, and a host of other places in order to take on Baghdad, Saddam and family, and Iraq's WMD.

In formulating this war plan, CENTCOM relied heavily on intelligence assessments of conditions in theater—analyses of both friends and foes—provided by the CIA. The basic working assumption was that Iraqi forces, perhaps with the exception of some Republican Guards and Special Republican Guards units, would not fight, and some might even assist the invading forces against the hated regime. CENTCOM received assurances that the CIA was running an elaborate operation to locate family members of Iraqi officers in the West and use them to influence their relatives in Iraq by promising postwar rewards. The CIA told the strategists that it had successfully convinced large segments of the Iraqi defense establishment that America had no interest in destroying their military if they cooperated or abstained from the fight. The CIA's unshakeable confidence bolstered General Frank's willingness to entertain the concept of a mini-invasion of Iraq.

From the very beginning, Turkey conditioned its participation in the war on being able to secure its own vital interests. Most of all, Ankara wanted to address "the plight of the Turkman," who were demanding autonomy in vast areas also claimed by the Kurds. Turkey insisted upon unique status for the two and half million. Turkman living in northern Iraq, mostly in a narrow strip extending from the Turkish border in the general direction of Mosul, Kirkuk, Dala, and the Iranian border. The Turkman area encompasses large Kurdish and Sunni-Arab pockets, including Tikrit, Saddam's birthplace and center of support. This area includes the bulk of Iraq's northern oil fields, and Iraq's main oil pipelines run through the middle of the Turkman strip. Turkish military intelligence and Special Forces had penetrated and maintained an active presence in the area for more than a decade. The Turkman population was supportive of Ankara, and if empowered would effectively isolate the purely Kurdish zone, now under de facto autonomy, from Turkey.

The Turkman would enable Turkey to exploit the oil-rich zones of Iraqi Kurdistan and could also prevent the Kurds from controlling a unified Kurdish area in northern Iraq, an irksome topic in eastern Turkey, where a large Kurdish population dwells. In early 2001, once the incoming administration began "talking Saddam" with Ankara, Turkish intelligence expanded training and transfer of equipment to Turkman guerrilla forces. In summer 2002, Ankara informed Washington that its support for the war was explicitly conditioned on establishing an autonomous strip for the Turkman population in postwar Iraq. Washington agreed, thus sowing the seeds of a major crisis to come.

The United States now markedly increased its requests for help and access from Turkey, and Ankara believed that the administration was fully aware of the cost of its cooperation. The first American project was refurbishing three abandoned Iraqi Air Force bases in Kurdistan. Under the supervision of American personnel, Turkish contractors and Kurdish workers fixed the runways so that they could accommodate heavy transport aircraft and A-10 Warthogs. These bases were to serve as the core of three military clusters inside Kurdistan: the western cluster in the Zako-Sinjar strip, the central sector in the Zako-Mosul strip, and the eastern sector in the Irbil-Sulaymaniyah strip. Although the CIA and U.S. Special Forces nominally owned these facilities, Turkish intelligence, by manipulating the local militias and workforce, actually controlled these clusters.

Meanwhile, Washington requested that Ankara accommodate a total of 25,000 troops. Some 7,000 soldiers arrived at Incerlik, and 3,000 of them deployed to the mountain region along the Iraqi border, ostensibly for acclimatization exercises. In reality, they were there to assist the rapid expansion of U.S.-sponsored Kurdish forces. Turkey was alarmed by the CIA's progress organizing its "secret army" in Kurdistan, and Ankara's woes increased when U.S. officials told their Turkish counterparts that the Kurds were to serve as the spearhead of the offensive. Turkish intelligence warned that regardless of Washington's assurances and orders, these U.S.-empowered Kurds would never cooperate with the Turkman autonomy plan.

Although relatively small and confined to northern Iraq, these developments touched a raw nerve in Ankara, as Turkey has had a historical feud with the Kurds spanning several centuries. At the core of this bitter conflict is Turkey's adamant refusal to recognize all Kurds—not just the community of eastern Turkey—as a distinct people. After the Second World War, a bitter armed struggle developed between Turkish Kurds and the government, in which the Kurds resorted to terrorism in the heart of Turkey, and the Turkish military and security forces repeatedly abused the Kurdish population. Since the Kurdish terrorist forces, especially the Kurdish Workers' Party (PKK), relied on safe havens in Iraqi Kurdistan, Ankara was most apprehensive about a Kurdish entity, recognized by the

United States, near the Turkish border. That Turkey was asked to contribute to these undertakings added insult to injury in Ankara.

The Iraqis were not oblivious to these developments. In July, Saddam ordered the deployment of commando and Special Forces—including elements of the Republican and Special Guards—into the Kurdish zones. Saddam then signed a presidential directive ordering these forces "to conduct secret, resilient, and protracted war until the annihilation of the enemy forces that invaded the Iraqi motherland." The Iraqis conducted irregular warfare, ambushing Kurdish patrols, raiding their bases, and inflicting casualties. The Iraqis also started building a network of secret caches of weapons, munitions, food, water, and medical equipment for the conduct of long-term irregular warfare throughout northern Iraq. The Iraqis ran their campaign from three headquarters—Sinjar in the northwest, Sumail (northeast of Ain Zalah) in the north, and Rost in the east, close to the Iranian border. Saddam ordered his commanders to demonstrate caution in order not to provoke the Americans and Turks into an insurmountable escalation. Iraqi military intelligence recruited a large number of Kurds—including Turkish Kurds—training and organizing them into special terrorist units to be deployed in the rear of the American-led forces. Ankara feared that these Kurds would be used against Turkey as well, inciting its problematic Kurdish population.

In August, Ankara resolved to take matters into its own hands. Not to be sidetracked, the United States decided to cooperate. On August 8, U.S. and Turkish Special Forces captured the Bamrani air strip at the heart of the Iraqi Kurdish and Turkman area, some 50 miles north of Kirkuk and Mosul. The Turks and their Turkman allies conducted a brief firefight with the Iraqi garrison. The Turks then deployed some 5,000 Special Forces to Bamrani, ostensibly to give cover to American forces working to repair the runway. Bamrani is a key position overlooking Mosul, Kirkuk, and facilities near Dowek. The United States quickly established electronic intelligence facilities in Bamrani, which were also guarded by the Turkish Special Forces.

At the same time, the United States accelerated land and air exercises with the Jordanian armed forces meant to boost cooperation between the two militaries. The exercises were held in southern and eastern Jordan and focused on the movement of Special Forces and air formations in terrain similar to that of the western Iraqi desert. The United States also funded the refurbishing and upgrading of several military facilities in central and eastern Jordan. In early August, the United States deployed some 4,000 ground troops to Roshaid, in northeast Jordan near the Iraqi border, ostensibly for joint exercises with Jordanian forces. However, Washington pressured Amman to let these forces lead a Jordanian task force to seize the H-2 and H-3 complexes in western Iraq—two major air bases and related military complexes along the old British oil pipeline and the main highway between Baghdad and Amman—so that they would then serve as a springboard for the assault on Baghdad.

Most important, however, was Washington's decision to quietly transform the policing of UN-mandated "no-fly zones" in southern and northern Iraq into a discreet but sustained air campaign aiming to destroy Iraqi air defenses. Starting in July, American and British aircraft capitalized on routine Iraqi challenges—such as radar-homing and sporadic light anti-aircraft fire—in order to systematically destroy missile batteries and command and control stations that could threaten air strikes against Iraq once the war started. An American strike on August 6 in al-Nukaib marked the beginning of the attacks against Iraqi air defense and military command, control, and communication facilities and particularly the fiber-options communications in southern Iraq.

The war hadn't started yet. But the battle lines were already drawn.

2
THE GATHERING STORM

Saddam Hussein was not oblivious to the gathering storm around Iraq. On August 7, he delivered a bellicose speech addressing the threat of war. Saddam's speech was overtly religious, strewn with Islamist themes and verses from the Koran. "Anybody who dares to attack Iraq is taking a huge risk," he declared. "We are not afraid of the various threats to attack us." Saddam warned would-be attackers that they were risking the divine retribution meted out to all previous invaders of Arab lands: "He who was blinded by his own might to dare to attack Arab land will be buried therein." Saddam also promised to help the Palestinians destroy Israel in the context of such a regional war.

On the night of August 8, Saddam made a major stride toward the implementation of these objectives. Escorted by a couple of loyalists, he traveled to Abu-Kamal, a small town on the Iraqi-Syrian border. There, the Iraqis met with Bashar al-Assad, his brother Maher, and a senior intelligence official for an all-night summit. First, Saddam presented Bashar with a historic token—the first rifle donated by Syria in 1920 to the nascent al-Shawwaf Revolution against British rule in Iraq. Saddam stressed that the return of the rifle was a symbol of both the Syrians' crucial help in saving Iraq at its hour of need, and Iraq's forthcoming rescue of Syria from a worse plight. With that, Saddam launched a lengthy monologue articulating his reading of the regional situation and urging a ferocious regional war against Israel (including the possible use of WMD) as the only viable way of preventing and averting the U.S. attack on Iraq and the region's other rogue states. Such a war would incorporate the Islamists instead of allowing them to move against governments in order to wrest power from them in the war's aftermath.

Saddam warned that he had learned from impeccable sources that the

Bush administration was committed to the suppression of all Arabs and Muslims—starting with a massive military blow that would bring down regimes and alter the history of the Middle East. It was imperative that the Arabs forestall these designs by uniting against and destroying America's regional springboard—Israel. Rumors of an American offensive launched from several Arab and Muslim states were disinformation, Saddam intimated, because no nation would allow its territory to be used in the service of an attack against a member of the Arab League. Israel, on the other hand, was eager and able to serve as America's springboard into the region. Thus, by destroying Israel, the Arabs would not only be liberating Palestine, but also depriving the United States of its ability to project power into the Arab world.

Saddam stressed that the American war was a personal matter. He said he had been informed not only that America's top targets were his sons and himself, but that its war plan aimed to destroy all Arab leaders resisting U.S. hegemony. Bashar and his Allawite clan were next in line, to be followed by Arafat and the Saudi royal family. Either the Arab leaders united to bring the war into the enemy's heartland, or they would be destroyed piecemeal by the American-Zionist conspiracy, Saddam warned. Iraq, he continued, was getting ready to play a major role in such a fateful confrontation. Two large Iraqi armies were already deployed in central and western Iraq ready to advance westward through Syria and Jordan respectively, and Iraqi military intelligence, together with Arafat's aides, had already prepared Palestinian terrorist teams in Jordan and the territories for the strike. The Palestinians would attack once the war began, neutralizing Jordan's ability to block the Iraqi advance and degrading Israel's ability to react in time.

Saddam then invited Bashar to take a major part in this historic endeavor. An all-out offensive, involving Syria and HizbAllah, from Lebanon and the Golan Heights, in tandem with an Iraqi drive via Jordan and a spate of Palestinian terrorism, would surely overwhelm Israel. Moreover, Saddam intimated that he had reason to believe that once the war started Mubarak would join in, sending the Egyptian army across the Sinai to attack Israel's southern border. A pan-Arab onslaught would not only destroy Israel, but cripple the Americans' ability to attack the rest of the Arab world, Saddam concluded. This victory would therefore be the beginning of the new era of Arab glory and triumph.

Bashar stayed quiet throughout Saddam's presentation, and then noted that he agreed with Iraq's threat analysis. Bashar concurred that it was imperative to destroy Israel and prevent the United States from un-leashing its anti-Arab crusade. However, he stopped short of committing to the war. Instead, he wanted further studies of the specific contingency plans drawn up by the Syrian and Iraqi military and intelligence commit-tees. Bashar also asked about which Arab and Muslim leaders Saddam had consulted with and whose support he already had. The next day, Bashar called Mubarak, Libya's Muammar Qadhafi, Crown Prince Abdallah, and Iran's Khamenei and Hashemi-Rafsanjani, inquiring about their impres-sions of Saddam's ideas.

Regardless, Iraq's actions matched Saddam's words. The entire Iraqi armed forces had been put on a higher level of readiness. Republican Guard divisions and other elite units withdrew from forward encamp-ments into the major cities, particularly Baghdad. Concurrently, the Iraqis deployed a new unit established to prevent insurgents from attacking regime interests in the major cities, and patrols were given orders to fire on suspicious people without warning. "In Baghdad, [Saddam] has distrib-uted weapons, and there are cells with instructions to impose basically a curfew and to fire upon anybody that is seen walking in the streets," Iraqi National Congress spokesman Sharif Al-Hussein said. Units designated ready to take on Israel were sent to reinforce forces in the H-3 area. The Iraqis also moved SAMs to key zones. Most worrisome was the intense ac-tivity at a biological weapons facility near Baghdad, where some sixty trucks brought equipment to forward storage sites. American national technical means closely monitored and recorded all these activities.

Most important were joint Iraqi and Syrian operations transferring and hiding Iraq's strategic reserves and weapons of mass destruction, as well as key production facilities in Syria. Iraq started the transfer in August as Iraqi engineers and technicians dismantled the pieces of equipment in the nuclear center in al-Qaim and moved them into storage at the Syrian military complex at Hsishi, part of the greater Kamishli area, in northeast-ern Syria near the Turkish border. Syrian forces established special defense positions and deployed additional air patrols around the site. By early Sep-tember, the Iraqis were also evacuating chemical weapon components and production facilities, as well as "nuclear material," all of which was also stored in the Hsishi area. Bashar, who had never been to Kamishli, visited the area a few times in August and September.

Israeli intelligence learned about the nocturnal summit and Bashar's deliberations almost immediately and quickly appraised Washington. Meanwhile, it watched pro-Iraqi Palestinians preparing mega-terror strikes against Israeli cities. According to Israeli intelligence officials, "the attacks are meant to target infrastructure, oil, and natural gas facilities and meant to cause hundreds of casualties." Israeli military intelligence warned that "Palestinian insurgency groups, helped by the Palestinian Authority, are designating targets throughout Israel deemed as prone to cause mass casualties and destruction." The aim was to draw Israel into a massive attack on the Palestinian Authority, thus creating the excuse for Saddam to attack. Most worrying were reports, confirmed by British intelligence, indicating that Iraq was preparing to give the Palestinians biological weapons for spectacular operations against Israeli and American targets. Baghdad's rhetoric gave credence to these reports: "If attacked, Iraq will strike United States interests all over the world," warned Iraqi Vice President Taha Yassin Ramadan on August 15.

The true meaning of the Palestinian preparations was clarified in August, when Israeli intelligence acquired sensitive data about conversations Saddam Hussein had recently had with a few confidants, mainly senior military officers, about what was next for Iraq. Without stating anything explicitly, Saddam opined that he had resolved to launch a preemptive strike against Israel and the United States rather than wait for the American attack. Only a surprise first strike would be able to breach Israeli defenses, he explained, and the consequent Israeli setbacks, even if temporary, would mobilize the Arab world behind Iraq. If, on the other hand, "the American-Zionist conspiracy" was launched as planned, it would be difficult for the Iraqi armed forces to endure the onslaught of the most advanced aircraft and missiles. Therefore, Saddam's logic dictated, Iraq must seize the strategic initiative and dominate events in the region. Iraq had two options for delivering such a first strike: either a ballistic missile attack from inside its territory, or sponsoring a mega-terror strike against Israel. He was in contact with Arafat, Saddam intimated, and Col. Tawfiq Tirawi, the chief of general intelligence in the West Bank, was already addressing practical issues. If the Palestinians were to fire the first shot, Saddam told his confidants, Iraq would be able to act as if supporting the Palestinians against Israeli aggression.

Saddam's assurances to Bashar regarding Mubarak's commitment to a military confrontation with Israel seemed to have been borne out when the Egyptian armed forces suddenly launched the *Tahrir* (Liberation) exercises. These division-level maneuvers aimed to test their ability to fight modern wars in the Sinai Peninsula against an advanced army in the mold of the Israel Defense Forces. At their core was a deep offensive involving

airborne and helicopter-borne assault landings, and swift assaults involving mechanized infantry, tanks, and artillery while attack helicopters and
fixed-wing aircraft provided close air support. The exercise emphasized
the introduction of a new military doctrine based around deep offensive
operations rather than on protecting Egyptian territory against an aggressor. Indeed, *Tahrir* was conducted under the command of the minister of
defense, Field Marshal Muhammad Hussein Tantawi, rather than one of
the senior commanders of the participating units, and the entire Egyptian
high command attended the maneuvers. *Tahrir* constituted a clear signal
of Cairo's readiness and willingness to participate in an attack on Israel.
Further evidence of how serious these exercises were can be found in the
code name they used: *Tahrir* was the name given to the exercises before the
1973 Yom Kippur War when Anwar Sadat launched a surprise attack across
the Suez Canal on the holiest day of the Jewish year.

Analyzing these developments, Jerusalem was extremely wary of an
imminent assault. "Israel should be prepared to face an Iraqi attack at any
moment," Science Minister and former deputy chief of staff Matan Vilnai
said on August 11. Iraq's movement of forces and WMD-related equipment from Baghdad to its western border, as well as the deployment of new
types of air defense systems, confirmed the heightened warning. Israeli experts noted that American bombing of command centers south of Baghdad had proved futile, and that Iraq was still capable of launching a
surprise attack by relying on untraceable fiber-optic communications. On
August 15, Jerusalem notified Washington that Israel would retaliate if attacked by Iraqi missiles. "Israel has both the capabilities and perhaps even
the freedom of action to do what is necessary to defend its population,
should Iraq decide to extend its war against the international community
to Israel itself," noted Dore Gold, a senior adviser to Prime Minister Ariel
Sharon. To demonstrate how serious it was, the Israeli Air Force conducted
visible exercises "for a rapid-response strike to an Iraqi missile attack." A
Patriot battery was also deployed to the Negev, bolstering Israel's antiaircraft and antimissile defenses.

When it learned of these developments, the White House decided to accelerate its march to war. In August the administration formally warned Arab
leaders "to prepare their people for an eventual U.S.-led war on Iraq."
Diplomatic sources told Steve Rodan of Middle East News Line (MENL), a
specialized Internet newsletter, that "the Administration has sent letters to

the leaders of Egypt, Jordan, Kuwait, Morocco, Saudi Arabia, and other Arab states in the Middle East. The letters, said to be nearly identical, assert that Washington is determined to topple the regime of Iraqi President Saddam Hussein."

The leaders learned that the United States was already deploying the necessary forces to bases and facilities in the region. "There will be no turning back from the military option," the letters said, according to an Arab official whose country received one. Taking stock of the American deployment, the Israel Defense Forces (IDF) briefed the cabinet that the war would begin between November 2002 and March 2003. The IDF estimated that Saddam was likely to preempt the attack using everything at his disposal because he had nothing to lose. The same approach applied to Syria and Iran because they would consider a U.S.-dominated Iraq an intolerable strategic setback, although the administration stressed in all communications with Israel, Turkey, and numerous Arab governments that the forthcoming war would be strictly limited to taking on Saddam's regime.

In August, the administration began emphasizing the urgency of disarming Iraq. Several senior officials went public, making the case for preempting Saddam. "This is an evil man who, left to his own devices, will wreak havoc again on his own population, his neighbors and, if he gets weapons of mass destruction and the means to deliver them, on all of us," National Security Adviser Condoleezza Rice told the BBC on August 16. "There is a very powerful moral case for regime change. We certainly do not have the luxury of doing nothing." She warned that Saddam constituted a looming threat Washington could not ignore. "Clearly, if Saddam Hussein is left in power doing the things that he is doing now, this is a threat that will emerge, and emerge in a very big way," Rice argued.

On August 21, the president summoned Cheney, Rice, Rumsfeld, and key military officers for "discussions" at his ranch in Crawford, Texas. By the end of the meetings, Bush asked the Pentagon for specific military options and detailed contingency plans, and meeting the media after the summit, Bush delved right into the Iraq issue, stressing that overthrowing Saddam remained a high priority of his administration. "Regime change is in the interests of the world," Bush said. "How we achieve that is a matter of consultation and deliberation, which I do. I'm a deliberate person." He played down speculations about an imminent strike, saying, "I'm a patient man. . . . We will look at all options, and we will consider all technologies available to us." Despite these words, virtually every leader in the Middle

East and Europe was convinced that the United States had committed to attacking Iraq, regardless of the effect on the rest of the Middle East.

Subsequent U.S. activities confirmed these impressions. In August, a high-level Department of Defense delegation led by Lt. Gen. William S. Wallace, the commander of V Corps, arrived in Israel to check the logistical and military support infrastructure and emergency stockpiles in place for the forthcoming war. The Americans told their Israeli counterparts that they were operating on the basis of a master schedule according to which the United States would attack Iraq before the end of November. The American officers briefed the IDF that the objective of the war was "the elimination" of both Saddam and his regime, and said that the United States would make every effort to ensure that Saddam did not attack Israel. On the basis of a wealth of technical intelligence (including both visual and electronic intercepts) collected during numerous exercises of the missile and rocket forces over the last few years, the DOD's working assumption was that Iraq had ballistic missiles and WMD capable of reaching Israel.

By September, "huge" quantities of U.S. military equipment—weapons, ammunition, and medical equipment—started arriving in Israel's seaports for storage in IDF facilities. Dozens of U.S. officers were on hand to supervise and store the equipment. "The quantities to arrive, and the quantities that had already arrived, are huge, because Israel is the only country we can really trust," explained a U.S. officer.

America also continued its military buildup in and around the Persian Gulf, aiming to place up to 100,000 troops within striking distance of Iraq. To that end, CENTCOM organized a special team of over a thousand military planners, logistics experts, and support specialists to oversee a rapid airlift of forces to the Middle East on very short notice. Given the sensitivities of the Gulf States, special attention was paid to ensuring a low "footprint" in the area. In August these planning teams deployed to various facilities in the Middle East, and soon afterward they completed a plan to ship up to 200,000 tons of heavy weapons and other equipment to the region. The activation of these plans would enable the United States to attack Iraq within a few weeks of a presidential decision. Coincidentally, CENTCOM headquarters deployed to Qatar on September 11.

Israel needed to prepare as well. On September 3, Prime Minister Ariel Sharon convened the cabinet to discuss their contingency plans, which were based on the premise that Iraq, Syria, Iran, and a number of terrorist organizations led by HizbAllah and al-Qaeda would be directly involved in operations against Israel. The cabinet also expressed great concern about demonstrable progress in Libyan nuclear and ballistic missile programs. (These were actually joint Iraqi-Egyptian programs conducted in Libya to preserve plausible deniability.) Israeli intelligence also noted the recent increase in both North Korean technical support and Saudi funding for these programs, and estimated that unless stopped by force, the Arabs would have operational nuclear capabilities by 2004. The cabinet was then briefed on plans for both defense and retaliation, with special emphasis on the air force. Through leaks and statements, the cabinet broadcast the impression that "Israel will retaliate against any Iraqi attack."

However, the primary reason for this meeting, as well as Israel's overall trepidation and uncertainty regarding Iraq, was highly sensitive data about Saddam Hussein. Israel learned that Saddam convened an August session with Iraqi provincial governors ostensibly in order to instruct them about war preparations. However, he instead lectured them about the importance of cleanliness in public places. Saddam seemed to the shocked governors to be hallucinating. Israeli intelligence analysts who studied the raw data could not decide if it was disinformation or a uniquely rare glimpse of the real Saddam Hussein. If the latter, analysts ventured, then "Saddam's mental state is so distraught that it is only a question of what will happen first, the American attack that will topple him for good or his own mental collapse . . . which can happen any moment. Under such circumstances there can be a situation where Saddam will collapse even without an attack by the United States. In other words, the United States will win the war even without having to fight a single battle."

In the briefing, Israeli intelligence analysts surveyed the latest changes in Iraqi military deployments in the context of the latest data about Saddam, noting the sudden concentration of Iraqi forces around the regime's key bunkers, the return of Iraq's Special Forces in Kurdistan, the reversal of a recent surge in Iraqi Air Force training, and the vanishing of Iraq's strategic weapons (especially ballistic missiles and strike aircraft) from their usual forward deployment zones. Most telling was the massive recruitment and deployment of home armies (citizen units comprised mainly of zealous, if poorly trained, volunteers and older recruits) to the center of Iraq's main cities. Israeli analysts noted that these untrained forces replaced highly capable Special Forces detachments that had virtually vanished. "Whoever planned on fighting protracted and costly urban guerrilla warfare inside the Iraqi cities," opined an Israeli expert who studied these developments, "has nothing to look forward to." Similarly, Israeli analysts raised questions about Iraqi commanders' willingness to fire ballistic missiles in the event that Saddam left Baghdad. If he did not appear to be leading the war effort, Israeli intelligence concluded, it was doubtful that ballistic missile commanders would launch anything at all on their own, regardless of written orders in their safes.

August also saw a buildup of Islamist forces in northern Iraq, primarily devotees of Osama bin Laden, working in cooperation with both Saddam Hussein's military intelligence and the Kurdish Islamists of Ansar al-Islam. The cooperation between the Mukhabarat and Ansar al-Islam was under the direct supervision of Colonel Saadan Mahmud Abdul Latif al-Aani of the special intelligence directorate in the Mukhabarat, who was known to the Islamists only as Abu-Wael. Significantly, his wife is Izzat Ibrahim al-Durri's cousin—which makes Colonel Saadan Mahmud part of Saddam's inner circle, and indicates the importance of the cooperation with the Islamists to the Iraqi leadership.

Hundreds of recent recruits arrived from Iran and Syria, and the primary objective of these terrorists was the destabilization of Arab regimes once the war erupted and moderate leaders refused to join the jihad against the United States and Israel. Furthermore, over 150 al-Qaeda terrorists arrived in northern Iraq to prepare for spectacular operations in Western Europe. Most of them traveled via Iran, although some arrived directly from Jordan, Syria, and Egypt, and they were initially based in camps supervised by Ansar al-Islam, but later moved to central Iraq. In September, Israeli analysts interpreted these sudden changes in Baghdad's preparations to mean that Iraq meant not to defend against an American invasion, but rather actively to participate in an offensive against Israel spearheaded by Iran. Unbeknownst to Israeli and other Western intelligence services monitoring these movements, the terrorists in Iraq would soon provide the United States with the indisputable argument for war the administration was so desperately seeking.

Tehran could take pleasure in the end of Saddam Hussein's reign, but it was seriously worried about the implications for Iran's national security. Tehran believed that the United States was adamant about profoundly tilting the balance of power by establishing Israel and a few Arab surrogates as America's regional policemen. American activities in Afghanistan, including incursions into the Herat region near the Iranian border—traditionally a zone of Iranian hegemony—as well as the bilateral U.S.-Russian discussions on how best to contain Iran, led to fears that the establishment of an Americanized Iraq would completely encircle Iran and stifle the mullahs' regime. The Iranian leadership resolved to undertake drastic steps to prevent the American onslaught from materializing.

In August, the Iranian defense establishment drafted contingency plans to repel the anticipated U.S. attack. "For America's recent threats, plans have been prepared, which are being studied and completed," Iranian Army commander Maj. Gen. Mohammed Salimi said. "The contexts of the plan to confront American threats by moving ground, air, and naval forces of the army and carrying out drills, tests, and war games have been prepared."

Iranian defense officials noted that these contingency plans had already been put through computerized simulations and command-post exercises to ensure their feasibility. At the core of these plans would be coordinated efforts by the army, navy, and air force to form a rapid-response force grouping. The scenarios studied included American attacks on Iran from both Iraq and Afghanistan. The Iranian high command was quite satisfied with the outcome of the exercises, particularly those conducted near the border with Iraq. "The American threat is not a new thing," Salimi said. "The army is only acting according to its duties. Whatever the threats are and by whoever they are made, we have lots of equipment to confront them."

Nevertheless, defense officials acknowledged, the mullahs were alarmed by the prospect of defending against simultaneous attacks along the Afghan and Iraqi borders. In September, Khamenei established a special national security committee to deal with the American threat. Khamenei himself was the chairman, and the other members were Yahya Rahim-Safavi (IRGC commander), Ali Akbar Velayati (former foreign minister and Khamenei's confidant), and Ali-Akbar Mohtashemi-Por (the founding father of HizbAllah and Iran-sponsored terrorism as a whole). The committee's working assumption was that once Israel and the United States realized the high cost of war against Iran and its allies, they could be deterred from embarking on such a painful adventure. The committee also agreed with Saddam's reasoning that even reluctant Arab states (such as Egypt and Saudi Arabia) would succumb to public pressure and join any war involving Israel. Khamenei approved initial plans to provoke Israel into an attack, by approving massive terrorist operations that would leave no doubt Iran and Syria were responsible.

On September 3, Mohammed Sadr, formally Iran's deputy foreign

minister and Khamenei's confidential emissary, rushed to Damascus to
brief the leadership about Tehran's assertive policy. Sadr met with Bashar
al-Assad and Mustafa Tlass, relaying the committee's conclusion that once
the United States committed fully, Iraq would "succumb" like Afghanistan.
Tehran was afraid America would then be able to place a "Karzai" in Baghdad, even if only temporarily, setting a dangerous precedent. Tehran could
not afford the risk and would work to preempt the attack. Sadr convinced
Bashar al-Assad that his rule also would not survive the emergence of a
pro-U.S. Iraq and American pressure to eradicate terrorism. Bashar,
swayed by Sadr's arguments, agreed to unify the Iranian and Syrian preparations to seize the strategic initiative by provoking a regional war against
Israel.

Iran recommended that HizbAllah, in association with fighters from
al-Qaeda, launch spectacular strikes that would elicit Israeli retaliation
against Syria, unleashing a chaotic war before the United States was ready
to intervene. Given the close cooperation between the HizbAllah and jihadist forces in Lebanon since the 1990s, Tehran could trust that they
could operate jointly. Sadr then went to the Bekaa Valley to inform leaders
of Palestinian terrorist organizations and HizbAllah of their roles in the
Iranian plan; Nasrallah, for one, enthusiastically supported the strategy.
On September 3, Iran moved to prepare Palestinian and HizbAllah leaders
for their operations, launching a special three-day training session in
Tehran supervised by IRGC experts. The great importance assigned to this
terrorism offensive by the leadership in Tehran could be gleaned from the
nomination of Imad Moughniyah—formally HizbAllah's chief of special
operations, now a senior operative of Iranian intelligence and close colleague of Osama bin Laden since the establishment of the HizbAllah International in 1996—to oversee the preparations. Indeed, Abdallah Safi
Izz-ad-Din, Imad Moughniyah's operational officer, chaired the sessions in
Tehran. Other training sessions aimed to train Palestinian commanders to
organize and run major operations in Israel from bases in the West Bank
and Gaza. For Israel, these threats were all the more credible and menacing
given Tehran's obsessively held position that the United States was unable
to properly react to crises, make decisions, or take drastic steps during
election years.

In August, there was a noticeable intensification in the Fatah-
controlled effort to conduct large operations in Jerusalem and elsewhere,
as Israeli intelligence pointed out Arafat's direct guidance and specific instructions. Arafat's determination to cause an eruption was driven by his

fear that Israel's discussions with Palestinian Authority security officials, including Muhammad Dahlan, over the "Gaza and Bethlehem First" deal might end positively. Arafat knew, particularly from Palestinian Authority minister Nabil Shaath's report on his visit to Washington, that the United States was serious about "democratization" and "reforms" that would make him irrelevant. Only a return to violence—especially in the context of an Iraq war—would force Washington and Jerusalem to concentrate on Arafat. The Iranian initiative thus provided Arafat and Tirawi with added incentives to strike out.

In September Israeli soldiers discovered a car loaded with 600 kilograms of high explosives on its way to central Israel from the West Bank, confirming the intelligence warnings. The enormous bomb was equipped with a cell phone detonator—the unmistakable proof of a Fatah nonsuicide operation, directly implicating Arafat. The bomb itself was designed to cause extremely heavy casualties among civilians on the eve of the Jewish New Year, thus provoking a massive retaliation against the Palestinian territories. The spasms of violence that would have surely followed would have been used by Saddam Hussein, the Iranians, and the Syrians as a justification to strike out in order to save the Palestinians from Israeli retribution. Simultaneously, any Israeli reaction would have stunted a joint Israeli-Jordanian effort to consolidate alternate, post-Arafat Palestinian leadership with which Israel would be able to make a deal, including the handover of populated centers in the West Bank. Such an attack would have been a lifesaver for Arafat and his coterie; it's not surprising that Israel's then foreign minister, Shimon Peres, commented that had the car bomb gone off, the entire Middle East would have changed.

While the car bomb operation failed, the Palestinians escalated their attacks on the Israel Defense Forces in the Gaza Strip, instigating several shooting incidents, an ambush of a patrol of one of the Givati Brigade, one of the IDF's elite infantry units near Dugit, and a bombing of a Merkava 3 tank near Kissufim. Apprehensive about the ramifications, Israeli retaliation was limited to a few helicopter gunship strikes against Palestinian Authority buildings—unremarkable reactions meant to preserve the "Gaza First" plan without causing a larger war.

The Bush administration knew of these developments, and on September 5 Deputy Secretary of State Richard Armitage assessed that in the long term the Iran-sponsored HizbAllah might be more dangerous than al-Qaeda: "HizbAllah may be the A-team of terrorists, and maybe al-Qaeda is actually the B-team," he said. "They're on the list and their time will come."

Armitage noted that HizbAllah's capabilities depended on the money and weapons they received from Iran and Syria. "They have a blood debt to us," Armitage stated. "And we're not going to forget it and it's all in good time. We're going to go after these problems just like a high school wrestler goes after a match: We're going to take them down one at a time." Tehran concluded that it eventually would not be able to escape a clash with the United States, as any attack on HizbAllah would inevitably lead to a confrontation with its chief sponsor and master—the Islamic Republic of Iran.

On the night of September 4, American and British forces launched a one-hundred plane air strike on Iraq—an attack that might have constituted the real beginning of the war. The air strike was launched on the H-3 and al-Baghdadi air bases some 250 miles west of Baghdad, near the Jordanian border. Nine U.S. Air Force F-15E Strike Eagles and three Royal Air Force Tornado GR4s flying from Kuwait dropped precision-guided bombs on selected targets. Fighter cover was provided by U.S. Air Force F-16 Fighting Falcons and Royal Air Force Tornado F3s from Saudi Arabia. Royal Air Force VC10 and U.S. Air Force KC-135 tanker aircraft flying from Bahrain provided aerial refueling. U.S. Navy EA-6B Prowlers shielded the bombers, while U.S. Air Force E-3A AWACS controlled the operation. RAF Tornados conducted the poststrike reconnaissance. The aerial strike opened the area to helicopters and Special Forces involved in SCUD reconnaissance and hunting. Although presented as a routine part of patrolling the southern no-fly zone, the strike on H-3 was a major development. Until then, American and British air strikes had been aimed exclusively at air defense sites, mostly in the south, around Basra, Amara, Nasiriyah, and Baghdad's southern approaches.

There were other allied military activities in and around Iraq during the first week of September. Operating out of the Bamrani air base, U.S. and Turkish Special Forces probed as deep as 15 miles north of Mosul and Kirkuk. They encountered no viable Iraqi presence, let alone resistance. In the south, the United States announced large-scale, "regular schedule" military exercises and moved weapons and equipment from deep storage in Qatar to forward sites in northern Kuwait. There were about 10,000 U.S. troops in Kuwait, along with combat aircraft, tanks, and armored personnel carriers, and the American contingent at Kuwait's Al-Jaber air base included F-16s, F/A-18s, F-117s, and A-10s. British Tornados were based in the Al-Salem air base, also in Kuwait.

Starting the weekend of September 7, the United States and Great Britain significantly raised the level of rhetoric about the necessity of removing Hussein, as well as the imminence of the attack. The slide toward war took a major step during the Bush-Blair summit at Camp David over the weekend, in which Blair committed the United Kingdom to actively supporting the United States in the war. The Pentagon had just completed the highly detailed set of military options Bush had requested in Crawford. The war would be "an attack on a government, not a country," explained a U.S. official.

"Our interest is to get there very quickly, decapitate the regime, and open the place up, demonstrating that we're there to liberate, not to occupy," one military planner told the *Washington Post*. The plan anticipated that the war would begin with massive aerial bombing using smart bombs and cruise missiles. The key targets would be in the Baghdad area, isolating Saddam Hussein from the rest of Iraq. The air campaign would be followed by an offensive surge of a relatively small ground force moving from three directions in order to quickly seize Baghdad. Special operations teams would attack "thousands of Iraqi targets"—from air defense sites to command and control headquarters—to expedite the advance of the main forces. The Pentagon defined January or February as the most suitable months for war, and expected to be ready forty-five to sixty days after the president gave the order.

The tight schedule, the list of bombing targets, and the relatively small size of the ground forces were based on the premise that the Iraqi military would not fight. Indeed, the air force bombing plan assumed that "most Iraqi troops" would run from the attack. U.S. intelligence was making lists of the Iraqi units most likely to turn; one of the intelligence officials involved predicted that "the major units around Basra, in the Shiite south, won't fight the Americans, and that some may join them. In the north, some Kurds are reporting contacts from Iraqi officers facing them eager to arrange private cease-fires." U.S. intelligence was so certain of its reading of the Iraqi military posture that, as one officer told the *Washington Post*, "as part of a series of changes in how U.S. warplanes enforce the 'no-fly' zones . . . the United States has avoided bombing certain units that possess antiaircraft weapons but are believed to be ready to change sides." This confidence in the Iraqi military's reluctance to fight for Saddam would continue to dominate U.S. contingency planning. There would be a price to pay for this miscalculation.

As the plan took shape, the military attacks on Iraq continued. Beginning on September 9, once again under the pretext of enforcing the no-fly zone, American and British aircraft bombed military facilities in southern and western Iraq that had nothing to do with air defense. Among the initial strikes was a Silkworm antiship missile site near Basra (the formal excuse was that an Iraqi radar battery attempted to lock on a ship transferring weapons and equipment from America's al-Udeid base in Qatar to Kuwait). The next day American planes bombed a military communications center at Al-Kut, 100 miles southeast of Baghdad, used by the Revolutionary Guards and related army units. Essentially, these bombing raids meant to chip away at the Iraqi military system even before "formal" hostilities began. The raids generated fear among pro-American senior officials in the region—both Arab and Israeli—that Washington was trying to provoke a Tonkin Gulf–type incident (for example, Iraqi troops downing an American jet) in order to ensure congressional and public support for the forthcoming war. At the same time, Special Forces detachments from the United States, United Kingdom, Jordan, and Israel were increasingly able to concentrate on western Iraq.

White House officials were by September openly stressing the need for "preemptive military strikes against any nation threatening the United States." In background briefings they stated that "President Bush would not stand by idly as dictators menaced the world with weapons of mass destruction." Special attention was paid to Iraq as the preeminent case for such a policy. "After September eleventh, nobody wants to take the risk that when you connect the dots on Iraq, that the first time that you see what that picture really looks like is when there's an attack on American soil or against American interests," explained a senior administration official.

President Bush used the same logic, although less explicitly, in his September 12 speech at the United Nations. Bush demanded that the UN take immediate action because Saddam might supply terrorists with weapons of mass destruction. Such a possibility, Bush stressed, was "exactly the kind of aggressive threat the United Nations was born to confront." Bush saw no mitigating circumstances for Baghdad. "Saddam Hussein's regime is a grave and gathering danger," Bush said. "To suggest otherwise is to hope against the evidence. To assume this regime's good faith is to bet the lives of millions and the peace of the world in a reckless gamble."

For the entire Arab world, Bush's speech at the UN was a declaration of

war, not only against Iraq but against all Muslims. Because of widely popular pan-Arab and pan-Islamic solidarity with Baghdad, no Muslim
regime could afford to openly endorse Bush's speech. Governments and
movements were now convinced that there was no way back for the United
States and that as far as Washington was concerned, the attack on Iraq was
only a question of time. They then scurried to prepare for the war, hoping
to actively forestall or preempt the American onslaught.

Most leaders of countries in the Middle East felt cornered. Though
many rely on American foreign assistance or trade, and happily get their
weapons from the United States, there were no discussions about cooperation. The only question was the degree to which they would actively support the object of America's ire. Not having any other way out of the war,
and clearly enjoying Arab endorsements, Saddam, Bashar, and Khamenei
were more and more inclined to launch a preemptive attack. They considered terrorism the most expedient method of instigating violence without
a direct attack on either the United States or Israel. At the same time, Baghdad was convinced—and not without reason—that once the Arab world
responded to the lure of finally destroying Israel and throwing the Jews
into the sea, it would no longer tolerate an American presence in its midst,
regardless of U.S. successes in a war against Iraq.

By September, as America discussed launching a devastating first
strike against Iraq, the regime became more desperate. On the one hand,
to buy time and international legitimacy, it announced its willingness to
let the UN weapons inspectors back into Iraq; on the other, it increased its
close coordination with Arafat in the service of attacking Israel. The discussions were conducted by Tirawi on Arafat's behalf, and the Iraqi pressure led to a suicide bombing in Tel Aviv and an overall escalation in
Palestinian violence.

In response, the Israel Defense Forces surged into the *Muqataah*—
Arafat's compound—in Ramallah. Israel confined Arafat to his office, cut
his communications, and insisted on Tirawi's extradition as a condition
for lifting the siege. Meanwhile, Arafat and the Palestinians kept advertising the crisis as an all-Arab event, attempting to lay the groundwork for an
Iraqi intervention. At the same time, Iraq accelerated its preparations for
three forms of surprise attack: spectacular terrorism using weapons of
mass destruction at the heart of Israel and the United States; terrorist
strikes in Gulf States, particularly against U.S. facilities; and the launching
of ballistic missiles at Israel. Israeli intelligence briefed the cabinet about
these preparations in great detail, relying on information gleaned from re-

cently captured Palestinian terrorists as well as Israel's unique outreach inside Iraq. Jordanian intelligence, with its own extensive network of sources
inside Iraq, shared the Israeli threat assessment.

As a result, the United States slowed its race toward war. Formally, the
administration agreed to give the UN a chance to send weapons inspectors; behind the scenes, though, the Joint Chiefs of Staff concluded that the
U.S. military was not ready for a war with Iraq and recommended that
they needed up to six more months to prepare for a realistic confrontation.
This reassessment was prompted by the lessons derived from the Millennium Challenge exercise conducted in August.

The exercise simulated, through the use of sophisticated computers
and expert role players, an American attack on Iraq. Under the command
of U.S. Marine Corps Lt. Gen. (Ret.) Van Ryper, the Opponent's Forces
(OPFOR) "decimated" the U.S. naval forces and stalled the ground offensive, succeeding by the use of primitive methods in evading high-tech
weaponry and repeatedly surprising the American forces. In the aftermath
of Millennium Challenge, the Joint Chiefs concluded that the military did
not have enough troops and aircraft for the type of war the White House
wanted, pointing specifically to an acute shortage in special operations
forces because of worldwide deployments.

Moreover, sharp disputes burst into the open within the U.S. intelligence community—mainly between the CIA and the Defense Intelligence
Agency—over the willingness and ability of Iraqi opposition forces to help
the U.S. war effort. While the disagreement prevented the drafting of the
National Intelligence Estimate on Iraq, Bush and the Pentagon's civilian
elite decided to go with the CIA's assessment that the Iraqi opposition was
a potent force the United States could exploit. Judging from the overall
pace of American activities in September, allied governments in the Middle East concluded, in the words of a senior intelligence official, that "there
will not be a war against Iraq this year."

3
CASUS BELLI

On January 14, 2003, British police and security forces raided a terrorist safe house in Manchester, ending a several-months-long investigation. A Scotland Yard detective was killed in this raid, which recovered a quantity of ricin—an extremely potent poison. The investigation, begun in fall 2002 in Israel, involved at its peak the intelligence services of more than six countries. The investigators' findings provided the "smoking gun" supporting the administration's insistence on Iraq's centrality to global terrorism, the availability of operational weapons of mass destruction in Iraq, and proof of the close cooperation between Iraqi military intelligence and al-Qaeda.

The data accumulated during this investigation could have provided the casus belli—the justification for war—and urgent imperative to take on Saddam Hussein. Yet in the first of several indecisive and self-contradicting political maneuvers, the Bush administration preferred to accommodate Blair's pressure to keep Israel at arm's length, not implicate Arafat, and placate Blair's fellow West European leaders rather than go public with the findings of the investigation. Despite mounting international criticism and skepticism in the media, the American public was not presented with one of the strongest and most explicit justifications for the war with Iraq.

On the night of September 13, 2002, Israeli Special Forces intercepted and captured a three-man squad attempting to cross the Jordan River and enter the Palestinian territories on their way to Arafat's compound in Ramallah. Their interrogation revealed that they were highly trained members of the Baghdad-based Arab Liberation Front (ALF), sent to conduct spectacular strikes under the banner of Arafat's Fatah. Specifically, they were dispatched by ALF Chief Muhammad Zaidan Abbas, better known as Abu-al-Abbas, to operate directly under the control of Tawfiq Tirawi, chief of the Palestinian Authority's General Intelligence Service and Arafat's closest confidant. Abbas and Tirawi were extremely close childhood friends, having grown up together in a village just north of Ramallah and ultimately joining Arafat's fledgling terrorist organization together in the early 1960s.

The three ALF terrorists were trained for several missions, including an operation that involved using shoulder-fired missiles to shoot down civilian airliners as they approached Ben-Gurion Airport and using anti-tank rockets and missiles to ambush convoys—including American groupings on their way to Iraq. They were also there to organize and train Palestinian terrorists—all trusted operatives of Tirawi's—to assist with operations and intelligence collection inside Israel. The three had been briefed in Baghdad that they would get the missiles, heavy weapons, and explosives they might need from Fatah via Tirawi.

The Israeli interrogators were most interested in what the three had to say about their training: During the summer, they had been trained along with other squads of ALF terrorists at Salman Pak—a major base near Baghdad—by members of Unit 999 of Iraqi military intelligence. They recounted that in an adjacent part of the camp, other teams of Unit 999 were preparing a select group of Islamist terrorists specifically identified as members of al-Qaeda. Although the training was separate, and individuals used code names exclusively, they were able to learn a great deal about the missions of their Islamist colleagues.

The three ALF terrorists told the Israelis that in addition to the myriad special operations techniques taught at Salman Pak, the Islamists also received elaborate training with chemical weapons and poisons, specifically ricin. Moreover, on their way to their operational deployment zones, the Islamists were taken to a derelict complex of houses near Halabja, in Kurdistan, where they conducted experiments with chemical weapons and poisons. The area where the training took place was nominally under the control of Ansar-al-Islam, Osama bin Laden's Kurdish offshoot. From there, the ALF terrorists recounted, Islamist detachments traveled to Turkey, where they were to strike American bases with chemical weapons once the war started, and to Pakinsy Gore in northern Georgia (on the border with Chechnya) in order to assist Chechen terrorists as they launched major terrorists operations against Russia. Others were dispatched to train Islamist teams arriving from Western Europe via Turkey in sophisticated terrorism techniques, including the use of chemical weapons and ricin.

Within a week of the capture of the ALF trio, a delegation of senior Israeli military intelligence officers traveled to Washington to brief the White House about their findings. By then, there had already been independent corroborations of the Israeli reports: Turkish security forces, acting on tips provided by Israel, arrested two al-Qaeda operatives studying plans to attack the U.S. air base in Incerlick with chemical weapons, and American intelligence also learned from its own sources about the activities of foreign mujahedin in Georgia's Pakinsy Gore. Then, on October 23, a group of Chechen and Arab terrorists captured a Moscow theater in the middle of a performance, taking over seven hundred people hostage, rigging the theater with bombs, and threatening to kill everyone in the building. When negotiations failed and the terrorists shot at least one hostage to demonstrate their determination, Russian antiterrorist forces broke into the theater after using a special knockout gas to neutralize the Chechens before they were able to detonate their bombs. The Russian operation was considered a great success, as all the terrorists were killed before they could blow themselves up; however, close to two hundred hostages died from secondary effects caused by the gas, including heart attacks and choking on their own vomit. In any case, the mere occurrence of a spectacular strike in Moscow meant that there could no longer be any doubt about the accuracy of the material provided by the three Palestinians in Israel's custody.

Still, the White House was reluctant to advertise this evidence because it demonstrated Israeli intelligence's major contribution to the war on terrorism. Nevertheless, Israel quietly shared the acquired data with several European governments, leading to the disruption and capture of several Arab and Chechen terrorist networks in Paris, London, and Manchester, as well as related support networks in Spain and Italy. Chemical weapons and ricin had played important roles in the thwarted operations of these networks, all of which had been trained in Georgia's Pakinsy Gore, and when ricin was discovered in Manchester and all the dots connected, the intelligence Israel had extracted from the terrorists in its custody was proved wholly accurate. Israel had in fact demonstrated to the Europeans why Saddam Hussein had to be toppled, and soon.

Still, most Western European governments adamantly refused to address Iraqi training of al-Qaeda terrorists in the use of chemical weapons and poisons. Acceptance of this evidence would also acknowledge the intimate involvement of Yasser Arafat and the Palestinian Authority in international terrorism. The European governments not only insisted on separating the Palestinians from the war on Iraq, but demanded that the Arab world be compensated for the American-led attack, by forcing Israel to accept a political solution favorable to Arafat, regardless of the extent of Palestinian terrorism. Moreover, in winter 2002, Tony Blair led a European effort to salvage Arafat and reward him with a Palestinian state, hoping to demonstrate that the war was not indiscriminately anti-Arab.

Having to choose between further alienating the Western Europeans, who insisted on keeping Arafat out of the war, and bolstering its case against Iraq by providing concrete Israeli evidence, the White House decided to go with the Europeans. On February 5, 2003, during his presentation at the UN, Secretary of State Colin Powell showed an aerial shot of the Ansar-al-Islam facility, which he called a "poison and explosive training center." When foreign journalists pointed to the derelict status, Washington remained mum rather than hint at evidence that would confirm Powell's claims but also prove Arafat's involvement with Iraqi terrorism and WMD and point to Israel's contribution to the effort to disarm Iraq.

Meanwhile, the ineffectiveness of American diplomatic efforts had little impact on the administration's resolve to swiftly bring down the regime of Saddam Hussein. On that level, the intelligence provided by Israel, including that received from further interrogation of the three ALF terrorists, was taken most seriously.

In September, U.S. and allied forces intensified their undeclared war against Iraq. The aerial bombing of military targets in southern and central Iraq was stepped up, including attacks on civilian objectives such as Basra Airport. Using their wide array of technical capabilities, U.S. Intelligence tracked Iraqis as they used barges and other river craft, particularly in northwest Iraq near the Syrian border, to transfer and store materials used in its WMD programs, laboratories, and technical facilities. The patterns of heavy security and specialized communications, as well as the shape and size of some of the cargo, strongly indicated the nature of this river traffic. Meanwhile, Jordanian intelligence learned from its own sources that Iraq had also converted barges into mobile launch platforms for ballistic missiles. Although any of the navigable areas of the Tigris and Euphrates river systems could now be considered launch points or support sites, the upriver zones were more likely locations because the barges could be hidden in the thick vegetation. In response, a growing number of Special Forces—from the United States, United Kingdom, Israel, and Jordan—kept crossing into western Iraq, conducting reconnaissance of potential targets, and probing Iraqi defenses.

It did not take long for U.S. Special Forces and Iraqi Republican Guard units to clash near H-3. On the night of September 28, Iraqi patrols opened fire on a U.S. team getting too close to H-3. Once the Iraqis successfully blocked their withdrawal, reinforcements were rushed from Rushaid, Jordan, while the Iraqis brought additional forces from H-2 and H-3. When American reinforcements failed to relieve the stranded patrol, a stalemate ensued during the day, and Baghdad decided to exploit the incident in order to demonstrate Iraq's resolve. On the night of September 29, despite the presence of U.S. patrols in their midst, the Iraqis moved SSMs, including chemical and biological weapons warheads, from concealed storage in the H-2 area to forward firing positions around H-3.

Throughout, U.S. forces had problems dodging Iraqi patrols in order to get sufficiently close to the Iraqi missiles to either collect irrefutable evidence of their presence or, if possible, attempt to destroy them. On October 1, Iraqi forces managed to surround the Americans stranded near H-3. It took a second wave of U.S. and Jordanian reinforcements to relieve the cornered troops and escort them back to Jordan. Fearing contamination if any of the CBW warheads were to be damaged, the United States refrained from using airpower throughout the clash. The Iraqis, therefore, were able to deploy missiles to forward positions and, after a few days, when American troops were no longer nearby, evacuate them back to concealed shelters.

Also, a close examination of Iraq's military posture concluded that the Americans and the British had achieved little in their repeated efforts to destroy the Iraqi air defense system, particularly the SAMs. American and British strike aircraft had difficulty locating the mobile antiaircraft assets—missile batteries, antiaircraft artillery, and radars—which had been camouflaged and concealed. "Now, those who have flown over antiaircraft artillery sites that are firing at you, it's very difficult to pinpoint them and to do anything about them," Joint Chiefs of Staff chairman Richard Myers told a Pentagon briefing. "We have been somewhat successful from time to time, but it's ubiquitous, so it's very difficult to defeat that."

The United States had better results confronting Iraq's strategic infrastructure. "We've also gone after their command and control headquarters and their communications buildings to try to degrade this," Myers said. "And we've had some success there. And we've had some success against their long-range radars. But, you know, any air defense system has redundancy."

But U.S. interception capabilities also needed improvement. On September 24, three Iraqi MiG-25s flew deep into the no-fly zone in southern Iraq, returning safely to their base long before U.S. fighters arrived. Israel, for its part, was very worried by these and other developments in September. Even before the violent encounter between American and Iraqi Special Forces, Israeli and Jordanian units operating in western Iraq had doubts about the Americans' ability to locate and destroy Iraqi mobile objectives—including ballistic missiles—in the vast zones of the desert. With tensions rising, Jerusalem asked Washington for urgent high-level consultations. The administration agreed, and to placate a reluctant and somewhat embarrassed Washington, Sharon instructed the Israel Defense Forces to comply with American requests to ease the siege of Arafat; on September 29, the IDF withdrew from Arafat's compound in Ramallah. Jerusalem also relented under massive U.S. pressure to disassociate Arafat from Saddam in order to cajole the Europeans and "friendly" Arabs, at the expense of Israel. "It is impossible to say no to our big friend [the United States]," Sharon told the newspaper *Yediot Aharonot.*

On October 1, Maj. Gen. (Res.) Amos Yaron, the director general of Israel's Ministry of Defense, rushed to Washington to coordinate cooperation on the looming threat of ballistic missile launches. Iraqi activities in the western desert were worrisome, and Washington anticipated a sudden preemptive move by Iraq pending congressional authorization for a strike on Iraq, a vote then scheduled for early October. Senior administration officials stressed to Yaron that the United States expected Israel not to become involved in any military campaign to topple Saddam, virtually regardless of any sort of attack on Israel. At the same time, they expected still more logistical help to be provided to their forces in the Middle East, including unique Israeli weapons systems developed for urban warfare. To further put Israel on the defensive, they also pressured Israel to show greater flexibility regarding the Palestinians.

According to State Department spokesman Richard Boucher, senior officials and Yaron met "to discuss a broad range of bilateral issues, including our policy on Iraq, our efforts to end violence and terror and advance a comprehensive institutional reform process in the region, in preparation for Palestinian statehood envisaged by President Bush. . . . As you know, we consult regularly with Israel regarding the ongoing threat that the Iraqi regime presents to its own people, its neighbors, and the region, and those discussions are ongoing."

On October 2, while Yaron was still in Washington, Israeli Special Forces entered Ramallah and seized Rakad Salam, Saddam Hussein's chief representative in the territories. A small detachment of Israeli soldiers entered an office building dressed as Arabs, their faces partially hidden by kaffiyehs (traditional Arab head scarves), grabbed Rakad Salam and files full of documents without uttering a word, and walked out to a waiting vehicle. Ostensibly the head of Arab charities, Rakad Salam was the underground ALF chief in the West Bank. He handled tens of thousands of dollars sent from Iraq, and supervised the activities of Iraqi emissaries. Retrieved documents showed that the Iraqi vice president, Taha Yassin Ramadan, was directly responsible for Iraqi support of Palestinian terrorism conducted via Abu-al-Abbas. "Indeed, the Intifada is a historic opportunity that will not repeat itself to build—mold from solid iron—the Baath organization and expand its organizational base," Ramadan wrote Salam in a personal letter. Ramadan urged Salam to do more to increase Iraqi influence and promised the required funds. Other documents showed that Arafat personally authorized attaching Preventive Security officers to Abu-al-Abbas's ALF squads in the territories.

Washington immediately requested any information gleaned from Salam's interrogation, especially concerning Iraqi coordination with Palestinian and other terrorist organizations. Publicly, however, the administration continued to pressure Israel for concessions to Arafat, and also loudly warned Israel not to do anything once the war started, even if Iraq launched missiles at the tiny state. Washington promised to commit large ground forces and an intense air campaign to neutralize the threat of SCUD-type missiles, as it had done during the first Gulf War.

Jerusalem would not be satisfied easily. Over the next few days, the two sides continued their deliberations about the extent of Iraq's capabilities to launch ballistic missiles with chemical and biological warheads at Tel Aviv. Israel was unnerved by the failure of the initial American operations in western Iraq to stem the tide of activities in the area, particularly the movement of forces and missiles. Israeli intelligence had great apprehension about Iraq's ability to launch a surprise attack and so briefed the kitchenette. Publicly, Israel put on a brave face, but behind closed doors, Israeli officials asked their American counterparts hard questions about their plans to destroy Iraq's strategic weapons.

Rather than resolve these issues professionally, the administration decided to ratchet up the pressure on Jerusalem. On October 5, Bush invited Sharon to the White House for special consultations. Israeli diplomatic sources acknowledged that they expected Bush "to press Sharon for a commitment that Israel will not retaliate against any Iraqi missile attack." Washington refused to accept Sharon's repeated warnings that Israel would not maintain restraint if it came under Iraqi attack: "Bush does not want any surprises and wants such a commitment from Sharon," a diplomatic source told Steve Rodan of MENL. In the meantime, Israel accepted the American demand to "lower the profile" on Iraq. Throughout, however, Arrow and Patriot crews conducted exercises in full WMD protective suits.

Washington was by then in the final phase of the national debate on the war, with or without UN consent. On October 10, both the House and the Senate overwhelmingly passed resolutions authorizing the United States to attack Iraq; at the same time, Congress urged that diplomatic efforts to obtain UN consent continue. As a result, the momentum for U.S.-led strategic moves against Iraq intensified, and detailed military preparations began to take shape. On the political front, Bush promised "no negotiations with Iraq. . . . Its days as an outlaw state are nearing their end." Baghdad, for its part, remained defiant: "If America attacks, we will be ready within an hour," Foreign Minister Tarik Aziz declared.

Osama bin Laden made it clear that al-Qaeda would not abstain from war while his Iraqi allies faced off against the United States. On October 8, an Islamist terrorist detachment ambushed American troops on Falaika Island off the Kuwaiti coast, killing one soldier and wounding a few others. Swift investigation of the attack unearthed a fifteen-member network closely affiliated with al-Qaeda, which at the time of their arrest was planning to launch at least five more attacks on Americans in Kuwait.

The signals from Iraq were both alarming and confusing. Starting on October 9, American and allied intelligence detected numerous indications that some members of Saddam's inner circle had started to look for escape routes, particularly to evacuate their families and property. They now believed that the regime might collapse if the United States attacked, and they were not alone. In October, Iraq started moving gold bars and valuable works of art from Baghdad and Mosul to Abu-Kamal, so that they could be moved across the nearby Syrian border on very short notice.

Saddam himself reexamined the threat of an internal military rebellion against the regime. To guard against this contingency, a senior Arab military official noted, Iraq moved the bulk of the army, including key Republican Guard units, out of Baghdad, mostly to the extreme west of the country, near the Jordanian and Syrian borders. Ostensibly ready for a rapid military move against Israel, the official noted, these forces could no longer move against Saddam. Arab intelligence services also warned the CIA of the horrendous aftereffects that would result from Saddam's swift collapse, the occupation of Baghdad, and the ensuing rise of Islamist militancy.

Arafat, however, remained convinced that the Iraqi deployment near the Jordanian border was coming to his aid. He ordered hectic preparations for an escalation of the intifada, including the use of missiles, and terrorists carrying WMD. In a series of meetings, Tirawi and other senior Palestinian officials assured regional terrorist commanders that they would soon receive these weapons from Iraq. Washington knew that Tirawi's threat was viable because Lieutenant Colonel al-Dabbagh had reported that his unit, then deployed in western Iraq, had just received rocket-propelled grenade (RPG) shells filled with WMD. "They were either chemical or biological weapons; I don't know which, because only the fedayeen and the Special Republican Guard were allowed to use them. All I know is that we were told that when we used these weapons we had to wear gas masks," he later told Con Coughlin. These weapons were to be used by officers wearing civilian clothes in case Iraq's defeat appeared imminent. Al-Dabbagh and other human sources reported that many of these WMD-filled RPGs were deployed to forward sites adjacent to the Jordanian border and could be easily smuggled into the West Bank.

On Friday, October 11, and Saturday, October 12, the Iraqi government signaled for "emergency activities" on Saddam's instructions. Both the Iraqi media and the imams of the government-approved mosques intensified their vitriolic attacks on the United States. As an indication of Baghdad's seriousness, the Revolutionary Command Council formally approved Qusay Saddam Hussein as Saddam's successor if anything happened to his father. There was no surprise in this move, but the decision added to the melodrama prevailing in Baghdad. On October 15, the Iraqi people voted on a referendum to extend Saddam's tenure by seven years, through 2009. Saddam happily accepted the results; according to the official tally, not a single vote was cast against him.

Regardless of the political and diplomatic activities, America's undeclared war on Iraq continued throughout the first weeks of October. In northern Iraq, U.S. Special Forces bolstered the line held by a combination of Turkman and Kurdish militias and Turkish Special Forces and intelligence operatives. The line stretched from west to east, incorporating the cities of Sinjar, Mosul, Irbil, Kirkuk, and Sulaymaniyah. In the east, forces of the al-Badr Brigades coexisted with the U.S.-sponsored Kurds, while in western Iraq, U.S. and allied Special Forces continued their repeated probes toward the H-2 and H-3 complexes. Many of these surges were blunted in fierce skirmishes with Iraqi commandos.

On October 2 the Iraqis once again deployed SSM batteries from the Baghdad areas, and attempts by U.S. Special Forces to take out the batteries failed. Iraqi patrols discovered the Americans far away from the bases and subjected their immediate vicinity to intense artillery fire. The accuracy of the shells suggested that the Iraqis knew where the American soldiers were and were surrounding their location. This cat and mouse game extended over three nights. Then on October 5, the Iraqis tacitly opened a corridor for the Americans to withdraw into Jordan by daylight, which they quickly used. Baghdad seemed to have decided to quietly defuse the crisis before the United States committed reinforcements and turned the clash into a major confrontation for which Iraq was not yet prepared.

Although the United States was formally committed to waging war alone, without an endorsement from the UN or any other international body, the Bush administration embarked on an all-out effort to convince both Egypt and Saudi Arabia to support the offensive. In the Middle East, the mere fact that the United States attempted to persuade the two nations demonstrated to friends and foes alike just how little Washington understood or cared about the vital interests of countries America considered its friends and allies.

However, the Bush administration first had to contend with an eruption of instability in Qatar, home to al-Udeid, the largest U.S. air base in the region and CENTCOM's in-theater headquarters. In October, the Qatari security authorities arrested numerous officers, especially in the tank corps, and initial reports attributed the arrests to an aborted coup attempt by a number of sheikhs in the al-Thani ruling family. They were, explained a Gulf security official, "adamantly opposed to Qatari policies, especially Doha's special relationship with Israel, its decision to allow the construction of a new U.S. base in the country, and turning Qatar into the largest depot for U.S. weapons outside the United States." Qatari officials acknowledged brewing tension with the military elite but insisted that there had not been any attempt to overthrow Emir Hamad. The Qatari security forces did arrest mid- and senior-level officers because they had "plotted to end the U.S. military presence in the emirate," a Western intelligence source told Steve Rodan. The source added that "the officers did not plan a coup, rather [they planned] to confront the emir and force him to abandon Doha's alliance with the United States." Either way, the crisis in Qatar was not a good omen for things to come throughout the Arab world.

In the fall, Hosni Mubarak was immersed in a crisis of legitimacy; Mubarak was adamant about handing over the reigns of power to his son Gamal despite mounting public opposition. As the Iraq crisis intensified, Mubarak feared that the U.S. intervention and removal of an Arab leader and would-be successor might create a precedent to be followed in Egypt. Mubarak had long been using—many Egyptians say *abusing*—lavish U.S. aid, to help those who would assist Gamal as he consolidated his power. To the American officials, primarily on Capital Hill, who criticized Egypt's domestic and economic policies—the cold peace with Israel, the missile deals with North Korea, and other objectionable practices—Mubarak for years answered that in helping Egypt, America was first and foremost subsidizing its own gateway to the Arab world. Now, Mubarak knew, a post-Saddam Iraq allied with the United States would inevitably become America's primary gateway, making Egypt superfluous. Any close inspection of Egypt's practices would most likely result in a massive reduction in American foreign aid, jeopardizing Gamal's ascent. In response to these developments, Egypt resolved to undermine the American war effort as much as possible—without prompting a direct confrontation with Washington.

Demonstrating its displeasure with the situation in the Middle East, Cairo ordered the Egyptian Third Army to launch a ten-day major exercise in the southern part of the Sinai Peninsula. Defense Minister Hussein Tantawi, as well as senior military commanders and several parliamentarians, attended the Aasar-2002 exercise in October, highlighting its political significance. Egyptian military officials described the maneuvers as "a joint air-ground exercise" comprising two phases. In the first phase, the Third Army conducted "a rapid crossing of the Suez Canal by ground forces backed by fixed- and rotor-wing aircraft." In the second phase, the Egyptian forces conducted "an offensive against mock enemy positions in the eastern part of the Sinai." In Cairo, Western diplomatic sources told MENL's Steve Rodan that "Egypt has been training its ground forces in rapid-response missions and offensive tactics."

The sources said the focus of the latest exercise was on "mobility under air defense cover for Egyptian infantry and tanks." Egyptian officials would not address the potential threat such exercises constituted to Israel. "We are making all efforts to achieve a permanent and comprehensive peace," Tantawi quipped while attending the exercise. In Cairo, Egyptian officials stressed the timing and location of the Aasar-2002 exercise. The exercises peaked just as CENTCOM chief Gen. Tommy Franks arrived in Cairo to discuss Egypt's participation in the forthcoming war against Iraq. The Aasar-2002 exercise bluntly demonstrated to Franks, and his bosses, Cairo's real national priorities and security interests.

Just to emphasize the point, Egypt conducted another live-fire air defense exercise in the Sinai Peninsula shortly after Assar-2002. Egyptian officials stressed that the exercise was meant "to commemorate the anniversary of the 1973 Arab-Israeli war," as well as send signals to both Washington and Jerusalem regarding Cairo's resolve. "What we witnessed today increases our confidence in the combat-readiness of the air defense forces, which are equipped with advanced equipment and weapons," Tantawi said. These were not empty words, as in November Cairo rejected Washington's request for special security measures in the Suez Canal during the passage of navy warships on their way to the Persian Gulf. Formally, Egypt said it could not provide the additional manpower requested by the United States, and instead permitted the navy and marines to conduct flights in Egyptian airspace and take other special measures to enhance their ships' security. Privately, Egyptian officials confided to their Arab colleagues that there was no way Cairo would provide even the most rudimentary and indirect help to the U.S. war effort against "brotherly Iraq."

For the Saudis, any semblance of cooperating with the United States in the occupation and destruction of Baghdad—regardless of the fact that they hated Saddam Hussein—was sacrilegious. Immersed in a succession struggle, the House of al-Saud could ill afford to risk further confrontation with its increasingly Islamist population. Moreover, if the Arab world accepted the legitimacy of replacing one Arab leader—even a leader feared and despised—why shouldn't the Arab world be expected to sanction the removal of the House of al-Saud as well?

In October, the succession struggle in Riyadh gained preeminence as the country prepared to cope with the reverberations of the war in Iraq. Resigned to a short conflict—two to three weeks long—and expecting the subsequent restoration of Iraq's oil industry within a few months, Riyadh also expected a drastic reduction in world oil prices as the United States and the new government in Baghdad tried to grab as large a share of the market as possible to finance the war and Iraq's rehabilitation. Additionally, Riyadh expected the existence of a new American-dominated Iraq to reduce the influence and importance of Saudi Arabia in Washington. The Saudi policy enacted to cope with these crucial trends had direct bearing on the succession struggle.

As the struggle deepened, King Fahd moved from Geneva to his summer home in Marbella, Spain. Here, debate centered on questions of how Saudi Arabia should react to the war with Iraq, to what degree it would cooperate with the Americans, and if Riyadh would grant them permission to use Saudi bases and facilities when the predominantly Islamist population was adamantly opposed to any such cooperation. The two main camps in the succession struggle held diametrically opposed opinions on all these points. Crown Prince Abdallah's camp wanted to pacify the Saudi "street" by distancing Riyadh from Washington, particularly on issues as controversial and sacrilegious as the sacking of Baghdad; supporters of Defense Minister Prince Sultan argued that by helping America in an unstoppable war against a regime that also threatened Riyadh, they would be able to commit Washington to helping their own ascent to power against both the Abdallah camp and the largely hostile Saudi population.

Because the Bush administration insisted on access to military bases and facilities, Saudi officials believed it was only a question of time before Washington toppled Crown Prince Abdallah and empowered Prince Sultan. Therefore, Crown Prince Abdallah moved to consolidate King Fahd's support against his rival by empowering Fahd's fourth and beloved son—Prince Abdulaziz bin Fahd—as the next in line. In practical terms, Abdallah hoped to replace Sultan as third in line for the throne, so that soon after King Fahd's death, Abdulaziz would emerge as the new Crown Prince. Abdallah justified the urgent imperative to sideline Sultan by warning about the dire ramifications of closer military cooperation with the United States.

The bombings in Riyadh in October influenced the succession struggle further. Crown Prince Abdallah was the driving force behind the firing of Tahah Sufyan—a senior security official in the Ministry of the Interior—which shifted blame for not preventing the attacks away from Prince Salman, the powerful governor of Riyadh. As a result, Prince Salman became beholden to Crown Prince Abdallah.

But these maneuvers had nothing to do with improving internal security in Saudi Arabia. The growing tension emanating from the street's reaction to the brewing Iraqi crisis was reflected in the deteriorating security situation within the kingdom. While the spate of bombing attacks against Western targets in Riyadh made headlines, far more important were the clashes between internal Saudi security forces and indigenous Islamist gangs. The November 16 skirmishes in the al-Shafaa district of Riyadh provided a good indication of the extent of the Islamist threat. The security teams encountered at least fifty al-Qaeda terrorists, well armed and hiding in a single house. Lengthy firefights ensued, and both sides sustained numerous casualties. Many of the Islamist terrorists escaped before the security forces broke into the house in the aftermath of two days of fighting, and only one of the leaders, betrayed to the authorities by a protector, was taken into custody. For the Saudi elite, the clashes in al-Shafaa served as a grim reminder of the grassroots threat they faced if they cooperated too closely with America.

The other regional power the Bush administration hoped to entice into supporting the war was the Islamic Republic of Iran. In October, Washington reached out to Tehran, hoping to get its tacit support. To demonstrate its absence of hostile intent, Washington looked the other way as Iranian intelligence, Special Forces personnel, and al-Badr squads—composed of Iraqi Shiites, Iranians, and *Hazara* (Shiite Afghans) mujahedin—entered Iraqi Kurdistan. While exploiting the gesture, Tehran was convinced that a U.S. victory in Iraq would constitute a mortal threat to the mullahs' regime. Therefore, Iran launched a major military exercise near Qom in order to deter the United States. "The three-day exercise consists of maneuvers by various units of ground forces aimed at displaying the country's latest military achievements, as well as promoting defensive capabilities," Iranian army commander Brig. Gen. Nasser Mohammadi-Far said. "The enemy should know that we will retaliate to any move from their side. We are preparing so that no enemy will dare to attack us."

Although America does not have formal diplomatic ties with Iran, Washington warmly endorsed British Foreign Minister Jack Straw's trip to Tehran on October 15. Iranian leaders confronted Straw with a lengthy diatribe about the inherent danger of an American invasion and argued that there must be other ways to get rid of Saddam Hussein. They proposed that IRGC Chief Safavi lead a secret delegation to Iraqi military and intelligence elites in Baghdad to see if they would agree to a military coup against Saddam or any other form of regime change to prevent post-Saddam Iraq being subjected to American occupation and hegemony, and Straw agreed.

The CIA, though, decided to counter the Iranian initiative by reaching out to powerful Iraqi Sunnis through Arab intermediaries, warning them that any coup instigated by Iran would lead to a Shiite-dominated regime that would surely deprive the Sunnis of power and perks. The Iraqi leadership did not address the Iranian pitch, fearing it was part of a CIA conspiracy. Only on the eve of the war did Tehran learn that there was interest in the Safavi initiative because Iran has impeccable anti-American credentials. However, once the CIA became involved, the potential conspirators lost all interest.

Ariel Sharon arrived in Washington in mid-October, and after their meeting in the Oval Office, Bush called Sharon a "close friend" and said he "understood" Israel's intent to defend itself against Iraq. "If Iraq attacks Israel tomorrow, I would assume the prime minister would respond. He's got a desire to defend himself," Bush said. He stressed the Iraqi threat to Israel and Israel's right to self-defense.

At the same time, Bush urged the revival of the peace process with the Palestinians. In his response, Sharon praised Bush's determined stance against international terrorism and stated that Israel had never had a better friend in the White House. "As far as I remember, as we look back toward many years now, I think that we never had such relations with any president of the United States as we have with you, and we never had such cooperation in everything as we have with the current administration," Sharon said, facing Bush.

But regardless of public statements, the United States demanded that Sharon take no action against Iraq, receiving in return an American commitment to do its utmost to protect Israel. Moreover, Sharon came out of the Oval Office deeply insulted and personally hurt when, at the last minute, a six-page "position paper" on the future of the Middle East that included veiled threats to Jerusalem was stuffed into his hand. Sharon had not expected "his friend" Bush to sandbag him, especially in light of Sharon's close cooperation with America, even at the cost of Israeli lives. Despite Sharon's indignity, Israel made unilateral concessions to the Palestinians that enabled greater movement to would-be martyrs and bomb makers. As a result, Israeli citizens suffered some of the most lethal strikes in recent memory, including, on the morning of Sharon's meeting with Bush, a bus bombing in which fourteen civilians were killed and close to fifty wounded.

Sharon returned from Washington convinced there would soon be war. He anticipated tremendous U.S. pressure regarding both the Palestinian issue and Israel's ability to retaliate. He was particularly apprehensive about the public impression of a loss of Israeli deterrence that the American demands would surely foster. The Arab world, Sharon knew, would not miss the signals that the United States did not care deeply about Israel, which their negotiations had suggested. Although Israeli officials tried to articulate the problem, senior U.S. officials did not grasp the complexity and importance of Middle Eastern policy based on perception rather than the mere analysis of facts. As a reaction, Sharon established a mini-kitchenette—a specialized decision-making and crisis-management body—to address the quintessential issues of Israel's security. The kitchenette members included Sharon, Mofaz (who was formally nominated minister of defense on November 4), Yaalon, Halevi, Dagan Dichter, and Kaplinsky (the commander of the Israel Defense Forces' Central Command). It was a very pragmatic group of people who, while working closely with the White House, were ultimately determined to save Israel from the forthcoming crisis. The IDF prepared for a regional conflict, acting as though it would not require American protection in the event of a wider war. The entire Israeli Air Force conducted exercises on a full war footing during the week of November 3.

But whatever their own plans for the crisis, the Israelis assisted America's preparations throughout the fall. The IDF expanded their training programs—especially for U.S. Special Forces and Marines—in urban warfare, based on Israel's latest experiences. American forces gained access to Israel's own highly sophisticated urban warfare training centers, and the IDF shared locally developed unique weapons and systems optimized for urban and desert warfare of the type the United States was likely to encounter in Iraq. At America's request, some of these weapons were supplied even at the expense of Israel's own fighting forces. Israeli security officials also taught their American counterparts the art of interrogating Arab suspects. Israeli intelligence provided a huge amount of material, particularly from its unique human sources. Meanwhile, Israeli Special Forces continued their clandestine surveillance missions in the western Iraqi desert to help the United States identify targets for future bombing. Using their intimate knowledge of Iraqi military practices, the Israeli teams mapped potential launch pads and possible attack routes.

At the same time, Israel went out of its way to ensure the low profile of this cooperation. Washington feared for its shaky relationships with its Arab friends, and Israel was ready to accommodate. "The Americans have asked us to keep a low profile, and we accept that," an Israeli official told

USA Today. In November, America and Israel conducted another round of military consultations. Gen. James Metzger and his U.S. military delegation arrived in Israel to check on American military equipment stored in Israeli facilities and the avenues for further cooperation with the Israeli defense establishment.

Formulating his own plans, Arafat ordered the establishment of new terrorist forces to help Iraq; in November he and Tirawi organized an elite group, based in Nablus and Ramallah, comprising the best men from all the intelligence and security organs of the Palestinian Authority. Carrying out martyrdom and nonmartyrdom spectacular strikes, the new force would deliver the provocation Saddam needed to justify his attack. The terrorists were also trained and organized to conduct strikes, lay ambushes, and sustain guerrilla warfare against American forces expected to operate out of Israel and Jordan. Tirawi was in direct control of these preparations, while Abu-al-Abbas sent Iraqi terrorists, funds, and specialized equipment. Israeli intelligence learned about these decisions and preparations and promptly notified the United States.

Around the same time, the United States continued its attacks on Iraqi defense facilities, air bases, and command posts. On October 23, the United States launched two major strikes on the air bases and military complexes in Tallil and al-Jarrah, to the north and southeast of Baghdad respectively, and also unleashed air attacks on the Mosul area from bases in Turkey. In November, aerial and Special Forces units escalated their activities in southern Iraq, advertising their operations by dropping leaflets along a strip stretching from al-Kut to Basra—an area determined to be the primary gateway to Baghdad in the forthcoming war. In words and pictures, the leaflets urged Iraqi troops and citizens to stay away from military objectives because they would soon be bombed from the air. American and British aircraft carried out intermittent bombing and leaflet dropping on key military deployments and concentrations in the areas of Al-Halafyah and Mussalan, as well as Al-Qurnah and Al-Muzayrah.

Meanwhile, American and British Special Forces teams advanced from Kuwait and raided key objectives between al-Ghabi and al-Qurnah, constituting a considerable chunk of southeast Iraq. The primary objective of the raiding Special Forces was to attack the Babel Republican Guard division and ultimately force it to withdraw north toward Baghdad. In November, the Babel was forward deployed and in excellent positions to block the U.S. and British invasion from Kuwait.

The units also checked axes of transportation in the Har-al-Hammar sector of the Iraqi marshes, just in case main ground forces had to use the corridor to get to Baghdad if the Basra-al-Amarah highway was untenable. The patrols kept bouncing into Iranian teams working with the local Shiite tribes, and both sides observed a tenuous coexistence in which neither side interfered with the others' activities.

The Special Forces groups also established observation points in Al-Halafyah and Mussalan, near the key bases of al-Amarah, to monitor Iraqi military activities. These posts had the ability to call in airpower once the war began, and on-site Special Forces would be able to expedite the advance on Baghdad along the wide river roads without getting into the key Shiite cities in the west. Reconnaissance was also carried out along the rivers as the U.S. Marine Corps studied the possibility of moving material along the rivers in case the Iraqis blew up the numerous bridges on the main roads to Baghdad.

In the fall of 2002, there were three developments on the global scene that would have direct bearing on America's management of the Iraqi crisis. The first event was the North Korean nuclear challenge. While North Korea's nuclear capacity had been known for nearly ten years, the manner in which Pyongyang boasted of it was worthy of note. On October 17, 2002, the Pyongyang Broadcasting Station carried a lengthy commentary, attributed to the Party's newspaper *Nodong Sinmun*, accusing the United States of abrogating international agreements and conventions, specifically regarding nuclear nonproliferation. "Recently, the U.S. belligerent forces are advocating preemptive attacks against the DPRK [Democratic People's Republic of Korea] on the assumption of using nuclear weapons. This is a declaration of war and an announcement of a nuclear war against us." The commentary virtually repeated Pyongyang's usual accusations, but they were followed by a new assertion: "In coping with mounting nuclear threats from the U.S. imperialists, we have come to have powerful military countermeasures, including nuclear weapons, in order to defend our sovereignty and right to existence."

At the close of 2002, sensitive internal documents of the Korean Peoples' Army covering the period between summer 2000 and fall 2002 were obtained through Japanese sources. They conclusively demonstrated that the entire political process, including the Worker's Party of Korea's policy statement, was actually part of a cynical but highly effective strategic deception launched and run by Kim Jong-Il himself. Singularly important is the officers' *Haksup Chegang* (Study Manual), a sixteen-page pamphlet of very poor-quality paper. The *Haksup Chegang* is Pyongyang's primary instrument of distributing top-secret directives of a political or ideological nature to ranking officers in the front line units, and these manuals constitute a uniquely important source of information on the KPA's internal thinking. The copy of the *Haksup Chegang* obtained is a special edition published in September 2002 to address issues pertaining to the first anniversary of the September 11 strikes and the beginning of America's war against the "Axis of Evil," which includes the DPRK, according to Bush's 2002 State of the Union Address.

The conclusion of this *Haksup Chegang* suggests that in fall 2002, the upper echelons in Pyongyang were genuinely convinced that Pyongyang's turn would come after Baghdad's. Kim Jong-Il believed that President Bush was serious when he declared his resolved to topple rogue regimes. To avert this fate, the DPRK needed to act resolutely and audaciously and strike out before it was too late. Indeed, Kim Jong-Il seemed to have resolved to go to war and was waiting for the most opportune moment to make his move.

The final paragraph of this *Haksup Chegang* ominously reflects his state of mind: "All military personnel must understand the importance of Dear Supreme-Commander Comrade Kim Jong-Il's enemy force breakup operation as a strategy for the unification of Korea by force. Once the Supreme Commander Comrade issues an order, all of you must charge ahead and accomplish the historic task of liberating the southern half by sweeping out all the U.S. imperialists and their pawns, leaving no one out." Unfolding events on the Korean Peninsula closely fit the doctrine outlined by the KPA ideological document, marking the beginning of a continuing campaign aimed to unnerve the United States, Japan, South Korea, and the rest of the world, compelling them to succumb to the DPRK's ultimatums.

The second such event was the November 3 national elections in Turkey. To the surprise and dismay of most, the Islamist Justice and Development Party (AKP) of Recep Tayyip Erdogan won an overwhelming (34.2 percent) electoral victory. Because of the 10 percent threshold in the Turkish Parliament, the AKP actually won enough votes to become Turkey's first single-party government in more than a decade. Erdogan has since overcome numerous legal challenges and became the country's prime minister. Significantly, the new political situation paved the way for unprecedented cooperation between the politically powerful Turkish General Staff (TSK) and the moderate Islamists of the AKP. In the past, the TSK's commitment to Attaturkism (and therefore Westernization) meant that it was diametrically opposed to Islamism (which had largely meant a retreat from Western bias and a return to an oriental understanding). Now, a growing pan-Turkism—an ideology calling for the reestablishment of Turkish influence over Turkish areas of Central Asia and the restoration of Turkey's original borders—popular among the younger members of the Turkish armed forces has been married to Turkish Islamism.

The new political reality had a direct impact on Turkey's relations with the United States because the pan-Turkists and the Islamists had a common cause in questioning regime change in neighboring Iraq. For Ankara, the question was not the removal of Saddam Hussein but rather America's determination to reaffirm Iraq's territorial integrity within its current boundaries. The pan-Turkists had already indicated that they wanted the Kurdish part of Iraq restored to Turkey. Any American action that legitimized a "new Iraq" in its present borders would prevent Iraqi Kurdistan from being restored to Turkey—a development ideologically unacceptable to both the Islamists and pan-Turkists.

Washington got a sense of the new Turkish consensus within a few days when the newly appointed chief of the Turkish General Staff, Gen. Hilmi Ozkok, visited the United States between November 4 and 10. Ozkok's visit did not go well, and his American hosts failed to take much notice of that. He was lectured by defense officials (most of whom consider themselves friends of Turkey), who told him that his country must stand beside America's planned regime change in Iraq. Ozkok attempted to remind his hosts that although Ankara had reluctantly supported Washington's Iraq policies since the Gulf War, the new government and armed forces would have none of it, but his warnings fell on deaf ears. The Defense Department simply did not comprehend the gravity of the changes Turkey was going through.

The third major event affecting the formulation of America's Iraq policy was the resounding victory of the Republican Party in the November 5 midterm elections, in which the Republicans regained control of the Senate and improved their majority in the House of Representatives. The victory gave the administration two years to make meaningful gains in strategic and economic arenas before facing the next round of presidential and congressional elections. The public was still shaken by the reverberations of September 11 and convinced of the need for a mighty Homeland Security Department. The White House "spin masters" addressed these issues by transforming the elections into a referendum on the president's desire to attack Iraq. In short, Americans were asked to vote Republican if they thought war with Iraq was the most important item on the national agenda, and vote Democratic if they thought the sputtering economy took precedence. The resounding Republican victory—all the more impressive because traditionally the party in the White House loses the midterm elections—was perceived by the White House as an endorsement of the war. The administration eagerly waited for the opening session of the new Congress, looking to gain support for implementing the president's policy.

In November Saddam Hussein conducted both secret and highly publicized meetings with the Iraqi high command as well as leading intelligence and weapons industry officials. The meetings covered by Iraqi TV reflected Baghdad's defiant mood and real intent, and in one such session on November 3, Gen. Hamid Raja Shilah, an Iraqi Air Force commander, clarified Iraq's strategic objectives. The coming war, he assured Saddam, would be first and foremost for the liberation of Palestine and not merely to resist the American onslaught on Iraq. Shilah expected Saddam to "fulfill the ambitions and hopes of the Arab masses, and lead them to liberate Palestine and its crown, Holy Jerusalem, from the claws of the Zionists."

Baghdad's expectations were neither illogical nor impractical. The Iraqis knew they could not match American military might—the first Gulf War had demonstrated that, and Iraq's military had not improved since then—and understood that once hostilities commenced the Iraqi armed forces would be destroyed. However, regardless of the extent of the destruction, Baghdad was convinced that any outcome in which Saddam and Qusay remained alive and capable of issuing sporadic communiqués was a victory over the United States. The key to Saddam's strategy was not victory itself, but rather the perception of victory throughout the Muslim and Arab world. Saddam merely appropriated the widespread perception of Osama bin Laden's enduring ability to elude capture by the United States while sustaining communications with his followers all over the world. As in Afghanistan, prolonged guerrilla warfare—even if sporadic and largely symbolic—and his own escape would help Saddam's cause.

With the confrontation looming, the Iraqis developed two master contingency plans: an assertive strategy intended to ignite a regional jihad against Israel; and a defensive strategy intended to ensure Saddam Hussein's survival while ensnaring the United States in a war of attrition that would place it in the position of killing Iraqi and Arab civilians, making the war unpopular to both the American public and the Muslim world. Intentionally subjecting the Iraqi civilian population to heavy fire was an integral part of Saddam's designs; like many tyrants, his self-preservation was far more important than the well-being of his countrymen.

The contingency plans of the Iraqi armed forces were a blend of offensive and defensive operations. Iraq's strategic arms—the missile regiments and the air force—prepared for offensive operations primarily against Israel but also against the Gulf States that might support the American war effort. According to senior Arab security officials who visited Baghdad in July, Saddam had already "put the final touches to a plan for a counterattack that involves the use of biological and chemical weapons. The plan calls for launching attacks in the whole of the Middle East." The Iraqi Air Force intensified its training, particularly with long-range strikes and aerial refueling hardly attempted for a decade. In July, Special Unit 223—Iraq's preeminent ballistic missile force—was put on high alert with experts conditioning its chemical and biological warheads for imminent use.

In mid-September, an Iraqi brigadier general on the General Staff warned Arab colleagues about Iraq's military posture and preparations for the war. He noted "Iraq's tremendous supply of surface-to-surface missile warheads," filled with weapons of mass destruction. "Inspection teams destroyed only a small number of them," he gloated. Iraq's ballistic missiles and warheads "are controlled by the Surface-to-Surface Missile Command based in al-Taji, north of Baghdad," the general explained.

Because there had been no effective attempt to destroy Special Unit 223 since July, Iraq activated and deployed all four missile units in mid-September—Special Units 222, 223, 224, and 225. "They are deployed in various locations in Iraq, permitting them to hit predetermined targets and carry out direct orders from Saddam himself," the general stated. This strategic effort was supervised and coordinated by Iraq's deputy prime minister and minister of military industrialization, Abd-al-Tawab al-Mulla Huwaysh, who received his instructions directly from Saddam in person.

The other key issue raised by the Iraqi brigadier general was the evolving role of the Republican Guard. The last decade, and especially the last couple of years, had seen elaborate preparations and active deployment of Iraq's al-Quds (Jerusalem) Forces to the Syrian and Jordanian borders.

Now under Qusay's direct command, these forces conducted offensive exercises in close cooperation with the Syrian armed forces in preparation for a future war with Israel. At times these exercises, which involved forward deployment of ballistic missiles, were so realistic that both American and Israeli forces were on the verge of launching preemptive air strikes.

The Iraqi general further stressed the role of Iraq's eight Republican Guard divisions—Baghdad, Hammurabi, Nebuchadnezzar, Allah-hu-Akbar, Adnan, an-Nida, al-Fath al-Mubin, and al-Madina al-Munawwarah—in both offensive and defensive operations. Under Qusay's personal command, these divisions were shifting between protecting the regime in two force groupings north and south of Baghdad and spearheading the onslaught on Israel via Jordan and Syria as the elite core of Qusay's Al-Quds Forces. Under the latest adaptation of Iraq's contingency plans, as disclosed by the general, all or most of the eight Republican Guard divisions would join the five to six regular divisions and an assortment of special operations and irregular terrorist forces already in the Al-Quds Force, creating a formidable assault grouping to take on Israel via Syria and Jordan. Baghdad was convinced that since the bulk of the Jordanian population is Palestinian, they would rise up against the Hashemite rulers in case of war, and that under such conditions the Iraqi armed forces would have no problem defeating the few Bedouin units still loyal to the King of Jordan.

In October, the Iraqis moved many of their operational fighter-bombers, particularly long-range Mirage F-1s, to the Jal al-Batan air base in southwestern Iraq. There, the aircraft were dispersed in numerous underground shelters over a vast area, making them harder targets for would-be attackers. Toward the end of October, the Iraqis also moved a few L-29s converted into unmanned delivery vehicles for biological weapons to Jal al-Batan. Overflying northern Saudi Arabia and southern Jordan, Iraqi strike aircraft would be within range of the entire southern part of Israel, thus constituting a potential threat to some of Israel's most sensitive strategic objectives.

Concurrently, Saddam Hussein ordered the activation and forward deployment of Iraq's own elite terrorist forces operating under Unit 999 of military intelligence; slightly over 2,000 Special Forces operatives were organized into seven battalions, each of which was then divided into numerous highly trained teams and detachments. Most of these deployments, each of them roughly 300 strong, were completed in early November. The key elements of the deployment were as follows: the Persian Battalion fanned out along the border between Iran and Iraq's Shiite areas; the Saudi Battalion deployed between Nasiriyah and the Saudi border; the Turkish Battalion took up positions along the key mountain passes from Iraqi Kurdistan into Turkey; the Naval Battalion deployed near the Kuwaiti border; the Palestinian Battalion was sent to refugee camps in Jordan and joined Arafat's terrorist forces in the West Bank; the Opposition Battalion deployed throughout Western Europe in order to assassinate Iraqi opposition leaders and terrorize their supporters; and the United States Battalion, of some 500 men, deployed into the United States and Canada. Arab and Israeli security officials estimated at the time that several Unit 999 teams—totaling 60 to 80 highly trained operatives—were in the United States and Canada by November.

The threat of Iraqi terrorism was quite serious, and several intelligence sources in the region—both Israeli and Arab—reported almost simultaneously about the activation, on Saddam's order, of the entire terrorist force under Unit 999 of military intelligence. Baghdad's original order was all-inclusive, applying equally to all seven battalions. Subsequently, different sources in different countries began reporting about the localized implementation of these orders in their own countries and regions. For example, the intelligence and security services of Saudi Arabia, Kuwait, and other Gulf States noted on their own the arrival of Iraqi operatives near their borders and, soon afterward, their crossing deep into Saudi Arabia on reconnaissance and sabotage missions. The Saudi security forces clashed with the intruders and some were either killed or captured. Most of them, however, eluded their Saudi pursuers. The Kuwaiti security forces had a similar experience with Iraqi intruders, particularly in the various islands in the northern tip of the Persian Gulf. Similarly, the Turkish security authorities acknowledged the arrival of Unit 999 operatives in the ranks of Iraq-sponsored Kurdish insurgency networks—first in eastern Turkey and eventually in Istanbul as well. There, the Iraqi operatives surveyed the Bosporus bridges, port facilities, and other strategic objectives as targets for sabotage. The Turks were able to neutralize some of these cells—learning from the interrogation of captured Iraqi agents and their local supporters about their overall activities and tasks. Meanwhile, Israeli and Jordanian security forces learned about the arrival of operatives from Palestinians in both countries, and several of the Iraqis' local helpers were apprehended or killed in a series of raids. The interrogation of the captured Palestinians enabled the neutralization of a few, but far from all, of the Iraqi cells in both Jordan and the territories.

Additionally, the arrival of Iraqi intelligence operatives was identified by the intelligence and security forces in several Western European countries, after the terrorists made contact with local supporters in the Arab expatriate communities. Some of these Iraqis communicated with either Baghdad or institutions in other Arab countries known to be fronts for Iraqi intelligence. It did not take long for the Iraqis to begin threatening opposition leaders, and subsequently there were some assassination attempts. Although little progress was made in the attempt to disrupt these networks, largely because local Muslim communities refused to help intelligence services, enough all-around pressure was put on the Iraqi-led networks to prevent major operations in Europe. Meanwhile, the United States was warned by several friendly intelligence and security forces about the arrival of Iraqi operatives in North America. In addition, several Latin American governments mentioned to the United States that Iraqi operatives had passed through their countries on the way to the United States. However, given the strategic significance of operations at the heart of the United States—essentially, the realization that such strikes would provide Washington with its long-sought-after casus belli against Iraq—these operatives were ordered by Baghdad to lie low until activated—and they never were. After the fall of Baghdad, some of these operatives simply melted away into the vast community of illegal immigrants in the United States, while others made their way back to the Middle East through Latin America and Africa. At the time of this writing, most of these ex-operatives are wandering around Europe in search of refuge and political asylum.

To wage this war, Saddam established a special high command in October under the direct command of himself and Qusay. The key members of this high command were Abd-al-Tawab al-Mulla Huwaysh; Uday Saddam Hussein; Staff Gen. Sultan Hashim Ahmad, the minister of defense; Muyassar Raja Shalah, minister of industry and minerals; Dr. Fadil Muslim al-Janabi, head of the Atomic Energy Organization; Staff Lt. Gen. Muzahim Sab al-Hassan, commander of air defense; Staff Lt. Gen. Hamid Raja Shilah, commander of the air force; and Staff Maj. Gen. Kamil Ismail Mahmud, dean of the Military Engineering College. According to Iraqi senior officials, Saddam's high command also included several "specialized mujahedin and fighters" with unique skills and responsibilities. Saddam intended to rely on this high command for the conduct of offensive operations in the context of both a regional war against Israel, and preemptive strikes in the Persian Gulf area in connection with American preparations for the attack.

*   *   *

In case it proved impossible, or inadvisable, to launch a war against Israel, Baghdad devised a comprehensive, multilayered defense plan with assistance from U.S.-educated Egyptian senior officers, most of whom were recently retired. The pragmatic plan assumed the gradual capture of most of Iraq's cities and the destruction of its known military infrastructure. To reduce the pace of collapse, Iraq mobilized "Saddam's Fedayeen" in July—a 35,000-member-strong personal guard composed solely of men from Saddam's own Tikriti tribe, serving under Uday's command. The martyr force served as the regime's last-resort defense and was the primary instrument of ruthlessly purging the defense establishment's ranks of traitors. The martyrs' activation signaled Saddam's resolve to forestall any possible cooperation between elements of the Iraqi Army and the U.S.-sponsored Iraqi opposition.

In early October, senior Arab officials in contact with Baghdad noted that Saddam's defensive plans "proceeded from the possibility of a quick military defeat for the Iraqi regular forces, the fall of major cities in the north and the south, and even the surrender of scores of military barracks and divisions and the desertion of thousands of soldiers." They explained that Baghdad's working assumption was that "the U.S. invasion would take place at any time and would be aimed at Saddam personally, his family, and the narrow ruling circle around him." Saddam was convinced, they elaborated, that "the sole victory, which he could achieve and defeat Bush with, is staying alive and preventing the U.S. forces or their military and civilian Iraqi collaborators from achieving the aim of arresting or assassinating him, even if they succeeded in occupying Baghdad and appointing a bogus 'Iraqi Karzai.'" The essence of the Iraqi defensive plans was to facilitate Saddam's "victory" regardless of the price Iraq would have to pay.

The outer layer of the defense plan relied on the Iraqi regular army and civilians recruited into the al-Quds militias (Baghdad boasted of seven million volunteers for these militias). The defensive effort was divided into two distinct zones in northern and southern Iraq. In the north, the defense zone was very shallow and covered the area between the Kurdish-controlled areas and the forward positions of the Republican Guard forces. The objective of these defense lines was to buy time for the Republican Guard. In the south, the forward defense zone covered the entire Shiite area from the border with Kuwait and Saudi Arabia all the way to the Republican Guard positions just south of Baghdad. Indicative of Saddam's plans for this region was the nomination of Lt. Gen. Ali Hassan al-Majid as the commander of the south with headquarters in Nasiriyah. Commonly known as Ali Keemawi—"Chemical Ali"—he arrived in southern Iraq "authorized [by Saddam] to use chemical weapons against any popular insurrection there." In case Baghdad decided to implement the defensive strategy, al-Majid's instructions called for buying time for the defenders of Baghdad by inflicting at least a thousand American fatalities and ensuring popular resistance to the invading forces, which would kill thousands of Iraqis—mainly members of the al-Quds militias—in front of Western TV. Saddam was convinced, the senior Arab officials stressed, that the aggregate impact of heavy American casualties and the gore of Iraqi civilian casualties "would lead to international and U.S. pressure for withdrawal from the 'Iraqi Vietnam.'"

The second layer of the Iraqi defense consisted of the Republican Guard forces covering an area that included Baghdad, Tikrit, and Qusay's forward headquarters at the al-Baghdadi air base. Under Qusay's command, the Republican Guard's eight divisions, along with an assortment of artillery, missiles, and Special Forces, were expected to put up a protracted fight against American units. These forces were well equipped, constantly trained, and fiercely loyal to Saddam and Qusay. While they were expected to demonstrate long-term endurance against the Americans as well as to inflict heavy casualties, they were not expected to defeat the U.S. Army. Ultimately, the Iraqi contingency plans predicted, "the Republican Guard would not be able to resist the military and psychological warfare pressure," and fighting would move into Baghdad. Saddam, the Arab officials noted, was convinced that "the real battle of [Iraq's] existence and destiny would be fought in and around Baghdad." For the Battle of Baghdad, Qusay established a special force of some 40,000, made up of special units from the Republican Guard whose loyalty was not in doubt, regiments of the Republican Palace's special defensive companies, and protocol and guard forces. They were expected to conduct urban warfare and terrorism at any cost to themselves and without regard to the plight and losses of the civilian population.

Iraq's defensive war plan anticipated that Saddam, Qusay, and a host of key officials would ultimately move to shelters in the heart of the Iraqi desert to conduct the next phase of the war, which was heavily dependant on irregular warfare and terrorism. Of special significance was the transition period from urban warfare to desert-based guerrilla fighting. To oversee this phase, Saddam nominated Abu-Karmi, who, along with Abid

Hamid Humud, Saddam's private secretary, was considered one of the two nonfamily members closest to Saddam and Qusay. According to a high Arab official actively involved with the leadership in Baghdad, Abu-Karmi's mission was "to open the doors of hell on U.S. forces' positions and bases in the neighboring countries, especially Qatar and Kuwait, and even Jordan, if U.S. operations were launched from there, with all the missiles and biological and chemical weapons Iraq possesses."

Preparations for the wartime transfer of Saddam and his coterie to the desert and the activation of the guerrilla phase of the war were entrusted to Abid Hamid Humud. Over the previous few months, ever since Baghdad became convinced that President Bush was certain to topple the regime, Humud had been working on the "underground resistance" plan. He identified the areas in which the resistance would be active and appointed local Baath Party and tribal officials as local commanders. He also oversaw the construction of long, deep tunnels in safe areas in the Sunni region and near the Syrian and Jordanian borders. These tunnels were filled with cash, provisions, weapons, and explosives in quantities that could sustain a guerrilla war for three years.

For the long-term guerrilla war, Saddam established jihad leadership consisting of Saddam, Qusay, Ali Hassan al-Majid (Saddam's cousin), Abd-al-Tawab Mulla Huwaysh, Mustafa Kamil (Saddam's brother-in-law), Sultan Hashim, Lutayyif Nusayyif Jasim, Tariq Aziz, and Watban al-Tikriti (Saddam's brother). The guerrilla war would be waged by a force of over 100,000 troops, all of whom were from the Tikrit and Al-Bu-Nassir tribes. Most of them were drawn from the tribes' own defense force, the Republican Guard, the intelligence services, and the Baath Party militias. About 5,000 troops were experienced commandos from the Republican Guard, special security, and intelligence organizations, especially Unit 999—Iraq's primary terrorism training and control force, which was now entrusted with setting up martyrdom squads to strike American objectives throughout Iraq. By fall 2002, Saddam was convinced that these forces would be able to sustain a terrorist campaign throughout Iraq and a lengthy, bloody struggle for Baghdad, thus transforming Iraq into a new Vietnam.

Saddam, in a November conversation with Sayyid Nassar, a long-time Egyptian friend and journalist for *al-Usbu,* insisted that Arab leaders grasp that "Iraq is not the only Arab country facing the plots. The United States wants to impose its hegemony on the region. In trying to achieve that, it is directing its hostility to the Arab states, especially the key ones. This serves the interests of the Israeli entity and World Zionism. . . . The United States wants to destroy the centers of power in the entire Arab homeland, whether Cairo, Damascus, or Baghdad." Saddam articulated his view of a coherent U.S.-led conspiracy against the entire Muslim world. "The United States wants to impose its hegemony on the Arab homeland and as a prelude it wants to control Baghdad and strike at the rebellious capitals that reject this hegemony. Once Baghdad is placed under military control, it will be Damascus and Tehran's turn to be struck at and split up." Saddam warned that the United States intended to take on "Saudi Arabia by splitting it up into small entities to be ruled by sentries and guards working for the United States. Thus, there will not be any state bigger than Israel in size and population. Arab oil will be under U.S. control and the region, especially the oil fields, will be, after the destruction of Afghanistan, under the full hegemony of the United States." Washington's ultimate objective, Saddam stressed, is "for Israel, under this strategy, to become a great empire in the region. Iraq's problem in all of this is that it is confronting all these plans without the others [Arab states and leaders] realizing that it is fighting on their behalf. . . . All [Arabs] are the same in the U.S. and Israeli view. What is taking place and planned against us now will also take place and be planned against the others tomorrow."

At the same time, Saddam demonstrated pragmatism regarding the possibility of a U.S.-led invasion of Iraq:

> We are getting ready as if war would take place within an hour. We are prepared psychologically for that. The daily U.S. attacks and attempts to exhaust us and kill our civilians daily with the missiles and bombs of its aircraft, which take off from bases in the neighboring countries, have made us feel we are in a continuous war. The attacks have not stopped since 1991. Therefore, we are prepared for war. But Iraq will never be like Afghanistan. This does not mean that we are stronger than the United States. It has fleets and long-range missiles. But we have faith in God, the Homeland, the Iraqi people, and more important also faith in the Arab people. We will never make it a picnic for the U.S. and British soldiers. The land always fights with its people.

Ultimately, however, Saddam Hussein did not take any chances with the conservative Arab leaders. Starting on November 5, senior Iraqi emissaries quietly delivered ultimatums to the leaders of Saudi Arabia, Kuwait, Qatar, and most likely other Gulf States. Saddam's emissaries told the Arab leaders that Iraq was resolved to preempt any American buildup rather than face a major onslaught. Toward this end, they stressed, Iraq would not hesitate to invade and occupy Kuwait, invade Saudi Arabia, and decisively strike out at Qatar. The Iraqi military in southern Iraq was already deployed accordingly. Moreover, no American installation and no American ally would escape Iraq's wrath and long arm, the emissaries stated, alluding to the planned use of Islamist terrorists. Moreover, the emissaries stressed, Saddam was adamant about striking Israel the moment hostilities erupted, and the required deployment of Iraq's key military groupings was already completed in western Iraq near the Syrian and Jordanian borders.

Asked about the threat of Israeli retaliation, the emissaries stated that Iraq would use a "surprise weapon" against Israel, reducing such a threat. Senior Arab officials who dealt with the Iraqi emissaries, as well as Arab leaders, considered these ultimatums to be very credible and serious. The Arab leaders contacted were seriously studying the Iraqi message, and profound policy changes regarding the American war were not ruled out.

In late November the coalition's military preparations for a large-scale conflict with Iraq appeared to be moving ahead. Because of the growing involvement of the UN in the hunt for Iraq's WMD, the American timetable was pushed forward again and again in order to accommodate the Security Council. At the same time, the inspectors' inability to discover any evidence of WMD and the mounting hostility to the war worldwide were adding to the Bush administration's sense of urgency. The acceleration in preparations for war, including preparatory special operations, was clearly reflected in the fact that coalition Special Forces operating inside Afghanistan were being replaced by regular forces in that country and reorganized as teams for operations inside Iraq.

Of the international reaction and mounting criticism of the administration, most important was Russia's position. Given the centrality of Russia's contribution to the war in Afghanistan, particularly in intelligence and special operations matters, and the extent of Russia's long-term involvement in and intimate knowledge of Saddam Hussein's Iraq, Moscow was not to be trifled with. November saw the beginning of U.S. tension with Russia over the war in Iraq; at the core of the administration's annoyance with the Kremlin was Putin's advice to Bush that the United States should first concentrate on the real sponsors of Islamist terrorism, specifically Pakistan, and stop Saudi funding of extremists, instead of going after Iraq. In contacts with their American counterparts, Russian experts wondered loudly if the Americans took into consideration such issues as the Islamic character of Palestinian terrorism or the escalation in Chechnya, when planning for Iraq. The radicalization of the Muslim communities in Western Europe that are closely cooperating—among other things—with Chechen Mafiya and terrorists—was also an issue of great concern for Moscow.

Putin himself warned Bush that America's cajoling of Turkey in order to win access to Iraq amounted to looking the other way regarding Turkish support for anti-Russian Islamist terrorism in the Caucasus. Russian experts warned that the problem in Iraq was not just Saddam Hussein and his weapons of mass destruction, but rather the prevailing radical militant trends. They urged the Americans to be ready to deal with radicalized populations, Sunni Islamist militancy, a radical Shiite population under Iranian influence, the flow of al-Qaeda operatives, and Kurdish-Turkish and Turkman-Arab hatred—all of which were likely to intensify in reaction to an American invasion of Iraq. "The insistence of the administration on connecting the war against Iraq to the war on terrorism not only endangers and undercuts the American achievements to date, and these are not that great, in the global war against terrorism, but actually creates and opens new venues for terrorism," opined a Russian expert, reflecting the Kremlin's position. The Kremlin was baffled when the White House regarded these professional points as political criticism and antiwar policies.

The communications with Washington convinced the Kremlin that the war was a foregone conclusion. Moscow was most apprehensive about the adamant refusal of the administration to address the issues of the huge Iraqi debt to Russia (a carryover of some ten billion dollars from the days of the USSR) and Lukoil's numerous contracts in Iraq, all of which were approved and supervised by the UN under the oil-for-food program. While asking for Russian help in confronting Saddam's regime, the United States would not guarantee that post-Saddam Baghdad would recognize either the debt or the oil contracts. On the contrary, the Russians sensed that Washington was adamant about American companies benefiting economically from the rebuilding of a U.S. occupied Iraq. And it was this insensitivity to Russia's economic interests in Iraq—rather than political disagreements about the postwar strategic posture—that set off alarm bells in the Kremlin.

By now, Washington was pleading with Moscow for intelligence assistance in Iraq. The United States wanted access to the huge and comprehensive archives of the KGB and the GRU regarding the Iraqi elite and whatever connections the Russians still had with the Iraqi military and intelligence leadership. Russian intelligence was indeed intimately familiar with the structure of the Iraqi regime—from the institutions of the uppermost elite to the actual deployment of weapons and barracks. The Kremlin could also rely on the help of numerous generals and intelligence officers, both retired and still on active service, who had strong ties—sometimes on personal and family levels—with Iraqi military and intelligence figures. Russian intelligence maintained voluminous files on the thousands of Iraqis who had undergone military and security training in Soviet, Soviet bloc, or Russian military and intelligence facilities. The Kremlin also had access to former Soviet-era generals and KGB officials who, after retirement, switched to selling arms on the black market. Having established and maintained close ties with the Iraqi military and intelligence elite, these Russians provided the Kremlin with their most up-to-date files and intimate knowledge of Iraq. The governments of Belarus, Ukraine, and Yugoslavia maintained comparable relations with Baghdad, and their intelligence services now closely cooperated with Moscow.

In the late fall, in the aftermath of the rebuff by the United States, the Russian National Security Council (RNSC) raised with the Kremlin the idea of putting this wealth of knowledge and access to use for Russia's benefit even if at the expense of the United States. The RNSC suggested that Moscow engineer a "preemptive coup" in Baghdad, which would topple the Saddam Hussein regime and establish a military elite friendly to Russia. The Kremlin decided to further examine the idea, and Russia's military and intelligence leadership prepared a detailed plan to unseat Saddam with a military coup, which might include the assassination of Saddam's inner circle. The plan was most detailed, and drafted with utmost seriousness. The Russians identified the key individuals and military formations that could be trusted to successfully carry out the coup, and Russian intelligence was confident that it could ensure the secrecy and safety of such preparations.

Then the leadership made a cardinal error. On behalf of the Kremlin, Russian intelligence notified the CIA of its plans, to make sure that no U.S. asset was killed and no U.S. intelligence activities were thwarted as a result of the Russian-inspired coup. Moscow also asked Washington to recognize and support the new government in Baghdad.

The administration was horrified by the Russian plans—particularly by the domestic political ramifications of somebody else taking credit for toppling Hussein's regime. Hence, Washington betrayed the Russian plans to, reportedly, Egyptian intelligence, with the full knowledge that Baghdad would be forewarned. It did not take long for Russian intelligence to learn about the American perfidy. The coup plans were immediately shelved before any Russian asset was harmed, but Moscow no longer saw itself obligated to help and save U.S. assets. Hence, Russian intelligence stopped warning its American counterparts when Iraqi surveillance focused on individuals suspected of ties with the Iraqi opposition in exile or American intelligence. For American intelligence, the Russians' hands-off approach would prove detrimental, as the United States was about to embark on a major clandestine undertaking inside Iraq.

Meanwhile, Islamist terrorism continued to escalate. In Kuwait, two Americans driving on a highway between the American military base of Camp Doha and the town of Arifjan were seriously wounded by a gunman, and other Americans—both civilian and military—were reporting a growing numbers of shooting incidents, albeit without casualties, as well as overall hostility and stone-throwing.

Early in the morning on November 21, a HAMAS suicide bomber blew up a bus in the Kiryat Menahem neighborhood of Jerusalem, killing eleven and wounding over fifty. What made this incident uniquely horrific was that the bus was packed with children on their way to school—something that the bomber must have noted before blowing himself up. Israeli security authorities quickly ascertained that he came from Bethlehem, which had recently been transferred back to Palestinian Authority control in the framework of a plan the administration pressured Jerusalem into implementing. "The transfer of Bethlehem to PA security control was that which enabled the attack to be prepared and the terrorist to enter Kiryat Menachem, only a few hilltops away," stressed a senior Israel Defense Forces officer.

The suicide bombing in Jerusalem corroborated accumulating intelligence evidence that the bus bombing was the first of numerous strikes—all sanctioned by Arafat—aimed to provoke Israel. Arafat won commitments from *every* terrorist organization—from HAMAS and Islamic Jihad to the radical leftists—that they would closely cooperate in a joint onslaught on Israel in order to start a regional war. The Palestinian leadership now anticipated a major escalation that would cause "unprecedented pain and suffering" to the Israelis. Jerusalem shared this information with Washington, which kept pressuring Jerusalem to avoid retaliation and instead "demonstrate responsibility and self-restraint." When Israeli officials pointed out the intentional killing and maiming of schoolchildren, the White House unleashed tremendous pressure on Jerusalem not to do anything that might interfere with the ongoing preparations for the war on Iraq. The United States also criticized the enduring presence of Israeli Special Forces, including experts on target identification and marking for smart munitions, in the western Iraqi desert. The Israelis, however, actually intensified their SCUD hunting in order to prepare war plans for both the war on Iraq and, should the need arise, Israel's own retaliation. The administration did not hide its displeasure.

Israeli intelligence also learned that HizbAllah and Iran had intensified their involvement with the Palestinian Authority security authorities in planning a terrorism campaign against Israel. Tehran was adamant about controlling or at the very least influencing the escalatory process. Toward this end, the Iranians increased their support for and influence on a myriad of Palestinian organizations, both directly and via HizbAllah. Arafat blessed this involvement because the Iranians were balancing the Iraqi influence in Ramallah, pouring more money into Palestinian Authority coffers, and facilitating even more spectacular strikes against Israel and the West. The growing influence of HizbAllah was corroborated by the discovery of HizbAllah-style bombs and other terrorist equipment in Nablus and elsewhere in the West Bank. Israeli forces also recovered Iranian-made fuses while raiding terrorist targets in the Gaza Strip. These were indicators of Iran's moving to the center of the Arab world's preparations to confront the United States.

4
ADVANCE PREPARATIONS

With the invasion sure to take place, Tehran and Damascus embarked on an audacious plan aimed at creating a strategic posture in the Middle East that would compel Israel to attack Syria and Lebanon regardless of the outcome of the war. Even if Saddam failed to provoke an Arab-Israeli war, and even if the United States convinced Israel to exhibit passivity during the war with Iraq, ultimately it might be impossible for Israel to refrain from an attack on Syria and Lebanon. Any such attack would involve Iran directly in the war, which would ultimately reverse the American gains in and against Iraq without their having to confront the United States directly.

Neither Damascus nor Tehran was ready to commit suicide in order to prevent Washington's triumph over Saddam Hussein. At the same time, both nations were cognizant that once the United States began its effort to remove Saddam Hussein, it would swiftly occupy the bulk of Iraq and establish a friendly regime, even if Saddam survived in hiding and some terrorism and guerrilla warfare continued. Significantly, both countries were convinced that the passing of UN Security Council Resolution 1441 would have no impact on America's regional designs. If anything, Syrian and Iranian officials intimated, the Security Council had just provided "a fig leaf of legitimacy to the preordained American aggression."

As American pressure on the UN Security Council (of which Syria is a temporary member) increased, Syria and Iran accelerated their preparations for the destabilizing provocation. At the core of the Iranian-Syrian grand design was the deployment in southern Lebanon of a large number of long-range missiles and rockets, some of which are capable of reaching anywhere in Israel from Mount Hermon in the north to Beer Sheva in the south. Ostensibly in the hands of HizbAllah, the long-range missiles would actually be controlled by Iranian Pasdaran (Revolutionary Guard) crews.

Both Tehran and Damascus were convinced that Jerusalem would not be able to tolerate such a threat for a long time, but to speed up Israeli reaction, Syria launched, and directly oversaw, operations against Israel's vital water resources—both diverting spring water and contaminating other supplies with sewage. With the aggregate impact of these provocations affecting well over 15 percent of the country's drinking water, Israel would eventually have to act—at the very least in southern Lebanon—thus instigating the regional war Damascus and Tehran aspired to.

In fall 2002, Tehran embarked on a dangerous gambit. Iran's ruling mullahs considered the outcome of the U.S.-led war with Iraq a matter of life or death for their regime, but their interests in the current crisis were complex. In principle, the toppling of Saddam Hussein was in Tehran's interest; however, Tehran had a greater interest in the dismemberment of Iraq, so that Tehran might, by capitalizing on its influence over Syria's Allawites and Lebanon's HizbAllah, consolidate the Shiite belt all the way to the Mediterranean. Therefore, starting that summer, Iran revived the Badr Corps, comprising a few thousand Iraqi Shiite followers of Imam Sayyid Muhammad Baqir al-Hakim, leader of the Supreme Council for the Islamic Revolution in Iraq (SCIRI). Nominally Iraqi, the Badr Corps is under the command of Pasdaran officers. To expedite preparations, a special training base was established for the Badr Corps in Qasr as-Shirrin, in western Iran, under the command of Col. Hosni Merza Khalil of Pasdaran intelligence. In August, al-Hakim met his commanders to discuss the forthcoming war, and declared that "the Badr forces will be assigned an important combat role during the expected U.S. military strike against Iraq," in order to safeguard the interests of the Iraqi Shiites. Special attention was paid to the ongoing activities of "the jihadist formations" that, according to their chief, Hassan Abdallah, already had around thirty secret operational centers in Baghdad and other Iraqi cities. In September, Imam Baqir al-Hakim issued a fatwa ruling that "any cooperation with the United States is religiously prohibited."

However, it was impossible to ignore the mounting United States threat—from expanded regional presence, to the profound, long-term ramifications of an attack on Iraq. Therefore, Tehran embarked on a very sophisticated game aimed at furthering its inherently anti-American interests without risking direct confrontation with Washington. It was an audacious and dangerous gambit because it was based on a deception of the

United States based on the pretense of tension with Damascus—Tehran's closest ally—as well as the sponsorship of deniable anti-Israeli terrorism.

The Iranian goal was to divert American attention away from Iran while, in concert with Syria, preparing HizbAllah and Palestinian terrorists to launch a major war against Israel from southern Lebanon. Teheran's ultimate strategic objective was *not* to prevent the American assault. While Tehran might prefer such a development, that was not in its power. Being pragmatic, Tehran therefore adopted a realistic and practical objective—to disrupt the American antiterrorism initiative and, most important, destroy America's ability to consolidate a pro-American regional order in the Middle East—all without a direct confrontation between the United States and Iran. Tehran was convinced that any major flare-up of Arab-Israeli fighting, particularly in and around Lebanon and Syria, would serve its ultimate objectives to perfection while keeping the war away from Iran. Significantly, although the actual fighting would involve a host of "allies" and "partners," the ultimate command and control authority remained solely in Tehran's hands; Iran controlled the operation, and only Iran had the authority to reignite the region, attack Israel, and disrupt Washington's grand design.

At the same time, Iran knew it had to operate through local venues, if only because it was hundreds of miles from Israel and did not have a common border. In Bashar al-Assad's Damascus, Tehran found an eager and ready partner to help implement its grand design. Bashar had long been committed to the empowerment of HizbAllah over Lebanon, and considered the eruption of violence along the Lebanese-Israeli border a key to Syria's strategic posture. In the fall, Syria began changing the top level of its security apparatus in order to expedite cooperation with Iran. Most crucial was the rise of Assaf Shawkat—Bashar's brother-in-law and closest confidant—to the post of deputy chief of military intelligence. This made Shawkat the strongest man in Syrian intelligence because his ostensible chief, Hassan Hallil, though an important figure in Damascus, was significantly weaker than the almighty Ali Duba, Hafez al-Assad's fierce loyalist. Whatever the military outcome, Assaf Shawkat had long argued, a war with Israel would serve the long-term interest of Bashar al-Assad because it would provide for the cementing of a new Jamaah (group of inner-circle loyalists)—much like the role of the 1967 Six Day War in the consolidation of Hafiz al-Assad's Jamaah and regime. Another manifestation of the changes in Damascus was the October 9 replacement of the ubiquitous Maj. Gen. Ghazi Kanan by Brig. Gen. Rustum Ghazali—a Shawkat loyalist and a staunch supporter of HizbAllah—as chief of the Security and Intelligence Agency of the Syrian armed forces in Lebanon.

Iran's national policy on the connection between the American threat to Iraq and the liberation of Palestine was publicly articulated in October. Two Friday sermons delivered on October 11 provided an authoritative statement. In the first sermon, Speaker of the Majlis Mehdi Karrubi stressed that only the destruction of Israel would bring an end to the Palestinian crisis, and that the American threat to Iraq was but one minor aspect of the U.S. threat to Islam. "The United States is trying to impose its will in the Near East by making al-Quds the capital of the Israeli regime. Beyt-ol-Moqaddas [the Temple Mount in Jerusalem] is the Muslims' first Quibla [direction of Muslims' praying]," Karrubi stated, "and the revolutionary Muslim generation will not remain silent in the face of this problem."

In the second sermon, IRGC commander Yahya Rahim-Safavi called for the creation of a pan-Muslim army to reverse the American gains and destroy Israel. "If only one-tenth of the billion Muslims who make up the Islamic world join this army, the Zionist state might be overthrown," he said. "The only way to topple the Zionist regime is to create an Islamic army with the help of all of the world's Muslims." Moreover, the defeat of America in Iraq would be the first step toward the destruction of Israel: "The American goal in attacking Iraq is not to overthrow the regime of Saddam Hussein, but to safeguard the Zionist state," Safavi stated. "If just one-tenth of the world's Muslims took part in this army of one hundred million mujahedin, then every Muslim would take part in the jihad to liberate Palestine."

The key Syrian-Iranian strategic coordination was completed on October 18, during a visit to Damascus by Iran's minister of intelligence, Ali Yunesi. The visit took place immediately after the completion of the first phase of the Iranian buildup of strategic capabilities in Lebanon and on the eve of a deception and disinformation campaign suggesting tensions between Damascus and Tehran regarding the future of Iraq. According to senior Lebanese officials, Yunesi's visit "was decisive in achieving 'full' Syrian-Iranian understanding over the Iraqi issue."

Yunesi met at length with Bashar al-Assad and other key Syrian senior officials and the senior leaders of HizbAllah. In their meeting, Bashar al-Assad stressed that conditions in the region were "dangerous" and that "strategic cooperation" between Iran and Syria would be "very beneficial and important at this sensitive point in time." Reporting to Tehran, Yunesi summed up his meeting with Assad as a "very good meeting" leading to joint undertakings. Yunesi reported that "the most important points raised concerned the question of a possible American attack on Iraq and current developments in Palestine. . . . Fortunately, on all issues, there was like-mindedness. Both countries are anxious about America's aims and intentions in the region and both countries are anxious about the fate of Palestine, and they will use all their efforts to this end." Regarding the impending invasion, Yunesi reported, he and Bashar "decided that the two countries should do their utmost to prevent this attack."

Senior Lebanese officials who were briefed by the Syrians relayed additional details about Yunesi's other meetings in Damascus. On the eve of Yunesi's visit, Damascus "had expressed a kind of concern about statements that emerged from Tehran from time to time about Iraq," the officials noted. In Damascus, they added, Yunesi managed "to dispel this concern in a decisive way." He conveyed to the Damascus leadership Tehran's conviction of "the danger of the American war on Iraq and, subsequently, the American presence in that country," and convinced Damascus of the imperative need to formulate a common anti-American strategy. Yunesi briefed the Syrians on Khamenei's recent guidance to the National Security Council, which led to a formal resolution that "it is 'not allowed' to offer any assistance to the American war against Iraq and that the Shiite and Kurdish opposition groups on which Iran and Syria have any amount of influence are 'not allowed' to be part of the American plan." Tehran had already resolved, Yunesi said, that "the pro-Iran Iraqi Shiite opposition will not be part of the American military strike." The Lebanese officials concluded that "Yunesi's visit provided an opportunity for the two sides to reach an understanding over strategy and ways of dealing with [regional] developments," and that "Syria and Iran 'might take major joint steps' to prevent, or at least delay, the American strike [on Iraq]."

Yunesi and Bashar agreed that their primary instrument for forestalling and defeating the American designs against Iraq and the Middle East as a whole was what they called "the development of relations among the Syria-Iran-HizbAllah triangle" in the current "sensitive" circumstances. The senior Lebanese officials stressed that the agreement between the members of what the Syrians called "the strategic triangle" was so close that "it is now difficult, indeed impossible, to separate the three parties or disengage the three tracks." Yunesi and Bashar resolved to use "HizbAllah's regional dimension" as the primary instrument for disrupting the region's stability. Indeed, Sheikh Hassan Nasrallah and other HizbAllah leaders who were summoned to Damascus for meetings with Yunesi, Bashar, and other senior officials were told that HizbAllah must now stress its "regional role" at the expense of its current "Lebanese role and dimension." Hizb-Allah would be instructed "at the right time" when to begin implementing "HizbAllah's regional role in cooperation with Syria and Iran."

Given their close relationship and frequent meetings, neither Bashar al-Assad nor Sheikh Nasrallah needed any encouragement from Tehran. Starting in October, Bashar assumed direct control over HizbAllah's buildup and activities along the Israeli-Lebanese border. He directly called both Lebanon's President Emile Lahud and HizbAllah's Sheikh Nasrallah, giving them specific and precise instructions. On the basis of these instructions, HizbAllah started to sporadically ambush patrols, shell Israeli strong points, place roadside bombs on Israel Defense Forces' patrol routes inside Israel, and dispatch reconnaissance teams deep into Israeli territory. Assad continued to do this even when, acting on specific intelligence, Undersecretary of State William Burns visited Damascus to deliver a warning from Washington. Damascus shrugged off the American warnings and intensified HizbAllah's provocation of Israel and prodding of its defenses in order to gauge Israel's reaction to a major escalation once America attacked Iraq. Meanwhile, Bashar started summoning Nasrallah to Damascus more often to consult on the next activities, as well as to give him specific instructions on operations ranging from firing antiaircraft guns at passing Israeli jets to the diversion and contamination of Israel's drinking water.

Although Damascus ignored Burns's warnings, they nevertheless prompted it to take precautionary steps. In November, Damascus launched a disinformation campaign aimed at portraying a conflict between Syria and Iran over the Iraqi crisis. A fabricated message was leaked to the Arab world's elites through a November 7 article in *al-Hayah* by Ibrahim Hamidi, Syria's unofficial spokesman in the Arab world. Hamidi argued that despite the enduring "strategic" relations between Syria and Iran, the gap between them over reaction to the American threat was "widening." There are points of agreement between Damascus and Tehran, Hamidi explained and quoted Syrian officials as listing these: "Opposition to the military strike, concern about the emergence of a pro-Washington regime in Iraq close to their borders, opposition to a Kurdish state in northern Iraq, satisfaction with the 'containment' of President Saddam Hussein's regime, and the growing feelings about the U.S. post-Baghdad targeting." The differences were on the basis of divergent economic interests in Iraq and fear of the impact of a pro-U.S. Iraq on Israel's strategic posture.

Damascus, Hamidi wrote, was apprehensive about Tehran's professed policy of "positive neutrality" and the assertion that Tehran "will not shed tears" over Saddam. Damascus was also reacting to intelligence reports about U.S.-Iranian negotiations in Europe on methods of tacit cooperation against Iraq. Yunesi came to Damascus "to dispel this concern and discuss the common points," Hamidi wrote. According to Hamidi, Yunesi had told Bashar, "What this means is that Iran will not be a soldier in the U.S. Army and we will not stand with Saddam Hussein."

Yunesi had added that "the public positions of Syria and Iran do not mean defending and standing with Saddam but opposing the policy of power and arrogance that the United States is pursuing against the countries of the region and which will lead to a real disaster." Nevertheless, an Arab diplomatic source explained, "the Syrians have been left out of this [contacts between America and Iran] and feel vulnerable." Therefore, not to be left out, Syria would have to also moderate its opposition to the strike. The Syrian vote in support of UN Security Council Resolution 1441 should be seen in this context—as a way to further the appearance that Syria was placating the United States in order not to be maneuvered by Iran.

The reality of Iranian and Syrian cooperation was completely different. While these political maneuvers were taking place, Iran and Syria completed a major military buildup in southern and eastern Lebanon. Damascus and Tehran closely cooperated in the consolidation of both direct and deniable strike capabilities against Israel in order to provoke a major Israeli attack on Syria, thus instigating a regional war regardless of Baghdad's position.

The Iranian infrastructure included three defense lines established earlier in the summer. In June and July, Bashar ordered the acceleration of the terrorist buildup in southern Lebanon in accordance with the resolutions of the Tehran conference, including Imad Moughniyah's nomination as the local supreme commander. By the middle of July, Moughniyah's command included some 12,000 trained Shiite fighters and an arsenal of heavy weapons, including over ten thousand missiles and rockets, as well as 10,000 Palestinian fighters and between 120 and 150 al-Qaeda veterans who arrived via Pakistan and Iran. Moughniyah's forces were deployed in a series of fortifications covering an up to 15-mile-wide sector north of the Israeli-Lebanese border, with a central headquarters in an underground bunker complex under a hill in an eastern neighborhood of Sidon overlooking the Mediterranean. The new command enjoyed lavish logistical, intelligence, and financial support from Iran and Syria, including an expanded and dedicated training infrastructure in Lebanon, Syria, and Iran. Indeed, some officials considered this buildup a more urgent threat to America than that presented by Saddam.

Subsequently, HizbAllah was supplied with new types of missiles with a longer range and bigger warheads. First to arrive were several hundred long-range Iranian-manufactured 240-mm Fajr-3 rockets with a range of 25 miles and 333-mm Fajr-5 rockets with a range of 45 miles. Both missiles have a standard 220-pound warhead. These were supplemented later in the fall by the delivery of over three hundred 220-mm rockets with a range of 45 to 50 miles but smaller warheads. This was a politically important development primarily because these rockets are produced by Syrian military industries for the sole use of the Syrian armed forces. Hence, the delivery of these rockets amounted to Syria's direct involvement in any future use by HizbAllah—a first of great political significance.

In November, Damascus promised to supply HizbAllah with long-range 330-mm rockets the Syrian military industries have yet to put into production. Strategically more important were the September and October deliveries of numerous Zalzal-2 missiles to the Pasdaran contingent in southern Lebanon. Although not accurate, the 610-mm Zalzal-2 has a range of 130 miles with a standard 1,323-pound (600-kg) warhead—thus covering all of central Israel to the northern Gaza Strip. The Zalzal-2 is thus capable of easily reaching the greater Tel Aviv area. With a smaller warhead, the Zalzal-2's range can be extended to at least 200 miles—which means covering Israel's Dimona-area nuclear facilities. The Zalzal-2 missiles are hidden in underground storage bases in the Tyre and Sidon areas under Pasdaran control.

In October, immediately after their meeting with Yunesi, HizbAllah leaders and Iranian senior officials became far more audacious in their rhetoric to Israel, alluding to the new long-range weaponry. On October 20, Sheikh Mohammed Yazbek, the Lebanese representative of Iran's supreme leader, Ali Khamenei, said, "All sensitive areas of the Zionist entity are within the range of our fire." Appearing on HizbAllah's al-Manar TV two days later, Nasrallah gloated about the organization's new reach: "In 1996 . . . with Katyushas alone, the resistance was able to displace two million people and [the Israeli government] had to look for places in central Israel to settle them," he explained. "[Since] HizbAllah's missiles can now reach all population centers in Israel, where can they [the Israeli people] flee?"

By now, HizbAllah's rhetoric emphasized the organization's growing commitment to solidarity with the Palestinians, sustenance of the intifada, and total victory over Israel—that is, the destruction of Israel. HizbAllah senior commanders in southern Lebanon openly talked about a massive attack on Israel in conjunction with an American attack as an expression of "solidarity with the Iraqi people." Toward this end, a force of well over 1,000 highly trained HizbAllah elite was deployed on the border with Israel, ready to strike at a moment's notice. HizbAllah also started the deployment of rockets from storage sites in the Bekaa to forward positions near the Israeli border. As well, a large number of Syrian forces mixed with these HizbAllah formations—ensuring that any Israeli retaliation would inevitably injure Syrians. In November, Israeli senior defense officials noted that HizbAllah was "one decision away from striking out" and pushing the whole region into war involving at the very least Syria, Iran, and Iraq.

The high-profile involvement of Iranian intelligence and HizbAllah in Palestinian terrorism was of great strategic importance—exceeding by far the impact of the carnage on the Israeli public and government. The primary objective of the joint support for Palestinian terrorists was to prove to Baghdad that Tehran had its own reach into the heart of Israel and the Palestinian Authority areas—and that it did so with Arafat's blessing and active support. Indeed, all the major terrorist strikes since November 2002—from the Hebron ambush, through the bus bombing in Jerusalem, to the Israeli advance neutralization of a huge HizbAllah-type bomb in Nablus—had the fingerprints of Iran and HizbAllah on them. Although claimed by a myriad of Palestinian organizations, these operations were actually conducted by many ad hoc teams made up of Iranian-sponsored Palestinian Islamists and Syrian-sponsored Palestinian radicals supervised and controlled on-site by HizbAllah operatives long active inside the territories. (Incidentally, the cache of documents and weaponry captured by Israel in Muhammad Dahlan's old compound in Gaza provided confirmation of the prevalence of the Iranian and HizbAllah presence in the ranks of the Palestinian Authority leadership.) Thus, when Sheikh Nasrallah bragged on November 21 about the spread of "the martyrdom culture" worldwide and HizbAllah's meaningful solidarity with the Palestinians, he was referring to the organization's recent contribution to the spate of terrorism in the heart of Israel.

Although dominated from Tehran, HizbAllah's buildup was progressing in intimate cooperation with the highest authorities in Damascus. Bashar considered himself the patron and friend of Nasrallah and Hizb-Allah and was committed to empowering Nasrallah over Lebanon. Given these relations, Bashar was convinced he was in position to unilaterally ignite a regional war that would draw Iran into active participation if only because of the inevitable destruction by Israel of the Iranian expeditionary presence in Lebanon and Tehran's determination to prevent the destruction of HizbAllah. However, the mullahs could not afford to hand over such a strategic victory to Damascus or to lose their dominance over the strategic dynamics in the region. Hence, Tehran was adamant about retaining the strategic initiative. Therefore, Iran sought to avoid unnecessary clashes with the United States in order to reduce the threat of the United States taking on Iran before Iran could unleash the strategic surprise—a surge from Lebanon toward Jerusalem.

In November, Tehran's strategic calculations were firmed up, defining its best-case scenario: Saddam's collapse, but a chaotic aftermath that would prevent America from consolidating its victory and effectively governing Iraq. The key measure of success would be America's ability to establish a viable and legitimate post-Saddam regime in Baghdad; in this context, Tehran was encouraged by Karzai's enduring plight in Afghanistan. Under such circumstances, the mullahs were convinced that a larger war against Israel would force America, humiliated, out of the region. The Iranian and HizbAllah strategic priorities, including the specter of an Israeli war against Syria and Lebanon, aimed to deliver such an outcome. Subsequently, a weak Iraq, even if ostensibly unified, would serve as a venue for the Shiite corridor to the Mediterranean. Iran would then emerge as the strategic winner of the regional war and upheaval.

The other alternative—namely, a clear American victory and the establishment of a pro-U.S. government in Baghdad—was deemed a profound threat to Iran's vital interests. In November, Pasdaran commander Brig. Gen. Yahya Rahim Safavi explained that by invading Iraq, the United States sought to undermine Iran's security. "America is intending to endanger Iran's security by occupying Iraq and creating crisis and tensions in Tehran's relations with other countries of the world," he told Iranian officers. The entire Iranian defense establishment "must play a leading role in establishing enduring security in the country by boosting its power and defense readiness so that it could resist threats of America and the Zionist Israeli regime," he added.

Similarly, Deputy Interior Minister for Security and Disciplinary Affairs Ali-Asghar Ahmadi noted that "Iran is the only deterrent to the U.S. in the Middle East" and it was therefore only logical that "the U.S. also considers Iran as the main obstacle to advancing its policy against the Palestinian Intifada." Iran's main challenge would come only in the aftermath of the U.S. invasion, Ahmadi explained, and Tehran "should wait and see how the Americans treat Iran after the invasion of Iraq."

In the meantime, Tehran resolved to refrain from both provocations along the border with Iraq and any semblance of assistance to the Americans. "The border with Iraq will remain secure and calm even if the ruling regime in Baghdad collapses as a result of the anticipated U.S. campaign," Iran's defense minister, Adm. Ali Shamkhani, told a meeting of senior officers. Senior Pasdaran commanders instructed commanders of the Badr Corps that they "must not establish any cooperation with the American forces if a U.S. attack is launched against Iraq." Tehran's priorities and preferences were best defined by SCIRI leader Imam Baqir al-Hakim. He told commanders of the Badr Corps that "war on Iraq is unavoidable" because "the internal situation in Iraq and the position of the Iraqi regime are all indications of the war." Rather than help America take on Saddam's regime, al-Hakim stated, "The Iraqi opposition was ready to play a major role to fill up the political vacuum that would occur when the Iraqi regime is overthrown."

Meanwhile, preparations in Lebanon for the forthcoming crisis and war accelerated. In November, Iranian emissaries told the HizbAllah leadership that "the American war against Iraq is inevitable and its justification is ready" and that Tehran "expects the war to start between 20 and 30 January." Tehran had learned from its Western European allies and passed on to HizbAllah the information that "the United States will prevent Israel from opening a front against HizbAllah in south Lebanon before or during the military attack against Iraq. The United States believed that Israel should not take advantage of its war against Iraq to attack HizbAllah and Lebanon's vital installations." However, the Iranians had no faith in these assurances, and Tehran's working assumption was that Israel would "defy the American demand."

HizbAllah's take on the Iranian instructions was expressed in a November 27 lecture by Sheikh Nasrallah at the university breakfast in Burj al-Barajinah. Nasrallah stressed the fatefulness of the time, and the profound implications of any undertaking by the HizbAllah. "We want to defend our country. Any step forward or backward will be of a historic nature at this stage, and any effort will have fateful results," he said. Nasrallah told his audience that "what we are warning of is the possibility of the Israeli enemy attacking Lebanon and Syria concurrently with the U.S. military attack against Iraq. This possibility is getting bigger and bigger, and therefore we must be cautious." HizbAllah had no intention of remaining passive under such circumstances, and its ongoing buildup was intended to meet this challenge. "The enemy will not know the capabilities, numbers, plans, or ideas of the resistance. It will not know how far the resistance advanced and how prepared it is. These things will remain secrets," Nasrallah said. He added that the enemy "does not know any small detail about these things because it failed to penetrate any HizbAllah cadre." He stressed that the ultimate objectives of HizbAllah in confronting Israel were of a historic nature: "In the face of the new threats, we are not talking about standing fast or about obstructing the objectives of the Israeli aggression. We are talking about something much bigger and looking forward to achieving a victory greater than the victory that was scored on 24 May 2000 [the pullout of the Israeli forces from south Lebanon]. The victory we are looking forward to will have bigger and more serious strategic consequences for the existence of this entity [Israel] and for the entire Zionist project in the region," Nasrallah declared.

The next day, Tehran joined the public threats to Israel, calling for a new front to be opened against Israel so that "Zionists" would no longer feel safe anywhere in the world. "After the lightning success of the Intifada against the Zionists, more and more Muslim revolutionaries have reached the conclusion that we should open a front outside occupied Palestine that targets the security of the Zionists and their protectors," *Kayhan*'s editor Hossein Shariatmadari wrote in a front page editorial. "They should all be killed and expelled from the areas where they have expelled you." In the editorial, Shariatmadari noted that the breaking news of the terrorist attacks on Israeli targets in Kenya came after he had written his piece, and that these attacks were in agreement with his call to arms.

In late November, Saddam and his confidants determined to cooperate closely with the Islamist networks in Iraq and the Persian Gulf in order to go underground once the war began and to be able to rely on the Islamists to resurrect the anti-American jihad. Therefore, senior Iraqi intelligence officials in several Muslim countries—most notably Pakistan, Turkey, Sudan, and Algeria—reached out to local Islamist leaders known to have close ties to bin Laden's inner circle and asked them to intercede on Baghdad's behalf. In their conversations with these Islamist leaders, the Iraqis stressed that they were convinced that only the Islamists had real reach and grassroots support throughout the Middle East. The Islamists also had the motivation and tenacity to persevere in the jihad despite arduous conditions. On more practical and pragmatic terms, the officials noted, the same people who had kept Osama bin Laden and his confidants concealed and safe since September 11—that is, bin Laden's security officials—must know how to hide and shield people from American intelligence. In these conversations the Iraqi intelligence officials stressed that "there is a near consensus [among Iraq's leaders] that Iraqi President Saddam Hussein's escape of assassination at the beginning of an attack will be a landmark in the Iraqi response to a U.S. aggression." This notion was shared by Saddam's foes. A leading national opposition member told *Al-Quds al-Arabi* that "the Iraqi president's survival, as was the case with Sheikh Osama bin Laden in Afghanistan, will trigger a fierce resistance to any U.S. attack because the regime's men will continue to resist and will not lay down their arms either to show their allegiance and defend themselves and their interests or out of fear of revenge at a later stage if the U.S. aggression fails to achieve its goals."

Meanwhile, Saddam and his inner circle kept refining Iraq's "emergency plans" for confronting the invasion. A key Baath official discussed the tenets of these plans with *Al-Quds al-Arabi*. He explained that "the Iraqi regime laid down emergency plans to confront any U.S. aggression" based on three key components: The first was the deployment of the Republican Guards forces to the outskirts of the main cities, especially Baghdad, in order to confront both offensive and domestic rebellions. The second was the deployment of the Special Forces consisting of the "elite of the elite" inside Baghdad to engage in street fighting once U.S. forces arrived, and then "embark on ferocious resistance operations like those carried out in occupied Palestine" for as long as the U.S. forces remained. The third was the deployment of groups of Saddam's Fedayeen (commandos) inside Baghdad and other cities "to control the domestic situation" after the occupation and "engage in resistance actions." A senior Iraqi official opined that Iraq would "not hesitate to use all the weapons of mass destruction in its possession" in order to "defend its existence and also its reputation." He stressed that nobody should "expect us to stand with hands tied against any aggression that seeks to annihilate and remove us not only from power, but also from life."

Ultimately, both Iraqi security officials and Islamist activists anticipated a protracted war in which the United States would occupy Iraq relatively quickly and then face protracted insurgency and terrorism by both the Islamists and Saddam's diehard loyalists. The full resistance would take time to gestate, they agreed. "The overwhelming majority of the Iraqi people believes that the presence of U.S. forces on Iraqi soil will prompt the Iraqis to step up their resistance a few months after the U.S. forces enter Iraq because the Iraqis will have overcome the 'shock,' opened their eyes to the new situation, and begun to act to avenge their national dignity and sovereignty over their land," explained an Iraqi security official. Saddam and his inner circle were actively preparing to ride and exploit such popular resistance and the ensuing terrorism campaign.

Strange developments that took place in Baghdad during the Thanksgiving weekend of November gave credence to the reports about Iraq's active preparations for a protracted war. First, Saddam Hussein suddenly left Baghdad for a fortified hiding place somewhere on the outskirts of Al-Habbaniyah (50 miles northwest of Baghdad), along with Latif Nasif Jasim, Ahmad Habbushi, and elite forces from the army and the air force. Concurrently, Saddam's son and heir, Qusay, Taha Yassin Ramadan, Izzat Ibrahim al-Durri, Tariq Aziz, and Lt. Gen. Kamal Mustafa moved together to another secret location just west of Baghdad. No explanation was given for the sudden moves. According to Iranian sources, there was no contact with Saddam and his immediate entourage. Iraq was effectively controlled by Qusay and the leadership team hiding with him.

Meanwhile, Saddam Hussein's half brothers Barzan and Watban (who controlled the family money hidden in the West and maintained Saddam's emergency contacts with Western European governments) arrived in Amman from their postings in Western Europe. There, they met with emissaries of a few European governments to discuss emergency relocation of key family members and a lot of cash. These developments were noteworthy if only because the West's worst-case scenario was based on an Iraqi surprise attack on Israel while the UN weapons inspectors were still in Iraq and thus constituted a human shield protecting Iraq against the anticipated vicious Israeli retaliation. American and Western intelligence services identified the sudden evacuation of the families of the Iraqi elite and their funds as one of the most reliable indicators of an impending surprise attack.

By late November, Iraqi senior officials had begun circulating reports throughout Arab capitals about what they termed Saddam's worst-case scenario. Senior Saudi, Egyptian, and other Arab officials briefed Washington about it. The guiding principle behind this "horror scenario" was Saddam's known fear of an Israeli nuclear retaliation. According to these officials, Saddam was convinced, first, that he could evade and dodge virtually all external threats short of an Israeli nuclear strike, and second, that only the Mossad could locate him, thus enabling Israel to accurately direct the nuclear-tipped missiles aimed to get him. At the same time, Saddam concluded that there could be no compromise with the U.S.-sponsored UN inspectors because they were now accepted by the United States and therefore unlikely to adopt policy contradictory to Washington's demands. Saddam's agreement to let the UN inspectors into Iraq was merely a ploy to buy time and enable him to address his worst-case fears. Saddam's "horror scenario" would unfold as follows: The Iraqis would launch a WMD strike at Israel (ballistic missiles, air strikes, terrorists) while the UN inspectors were still in the country. Saddam believed Israel would refrain from retaliating with a nuclear strike, fearing they'd kill the inspectors. At the same time, the rest of the Arab world, as well as Iran, would be emboldened by Israel's anguish and rally behind Iraq for the decisive final onslaught on Israel, in the process recognizing Saddam Hussein as their supreme leader. All these Iraqi senior officials were convinced that Saddam would not hesitate to implement his plan the moment he decided it would save his life.

By December, hunting Iraqi weapons of mass destruction had become the singular priority of the clandestine war at the heart of the Iraqi western desert. There was a marked intensification of Special Forces operations— from the United States, United Kingdom, Israel, Jordan, and Turkey— exploring the western desert and other parts of Iraq in an effort to locate and monitor Iraqi WMD and ballistic missiles. Baghdad could not ignore these activities, for there was an increase in the number of Iraqi nuclear and other WMD scientists, some wanted by the UN for questioning, who escaped to Syria. As well, incriminating equipment and even backup weapons systems were removed from their storage sites inside Iraq and also transferred to Syria.

In Washington, there was overconfidence in U.S. ability to monitor these activities. "We are sitting on them," a senior officer assured his Israeli counterpart. The Americans were certain they'd be able to actively prevent launches and destroy weapons even if Saddam gave the order. American officials pointed to the availability of massive airpower in constant readiness for swift-reaction strikes against objects identified by Special Forces. Testing and simulations conducted by the military convinced Washington it would be possible to destroy Iraqi launchers within ten minutes of detection. This data was all the more impressive as U.S. intelligence suggested that it would take some ninety minutes for a SCUD to be removed from its concealed site and made ready for launch—thus giving ample time for the multitude of sensors and Special Forces teams to detect the missile and home devastating air strikes on it.

Meanwhile, the flow of U.S. equipment to Israel continued at a greater clip through December, and included a shipment of two Patriot batteries. These batteries first participated in joint training with the Israel Defense Forces in the Negev and were then deployed in the greater Tel Aviv area. American officials coordinated with the IDF, providing expanded security for American convoys that ran from Israel through Jordan to western Iraq. Intelligence data collected by the United States, Israel, and Jordan, including specific data about ambush exercises by the Palestinian Authority security forces and consultations among senior Palestinian commanders, left no doubt that Palestinian forces were getting ready to ambush the convoys, and Washington expected the IDF to operate resolutely against such threats. Elite American forces also arrived for intense training in Israel's own urban warfare center, studying the unique Israeli equipment being transferred to their units. U.S. Israeli intelligence-sharing sessions expanded as well.

American planes also intensified their air raids in southern Iraq—particularly the approaches to al-Amarah from the direction of Basra, a highly fortified area ground forces would have to traverse to get to Baghdad. On December 11, for example, the United States bombed upgraded SA-13s modified to intercept cruise missiles. And on December 14, American and British aircraft conducted a series of major strikes along the entire eastern axis to Baghdad—hitting military installations in al-Kut, Qalat Sukkar, and al-Amarah.

There was an escalation in Kurdistan as well. On December 4, the Islamists undertook preemptive moves against American allies. A combined force of al-Qaeda, Ansar, al-Islam, and Iraqi commando fighters attacked

Kurdish Patriotic Union (PUK) forces through the Suren Mountains to Halabja. At first the Islamists succeeded in destroying PUK's forward positions, forcing the PUK fighters away from positions overlooking access roads to Iran and Iraqi military positions. This withdrawal had an adverse impact on America's ability to monitor regional buildup on the eve of the war because ground-based systems and personnel had to be removed from topographically advantageous terrain.

Meanwhile, emergency supplies were rushed by U.S. and Turkish intelligence and Special Forces from stockpiles in Turkey. Invigorated, PUK forces launched counterattacks on December 9 and after a series of brief but fierce firefights were able to seize the hills overlooking Halabja from the Islamists. Heavy fighting continued for the next several days, with both sides sustaining many casualties. On December 18, Abu-Abdallah al-Shafi, one of the chiefs of Ansar al-Islam, was killed in the fighting in the Halabja area. His death was a major setback for the Islamists because of his skills and popularity with both the Kurds and the Arab mujahedin.

By now, Tehran had concluded that there was no way to stop the United States from attacking Iraq and that American forces would occupy Baghdad shortly afterward. There was nothing Tehran could do to save Saddam's regime. Their great challenge, therefore, would be the building of postwar Iraq as a pro-Iranian, and therefore implacably anti-American, country and society. Toward this end, on December 10—the eve of yet another U.S.-organized opposition summit in London —Tehran hosted a three-day summit of the Iraqi opposition leaders Chalabi (Iraqi National Congress), Hakim (Supreme Council for the Islamic Revolution in Iraq), Barazani (Kurdish Democratic Front), and Talabani (Kurdish Patriotic Union). The Iraqi leaders not only discussed among themselves issues pertaining to the future of Iraq, but also met with top Iranian leaders who promised support and made sure the Iraqi leaders understood Tehran's own concerns. Hashemi-Rafsanjani elucidated Iran's perception of the crisis. "America does not seek the establishment of a free and independent government in Iraq. Instead, it seeks to safeguard its and the Zionist regime's interests by installing another dictator in that country," he explained. "Everyone must pay heed that another dictator who is an American agent and dependent and an ally of Israel is not imposed on the oppressed people of that country and the region in the place of the Baathist Iraqi regime."

Tehran played a key role in the creation of the Shiite-Kurdish alliance, which was inherently anti-American although also anti-Saddam. A member of the Supreme National Security Council—Iran's highest decision-making body—noted that the leaders of the Iraqi opposition committed to "the actual implementation of a decision taken by the council at one of its recent meetings in the presence of the two leaders, [Spiritual] Guide Ali Khamenei and President Mohammad Khatami." The council resolved that because of its ethnic-national tapestry, Iraq was not suitable for the establishment of a Khomeini-style Islamic republic or any other form of "a Shiite theocratic regime." Instead, the council decided to take a pragmatic approach to the recent developments in Iraq and support any form of government that would recognize and cooperate with Iran's strategic interests, which convinced the two Kurdish leaders and Chalabi to commit to Iran's sponsorship rather than face "occupation, colonialism, and Westernization" on their own. In practical terms, Iran promised and delivered funds and weapons and even "volunteers" for any confrontation with Saddam for as long as it did not help the war effort.

The administration learned of the Tehran summit from the CIA, rather than Chalabi, Barazani, or Talabani. With the war so close and with the United States on record as supporting Chalabi, there was little the administration could do but grind its teeth in private.

In London, Chalabi, Barazani, and Talibani raised an Iranian-driven agenda as if it were their own. Most Iraqi leaders were aghast when the American representatives refused to address the idea of a federation and the structure of the interim Iraqi government. "Despite this," explained an Iraqi participant, "the 'Kurdish-Shiite Alliance' has continued to step up its demands of endorsing a federal system for Iraq to give the Kurds autonomy, with broad powers, and also end the 'discrimination' against Shiites."

Following Tehran's recommendations, the opposition leaders insisted on a quick national election. Essentially, given Iraq's demographic composition, any national-level election system would immediately empower the pro-Iranian Shiites and Kurds at the expense of the Westernized Sunni and Shiite urban population. Having committed to "establishing democracy" in post-Saddam Iraq, there was precious little Washington could do against such a demand.

The North Korean issue took center stage in the Middle East crisis on December 11, when Spanish and American Navy ships intercepted an unmarked ship in the Arabian Sea not far from Yemen. The vessel had sailed from North Korea, ostensibly delivering cement bags. A search of the ship by Navy SEALs netted twelve NK-SCUD-C and three NK-SCUD-D ballistic missiles, as well as eighty-five tanks of chemicals—all concealed under the cement bags. The ship's crew knew nothing about the missiles or their ship's ultimate destination, beyond a forthcoming stop in Yemen. Multiple-source intelligence, however, knew that the missiles and the chemicals were on their way to Iraq. They were to be unloaded in Yemen, put on an Egyptian ship, unlikely to be stopped by the U.S. Navy, and taken to a Syrian port via the Suez Canal. From there, the missiles and chemicals would have been transported to Iraq by trucks.

The moment the capture of the ship was announced, Pyongyang passed an ultimatum via Beijing and Tokyo. Stripped of its diplomatic niceties, the North Korean ultimatum told the United States that it must "release the boat or we launch a war against South Korea, not excluding the use of nuclear weapons." Both Beijing and Tokyo notified Washington that they were taking the ultimatum very seriously and urged Washington to expedite dealing with Pyongyang. Because the ultimatum had no deadline, the administration decided it could ignore it. Instead, Washington rushed to embrace the Yemeni claim that "the [missile] shipment is part of contracts signed some time ago," and their "guarantees" that Yemen would not purchase North Korean ballistic missiles again. The boat was let go, and America did not have to respond directly to the ultimatum. (Incidentally, in 2003, when Muammar al-Qadhafi opened his country's ballistic missile and WMD stockpiles for British and American inspections as part of Libya's effort at rapprochement, the inspectors discovered the "Yemenite" NK-SCUD-Cs and NK-SCUD-Ds. These missiles had been smuggled out of Yemen in accordance with the original plan, except that from Egypt they were taken to Libya instead of their original destination—Iraq.)

Pyongyang was pleased to see just how afraid Beijing and Tokyo were of a North Korean nuclear strike. Yemen got to keep the missiles, and Iraq still paid for them. The Bush administration had one less crisis to contend with. The White House had been inclined to comply with the North Korean ultimatum from the very beginning because the United States did not want any distraction from Iraq. The Pentagon briefed the White House that brave rhetoric notwithstanding, America was incapable of fighting in Iraq and in Korea simultaneously with the forces at hand. It would take a major mobilization—perhaps even restoring the draft—and crash procurement and production programs before the United States was ready, the White House was told. Meanwhile, intelligence experts urged the White House not to release the boat and to issue Pyongyang a counterultimatum—arguing that a demonstration of weakness, even if motivated by pragmatism, would be exploited by North Korea, Iran, and Iraq, as well as scare Tokyo and Seoul regarding America's resolve and commitment. They were overruled. Pyongyang kept raising the ante, and America was increasingly isolated and on the defensive in its Far East politics.

Indeed, on December 13, Iran announced that it had made major strides toward the development of nuclear weapons. The announcement was aimed at deterring American intervention—using both Pyongyang-style nuclear brinkmanship and Russian diplomatic support.

Alarmed by criticism from the Arab world declaring that the United States was intentionally sabotaging the possibility of a negotiated settlement with Saddam, Bush asked Blair to attempt a go-around maneuver. Toward that end, Bashar al-Assad was invited on December 17 to a special visit at 10 Downing Street. There, he was presented by the British with the particulars of a political initiative to resolve the Iraqi crisis. This was the final American ultimatum and Saddam's last chance to avert a major war, Bashar was told.

First, Saddam must appear in public, acknowledge that he had lied about Iraq's weapons of mass destruction, provide details about the programs and arsenals, and then announce a framework for handing these over to the UN by January 2003. In return, the United States committed to stopping all preparations for war the moment Saddam showed up on TV. Furthermore, the United States guaranteed it would not use Saddam's public admission as an excuse for attacking him and Iraq. The United States would also provide guarantees for the handing over of power from Saddam to a government acceptable to Washington and would guarantee Saddam's safe passage into exile—but only after Iraqi WMD were handed over to the United Nations.

As a gesture of goodwill, Blair said, the United States would freeze the deployment of forces to the Persian Gulf until after January 1, giving Baghdad a period of time to reflect and comply. At the same time, Blair stressed, there would be no negotiations over the ultimatum and its conditions. Either Saddam started implementing or war began. The United States and the United Kingdom would resume moving forces to the region the moment they concluded that Saddam had no intention of complying with this latest offer—at which point war would be irreversible. Significantly, the United States offered no guarantees about prohibiting the international court or the UN from going after Saddam in the future.

Bashar returned from London on the night of December 21–22, and immediately called Saddam. They met the next night near the border, in the al-Qaim region. At the meeting, Bashar ridiculed the American and British offer—telling Saddam he was convinced that this was a trap. In so doing, Bashar confirmed Saddam's own reading of the situation. Both leaders concluded that this was a conspiracy designed to first humiliate Saddam in front of the entire Arab world and then, when he was no longer a revered leader, lure him into an exile area where he could be snatched by American and British agents and brought to The Hague. The two leaders also discussed the transfer and deployment of additional Iraqi resources and weapons to safe havens in Syria. War was inevitable and quite imminent, Bashar and Saddam concluded.

Still, a few days later, several Arab states, led by Qatar, offered Saddam their services in persuading the United States to cancel the attack on Iraq in return for his abdication and safe exile. Iraq wondered initially about guarantees from Washington that Saddam would not be arrested and brought to trial in The Hague. The Bush administration ridiculed the idea of such guarantees when the Qataris and Kuwaitis raised the issue with senior officials, and Baghdad cut all contacts. Saddam had convinced many that the forthcoming war was indeed the revenge of the Bush family, to be waged ruthlessly regardless of the political compromises that might come up. Senior Arab diplomats involved in high-level discussions with the United States noted that their American counterparts stuck to their positions regardless of the dire consequences for the Arab world—namely, an Islamist upsurge—and the immense threat faced by the pro-U.S. Saudis, Egyptians, and Jordanians.

Still, Saddam's confidants began to seek a suitable site near Tripoli, Libya, to build and/or refurbish a neighborhood as an exile site for the Iraqi elite. The luxury items sought ranged from swimming pools to elaborate protection. Work started in December, and the region became commonly known as "Saddam City." In late December, once the Qatari initiative failed, the work on "Saddam City" accelerated, with at least five major houses or palaces virtually ready by the year's end, as were half a dozen support buildings. By then, the Libyans had placed air defense units and heavy guard forces around the entire compound.

*   *   *

The actions of both Iraq and the United States now clearly indicated their anticipation of an imminent eruption of hostilities. Baghdad moved to ruthlessly stifle the UN weapons inspections. Iraqi opposition sources reported that Iraq executed a few scientists and technicians the UN wanted to interrogate and who seemed willing to go overseas with their families. The rumors about the disappearance and fate of these scientists immediately served as a lesson to all concerned.

Nevertheless, American and British intelligence, working in cooperation with the Jordanians, tried to exploit new cracks in Iraqi society. Special Forces and CIA operatives crossed into southern Iraq carrying millions of dollars in cash with which to bribe tribal chiefs to rebel against Saddam once the war started. The operation was based on the CIA's perceived success in Afghanistan. At the recommendations of the British, the Jordanians, and the Saudis, the CIA approached the leaders of Sunni Arab tribes traditionally threatened by the ascent of the Shiites. These tribes are close by blood and tradition to the Saudis. Hence, the CIA hoped they would change sides at the right moment. Moreover, Saddam had maintained complex relations with the key sheikhs—showering them with bribes, gifts, and honors on one hand, but also sending security forces to clash with the tribal forces every now and then to remind them that Baghdad was ultimately in charge. Thus, in 1999 members of the al Dulaimi tribe revolted in northwest Iraq after suppression by the security services, and in 2001 members of the Bani Hassan tribe clashed with the security services in southern Iraq. Ultimately, the sheikhs took the CIA's money but gave only vague assurances about future cooperation with the United States.

The growing assertiveness of the Iraqi armed forces, particularly the air force, was one of the main reasons for Israel's growing apprehension. With the flow of spare parts via Syria growing during the fall of 2002, the Iraqis were able to make about 80 percent of their air force combat-ready. There was a corresponding increase in the number and frequency of their flight trainings. By winter, the Iraqis began daring the American and British aircraft in the air—usually by dashing deep into the no-fly zones and even into northern Saudi Arabia. On December 23, an Iraqi fighter chased and shot down a Predator unmanned airborne vehicle (UAV) over southern Iraq.

Meanwhile, Israel's continued presence in western Iraq alarmed the White House, which feared that Jerusalem might after all launch its own

SCUD-hunting operations once hostilities commenced. Senior U.S. officials told Mofaz that Washington had "decided that Israel will not be involved in the war against Iraq" even if Israel were to be attacked. "They [the United States] are willing to give us all the necessary aid," Mofaz said, putting on a brave face. "I think the state of Israel is better prepared than it was in the past in the face of threats to the safety of the state of Israel if and when there will be an attack against Israel and if Iraq will respond with a missile attack against the state of Israel." In return, America promised to postpone the formal submission of the "Road Map" that articulated the establishment of an independent Palestinian state under Arafat and in disregard of some of Israel's most vital security considerations.

As December came to a close, Jerusalem and Washington continued to disagree over the prospect of an Iraqi ballistic missile attack. There emerged a wide gap in the intelligence reading and interpretation of the data regarding Saddam's intentions and capabilities. At the core of the dispute was assessment of the likelihood of Saddam's "horror scenario" and Israel's reaction. Jerusalem insisted that in the case of an Iraqi preemptive strike on Israel, particularly if defined as Iraqi intervention on behalf of the Palestinians, Israel would have to retaliate immediately or face unacceptable erosion to its deterrence posture. The United States insisted that it was very unlikely Saddam would attack Israel, and even if he did, American forces would immediately strike out so that there was no need for Israel to retaliate at all. U.S. officials warned the Israelis that any retaliation—even in response to an Iraqi intervention in the Israeli-Palestinian conflict—"would derail the entire effort to destroy the Saddam regime."

At the same time, also at the urging of Washington, Israel accelerated the preparations for war, particularly on issues of homeland security and civil defense. The latest American intelligence analysis anticipated that Iraq would launch ballistic missiles at Israel the moment hostilities commenced. The experience of the Israeli Special Forces in western Iraq had further eroded Jerusalem's confidence in America's ability to locate and swiftly destroy all missiles aimed at Israel. This realization prompted greater apprehension in Jerusalem and quiet talks in the kitchenette about potential operations—both retaliatory and preventive. Sharon decided that the Iraqi threats to Israel constituted far greater risks than American retribution for unilateral Israeli actions. Mofaz rushed to Washington to air Israel's concerns and better coordinate with the United States. Instead, he was met by additional demands for Israeli "responsible behavior." Essentially, Mofaz was told, the Bush administration expected Israel to undertake additional risks by completely foreswearing any preemptive or retaliatory act against Iraq regardless of casualties and damage. The administration stressed that Israeli sacrifices were crucial in order not to complicate the war.

Undaunted, Sharon publicly acknowledged the existence of the Iraqi threat but insisted that Israel had the means to overcome it. Sharon sent a message to Washington reiterating Mofaz's message. Israel might be reluctant to retaliate, and in cases of little or no damage would even refrain from retaliating, but if the Iraqis crossed a certain red line, Israel would strike out. Quietly, the IDF high command refreshed the "Iraq File"—that is, the contingency plans for retaliation against Iraq, the lists of target updates, as well as modalities for air strikes and raids by Special Forces. Relevant exercises of air force and ground forces were accelerated. Aware of Jerusalem's growing anxieties, the Pentagon briefed the IDF that there would be no move before the January UN report. America would embark on a series of swift and resolute moves soon afterward, the IDF was told. Israeli military intelligence suggested that the kitchenette operate on a working assumption that the war would be launched in early February, immediately after the Israeli elections scheduled for January 28, 2003.

CENTCOM used the last days of 2002 to refresh its contingency plans, responding to growing pressure from the White House and the secretary of defense to shorten the anticipated duration of the war and reduce the size of the ground forces involved. The politicians wanted the war to be over within a few days, and the new panacea, CENTCOM was told, was a large number of special and light forces operating from numerous bases in Turkey, overflying Kurdistan—to be dealt with by Kurdish forces assisted by American special operations units and airpower—and landing on the northern approaches to Baghdad. This deep surge would thus isolate Saddam and the Iraqi elite from their safe havens and friendly population base in the Tikrit area.

Toward this end, the United States wanted access to four air bases—Incirlik, Diabkir, Batram, and Van—and a total of seven land force bases, if the use of the heavy 4th Infantry Division—now earmarked for a consolidating siege on Baghdad from the north—was taken into consideration. The United States planned to airlift combat helicopters from Turkey to the forward strips already in Iraqi Kurdistan in order to sustain the swift surge southward. Meanwhile, American and British assault forces would surge from Kuwait in the south and reach Baghdad in a wide pincer move from the southwest and southeast, thus overwhelming the Iraqi defenders and avoiding a clash with the large Iraqi forces arrayed to block the invasion from the south. These plans assumed that Iraq would be in a state of shock, perhaps decapitated, and that the national communications would be disrupted by the opening "shock and awe" air and cruise missile strikes.

Ankara was most worried by these developments because of, first, the American plans for Iraqi Kurdistan, which completely disregarded past promises to Ankara that there would be no independent or even Kosovo-style autonomous Kurdish entity in post-Saddam northern Iraq, and second, America's lack of interest in Iraqi activities in Syria, still the preeminent sponsor of anti-Turkish Kurdish terrorism. Also, there was growing apprehension in Ankara because of intelligence data acquired by both Ankara and Jerusalem (from separate sources) that Saddam had instructed his forces to immediately launch strikes on the Gulf States and Israel in case of war. Ankara considered that the possible emergence of a viable Iran-Iraq-Syria axis in the aftermath of such a war would constitute a major setback to Turkey's vital strategic interests. Moreover, Syria promised to help in this endeavor, which also meant a potential threat to Turkey's stability, given Syrian sponsorship of Kurdish and Islamist terrorism. Ankara wanted to consult with Jerusalem over how to avert the regional flare-up.

On December 24, IDF Chief of Staff Bogy Yaalon and a small delegation of senior officers traveled to Turkey for a quick consultation with Hilimi Ozkok and the high command on joint contingency plans. High on their agenda were the coordination of bilateral, mutual air defense, air operations, and naval operations in the Mediterranean. Special attention was paid to a possible regional flare-up instigated by Syria and HizbAllah. The United States was brought into these arrangements only later.

Ankara was increasingly panicked about the prospect of grand strategic setbacks if America implemented its plans for Iraqi Kurdistan. Hence, Turkish intelligence initiated contacts with both prominent Kurdish leaders—Talabani and Barazani—in order to discuss the preemptive deployment of Turkish forces into northern Iraq. The Turkish officials assured the skeptical Kurdish leaders that Ankara would like Kurdish consent for this deployment. The Turks offered a plan according to which some 70,000 Turkish troops from the 2nd and 3rd Corps would enter Iraq and seize Mosul and Kirkuk and a few strategic sites. Turkey would then recognize and support a Kosovo-style "wide autonomy"—de facto independence—of the Kurds in their current enclave plus small expansions to the south and west. Although the oil fields would be controlled by the Turkish-sponsored Turkman, the Kurds would be assured their fair share of income. Finally, Turkey would also sponsor the establishment of a Turkman "wide autonomy" in the areas claimed by the Turkman. Turkey, the United States, and Europe would all guarantee the Kurdish autonomy and oil income, Ankara stressed.

The Turks added an explanation and warning—namely, that the Kurds would not receive the same level of independence and oil revenue in the context of the "new Iraq" the United States planned to establish. Moreover, if Ankara felt threatened by developments in Kurdistan, Turkey would not hesitate to invade northern Iraq and crush everybody standing in its way. Then, Turkey would consider itself released from abiding by the current generous offers. Both Talabani and Barazani asked for some time to further study the Turkish offer. However, having learned about the Turkish offer, Washington scared the Kurds into ignoring it but still refused to allay the Turkish fears. Washington also pressured Israel into ignoring its understandings with Turkey regarding joint military strategy and, should the need arise, even joint military operations, thus sending Ankara further into the corner.

Baghdad was taking these latest developments very seriously and, between December 25 and 27, deployed Republican Guards, medium-range ballistic missiles (mainly Sumud-2), and other elite units to the area where the borders of Syria, Iraq, and Jordan met and to the southwestern border with Saudi Arabia east of the border with Jordan. From both deployment areas, the Iraqis could strike at both Israel and Saudi Arabia. Moreover, the Iraqi Air Force completed the redeployment of almost 120 military planes—including some of Iraq's most modern fighters—to Syria, a transfer that took a few weeks to complete clandestinely. The Iraqi planes were dispersed between five Syrian military air bases next to the Iraqi-Syrian border, two Syrian military air bases near the Turkish-Syrian border, and two Syrian military air bases in the Damascus suburbs where ten to fifteen fighters were kept as Iraq's contribution to the defense of Damascus. These aircraft arrived with their pilots, ground crews, spares, and weaponry. The deployment was considered a temporary measure to protect the Iraqi Air Force from preemptive strikes until conditions were ripe for committing it to war against either Israel or America. The Iraqis demonstrated a blatant disregard for American activities in Kuwait and the other Gulf States, even though heavy bombing of Iraqi facilities in southern Iraq was resumed, ostensibly in retaliation for the shooting down of the Predator.

In December, Israeli intelligence learned about intensified preparations by Iraqi intelligence—specifically Unit 999—to prepare and deploy detachments of the Palestinian Liberation Front and the ALF back to the territories in order to carry out preemptive and preventive operations on the eve of the war. This program was personally supervised by Abu-al-Abbas and his deputy Bassam al-Ashkar (the commander of the attack against the cruise ship *Achille Lauro*). They were working closely with Tirawi in order to capitalize on the latest intelligence from Israel and Jordan in preparing specialized and superlethal operations. Taha Yassin Ramadan still oversaw the flow of millions of euros and dollars to the territories in order to recruit resources, build support, and otherwise prepare for the megastrikes. Working in close coordination, Abu-al-Abbas and Tirawi were in charge of implementing Iraqi plans in the West Bank.

Meanwhile, the entire spectrum of Palestinian political parties began preparations for a wide scope of actions—from demonstrations to terrorism—once the United States attacked Iraq and Iraqi missiles started falling on Israel. These activities would be run by an ad hoc leadership—called the Palestinian Popular Support Committees—comprising senior commanders of the Fatah and al-Aqsa Martyrs' Brigades, HAMAS, Islamic Jihad, and Iraq's ALF/PLF. Initial statements and leaflets attributed to the committees had strong Islamist/jihadist terminology and virulent anti-American and anti-Israeli rhetoric. The first public show of force by the committees took place on December 27 during a rally organized in Gaza by HAMAS activists but attended by all. American flags were burned in the rally, and each speaker urged Saddam to destroy Israel and the United States.

On December 30, Abu-al-Abbas arrived in Cairo to join the negotiations between Fatah, HAMAS, and Islamic Jihad, ostensibly on conditions for the resumption of the peace process. In reality, they were discussing a major provocation in conjunction with the war. On the night of December 30, the IDF attempted but failed to capture a major emissary from either HizbAllah or al-Qaeda with instructions for upcoming operations from the Moughniyah–bin Laden headquarters in Lebanon.

Thus, by the end of 2002, the United States was rushing to complete the preparations for war and committing to the deployment of additional forces to the Middle East. In Israel, Mofaz and the high command visited the Hatzerim air base—home of Israel's F-151 long-range strike aircraft—to discuss the specifics of the Israeli Air Force's operational plans for retaliatory strikes into the heart of Iraq. "The air force is arrayed better than ever before—both offensively and defensively," Mofaz stated at the end of the briefing.

5
END RUN

By early 2003, the United States was desperately trying to wiggle itself out of the quagmire of UN Security Council politics and the UN weapon inspections in Iraq, as well as the ensuing conflicts with numerous European countries—mainly France, Germany, and Russia—over the quintessence of the Bush administration's Iraq policy. Yet it was clear to all—friends and foes alike—that the White House had already resolved to go to war. All that remained was to determine the proper date and circumstances for the hostilities to commence.

On January 1, America started mobilizing nearly 250,000 soldiers, bringing heavy ground force units into position to spearhead assaults into Iraq. Saddam knew that the ultimatum delivered via Bashar was no longer valid, and the United States was gearing up for war. On January 3, President Bush traveled to Fort Hood, Texas, for a formal send-off of the 3rd Infantry Division. "You'll be fighting not to conquer anybody but to liberate people," an emotional Bush told the troops. "Wherever you serve or wherever you may be sent, you can know that America is grateful and your commander in chief is confident in your abilities and proud of your service . . . I also know without a doubt that every order I give will be carried out with skill and unselfish courage," he added. "We know the challenges and the dangers we face. Yet this generation of Americans is ready. We accept the burden of leadership. We act in the cause of peace and freedom and in that cause we will prevail."

At the same time, Israel and the United States began their emergency deployment of Patriot batteries all over Israel. At first the systems were deployed in the southern parts of the Negev in anticipation of an Iraqi air strike from the south, but aware of intense Iraqi activities in the southwestern desert, Israeli Air Force fighters also conducted long-range patrols above the Red Sea—first only at night, but within a few days, around the clock. Israel also completed the operational deployment of its antimissile Arrow batteries. On January 5, the Israeli Air Force conducted a major test of its first Arrow operational battery. The test included the simultaneous handling of four different targets—incoming ballistic missiles—by the quick-succession launches of Arrow missiles to intercept them. In the exercise, Israel launched one operational missile that intercepted a target missile, and three training missiles that flew in the direction of simulated targets. The exercise proved a great success. Israel's leaders were visibly relieved.

One reason for the leaders' concerns was the new intelligence assessment they'd just received. On January 2, Israeli military intelligence told the cabinet that Iraq had four to six mobile launchers and twenty to sixty SCUD-type SSMs in operational status, an arsenal large enough to cause major damage and debilitating casualties in Israel's densely populated coastal plains. However, the briefer opined, on the basis of the most recent consultations with the Americans, the real SSM danger would last "only a few days" because by then Baghdad would have been encircled and Iraqi communications collapsed.

The cabinet was also offered reassurance on the question of lone suicide strikes by Iraqi aircraft. While Israel has a multiple-layered air defense, America had promised that any such aircraft would have to get past U.S. Air Force fighters from Saudi bases and then U.S. Navy fighters from a carrier in the Red Sea before there was a need for interception by the Israeli Air Force. Nevertheless, the Israeli intelligence experts were apprehensive, and so briefed the cabinet, considering that the Americans were too optimistic regarding the situation in Iraq. "Anybody who thinks that the Americans are facing a short and sweet stroll in Iraq is bound to face a nasty surprise," opined a senior defense official.

There was no need to remind the cabinet of the ever-present threat of a Palestinian provocation aimed at igniting a regional war. On January 5, two martyr bombers blew themselves up in southern Tel Aviv, killing 22 and wounding 115. It was a joint operation of the Fatah's al-Aqsa Martyrs Brigade and Islamic Jihad. The operatives came from Nablus—one of the centers of the Abbas/Tirawi forces. The Bush administration immediately claimed that the attack was a desperate effort to derail the peace process and that Bush was determined to persevere on course. Quietly Washington issued stern warnings to Jerusalem not to do anything to provoke escalation and spoil Bush's war plans. Indeed, the Israeli reaction was lukewarm—a few helicopter raids on largely empty buildings in the Gaza Strip. Despite a public outcry for revenge, Sharon came out of a kitchenette meeting with senior political sources stating that "there would not be far-reaching moves" by Israel given the unique strategic posture in the region. Jerusalem assured Washington that Israel would only undertake measures directly related to the bombing.

Throughout, there was an increase in the number of American officers and senior NCOs visiting Israel and following IDF units in the territories to better understand the Israeli tactics for urban warfare—particularly the combined use of tanks, helicopters, UAVs, and elite forces. The visitors also closely studied the IDF's siege of Arafat in the *Muqataah* just in case it would be impossible to seize Saddam Hussein and the United States had to besiege a presidential compound in Baghdad or Tikrit. In return for Israel's comprehensive military assistance and cooperation, as well as Jerusalem's self-restraint vis-à-vis the Palestinians, Bush and Sharon expanded their strategic dialogue, particularly on the nature of the postwar Middle East, the role of Israel, and the extent of Palestinian independence. Although the White House seemed forthcoming to many of the Israeli perceptions, Bush ultimately remained noncommittal about the extent of his administration's support for Israel's positions and concerns. For Sharon—who was at the time in the last sprint of the election campaign scheduled to end on January 28, the absence of immediate and embarrassing American pressure was a satisfactory return for Israel's self-restraint.

Still, the intelligence indicators of an Iraq-inspired spectacular terrorist strike against Israel kept mounting. In January, for example, Palestinian security forces in Jericho were observed preparing remote-controlled model aircraft (purchased with European Union humanitarian funds) as flying bombs and flying dispensers of biological weapons. The expertise came from Iraqi intelligence, which had been deploying such weapons on various cargo ships and tankers for use against coastal areas of Western Europe and the American Atlantic coast since the late 1990s. This was not a negligible threat, as, depending on the quality of the spur—the type of disease and the fineness of the powder—and climate conditions, a single UAV could inflict anywhere from thousands to hundreds of thousands of civilian casualties.

Israeli intelligence learned, and so reported to the cabinet, that Tirawi called Jericho from Ramallah to inquire about the progress on behalf of Arafat. Meanwhile, the major U.S.-Israeli air defense exercise in the Negev continued, with both armed forces learning how to smooth close cooperation and coordination between their respective Patriot batteries, as well as the Israeli Arrow system. By now, Israel had completed the operational deployment of a second battery of Arrows about midway between Tel Aviv and Haifa.

Meanwhile, the United States increased its bombing of Iraqi military installations. The first objective was to destroy the antiaircraft batteries and radar in southern Iraq near the Kuwaiti border before the war formally began. In the second week of January, special attention was paid to command and radar installations near al-Amarah. The United States once again bombed Iraqi antiship missile launchers near the Persian Gulf because they constituted a threat to the naval buildup, and also attacked four communications stations deep inside Iraq in an effort to paralyze the country's overall command and control system. By now, some 100 Special Forces and 50 CIA operatives were operating all over Iraq. A small number of Jordanian, British, and Australian Special Forces also participated in these operations. They maintained real-time observation of the oil fields and a host of strategic objectives they were determined to either destroy or preserve in the opening phase of the war. Special Forces were also trying to locate SCUD launchers. As the bombing raids got closer to Baghdad, Special Forces used laser designators to illuminate targets for American aircraft. Another major goal of these operations was funneling and supporting spies in the Baghdad area, who would both watch Iraqi military movements and sustain contacts with supportive Iraqis.

America's Arab allies were increasingly apprehensive about the rolling undeclared war. Kuwait, the primary site of the buildup, repeatedly questioned American preparations for a post-Saddam regime. Kuwaiti officials complained that they were being kept away from American discussions with the Iraqi opposition even though the character of any regime in Baghdad would have a major impact on Kuwait's own stability. Kuwait especially wanted Washington's assurances that any post-Saddam ruler would pledge to end Iraq's territorial claims against Kuwait—but came away thwarted. Moreover, the seemingly preeminent role accorded by the American negotiators to both Shiite leaders and former Iraqi senior officers alarmed the entire Arabian Peninsula—long the target of Shiite subversion and Baathist conspiracies. Hence, Riyadh kept pressuring Washington to let the Saudis convince Saddam to find a way out of the crisis and still avoid war at the last moment. Riyadh was convinced that Saddam would ultimately accept voluntary exile rather than face the destruction of his regime and Iraq. Qatar joined Saudi Arabia in urging the

Bush administration to give Arab politics a chance. Washington, they were told, now believed that all political options had already been exhausted. It was time for war. "Among Arab leaders there's the feeling that the United States wants Saddam's head, not the disarming from weapons of mass destruction," opined a senior Arab official.

Baghdad, meanwhile, remained defiant. On January 6, Iraq's Armed Forces Day, Saddam held key meetings commemorating the day, stressing the importance of the commanders and fighters of the popular forces earmarked for fighting the United States in case of an invasion, particularly the al-Quds Forces. The delegation of senior officers was composed of Qusay Saddam Hussein in his capacity as supervisor of the Republican Guard, Staff Gen. Abd-al-Jabbar Shanshal (minister of state for military affairs), Staff Gen. Sultan Hashim Ahmad (minister of defense), and Staff Gen. Iyad Futayyih al-Rawi (chief of staff of the al-Quds Forces). This meant that the al-Quds Forces—the civilian volunteers earmarked to die as human shields in the defense of Iraq's cities and the forces slated to attack Israel—were elevated above such elite services as the air force and the missile forces. In the main reception, Saddam received fighter commanders and staff officers of the Republican Guard, al-Quds Forces, and Saddam's Fedayeen.

The main editorial in *Babil*—Uday's newspaper—carried an article by Dr. Abd-al-Razzaq al-Dulaymi—Uday's pen name—titled "The Iraqi Army Is the Army of Palestine and Pan-Arabism." The article stressed the central role played by the Iraqi Army in all the Arab wars against Israel, rather than the war with Iran and the Gulf War. Building on the heritage of "our army's epics in defense of the Arab nation and in defense of its central issue Palestine in the 1948 war of liberation," the editorial stressed, "the Iraqi Army looks forward to the day when it will take its revenge on the evil Zionists and enter the Holy Mosque as our forefathers entered it as liberators [during Israel's War of Independence in 1948]." The article noted Iraq's participation in all the Arab-Israeli wars and clashes in which the Syrian and Jordanian fronts—Iraq's gateway to the Israeli frontlines—were active. The piece concluded by hailing the army's role in confronting "the neobarbarism that is led by the forces of evil" (the United States and the United Kingdom) whose sole purpose was "to support the Zionist entity which has always considered the brave leadership of Iraq and its victorious army as a source of real danger to its aggressive plans. How else could it be since the Iraqi Army is the army of Palestine, Arabism, and Islam." Baghdad's preoccupation with Israel on the eve of a fateful war with the

United States was most significant because it reflected the mood of Saddam and his inner circle.

The Palestinians warmed to the Iraqi incitement, and even Islamist HAMAS issued a call to establish a pan-Arab army of martyrs to confront America and defend Baghdad. The call was by HAMAS leader Abdul Aziz al-Rantisi, and constituted the first major Islamist analysis of the war. HAMAS stressed that the challenge was confronting the buildup of "Crusader forces" on Muslim soil rather than saving the Iraqi regime. On the contrary, HAMAS criticized Baghdad's failure to adopt Muslim ways and its attempt to rely on as diverse a group as the Arab states even though "the Arabs are helpless right now, and they think that the smartest thing for them to do is surrender," as well as on Russia, France, and China, which not only "cannot help Iraq" but actually "prefer their national interests to Iraq's interest."

The key to Iraq's victory, Rantisi argued, lay in the profound difference between the Muslims and the West where "the enemies of Iraq crave life, while Muslims crave martyrdom. The martyrdom operations that shock can ensure that horror is sowed in the [enemies'] hearts and horror is one of the causes of defeat." To defeat the United States, the Muslim world must "establish thousands of squads of martyrs, in a secret apparatus, who, from now, have at their disposal the capability, as well as thousands of sophisticated explosive belts with powerful explosives, to cause great damage."

Rantisi urged Baghdad to closely cooperate with the various Islamist jihadist organizations and train and support their fighters so that they could better contribute to the war against the West. He urged the Iraqis to "open your gates to the mujahedin. . . . The mujahedin must advance from everywhere to defend the land of Iraq. Had we not been in battle against the [Israelis] in Palestine, our people in Palestine would be the first to come to the aid of our people in Iraq," Rantisi stated.

Emboldened by the mounting opposition to the war, Saddam revived his political dealings with Arab leaders—most notably Mubarak. Around January 10, Baghdad notified Cairo of Saddam's agreement to send a senior envoy to discuss an Arab plan to prevent the war that included his going into exile. On January 14, Saddam sent Ali Hassan al-Majid, a confidant and the commander of Iraq's southern front, as an envoy to Cairo. Baghdad tried to imply that it considered the Arab plan a reliable measure for preventing—at the very least postponing—the offensive. The public message from Baghdad was contradictory, though. "Saddam Hussein will never leave his country, but will stay there until the last Iraqi shot is fired," Tariq Aziz told the BBC. "The danger will be greater for Iraq if the president leaves."

Arab officials later noted that subsequent Iraqi messages clarified that Ali Hassan's mandate would only cover "internal relocation." However, a few days later, on January 19, Baghdad informed Cairo that Ali Hassan would not be arriving after all, even though he had been given permission by Saddam to discuss "personal issues" with Mubarak. Instead, Mubarak sent a midlevel diplomat to Baghdad with a message of regret blaming America for the failure of his initiative. "The United States refused to guarantee that Saddam would not be arrested for war crimes once he enters exile," lamented an Egyptian senior diplomat, "[even though] publicly, the United States encouraged efforts to convince Saddam to go into exile."

Undaunted, Arab leaders launched a new cycle of intense political maneuvering, in both the Arab world and the West, intended to prevent the war. Heads of state and senior officials stressed to Washington that their objective was not saving Saddam. The Arab leaders were desperate to prevent both the rise of a Shiite Islamic republic in Iraq and an upsurge of Islamist and jihadist subversion and terrorism throughout the Arab world in the aftermath of the occupation of Baghdad. A personal emissary of Saddam shuttled between Cairo and Riyadh, providing assurances of Iraqi cooperation with the Arabs. However, Saddam's adamant refusal to step down and leave Iraq prevented the Arab leaders from making any tangible progress. The situation was further complicated when Iraqi emissaries began delivering veiled threats that Saddam would ignite the region in case of war—taking everybody down with him.

On January 17—the anniversary of the Mother of All Battles, which Iraq celebrated by reasserting its unyielding hostility toward and defiance of the United States—Saddam delivered a militant Islamist speech, vowing to defeat the Americans at the gates of Baghdad the same way previous invaders of Mesopotamia had been defeated. "Everyone who tries to climb over [Baghdad's] walls . . . will fail in his attempt," Saddam declared. He urged all Iraqis to "let your guns wait in ambush" for the enemy while holding fast to "the banner of God the Greatest"—a reference to both the traditional banner of jihad and Iraq's national flag. "The people of Baghdad have resolved to compel the Mongols of this age to commit suicide on its walls," Saddam said. He urged all Iraqis to rise to the challenge because "our enemy has mustered a great force against you," but, Saddam stressed, Iraqis should have "no fear of them" because of their faith in the triumph of Islam. Saddam added that the Iraqi military, people, and leadership were all "fully mobilized" to fight American aggression so that any attackers would be "defeated at the gates of Baghdad."

Over the next couple of days, Saddam had several key meetings with members of his high command. He expressed confidence in Iraq's ability to triumph and inflict extremely heavy casualties. Saddam attributed his confidence to newly acquired weapon systems but did not identify them further.

The U.S.-Turkish crisis kept escalating. In late December and early January, the Turkish military completed a new line of fortifications along the Iraqi border in order to protect the military buildup. Large quantities of equipment and supplies, including kits to protect against chemical and biological weapons, were transported to the Turkish troops on both sides of the border. Alarmed by the pace of Turkish preparations, the Bush administration intensified its pressure on Ankara to agree to the deployment of American troops, warning the Turks against any further delay in meeting this demand.

In response, Turkey put its foot down and refused to play a central role in the war. Essentially, in a few days Ankara reversed almost two years of U.S.-Turkish coordination and planning. Ankara resolved that Turkish forces would not open a second front in the north, thus reversing the Bush administration's anticipation of a large Turkish expeditionary force overwhelming the Iraqi forces and facilitating the swift race of U.S. units to Tikrit and Baghdad without having to fight their way into central Iraq. Moreover, Turkey would not permit U.S. aircraft and combat units to operate from bases in Turkey against Iraq. Ankara also established strict conditions for the passage of American forces through Turkish territory—including giving Turkey control over the cities and oil fields of Kirkuk, Mosul, and the Turkman belt, as originally discussed.

Most significant was the elucidation of Ankara's view of the Kurdish problem. Ankara notified Washington that any type of Kurdish autonomy was not only unacceptable to Turkey, but would be defined as a threat to Turkey's vital interests. Hence, Ankara did not rule out anything—particularly the use of force—in order to prevent this threat from being realized. That threat meant that the American forces in Iraqi Kurdistan would not only have to fight the Iraqi forces, but also create a buffer separating the Turks and the Kurds. In addition, Ankara notified Washington that Turkey must be an integral and key member in any negotiations on the future of the Kurds of Iraq. To demonstrate that they were serious, the Turks sent armored units to block all the main roads into Iraqi Kurdistan. They also rushed reinforcements to the 2nd and 3rd Corps near the Kurdish border. Several Turkish units crossed the border and seized key positions overlooking the main axes into the heart of Kurdistan. Most importantly, the Turks advanced into Iraqi Kurdistan and seized positions along the main roads from Zako to Ammadiyah and on to Dahuk and Aqrah. When the United States complained, the Turks blocked their access to American officials and impeded the passage of food and humanitarian aid to the Kurds. Turkish Special Forces popped up deep inside Kurdistan, setting roadblocks and searching cars. As far as Ankara was concerned, settling the Turkish-Kurdish confrontation took precedence over anything to do with Saddam Hussein's Iraq.

In response, Barazani and Talabani moved some 45,000 troops to face the Turkish Army—forces that had been deployed on the southern lines facing the Iraqi armed forces. Meanwhile, both Barazani and Talabani notified Washington that they would not permit the entry of Turkish forces into Iraqi Kurdistan, and if they had to choose, they'd fight the Turks before they fought the Iraqis. They also demanded that the United States arrange for the immediate withdrawal of all Turkish presence—particularly Special Forces and intelligence operatives—from Iraqi Kurdistan or else they would attack them—thus instigating a Turkish invasion.

Still hopeful of having forces open a northern front from Turkish bases, Washington urged the Kurds to reach a compromise with the Turks. Hence, the pragmatic Barazani arrived in Ankara on January 7 for unpleasant talks that included outright threats. The Turks told Barazani not to forget that the Americans were coming from the other side of the globe and would one day, not that far off, return home. Turkey, however, was here to stay, and the Kurds should not forget that distinction. Turkey was adamant about securing its vital interests at all cost, Barazani was told, and the Kurds should not be in the way. At the same time, the Turks reiterated that they were not against some kind of Kurdish autonomy in the east for as long as Turkey was the recognized power in the area and in control of strategic and economic resources. However, according to Ankara's plans, the Kurds would get their fair share of oil revenues only if they cooperated. Barazani internalized the threats, realizing that the Turks were very serious and that one must not play with them, or even irritate them.

By now, American and British senior officers—including the chairman of the Joint Chiefs of Staff, Gen. Richard Myers—were trying to gauge Ankara's military plans but were unable to get any answers from their Turkish counterparts. Nor were the Turkish senior officers friendly. The Turks repeated accurately that Iraqi Kurdistan was an integral part of Turkey until Churchill tore it away to create Iraq back in the early 1920s. All this time, pro-Turkey senior officials in the Department of Defense remained convinced that Ankara's posture was the opening phase in the "Great Turkish Bazaar" (as the negotiations were known), and that, given Turkey's economic plight, Ankara was actually trying to squeeze more financial aid from the United States.

Ankara resolved to ensure that Washington understood where Turkey was standing, and on January 13 the Turkish minister of state, Kursad Tuzmen, arrived in Baghdad and immediately met Saddam Hussein for two hours and twenty minutes. Turkish and Iraqi officials defined the talks as "friendly and mutually beneficial." The talks focused on jointly addressing the Kurdish (and American) problems without "stepping on each other's toes," explained a Turkish official. He added that Iraq offered concessions regarding the northern oil fields if Turkey blocked America's ability to open a second front.

Meanwhile, then prime minister Abdullah Gul left on a quick trip throughout the Arab world and, pointedly, Iran. At each and every stop, Gul emphasized publicly and in private talks with the local leaders that Turkey would not permit the use of Turkish territory as a springboard for U.S. aggression against Iraq. Turkey urged a unified position of the region's Arab and Muslim countries to prevent the United States from launching the war on Iraq. America was far off the mark in reading Turkey's position. U.S. diplomats in several Arab countries tried to find out about Gul's discussions with his hosts, and had one basic question: Were the Turks trying to get more financial help than that offered by the United States from the Arabs and Iran in return for not facilitating the northern front? On January 18, Turkey and Syria launched separate though similar efforts to prevent the war against Iraq by convening the foreign ministers of Middle East countries over the coming week. Ankara was adamant about Saddam's removal from power. "Saddam Hussein must stop being a threat to the region and the world," Gul said. "And he has to prove that. Our primary objective as countries in the region is to exert pressure on Saddam in this direction."

In order not to deepen the U.S.-Turkey crisis, Ankara gave its consent for a small group of American logistics experts to start a survey of Turkish bases the United States might want to use. Ankara stressed that this had nothing to do with permitting U.S. use of these bases—a fine point Washington refused to hear. Starting on January 20, a parade of American leaders and senior military officials arrived in Turkey to try and convince the government to accept U.S. forces. The Americans kept increasing their offer of financial support and weapons supplies. Unfortunately, they demonstrated complete misunderstanding and disregard of Turkish national aspirations and strategic concerns. The Turks were not pleased by this. They were even less happy when around January 25, officials leaked that an agreement had been reached with Turkey.

Meanwhile, Israeli intelligence kept acquiring data suggesting that Saddam had resolved to strike before the United States had a chance to attack Iraq. U.S. intelligence, from its own sources and assessments, concurred. In Washington, the Pentagon urged Bush to move quickly to prevent the preemptive strike. Jerusalem was notified of these ideas. Hence, on January 19, the Israeli kitchenette met. Mofaz briefed them on the latest developments, stating that "Israel should be ready for an attack on Iraq in the next few weeks." In another meeting a few days later, Major General Gilad predicted that "Saddam will not survive in power by his next birthday"—that is, April 28, 2003. By now, the kitchenette had already ordered the Israeli Air Force to initiate reconnaissance sorties and combat patrols over western and central Iraq in order to emphasize Israel's long reach and determination. The Israeli Air Force was overflying Syrian airspace with impunity in order to reach Iraq—a point that was not lost on Damascus.

Apprehension grew on January 19 when Iraqi TV broadcast a meeting of Saddam, Qusay, and key generals. "Victory has become certain. It is within the reach of our weapon systems and hearts. When the forces of evil arrive, we must protect our people and materiel so that they suffer the least possible losses—a decisive factor in our victory," Saddam told his generals. "The American surprise attack will be the decisive campaign, because the Iraqis, who know the land and the terrain better, have the advantage. Therefore, they can push the enemies who arrive from the other side of the ocean." Baghdad urged the Palestinians into action, and on January 22, a huge car bomb—consisting of some 300 kilograms of high explosives— was captured and blown up harmlessly inside Israel. The Israeli security forces were acting on intelligence that a "megastrike" had been planned for a major city in the coastal plains in order to destabilize the Middle East. As well, HAMAS launched a barrage of Qassam rockets into southern Israel.

Since there were no casualties and little damage was sustained, Jerusalem showed self-restraint.

The flow of intelligence included details of a recently drafted operational plan on how to thwart any American attack on the regime in Baghdad. Saddam was repeatedly briefed on this plan by his high command in the third week of January. The plan stressed protracted defense around Baghdad and the grounding of all Iraqi combat air missions so that the air defense could fire at will. The Iraqi strategy called for the military to channel American troops into urban areas where they would be pinned down by Saddam's elite units and zealous irregular forces. Iraqi intelligence reached an agreement on the tactics to be employed by the al-Qaeda and Ansar al-Islam terrorists to slow down the forces arriving from Turkey. The strategic principles of the cooperation were reached between senior officers of Iraqi intelligence and senior al-Qaeda commander Abu-Musab al-Zarqawi who was then in Baghdad. It was agreed that specific tactical arrangements, particularly the location of the Islamists' ambushes and roadside bombs, would be made on-site by local commanders of both sides. Soon afterward, Zarqawi traveled to northern Iraq.

The Iraqis also arranged for numerous volunteers-for-martyrdom— particularly commando troops and fighter pilots—who would employ WMD on last-resort suicide missions. Pilots were expected to crash aircraft carrying tanks filled with chemical weapons into American force concentrations, particularly choice objectives such as aircraft carriers, while commando solders were to attack advancing forces with RPGs tipped with chemical warheads and backpack bombs filled with chemicals. Defense Minister Sultan Hashem Ahmed discussed the new military strategy with both Saddam and Qusay, stressing that the war would be decided in attrition-heavy ground battles. "The occupation of countries is not achieved by air battles, rather by men on the ground," Hashem said. "The United States will not be able to occupy Iraq, because the Iraqis have faith in their soil and home and have sworn not to allow the enemy to pass. Accordingly the Americans will be unable to achieve anything but destruction."

On January 27, Saddam and Qusay Hussein met with the Iraqi high command to discuss the status of the Iraqi military manpower. According to Iraqi sources, they talked about "the fighters' morale and the preparations of their units and formations in terms of personnel, equipment, training, defense lines, and supplies." The commanders assured Saddam and Qusay that "they are all proceeding in accordance with a well-charted and accurate plan and in a manner commensurate with the requirements of the current circumstances facing Iraq." Most significant, the sources emphasized, was the reported progress to "achieve harmony and fateful cohesion between the army and the [Baath] Party . . . so that the fighters will be able to perform their combat duties, actively confront the remnants of the evil aggressors, crush them, and thwart their conspiratorial plans." This meant the further integration of the Baath Security Service into the military to ensure loyalty, purge Saddam's enemies, and attempt to prevent the collapse and surrender of military units through sheer terror. During the war, the Baath cadres would assume leadership of the irregular warfare against American and British forces. Meanwhile, January saw a growing number of intelligence reports that Iraq was accelerating its preparations for martyrdom operations, as well as preparing to sabotage the fifteen hundred oil wells in southern Iraq.

In both an al-Jazeera interview and a *Babil* editorial, Uday warned America of the dire consequences of the war and then offered an olive branch. "September 11 will be a walk in the park when compared to the blood they will spill if they launch a large-scale attack on Iraq," Uday wrote in a pseudonymous editorial. "If the Americans decide to commit another stupidity, it will cost them a lot, even beyond their calculations and expectations. It will be a big political defeat, which will be a further step toward the end of U.S. hegemony."

In the al-Jazeera interview, Uday went further—hinting that Iraq was willing to consider a negotiated settlement. "It is better if the Americans keep themselves far away from us. They will benefit much more from Iraq through dialogue and without resorting to force and war," he said. Uday also predicted that the United States would collapse if it attempted to overthrow Saddam.

On January 29, Iraq raised the ante in public diplomacy. Tariq Aziz warned that if war was inevitable, Iraq would consider a preemptive invasion of Kuwait in order to destroy the foreign bases. Still, he claimed, Iraq was interested in finding a negotiated way out of the crisis rather than going to war. In a meeting with the Iraqi high command, Saddam demanded ruthless uprooting of any sign of treason.

In January, Damascus positioned itself as the leader of an Arab camp determined to save Saddam Hussein and his regime. On January 17, Bashar met Ali Hassan al-Majid in Damascus, who arrived with a special message from Saddam. Damascus than called for a summit of foreign ministers, inviting Egypt, Jordan, Saudi Arabia, Iran, and Turkey to attend.

Syrian Foreign Minister Farouk A-Shaara embarked on a tour of Arab capitals to mobilize support for the summit. Although not having a common border with Iraq, Egypt was invited to Damascus because of Cairo's unique relations with Washington. Now, at the behest of Baghdad, Cairo convinced the Bush administration to permit the safe travel of Ali Hassan al-Majid—despite being wanted for war crimes—so that the possibility of Saddam's going into exile could be further pursued. However, by late January, Saddam would not permit Ali Hassan al-Majid to travel beyond Damascus. Officially, the reason was Baghdad's growing fears that the United States would not honor its commitment to Ali Hassan's safe travel and would try to capture him. The real reason, however, was Saddam's decision to cut off negotiations on going into exile. Meanwhile, the American embassy in Cairo notified the foreign ministry that the embassy would submit legal papers demanding Ali Hassan's detention and extradition to The Hague if he arrived in Egypt. This futile move served only to strengthen Saddam's fig-leaf excuses.

On January 28, all eyes were focused on Israel where fateful elections were taking place. With the intifada having dragged on for more than two years, with several radical states committed to the acquisition of WMD and ballistic missiles, and with the Iraqi threat increasing the Israeli public considered the elections a referendum on the direction Israel should take in formulating its national security policy. The magnitude of the political earthquake was clear by the time the votes were counted. Sharon's Likud won 38 seats (later to rise to 40) out of the Knesset's 120, while Labor sank to 19 seats, the lowest in its history. The overall balance was to be 70–50 for the hawkish nationalist parties. With the 14 members of the centrist Shinui party (which later joined Sharon's government) taken into consideration, Sharon's majority stood at an unbeatable 84–36. That night, Sharon was magnanimous, stressing the national challenges ahead rather than outstanding political disagreements. "We can be happy, but there is no room for celebrations: terrorism has not ended, the Iraqi threat remains over our heads, an economic and social crisis is still threatening our economy. This is a time not for celebration, but a time for reckoning and the unification of all our forces in order to bring true victory—victory over terrorism and the beginning of diplomatic process, and victory over unemployment and the growth of our economy," Sharon told Israel.

* * *

By the end of January, the administration had made up its mind to go to war. Although the political process seemed to be unfolding, the UN inspections were on track, and international opposition was on the rise, the White House resolved it was time for action. "This will not go on much longer," a senior administration official said. "This process is coming to a close."

America's resolve and commitment were articulated by President Bush in his State of the Union Address, delivered on January 28. "The gravest danger facing America and the world is outlaw regimes that seek and possess nuclear, chemical, and biological weapons," he said. "These regimes could use such weapons for blackmail, terror, and mass murder. They could also give or sell those weapons to their terrorist allies, who would use them without the least hesitation."

Bush singled out Saddam Hussein as the primary threat among the rogue terrorism-sponsoring leaders. Saddam, Bush said, a "brutal dictator, with a history of reckless aggression, with ties to terrorism, with great potential wealth, will not be permitted to dominate a vital region and threaten the United States."

Bush stressed Washington's resolve to address the Iraq challenge on its own if need be. "The course of this nation does not depend on the decisions of others," he stated. "Whatever action is required, whenever action is necessary, I will defend the freedom and security of the American people."

Bush concluded by eloquently articulating the overall approach of the United States to fighting the war on terrorism: "We strive for peace. And sometimes peace must be defended. A future lived at the mercy of terrible threats is no peace at all. If war is forced upon us, we will fight in a just cause and by just means—sparing, in every way we can, the innocent. And if war is forced upon us, we will fight with the full force and might of the United States military—and we will prevail."

There followed close consultations with Tony Blair, Bush's principal ally in the war. On February 1, they agreed that the solution for the Saddam problem must come within weeks, not months. And since Baghdad was not showing any inclination to genuinely disarm and cease the sponsorship of terrorism, there was no turning back from war.

Still, the United States and the United Kingdom had to cope with widespread skepticism and outright hostility to the war. In a desperate attempt at gaining international legitimacy, Colin Powell addressed the UN Security Council on February 5. With George Tenet sitting right behind him to add credence to the intelligence he was about to present, Powell delivered a lengthy presentation of the administration's case against Iraq. He presented numerous satellite photographs and intercepted phone calls demonstrating how the Iraqi authorities had repeatedly schemed to hide their banned weapons from UN inspectors. He showed pictures of trucks evacuating equipment on the eve of inspections, played telephone conversations between Iraqi officers discussing the concealment of items, and provided details about Iraq's methods of cheating on the UN. "How much longer are we willing to put up with Iraq's noncompliance?" Powell asked. The United States, he made clear, was not willing to wait any longer.

By now, the Pentagon and CENTCOM had presented the White House with the final war plan for approval. The working assumption was that the war would start in the last week of February. An intense air campaign would be conducted in the first forty-eight hours. The United States and the United Kingdom had assembled an armada of over five hundred land-based combat aircraft, as well as four or five aircraft carriers, in the region. The plan called for the delivery of some three thousand smart bombs and cruise missiles during the air campaign in order to overwhelm the regime, paralyze its reaction capabilities, and expedite the ground forces' surge northward. Special attention was paid to "leadership targets"—palaces, bunkers, and the like—with the aim of decapitating the regime. The Pentagon was convinced the intense bombing would break the will and ability of the Iraqi military to fight by demonstrating the fury and reach of American firepower. With the Iraqi leadership isolated, the rank and file would find it expedient to surrender rather than fight a losing battle for a doomed regime.

The projected swift encirclement and ultimate capture of Iraq's two main cities—Baghdad and Basra—was the best example of the ground campaign. American forces were to carry out a three-pronged assault on Baghdad: Originating in Kuwait, the U.S. Marine Task Force would advance from the southeast (via al-Amarah and al-Kut), and the Army's 3rd Infantry Division would advance from the southwest (via Nasiriyah and around the Shiite heartland). Coming down from Turkey, the Army's 4th Infantry Division would reach Baghdad from the north (via Iraqi Kurdistan). The mission of the British expeditionary force was the capture of Basra and the nearby port of Umm Qasr. Significantly, the Pentagon remained convinced that Turkey would ultimately relent and allow American use of its bases. In addition, the United States would deploy elements of the 82nd Airborne and 101st Air Assault Divisions, as well as an assortment of Special Forces, for special operations, SCUD hunting, and theater-level reserves. America promised Israel that Special Forces and some 120 combat aircraft would be dedicated to SCUD hunting in western Iraq. As well, armored elements of the 101st would deploy to all major roads and axes in western Iraq to prevent movement of missile launchers.

Indeed, America's allies in the Middle East were convinced there was no way back for the United States and that the countdown for war had begun. The entire Middle East expected a war in a matter of weeks. The Israeli Air Force, including air defense, was put on high readiness in the context of "Red Hail"—Israel's code name for the set of contingency plans and procedures for the Iraqi crisis. Tens of fighters began patrolling the Israeli skies on a daily basis and the pace of Israeli reconnaissance patrol sorties over Iraq increased. On February 4, the U.S.-Israeli air defense exercise peaked with the launch of fourteen live Patriot missiles under warlike conditions. Nevertheless, in addition to the three Patriot batteries deploying to Israel, Israel borrowed two more batteries from the German Army. On February 9, the German batteries arrived at the port of Ashdod in Israel. Kuwait also closed the northern half of the country as a military zone where civilian traffic was forbidden.

America's continued belief in the ultimate availability of a northern front opened from Turkey was all the more inexplicable given the position of the Turkish military elite—and particularly the all-powerful General Staff (TSK). Traditionally, the TSK was considered the most pro-American element of the Turkish power elite. In early 2003, the TSK was, in the words of staunchly pro-Turkey U.S. officials, "largely complacent over the U.S. request for cooperation in any war against Iraq." On-site observers, however, defined the TSK's position as "overtly hostile" to the United States. Once the military refrained from using its clout in Ankara, the Turkish government felt free to refuse American requests. Once again, rather than definitively refuse the entreaties, Ankara sought to come up with complex sets of preconditions they were certain Washington would refuse.

On February 7, Turkey started concentrating forces along its border with Iraq. Gul informed the Bush administration of Ankara's insistence that the Turkish forces deployed into northern Iraq be significantly greater in number than the Americans. Ankara demanded that there be no limitations on the movements of the Turkish forces, now estimated to be 80,000 strong, and that they would act to assume control of the northern oilfields with an American endorsement. The United States floated a compromise according to which all forces in northern Iraq—including Turks and irregular Kurds—would operate under a unified American command. Both the Kurds and the Turks would refrain from capturing Mosul, Kirkuk, and the oil fields, the United States suggested. In return for Turkish cooperation, the United States promised, the Kurds would refrain from declaring independence, or even Kosovo-style autonomy, in Iraqi Kurdistan.

Washington could not guarantee such a profound concession in the name of the fragmented Kurds, and Ankara knew it. Little wonder that a few days later Turkish and Kurdish forces started improving their advance deployments for speedy capture of key positions and terrain features.

The Iraq-based Islamist terrorists were also posturing in anticipation of the war. In southern Iraq, al-Qaeda cells began deploying into Saudi Arabia, bringing with them weapons and explosives. In January, Saudi Special Forces pursued numerous small detachments trying to infiltrate desolate sectors of the kingdom's long border with Iraq. The security forces also raided houses of known Islamist activists, capturing terrorists and weapons. Many clashes took place between the Saudi forces and the terrorists both in the desert and during raids.

In February, terrorists affiliated with al-Qaeda, Palestinian networks, and Unit 999 of Iraqi intelligence intensified their activities. The Iraqis were preparing teams for operations worldwide—with priority given to the Gulf States, Turkey, and Israel, as well as contested areas such as Kurdistan. Most important were the preparations at the main secret intelligence facility in Tajdari (100 miles northeast of Baghdad) and the Salum air base (10 miles to the north), which now increasingly served as the gateway for clandestine shipping of people and small goods in and out of Iraq. The new operational base was under the command of Col. Abu-Wael.

On the night of February 8, Iraq attempted to seize the initiative in Kurdistan through covert operations and terrorism. Operating on the basis of excellent information provided by Iraqi military intelligence, a strike team of Ansar al-Islam penetrated the outskirts of Sulaymaniyah and ambushed four senior officers of PUK on their way to an ostensibly secret meeting. The raiders killed Gen. Shawkat Mushir (commander of PUK forces on the eastern front along the Iranian border area), Sheikh Jaffar

Mustafa (commander of PUK forces in Halabja and the city's de facto governor), Hekmat Osman (commander of PUK forces in Sirwan), and Mohamad Tawfiq (chief of PUK intelligence in Sirwan). The chief of PUK intelligence in Halabja was critically wounded. Reportedly, an Ansar al-Islam "defector" promised to arrange a meeting with a like-minded Islamist Kurd who—as a gesture of good will—would be bringing in a couple of al-Qaeda terrorists. A meeting was arranged with the local chiefs who were known to be in Sulaymaniyah. Approaching the meeting, the "defectors" and "prisoners" pulled out guns and grenades and hit all the VIPs. All the attackers escaped in the ensuing melee. The strike was a devastating hit to the pro-U.S. Kurdish high command in the most active front in Iraqi Kurdistan, putting in doubt PUK's control of the main road to Kirkuk from the Turkish border. Analysts in the region noted that with the Sulaymaniyah attack, "Iraq fired the first shot in the war."

Most significant were the adventures of Adib Shaaban, the personal chief of office of Uday Saddam Hussein, an old friend and close confidant on professional and personal matters. Shaaban suddenly arrived in Jeddah on February 9, ostensibly to arrange for the smuggling of Uday's gold and jewelry out of Baghdad. The next day he traveled to Beirut again in order to manage Uday's numerous bank accounts and safe deposit boxes. Yet he "vanished" while in Beirut, only to reemerge in Damascus. Shaaban was seen on and off in Beirut, Bekaa, and Damascus until February 17. He now coordinated additional smuggling of Iraqi oil to Syria, ensuring that both oil and revenue would be available to Syria and Iraq as the war progressed. The actual sale of the oil would be handled by front companies under the control of Firas Tlass and Maher al-Assad.

At the same time, Shaaban was also making efforts to establish better coordination with HizbAllah and the Iraqi contingent in their midst—relations that had soured since an Iraqi missile accidentally exploded in the Bekaa in late December 2002. The missile was being moved out of storage for a test launch operated by Iraqi military technicians and the HizbAllah fighters they were training when it exploded, causing heavy HizbAllah casualties. Both sides have since blamed each other for the accident. Shaaban also delivered a message from Uday to leaders of HizbAllah and other terrorist organizations in Lebanon, urging them to coordinate with Saddam's Fedayeen and launch a wave of terrorist operations in the Middle East and worldwide.

While in Lebanon, Shaaban met with the leaders of Arafat's terrorism establishment—particularly Colonel Aynayn, who was instrumental in reviving "Black September" in 2002—to discuss the Palestinian role in the forthcoming campaign. According to Lebanese intelligence and security sources, Shaaban also oversaw the transfer of Iraqi WMD, mainly a few dozen chemical warheads for 122-mm Katyusha rockets, to HizbAllah and pro-Iraqi Palestinians, mainly Arafat's Fatah, in southern Lebanon. The warheads themselves were delivered shortly afterward by Syrian forces and stored in HizbAllah bunkers in central Bekaa under the supervision of Syrian commando forces from Anjar. The Syrians thus ensured that Hizb-Allah would not be able to launch these weapons without the approval of, and facilitation by, Damascus. Meanwhile, as Shaaban was moving fast, rumors began to spread about his defection to the United States with a "smoking gun." On February 15 he met with a few Arab journalists in Damascus to deny all rumors. He then returned to Baghdad and vanished once again.

A major aspect of these developments was the growing presence of HizbAllah terrorists with the Palestinian security authorities in the Gaza Strip and the Judean mountains. The HizbAllah representatives brought expertise—such as sophisticated bomb-making techniques and tactical skills—and unique systems—including sophisticated remote-control fuses and electronic sensors—which could facilitate a major escalation in the terrorist strikes at the heart of Israel. These activities took place in close cooperation with Arafat's and Tirawi's senior commanders. Baghdad grew afraid of a consequent reduction in its influence in the territories, particularly because Baghdad had not launched the long anticipated and desired war against Israel. Now, one of the main challenges facing Shaaban was to better coordinate all activities with Nasrallah so that Iraq would not lose out completely. For their part, Arafat and Tirawi wanted a fallback position from which to continue the intifada even after the anticipated collapse of Iraq and the cessation of funding from Saddam; closer cooperation with Iran, Syria, and HizbAllah would ameliorate the loss of Saddam's patronage.

Cognizant of the intense preparations in the territories, on February 10 Mofaz imposed a total and hermetic closure on the territories. Jerusalem pointed to "hot" intelligence about a forthcoming series of megastrikes—of "unprecedented magnitude"—at the heart of Israel aimed at instigating wrathful retaliation. Israel's sense of urgency intensified after the IDF intercepted and arrested four Palestinian would-be bombers on their way into Israel carrying large bombs.

Meanwhile, HAMAS urged an Islamist jihad as a response to the war against Iraq. Sheikh Yassin urged all Muslims to attack Americans and other Westerners the moment the United States attacked Iraq. "Muslims should threaten Western interests and strike them everywhere," Yassin wrote, because the Muslim world was facing a new Crusaders' war against Islam. He also asserted that any method of attack was permitted, saying, "As they fight us, we have to fight them."

During the first half of February, Saddam profoundly altered the Iraqi doctrine and war plans. The emphasis shifted from offensive strikes aimed to expand the conflict, to a defensive posture centered on the greater Baghdad area. Toward this end, Iraq suddenly withdrew its military—that is, tens of thousands of troops and hundreds of tanks, armored personnel carriers, and artillery—from the borders with Jordan and Kuwait. The bulk of these forces were arrayed in a new ring covering the southern and western approaches to Baghdad. Additional units were deployed in the Kirkuk area. Iraqi TV began broadcasting a series of reports showing Saddam meeting senior officers to get updated reports on the situation and preparations for war in various fronts and parts of the country. Saddam was seen giving the officers instructions, from adding machine guns to tanks (pointedly imitating what the Israelis were doing in the territories) to organizing battle lines against the invading forces. Saddam urged Iraqi forces to keep their cool, patiently wait until U.S. forces came in close range, and then devastate them with well-aimed fire. Throughout, Saddam exuded confidence, telling the commanders that even if the Americans sent a million troops to Baghdad, "the *shabab* [youth] will kill them."

In retrospect, Saddam's was a momentous decision, because this was the last time Baghdad would switch priorities in its war strategy, and Iraq stuck with the defensive strategy into the war. Still, it is not clear what made Saddam suddenly commit to this kind of a defensive strategy. Although he had wavered between regional offensive and Iraqi defensive strategies from the very beginning of the crisis, he had never decided to abide by only one option. Furthermore, there were virtually no deliberations within the Iraqi elite—none of Saddam's usual speeches, meetings called, or declarations suggesting that contemplation of a new policy had taken place came to the fore. There were no indications that Saddam was deliberating a momentous decision of the kind that was taken. Similarly, there were no briefings of or consultations with Saddam's allies in the Arab world; his friends and foes learned about the decision when the Iraqi forces suddenly began redeploying. Hence, it is difficult to assess, even in retro-spect, what prompted Saddam to make this fateful decision. He seemed to have internalized the debate and made the decision himself, perhaps in consultations with Qusay. In retrospect, Saddam must have been sure in his conviction or he would not have kept to this strategy into the war and the ultimate fall of Baghdad.

That Saddam decided to stay in Iraq rather than accepting any one of the exile offers was explained by Professor Amatzia Baram, Israel's leading expert on Iraq. "Saddam Hussein always believes that things are going to turn out in his favor, no matter how bad they might look to others," he said. "Saddam's insurmountable optimism rests on his life of achievements in the face of overwhelming odds."

Baram noted that Saddam was genuinely convinced that "he is uniquely lucky and that his fortune will never forsake him." That world-view dominated Saddam's reading of the developments around him. "In-deed, the offers of asylum from foreign leaders and the stream of antiwar activists to Baghdad in recent weeks almost certainly have further con-vinced Saddam that Americans do not want to go to war and are desper-ately looking for a way out," Baram said.

Where Saddam would not relax was the issue of personal security. De-spite the comprehensive security system, Saddam's fear of conspiracies, treason, and coups only intensified. In February, he started putting extra guards on the houses of leading national security officials and senior offi-cers so that they could carry on official functions but remain effectively under house arrest for the rest of the day. These were pillars of the regime Saddam could not do without but no longer trusted fully. Among them was Sultan Hashem al-Jaburi, the Iraqi minister of defense, whose daugh-ter was married to Qusay.

Saddam's apprehension about the loyalty of the defense establishment was not without merit. Since February there had been an increase in the number of mid-ranking officers defecting to America via Kurdistan. They brought with them updated intelligence and a willingness to get in touch with friends and superior officers to convince them not to fight. The most revealing phenomenon was that small groups of ten to twelve officers were now arriving together, which indicated prior coordination and no fear of the fedayeen or internal security organs among the officers. The wave of defections was accelerated by an effort on the part of U.S. intelligence en-couraging American and British Iraqis to call family members still in the military and urge them to defect or at the least stay out of the war. Meanwhile, Jordanian security authorities claimed that aides to the Iraqi leadership appeared edgy and might begin to flee Baghdad as war drew closer. A few aides to leading ministers made discreet inquiries in Amman regarding defection and asylum for themselves and their bosses. They all claimed they knew the Iraqi regime would not survive an American attack and wanted out before the end.

The growing instability and uncertainty in Baghdad were duly felt in most Arab capitals. Several Arab leaders—led by Saudi Arabia's Crown Prince Abdallah—thought there was still a chance to prevent the war by convincing Saddam to go into exile. Riyadh and Doha started organizing a high-level commission to persuade Saddam to agree to exile in exchange for immunity from prosecution for war crimes. Several regional leaders agreed to travel to Baghdad and attempt to persuade Saddam to accept this offer. At this point, Cairo suddenly intervened and effectively scuttled the initiative. The Egyptians warned that any Arab effort to persuade Saddam to abdicate would be tantamount to creating a precedent for outside intervention in the legitimization or removal of Arab leaders—an issue Egypt was most sensitive about. "I don't think any Arab country would interfere in Iraq's internal affairs," Egyptian Foreign Minister Ahmed Maher said. "It is the Iraqi people who should decide who rules over their country." With that, the Arab League's initiative was effectively dead on arrival.

By now, most Arab capitals—particularly Riyadh—were resigned to the fact that the offensive was irreversible, and their priorities shifted to preparing for the postwar Middle East. In February, Iran, Syria, and most other Arab countries secretly committed to sponsoring an "Iraqi *Taif*"—a conference of national reconciliation named after the original *Taif* conference that ended the Lebanese civil war. The declared objective of the Iraqi *Taif* was to "set down the principles and the basis for a comprehensive national reconciliation . . . which should give birth to an Iraqi government of national consensus." The Iraqis would be participants, and international organizers stressed that the implementation of this reconciliation would deprive America of an excuse to attack "sisterly Iraq." Both the Arab League and the Organization of the Islamic Conference readily committed to assisting the Arab-Iranian initiative.

The Saudis were most apprehensive about the Islamist backlash an American occupation of Baghdad would engender, as Saudi intelligence warned of accelerated Islamist subversive activities. Indeed, in late February Saudi security forces discovered jihadist terrorist training camps containing special training equipment, weapons, sandbags, and trenches. The camps were located in the Asfan area between Jeddah and Medina near the Red Sea. Back in mid-February, Riyadh wanted to defuse the primary accusation of bin Laden's followers—that Saudi Arabia welcomed the presence of U.S. forces on its soil. Since officially these forces were in Saudi Arabia to meet the Iraqi threat, the removal of Saddam provided Riyadh with a perfect reason to ask the Americans to leave.

"The presence of American, British, and French forces in the Prince Sultan air base in Al-Kharj was for a precise reason, that is the control of the southern exclusion zone," Saudi Deputy Defense Minister Prince Khaled bin Sultan said in February. "If that reason goes away, the presence of U.S. and other forces will end." The Bush administration had long thought that such a request would be coming and decided not to fight the inevitable.

However, when Crown Prince Abdallah discreetly raised the subject with the White House, the administration had long assessed that such a request would be coming and decided not to fight the inevitable. It was decided that no formal announcement would be made until after the war, and Abdullah agreed. In the meantime, Saudi Arabia relented, permitting American use of Prince Sultan air base for command and control of air operations, to conduct noncombat flights from Saudi bases, and to launch special operations across the Iraqi border. Moreover, Riyadh stressed that it would continue military and security relations with the United States after the withdrawal of American forces.

Nevertheless, most Arab governments were terrified by the prospect of a consolidated U.S. military and political presence in postwar Iraq. While the shifting of the U.S. military presence away from several Gulf States would be a welcome development, the fact of an enduring U.S. presence in Iraq would not. Many Arab regimes were convinced that with the United States in control of Iraqi oil, it would no longer be that dependent on oil from the Arabian Peninsula and therefore was likely to be less tolerant of the transgressions of local governments—from human rights violations to the funding of Islamist charities and terrorism. While Saudi Arabia would be rewarded with an American withdrawal, other regimes could see no redeeming development.

The untenable position Egypt would find itself in if the United States built a sympathetic regime in Baghdad compelled Cairo to form an activist group under the auspices of the Arab League to undermine America's efforts. That way, Egypt would be able to remain the key to America's standing in the Arab world, assuring that the United States would continue to ignore Egypt's bad behavior, and bad faith.

6
THE DIE IS CAST

All these regional developments prompted another round of consultations between Washington and Jerusalem about the war and its aftermath. In mid-February, in the aftermath of the latest round of such discussions, Israeli senior defense officials were alarmed by what they described as the Americans' confidence in their winning strategy. Nobody had any doubt that the United States—being a superpower—would win the war. However, the Israelis were perplexed that the Americans had no well-defined contingency plans for, or even conceptual approaches to, possible entanglements or worst-case scenarios. In high-level meetings, the Israelis raised numerous hypothetical questions and got no answers from the Americans. These questions included such scenarios as America failing to kill or capture Saddam Hussein or even silence his messages; America becoming entangled in protracted and casualty-heavy urban warfare, causing the Arab world to erupt in rage; Israel being hit by Iraqi WMD and, despite American pleas for restraint, striking out with tremendous might; the Turkish Army invading Iraqi Kurdistan in order to prevent the emergence of a Kurdish entity; Iran exploiting the chaos in Iraq in order to exacerbate and empower the Shiite population; America extending its stay in Iraq, and an "enlightened occupation" becoming the source of grassroots hatred and uprising; and the American military failing to discover WMD on Iraqi soil, resulting in the eruption of a political crisis in the Muslim world.

The Israelis urged the Americans to learn from the Israeli experience that everything always goes wrong and takes longer than anticipated. Israeli officials fretted that their American counterparts were not receptive to their ideas and recommendations.

* * *

By February, Ankara had concluded that the realization of American designs for a postwar Iraq would be detrimental to Turkey's long-term vital interests. Unless the United States changed its plans, there was no escape from direct intervention in northern Iraq. The TSK drafted operational plans for a major invasion of northern Iraq according to which a force of up to 80,000 troops would enter Iraq, capture northern oil-rich areas, and establish "safe haven areas" for the Turkman roughly identical to the Turkman strip originally agreed upon by the United States. The TSK examined plans for a two-phase operation in northern Iraq that would both prevent the rise of a Kurdish state and secure a Turkman "entity" in control of the oil fields. Ankara had attempted to brief Washington about these concerns during the negotiations about granting U.S. access to Turkey's military infrastructure but to no avail. In February, Turkey quietly began implementing the first phase of its plan, deploying about 20,000 Turkish troops to the immediate border area, including a cross-border presence. The rest of the Turkish forces deployed in forward positions ready to penetrate as deep as 150 miles once hostilities erupted and America did not act to prevent anti-Turkey developments. Moreover, the TSK notified the government that Turkish forces must not come under American command or they would be diverted away from safeguarding the vital interests of both Turkey and the Turkman.

When Washington kept pleading for a compromise, the TSK proposed that the United States establish two military commands to determine their cooperation during the war against Iraq. The first command would be in Doha, Qatar, and through it the United States would unilaterally control all military activities in southern and western Iraq. The second command would be in the major Turkish air base of Diyarbakir—an installation high on the American list of coveted facilities—and would serve as a joint U.S.-Turkish command for the conduct of military operations in northern Iraq. This way, Ankara argued, Turkey would have no impact on America's ability to topple the regime of Saddam Hussein, while the vital interests of Turkey would not be harmed.

However, Washington adamantly denied Ankara any presence or role in postwar Iraq. Formally, the United States was reluctant to harm its long-term relations with the Kurds—an inevitable outcome of any Turkish military intervention. Moreover, the Bush administration was increasingly afraid to offend the Saudi royal family and other key Gulf sheikhs and emirs who were fiercely opposed to any Turkish role in postwar Iraq—a power position they believed would come at the expense of their influence in Washington. The administration accepted the concerns of the Arab ruling elites.

On February 18, when Washington refused to seriously consider the latest Turkish proposal, President Sezar formally announced that Turkey would not permit the United States to land and use Turkey's territory unless there was a UN resolution authorizing the war on Iraq. Efforts by American "friends of Turkey"—several Washington insiders in and out of government who were very close to the administration and who had long championed close relations with Turkey—to convince Ankara to change its mind and accept six billion dollars in direct aid failed. The possible absence of Turkey dawned on CENTCOM. The initial reaction of CENT-COM was to postpone the war to the fall, by which time it would be possible to deploy the necessary forces to the Gulf (while skipping the horrendously hot summer). The administration, including the Pentagon's civilian elite, demanded that the war be launched in the spring—in March, for example—even if only with a southern front. The White House was convinced that any further delay of the war would subject the United States to mounting international pressure to reach a political compromise with Saddam, which Washington might not be able to ignore or resist.

CENTCOM, though, insisted it needed a northern front, so Washington "took off the gloves" with Ankara. The administration threatened to review the entire strategic relationship with Turkey unless the latest requests for access to bases and the deployment of up to 40,000 American troops were promptly met. Meanwhile, CENTCOM would not change the overall contingency plans. "The United States has thousands of troops on ships waiting outside of Turkish ports, and Ankara won't come to a decision," a Western diplomatic source told MENL's Steve Rodan. "This situation is quickly coming to a head. It's a matter of hours and days."

Still the administration refused to address the Turkish concerns, limiting the discussions with Turkey to issues of money and raw pressure. The source said Washington was now threatening to review its overall strategic relations with Ankara unless it quickly decided to allow American combat troops and aircraft in the country. "If [the Turkish] parliament doesn't pass the proposal, we will review our relations and they could suffer enormous damage," an American official told the Ankara-based *Hurriyet*. "We wouldn't forget such a thing." Undaunted, Turkey stuck to its guns. On February 21 and 22, the Turks reinforced their Second Army to over 100,000 troops (up from 70,000 to 80,000 a week before). The Second

Army was in offensive positions on the Iraqi border with numerous advance units deep inside Iraqi Kurdistan.

Toward the end of January, Iran's supreme leader, Ayatollah Seyed Ali Khamenei, convened a secret high-level meeting in a building not usually associated with the Office of the Iranian Guide. The participants included fiercely loyal conservative clerics, representatives of the National Security Council, members of the intelligence community affiliated with radical currents, and Lebanese representatives of HizbAllah's security apparatus. Khamenei made every effort to ensure the complete secrecy of the meeting so that reform-minded officials or clerics could be excluded. The topic of the meeting was the future of Shiites in the Middle East—not just in Iran, but also in Iraq, the Arabian Peninsula, and Lebanon.

A senior official from Khamenei's office briefed the meeting that "the ultimate aim" of the American conspiracy against Shiite Islam "would be not only the collapse of the mullahs' regime in Iran but also the removal of the seat of Shiite authority from Qom to Al-Najaf in Iraq." Senior IRGC and intelligence officials stressed that this development "greatly embarrassed" official Tehran and especially Khamenei, since he had personally instructed the Iranian negotiators to notify Ahmad Chalabi during a recent visit to Tehran that Ayatollah Muhammad Baqir al-Hakim and the Supreme Council of the Islamic Revolution in Iraq (SCIRI) would be authorized "to open all channels of alliance with the Americans against Saddam Hussein." That move was to lead to secret negotiations with Washington "over a deal regarding the future of Shiites in and outside Iraq" in an American-dominated Middle East. The Iranian security elite felt betrayed by America's policy and regional plans.

The meeting resolved to reach out to Baghdad in order to jointly examine methods of resisting the American conspiracies. On February 9, Iraq's foreign minister, Dr. Naji Sabri, arrived in Tehran at the head of a delegation made up of intelligence officials at the invitation of Iran's foreign minister, Dr. Kamal Kharrazi. The declared objective of the visit was "talks on bilateral relations and means of promoting them between the two neighboring Islamic countries based on good neighborliness and joint interests." Both Iranian and Iraqi officials involved in the talks stressed that the real goal of the visit was "to discuss developments in the regional and international situation in light of American threats to carry out an aggression against Iraq and the region, as well as the dangers posed to the region's

security." Significantly, Sabri convinced Tehran that Saddam's Iraq constituted a far lesser threat to Iran than America's schemes and machinations.

Iran's new strategic priorities were first elucidated by Hashemi-
Rafsanjani, the country's chief strategist. In a few sermons and speeches
delivered to select audiences on February 12—during the holiday of Eid
al-Adha—Hashemi-Rafsanjani repeatedly stressed that for Tehran "the
worst scenario [is] Iraq ruled by a U.S. 'puppet,' " and therefore, everything
must be done to ensure that "the United States [was] not allowed to remain in the region" in the aftermath of the war with Iraq. The alternative—the stifling and collapse of the mullahs' regime—was inconceivable
to Tehran, and all available means, from terrorism to sparking a regional
war, must be utilized in the desperate struggle to prevent Khomeini's
dream-state from withering away.

The intensity of Tehran's alarm was best expressed by Khamenei in an
address to Hajj officials—mostly intelligence officers—who had just returned from Saudi Arabia. He described the overall strategic and historic
threats looming over Iran as a result of the imminent war in Iraq: "Global
imperialism—that is, the closely knit network of oil cartels, arms manufacturers, world Zionism, and their ally governments—threatened by the
awakening of the Islamic *Ummah* [Nation], is in a state of aggression accompanied with panicky moves. This aggression, which has political, media, military, and terrorist dimensions, is today clearly visible in the violent
and unabashed conduct and statements of the militarists in charge of the
United States government and the Zionist regime," Khamenei continued.

According to Khamenei, American aggression was being manifested
through a coordinated effort at three focal points. In the first, "Palestine,
oppressed and drenched in blood, is a daily victim of the most ruthless
measures of the usurper regime." In pursuit of the second, "the people of
Iraq receive threats of war because the U.S. regime considers it necessary to
establish itself in Iraq and take the destiny of its people into its hands and,
as a consequence, the destiny as well of all countries of the Middle East, in
order to establish its control over the vital flow of oil and to plunder the remaining oil resources of this region and to establish an effective presence
close to the borders of Palestine, Iran, Syria, and Saudi Arabia." And in the
third focal point, "the people of Afghanistan were made to feel the brunt of
American and British bombs and weapons of mass destruction for the
past year and several months with their soul and body and to suffer the
humiliating presence of their occupying forces because the U.S. administration has chosen to define its illegitimate interests in these terms."

Khamenei stressed that these three concentrations constituted the spring-board for America's quest "to be the absolute sovereign and dictator of the Muslim countries of the region in the current half century. The extravagant international objectives and plans of the United States are all indicative of this arrogant yet stupid ambition."

Although Khamenei had no doubt about the ultimate outcome of this confrontation, he urged resolute action by all Muslims. "There is no doubt that the United States and its allies will fail, and once again the world will witness the collapse of a powerful yet drunken emperor, as we saw that his miscalculations came out wrong in Palestine and Afghanistan. However, if the Muslim *Ummah,* the states and the peoples, do not take timely, wise, and courageous decisions, they will suffer heavy damages that will take a long time to remedy. . . . With the pretext of defense of democracy and war against terrorism [the United States] addresses a tirade to Muslim nations condemning chemical arms and weapons of mass destruction." The initial results of the Muslim world's reaction were encouraging, Khamenei noted. "The arrogant and imperialist United States has not realized its objectives in Palestine and Afghanistan, and its stupendous financial and human outlays have brought it nothing but loss. It will be the same story in the future, God willing."

America's forthcoming attack on Iraq should be assessed in the context of this greater conspiracy, Khamenei emphasized. He stressed that "in the case of Iraq, the U.S. claims that its objective is elimination of Saddam and the Baathist regime. This is, of course, a lie. Its real aim is to appropriate OPEC and to swallow up the region's oil resources, to offer a closer support to the Zionist regime, and to plot more closely against Islamic Iran, Syria, and Saudi Arabia. That which is certain is that in case of American control of Iraq, with or without war, the primary victim of this hostile occupation will be the Iraqi people and the honor, dignity, and wealth of that historic nation. But if the people of Iraq and the neighboring nations are vigilant, the United States will not attain these objectives either, God willing." In mentioning "neighboring nations," Khamenei for the first time alluded to Iran's direct role in confronting the United States.

Khamenei concluded his address with a passionate statement of the inherent danger to all Muslims and Islam from the rise of American presence and influence in their midst. "Islam is a religion of freedom, justice, and quest for truth. Real democracy is religious democracy established on the basis of faith and the sense of religious duty. As witnessed in the case of Islamic Iran, it works in a manner much more reliable, sincere, and democratic than in democracies such as that of the United States. The democracy that the Americans claim they want to offer to Islamic and Arab countries is as destructive as their bombs and missiles. When the enemy offers us even a date, one cannot be sure that it has not been soaked in fatal poison. The Muslim *Ummah* has experienced the truth of this in Africa, the Middle East, and West Asia recurrently in the past as well as in more recent years," Khamenei concluded. His listeners—all veteran intelligence officers—knew there was no turning back from such a sermon.

Khamenei reiterated his position forcefully on February 17 in a public speech. Referring to the unfolding Iraqi crisis, he declared:

> You can see what is happening on the issue of Iraq. The Americans are explicitly saying that they want to go to Iraq and put in power an American ruler at least for a period of two years. This reveals the Americans' true character. That is what they want in their heart of hearts. They are not satisfied with less than that. They will not be satisfied with installing an Iraqi ruler who is their own puppet. They want to feed an entire nation, country, and collectivity which contains human, monetary, and financial resources to the greedy and avaricious Zionist companies and world power centers. They are not satisfied with anything less than that. That is what they want. Of course, these days, their demands cannot be met. Yes, perhaps one hundred or one hundred and fifty or seventy years ago the colonialists could do such things. They were capable of doing such things. They did such things in Africa and Asia. They took advantage of the ignorance of nations, their lack of information and backwardness. They did that in India, Algeria, and Latin America. They could do that in those days. However, today they are making a mistake. American rulers are making a mistake. One cannot talk about such things today.

By now, the Iranian defense establishment was already implementing the leadership's orders. "Iran is faced with a wide spectrum of threats, including a foreign military aggression, which requires the Islamic Republic to adopt appropriate security measures to defend itself," Defense Minister Rear-Adm. Ali Shamkhani told the Tehran newspaper *Siasat-e Rouz* on February 18. "Some of the threats before the Islamic Republic are a foreign aggression, war, border skirmishes, spying, work of sabotage, regional crises falling out from the proliferation of weapons of mass destruction, organized crime, and state terrorism. Thus, the Islamic Republic of Iran, in its defense and security doctrine, has put 'confronting threats' and 'defusing them' as the key basis of its policies." Shamkhani added that "the deterrent defense [policy] means that we will never take any offensive step. . . . We are trying to boost our resistance against the first strike of the enemy . . . and then maintain this resistance. Thus, the Islamic Republic's objectives are defensive." It was in pursuit of this defensive doctrine, Shamkhani stated, that Iran was "fiercely opposed to any military showdown in the region, including a probable U.S. attack on Iraq."

The next day, Shamkhani ordered that "Iran's airspace and land borders would remain closed to America, even if the UN should endorse [the American attack on Iraq]." Alluding to a decision to intercept by force American violators of Iranian airspace, Shamkhani told senior officers that Iran would "not allow any American mistake to take place over our country's airspace. In view of the fact that the Americans are economical with the facts on their technical capabilities, we shall stop their mistake promptly and decisively, should it occur over the Iranian airspace."

Most significant was the change in the position of SCIRI regarding the forthcoming war and its aftermath. On February 17, SCIRI leader Ayatollah Muhammad Baqir al-Hakim declared that Iraq's Shiites "will not back the United States" in the confrontation with the hated Saddam Hussein regime. "We reject the idea of a regime of the infidels governing Iraq," he stated. "We categorically reject this form of administration for our country. If the United States respects the opinions and aspirations of the Iraqi people, it must set aside its plans." Another leading member of SCIRI, Abdulaziz Hakim, stressed that there would not be any confluence of interests between the United States and SCIRI. "Even if the regime in Baghdad is not toppled, we will continue with our resistance. America's plans for Iraq are different than ours. We have our own strategy and tactics in resisting the Baathist regime," he stated.

With that, Tehran went into action. Starting in February, some 5,000 Iraqi-Shiite and Iranian-Arab troops of Imam Baqir al-Hakim's al-Badr Corps crossed into northern Iraq from Iran. This unit—highly trained, well armed, and totally controlled by the Pasdaran—changed the correlation of forces in Kurdistan. Even before the United States or Turkey could attempt to seize control of Iraqi Kurdistan, Iran had a trustworthy proxy force already in place at the heart of Kurdistan. Significantly, Iraq's armed forces did not intervene as the al-Badr forces moved around.

On February 18, Abdulaziz Hakim strenuously denied reports that the al-Badr Corps would cooperate with the American military once the war started. "The al-Badr Corps is active in Iran, Northern Iraq, as well as Iraq proper in underground cells. Their aim is the long-held desire of the Iraqi people, which is the liberation of their country from the menace of Saddam Hussein. However, the al-Badr Corps is dependent on Iranian policy. We abide by the decisions of the Iranian government," Hakim explained. He stressed that the al-Badr Corps "would not join the U.S.-led coalition for invading Iraq" but instead "would become active when it is appropriate to prevent further harm to the Iraqi people and toward the realization of Iraq's national security and other interests."

Saddam Hussein was also modifying the Iraqi contingency plans in accordance with the prevailing circumstances in the Middle East. By late February, Iraq seemed to have completed the last phase of war preparations. These preparations went beyond a new cycle of redeployment of troops and assets to include the nomination of senior commanders and additional arrangements by Saddam in the case of a major U.S.-led offensive. Around February 10, to buy time for the forthcoming reorganization of the Iraqi military deployment, Baghdad began dispatching detachments of agents from the al-Rasafah Regiment of Saddam's Fedayeen—under Uday's command—to carry out sabotage operations when military strikes began. Fedayeen teams were already known to be in Jordan, Turkey, the West Bank, and a few Gulf States. According to a knowledgeable Arab intelligence officer, some 180 terrorists and operatives from the al-Rasafah Regiment were dispatched to each of those locations in February.

The Iraqi military preparations were based on the latest round of instructions by Saddam Hussein during the weekend of February 7–9. Saddam gathered his most senior aides and told them that the UN Security Council session on February 4 had convinced him war was inevitable and imminent. He stressed that one of the primary American objectives would be his assassination. Therefore, senior Arab officials disclosed, he intended "to disappear immediately once the war broke out and would cut off completely his contacts with the leadership" so that neither electronic monitoring nor human traitors could betray him to the Americans. At the same time, the officials noted, Saddam gave his senior aides instructions to "enable the commanders of corps and divisions to deal with the developments of a U.S. war without waiting for his orders." Saddam also implied that "he has chosen Qusay as his successor if he disappears totally and for good," and that both the aides and the senior commanders could "refer to . . . Qusay as the final authority during the period of his absence." Saddam informed his aides that only Qusay would have the means of knowing Saddam's whereabouts as necessary.

In the first phase of redeployment war preparations, completed around February 18–19, Iraqi forces were withdrawn from the areas close to the Jordanian and Kuwaiti borders. The new force deployment was in accordance with Saddam's latest "confrontation plan," which focused on Baghdad, the oil region in Kurdistan, and Saddam's hometown of Tikrit, from which most of the Republican Guard had been recruited. The senior Arab officials added that "the elite forces, specifically the Republican Guards, would be deployed in Baghdad and the sensitive points outside it."

Former Iraqi generals concurred, assessing that "a U.S. war may have a devastating effect on the Iraqi Army, dividing it on the basis of region, tribe, and sect. This will deny the country the only institution that guarantees its unity and prevents civil wars from breaking out." They expected the regular army of about 300,000 troops to collapse without much fighting, while the elite forces—the Republican Guard of approximately 100,000 troops and especially the Special Republican Guard of approximately 40,000 troops—would remain loyal and fight in Baghdad and in a protracted insurgency afterward. These highly trained elite forces were completely and fiercely loyal to both Qusay and Saddam, and their morale was high. According to a wide variety of sources, ranging from Arab intelligence officials and Iraqi defectors to Western technical intelligence, Saddam also prepared a "chemical defensive belt" around Baghdad with the weapons concealed in underground shelters, ready to be used once American forces crossed a specific "red line" on their way to Baghdad. (As of this writing, U.S. authorities have failed to locate these facilities. The shelters, which were reportedly exceptionally well concealed, may remain hidden— along with whatever chemical weapons Saddam's forces managed to store there—until knowledgeable former Iraqi officials come forward to identify their specific location.)

Most significant were the changes made to the Iraqi high command in the north, which were completed by February 21. Saddam nominated his key confidants as commanders of the key sectors in Kurdistan. Deputy RCC Chief Izzat Ibrahim al-Durri was made commander of the Mosul military sector, Hisham Ali Hassan (the son of Ali Hassan al-Majid, the commander of southern Iraq) was made commander of the forces in Kalak Yassin Agha (halfway between Arbil and Mosul), and Vice President Taha

Yassin Ramadan was made commander of the forces in Kirkuk. These nominations came at a time of markedly intensified activities by Turkish military intelligence and Special Forces among the Kurds and Turkman of northern Iraq, as well as the deployment of the Iranian-controlled Shiite brigade inside Iraqi Kurdistan. By February 23, Turkish military intelligence and Special Forces were distributing weapons to the Turkman in northern Iraq and organizing their own anti-Kurdish militias; the Turks actively challenged Kurdish forces supported by the United States and expected to fight the Iraqi armed forces. To a great extent, the Turkman forces have created a buffer area between Saddam's forces and America's Kurds.

Meanwhile, the Iran-sponsored Shiites intensified their activities in southern Iraq as well. "Shiite Muslims of southern Iraq will mount an uprising against Saddam Hussein as soon as the American and British troops invade," noted a well-connected Shiite traveler from Najaf. He stressed that "the [Shiite] intifada in the towns and villages of the south" would be "largely spontaneous" and as much anti-American as anti-Saddam.

Starting on February 20, the local forces had been increasingly helped by the infiltration of the 2nd Brigade of the Iran-sponsored al-Badr Corps. The Iranian-Arab and Iraqi troops brought with them large quantities of weapons and supplies for the popular forces throughout southern Iraq. On February 24, Ayatollah Muhammad Baqir al-Hakim warned the West against equating the Shiites' fervent hatred of Saddam with pro-Americanism. He expected the Shiites to rebel against both the Iraqi and the American forces. Addressing the prospects of a U.S.-nominated government in postwar Baghdad, Ayatollah al-Hakim warned that "a U.S.-led government would offend the national and religious sensitivity. There would be violence."

Most intriguing, however, was the concurrent deployment of the Iraqi Air Force. Most of the Iraqi tactical combat aircraft usually deployed in the greater Baghdad area were transferred to the forward air bases near H-1, H-2, H-3, and Ghalaysan—all close to the Jordanian border. This was the first major deployment of the Iraqi Air Force since the forward deployment, in October 2002, of operational high jets, particularly long-range Mirage F-1s, as well as a few L-29s converted into unmanned delivery vehicles for biological weapons, to the Jal al-Batan air base in southwestern Iraq. These aircraft were concealed in deep underground tunnels where they were supposed to remain until minutes before the strike.

The new disposition of the Iraqi Air Force was optimized for the

launching of swift surprise attacks against the center and southern parts of
Israel. Because the attacking Iraqi planes would have to fly over Jordan and
Saudi Arabia before reaching Israel, Baghdad hoped that political considerations—for instance Israel's desire not to irritate America by sending
fighters through Saudi airspace—would slow down the response of the Israeli Air Force, giving a few of the Iraqi planes a chance to complete their
missions. Baghdad was convinced that any such surprise strike, regardless
of its ultimate success, would ignite an Arab-Israeli war because the Israeli
Air Force would, at the very least, retaliate against forward Iraqi air bases.

The viability of the aerial strike option as a catalyst for war against Israel was reinforced on February 23 with the sudden publication in all Iraqi
media of a congratulatory letter that Arafat had sent Saddam Hussein in
commemoration of Eid al-Adhah (February 12–13). In the letter, Arafat
wrote that the Palestinians "pray to God to enhance the ties of fraternity,
solidarity, and cooperation that serve our interests, rights, nation, and the
future of our generations and spare us all the dangers that threaten us in
our region." Arafat called on Saddam and the Iraqis

> to alleviate the suffering of our steadfast and enduring people and
> enhance our firm and continuous steadfastness to confront the Is-
> raeli war, aggression, killing, and machine of destruction. The sup-
> port of our brother [Saddam] will enable us to foil all attempts and
> plans of the government of Israel, the occupying power that aims
> to destroy the peace process and the structures, foundations, and
> institutions of our Palestinian National Authority. . . . All forms of
> support from you at these difficult and critical times will enable us
> to continue our endurance and steadfastness until we end the oc-
> cupation of our holy Jerusalem and our Islamic and Christian
> places. Your support will also enable us to practice our legitimate
> and firm rights according to the pertinent international resolu-
> tions, foremost of which is the right of self-determination, the
> right of return, and the establishment of our independent state
> with Jerusalem as its capital."

The Iraqi coverage of the letter noted approvingly that Arafat hinted at
the imperative of military intervention—"*all* forms of support"—and the
goal of destroying Israel by unconditionally implementing "the right of return." To Baghdad, Hans Blix's demand to destroy the Samud-2 ballistic
missiles was a lose-lose option: if Iraq destroyed the missiles it would both

deprive itself of a major element in its arsenal on the eve of a war, and provide the Bush administration with a smoking gun regarding major violations and thus provide the excuse for war. Refusal to destroy the Samud-2 missiles—most of which were currently arrayed against Kuwait with at least one battery equipped with chemical warheads—would certainly lead to war.

Alarmed by the dire ramifications of an eruption of violence in the Middle East for the entire Muslim world, Russia decided on yet another attempt at defusing the crisis. On February 22, Yevgeny Primakov arrived in Baghdad on a special flight as a special representative of President Putin. The next day, Primakov spent ten hours with his friend Saddam, discussing a variety of ideas Primakov had for resolving the crisis. Saddam wanted to think over some of these ideas overnight, and on February 24 Primakov and Saddam had a follow-up talk before Primakov returned to Moscow. Primakov reported that Saddam did not react to his proposal but left the door open for further talks about the Russian initiative.

The Primakov initiative, which Putin endorsed, stipulated that Saddam hand over Iraq's WMD and SSMs to the UN in a reliable and verifiable manner. America would withdraw from the Gulf once disarmament started. The plan also called for the establishment of a UN supervised transition government that would oversee the de-Baathification of Iraq, with Saddam remaining as the titular head of state. The UN, meanwhile, would organize free elections within a year and write a new Iraqi constitution that the new elected government would be committed to. After the election, Saddam would hand over power to the new president (*not* Uday, Qusay, or key members of the current regime), and the entire Baath elite would retire to a compound near Lake Tharthar, north of Tikrit, under international protection and supervision. The international supervision was designed to ensure that Saddam could not influence Baghdad even indirectly and that the Americans could not grab him for war crimes and force him to stand trial in The Hague. Practically, Saddam would have retained a certain influence along with access to his stolen fortunes. However, there would have been an internationally supervised new government in Baghdad, and by all estimates Saddam's influence would have diminished in time.

Briefed by Moscow about the Primakov mission, Arab governments liked the plan because Saddam was likely to accept it, and because its implementation would keep the Shiites from establishing an Islamic republic in Iraq. Ankara liked the plan because it guaranteed that no Kurdish state would be established. The Western Europeans liked the plan because the Iraqi economic recovery would start from the current oil-for-food programs—which gave advantage to the European (primarily French and Russian) companies already active in Iraq under UN supervision.

However, as the Kremlin expected, Washington would hear nothing of Primakov's ideas, and instead reiterated its commitment to commencing hostilities soon. The administration would not consider any alternative to the toppling of Saddam Hussein by force and the establishment of a U.S.-dominated "democratic" government in Baghdad. Moscow concluded that war was inevitable. The next day, Russia started sending chartered planes to evacuate families of diplomats and other Russians working in Iraq—oil people, UN personnel, and the like.

By late February, Washington was growing increasingly exasperated with Ankara. CENTCOM's inability to come up with a viable contingency plan to substitute for the northern front created palpable pressure on an administration adamant about going to war within a few weeks. The Pentagon alerted the White House that it would have problems sustaining the naval deployment off the Turkish coast—at least four navy ships waiting just outside Turkish territorial waters and another twenty to thirty ships a short distance into the Mediterranean—for more than a few days. These ships were carrying troops, tanks, armored personnel carriers, munitions, and supplies of the 4th Infantry Division. On February 19, Washington interpreted as a sign of progress Ankara's permission to unload 522 military vehicles in the port of Iskenderun. However, these vehicles—trucks, radio transmission vehicles, and troop transporters—were for a project to modernize Turkish bases and ports and had little to do with the war with Iraq. On February 21, rumors began circulating in Washington that Turkey would after all permit the transfer of U.S. forces, and that the 4th Infantry Division had already started unloading the first ships and transport aircraft. Reportedly, Ankara was apprehensive that once Washington started talking about "another way" to wage the war, Turkey would miss out on all the financial aid offered and therefore came around.

In reality, these rumors were floated by Washington without any foundation in order to sustain the pressure on the Iraqis and perhaps confront the Turks with an illusory fait accompli they would have to swallow.

The trial balloon did not work. Instead, on February 23, Ankara reiterated its demand to deploy an 80,000 strong expeditionary force in northern Iraq as a precondition to letting the American forces pass through Turkey. In response, both PUK and KDP announced that if the Turkish forces crossed into Iraq, the Kurds would fight them rather than Saddam's forces.

Finally, on February 24, Ankara notified the United States that the Turkish Parliament would convene on February 26 to vote on permission to use Turkish facilities. Gul did not have much hope that there would be approval. Nevertheless, on February 25, American aircraft from bases in Turkey bombed three batteries of SSMs in the Mosul area. It was the first case of expanding the undeclared air war, already in progress in southern Iraq, to the northern no-fly-zone area. Ankara was furious about America's violation of the no-fly-zone terms of using Turkish air bases, and closed all traffic into and out of Iraqi Kurdistan. Turkish military roadblocks stopped even the limited activities of American personnel, such as base inspection and improvement projects. Meanwhile, after several days of bitter disputes and deliberations, NATO finally sent defensive weapons to protect Turkey against a possible Iraqi attack. Turkey's doubts about America's ability to control and utilize the Kurdish irregular forces were reinforced on February 26, when an Ansar al-Islam martyr bomber almost entered Talabani's headquarters in Halabja when the U.S. special envoy, Zalmai Khalilzad, was expected. The terrorist was stopped by a guard at the door and blew himself up, killing three elite troops. Turkish intelligence gloated about yet another security and intelligence failure of the Kurds.

After repeated and bitter political maneuvers, on March 1 the Turkish Parliament cast 264 votes for helping the United States, 250 against, with 19 abstaining. The tally came 4 votes short of the "absolute majority" the Turkish constitution requires for such decisions. Hence, there would be no U.S. forces or bases in Turkey. Washington was stunned by the results. "What more do you want?" Tayyip Erdogan asked. "It was a completely democratic result. Maybe it's for the best." On March 3, Parliamentary Speaker Bulent Arinc ruled out the reintroduction of the government request for a vote. "The motion regarding the dispatch of Turkish soldiers abroad and deployment of foreign armed forces in Turkey should not be submitted to Parliament again in the same way," he said, effectively killing America's chances of operating in, through, and out of Turkey.

In the Persian Gulf, the buildup and preparations for war continued unabated despite the setbacks in Turkey. By February 22, the United States and the United Kingdom had sufficient forces deployed to go to war at any moment. American and British ground forces were undergoing intense urban warfare training in the specialized training center built in Al-Zawr, on Faylakah Island, off the Kuwaiti coast. It was not a simple undertaking because of the increase in Islamist terrorism. For example, around March 1, the Kuwaiti security forces arrested numerous Kuwaiti "Afghans" with fire bombs, sabotage equipment, and automatic weapons in the Kuwait Hilton and elsewhere. They were ready for terrorist strikes against Americans.

Meanwhile, the Special Forces expanded their operations in southern Iraq, launching probes into the southern oil fields to ascertain if the United States would be able to prevent sabotage of the pumps and other key installations, conducting an up-to-date survey of the key approach roads and venues to be used by the main forces moving toward Basra and Baghdad, and escorting and providing protection to CIA operatives trying to talk key Iraqi units and formations into staying out of the war. In March, American and British Special Forces got a boost with the establishment of "Task Force 22" in Jordan, which was optimized for sustaining special operations into western Iraq. Task Force 22 was essentially a centralized, U.S.-dominated command for American special operations teams, as well as British and Australian Special Air Service (SAS) units already operating in western Iraq, particularly on SCUD-hunting patrols. The key bases were Ruwaished and Abu-Tarha. On the eve of the war, the Jordanians allowed the United States to deploy a composite squadron of F-16 fighters so that the Special Forces could have timely air support.

Lingering concerns regarding the possible use of WMD against American and British forces were revived by an Iraqi defector—an officer who was fairly senior in the air force hierarchy before fleeing to Jordan in 2002. He claimed that Iraq had developed and fielded systems for dispensing chemical weapons from the air that were far more sophisticated than those the UN knew about. Most effective were binary-type nerve agents—a new generation of highly lethal nerve agents capable of penetrating most protective equipment (including gas masks)—installed in a new generation of weapons. He was sure the Iraqis would use WMD only as a last resort. "Saddam will never surrender these weapons," the defector insisted. "They are as much a part of his life as eating and drinking." Significantly, information about the Iraqi Air Force that this defector provided was vetted through independent sources and found to be very accurate.

Concurrently, Iraq also amended its force deployments in preparation for the coming war. First indications of renewed movements of Iraqi forces came when Republican Guard units were observed moving to the Tikrit area from northern Iraq. Several large truck convoys—one hundred trucks at a time—moved weapons, ammunition, heavy equipment, and troops to the vicinity of Tikrit. These troops could deploy into the city for urban warfare from their new deployment sites. On March 2, Iraq deployed batteries of Sumud-2 and Ababil-100 SSMs southward to forward positions from which they could strike American and British concentrations inside Kuwait. Multiple-source technical intelligence provided solid evidence that at least one SSM battery was equipped with chemical warheads. For example, the battery's communications system with the Iraqi high command in Baghdad was known to be a dedicated system for the delivery of commands directly from Saddam and his inner circle to units using WMD; conventional missile batteries did not have this kind of communication system. Moreover, chemical decontamination vehicles and added security were observed in the battery's compound—strong indications that chemical warheads were present.

The same day, the Iraqis conducted a major provocation of and signal to Riyadh. A MiG-25, flying at 70,000 feet, penetrated the Saudi airspace and surged toward Prince Sultan air base. U.S. Air Force F-15C fighters scrambled for a head-on intercept and reported to the AWACS [Airborne Warning and Control System] that they had locked on target and were two minutes from launch of air-to-air missiles. The Iraqis, who monitored the exchange, instructed their pilot to abort the sortie and race to the safety of Iraqi airspace. The incident was both a test of American and allied air defenses and a reminder to Riyadh of the Iraqi threat.

Also on March 2, Baghdad attempted a last-minute game of brinksmanship, suddenly threatening to stop the destruction of Sumud-2 missiles—in itself a deception because the missile's Volga-type engines were replaced with old SA-2 engines before the UN-supervised destruction—unless the United States reversed its war preparations. Moreover, Iraq claimed to be discovering "discarded" weapons, enticing continued cooperation with the UN and increasing European and Arab pressure on the United States to postpone the war and give the UN inspectors more time.

Tehran was not oblivious to these developments. On February 26, Iran closed the border with Iraq and declared a state of "national emergency" in the western provinces of the country. Army and IRGC units were put on a high state of alert and began deploying to forward positions near the border with Iraq. On March 1, large units of the Iranian Army moved close to the border at heightened readiness. By March 3, Iran had already deployed eight hundred tanks near the Iraqi border organized in two armies, in Qasar Shirin and Khorramshar. The Iranian forces were kept ready to move into the Shiite heartland. Meanwhile, Syria intensified the last-minute supplies of weapons from Slovakia, Belarus, Hungary, and Ukraine to Iraq—a major national-level undertaking organized by Firas Tlass, the son of Syria's minister of defense, and funded through an elaborate smuggling of Iraqi oil via Syria.

On March 1, Mubarak called for an emergency summit in Sharm el-Sheikh to demonstrate Arab solidarity with Iraq, as well as try to find a negotiated solution to the crisis and avert the war. The summit "completely rejected" any U.S.-led war on Iraq or the participation of any Arab state in the anticipated conflict. Most Arab leaders urged the Arab world to directly confront American and British "aggression" against Iraq, and called on the Arab League to secure a peaceful solution to the Iraqi crisis. They publicly demanded and privately pressured the Gulf States to evict the United States and prohibit operations from their territory.

The United Arab Emirates called on Saddam to resign in order to prevent war and urged other Arab leaders to come up with an initiative not too different from Primakov's. Mubarak publicly stated that he would give political asylum and protection to Saddam and the Iraqi leadership. Bashar bitterly complained about the Arab world's betrayal and abandonment of Iraq, and alluded to Syria's active support of the Iraqi war effort. Despite the Arab criticism of the war, however, Kuwait stated that, barring a decisive solution of the crisis, it would continue to allow the deployment of more than 140,000 American and British troops on its soil, and Qatar was also hosting invasion forces. Bahrain had deployed air and ground units to Kuwait in advance of the anticipated conflict with Iraq.

Throughout the summit, Crown Prince Abdallah was desperately attempting to consolidate a consensus that would include a resolute Arab position against Saddam Hussein, with support for the war as a last resort, but at the same time provide Saddam with an honorable exit to be supported by the entire Arab world. This effort came to naught when Libya's Muammar Qadhafi lashed out at Abdallah during a session broadcast live on Arab satellite TV. Qadhafi claimed that Saudi Arabia was in no position to consolidate an all-Arab position since King Fahd had been ready to "strike an alliance with the devil" to defend the kingdom after Iraq's 1990 invasion of Kuwait.

Crown Prince Abdallah then cut in, saying, "Saudi Arabia is not an agent of colonialism," referring to Saudi Arabia's accommodation of the American military. He then said to Qadhafi, "Who exactly brought you to power? . . . You are a liar and your grave awaits you."

With this question, Crown Prince Abdallah publicly acknowledged that Saudi Arabia had backed the 1969 coup by Qadhafi against then king Idris al-Senussi of Libya. He also implied that he knew Qadhafi was terminally ill. While Qadhafi subsequently apologized for his outburst, the exchange was the excuse everybody was looking for to avoid meeting the challenge of formulating an all-Arab position regarding the war all Arabs were dreading but incapable of preventing. "The Arab Nation with all its capabilities, its strategic position, and its active influence in the world economy should have an audible voice based on wisdom and logic," Bahraini King Hamad Bin Khalifa lamented.

The turmoil in the Arab world was a major issue brought up in periodic American and Israeli military and intelligence consultations conducted in March. The main topic, however, was tactical and military approaches to the Iraqi theater. Israeli experts warned against a frontal entry to Baghdad with massive forces. Instead, they suggested, the United States should encircle Baghdad while taking over Tikrit and other key objectives. U.S. and Israeli intelligence agreed on an estimate of 60,000 elite Iraqi troops inside Baghdad.

The assessment that Israeli military intelligence shared with Washington was that "the north and the south will be occupied easily, and the Iraqi forces in these areas will be annihilated. In Baghdad, the story will be different." In the Tikrit area, the challenge would be a large number of officers and former soldiers now joining special defense units, which constituted the last-resort protection of the regime after the fall of Baghdad. The Americans acknowledged that they would most likely delay their war against Iraq for at least another two weeks in order to complete their troop deployment throughout the theater. A senior Israeli military source told MENL's Steve Rodan that "the administration is not expected to launch a war against the regime of Iraqi President Saddam Hussein until after March 15."

Israel was urged to stay out of the war under any circumstances, and Jerusalem agreed in principle. "It is not our war," Defense Minister Mofaz said. "The extent of the threats is very low. We are taking all required steps to prepare." Jerusalem was now increasingly convinced that Baghdad was not likely to change its defensive strategy at the last minute. Although the Iraqi ballistic missiles and strike aircraft remained the most strategically significant threats because of their WMD warheads, there were other threats Israel could not ignore and so informed the United States. Meanwhile, Israel was concerned about the continued forward buildup of HizbAllah along the Lebanese border. Recently acquired intelligence suggested that Israel did not need to fear a massive attack by HizbAllah along the border with Lebanon, because the terrorist group had received instructions from Tehran and Damascus not to provoke a war with Israel. However, intelligence did warn about a major HizbAllah or Islamist terrorist attack inside Israel or against Israeli interests abroad. The warnings proved right on March 5 when a suicide bomber blew himself up on a Haifa bus, killing fifteen and wounding over forty—mainly teenagers. The martyr bomber, Shadi Kawasme, was a student in the Arab Polytechnikum University in Hebron—a known HAMAS stronghold. HAMAS blessed the operation, but Israel kept quiet because of the war's imminence.

Meanwhile, Saudi Arabia enabled the United States to make the latest adjustments to the forces deployed there. The U.S. Air Force refined the use of Prince Sultan air base facilities—especially the command, control, and communication center. The Saudis also agreed to the forward basing of SAR [Search and Rescue] helicopters and "specialized teams," which was an agreed-upon euphemism concealing the presence of clandestine Special Forces and CIA teams. The main center of special operations was the Araar Airport, some 10 miles from the Iraqi border. In addition, American troops landed at the Saudi air base at Tabouk, located near the border with Jordan and Saudi Arabia, and established another support base for SCUD-hunting operations. Iraq noticed some of these activities and, in March, sent Riyadh a harshly worded warning. Saudi forces were put on heightened readiness on March 3. Intriguingly, Saudi forces deployed to forward positions near the Iraqi-Kuwait-Saudi Arabian border to prevent U.S. forces from circling far behind Iraqi defenses, in a maneuver reminiscent of 1991's deep American offensive into Iraq through the Saudi desert.

On March 5, the Bush administration finally resigned itself to the long-obvious reality, namely that Turkey would not serve as a major front in the war. The Pentagon ordered CENTCOM to consider options for either an alternate northern front or a war based solely on ground troops originating from Kuwait. The White House put on a brave face as spokesman Ari Fleischer pointed to the existence of a Plan B excluding the use of Turkey, as distinct from the Plan A that included a northern front originating in Turkey. "The preferable is Plan A for a variety of geographic reasons," Fleischer said. "But Plan B is also a very militarily viable option, which will be successful. So I think it rather speaks for itself." A senior U.S. officer had quite a different opinion. "Yeah, 'B' as in bullshit," he quipped in response to a question about Plan B.

Actually, CENTCOM and the Pentagon did think about a fallback contingency plan for a northern front in case Turkey lived up to its refusal to let the United States use its facilities. However, the confidence of the Pentagon elite in resolving the Turkey problem was so absolute that only a few dared whisper about alternate solutions. Essentially, the fallback plan used the British air base in Akrotiri, Cyprus, as the main substitute for the Turkish air bases. The plan envisioned landing the 4th Infantry Division's equipment in an Israeli seaport and moving it in convoys to northern Jordan, with the division's troops being flown directly from Texas to Jordan. From northern Jordan, the division could cross into northwestern Iraq and still participate in the assault on the Sunni heartland and Baghdad as originally planned.

Cyprus, Israel, and Jordan gave their tacit approval to the plan. Hence, about ten ships laden with military equipment that had been waiting outside Turkish territorial waters were moved to a loitering area off the Israeli coast. Just to be on the safe side, CENTCOM quietly inquired with the Gulf States and Saudi Arabia about the transfer of troops and equipment through Israel and was assured that if the transfer were kept secret, these countries would simply ignore the move. However, on March 4, the White House vetoed this option, fearing that even "a whiff of a rumor" about using Israeli roads and ports would derail Arab support for the war. Instead, Bush called Mubarak and asked him to expedite the transfer of American ships via the Suez Canal on the way to Kuwait. Mubarak was noncommittal. "We are expecting the Egyptians to cause problems or just plain delays," a Pentagon source told MENL's Rodan. "It's clear that after the Turkish episode, the Egyptians will want guarantees for additional aid and other incentives."

Meanwhile, Ankara was adjusting to the new strategic realities. Back on March 4, a senior Turkish official had confirmed that "The National Policy

Document for Iraq, which considers the establishment of a Kurdish entity/state in northern Iraq as a reason for [military] intervention, is continuing without change." Given the policies on Kurdish autonomy espoused by the United States, the official concluded that "war will break out" between Kurdish and Turkish forces.

The TSK warned its government that in operating in northern Iraq, Turkey should now take into consideration American hostility. "If Turkish troops enter northern Iraq, this would cost Turkey," Ozkok told Gul. "It wouldn't be appropriate for the TSK to enter northern Iraq under these conditions as it didn't get enough support from the United States."

At the same time, all were in agreement that Turkey could not permit the rise of a Kurdish entity on its eastern border. Hence, Turkey first consolidated the positions of the division (about 20,000 troops) already in northern Iraq. Preparations were also made for the speedy insertion into northern Iraq of an additional four divisions, or 80,000 troops, now deployed on the Turkish side of the border. Special Forces detachments were dispatched to bolster the Turkman forces deep inside Iraq.

On March 6, a convoy of some two hundred military trucks reached the Iraqi border and soon afterward crossed into Iraq. The trucks were loaded with munitions, communications equipment, and other supplies. Ankara termed these movements routine. "The measures, which have been taken under totally normal procedures, are reflected as cross-border movements," the General Staff said. "All movements of the Turkish armed forces are initial measures regarded with security, which takes place within purview of the TSK. They should not be misconceived." TSK sources acknowledged that Ankara planned to deploy 80,000 troops into northern Iraq "to protect oil fields, protect the Turkman minority, and prevent the establishment of a Kurdish state."

On March 5, 2003, Saddam Hussein delivered a message to the Iraqi people at the advent of the Islamic New Year. Significantly, the speech was read on Iraqi TV and radio by an announcer and not Saddam himself, as had been customary for such speeches. Saddam's was an Islamist speech of the kind Osama bin Laden would have delivered. Therefore, the key to understanding Saddam's message is in the Islamic metaphors he used.

The timing and occasion of Saddam's speech were not accidental. The Islamic New Year is celebrated on the anniversary (by lunar calendar) of the Prophet Muhammad's forced migration—the *Hejira*—from Mecca to

Medina. It was in Medina that Muhammad built his forces and consolidated his base, and then returned triumphantly to Mecca—thus starting
the ascent of Islam.

In the first part of his message Saddam delved into the relevance of the
lessons to be learned from Muhammad's experience. He emphasized that
present-day Iraqis "also feel the determination of early believers . . . not to
relinquish their faith" either in word or in action, for like their historic predecessors, "they had rejected despotism and pruned the path of faith as
their own course." Muhammad's original followers, Saddam declared,
"fixed landmarks for all coming generations until faith and Islam have assumed their current status." Saddam stressed that this legacy is "what early
believers wished for us and aspired for so that we can be on the right, in-
fallible path, the path of faith with all the implied sincerity, zeal, and the requirements of jihad."

Saddam then went to great lengths to articulate the lessons of Muhammad's *Hejira*. Prophet Muhammad and his followers "left behind their
homes, families, and possessions." They were forced to leave Mecca
"haunted by the devil and tyranny," which included the people of Mecca
who had succumbed to "the influential tyrants and those who were driven
away by their superiority in number." Muhammad elected to migrate not
only to save his followers, Saddam stressed, but primarily "to establish a
capital for true Muslims and a center for their faith." He found this refuge
in Medina.

In Medina, Saddam explained, Muhammad consolidated "the umbrella of the glorious fraternity between *muhajirin* [migrants from Mecca]
and *ansar* [supporters from Medina]" that confronted the local Jewish
tribes, and through whose exploits "the early steps of building the army of
jihad were taken." These experiences defined the quintessence of Islamic
struggles. "The great values of faith, the ability to hold out and be determined to maintain jihad which were infused in the souls of believers, all
combined with the momentum of the right to seek a return to their homes
which they had left, to their families and beloved ones," Saddam explained,
shifting to contemporary issues. "Sincere Iraqis, men and women, brave
Palestinians and believers everywhere, when we recall all that within this
very brief account, we may ask: What is the despot of this age after?"

Saddam quickly answered the question, unifying in the process the
Iraqi cause with the Palestinian. He addressed his response to the "patient,
jihadist, sincere Iraqis, Palestinians, and all jihadists in our [Muslim] Nation." He highlighted all the sacrifices and suffering endured by both Iraqi

and Palestinian individuals as the foundations of the resurgence of the Muslim Nation. He emphasized that both Iraqis and Palestinians "are victorious by virtue of faith, through the course of justice against injustice, virtue against vice, sincerity against betrayal and the fight of the mercenaries and aggressors. The despot, along with his models, no matter how tyrannous he grows, is defeated." Saddam drew direct parallels between the trials and ultimate triumph of Muhammad's followers and those of contemporary Arabs. "Just as early believers who struggled and put up with harm to win God's reward," Saddam declared, "you would reap the gains of your patience, faith, God's satisfaction, and what you expect God to reward believers with. It is victory over your enemy."

Ultimately, the great quandary Saddam's speech failed to resolve was the significance of his emphasis on the legacy of the *Hejira*. Saddam's speech was delivered at the commemoration of Muhammad's original *Hejira*, and thus the mention of the subject was in place. However, these were not ordinary times. Iraq was on the eve of an invasion explicitly aimed at wiping out Saddam Hussein and his regime, and as a result, there was reason to read more into Saddam's historical-religious allegory. In his message to the Iraqi people, Saddam might have been telling the Iraqis that his disappearance in the aftermath of the invasion, as well as any discernable setback to the Baath regime, were really the initial phases of a modern-day *Hejira*—an escape and exile under adverse conditions—which like Prophet Muhammad's original *Hejira* would be the precursor of a historic return and triumph over the contemporary "despots" and "tyrants."

In early March, the White House had to make the final decision on going to war. While America's commitment to removing Saddam by force had been clear for all to see for several months, the formal and abiding decision was yet to be made. Hence, on March 5, Bush convened the national security leadership for the last round of deliberations regarding the war. He was briefed in great detail about the status of American forces—their deployments, capabilities, and war plans—and was also briefed on the progress of the UN weapon inspections and the latest political maneuvers at the UN. Bush resolved that the United States would no longer wait for the UN's endorsement; it would initiate military operations soon. Bush gave his approval to the existing force deployments and contingency plans. The ball started rolling.

The next night, Bush delivered a brief speech at the beginning of a press conference at the White House. It was a thinly veiled ultimatum to Iraq and the rest of the world. Facing the American people and the rest of the world, Bush looked and sounded like a commander in chief who had already made up his mind. "It makes no sense to allow this issue to continue on and on," he said. He flatly stated that Saddam Hussein's Iraq posed a direct threat to American security. The United States would unilaterally undertake all that was necessary to remove the threat, Bush stated, because "we don't need anybody's permission" to defend the United States and its interests. "I will not leave the American people at the mercy of the Iraqi dictator and his weapons," Bush reiterated. At the same time, bowing to mounting international pressure, Bush agreed to give Saddam Hussein until March 17 to comply with all pertinent UN Security Council resolutions.

The next day, March 7, CIA Director George Tenet arrived in Israel for a secret visit that would last only a few hours. In conversations with Sharon and senior defense and intelligence officials, he confirmed that war would begin on or immediately after March 17. Tenet demanded Israeli restraint regarding the Palestinians and Iraq and declared America's right to veto Israeli massive retaliation if Israel were attacked. Sharon stressed that Israel would retaliate if attacked, but agreed to honor a U.S. veto in the unlikely case that "uniquely extreme" retaliation were to be considered by Israel.

Over the next few days, there was growing apprehension in Washington that Saddam might come out at the last minute with sufficient concessions, exciting the Europeans and Arabs and complicating America's ability to strike out on time. Sudden moves of key units in southern Iraq added to the worry. Most significant was the redeployment of two Iraqi armored brigades—the 41st and 624th—in the marshes of Abu Ghorab Slam, Meymouneh, Juraygah, Gusara, and Sida, all in Meysan Province near the Iranian border. This marshy area was the bastion of Iranian-backed Shiite opposition forces. The redeployment of these brigades implied a shift in Iraqi priorities away from confronting the invasion to dealing with internal instability.

Tehran contributed to Baghdad's growing agitation. On March 5, Hashemi-Rafsanjani warned of a wave of terrorism in the aftermath of an attack on Iraq. "The continuation of pressure on the people of Iraq will promote terrorism in the region and the world. Terrorism is a consequence of coercion and bullying. If America occupies Iraq and the Iraqi people feel they cannot seek justice, it is possible that they will resort to terrorism and clandestine violence," Hashemi-Rafsanjani stated. Concurrently, Iran launched a major IRGC exercise in the province of Khuzestan, near the Iraqi border. The exercise involved 20,000 troops operating in four different areas of Khuzestan. Brigadier General Zahedi, acting deputy commander of the IRGC, said the exercise would train forces in such areas as asymmetrical warfare in order to increase Iran's capability to defend "against any type of modern weapon."

On the night of March 11, Michael Gurdus, who works for Israeli radio and television and has long been regarded as the leading communications monitor in the Middle East, told Israel's Channel 2 TV that the U.S. military had been ordered to launch a war against Iraq on March 18. He reported that the order had been relayed by U.S. Central Command to all American forces in the Persian Gulf. Gurdus explained that he heard the order being relayed to American pilots and others over radio communications he had intercepted earlier that day. Gurdus's scoop came a day after Israeli media reported Washington's demand that senior Israeli officials stop issuing predictions of when the war would begin.

7
THE RACE TO BAGHDAD, PART 1

I t was the stuff fictional thrillers are made of. The director of Central Intelligence suddenly breaks into the chambers of the secretary of defense in the Pentagon holding extremely hot raw intelligence. After a brief consultation and a call to the Oval Office, both senior officials rush to the White House for an unscheduled emergency meeting with the waiting president. As a direct consequence of this meeting, America's meticulous contingency plans for the opening phase of the war with Iraq are drastically changed at the last minute, and stealth aircraft and cruise missiles are diverted to make a "decapitating" strike on Baghdad—an audacious gambit that would ultimately prove futile.

But that's exactly what happened on March 19, 2003.

That morning, President Bush went to the situation room of the White House to be briefed about the latest update and status of the war plans—officially designated "OPLAN 1003 V." The plan covered the overt contingencies to be undertaken once the United States was officially engaged in fighting with Iraq. This was a somewhat thin line of legalese, for the real—albeit undeclared and unacknowledged—war with Iraq had already begun almost two weeks before. Around 10 A.M. Bush approved "OPLAN 1003 V" and instructed that it be put into action. The plan would remain intact for about six hours.

Shortly before 3 P.M. (11 P.M. Baghdad time), the schedule of CIA Director George Tenet was interrupted by the arrival of fresh data from Baghdad. An intelligence source there had identified in advance the bunker where Saddam and his two sons were going to spend the night, at a Baghdad complex called Dora Farm. The source had been deemed very reliable, and some of his data was checked independently against other sources—particularly data collected by American sources through technical means. Therefore, Tenet concluded that this intelligence warning should be capitalized on. He immediately rushed to the Pentagon and, around 3:30 P.M., burst into the offices of Defense Secretary Donald Rumsfeld, who at the time was discussing the forthcoming air war with his deputy Paul Wolfowitz. The opening phase of the air war was scheduled to begin the next night. Now, Tenet argued, presenting the latest intelligence from Baghdad, there was a possibility of ending the war in a single "decapitating strike"—that is, by killing Saddam and his inner circle before major fighting erupted. Rumsfeld agreed, and Tenet called the White House from the Pentagon, requesting an emergency meeting with the president.

Around 4 P.M. Tenet and Rumsfeld entered the Oval Office and told Bush that the CIA believed it had a fix on Saddam and that the Pentagon was convinced it could deliver the decapitating strike. They now needed presidential authorization to go into action. This was not a simple demand, for carrying out the proposed decapitating strike amounted to completely altering "OPLAN 1003 V"—the carefully orchestrated and detailed war plan CENTCOM had been working on for several months. Hence, Bush called in other members of his national security team—Vice President Cheney, Secretary of State Colin Powell, National Security Adviser Condoleezza Rice, White House Chief of Staff Andrew Card Jr., and Air Force Gen. Richard Myers, chairman of the Joint Chiefs of Staff. Bush let Tenet and Rumsfeld repeat their suggestion. Army Gen. Tommy Franks joined in from his headquarters via secure video link. There ensued a debate about the practical, political, and legal implications of launching the decapitating strikes.

By 6:30 P.M., once the military contended they could improvise and run the war in accordance with the new schedule, Bush signed the launch order, authorizing initial preparations for the strike to commence. Two F-117A stealth strike fighters, each armed with a pair of 2,000-pound bunker-busting bombs, were launched from the Al-Udeid air base in Qatar. On several navy ships and submarines, new targeting data was inserted to some forty Tomahawk cruise missiles. In the Oval Office, meanwhile, the debate continued on whether to implement the new plans, taking into account the strict 7:15 P.M. deadline set by General Franks. At 7:12 P.M. Bush said, "Let's go," and a few minutes later, the two F-117As slipped undetected into Iraqi airspace on their way to Baghdad. Sometime after 9 P.M. a CIA spy on-site reported that Saddam was inside the bunker.

At about 9:30 P.M.—5:30 A.M. Baghdad time—the two fighters dropped their bombs on the main building of Dora Farm. Within minutes, some forty cruise missiles had blanketed the general area. "Coalition forces have begun striking selected targets of military importance to undermine Saddam Hussein's ability to wage war," Bush said in a televised address later that night. "These are the opening stages of what will be a broad and concerted campaign."

In Baghdad, surprise was complete. It took almost half an hour—until around 6:00 A.M. Baghdad time, 10:00 P.M. Washington time—before sirens, as well as heavy bombing, were reported in Baghdad and Saddam's hometown of Tikrit. Radio Baghdad went off the air. Soon afterward, UK-based B-52s and various strike aircraft from bases in the Gulf and aircraft carriers attacked a few additional targets in three distinct waves of attacks launched to obscure the real focus on the Dora Farm compound. The B-52s used Israel's airspace to get to Iraq from the west. Radio Baghdad went back on the air at 6:30 A.M.—10:30 P.M. Washington time—despite the bombing. A brief message was read by an announcer. "The sons of the great Iraq, the sons of the great leader Saddam Hussein, who will triumph, with God's help . . . Glory to the valiant men, the lions of Iraq the nation, the lions of the Iraq of Saddam Hussein, the victorious heroic leader, and the bastion of jihad . . . Glory to you, O sons of our great, heroic armed forces, the soldiers of the great redeemed leader, Saddam Hussein."

On March 20, Iraqi state radio and television broadcasts were repeatedly interrupted by new appeals to the military to fight for Saddam. A few hours after the strike, a defiant Saddam appeared on Iraqi television. He was disheveled, his moustache showed signs of gray (he had not colored his mustache properly), and he was wearing big square reading glasses (rather than his customary contacts). He read his speech from a steno pad rather than facing the camera. All of these features indicated a fairly impromptu production—a quick reaction to the failed decapitation strike—aimed at convincing the Iraqis he was alive and in control. He urged all Iraqis to escalate the fighting. "Unsheathe your sword," Saddam said. "Nobody will be victorious unless he is a brave man." Saddam concluded with a call to jihad in the name of all traditional causes. "Let Iraq live, long live jihad, and long live Palestine," he declared. And although "intelligence sources" and "senior officials" in both Washington and London kept alluding for a few more days to the possibility of Saddam's being either killed or wounded in the "decapitating strike," decision-makers had no such illusions. The silver bullet strike had failed. Moreover, the massive "shock and awe" air and missile strikes had now been postponed to the point where the surprise factor was largely diminished by Baghdad's anticipation of further hostilities.

Meanwhile, U.S. intelligence continued to receive a flow of data from Baghdad. The CIA's spy, who was somewhere outside the bunker, reported that Saddam and his two sons "definitely were" inside one of the three buildings of the Dora compound at the time of the strike. He sent numerous reports from the scene of rescue workers furiously digging in the rubble and said that Saddam had been wounded. The United States intercepted hysterical phone calls for medical help and emergency services. The initial reports reaching the CIA, ostensibly from agents on the scene, stressed that Saddam was either dead or had been removed on a stretcher, his face covered with a big oxygen mask. After Saddam's appearance, a CIA source still insisted that Saddam was believed to have "sustained two burst eardrums" during the attack and "also sustained damage from concussion" and was "extremely disoriented . . . almost in a vegetative state" for a time. Saddam's TV appearance, CIA officials intimated, was a prerecorded tape. For the next several days, U.S. and British officials would keep arguing that Saddam had been either killed or wounded in the air strike.

By contrast, the Kremlin had no illusions about the outcome of America's targeted strike. The March 20 Daily Intelligence Survey of the GRU reported on the strike's outcome: "According to the information received from Baghdad, the air strikes directed against the Iraqi leadership did not achieve their goals. Saddam Hussein and all key members of his cabinet are alive and distributed across several different locations." The GRU expected the Iraqi leadership to activate emergency procedures. "It is likely that Iraq's political and military leadership will be organized in accordance with the so-called 'network' principle," the GRU opined. "Iraqi political and military leadership will be constantly moving across a network of bunkers and other secure locations, conducting all communications using only secure lines and refraining from concentrating in one place more than two key leaders." This "network" leadership protection system would remain functioning until after the fall of Baghdad.

Subsequent reports from highly authoritative intelligence sources confirmed that Saddam and his sons had not been anywhere near Dora Farm at the time of the strike. "Within the [U.S. intelligence] community there is a general belief that Saddam is still alive, and the rest is wishful thinking," conceded a senior intelligence official. Indeed, a postwar search of the area by a U.S. Army team failed to find any corroborating evidence of Saddam's presence. Col. Tim Madere, the team's commander, told CBS News that "basically what [the team] saw was giant holes created. No underground facilities, no bodies." He added that people hiding in the main palace at Dora "could have survived" the strike. But there was more to the incident: Highly reliable Iraqi opposition sources subsequently revealed that "five Iraqi senior officials were killed as they were waiting for Saddam to arrive for a scheduled meeting." The sources stressed that "neither Saddam nor his sons arrived." This was a major point that did not receive attention in the immediate aftermath of the decapitating strike. Saddam's last-minute failure to show up meant that not only was the data sent to the CIA totally false, but in all likelihood it had been intentionally planted to confuse and mislead Washington. The fact that Iraqi officials were killed in the bombing should have meant nothing to American analysts. Given his ruthless purge of the Iraqi elite for several decades, Saddam would have had no qualms about sacrificing senior officials as bait to enhance the believability of the disinformation. This realization brought to the surface a major debate on the reliability of the raw intelligence used in formulating American policy and strategy toward Iraq.

In April, senior security officials in Amman long involved with Iraq reported that their sources inside Baghdad confirmed that two days before the bombing, Saddam Hussein had already disappeared into a hidden command center the location of which remained unknown even to his innermost circle. Since then, the Baghdad sources reported, Saddam had not met anybody in person or even talked to any senior official directly by telephone. By April 3, he was still sending his instructions through a few loyal messengers in writing or in video-and audiocassettes. The Baghdad sources believed that Qusay was the only person to know exactly where Saddam Hussein was hiding at any given time.

The specific material that prompted the March 20 decapitation strike came from a single spy in the heart of Baghdad. He was a relatively recent "walk-in"—a volunteering spy. Since early 2003, the United States had maintained a small team of CIA and Delta Force operatives either inside or just outside Baghdad—searching, in the words of American intelligence officials, for a way "to penetrate Saddam Hussein's inner circle." On the eve of the war, the CIA was approached by a senior Iraqi official who claimed to be in a position to know the schedule and location of the hideaways Saddam was using each night. The Iraqi official claimed that he had compared the risks of having Saddam discover his betrayal against the ramifications of being put on trial once the American military reached Baghdad.

He decided to take his chances with the Americans, he told the CIA operatives, and provided numerous tidbits about the workings of Saddam's inner circle. Shortly afterward, he told his handlers about the plans of Saddam and his sons for the night of March 19–20. By now, some of the earlier material provided by the spy had been verified independently as a result of a major achievement by a small group from Delta Force who had infiltrated a fiber-optic communication center in Baghdad. By monitoring these secure communications, the United States could intercept several calls that ultimately confirmed details provided by the Iraqi spy (who, the CIA believes, could not have known about the communications breakthrough). The possibility that both the spy and the intercepted communications were coordinated parts of a single deception plan was not even considered by the CIA.

Events in Baghdad immediately after the initial shock of the decapitation strike waned should have set off alarms in Washington. Three Iraqis who had assisted the CIA in the operation were immediately rounded up and executed. Iraqi counterintelligence shot two of them and cut out the tongue of the third—leaving him to bleed to death. The speed and efficiency of the Iraqi dragnet should have been contrasted with the near immunity enjoyed by the CIA and Delta Force operatives for the previous few months. Unless the CIA could identify a precise and convincing reason for the sudden capture of the three Iraqi spies, it should have assumed that the Iraqis chose not to round up the Americans in their midst. In other words, much of the intelligence collected by the Baghdad-based networks could have been compromised or even intentionally planted from the very beginning. As it was, the overall reliability of the espionage networks in Iraq was not challenged, nor were the basic intelligence assumptions made on the basis of material arriving from Iraq revisited. The administration went to war convinced that its reading of Iraq was accurate.

By the time fighting began, the United States had long been immersed in an all-out intelligence effort to recruit and subvert members of the Iraqi leadership. The intelligence community's quest to flip Iraq's senior officers both reinforced and was reinforced by the firm belief of the key proponents of the war in the Pentagon and their friends in the Iraqi opposition that there was widespread opposition to Saddam in the ranks of the military. There was a conviction in Washington that since the Iraqi military leadership had long been victimized by Saddam, it would therefore be inclined to participate in, or at least contribute to, Saddam's downfall. In the fall of 2002, senior Pentagon officials, particularly Secretary Rumsfeld and his closest civilian aides, were convinced that discontent among Iraq's military elite had reached the point of mutiny given the right circumstances—circumstances that an American invasion would create.

The intelligence drive was also motivated by military considerations. One of the panacea "combat multipliers" designed to enable the United States to take on Iraq with a minimal force was convincing the Iraqi Army—that is, the senior commanders—to stay out of the war. By early 2003, the United States had embarked on a new round of contacts aimed as much at persuading Saddam's inner circle to avoid war at the last minute as at inducing Iraqi senior officers to surrender and stay out of the war. This effort included Special Forces and CIA operatives bribing a number of senior officers with millions of dollars each to keep themselves and their units from resisting the advance of the American and British forces.

The American relationship with the Iraqi military elite, as well as with the various opposition groups that facilitated access to most of its members, has been excruciating at best, and by 2002, much hinged on interpretation of the events of 1996. In Amman, Ayad Allawi, the chief of the Iraqi National Accord, which had long received funding from the CIA, claimed he could orchestrate an anti-Saddam military coup. Allawi claimed to be leading a network of current and former military officers, as well as Baath officials, called *Wifaq* ("Trust" in Arabic), which he now intended to activate against Saddam. The coup attempt failed miserably and led to the slaughter of many patriotic Iraqi officers and their extended families by the Iraqi security services. Throughout the coup's preparatory phase, Ahmad Chalabi, chief of the Iraqi National Congress—which received aid from the CIA—warned that the coup had been penetrated by Saddam's agents and was thus doomed to fail. The CIA, and subsequently other key elements of Washington, had not forgiven Chalabi for being right. The subsequent near total disengagement from covert operations inside Iraq by the Clinton administration did not improve American intelligence in Iraq.

By the time Bush took office, the American intelligence community found itself increasingly dependent on material from Israel and Jordan, since both countries had been maintaining extensive human intelligence (HUMINT) resources inside Iraq. In early 2001, with a major confrontation with Iraq fast becoming a major objective of the fledgling administration, the CIA rushed to catch up and acquire sources and capabilities of its own. The haste, coupled with an endemic absence of deep skills in handling HUMINT, had a direct impact on the quality and reliability of the sources recruited by the CIA. "The Agency has been working for months to hook up with Iraqi dissidents in-country," an administration official told UPI's Richard Sale. Indeed, the fragmented and self-devouring Iraqi opposition provided many of the CIA's initial impressions of, and contacts with, members of the Iraqi military elite. And the number one objective of any opposition faction was to further its own agenda in Washington—at times through the dissemination of self-supporting disinformation and at times by concealing its own shortcomings—rather than to ensure Washington's objectives and comprehensive knowledge of Iraq. By 2002, key members and leaders of Iraqi opposition factions had adapted to telling Washington what they believed it wanted to hear. In the absence of indigenous intelligence capabilities inside Iraq, and with the some of the CIA inherently hostile to and distrustful of intelligence provided by Israel (because the CIA's Arabists feared Israel was tainting intelligence to further its own policies), the administration had no independent body of knowledge of Iraq against which to check the claims made by the opposition factions and their contacts and sources inside Iraq.

In fall 2002, with the United States intensifying its preparations for a major confrontation with Iraq by ordering intelligence and special operations inside the country, the opposition factions rushed to provide opinions and recommendations. Many aspiring leaders claimed they would be able to acquire control of some components of the Iraqi military before or during the initial phases of an American war. "Nobody in Iraq will defend that regime, including the military, both the regular army and the Republican Guard, elements of the security forces, and the general population," INC's al-Hussein said. "All of Iraq has suffered for many years from the oppression of Saddam Hussein's regime, and there is not a single person out there in Iraq that will fight or defend him." The majority of opposition leaders and former military officers insisted that the bulk of the Iraqi forces—including the Republican Guards and Special Republican Guards—would not fight for Saddam. "I don't think they will fight fiercely for Saddam," Najib Salhi said. "Even those closest—we know them quite well—are disgruntled. A few hundred, isolated from news of the outside world, will fight for the first couple of days." All these exiled former officers pointed to their extensive connections with former colleagues and friends inside Iraq as their sources of unique knowledge and ability to implement their plans. They asked for, and received, lavish financial aid from the

United States in order to improve and expand their communications with their Iraqi contacts and sources.

Baghdad was paying very close attention to these dynamics. Iraqi intelligence had long been tightly monitoring all communications with the West, officials' travels to neighboring countries, and signs of sudden wealth. That close supervision of society enabled Baghdad to quickly identify the mounting American efforts to build contacts with the military elite. Starting in September, dozens, if not hundreds, of intelligence officers—mainly from Sadam's Fedayeen—began to penetrate and subvert the effort. These agents approached Iraqi commanders and officers, claiming to be representatives of American-sponsored opposition groups. They offered huge sums of money, badly needed medicine for family members, and even shelter in the West in return for commitment to cooperate with the United States by avoiding the fight once the war began. There followed immediate public executions in the middle of Iraq's main garrisons of anybody showing even the slightest inclination to cooperate with the United States. At least thirty-five such executions were confirmed within the first couple of weeks of September. This ruthless counterintelligence initiative constituted a major blow to the efforts of the legitimate opposition to penetrate the Iraqi establishment.

Meanwhile, Iraqi intelligence vastly expanded its infiltration of the various opposition movements cooperating with the CIA, by activating numerous long-term plants in the West. For example, students and would-be refugees who had been permitted to leave Iraq in return for future cooperation with Iraqi intelligence were now called upon, with their families in Iraq serving as hostages to assure their good behavior. To ensure that nobody resisted the Iraqi overtures, the extended families of the first few hesitant plants were arrested, tortured, and executed. Baghdad's message was received. In many cases, Iraqi intelligence capitalized on newly established contacts between the exiled officers and their friends in Iraq to extort the opposition members into cooperating with Baghdad. Captured documents of Iraqi intelligence confirm the extent of the infiltration and subversion. For example, an October 29, 2002, a memo from Directorate 14 (in charge of special operations and assassinations) reported that "one of our sources in the United States, with a high level of reliability, says the CIA and the so-called opposition have a joint plan to bring 'quislings' to Iraq from the north and south to gather information and await future missions. Our informant will be one of them." Ultimately, Iraq used its vast network of agents both as spies and as conduits of disinformation to the United States. The latter role would have a lingering impact on Washington.

The pinnacle of the Iraqi counterintelligence effort was the *al-Tajammua* ("the Grouping") episode. It was built on the long traditions of the Soviet intelligence system—for a quarter of a century the source of knowledge, expertise, and support of Iraqi intelligence—in both creating and subverting indigenous opposition organizations in order to undermine efforts by foreign intelligence services. Indeed, the *al-Tajammua* was tailored after the great success of the mother of all deceptions—the NKVD's Trust of the early 1920s. (See "Notes: The Historical Record," p. 517.)

In the fall of 2002, with the CIA encouraging anybody they could to make contact with their relatives and acquaintances in Iraq in order to turn on Saddam, emissaries from Iraq suddenly arrived in Western Europe—seeking contact with the CIA. The emissaries claimed to represent a new faction aspiring to power in a postwar Iraq, all members of the Iraqi elite still inside the country. They claimed the *al-Tajammua* included a cabinet minister, military officers, university professors, tribal sheikhs, and other elite members of Iraq's Sunni, Shiite, and Kurdish factions, all of whom were united in their opposition to Saddam and the Baath Party and committed to the establishment of a pro-Western pluralistic government. In return for American support, the emissaries said, the military members of the group would disband the Republican Guard before it could confront the advancing forces and, immediately after the war, hand over all weapons of mass destruction to the American authorities. Sporadic contacts continued over the next few months, with *al-Tajammua* providing tidbits of intelligence to demonstrate its presence in the highest echelons of power. At the same time, the emissaries refused to divulge the identity of their key membership, citing the oppressive and pervasive nature of Iraqi counterintelligence.

By winter, the emissaries had one request for their CIA contacts. With the sweeps by Iraqi counterintelligence intensifying in response to the American outreach, the leaders of *al-Tajammua* were facing growing risks to their safety. They were fearful that a counterintelligence operation against one of the Western-based opposition organizations would result in their discovery and fall. Therefore, the emissaries urged the CIA contacts, there should be some form of coordination between them and the opposition activities so that they could both help the opposition representatives and, more important, avoid being implicated by their dangerous follies.

The United States urged various opposition groups to cooperate and assist *al-Tajammua* until American troops were actually inside Baghdad.

In early 2003, *al-Tajammua* and related individuals were instrumental in assisting the CIA and Special Forces operatives reach and operate in the greater Baghdad area. On one hand, they provided tremendous assistance and shelter; indeed, no American operative was captured or killed during this period. The operatives got inside help in entering communications centers and other strategic facilities, which enabled them to identify and mark crucial targets for the bombing campaign. At the same time, the Iraqi "hosts" had a fairly good knowledge of what the operatives did and saw, and in many cases were able to dissuade them from taking certain actions by citing security risks. Significantly, the Iraqi spy who would pinpoint Saddam's whereabouts on the night of March 19–20, profoundly changing the opening phase of the war, approached the American operatives in the context of these relations.

American cooperation with *al-Tajammua* peaked in February, when its representatives subverted a meeting between retired general Anthony Zinni and "two Iraqi generals close to Saddam." The meeting was organized by Greek Defense Minister Yanos Papandoniou in order to allow Zinni to clarify to the Iraqis just how determined the United States was to get rid of Saddam. Papandoniou was convinced that once confronted with the full extent of the Americans' resolve, the Iraqi military elite might either convince Saddam to give up or instigate a military coup, thus alleviating the need for a destructive war. Suddenly, *al-Tajammua* emissaries intimated that the two generals were somehow connected to their organization, although they were not members or even aware of its existence as an entity. Therefore, they recommended, Zinni should be forthcoming and encouraging rather than threatening. And so, when he met in Athens with the two Iraqi generals, Zinni urged them to work together to prevent the war. If that could not be achieved, Zinni urged them to deliver his message to the Iraqi high command to stay out of the war and survive. The American ultimatum, which might have affected the Iraqis, was not delivered.

Ultimately, after the liberation of Baghdad, all contacts were suddenly broken with *al-Tajammua* emissaries. No *al-Tajammua* members showed up to participate in the establishment of a postwar government in Iraq. No *al-Tajammua* member was there to hand over Iraq's weapons of mass destruction. Actually, members of *al-Tajammua* did not reveal themselves to the authorities at all. In other words, it seems clear that *al-Tajammua* was an audacious and largely successful anti-American provocation by Iraqi intelligence, which not only gained the Iraqis invaluable data about the CIA's activities in and against Iraq, but helped skew American intelligence's view of the potential challenges in postwar Iraq.

A sideshow related to the *al-Tajammua* episode was the case of Gen. Nizar al-Khazraji, a former Iraqi Army chief of staff who defected in the mid-nineties. By that time he had already been implicated in the gassing of the Kurds in the late 1980s, the occupation of Kuwait in 1990, and the ruthless suppression of the Shiite revolt in 1991. Indeed, he was indicted for war crimes by the international court. But by the late 1990s, as Khazraji quietly moved around Europe—finally settling in a small out-of-the-way Danish town—the CIA was viewing him as the key to post-Saddam Iraq, believing that he would be able to use his enduring influence in the Iraqi military to consolidate a post-Saddam military regime strongly influenced by the United States. Khazraji played the part. "I am sure that as soon as we set foot in Iraq, military units will join us. There are a large number of officers and soldiers who are ready to work with the United States so that we can fight our way to Baghdad," he told *Al-Hayah* in an interview on December 2, 2002. To his many detractors, Khazraji was known as "the CIA's General Karzai"—a disciplined puppet dictator to be empowered and controlled by Washington.

By fall 2002, at the behest of the CIA, Khazraji began reviving old military contacts in Iraq. He soon reported that there was a clandestine group among the senior officers that was both fiercely nationalist and staunchly anti-Saddam. That group wanted him—Khazraji—to be their go-between with a receptive Washington. What these Iraqi officers really needed, Khazraji told the CIA in the winter of 2002–2003, was extensive financial and political assistance so that they could organize their own coup against Saddam. When the United States was reluctant to oblige, fearing that the proposed coup in Baghdad would precipitate a rash of assassinations, which the CIA is legally prohibited from supporting, Khazraji went public with his warnings against the dire ramifications of a war with Iraq. "If a military confrontation takes place, the allied forces will use all their efforts to ensure success and to ensure they sustain no casualties. Hence, these forces will use their best equipment. It is possible that this equipment would destroy the environment and future Iraqi generations, similar to what happened during the Gulf War and in Afghanistan. Furthermore, tearing the Iraqi people apart and destroying their infrastructure and armed forces will lead to chaos. This could also lead to endless civil war," Khazraji told Al-Jazeerah TV on January 19, 2003. Instead of an American war, Khazraji urged that he be provided with the necessary assistance to return to Iraq and lead a military revolt against Saddam. "I feel like a caged lion. I should be in Iraq leading the people and the military against Saddam. I am certain that my presence in Iraq would convince the military to change the direction of its cannons and weapons, so that they would point toward Saddam," Khazraji said on February 21, 2003. "It is only natural for the people to turn against an American army of occupation, which will bomb the infrastructure and the military forces, remain in Iraq for a long time, and install a puppet government, while the cost of the war would ultimately be paid by Iraq's own wealth and oil."

Despite all this bravado, Khazraji retained his dependence on, and close cooperation with, the CIA. The handling of his case at the international court was progressing, and in early 2003 Copenhagen warned him that once an international arrest warrant was issued, the Danish asylum would be revoked and he would be extradited to The Hague. On March 17—the eve of the war—Khazraji vanished from his home in Denmark. His CIA friends moved him to the Persian Gulf via a few stops in Europe, and once hostilities commenced, Khazraji resurfaced at the head of what a senior Arab official called "a team of negotiators—with the participation of CIA elements—to hold direct talks with field commanders in the Iraqi armed forces in order to persuade those field commanders to stop fighting the U.S.-UK coalition forces." Furthermore, according to Iraqi opposition sources, "contacts with Iraqi field commanders, which are being supervised by the CIA and U.S. Special Forces in Iraq, aim to research the possibility of large numbers of Iraqi soldiers laying down their arms and maybe even the participation of Iraqi elite forces in capturing Saddam Hussein alive and handing him over to the U.S. forces."

On the eve of the war, Khazraji and his team clandestinely crossed into southern Iraq to expedite their mediation efforts with the military elite. Khazraji claimed to have established contacts with a few senior officers with whom he had long-standing ties. He conveyed Washington's offer for cooperation during and after the war. Senior Iraqi opposition officials in Beirut explained that Khazraji was urging his friends "to intervene to persuade President Saddam to show flexibility toward suggested mediation to spare the country the risk of mass destruction and guarantee his personal safety." In return, the officials added, "These commanders are promised a major role in the postwar era. They are to continue to have the same privileges they have at present and the option to carry out a military coup against Saddam to end the war." When the Iraqi senior officers declined to commit to a military coup or actively assist the American "invading troops," Khazraji offered his own plan to avoid war. According to these officials, Khazraji's "plan involves a safe refuge for President Saddam outside the country on condition that the Republican Guards do not use chemical weapons to abort any agreement between the army command and the U.S. troops. However, if Saddam insists on fighting even after such an agreement is reached, these army commanders are to ensure that no large number of units would take part in the fight, so as to weaken Saddam's front considerably and make it less difficult to handle militarily." Throughout, Khazraji insisted he had Washington's backing and authority to make such offers and deals.

As fighting escalated, the Khazraji team expanded its communications via cell phones, radios, and even couriered messages. Most of the communications were conducted through third parties meeting members of Khazraji's team in remote places. On March 24, senior American intelligence officials told the *Washington Post* that "covert contacts with Iraqi leaders were continuing in hopes of bringing about the surrender of Iraqi military forces, defections of key individuals, restraint in using chemical and biological weapons and eventually the downfall of [Saddam] Hussein." Once again, the emissaries of the Iraqi military interlocutors asked for a demonstration of faith from the United States—steps that would enable them to continue negotiating without arousing the suspicion of Saddam's security forces. With that in mind, the United States held off bombing the Iraqi Ministry of Defense because that was where the officers negotiating with Khazraji were reportedly hiding. As a result, the Iraqi high command was able to sustain some communications with its fighting units throughout most of the war.

As in the case of *al-Tajammua*, Khazraji's most promising contacts did not show up once the United States occupied Baghdad, and he remains one of the greatest enigmas of the CIA's relentless efforts to subvert Saddam's inner circle. It is still not clear where his real loyalties lay. While it is clear that he was not loyal to his CIA patrons, there is an enduring debate about whether he was a power-hungry, unscrupulous general who made expedient deals to further his own personal agenda, or a pragmatist who reached an agreement with Saddam assuring his personal safety in return for his assistance in Iraq's secret war against America.

By now, the Kremlin had an unambiguous picture of the situation in Baghdad. The GRU's March 20 Daily Intelligence Survey addressed the reliability and loyalty of the Iraqi high command in the context of the effectiveness of American covert operations. "In the next 24 hours Americans are anticipating news of 'sharp political changes' in Iraq. Analysts believe that an overthrow plot against Saddam Hussein prepared by the CIA during the past few months is the reason behind such expectations. However, Russian agents are reporting that this plot was either uncovered in time or was under control of the Iraqi security agencies from the very beginning. This information is confirmed by a certain air of unease within the CIA command center in Qatar, as the expected overthrow of Hussein was supposed to take place several days ago." In retrospect, the GRU's reading of the situation and analysis proved highly accurate.

Ultimately, the aggregate impact of all these relations and contacts with the Iraqi opposition, including the vast majority of Iraqi defectors, was the emergence of a completely skewed understanding of the situation in Iraq. That this intelligence analysis suited the political interests of the upper echelons of the Bush administration made it very tempting to adopt. As a rule, politicians are disinclined to challenge or doubt an intelligence analysis that confirms policies they have already committed to. Hence, as American operational plans were being drawn with emphasis on use of the smallest possible number of ground forces, the state of the Iraqi Army was a major factor in justifying an essentially political decision. "I don't believe we have to defeat Saddam's army. I think Saddam's army will defeat Saddam," opined Richard Perle, one of the more influential Pentagon advisers and proponents of the war.

The same logic applied to the need for a comprehensive system of controlling postwar Iraq and mopping up terrorism and subversion. The Iraqi opposition led Washington to believe that the newly liberated Iraqi people would be grateful to the American forces and would not constitute a security threat. "An explosion of joy will greet our soldiers," said Deputy Defense Secretary Paul Wolfowitz. Even as intelligence reports kept arriving, some from in-country Special Forces, about the active preparations of the Iraqi Army, there was a systemic reluctance to abandon the belief in the self-induced collapse of the Iraqi military system. "There may be pockets of resistance, but very few Iraqis are going to fight to defend Saddam Hussein," Perle suggested in February.

This conviction about the situation in Iraq would ultimately dominate America's war plans, affecting both the size and composition of deployed forces and preparations for handling postwar Iraq. On March 13, Donald

Rumsfeld, Richard Myers, and Peter Pace outlined the administration's thinking on the war to a group of former senior officers, think-tank strategists, and intelligence experts. The Pentagon envisioned a limited ground force of around 70,000 troops embarking on a "lightning drive" to Baghdad in which Iraq's cities would "be bypassed." The race to Baghdad would be facilitated by a "spectacular but precise" bombing campaign generating "shock and awe"—that is, debilitating and perhaps even decapitating the Iraqi leadership. "A hated regime could be removed without waging war on an entire country," Rumsfeld argued. The Pentagon expected Iraqi forces to desert Saddam and the "Iraqi people" to rise up against the Baath regime. This way, the Pentagon insisted, the war would be over "in weeks or even days" with little bloodshed by either Americans or Iraqis. Retired Gen. Barry R. McCaffrey, who commanded the 24th Infantry Division during the 1991 Gulf War and attended the March 13 briefing, warned at the time that planners were risking a "political and military disaster" if the Pentagon's assumptions regarding the Iraqi resistance proved incorrect. "They chose to go into battle with a ground combat capability that was inadequate, unless their assumptions proved out," McCaffrey said.

Meanwhile, desperate last-minute mediation efforts were taking place to make sure Saddam comprehended the gravity of the situation. Several individuals—mostly Arabs—who had established personal relations with Saddam took part in these efforts. They included a Jordanian business partner of Saddam's sons, an Egyptian businessman, oil trader, and sanctions buster, and a Jordanian minister. According to Jordanian officials who monitored some of these contacts, they were really nonstarters because "the U.S. administration insists on one condition in order to end the war; namely, for President Saddam Hussein to abdicate and depart Iraq. Baghdad absolutely rejects that condition and conceives the possibility of other arrangements." But Iraqi sources in Beirut and Cairo kept insisting a solution was possible and leaked the compromise Baghdad was willing to accept. Baghdad's solution was based on "Saddam's staying as president of Iraq in the context of a parliamentary system, where a prime minister is the actual executive official and the presidency becomes an honorary position that involves no actual powers." The Iraqi sources were convinced they had found a way to entice Washington to support the proposal. "The United States is to be given special undeclared privileges in terms of oil and military facilities in the framework of a broader deal to reintegrate Iraq in the

international community and resolve all the political disputes Saddam created locally and internationally, under an honorary UN umbrella," the
Iraqi sources explained.

A uniquely important last-ditch effort to avert the war was made by
former Lebanese president Amin Gemayel, a close acquaintance of Saddam since the 1980s. Gemayel convinced Saddam to meet an official on
March 8—an elderly colonel who was instrumental to America's clandestine support for the Iraqi war effort in the 1980s and who befriended Saddam at the time. Indeed, Saddam was very friendly when Gemayel ushered
the colonel in. However, the discussion turned terse when the colonel assured Saddam that the United States intended to assassinate him after the
March 19 deadline passed. The only way to avoid the assassination attempt
was for Saddam to go into exile in Egypt, Sudan, Syria, or any other country that would invite him. Saddam retorted defiantly, "I will die before I
surrender." The colonel reiterated the threat, at which point Saddam
threatened to send the colonel's head back in a box as a message to Bush.
This would start the war immediately, the colonel assured Saddam. "I have
no fear of death," Saddam repeated. The colonel still tried to convince Saddam that he would not be able to hold out indefinitely either in his bunkers
or among the Iraqis once they were subjected to the bombing. A dismissive
Saddam just waved his hand. He then bid the colonel and Gemayel good-
bye very warmly, asking Gemayel to stay a little longer in Iraq. He would
stay until March 12. Both Gemayel and the colonel concluded that Saddam
had made up his mind to fight.

On March 14, the GRU reported to the Kremlin that American forces
in the Persian Gulf area had assumed a state of high combat readiness and
would be capable of initiating combat operations within three or four
hours of receiving their orders. They further insisted that all the necessary
combat plans and orders had been delivered to all pertinent levels of the
command structure down to the battalion-level commanders. These intelligence reports came on top of the political impression at the Kremlin that
the Bush administration would go to war without waiting for a UN Security Council endorsement. Hence, Moscow resolved to make a final attempt to prevent the war. On March 17, Putin dispatched Primakov back
to Iraq to meet with Saddam and urge him to step down. At the meeting
Primakov told Saddam he was in Baghdad to convey an oral message from
Putin. "The message was that he [Saddam] must step down to prevent the
suffering of the Iraqi people, which would be serious in case of a war," Primakov said. At first, Primakov and Saddam met alone, having a long and

personal conversation in which Saddam dodged the reason for Primakov's visit. Saddam then insisted that Primakov repeat Putin's oral message in the presence of Tariq Aziz. Primakov later noted that Saddam never really reacted or responded to the message. "Saddam tapped me on the shoulder and went out of the room," Primakov recalled.

A few Arab foreign ministers who were planning trips to Baghdad to urge Saddam to leave the country were not even allowed into Iraq. Ever the survivor, Saddam was convinced he could outfox all his enemies. Saddam was now waiting for the Arab world to grow desperate to the point of tolerating his remaining in power and pressuring Washington to stop the war before the entire region went up in flames. "Saddam has relayed signals that he is ready to discuss giving up power," a senior Western intelligence source told MENL's Steve Rodan. "But so far this is purely tactical. Once the war begins, Saddam could urge his Arab allies that he is willing to end the war and refrain from any WMD attacks in exchange for safe passage out of Iraq. His military deployment is meant to give him enough time for international pressure on the United States to halt the war." Washington had other plans.

On March 17, President Bush delivered a TV address in which he gave Saddam and his sons forty-eight hours to leave Iraq without any immunity or protection. "Their refusal to do so will result in military conflict, commenced at a time of our choosing," Bush said. The president reiterated the offer to the Iraqi military to avoid resistance and instead be supplied with food and medicine but promised that any resistance would be met with destructive force. "It is too late for Saddam Hussein to remain in power," Bush said. "It is not too late for the Iraqi military to act with honor and protect your country by permitting the peaceful entry of coalition forces to eliminate weapons of mass destruction." Bush reiterated his call for the Iraqi defense establishment to cooperate with the American and British forces for their own benefit and for the future of Iraq. "I urge every member of the Iraqi military and intelligence services, if war comes, do not fight for a dying regime that is not worth your own life," Bush stressed. Saddam rejected the ultimatum outright—leaving no option but war.

Despite Bush's ultimatum, however, the United States was already actively engaged in warfare. In fact, by March 7 Kuwaiti sources insisted that the war was already in progress. American and British aircraft conducted heavy bombing of strategic objectives in the southern approaches to Baghdad, ostensibly in reaction to a flimsy no-fly-zone violation. However, the Kuwaiti sources noted, some of the raids were against strategic objectives north of the zone. On March 9, U.S. Marines started dismantling the protective fence along the Iraqi-Kuwaiti border. The fence was removed in thirty-three sectors, allowing armored units to roll quickly into southern Iraq. A growing number of fighter aircraft were also patrolling Kuwaiti and Iraqi skies. The next day, American and British aircraft launched a series of bombing raids on five key communication centers in southern and central Iraq—including in the Baghdad area. All the targets were automated control units for fiber-optic communications, which constantly monitored traffic and redirected communications from damaged lines to secure ones. The aircraft also dropped leaflets warning Iraqi units to stay away from cities, mainly Baghdad, or risk destruction from the air.

By March 11, CENTCOM assessed that the United States had completely destroyed all the stationary antiaircraft batteries in southern and northern Iraq. The latest sorties in this drive were aimed at assets located along the Jordanian and Syrian borders—namely, air defense systems that had nothing to do with the no-fly-zone issue but could affect American and British air operations during the war. The United States no longer even attempted to pretend the air operations had anything to do with enforcing the UN mandate. "In order to keep the pressure on the Iraqi regime to disarm we have stepped up Southern Watch operations," General Myers explained, "flying several hundred sorties a day, with two or three hundred [of them] over the southern no-fly zone." On the night of March 14, the United States used two B-1 bombers as part of a large strike formation against military objectives in western Iraq, mainly the H-3 complex. The air strike, which met with virtually no resistance, intended but failed to destroy Iraqi systems and facilities associated with the SCUDs deployed in the area to launch against Israel.

Meanwhile, the Iraqi reaction to the escalating attacks was intriguing, for on March 15, Baghdad ordered the Tawakalna Republican Guard Division to redeploy from southern Iraq to the vicinity of Baghdad. At the same time, U.S. and Israeli intelligence noted the reappearance of "signatures" of Iraqi ballistic missiles in western Iraq, but no specific location or multiple-source confirmation could be defined. On March 16, Saddam took over direct command of the Iraqi Air Force, air defense forces, and ballistic missile forces. Baghdad provided no explanation for the move. On the night of March 17, U.S. and Israeli intelligence noted the electronic sig-nature—that is, detectable, distinct patterns of electronic communica-tions—of the delivery of chemical and biological warheads and shells to operational units in southern and western Iraq. The Iraqis left this "signa-ture" in order to threaten and deter the Americans.

Starting in mid-March a growing number of Special Forces and CIA teams crossed into Iraq every night, meeting specific intelligence needs, looking for ballistic missiles, weapons of mass destruction, and other im-portant objectives. A concentrated anti-SCUD operation took place in the area of the derelict Shab al-Hiri base complex in western Iraq, a favorite deployment area for Iraqi ballistic missile units. Special Forces also stud-ied and closely monitored the routes of the main ground forces to ensure that there would be no surprises. On the night of March 19, the United States pushed a total of thirty-one U.S. Special Operations teams into Iraq—over 300 men—along with a few British and Australian SAS units. This was a major insertion, with some detachments driving from Jordan and Saudi Arabia, while others were flown in by specially modified heli-copters and landed in the deep rear of the Iraqi forces. Some of the teams linked up with and reinforced the smaller contingents of Special Forces and CIA operatives already in Iraq. Others were entrusted with their own missions. Over the next couple of nights, additional Special Forces teams—U.S., British, and Australian—were landed deeper and deeper in-side Iraq, particularly in remote areas of Kurdistan and near the Syrian border.

Although the Special Forces insertion and operations were to be clan-destine, their existence was known to the Russians from the very begin-ning. "Already around 30 diversionary and reconnaissance units have been airdropped in Iraq by the U.S. and Britain. The primary task of these forces is to provide targeting information for the upcoming initial waves of air strikes," the GRU reported to the Kremlin on March 19. Moreover, that night (Iraq time), the Iraqi high command in Nasiriyah ordered the popu-lation to seek out "U.S. Special Forces [that] have infiltrated into a border area in the most remote southeastern part of Iraq." The message warned that, unless stopped, the mission of these forces would be "exploring the territory for launching military ground operations." But despite wide-spread raids by Iraqi military units and intense patrolling by village secu-rity detachments, no U.S. or allied Special Forces detachment was discovered and no mission was aborted.

During the day of March 19, despite a heavy sandstorm, American and British forces began to gradually escalate ground operations along the Kuwaiti border. Advance forces captured the bulk of the 10-mile-wide no-man's land between Kuwait and Iraq, including the large Rumeila oil fields. Small contingents of American troops also crossed the Iraqi border near Iraq's sole naval base, in Umm Qasr. The "excuse" was a clash between Iraqi smuggling boats trying to drop mines and a Kuwaiti patrol boat the night before. During the day, the navy conducted a hunt in the Persian Gulf and the mouth of the Shat-al-Arab for suicide speedboats deployed to crash into American and British warships. Meanwhile, in the early morning, larger forces of British and U.S. Marines advanced to the eastern parts of the zone and all but crossed into Iraq. During the day, advance elements of American and British forces penetrated about 10 to 15 miles inside Iraq, moving north despite the heavy sandstorm. They probed along two discernable axes—to Basra and to Nasiriyah. Sporadic air support was provided by aircraft from the USS *Lincoln*. It was a good beginning, as key elements of two Iraqi battalions north of the demilitarized strip surrendered when they saw the forces coming at them. Meanwhile, F-18s bombed Iraqi facilities and forces not far from the Jordanian border in western Iraq.

That evening, the first major land engagement of the war took place on the road toward Basra. U.S. Marines attacked an Iraqi battalion-level defensive perimeter protecting the main highway some 12 miles from the Kuwaiti border. The Iraqi forces included some forty tanks and roughly twenty-five heavy artillery pieces. The marines attacked the Iraqi first line of defense, while American and British aircraft bombed the artillery units supporting the Iraqi forces. The battle was decided in a complex engagement taking place after dark in which superior American training in nighttime operations, as well as American fluency with night-vision and battlefield-awareness systems, proved crucial in defeating the well-entrenched Iraqis. The main coalition ground forces then turned eastward, consolidating a front line in the direction of Umm-Qasr and Basra. They were pushing the main Iraqi defending forces back toward the cities and away from the coastline and harbor facilities in order to facilitate the landing of reinforcements. The main challenge was still the large Iraqi artillery forces, which were organized in multilayered positions. U.S. intelligence indicated that some of these artillery batteries were provided with chemical shells. During the night, American and British aircraft continued bombing the Iraqi artillery positions, but these attacks were less than effective because of the sandstorm. Attack helicopters could not be used at all during the storm.

Overnight, representatives of the Iraqi 11th Infantry Division and the 51st Mechanized Division approached advance American units and offered to negotiate their surrender. These divisions were protecting the southern approaches to the southern oil fields. As would be discovered over the next few days, this approach was part of an Iraqi deception designed to confirm American intelligence's conviction that the Iraqi military would not fight.

Although the American decapitation strike on Baghdad on the morning of March 20 (Baghdad time) officially started the war, the ground operations continued to unfold in accordance with the original timetable, which called for the war to erupt on the night of March 20. In Kuwait, U.S. defense officials said that "a massive attack on Iraq is expected to begin later on Thursday [March 20] or early Friday [March 21]" and that "the attack would comprise strikes on Iraqi targets from air, land, and sea." But on-site American and British commanders were not oblivious to the strike on Baghdad, and immediately tried to accelerate the pace of advance. These first surges were met with heavy Iraqi artillery fire, the suppression of which necessitated air support. In retrospect, Iraq's first military reaction was ominous. According to excellent sources in the Gulf States, "Uday Saddam Hussein called on Saddam's Fedayeen to prepare for martyrdom." The significance of this order would become clear in the next several days, as American and British forces advanced deeper into Iraq.

In the afternoon, Iraqi forces fired five or six Al-Samoud and SCUD-type missiles in three salvos toward U.S. Army positions in northern Kuwait. The SSMs were launched from two sites—on the Faw Peninsula and south of Suq ash-Shuyukh. Patriot missiles were launched at the Iraqi missiles, but only one Al-Samoud missile was intercepted. Although nobody was hurt in the first missile attack, the Kuwaiti authorities sounded civil defense sirens in Kuwait City to warn of a possible biological or chemical weapons attack. The Kuwaiti authorities also called on residents to wear their gas masks. Minutes later the capital was rocked by an explosion from a second salvo of Iraqi missiles the Patriots failed to intercept. There were no casualties this time either. Still, most observers in the region considered the Iraqi missile attacks the beginning of a more intense campaign. The opinion of a very senior Iranian defense official was indicative of the prevailing analysis. "Since the United States enjoys electronic warfare superiority, Iraq has hidden its missile sites in order not to be identified by the United States. So it looks for a moment to unleash missile attacks against U.S. targets including Israel," he said. "Iraq will absolutely attack Israel."

8
THE RACE TO BAGHDAD, PART 2

The real ground offensive finally began on the evening of March 20, once the main formations of the American and British ground forces arrived at the front from their forward concentration areas. When they left Kuwait, the American forces carried with them vital supplies—food, water, ammunition—for four to five days of moderate fighting; these supplies would prove insufficient and ill suited for the clashes that would ensue.

The initial engagements did not unfold as expected. The original war plan called for a wide pincer movement toward Baghdad from the south and a single push from the north. Though the offensive from the northern front had to be cancelled because of the Turkish refusal to let the United States use its territory, the southern component remained largely unchanged. The general principle of the plan was a wide envelopment of the Shiite heartland from the west and the east, with the two columns converging on the greater Baghdad area. (A combination of air assault forces, Special Forces, and Kurdish troops was to substitute for the absence of the Turkey-based column.) The western pincer would advance west of the Euphrates (west of the Nasiriyah-Najaf road), and the eastern pincer would swing east of the Tigris (Basra-Amarah-Kut), until they finally closed in on Baghdad.

The underlying logic of this plan lay in the intelligence assumption that the Iraqi regular forces—largely deployed in the areas the two columns were expected to travel—would not fight. The pincer attack would encircle but avoid the radicalized Shiite civilian population—which is concentrated between the Euphrates and the Tigris—for fear of popular resistance incited by pro-Iranian elements. U.S. intelligence also feared that Iraqi terrorist and commando forces might blow up the main bridges on the two rivers, and the Republican Guards forces could destroy the al-

Hindiya Dam on the Euphrates and the Misan Dam on the Tigris in order to slow the advance.

The wide pincer route also allowed the Americans to avoid the central roads that exit into the Baghdad area, which the Republican Guard divisions controlled through established artillery kill zones, with ordinance including chemical shells. During the months leading to the war, combat aircraft had systematically bombed the key military facilities overlooking these axes of advance; whether the bombing was effective is still being debated by the military.

On the evening of March 20, there was a slowdown in the conduct of coalition air support operations, particularly by attack helicopters, because of the weather. This had an impact both on the confidence of the Iraqi forces and on America's ability to provide air support for the ground forces. On the Iraqi side, regular ground forces units proved tougher and more resilient than expected. They had a good defensive disposition with excellent artillery cover of all approaches. It would take the United States longer than expected to breach these lines without heavy casualties. All reports from the front line mentioned that the Iraqi resistance was significantly heavier than anticipated.

During the night, a "race" to get to the key oil fields and installations in the area developed. Some oil fields—including sectors of the Rumeila thought to be secure—caught fire. Some of the fire could be attributed to artillery fire, while other pumps were definitely set ablaze as the result of sabotage. Overnight, the Iraqis brought more heavy artillery to the area, and—with the weather improving—the possibility of chemical weapon shelling increased. Nevertheless, in fierce overnight fighting, the British division-size force, led by the 7th Armored Brigade, and elements of the U.S. 1st Marine Expeditionary Force captured the approaches to Umm-Qasr (both the city and the naval base) and were heading toward Basra. Even though resistance remained tough, the Iraqis were being pushed back. Meanwhile, massive air and cruise missile strikes on Baghdad started about 9 P.M. (local time), causing large fires and heavy damage to key government buildings.

The next morning saw little-noticed but nevertheless major developments of strategic significance. A few hundred Kuwaiti soldiers entered some of the outlying suburbs of the city of Umm-Qasr on the Persian Gulf coast and accepted the surrender of the Iraqi civilian authorities. Although the fighting in the area was done by the U.S. marines, the flags flying over these suburbs of Umm-Qasr were Kuwaiti. However, most of the city was still held by Iraqi elite forces of the 45th Brigade who did not make much noise but would not surrender either.

Meanwhile, the British 42nd Commandos began a helicopter-borne assault on the Faw Peninsula from the northeast. Simultaneously, British 40th Commandos and Queen's Dragoon Guards conducted an amphibious landing on the southern tip of the Faw Peninsula. Once again, Kuwaiti military patrols accompanied the British. Since Kuwait has irredentist claims to the Iraqi coastline, the Kuwaiti activity should be seen as the beginning of the Kuwaiti claim. If Kuwait's claim were met, Iraq would become a landlocked country. While this move boosted the morale and resolve of the Kuwaiti government, particularly the House of al-Sabah, the news of the Kuwaiti presence touched a nerve with the Iraqi population and forces, strengthening the resolve of both regular and irregular forces to resist the American and British advance.

By the afternoon of March 21, American and British forces had consolidated their hold over the outskirts of Basra, and small probing forces attempted to enter the city, although the extent of the coalition's hold remained uncertain, and nothing tangible would be decided until daylight in any case. Later that night, CENTCOM hoped that the positions held by the British advance units would allow U.S. marine columns to advance on the main road northward, toward al-Amara, without threat from the defenders of Basra. The hope for a speedy surge toward Baghdad was reinforced when the commander of Iraq's 51st Division and his top deputy surrendered to U.S. Marine forces. The surrender came after lengthy negotiations, while the vast majority of the division's soldiers and equipment—including tanks and other combat vehicles—simply left their posts and the 51st Division "melted away."

Fighting on the Faw Peninsula escalated, as Iraqi forces concealed in the marshes bounced back. According to an Iranian eyewitness, "American and British forces were forced to retreat from Al-Faw this afternoon after they were the target of heavy artillery fire by Iraqi forces. The invading forces were stationed near the salt factory in Al-Faw. However, they were forced to retreat with their weapons after a counterattack by Iraqi forces." The Iranian claimed that the Al-Faw area was quiet overnight. Radio Baghdad also alluded to heavy fighting. "The enemy landed its forces and armor in the Al-Faw, the city of sacrifice and the gate of the great victory. The enemy's bad luck led him to the [word indistinct] to be under our brave artillery fire. The enemy forces continue to receive devastating blows from our brave forces," Radio Baghdad reported. Interestingly, the Iraqis did not claim a American and British withdrawal as described by the Iranians.

Meanwhile, just as air strikes were beginning, Arab TV stations broadcast a briefing by Iraqi Defense Minister Sultan Hashim Ahmad. He claimed that events were "accelerating"—particularly attacks on Baghdad and the Al-Rutbah area in western Iraq (further east and deeper than America had claimed). "At the beginning, the U.S. military deployment was very close to the Jordanian border. Then the deployment expanded in the area. The areas in which they expanded were in the desert where our units are nonexistent," Ahmad explained. The American "aim was to look for missile launching pads to ensure that Israel would not be hit by missiles that they claim to be still in existence and with which they said we might attack Israel." Ahmad also claimed that the 45th Brigade was "still steadfast in its positions" at the heart of Umm-Qasr (the city) and that "the enemy is stationed in front of the 45th Brigade," and "clashes now are carried out with artillery."

Hopes for safely enveloping Basra and making a rapid dash toward Al-Amarah were thwarted on the morning of March 22. Despite intense fighting overnight at the outskirts of Basra, British and American forces failed to overwhelm the defenders or consolidate a safe line. According to an Iranian eyewitness, "the city of Basra had been attacked thirty-seven times by invading forces until this morning," without coalition forces gaining control of the region. However, the combination of bombing and cruise missile strikes all over the city caused heavy damage, and a renewed British-led ground assault resumed during the morning. In the afternoon, the bulk of the invading forces continued to move slowly. The main problem remained the continued fighting in the Basra area. The surrender of the Iraqi 51st Division provided for a relatively safe road to the north. However, the Iraqi 11th Division broke communications, and the 6th Tank Division—the main force in Basra—would not respond to offers for negotiations. Both Iraqi divisions had offensive capacities and a safe rear (against the Iranian border), posing viable threats to the advance toward Baghdad. On the ground, both divisions, as well as reconstituted elements of the 51st Division, held the line. The center of the 6th Tank Division was in the Majnun area, controlling the approaches to the Iranian border and southern oil fields. By evening, the British and U.S. marine forces were still incapable of consolidating a tight siege on Basra that would permit the marines' main forces to break around the city and move northward.

The situation in the Umm-Qasr area also remained in limbo. In the city, small American and British forces contained the Iraqi 45th Brigade and other defenders of the city to the point where they could no longer affect the coalition's traffic toward Baghdad. In the afternoon, elements of the U.S. 15th Marine Expeditionary Unit and the 3rd Commando Brigade of the Royal Marines thought they had secured the port of Umm-Qasr so that humanitarian aide could be delivered. However, Iraqi commando and fedayeen forces remained in the area, and their continued harassment strikes, sporadic mortar shelling, sniping, and ambushes made it virtually impossible to use the port. In Faw, there remained major Iraqi pockets of resistance. Captured soldiers were carrying gas masks, which alerted the allies that chemical shells or warheads for artillery and missiles might be nearby.

By evening, the British and U.S. marine forces besieging Basra were able to push the Iraqis farther away from the main road system to Baghdad. Still, Iraqi resistance in the city remained fierce, and both American and British forces were reluctant to get entangled in casualty-heavy urban warfare. Overnight, the Iraqi forces in Basra attempted a major counterattack. First, an Iraqi armored convoy moved toward the port of Umm-Qasr to bolster the besieged 45th Brigade and launch a counterattack. The Iraqi forces moving toward Umm-Qasr included several columns of armored vehicles, tanks, and artillery pieces, as well as over 1,000 infantry soldiers.

U.S. and British combat aircraft pounded the Iraqi column. Nevertheless, the Iraqi effort to stop the coalition advance on Baghdad continued to intensify. According to Iranian observers on the scene, Iraqi heavy artillery fire was "targeting the lines of communication of American and British forces that are trying to capture Basra" as well as advance toward Baghdad. The Iranian observers also reported that "Iraqi forces were trying to block the paths of American and British forces by digging trenches and filling them with oil in some parts of Basra. They have set fire to them and a massive fire and plume of smoke have covered the area as a result." The intense heat and thick smoke hampered the effectiveness of the various sensors that are integral to the accuracy and effectiveness of American bombing and artillery fire. To negate this tactic, between 12:30 and 1:40 A.M., the Iranians reported, "American and British aircraft fired their flare guns in the Basra general area." This was an effort to use the old and proven method of floating (by parachute) visual markers to be used as points of reference for both aerial bombing and artillery fire, a method going back to the Second World War.

By the morning of March 23, the fighting on the southeastern front had stabilized. Heavy Iraqi resistance continued around both the city of Basra and the city of Umm-Qasr (in the latter despite repeated claims that it had been captured). Except for a few probing patrols, the U.S. and British forces refrained from entering Basra for fear of heavy attrition and protracted urban warfare. During the day, the U.S. 15th Marine Expeditionary Unit attempted a breakthrough from Rumeila toward Qurna (north of Basra, overlooking the area where the Euphrates and the Tigris merge into the Shatt-el-Arab) in order to gain access to the main road to Amarah. However, the marines were met by stiff resistance and their advance stalled.

The slow progress on the eastern front stood in sharp contrast to the swift and smooth operations of the V Corps on the western front. The 3rd Infantry Division, along with a myriad of special operations, surged throughout western Iraq.

The initial success of V Corps clearly gained Baghdad's attention. On March 21, the GRU reported that "the elements of the 3rd Infantry Division were purposefully provoked into fighting by the Iraqi mobile units, which from the first hours of the ground campaign used 'pinprick' tactics by launching more than 20 artillery attacks against the positions of the coalition forces. To prevent further such attacks the coalition command ordered its troops to pursue all attacking Iraqi units." In retrospect, these pursuits consumed resources and slowed down the V Corps.

The GRU further elaborated on the strategic significance of the American tactics, noting that "the Iraqi command is organizing defenses in the central regions of the country. All main Iraqi forces have been pulled toward central Iraq leaving huge mine fields and many ambushes on the path of the advancing U.S. forces." The Iraqi delaying tactics were working to some extent, the GRU analysts concluded.

On the morning of March 21, soon after the 3rd Infantry Division picked up its pace, Baghdad reacted to the beginning of the war by issuing a decree from Saddam offering very large rewards for inflicting casualties on the American and British forces. The decree read:

leader President Mujahid Saddam Hussein, may God watch over him, has ordered the following:

1. Any stalwart Iraqi fighter who shoots down a hostile combat aircraft shall be awarded 100 million dinars.
2. Anyone who shoots down a hostile helicopter shall be awarded 50 million dinars.
3. Anyone who captures a hostile soldier shall be awarded 50 million dinars.
4. Anyone who kills a hostile soldier shall be awarded 25 million dinars.
5. Anyone who shoots down a hostile missile shall be awarded 10 million dinars.
6. Anyone who causes a hostile plane or a helicopter to crash shall be awarded 50 million dinars if he captures its pilot or 25 million dinars if the pilot is killed.

During the night of March 20, U.S. forces from the 101st Airborne, along with British, Australian, and other Special Forces arriving from Jordan, seized the huge military complexes H-2 and H-3 in western Iraq. These complexes constituted the key to Iraq's ability to strike at Israel and Jordan. The attack took place as the vast majority of the Iraqi forces in the area were deployed in the desert, and as a result there was no engagement with them beyond sporadic bombing by aircraft operating from aircraft carriers in the Mediterranean and inside Jordan. Most significant was a raid by Task Force 20 on a military base in the al-Qaim area suspected of being a potential SCUD launch area against Israel. No ballistic missiles were found, but the raiding forces killed the Iraqi guards and destroyed local facilities.

On March 21, the American hold over the H-2 and H-3 complexes was described by people on the scene as "tenuous." The ability to hold these vast complexes would depend on the Iraqi reaction and the availability of airpower, but if American troops could secure the area, it would significantly harm Saddam's plans for Israel.

Meanwhile, the lead elements of the 3rd Infantry Division crossed into the Iraqi desert from western Kuwait and began a surge of about 100 miles toward Nasiriyah, the center of Iraq's southern military forces, about 230 miles south of Baghdad. At first they advanced across the desert, but then shifted to traveling on Highway 8, which the Iraqis failed to destroy.

Throughout the advance, the Americans had to fight off ambushes and light strikes. The battle for Nasiriyah—a turning point in the ground war—began by the afternoon of March 21. Heavy fighting continued into the night, with the Iraqi 3rd Army Corp putting up stiff resistance. At first, the advance of the 3rd Infantry stalled as large forces were committed to fighting the defenders of Nasiriyah. However, within a few hours, the division started enveloping Nasiriyah and accelerating the race toward Baghdad, leaving behind holding forces to deal with the defenders. It was a major decision, for the Iraqi artillery units in Nasiriyah were known to have chemical shells and the authority to use them.

Indeed, the chief of SCIRI's "Jihadi office," Abdulaziz al-Hakim, warned that morning that the American and British forces "would soon discover that Saddam's regime possesses a weapon that they have not been able to discover until now. If the Iraqi regime can use this weapon, then the American and British forces will have to put up with its prolonged resistance. However, if it cannot do that, then the regime will be toppled rapidly."

During March 21, Iraqi and Arab media were predicting intense and protracted fighting. Iraqi TV showed Saddam Hussein in military uniform meeting with his son Qusay, Defense Minister Sultan Hashim Ahmad, and an unidentified secretary. But the story had only an announcer-read report over video; the footage itself could have been old. Several Arab TV stations carried a concluding remark by Defense Minister Sultan Hashim Ahmad during his press briefing, declaring that "no force in the world will conquer us, because we are defending our country, our principles, and our religion. We are, no doubt, the victors."

Heavy fighting continued through the night of March 21. Nasiriyah was subjected to a full night of shelling and bombing, from artillery to air strikes to a few cruise missiles aimed at the key government and military buildings. By 3 A.M. on March 22, most of the objectives were destroyed. However, the central garrison was still holding, and fierce artillery and tank fire exchanges were taking place around it. The forces of the 3rd Infantry Division were reluctant to storm the complex during darkness for fear of entanglement in urban warfare as well as delayed mines and booby traps that could have included chemical charges. Also holding was the military and intelligence communications center, although the extent of the damage to the relay equipment was unclear. However, the Iraqi artillery fire was sufficiently silenced to permit resumption of the advance toward Baghdad. By 4 or 5 A.M., it was possible for the first columns to rush past the smoking positions in Nasiriyah on the way toward Baghdad. Meanwhile, V Corps forces were convinced they had secured bridges over the Euphrates in the Nasiriyah area.

During most of March 22, small groups of the 3rd Division continued to put pressure on the defenders of Nasiriyah from the west, attempting to reduce their ability to threaten the road to Baghdad. However, the Iraqi defense was fierce, and the units were making little headway into the city. A lot of air support was called in to soften the defenders. Meanwhile, in an audacious, risky maneuver, the bulk of the 3rd Infantry Division took a road toward Baghdad that passes north of Nasiriyah and southwest of Najaf and Qarbalah—the militant Shiite heartland. This way, the 3rd Infantry Division did not have to fight the Shiites, but the Shiites, along with the Iranian forces hiding in their midst, were left untouched at the rear of the main American axis of transportation. When the 3rd Division captured the main bridge on the Euphrates, the forward units were roughly 200 miles from Baghdad's outskirts.

Throughout the day, the United States continued bombing Iraqi forces in and around Baghdad. The four Republican Guard divisions and one Special Republican Guard tank division protecting southern Baghdad suffered heavy casualties from overnight bombing and pulled back from their positions 30 miles south of the city to consolidate a new and tighter defense line 10 miles closer to Baghdad's outskirts. The units were in relatively good shape, maintained strong morale and discipline, and were expected to put up a considerable fight. Furthermore, Iran-sponsored Iraqi Shiite senior officials warned Tehran that "Iraqi President Saddam Hussein has ordered the destruction of the Darbandikhan dam in the northern part of the country if American and British forces approach Baghdad." Iranian experts opined that given "the amount of water in the dam and the size of its reservoir . . . the Iraqi action will flood vast parts of [Iraq]" as well as "parts of Iran's border strip."

By evening, the American and British were continuing the heavy bombing of Baghdad and six zones in the suburbs. The aircraft and missiles hit both national-level infrastructure and the latest defensive dispositions of the Republican Guard units as they were adjusting their positions to meet the advancing coalition forces. During the night of March 22 there were the first indications from numerous intelligence sources that the Iraqis had decided to concentrate the war in the Baghdad area. The various forces away from Baghdad were instructed to fight only delaying battles in order to slow down the American advance and prepare for a prolonged battle of attrition in the city itself—including the likely use of weapons of mass destruction. Overnight, on March 22, the move north continued at a slower pace as vanguard units of the 3rd Division encountered stiffer resistance.

While these battles were taking place, a major reassessment of the military situation in the theater was also assembled, as key building blocks of the Pentagon's strategy collapsed. The lack of a push from the north made it impossible for the United States to swiftly encircle Baghdad even if the Kuwait-based units were able to reach the capital unimpeded, and, at the time, the advance north of the eastern pincer was virtually stalled. Moreover, the initial fighting on the night of March 20 and most of the day on March 21 demonstrated that the Iraqi regular army was fighting tenaciously while the Shiite population was hostile and cool, and thus unsafe to pass through. This was a rude awakening for coalition intelligence, which had been convinced that once the invasion began, division-size units would surrender to coalition forces. "There were suggestions that large parts of the Iraqi armed forces might well come over at the appropriate moment," a key intelligence official told David Ignatius of the *Washington Post*. "It didn't happen in the way we hoped or encouraged."

On the other hand, V Corps, spearheaded by the 3rd Infantry, was moving through the desert, and also on Highway 8, at great speed. The 3rd Division was able to get close to Nasiriyah quite quickly. Since Highway 8 and the main bridges on the Euphrates were still intact, this route could sustain the advance of larger forces. Therefore, CENTCOM decided to shift the bulk of the 1st Marine Expeditionary Force—a force larger than a division—to a western axis that would run first behind and then parallel to V Corps. The new route the marines would follow was first in the rear of the 3rd Infantry to Nasiriyah, thus making up time, and then over the bridges on the Euphrates to take Highway 8 all the way to Kut—a shortcut that would permit the resumption of a wide pincer movement in the area of Baghdad. This reorientation was accomplished swiftly and smoothly, a major achievement given the chaos prevailing on any battlefield. Elements of the British forces filled in spots vacated by the U.S. Marines in the Basra and Safwan areas.

Abandoning the plan to surround Baghdad, even when the United States had to forgo the use of Turkish territory, was primarily a political decision dictated by Washington. Once it was clear that Turkey would refuse access to its territory, the United States could have landed the 4th Infantry Division in Israel and rushed it across Jordan straight into western and central Iraq. Jerusalem had long expressed its willingness to permit the transfer of American forces, and having permitted the clandestine deployment of a composite squadron of F-16s, Amman was willing to consider additional U.S. deployments as well. However, Washington was apprehensive that the Arab world would not tolerate this move and would use it as a catalyst for supporting Saddam. That was an error in judgment; by now most Arab governments were resigned to coping with—though not supporting—the war and would not have changed their position because of an advance from Israel. But instead of the more practical option, ships carrying the 4th Division's equipment started their long way through the Suez Canal and around the Arabian Peninsula, landing in Kuwait, in the hope that somehow the 4th Division could travel on land all the way to Baghdad. The division would miss the war.

Meanwhile, the assortment of Special Forces operating in western Iraq intensified the search for Iraqi ballistic missiles and weapons of mass destruction. To expand operations in western Iraq, about 1,000 elite troops were landed near al-Rutbah. On the night of March 22, the United States audaciously attempted to act on hot intelligence. Several sources, including a Moscow-based asset relying on a Russian eyewitness, reported that American Special Forces had tried unsuccessfully to seize Iraqi WMD in the al-Qaim area, in the northwestern desert not far from the Syrian border. The Americans were inserted by helicopter or parachute. Reportedly, a small force tried to storm the facility but was surrounded and overwhelmed by neighboring Iraqi ground units that were alerted by the facility's security force. A few Americans were killed and others were captured. The Russian eyewitness reported seeing a couple of American POWs.

March 23 was a day of coping with, and adjusting to, the reality of the Iraqi battlefield. It was a day of dogged advance northward despite the sandstorm by the 3rd Division, as well as the beginning of a standoff for the 1st Marine Expeditionary Force (1st MEF) at Nasiriyah. CENTCOM considered March 23 "the hardest day" of the war. To a great extent, the ground war could have collapsed that day due to the slow advance, with the key units starved for most basic supplies due to long and fragile supply lines.

"The situation in southern Iraq can be characterized as unstable and controversial. Heavy fighting is taking place in the Umm-Qasr-An-Nasiriyah-Basra triangle. Satellite and signals intelligence show that both sides actively employ armored vehicles in highly mobile attacks and coun-terattacks," observed the GRU's noontime report for March 23. Moreover, the Iraqis intensified their fierce resistance, seizing on the fact that the vast majority of Iraq's Army and population considered the Americans their enemies. Having to choose between the evil of Saddam and the evil of Westernization, they sided with Saddam, and fought tenaciously to defend the southern triangle. The urban population shielded, sheltered, and ac-tively supported the Iraqi forces in their midst.

Instead of rushing to Baghdad in a relatively benign environment—as originally planned—the V Corps had to fight repeatedly. Moreover, it had to peel off major units and leave them to contain significant pockets of resistance—all of them overlapping the main cities between the Kuwaiti border and Baghdad. Hence, although V Corps succeeded in advancing as far north as 60 miles from Baghdad, it actually controlled only the roads and narrow strips of land on both sides of the column. Meanwhile, since V Corps lacked the ground forces to occupy and hold the cities and the will-ingness to incur the heavy losses urban warfare entails, it resorted to heavy shelling and aerial bombing of both the defenders and the civilian popula-tion around them. Despite the reliance on smart bombs and precise ar-tillery fire, the Iraqi forces were so mixed among the supporting civilians that the United States could not avoid collateral damage and meet its ob-jective. While these measures kept the Iraqis from effectively challenging the hold over the roads, the predominantly Shiite population within the cities was further radicalized and alienated.

Terrorism and subversion were only a matter of time. And so the stretched-thin 3rd Infantry completely ignored the Shiite cities, trying in-stead to control a narrow wedge toward the western bridges leading to Baghdad. However, American forces increasingly ran into popular resis-tance and Iraqi commandos, incurring attrition in the process.

By the middle of the night of March 23, the situation had somewhat stabilized and new patterns emerged. The 3rd Infantry Division stalled due to heavy Iraqi resistance in Samawah, some 40 to 45 miles southeast of Na-jaf. The Iraqi forces launched a series of maneuvers in order to improve their defenses. Most important was the Iraqi forward deployment of Re-publican Guard divisions equipped with chemical shells to bolster the reg-ular units on the outer approaches to Baghdad. The Iraqis seemed to have decided to stall the coalition forces through entanglement in protracted battles. This approach reflected Baghdad's growing confidence in the loy-alty and fighting spirit of the regular units and their overall ability to take on the coalition forces. The first challenge was the advance of the al-Nida Republican Guard Division (RGD) toward Amarah—a major military complex and a city then protected by the Iraqi 10th and 11th Divisions. Any coalition forces advancing north of Basra were bound to engage these forces, thus reducing the likelihood of a wide pincer movement toward Baghdad. Closer still to Baghdad, the Iraqis positioned the al-Madinah RGD in the al-Kut area—another major city and military complex overlooking a series of road junctions and Tigris bridges converging from both Basra (via Amarah) and Nasiriyah. Reinforced by a special artillery unit with CW shells, the al-Madinah was therefore located in an ideal position to take on any axis of advance toward Baghdad.

On the morning of March 24, the GRU reported to the Kremlin, "The situation in Iraq can be characterized as quiet on all fronts. Attacking co- alition forces have settled into positional warfare, they are exhausted, have lost the attacking momentum, and are in urgent need of fuel, ammunition, repairs, and reinforcements. The Iraqis are also busy regrouping their forces, reinforcing the combat units, and setting up new defense lines."

The morning of March 24 saw the first clashes between elements of the al-Madinah RGD from al-Kut and the forward units of the 3rd Infantry southwest of Qarbalah, some 50 miles from Baghdad. The Iraqis tried to attack the 3rd Infantry's flanks through the gap between Najaf and Qar- balah, as well as block the road from Nasiriyah to al-Kut. In the predawn hours, the V Corps attempted the first deep strike by AH-64D Apache at- tack helicopters aimed at stalling the al-Madinah RGD. Instead, the heli- copter attack was beaten back by well-organized small-arms ambushes by both Republican Guard troops and fedayeen from the area's villages. The Iraqis managed to shoot down one Apache and riddle with bullets the other thirty-three to the point that the 11th Aviation Regiment was no longer combat ready. Significantly, the helicopter attack failed to slow down the al-Madinah's race toward Qarbalah. American commanders feared that, fully aware of the significance of this phase of the war, the Iraqis might attempt to use WMD to seize the strategic initiative. Indeed, U.S. intelligence intercepts and other information indicated that the al- Madinah was equipped with chemical shells and had the authority to use them once invading forces entered a designated red zone. By midday, de- spite the repeated air and helicopter strikes, the forward elements of the al- Madinah RGD held their ground not far from al-Hillah and thus continued to threaten the advance of the 3rd Division around Qarbalah. Meanwhile, the 1st MEF remained stalled in Nasiriyah. U.S. convoys were

also hit and stalled by well-planned ambushes of Iraqi infantry and fedayeen units.

Saddam took to the airwaves on Iraqi TV, looking, as usual, arrogant
and self-assured. The speech was Islamist in character, with Saddam again
using Koranic themes and metaphors usually associated with the likes of
bin Laden. He offered martyrdom and promised paradise in Islamist
terms, quoting the Koran throughout. There were three main themes in
the speech: (1) that Saddam himself was alive and well, unaffected by
American air strikes; (2) that the Baath regime was still functioning, with
Saddam in control—a point he demonstrated by recalling names of commanders and mentioning specific combat operations in Umm-Qasr and
Basrah (Saddam was, however, a day behind—an indication of the time of
the recording); (3) that Saddam was aware of the senior commanders, officers, and troops fighting for him and Iraq.

By mentioning the names of commanders, Saddam demonstrated his
awareness of their efforts (and hinted at the vulnerability of their family
members). He specifically mentioned Khaled al-Hashemi, the commander
of the 51st Division that had ostensibly surrendered to the Americans, as
still fighting. Later in the day, al-Hashemi appeared on al-Jazeera TV, prov-
ing that the man who had surrendered the division was not actually he. An
indication of the Iraqi decision to attack Israel could be found in the increasing frequency with which Palestinian issues were mentioned by Saddam and the Iraqi media as a whole. In his speech, Saddam hailed
"Palestine, free and Arab, from the [Jordan] river to the [Mediterranean]
sea," a reference to a future Palestinian state rising on the ashes of a destroyed Israel. Ultimately, Saddam Hussein projected confidence, demonstrating to the Iraqis that the war for Iraq was far from over.

During the day, irregular warfare and terrorism at the rear areas intensified markedly. American troops were routinely subjected to ambushes by
well-trained Special Forces equipped with small arms and rocket launchers. These Iraqi "irregulars"—members of fedayeen units, Baath militias,
and Iraqi commando squads—enjoyed widespread support and sheltering
from the civilian population. Such ambushes took place in areas, including
oil fields, in close proximity to the Kuwaiti border that had ostensibly been
under American control for some time. These ambushes complicated V
Corps' ability to push forward and sustain the drive toward Baghdad, and
slowed other advances considerably after nightfall.

The 1st MEF intensified the offensive on Nasiriyah, since the United
States was already behind schedule for the main offensive and advance on

Baghdad. Long convoys of U.S. Marine fighting vehicles needed for the surge jammed the roads south of Nasiriyah waiting for the suppression of Iraqi artillery fire so that they could take the road toward the main bridges on the Euphrates and then the direct road to al-Kut. Fighting also flared up between U.S. Special Forces and Iraqi forces in al-Rutbah, near the Iraqi-Jordanian border.

At the strategic level, the Iraqi high command continued to function and run the defense of Baghdad. Despite the intense bombing, the high command sustained fairly good levels of communication with the outlying units. The GRU's report of March 25 noted that "during preparation for the war the Iraqis were able to create new, well-protected communication lines and control centers." The GRU noted that "so far the U.S. electronic reconnaissance was unable to locate and to penetrate the Iraqi command's communication network, which is an indication of the network's high technological sophistication."

Indeed, the Iraqis demonstrated the ability to coordinate multiple-division maneuvers in bolstering the defense to meet the now narrow-front American push. Moreover, the Iraqis were able to reinforce the Nasiriyah garrison with several artillery battalions and a large number of antitank weapons. There was no real collapse of Iraqi units, mass surrendering, or cessation of fighting. The Iraqis, primarily regular troops and reservists, sustained dogged fighting and attrition.

Several senior officers at CENTCOM—and through them, the Pentagon—began to worry that at the current level of Iraqi opposition, the United States did not have sufficient forces to fight for Baghdad. Some officers suggested suspending the advance until the 4th Division arrived in Iraq. The new role of the 4th Division would be to act as reinforcements for the southern drive on Baghdad. To expedite its arrival in theater, the United States launched a major diplomatic effort in Riyadh to permit the 4th Division to disembark in Red Sea ports and rush by truck to Jordan and the war. The Saudis and Jordanians refused. Meanwhile, the 173rd Airborne Brigade based in Italy—NATO's strategic reserve, a quick-intervention force to be deployed in case of trouble in the Balkans—was ordered to prepare for imminent deployment to Iraq.

The perseverance of the Iraqi military despite massive bombing, and the population's support for active resistance emboldened Saddam and his inner circle. They now exploited the Islamist rejuvenation, a grassroots re-action to the presence of American forces in Iraq, as a demonstration of support for Saddam Hussein, which it was not. On the morning of March

25, an Iraqi spokesman announced that "The first martyrdom attack was carried out this night. . . . An Iraqi civilian penetrated behind enemy lines and destroyed a tank." The Faw Peninsula, where the attack took place, had been declared secured by the British and U.S. forces. Since morning, Iraqi TV had also been highlighting Saddam Hussein's special message to the chieftains of Iraqi tribes. The message urged them to continue their fight against the "aggressors" and to "inflict the gravest losses" possible, forcing them to flee in "panic." The tribal area is the southwestern desert, which American reinforcements were to envelop as the other units raced to Baghdad while avoiding the ambush-laden roads.

On March 25, V Corps forces maneuvered and reorganized in order to confront the al-Madinah RGD from a couple of directions while sustaining the advance toward Baghdad. Meanwhile, elements of the 1st MEF fought once again over the Euphrates bridges north of Nasiriyah as American airpower flattened neighborhoods threatening the road toward the bridges.

Most worrisome were the intelligence reports saying that Saddam had reiterated his order to his senior commanders permitting them to use chemical weapons if the U.S. forces crossed a certain line in the vicinity of Baghdad. At the rate they were going, V Corps forces would cross this line in two or three days. American intelligence was convinced the al-Madinah RGD received a fresh supply of chemical shells for its artillery on March 25. UAVs and satellites detected a well-protected convoy of ammunition trucks escorted by chemical decontamination vehicles arriving at the main compound of the al-Madinah RGD and then unloading munitions. By the end of the day, intelligence confirmed that most of the Republican Guard and Special Guard divisions in the Baghdad area, as well as the key artillery units in Nasiriyah, were provided with chemical shells. A few extra-large-caliber artillery pieces were also deployed in the southern suburbs of Baghdad. (In April, a U.S. Marine Corps unit would identify high concentrations of mustard gas and cyanide in the Euphrates near Nasiriyah and discover hundreds of gas masks and chemical warfare suits at a nearby military base, suggesting that the Iraqis dumped their WMD ammunition into the river once they realized the fall of the city was imminent.)

American apprehension increased when an announcer on Iraqi TV read a letter from "mujahid leader President Saddam Hussein" to "Saddam's heroic fedayeen," dated March 25. Saddam urged his fedayeen to continue their strikes on "this despotic cowardly enemy" anywhere and everywhere they could. Addressing his son Uday—the commander of the

202

fedayeen forces—Saddam asked him to remind the fedayeen of their pledge to commit to martyrdom and to tell them that today was "the day of sacrifice." Saddam called on the fedayeen to hit the enemy day and night, its front and rear units. "These are the days of the great victory, which is not awaited by the Iraqis only but also by all good believers in the world," Saddam's letter concluded.

March 25 was characterized by continuous fighting, attrition, ambushes, sporadic clashes, and shelling along the road to Qarbalah. Meanwhile, the 1st MEF finally stabilized the situation in the Nasiriyah area and crossed the Euphrates and the Saddam Canal. Heavy fighting continued in the outlying suburbs of Nasiriyah as Iraqis—with army artillery and fedayeen ambushes—made repeated desperate attempts to prevent the marines from reaching the bridges. By the end of the day, forward marine units were fighting at the approaches of Suway Ghazi on the road to al-Kut—a small but significant breakout. Concurrently, forward units of the 3rd Infantry Division stalled on the approaches to Qarbalah, hit by both intense Iraqi resistance and the sandstorm. V Corps was also facing mounting supply problems because of the escalating and expanding irregular warfare, particularly attacks on all axes of transportation. The supply lines were so stretched that senior commanders worried the 3rd Division would run out of water. British defense officials expected March 26 to be the "decisive moment" of the war, believing that unless U.S. forces resumed the rapid advance toward Baghdad, it was possible that the reinvigorated Iraqi forces would further stall the American advance and draw the relatively small American units into attrition-heavy combat the United States could ill afford.

Overnight, Special Forces located and destroyed what they believed to be two SSM launchers in western Iraq. However, further investigation showed they were only al-Babil launchers, whose maximum range is 45 miles. By the predawn hours of March 26, a few advance units of the 3rd Infantry were 40 miles from Baghdad. The main fighting was some 50 miles from Baghdad—a series of relentless ambushes and small attacks. While American forces sustained no real losses and the charging Iraqis suffered enormous casualties, the V Corps forces endured sufficient harassment to further slow down the 3rd Division's advance, as elements of the division were diverted overnight to quell Najaf, where Iraqi military and fedayeen activities proved too intense to be ignored.

On March 26, the forward forces of the 3rd Division were some 45 miles from Baghdad, with their advance further slowed down by a sandstorm and repeated attacks and ambushes. Despite the diversion of forces, 3rd Infantry Division units were still repeatedly attacked and ambushed in the Najaf area, being drawn into endless, fierce firefights with the Iraqis. Meanwhile, the 1st MEF's advance slowed to a trickle some 25 miles north of Nasiriyah because of fierce engagements with Iraqi regular army units. An Iraqi Republican Guard brigade of about 5,000 troops started moving from central Baghdad southward in the direction of the advancing units. This was the first indication of Saddam's resolve to defend Baghdad actively. By the evening, the Iraqis had launched a counterattack in the Nasiriyah area. The U.S. marines were subjected to barrages of mortar fire and close-range RPG attacks. The Iraqi aim was to disrupt the rush of marines charged with bolstering the 3rd Infantry Division's drive by protecting its flanks, as well as threatening the maneuvering of the Republican Guards with a pincer movement. Overnight, the 1st MEF forces were under pressure and virtually stopped. It took intense air support—despite the sandstorm—for the 1st MEF to be able to sustain advance despite the Iraqi fedayeen ambushes.

March 26 saw further intensification of the raids, ambushes, and light attacks on the entire 3rd Division. These clashes became a major problem affecting America's ability to move fast, and also consumed large fighting units needed to escort and protect the supply lines rushing from Kuwait with vital food, fuel, water, and ammunition. The main upgrading of the Iraqi threat was the introduction of the KORNET (AT-14) Anti-Tank Guided Missile (ATGM), which has a range of over 2.5 miles and the ability to knock out M-1A2 tanks. The Iraqis accomplished exactly that starting on March 26, when they knocked out two M-1A2s and one Bradley. The Iraqi irregular forces—fedayeen, Baath militas, and commandos—were improving their mobility with the deployment of about twenty-five hundred Nissan 4×4 pickup trucks (2001, 2002, and 2003 models) loaded with an assortment of weapons. The vast majority of these trucks were introduced into combat after March 28. Meanwhile, American and British Special Forces captured Al Rutba, a strategic complex near the Jordanian border, and cut off Highway 10 to Baghdad. Special Forces also exercised some control over western Iraq, particularly the areas of H-2 and H-3.

Having closely studied the situation on the battlefield in the first days of the war, the Iraqi senior officers in Saddam's inner circle were well satisfied with their ability to confront the American and British offensive. They interpreted the slowing down of the V Corps units as indicative of the dire state of American forces. Moreover, the Iraqi military's ability to withstand

numerous air strikes with acceptable casualty rates, and its capacity to severely damage a few U.S. helicopters, tanks, and armored personnel carriers (APCs), convinced Baghdad it was possible to even challenge the
Americans with a counterattack. By March 26, Saddam's inner circle was
seriously studying that option. Russian military experts concurred with
the Iraqi recognition of an American vulnerability. "It is difficult not to
notice the extremely overstretched frontline of the coalition," the GRU's
report of March 26 read. "If the Iraqis deliver a decisive strike at the base of
this front [in the Nasiriyah area], the coalition will find itself in a very difficult situation, with its main forces, cut off from the resupply units, losing
their combat readiness and mobility and falling an easy pray to the Iraqis.
It is possible that the Americans are relying on the power of their aviation
that should prevent any such developments. It is also possible that this
kind of self-confidence may be very dangerous."

During the night of March 26, these observations and analyses led to a
decision by an emboldened Saddam to move forces currently defending
Baghdad—particularly from a northern threat—toward an all-out clash
with the 3rd Infantry Division on the approaches of Baghdad. Using the
sandstorm as cover, overnight and during the early morning of March 27,
the al-Madinah RGD moved most of its units toward Najaf, and the first
brigade of the Nebuchadnezzar RGD (some 2,000 troops) moved from
north of Baghdad toward al-Kut to fill in the gap created by the maneuvering of the al-Madinah. By then, the Iraqi high command had determined
that two additional Republican Guard armored brigades—near Najaf and
Qarbalah—were properly deployed and combat ready. Baghdad was convinced they could pick off soldiers from the stalled 3rd Division into a
standstill—which would amount to a great victory for Iraq—and perhaps
even withdrawal.

Some one thousand combat vehicles of the Baghdad RGD started
moving toward Najaf and Qarbalah to bolster the defense for the major
clash. These forces were subjected to intense air strikes that destroyed quite
a few vehicles but failed to stop or even slow their advance.

On the morning of March 27, Baghdad attempted an audacious decapitating strike intended to shock the invading forces to a standstill. An
Iraqi battery just north of Basra launched an upgraded al-Samoud missile
toward Camp Doha in Kuwait. The Iraqi missile was aimed at the headquarters of the coalition ground forces—including the operations center
and war room—and was timed to impact in the middle of the morning
battlefield update, when Lt. Gen. David McKiernan and other senior offi-

cers were in the building. The Iraqi high command, in concert with the GRU's analysis, was convinced that a major shock might stall or perhaps even repel the offensive against Baghdad. However, the al-Samoud missile was intercepted by a Patriot battery. Debris fell on Camp Doha, illustrating the close proximity of the intercept.

Indeed, the Russian reading of the situation on the battlefield was fairly accurate. On March 27, American forces in Iraq reached a crisis point because of the extent of the Iraqi resistance, particularly in the Nasiriyah area, which held implications for the overall force posture of V Corps. The crisis was felt throughout V Corps from top to bottom. Lt. Gen. William S. Wallace, who, as commander of V Corps, was the army's senior ground commander in Iraq, warned on March 27 that the combination of overextended supply lines and the Iraqi's fierce rear-area operations had stalled the drive toward Baghdad. He attributed the situation to the unanticipated fierceness of the Iraqi Army. "The enemy we're fighting is different from the one we'd war-gamed against," Wallace said. He did not rule out the possibility of a much longer war.

Indeed, American commanders had to drastically modify their most basic tactics to meet the challenge of urban warfare. "We've already changed our tactics midstream," Marine Lt. Col. John Miranda acknowledged in Nasiriyah. The marines had to rely on the expertise of the British and other elite forces in order to quickly adapt to the situation in Iraq. "We've exchanged ideas with them already," Miranda noted in late March. "They've actually sent some of their experts over."

For the fighting units, the roads near Nasiriyah became "a shooting gallery for U.S. convoys" because of the unexpected ferocity of the fedayeen. "Nasiriyah was more difficult than we envisioned," acknowledged Col. Larry K. Brown, the U.S. Marine Corps' operations chief in Iraq. "I thought there would be a few of these knuckleheads out there and we would blow past them. It turned out there were more of them and they were more fanatic."

Arriving at a military hospital in Germany, a wounded young marine noted how he and his fellow soldiers were caught unprepared by the Iraqi resistance. "We were very surprised," said Marine Lance Cpl. Joshua Menard. "We were told as we were going through Nasiriyah that there would be little to no resistance." However, "when we got in, it was a whole different ballgame. . . . They weren't rolling over like we thought they would."

To break this deadlock, the United States committed the Kuwait-based

elements of the 101st Air Assault Division to the fight on March 27. Originally earmarked for filling in gaps in the siege of Baghdad and swift operations against Iraqi resistance, the 101st AAD was now part of an all-out
effort by V Corps to free the 3rd Infantry—still slugging it out with the
Iraqi ambushers—so that the pace toward Baghdad could be increased. V
Corps devised a twin pincer approach—the 101st AAD arriving from the
west of the 3rd Infantry Division, and two thirds of the 1st MEF peeling off
from the race to al-Kut and instead moving northward along the Euphrates
(east of the river, on Highway 8) in the direction of Diwaniyah in order to
strike the Iraqi forces ambushing the 3rd Infantry from the east. However,
implementation would take some time due to the acute shortages V Corps
had accumulated. By March 27, both the 3rd Division and the 101st AAD
had "paused indefinitely"—that is, until resupply lines could be restored
and they amassed a ten-day stockpile of vital supplies. Some shortages
were so acute that CH-47 helicopters had to brave the subsiding sandstorm
in order to deliver water, fuel, and some types of ammunition.

All through the day, American forces were subjected to a barrage of artillery shelling as well as hit-and-run strikes and ambushes by fedayeen,
Baath militias, and commandos—particularly in road sectors, cities, and
villages considered secure. This ongoing attrition and harassment, while
not causing heavy casualties, further bogged down the advance of the 3rd
Division. The 1st MEF kept pushing toward Diwaniyah in the hope of
reaching the road to al-Hillah, where they could relieve the Iraqi pressure
on the 3rd Division. For the 3rd Infantry, fighting continued throughout
the entire strip between the Samawah and Najaf roads to Qarbalah. There
was growing apprehension among American commanders about Republican Guard units getting through Hillah and attacking the eastern flank of
the 3rd Division before the marines could get to the area.

Weather was improving, though, and airpower could now be put into
better use, particularly close air support and attack helicopters. Still, repeated attempts to block the bridges in Nasiriyah were slowing down the
transfer of supplies. Ultimately, these readjustments in the movements and
priorities of the main forces operating on the road to Baghdad reflected a
profound revision of the war plans to cope with the prevailing conditions
in the theater. "We have seen, just over the last couple days, shifts both in
strategy that came out, and shifts in the fortunes on the battlefield," a senior Pentagon official told MENL's Steve Rodan. "And that's what ebb and
flow is about."

On the night of March 27, as Baghdad contemplated launching a counteroffensive, Iraq put the entire U.S.-led SCUD-hunting system to a test—and it failed. The Iraqis conducted a successful test to deploy and fire ballistic missiles against Israel. It was what Soviet doctrine calls a *probasila*—a move forward until there is a reaction, followed by a tactical withdrawal. Specifically, the Iraqis left a very clear electronic signature indicating that they were deploying at least one SCUD-type launcher with WMD warheads in western Iraq and preparing to launch them on Israel. According to the signature, the missile and warheads were deployed from Syria and returned there shortly afterward.

In retrospect, this could have been a test—with the Iraqis using only launchers or even trucks carrying the communications systems associated with launchers—to verify the reaction time of American electronic intelligence, the Special Forces roving in western Iraq, and airpower allocated to SCUD hunting. The Iraqi test succeeded; while U.S. and Israeli intelligence detected the Iraqi electronic signature, the U.S. Air Force F-15s and F-16s diverted to cover the deployment area were too late to catch any of the Iraqi vehicles. Hence, the Iraqis should have been encouraged, because the coalition could not launch any attack on the provocation vehicles. In Israel, this test served as a grim reminder that Baghdad could still initiate operational firings of missiles against Israel should Saddam give the order.

The morning of March 28 saw the American units making slow but persistent progress on all the lines of advance, although V Corps had difficulty in overcoming the Iraqi resistance and holding off the commando, fedayeen, and Baath forces. These Iraqis were making desperate efforts to buy time for the Republican Guard divisions to redeploy for the decisive battle in the greater Qarbalah area. Heavy aerial bombing in the predawn hours failed to dislodge the Iraqi forces. The first clashes between elements of the 101st AAD and the Hamurabi RGD, now redeploying in the greater Qarbalah area, took place in the afternoon.

The United States was acquiring a growing volume of intelligence from numerous excellent and highly reliable sources that the Iraqis planned on using chemical weapons if American forces breached their new defensive dispositions. U.S. intelligence even monitored the distribution of WMD shells and rockets to the forces deployed in the inner ring around Baghdad as part of the preparations for the decisive campaign for Baghdad. The Iraqi leadership readied for a siege on Baghdad, and Iraqi units were determined to conduct bloody urban warfare. "It will be no surprise that in five to ten days they will be able to encircle all our positions in Baghdad," Iraqi Defense Minister Sultan Hashim Ahmed said. "They have the capability to do so. But they have to come into the city eventually."

Meanwhile, after two days of intense fighting, the key elements of the 1st MEF began to breach the Iraqi defenses near Diwaniyah. The 3rd Infantry remained ensnared in clashes near Abu-Sukhayr (10 to 12 miles southeast of Najaf), and V Corps forces had to slow down in order to stabilize their formations, but forward units repeatedly launched localized attacks against the Iraqis. The intense air strikes that softened up the Republican Guard divisions as they deployed near Qarbalah helped the 3rd Infantry Division's ground attacks, but the GRU report of March 28 noted the haphazard character of these American attacks. "Today we can see that the U.S. advance is characterized by disorganized and 'impulsive' actions. The troops are simply trying to find weak spots in the Iraqi defenses and break through them until they hit the next ambush or the next line of defense."

The GRU noted the precarious state of V Corps' operations because of "its inability to hold on to the captured territory," due to shortages of men and materiel. The Iraqis, however, were not able to capitalize on the weaknesses of their enemies: "Among the drawbacks of the Iraqi forces is the bureaucratic inflexibility of their command, when all decisions are being made only at the highest levels. Their top commanders also tend to stick to standard 'template' maneuvers and there is insufficient coordination among the different types of forces. . . . At the same time commanders of the [Iraqi] special operations forces are making good use of the available troops and weapons to conduct operations behind the front lines of the enemy."

In light of the Iraqi test of the night before, on March 28 there was a marked expansion of Special Forces operations up to some 200 miles from the Jordanian border. The coalition forces did not control the territory but were able to deny the Iraqis the ability to operate there with impunity. Or so it was believed by CENTCOM and Washington.

In Jerusalem, senior defense and intelligence officials briefing the cabinet offered a grim assessment of the progress of the war. To that point, coalition forces had failed to build the momentum crucial for a swift decision of the campaign, the officials noted. The strategic command and control and national leadership structure of Iraq was still functioning and was capable of centrally controlling the war. The coalition air strikes had failed to decapitate the regime because virtually every valuable institution had been evacuated to emergency locations long before the bombing started. While the air strikes inflicted massive damage on the Iraqi forces near Baghdad, the experts acknowledged, the Iraqis had still been able to assemble their forces and maintained strategic maneuverability.

Senior American defense officials largely agreed with the Israeli assessment. Both Defense Department officials and senior military commanders now believed that V Corps' troop concentration and supply lines were inadequate for a sustained attack on Baghdad. Strong debates took hold in both Washington and CENTCOM about whether to suspend the race toward Baghdad to wait for the arrival of desperately needed reinforcements. The debate peaked on March 29, when the president invited several active duty and retired generals to Camp David for a conference on the situation in Iraq. Some of the retired generals stressed that the American concentration in Iraq was too small and that the offensive should be paused until the units could be reinforced by the 4th Infantry Division, then en route to the Persian Gulf. Privately, active duty generals concurred, but the White House resolved to accelerate the pace of the offensive with the forces on hand. "The meeting's conclusion," a presidential adviser told the *Washington Post*, "was that the campaign should remain 'Baghdad-centric,' and that the forces should push on to the capital as soon as possible, rather than try to secure their supply lines and consolidate their positions in southern Iraq." The White House reasoning, the adviser explained, "was that if you cut off the head of the snake, the rest of the snake wouldn't be able to eat you."

CENTCOM had been contemplating a four- to six-day hiatus to permit supplies to catch up with the main offensive forces and to divert large forces to secure the roads between Kuwait and the approaches to Baghdad. Facing Qarbalah, the United States had a force of some 20,000 troops, 200 tanks, 150 artillery pieces, and more than 250 helicopters. However, the position of these forces—now some 250 miles inside Iraq, far from the supply lines—remained precarious. Addressing the Iraqi rear-area operations, which targeted supply lines, also had a debilitating impact on the disposition of American forces. By late March, V Corps had little more than two divisions inside Iraq; out of these forces, three brigades—the rough equivalent of one division—were now devoted to protecting supply lines between Kuwait and Najaf. Even with this effort to broaden their control of territory around the main roads, the United States actually controlled only small pockets around V Corps' force clusters. The military had no lasting presence because of the acute shortage of ground forces.

This was a dangerous situation because of the growing hostility of the civilian population, especially Shiites, at the rear of the American forces. In addition, CENTCOM anticipated the need for large quantities of ammunition in order to cope with the continued dogged resistance of the Iraqi forces.

On March 29, the army's senior commanders in Iraq wanted to effectively restart the war. These commanders believed the United States could not launch and sustain a viable offensive on Baghdad without first securing their supply lines and building their own combat power by absorbing large-scale reinforcements. Some commanders now expected the war to run well into the summer. Continuing the war at the current force level was deemed imprudent, and most senior commanders anticipated a jump in American casualties.

The Bush administration, however, had other ideas. Washington kept insisting that CENTCOM expedite the resumption of offensive operations toward Baghdad with the forces at hand. Given the discontent among the senior commanders, Gen. Tommy Franks was dispatched to Iraq to convey Washington's message in person.

Meanwhile, the United States continued the air and helicopter strikes on Iraqi forces as they advanced toward the greater Qarbalah area. A small number of fedayeen detonated a car bomb near a Marine Corps roadblock on Route 9 near Najaf, killing five of themselves and five soldiers.

Marine Corps forces remaining in the area continued fighting with the defenders of Nasiriyah. The main element of the 1st MEF kept fighting its way through Qalat Sukkar on the road to Kut, while other elements advanced on Highway 8, finally breaking through the defense of Diwaniyah. However, despite a fierce all-night battle, the marines could not puncture Najaf's outer defenses while engaging the ceaseless raids against their rear. One brigade of the 3rd Infantry Division pulled away from the main axis of advance and crossed the Euphrates eastward so that it could advance north, parallel to Route 8, and assist the hard-pressed marines. The army brigade was quickly engaged by several raiding forces east of Najaf.

The main element of the 3rd Infantry continued its war of attrition with Iraqis arrayed between Abu-Sukhayr and Najaf. As the forward units of the 3rd Division got close to the Madinah RGD's defenses south of Qarbalah, the advance was further slowed by constant raids, ambushes, and close-range attacks. Commenting on the situation, Ralph Peters wrote, "the troopers of the 3rd [Battalion] of the 7th Cavalry [Brigade] . . . fought the longest uninterrupted series of engagements, in time and distance, in U.S. military history—while blowing sands reduced visibility to handgun range."

On March 30, there was another suicide strike against a U.S. road-block, and Iraqi Vice President Taha Yassin Ramadan threatened that the bombings would continue. "We will use any means to kill our enemy in our land and we will follow the enemy into its land," he told a Baghdad news conference. "This is just the beginning. You'll hear more pleasant news later."

Despite intense U.S. bombing, the flow of Iraqi reinforcements to both Republican Guards and regular army continued unabated, and as a result they were able to improve defensive positions in the Qarbalah area. The Iraqis had built a certain level of attrition into their war plans and there-fore could sustain operations despite the damage inflicted by U.S. air-power, and Baghdad saw the forthcoming battle for Qarbalah as the deciding event of the war. Iraqi Special Forces launched probing raids to gauge V Corps' preparations for the next phase of the offensive, and by contrast, V Corps was still short of forces to overwhelm the Iraqi defenses. Essentially, CENTCOM had expected the Iraqi command and control communication system to collapse, preventing the Iraqis from rushing forces to organize defensive positions. CENTCOM also had exaggerated expectations of the devastating effect air strikes would have on Iraqi ground forces before they reached the battlefield. Because of shortages of available aircraft, helicopters, and munitions, and the effects of the sand-storm, the damage caused by American airpower did not meet CENT-COM's estimates.

On March 30, with their stockpiles largely replenished, American forces were committed to reaching the outskirts of Baghdad within the next few hours. After three days of heavy, though largely static fighting, de-fense officials contended that the front units of V Corps were in position to "burst through Iraqi Republican Guard positions" and move toward Baghdad. Iraqi commanders considered their situation during the night of March 30 to be "critical" even though most of the American activities were merely probing operations.

On March 31, the 1st Brigade of the 3rd Infantry resumed its advance toward Baghdad after three days of constant, static fighting. After intense skirmishes, the brigade got within 50 miles of Baghdad but had to with-draw to stabilize its position. Sporadic clashes with forward Iraqi units continued despite the increased tempo of helicopter strikes—mainly by Apache elements of the 101st AAD—on Iraqi combat vehicles. Meanwhile, marine raids in the al-Shatrah area searching for senior officers and officials evolved into a series of clashes with local irregulars and Baath militias. Intense fighting also erupted in Nasiriyah. Throughout, the advance on Baghdad proved far more difficult than originally anticipated.

9
THE RACE TO BAGHDAD, PART 3

After its March 27 decapitation strike failed, Baghdad demonstrated the first signs of diminishing confidence. Though most evidence suggests they were still convinced that Iraq would ultimately contain or defeat the offensive, the Iraqi leadership suddenly asked Moscow for a second opinion about the state of the war. With that, a psychological barrier was broken and Saddam began pondering the unthinkable—that Baghdad would fall to the Americans. He immediately asked the Belarusians, who had long offered him refuge, to facilitate the urgent evacuation of his family members, senior officials, treasure, and archives. On both March 29 and 30, a chartered Belarusian IL-76 transport aircraft briefly landed at Saddam International Airport and took sensitive cargo and people straight to Minsk, Belarus. The aircraft departed through Iranian airspace, and Iran made no attempt to interfere with the Iraqi flights. Uday was sent to Minsk on the first flight out in order to prepare for the possible exile of the entire family. The commotion around the airport led to rumors that Saddam and his family had fled the country.

On March 30, Russian military experts delivered a devastating analysis of the war to Saddam Hussein and his inner circle. The gist of the Russian analysis was included in the GRU's March 31 report to the Kremlin:

> Russian military analysts are advising the Iraqi military command against excessive optimism. There is no question that the U.S. "blitzkrieg" failed to take control of Iraq and to destroy its army. It is clear that the Americans got bogged down in Iraq and the military campaign hit a snag. However, the Iraqi command is now in danger of underestimating the enemy. . . . For now there is no reason to question the resolve of the Americans and their determina-

tion to reach the set goal—complete occupation of Iraq. In reality, despite some obvious miscalculations and errors by the coalition's high command, the troops that have entered Iraq maintain high combat readiness and are willing to fight. The losses sustained during the past 12 days of fighting ... are entirely insignificant, militarily speaking. The initiative in the war remains firmly in the hands of the coalition. Under such circumstances Iraqi announcements of a swift victory over the enemy will only confuse its own troops and the Iraqi population and, as a result, may lead to demoralization and a reduced defensive potential.

Saddam Hussein took the Russian advice very seriously and immediately initiated profound policy changes, which altered the course of the war. On the morning of March 31, the first signs that Baghdad was rethinking its strategy became apparent: Overnight, elements of the Baghdad RGD moved north across the Tigris, without destroying the bridges, deploying north of Kut, away from the main battlefield zone. The Nebuchadnezzar RGD moved southeast toward Fallujah and then toward Qarbalah from the west to bolster the defense against the 3rd Infantry Division. At the same time, units of the 101st AAD attacked the Nebuchadnezzar RGD but could not stop its advance. Task Force 20 and elements of the 101st AAD reached Hindiyah Dam and after a brief but intense clash were able to prevent the Iraqis from sabotaging or opening the dam and flooding the Qarbalah salient. The 101st AAD forces operated near al-Musyyih in an effort to identify breaches and seams between the Iraqi units that the 3rd Infantry Division would be able to break through on its way toward Baghdad.

On March 31, while all of these engagements were taking place, the Iraqi high command, particularly in the Qarbalah salient area, was undergoing a profound crisis. During that day, high-level emissaries from Baghdad reached the key commanders with reminders that they had specific orders and were to follow them even if they did not hear from Saddam. In principle, these units were expected to hold the line until death. In retrospect, the mere arrival of these emissaries hurt the morale of the commanders, who until then had fought resolutely. Not without reason, the Iraqis interpreted Saddam's reminder as an indication that the leadership was about to flee, leaving them to die for a lost cause. Indeed, a few senior officers began to whisper about the previously unthinkable—breaking with Saddam.

The Iraqi commanders arrayed in the Qarbalah salient area received another major piece of news that day, this time from Shiite neighbors. During the weekend of March 28–30, fully aware of the crisis mood in Baghdad, Tehran made a profound decision regarding the war in Iraq, deciding not to intervene as the United States moved to topple Saddam's regime. Therefore, the Shiite population was instructed to postpone its own major "intifada" planned against the regime. At the same time, Tehran stressed that the Shiites were *not* to assist the United States in any way, let alone legitimize its presence in Iraq. Essentially, Tehran and the Iraqi Shiites would stand aside as the United States and Saddam's regime bled each other, and then would unleash fresh Shiite forces to seize power and evict the Americans. Iranian instructions reached the leadership in Najaf and Qarbalah on March 30 or 31—arriving at the same time as Saddam's emissaries. Iraqi senior officers concluded that the regime was doomed and that there was no point in dying for Saddam's cause—a realization that would drastically change the Iraqi resistance a few days later.

Numerous Arab and Iranian senior defense and intelligence officials now contend that around April 1, key Iraqi officers, both in the Qarbalah salient area and in the southern suburbs of Baghdad, were approached by emissaries of various opposition groups, including the ostensibly pro-Western organizations. These emissaries convinced the officers to reach an understanding with the Iranians through their emissaries among the Shiite community. The proposed deal was very much along the lines of the agreement reached in Tehran by Chalabi, Hakim, and the Kurdish leaders on the eve of the war. Essentially, Tehran struck a deal with members of the Iraqi high command to allow Saddam's removal, after which the remaining core of the high command would establish a new post-Saddam Islamic Iraq. Furthermore, with the blessing of Shiite leaders in Najaf and Qarbalah, several key Tikriti officers made contacts with the Islamist commanders affiliated with Osama bin Laden, who had established a clandestine forward position in the Fallujah area. They also looked into cooperating in a post-Saddam Islamic Iraq—albeit one without a Shiite character.

April 1 saw Iraqi commandos carrying out roving attacks and ambushes throughout the western desert, particularly in the general direction of the Syrian border. These forces were denying access to and impeding the movement of Western Special Forces. On the road to Baghdad, most of the fighting was related to probing attacks by both sides. American and Iraqi forces were still trying to determine the overall situation in what appeared to be the decisive battle of the entire war. The United States intensified its bombing of Baghdad, and two al-Sumud SSMs were fired at American concentrations near Najaf; one missile was intercepted by Patriots, and the other crashed harmlessly in the desert. With the threat of flooding removed, forward elements of the 3rd Infantry Division seized a major bridge and crossed the Euphrates near Hindiyah, some 50 miles from Baghdad. Aerial bombing of the al-Madinah RGD intensified to expedite the advance of the V Corps forces, although American claims that they had destroyed half the division's combat vehicles were grossly exaggerated. Moreover, the bulk of the 3rd Infantry was still mired in ambushes and could not exploit the seizure of the bridge. Still, the 3rd Infantry's crawl toward Baghdad resumed in earnest.

At this stage, the Iraqis—both Republican Guard and regular units, stretched along the Hillah-Hindiyah-Qarbalah defense line extending east to west—were still fighting fiercely. Units were rarely withdrawing but rather dying for Saddam. American progress was marginal at best, although V Corps units conducted several determined assaults in an effort to break through the Iraqi defenses on the edges of urban centers; the main push was in the direction of the strategic triangle including Qarbalah, Al-Hindiyah, and Al-Iskanderiya. The Americans were still struggling to move reinforcements and supplies, including a brigade of the 82nd Airborne Division, hampered by intense ambushes, firefights, and artillery shelling along the entire route from Kuwait. Most troubling were pockets of resistance in Nasiriyah, Samawah, Abu-Sukhayr, and Najaf.

"To move forward the U.S. units are forced to leave behind large numbers of troops needed to blockade the towns remaining under Iraqi control," the GRU observed. Furthermore, the 1st MEF units that were supposed to block the arrival of Iraqi reinforcements from Kut, as well as attack Iraqi eastern flanks, were still mired in their own debilitating fighting with the irregulars at Diwaniyah and weren't able to get to Hillah on time. The other marine units finally overcame the defenses of Qalat Sukkar and resumed their steady advance toward the still distant al-Kut.

On April 2, V Corps cemented its control over the main roads to Baghdad in order to sustain the advance even if large formations of Iraqi forces remained in their rear. CENTCOM reasoned that they had neither sufficient forces nor the time to deal with these pockets. V Corps was committed to drive into the center of Baghdad in the hope that the Iraqi units behind them would surrender once they realized that the war was over. In the meantime, aerial bombing of these pockets would continue. Ultimately, it was an audacious gamble by CENTCOM given its record of grossly underestimating Iraqi resistance. A jubilant Rumsfeld told CNN that U.S. forces got the green light to storm Baghdad, and CENTCOM had no way back.

Meanwhile, a 1st MEF brigade approached al-Kut but refrained from taking on the major forces defending it, including the Baghdad RGD. Small units of the 3rd Division passed between the Iraqis, trying to reach roads toward Baghdad. All these movements were beset by constant clashes, ambushes, and raids. As the marines started advancing from Kut toward Suwayrah, the site of a major Republican Guard headquarters, and forward elements of the 3rd Infantry Division moved toward Mussayib and on to Iskandiriyah, some worried the units were getting into densely inhabited areas where they could be ambushed easily. Given the size of the Iraqi forces in place, particularly those hiding inside the Shiite cities, the forward American units could be surrounded and decimated with no viable reinforcements in sight. V Corps was also gripped by renewed fear of a chemical attack after the United States intercepted a single-word transmission—"*Damm*" (blood)—to Iraqi units. Wind patterns were ideal for a gas attack. Nevertheless, V Corps was ordered to sustain, and even accelerate, its advance.

Meanwhile, British forces were desperately trying to end the protracted and so far indecisive fighting in southern Iraq. During the night of March 23, Iraqi commandos surging from Basra conducted a major ambush of the patrolling British forces, and on March 24, British forces in the area had to pull back and rethink their tactics. "Fierce Iraqi resistance—including attacks by irregular forces pretending to surrender and the use of women and children as decoys—forced British troops to withdraw from Basra to regroup," reported a senior British commander on-site.

Iraqi forces in Umm-Qasr also launched a major counterattack against the British. It was a nasty surprise, as the operation came more than a day after the city was supposed to be firmly in coalition control. Despite repeated shelling and bombing, the city of Umm-Qasr held, and the coalition forces—mainly British Marines—did not storm the city, fearing entanglement in costly urban warfare. By the night of March 24, the British controlled only the strategic roads going through Umm-Qasr, but fierce clashes continued in the residential districts.

The Iraqi resistance in Basra escalated the next day when fifty tanks with heavy artillery pieces surged out of the city to fight the British forces in the direction of Basra's airport. It was a fierce counterattack that initially pushed the thinly spread British forces back. Only massive air support, mainly from gunships stationed on the *Ark Royal* aircraft carrier, which destroyed seven tanks after chasing them by flying very low along the city's streets, punished the Iraqis into withdrawing to the safety of densely populated suburbs.

Elsewhere, static fighting continued. "The coalition forces in this area are clearly insufficient for continuing the attack and the main emphasis is being placed on artillery and aviation. The city is under constant bombardment but so far this has had little impact on the combat readiness of the Iraqi units," the GRU reported on March 25. Indeed, British forces had to pull back and readjust their positions in the Basra area. The main reason for the British setback was the unexpected popular resistance in the urban areas. "We were expecting a lot of hands up from Iraqi soldiers and for the humanitarian operation in Basra to begin fairly quickly behind us, with aid organizations providing food and water to the locals. But it hasn't quite worked out that way," said British military spokesman Capt. Patrick Trueman. "There are significant elements in Basra who are hugely loyal to the regime. We always had the idea that everyone in this area hated Saddam. Clearly there are a number who don't."

Once the Iraqi counteroffensive was pushed back, violent riots erupted in the middle of Basra. At first, coalition forces interpreted the Shiite riots to be anti-Saddam, and British artillery and helicopter gunships repeatedly attacked the Iraqi positions trying to suppress the Shiite revolt, but it did not take long for the true character of the unrest to emerge: The Shiite "rebellion" in Basra erupted after the Baathist security police executed a Shiite leader suspected of disloyalty to Saddam. There was nothing pro-Western in the uprising, and when a detachment of British Commandos reached the Shiites, they killed a British soldier. The British commanders' hope of capitalizing on the riots to destroy Iraqi forces and incite grassroots antiregime violence was soon dashed. Moreover, the Shiite community leaders in Basra called on the local residents to fight the "children of the Satan"—the Americans and the British. All the same, the Iraqis all but suppressed the Shiite uprising despite continued British help.

British activities along the Iranian border gave a good indication of strategic developments to come. British Marines and Naval Commandos began conducting patrols and raids along the border in order to intercept

Iranian agents, operatives, and Special Forces carrying large quantities of weapons, ammunition, explosives, money, and whatever was needed to accelerate the Shiite rebellion. When Iranian forces fired at the British patrols in order to prevent them from intercepting the Shiite convoys, British Commandos raided the Iranian positions, ensuring that they reduced their active support for the infiltration. Iraq was also extremely hostile to Iran's activities, and according to on-site Iranian observers, "Iraqi forces brought down an Iranian helicopter near Al-Faw yesterday afternoon [March 24]." The helicopter was over Iraqi territory—most likely delivering personnel, equipment, and weapons to the local Shiite mujahedin.

Meanwhile, the British operations in and around Basra devolved into a standstill. The GRU report of March 26 noted:

> Near Basra, the British forces in essence are laying a Middle Ages–style siege of a city with a population of two million. Artillery fire has destroyed most of the city's life-supporting infrastructure, and artillery is used continuously against the positions of the defending units. The main goal of the British is to maintain a strict blockade of Basra. Their command is confident that the situation in the city can be destabilized and lack of food, electricity, and water will prompt the local population to cause the surrender of the defending forces. [GRU] Analysts point out that capture of Basra is viewed by the coalition command as being exceptionally important and as a model for the future "bloodless" takeover of Baghdad. So far, however, this approach does not work and the city's garrison is actively defending its territory.

Over the next few days, the lines remained fairly static. The Iraqis controlled Basra and its suburbs as well as parts of the adjacent Faw Peninsula, while the British blockade was far from hermetic because the harsh, marshy terrain, crossed by numerous waterways, made it impossible to create a single front line. Both sides conducted sporadic raids in order to improve tactical positions. Under cover of the sandstorm, the Iraqis redeployed two battalions of the 51st Infantry Division to the Faw Peninsula to bolster the local defenders. The next day, the British attempted to completely take over the peninsula in order to complete the blockade of Basra. However, their advance along the Shatt Al-Arab stalled due to intense shelling and ambushes.

Finally on March 28, under continuous artillery shelling and aerial bombing, the Iraqi forces began pulling back toward Basra, relinquishing parts of the Faw Peninsula. That night, however, Iraq fired an upgraded Silkworm, with a range of over 50 miles, into Kuwait City. The missile hit the water just off the coastline, but still caused heavy damage to a shopping mall. Significantly, the Silkworm was fired from the Faw Peninsula— demonstrating again that the coalition's claims to have captured the peninsula were inaccurate. Shelling and ambushes also continued in the ostensibly secured Umm-Qasr area.

The GRU report of March 29 stressed the posture of the Iraqi population in Basra:

> The psychological levels among the city's residents, according to interviews, are far from critical. The Iraqi military made several public announcements to the residents offering them a chance to leave the city. However, most of the residents do not want to leave, fearing the fate of the Palestinian refugees, who, after losing their homes, gained pariah status in the Arab world. Basra's residents were extremely depressed by the video footage aired by the coalition command showing Iraqis in the occupied territories fighting for food and water being distributed by the coalition soldiers. The city's population views this as a sample of what awaits them if the Americans come.

By March 30 British forces all but surrounded Basra, leaving open a corridor leading south in the direction of Faw, permitting the Iraqis to withdraw from the city. British commanders assessed that, with their backs against the wall, the Iraqis had no option but to continue their ferocious resistance, and therefore decided to give them a way out. The British siege didn't finally yield results until the aftermath of Operation James, launched overnight by the Royal Marines Commandos in order to take the Abu al-Khasib neighborhood in the south of Basra and eliminate Baath leadership.

At the same time, the Iraqis launched an attack on the Basra Canal (also known as the Saddam Canal), damaging a British landing craft. The Royal Marines sank one of the Iraqi vessels with an ATGM. Clashes, ambushes, and exchanges of fire continued all around town. However, the Iraqis did not exploit the corridor and instead elected to remain and defend the city despite the worsening situation. The Iraqis put up stiff resistance, and repeated attempts by the British to break through their defenses along the

Shatt al-Arab failed. The British command concluded that it would require significant reinforcements before Basra could be stormed, in a decision that unnerved London. Having to wait for reinforcements, British forces around Basra adopted defensive tactics in an effort to maintain the tight blockade while avoiding further casualties. They launched small localized attacks and maintained pressure on the Iraqi positions on the Faw Peninsula.

The next day, March 31, British forces finally pushed the Iraqi line in northeast Basra farther back toward the Shatt al-Arab. In the west, a British attack from Basra Airport forced the Iraqis to pull back by several city blocks. However, the British attempt to advance along the Shatt al-Arab and slice Basra in two, separating Basra from the Iraqi-held part of the Faw Peninsula, failed. Localized fighting continued throughout the Basra area on April 1. The British attempted to capture the villages of As-Zubair and Suk-al-Shujuh under heavy artillery and air support but were forced to return to their original position, and an Iraqi counterattack that night near the village of Suk-al-Shujuh forced the British back about a mile from their original position. Over the next couple of days, the British resumed their efforts to breach the Iraqi defenses around Basra. They attempted a pincer assault northwest of Maakil Airport along the Shatt al-Arab, and from the southwest at As-Zubair toward the area of Mahallat-as-Zubair. The British advance was very slow, and largely failed to breach the Iraqi outer defenses. On April 4, the British seized the As-Zubair-Basra highway and established firing positions overlooking the opposite side of the river.

They continued their dogged advance on April 5, slowly pushing the Iraqi defenders away from their positions. However, the British still could not breach the main defense lines, and very heavy fighting took place at the outskirts of Basra. However, a fierce nine-hour assault by five British regiments on April 6 finished off the organized resistance. By the end of the day, British forces were nominally in control of the city except for a few pockets of fierce resistance, especially in the Ashshar neighborhood by the river and the city block including the headquarters of the Mukhabarat, Baath Party, and Basra's governor.

On April 7, the British finally claimed to occupy Basra. The situation stabilized largely because the local population ceased widespread resistance, and once again key Iraqi units melted away with most of their equipment before the British entered the city. Over the next couple of days, the Iraqis were able to expand their pockets of resistance in the Ashshar and Akina regions as well as a part of the Shatt al-Arab quay. Essentially, the British were reluctant to commit their forces to the prolonged and casualty-heavy urban warfare required to quell these pockets, but on April 8 the British forces were able to launch several local operations that reduced their size and intensity. Overnight, several Iraqi units abandoned their positions and either left the city or disappeared among Basra's citizens. Later in the month, active resistance, terrorism, and insurgency would resume throughout southern Iraq.

On the first day of April, as U.S. forces advanced north toward Baghdad on a rather narrow front, the military situation in the city still favored the defenders. Arab and other foreign officials interacting with the Iraqi population noted their resolve to actively resist the American invasion. Morale in the city was very high; the military remained loyal to Saddam and ready to fight for the capital.

These impressions were echoed after the war by an Iraqi brigadier general then hiding in Baghdad. "I was in command of an army division," he explained. "We were on the outskirts of Baghdad, and our job was to slow the U.S. advance to give the National Guard and the fedayeen militias time to organize for the final battle." The brigadier general then went on to stress the high morale of all Iraqis. "Since before the war began, the country seemed to be in thrall to collective euphoria. We were being threatened by the world's mightiest army. Everyone was demanding to fight, and the Defense Ministry decided to arm twenty-four million people. We were determined to fight to the last. We were fighting at home, and this would lead us to victory."

A Mukhabarat officer concurred with this description, stressing that for the entire Iraqi defense establishment, "Baghdad was like a castle. The Americans could never come close—we were sure of it."

Egyptian military experts who had long experience with the Iraqi armed forces also expected the defenders to "exhibit ferocious resistance" against the American invasion. In April, Gen. Saad Al-Shazli, a former Egyptian Army commander, predicted that the coalition forces would fail to capture Baghdad. "I believe the Iraqi people and army are at the peak of their morale," he said. "What many people do not realize is that the Iraqis are fighting for their homeland, dignity, and honor and I think this is enough for them to hold out and sacrifice everything. I know it is an unfair war, but it is a losing war for the allies."

Shazli explained that the Iraqi strategy was to preserve Iraq's air force and limit battles to urban areas. "The war could only be ended by the ground forces," Shazli stressed. "Storming Baghdad has to be done by the ground forces, not the air force. They have tried to capture Nasiriyah and other small cities but have not tried to enter them because they know they will enter a quagmire."

The defense of Baghdad was based on two tiers. The external defense relied on six Republican Guard divisions and an assortment of regular army units. Four of the Republican Guard divisions were in the southern part of Baghdad, in the path of the main American advance, while two (the Adnan and the Nebuchadnezzar RGDs) were deployed north of Baghdad. The four southern divisions were the Al-Madinah, deployed to the southwest of Baghdad, the Baghdad, deployed to the southeast of the city, the Hamurabi, deployed to the east, and the al-Nidah, deployed to the west. At the core of the inner defense were up to 25,000 elite troops of the Special Republican Guard, or the Golden Division. The Golden Division's 4th Brigade was deployed in the southern suburbs of the city, reinforced by two tank battalions of the Republican Guard; the 1st Brigade was deployed around the presidential complex at the center of Baghdad; the 2nd Brigade was deployed around the rest of the capital, and the 3rd Brigade, also largely deployed in northern Baghdad, acted as a quick reaction force and strategic reinforcement.

By late March, all of the Special Republican Guard's personnel were provided with civilian clothes, emergency hiding places, and concealed weapons caches so that they could quickly transform the defense of the city into a guerrilla war. Auxiliary forces inside Baghdad included 100,000 intelligence operatives, many of whom were highly experienced combat veterans of the anti-Saddam revolts, and roughly 40,000 police troops. Military intelligence organized a terrorist unit numbering in the thousands for the defense of Baghdad; the Baath militia had some 30,000 armed activists; and the Special Security Forces had 5,000 elite troops fiercely loyal to Saddam and the Tikriti clan. In addition, Sadam's Fedayeen, under Uday's command—operating completely outside the military-controlled central defense—had around 40,000 members, including death squads responsible for policing the loyalty of all the other units in the greater Baghdad area. Finally, hundreds of thousands of assault rifles, machine guns, and RPGs were distributed to the population, with a large number of those receiving guns elderly veterans of the war with Iran.

Although the various units arrayed in Baghdad seemed eager to defend the city, those at the top of the regime did not share their resolve. In the first days of April, Saddam's inner circle was beginning to crack under the war's pressure. The most significant manifestation of the growing strain was Qusay's assumption of direct command over the Republican Guards on April 2. Qusay took the reins because of Saddam's growing distrust of the military's high command, but Qusay, arrogant and unprepared for military command, quickly managed to alienate all his underlings, including unwaveringly loyal senior officers. According to former Iraqi generals and colonels, Qusay issued orders to specific units "despite his total lack of military skills."

One set of orders pushed thousands of soldiers, mainly of the Hammurabi RGD, into the open outside Baghdad. At Qusay's directive, the Republican Guards advanced in two columns toward Qarbalah and the far side of the Euphrates, encountering vicious American air strikes that killed most of the units' personnel. These orders, which the Iraqi officers believed to have been approved by Saddam himself, severely debilitated the defenses of Baghdad just as American forces were approaching the city. Given that state of affairs, many commanders resolved to protect their own forces through local redeployment rather than expose them to crushing air strikes.

By now, the doubt that had taken hold among Iraqi senior officers in both the Qarbalah salient area and the southern suburbs of Baghdad had filtered down to the fighting units. Gradually the Iraqi forces began showing less resistance; raids and ambushes against the V Corps forces occurred less often and lacked the former ferocity. Main Iraqi forces started pulling back into cities without much fire. Key units retreated away from American concentrations. No explanation was given for these developments, and no central communications or discernable instructions were detected by American or other intelligence services.

Similarly, in the aftermath of an American attack on Qarbalah, the April 3 GRU report explained that the "thrust came as a surprise to the Iraqi command," and as a result "the Iraqi headquarters [in Qarbalah] lost most of its communication facilities and has partially lost control of the troops. As a result the Iraqi defense units in the line of the coalition attack became disorganized and were unable to offer effective resistance."

But developments among the Iraqis were far more profound and not simply caused by a lack of communications. Under cover of darkness, Republican Guard and other major units began abandoning their strategic positions and quietly melting into the countryside. These developments stood in stark contrast to the parade of "determined" officers on Iraqi TV, who assured viewers that the fighting continued.

On April 2, Saddam failed to deliver a scheduled speech on Iraqi TV, despite repeated announcements that he would appear. Ultimately an announcer read a mediocre address attributed to Saddam. Rumors continued to fly around Baghdad that Saddam and his inner circle had left the city and gone to Syria or hiding places in western Iraq.

Fully aware of the growing tension and dissent among the Iraqi high command, and with the situation at the front worsening, Qusay called for an urgent meeting of his commanders on the morning of April 3; this conference irreconcilably strained both Qusay's and Saddam's relationship with the commanders. Wearing his usual suit and tie rather than a military uniform, and flanked by armed bodyguards, Qusay berated the attending senior officers. "Qusay blamed them for losing the war," Gen. Alaa Abdul Kader, a Baghdad-area commander of the Republican Guard, told Robert Collier of the *San Francisco Chronicle*. Although he had "avoided" this meeting, Alaa claimed to have been briefed in detail by the top aide he had sent. "One of the high command was crying, [and] said, 'My best soldiers were killed.' So everybody hated [Qusay]. But Qusay had a guard with him, and anybody who rejected what he said would have been killed."

Col. Khaled Tai, who attended the conference, stressed its detrimental effects on the high command's willingness to fight. "We were sick in our stomachs about what Qusay and Saddam had done," he told Collier. "We all talked and agreed, whoever wants to keep fighting, do it on their own, fight for the future of our children, fight for Iraq, but not for Qusay or Saddam. Or they can go to their homes. Most went home." This was the last formal contact between Qusay Saddam Hussein and the Iraqi military elite, although some senior officers claimed that Qusay was later seen in Baghdad.

Now allied forces started to move with unsettling ease. On April 3, forward marine units reached Aziziyah, which is only 45 miles from Baghdad, facing little or no resistance. In the west, forward units of the 3rd Infantry reached their position 25 miles from Baghdad. These units advanced along several axes that took them past major Iraqi formations that now hardly reacted. Other elements of the 3rd Infantry reached the Mussayib Bridge, 35 miles from Baghdad, without seeing any meaningful action. U.S. Special Forces also met little or no resistance during their infiltration of Baghdad's nearby suburbs.

After their meeting with Qusay, Iraqi senior officers started to gen-

uinely consider cooperation with the United States. Having concluded that
all was lost and hoping to soften the repercussions they'd face once the
United States occupied Baghdad, Iraqi officers now sought to capitalize on
their haphazard and convoluted contacts with American intelligence. On
the eve of the war, the CIA had ramped up a bribary campaign run in conjunction with allied intelligence services. What started as a trickle in January and was limited to the areas near the Kuwaiti border became a flood in
late March when defeat seemed inevitable. Local officers who had made
contact with Western intelligence organizations now brought colleagues
and fellow commanders in for follow-up arrangements, hoping to win
greater bonuses.

The United States had established a complex web of agreements with
local forces, particularly in the eastern approaches to Baghdad, expecting
the widespread collapse of the Iraqi defenses the moment hostilities commenced. Although a lot of money changed hands, the deals initially failed
to produce results, as demonstrated by the Marine Corps's inability to
break toward al-Amarah and on to al-Kut because of staunch Iraqi resistance. In all these agreements, the United States promised not to pursue
the commanders after the engagement, provided they had not committed
war crimes, and since the Iraqis remained uncertain about whether they
would be safe in an American-dominated Iraq, they were ultimately reluctant to change sides. However, by April 3 and 4, some of these initial contacts were suddenly revived, and this time the Iraqis genuinely wanted to
follow through on the agreements.

Most important was the major breakthrough with Gen. Waqil Massiri,
the son-in-law of Gen. Ali Hassan al-Majid (better known as "Chemical
Ali"). The CIA got to Massiri through Ezzedine al-Majid, Ali Hassan's
nephew, who lives in London. Without any specific command post of his
own, Massiri was one of a group of generals considered closest to Saddam's
inner circle and entrusted with "special services," including internal security and delicate overseas missions. Massiri promised "to bring in" the al-
Madinah, Hammurabi, al-Nidah, and Nebuchadnezzar RGDs defending
Baghdad. However, most of the officers initially contacted remained convinced that their loyalty was being tested by Saddam's Fedayeen and be-
haved accordingly. It seems that Massiri himself was not fully committed
until the first line of Iraqi units collapsed, the SAS guided a pair of bombing attacks meant specifically to kill Ali Hassan al-Majid (though neither
succeed, both came close), and the rumors of Saddam's flight from Bagh-

dad became prevalent and believable. Finally, after Qusay's April 3 conference, some of Massiri's original contacts became receptive.

The turning of General Maher Sufian al-Tikriti—one of Saddam's dearest cousins, who was considered "Saddam's shadow" because of their closeness—was Waqil Massiri's greatest achievement. Befitting Saddam's trust, Sufian was the head of the Republican Guards in the Baghdad area and thus the key to the city's defenses. A by-product of his friendship with Saddam, however, was that Sufian was fully cognizant of his cousin's unlimited wrath, ruthlessness, and cruelty and that of his sons as well. Sufian's own inner circle included the head of intelligence for the Republican Guard, General Taher Jalil al-Harbush al-Tikriti, and General Hussein Rashid al-Tikriti, whose son was the chief of Qusay's personal office. From the latter, Sufian's group learned about Qusay's fury and resolve to purge all the senior officers he held responsible for Iraq's military setbacks. Around April 3, Sufian and his colleagues resolved that only a deal with the Americans would ensure that they would not be blamed for the collapse of the Republican Guard, and they feared that if the regime survived, or even held Baghdad for a short while, they and most other senior officers would be executed to shift the blame away from Qusay's disastrous performance. Bearing that in mind, Sufian contacted Massiri again and asked him to revive contacts with the Americans and tell them that he would consider delivering Baghdad given the right circumstances.

Meanwhile, CENTCOM was still apprehensive about the forthcoming assault on Baghdad. The United States was committing virtually its entire ground force to the forward advance, while up to 100,000 Iraqi regulars and fedayeen fought behind the coalition's front lines. American and British military experts agreed that any assault on Baghdad would be a multipronged offensive staged under the umbrella of intense air strikes. The objective would be to divide the city into numerous war zones. Fighting would be protracted and intense, as organized surrender of Iraqi troops was not expected. "We are not expecting to drive into Baghdad suddenly and seize it in a *coup de main* or anything like that," Gen. Stanley McChrystal, vice director for operations at the Joint Chiefs of Staff, said on April 3. "So in regard to that, we are paying great attention to their ability to defend on the ground. They may just suddenly be effective on the ground."

On April 4, three thousand American combat vehicles were arrayed for the final assault on Baghdad, having covered more than 65 miles in the last thirty-six hours. As the Americans assembled, there was growing chaos among the Iraqi units in the city, and especially among those stationed in downtown Baghdad. Some units moved aimlessly, clearly without any defined mission or higher command authority; some companies and battalions simply parked their tanks and fighting vehicles while the troops sat and waited for orders to come.

There was no organized resistance in the approaches to Baghdad, but neither was desertion widespread. Some sporadic fighting continued against forward units of the 3rd Infantry at the edges of Saddam International Airport. But by the afternoon of April 4, a new quandary had emerged. Some 70,000 Republican and Special Republican Guard troops who were expected to defend Baghdad's southern approaches simply vanished. "There are virtually no abandoned or captured Iraqi combat vehicles," the GRU reported on April 4. "Iraqi troops are not demoralized and the Iraqi command is still in control of its forces." There was no logical reason for their disappearance and no clue to their whereabouts or that of their weapons—including tanks, artillery, and combat vehicles.

Against the background of puzzling and at times contradictory activities, Iraqi TV finally broadcast Saddam's long-expected speech on April 4. As in his last TV appearance, Saddam looked relaxed and confident, and in order to prove he had not fled, he visited his troops at the airport and boosted their resolve to continue the fight. According to a veteran Republican Guard NCO who was at the airport, Saddam arrived in a white Nissan escorted by only two motorcycles equipped with machine guns. Wearing his army uniform, Saddam climbed on top of his car and spoke to the troops using a handheld loudspeaker. "If you want to save your neck, you can bloody well go home. If you defy death, you can come with me," the NCO remembered Saddam declaring. "None of us left," he added. Saddam then held a conference with the officers for about fifteen minutes.

Troops of the 26th Special Commando Brigade—Saddam's personal guards—had been gathering at Saddam International Airport since the morning of April 3. There was no indication whether their mission was to protect Saddam or if they were summoned for a different reason. Nevertheless, that afternoon, forward units of the 3rd Infantry Division began entering the airport. At first, they established a small compound in the far reaches of the runways, away from the main terminals and the Iraqi forces.

Later that day, Iraqi TV also showed Saddam walking around Baghdad, inspecting bomb damage and interacting with the public. Intelligence concluded it was the real Saddam and not a double, and also determined, on the basis of the damage shown, that the footage had been shot earlier that day. After the war, one of Saddam's bodyguards, Muhammad Hamis, confirmed that the real Saddam indeed walked the streets and talked to the people. In the evening, Iraqi officials threatened a major operation overnight at the airport that would include the use of suicide bombers and unconventional weapons. They threatened that no American would survive the strike.

Indeed, fierce fighting raged that night at the airport compound: a mixed force of elite units, which now included three Republican Guard battalions, and mujahedin—including a few martyr bombers—attacked the Americans, pushing them away from the airport buildings. The battle, fought at close quarters, lasted for almost six hours. The NCO described intense fighting in the airport compound and nearby civilian neighborhoods, in which the Iraqis were able to inflict heavy casualties on American ground units but also suffered severe casualties from heavy bombing, especially when the aircraft dropped cluster munitions. Several Iraqi witnesses insist that Saddam personally fought for the defense of the airport, along with the 26th Special Commando Brigade. (While many such stories of Saddam's "heroic" adventures circulated in the months after the invasion—and there was always the chance that one of his body doubles was involved—this story was corroborated by too many Iraqi soldiers and officers to discount entirely.)

Buoyed, the Iraqis held their positions by daybreak. Throughout, the Americans kept control of their compound as well, and vigorously attacked the Iraqis, thinning their ranks. By daylight, airpower and a renewed ground assault had forced the Iraqis to withdraw from most of the airport's buildings. However, an attempt by the American units to penetrate Saddam's underground "cities" at the airport's remote edges failed. By now, as many as two regular Iraqi brigades and roughly 2,000 fedayeen, Baath militiamen, and mujahedin were fighting for the airport against less than 1,000 U.S. soldiers.

During April 5, around twenty-five tanks and twenty Bradleys belonging to the 3rd Infantry entered Baghdad for strategic purposes, but also to demonstrate American military dominance. The unit moved in from the south and advanced along the Hilla road into Umm-al-Tabul square, and then turned onto the Matar Saddam al-Dowli road (the main highway to Saddam International Airport). In this foray, the convoy skirted the Dora Farm and Yarmuk compounds, which both conceal major underground complexes, as well as the Special Republican Guards arrayed at the city's southwestern edge. The patrol engaged in a few firefights, but its advance was unimpeded.

While the American convoy moved through the city almost entirely without incident, another suicide bomber blew himself up near the airport, and heavy artillery fire was heard all over Baghdad. American attacks continued at the city's center against remnants of the Republican Guard. Heavy fighting also continued in the cities the United States had enveloped while rushing toward Baghdad. On April 5, the GRU observed that "extraordinary dispersion of the ground forces [that went unchallenged by the American military as they moved toward Baghdad] and their fragmentation (the biggest group contained up to 12,000 troops) create advantageous preconditions for Iraqi counterattacks, but the air superiority of the coalition severely complicates such projects."

Nevertheless, the fight for the airport took precedence. An Iraqi Army brigadier general stressed the crucial significance of the battle as the turning point of the war. He was convinced that "a general sold Baghdad to the United States" once he became disillusioned by the outcome of the engagement. On April 6, "two days before the fall of Baghdad, the order to drop everything came in from intelligence," the brigadier general recalled. "It happened when we lost the international airport, a point we regarded as strategic, and which was defended by Saddam himself, gun in hand."

The brigadier general vividly described the overall context of the events leading to the order to stand down.

> We fought for the first eighteen days, but losing the airport had a decisive impact. The orders we were getting were confused and contradictory, not least because Saddam had put his son Qusay in charge, and he had not a clue about military strategy. On two occasions he ordered the transfer of a number of divisions from the north to Baghdad, and on both occasions they were wiped out. The last few days were chaotic. The city was gearing up to defend itself to the last: trenches, passages, barricades, and sandbags. However, the townspeople were beginning to have doubts, and he [Saddam], old fox that he is, realized as much. He went out on his famous walkabout, and above all, he fought too at the airport. We held out for twelve hours, then we retreated. We saw hundreds of rifles abandoned, with knapsacks and uniforms, along the road to Baghdad. The troops had brought civilian clothes with them, and

when they heard about the airport being captured, most of them changed and made off.

On April 5, Saddam again failed to show up for an advertised address on Iraqi TV. Instead, an announcer again read a message. While heavy artillery fire resumed that night on the airport compound, the anticipated Iraqi ground offensive failed to materialize. Russian intelligence sources reported, however, that a group from the Republican Guard and other units of the regular army from the Tikrit area made their way to Syria in a daring operation including three hundred tanks, one hundred GRAD multiple-barrel rocket launchers (MBRLs), many of which had chemical warheads, and many other weapon systems, including Iraq's entire WMD arsenal. Lebanese sources with access to eastern Syria confirmed the arrival of the column.

According to an ex-Soviet "diplomat" with extensive experience in Iraq who was in Baghdad at the time of the invasion, the Iraqi column was led and escorted by captured Abrams tanks and other combat vehicles with friendly insignias. Indeed, several Apache helicopters surveyed the column but, having seen the American tanks with clear identification panels on top, did not open fire. By morning, the Iraqi column had crossed into Syria without any losses. The former diplomat and Arab officials based in Baghdad insist that Saddam, Qusay, and all key members of the Revolutionary Command Council traveled to Syria with the column. Contradicting that report, however, Iraqi TV showed Saddam walking the streets of Baghdad and later delivering a speech on April 6. Events would show that Saddam was not in the column, but Qusay might have been.

On that night, Saddam Hussein hinted at a hasty escape from Baghdad by joining a Russian diplomatic convoy. The Russian ambassador to Baghdad, Vladimir Titorenko, was to lead the convoy to Damascus, evacuating Russian and other diplomats from the Commonwealth of Independent States. The United States was notified in advance about the evacuation plans; although it strongly recommended that the convoy use the safer road to Amman, the Russians insisted on traveling to Damascus. As the convoy was getting organized in Baghdad, a thoroughly disguised Saddam Hussein recognized the ex-diplomat, whom he had known for a long time, and greeted him warmly. The official saw Saddam getting into one of the cars. Saddam's car joined the Russian formation, but broke away into the darkness right just outside of Baghdad. (The ex-Soviet official is convinced

Saddam then raced to link up with the Iraqi military column heading toward Syria.)

Twenty miles into the desert, the Russian convoy was attacked by U.S. Special Forces. The GRU report of April 6 noted that "this action [the ambush] was committed by coalition Special Forces and the column was shot using Russian-made weapons to conceal the origin of the attackers and to blame the Iraqis afterwards." Forensic examination of the slugs in the Russian vehicles and casualties confirmed the types of weapons used, and Russian communications intercepts left no doubt as to the identity of the attackers. The GRU report recounted that the convoy accelerated, although a few Russian diplomats were injured. A few miles down the road, unidentified military jeeps tried to block the convoy's progress, but when the Russians would not stop, the jeeps opened sporadic fire before vanishing into the desert. Several Russian sources claimed ignorance regarding Saddam's presence with the convoy when it left Baghdad but acknowledged that they evacuated highly sensitive Iraqi documents—"the archives of the Saddam regime," according to Russian sources—as well as, in the words of the GRU report, "secret devices taken from military equipment captured by Iraqis."

The next day Bush and Putin spoke on the phone, and Bush promised to investigate the incident. Later that day Condoleezza Rice arrived in Moscow to meet with Foreign Minister Igor Ivanov, and she apologized for the accident. Meanwhile, the Russian ambassador to Iraq suddenly returned to Baghdad from Moscow, via Damascus, on April 9. Hence, Titorenko must have had a special plane waiting for him in Damascus on April 6, and a plane returned him forty-eight hours later, another indication of the unique importance of the Russian convoy.

Meanwhile, larger groups of American forces poured into Baghdad on April 6. Together, there were roughly 20,000 U.S. troops in the area of the city, and up to an additional 5,000 available as reinforcements. Of these, 7,000 troops belonging to the 3rd Infantry were at the airport by the end of the day. Intense clashes continued in the streets, and the United States lost at least one tank. The Arab mujahedin—zealous and quite effective—were playing a growing role in the street fighting.

The first elements of the 101st AAD started to enter the city from the west, and marines from the 1st MEF came from the south. The 3rd Infantry Division sent another roving patrol through the center of Baghdad that endured repeated clashes with pockets of resistance as it crossed the Special Republican Guards' inner line of defense extending all the way to the Tigris River. The first U.S. Air Force C-130s landed at Baghdad International Airport later that day, and U.S. combat engineers began repairing the runways. That afternoon the Iraqis destroyed a bridge on the Tigris in southern Baghdad in order to prevent the marines from crossing. Heavy street fighting between fedayeen, Baath militias, Arab mujahedin, Iraqi commandos, and American soldiers, mainly marines coming from the south, ensued. During this fighting, U.S. forces came perilously close to a WMD attack. Lieutenant Colonel al-Dabbagh saw a group of fedayeen preparing to fire one of these RPG warheads on a U.S. position on the outskirts of Baghdad. "They were going to use this weapon, but then they realized that they would kill lots of Iraqis who did not have masks, so they put them in their cars and drove off," he told Coughlin. Elsewhere in Iraq, CENTCOM put pressure on the forces surrounding Nasiriyah, Najaf, Al-Kut, Al-Diwaniya, and Qarbalah to decide the battles quickly so that they could join the fight for Baghdad.

On April 7, American helicopter-borne forces—comprising elements of the 101st AAD, 82nd Airborne, and the marines—consolidated their hold over centers of resistance that had been ignored as American forces made their way to Baghdad. As a rule, the Iraqis had melted away at night with most of their weapons, and the United States found several abandoned and empty defensive positions. In the case of Qarbalah, the Republican Guard units received orders to abandon the town directly from Saddam Hussein after they reported to Baghdad that U.S. artillery was endangering the sacred grave of Hussein ibn-Ali. However, Nasiriyah, Najaf, Al-Kut, Diwaniya, and smaller towns in the south still remained under Iraqi control. Operating out of these cities, Iraqi fedayeen, Baath militias, and commandos continued their raids on American convoys traveling on the key roads.

Back in Baghdad, the 3rd Infantry Division and the marines enhanced their presence on city streets. American units still moved in heavy patrols of tanks and APCs under massive air cover, but although they encountered repeated clashes, their intensity had abated; the fiercest firefights were with mixed detachments of the Arab mujahedin and Saddam's fedayeen. However, many Iraqi fighters and Arab mujahedin opted not to put themselves in harm's way, simply moving to smaller streets when the American columns appeared and passed them by.

American forces searched for underground facilities, as well as missing garrisons and weapons. The 3rd Infantry Division dispatched a few patrols from the airport toward the southwestern compound near the Special Republican Guards' inner line, and in northern Baghdad, elements of the

101st AAD blocked the main road to Tikrit. The U.S. Marine forces that reached the Diyalah River and entered Baghdad from the south did so forty-eight hours behind the administration's schedule, and Colonel Dowdy was relieved of command, despite his successful performance in Nasiriyah.

Meanwhile, confidants of Saddam Hussein who fled to Damascus and other Arab cities assured the local leaders that Saddam was convinced the war had only begun. There was no way Iraq could withstand high-tech weaponry, they explained, which is why Saddam ordered his key forces to conserve themselves for urban warfare. In the meantime, Iraqi forces were to resist the U.S. onslaught within reason and then redeploy to predetermined secret locations. The confidants acknowledged, as reflected in Saddam's order that soldiers were to join other units if they couldn't return to their own, that some components of the Iraqi military had been hit badly. However, these were not crucial, war-winning elements of the Iraqi military. The time had not even come to use the readily available WMD, nor was the time ripe for a major strike on Israel, which, Saddam's confidants insisted, he could still deliver at will.

The Arab officials were genuinely convinced by the presentation of Saddam's confidants, and the leaders decided that they would continue to recognize Saddam's regime and refuse to accept a U.S.-imposed government in Baghdad. Arab intelligence services would also continue to provide active support for Saddam and his people in and out of Iraq.

During April 7, there were several multiple-source intelligence reports of sightings of SCUD-type launchers in western Iraq, near the Syrian border. Several Special Forces detachments launched an intense, though ultimately futile search and pursuit. The intelligence acquired was not sufficient to determine whether the Iraqis were attempting to launch missiles at Israel and were disrupted by the American patrol, or if the Iraqis were simulating launch-related activities in order to once again gauge the coalition's ability to react.

In the afternoon of April 7, the United States attempted once again to assassinate Saddam Hussein and his two sons. An agent reported that Saddam was seen entering a restaurant, or a nearby bunker, in the al-Mansur district of Baghdad. Saddam was to attend a meeting with some thirty Iraqi senior officials, the agent reported; a B-1B loitering on call over western Iraq was diverted to deliver the strike, and within twelve minutes dropped its payload. U.S. Air Force F-16CJs were sent to suppress any Iraqi antiaircraft batteries that might pop up, while an EA-6 Prowler accompanied the B-1B to provide surface-to-air radar jamming. The B-1B dropped two 2,000-pound GBU-31 bunker-busting JDAM bombs from 20,000 feet, followed by two 2,000-pound area-impact JDAM bombs. The bombing raid was a great display of both intelligence analysis and command and control of airpower. The four bombs destroyed the two bunkers and flattened the city block above them. However, neither Saddam nor his sons, nor any other leader of the regime was among the many civilian Iraqis killed or wounded.

The United States had once again been misled by Iraqi deception. On this occasion, Saddam decided to present himself as a potential target in order to determine conclusively if he had been betrayed by someone familiar with his movements. "Saddam Hussein knew he had been betrayed and that information on his whereabouts had been handed over to the Americans," a senior Iraqi security official told the Jordanians. On April 6, Saddam extended invitations to various groups of loyalists to rendezvous in Baghdad, asking many to join him at a restaurant in al-Mansur the next day. Saddam arrived slightly ahead of time, using an ordinary taxi. He went into the restaurant, leaving his guards behind. He then rushed through the building and exited through a rear door. American bombs hit the building soon afterward, "but Saddam emerged unscathed," the official noted.

The bombing happened so quickly that some of Saddam's guards could not clear the area. "Saddam Hussein no longer needed proof and ordered the execution of these officers who were known to be among those most faithful to him," another source told the AFP, the French news agency. Several Arab officials throughout the region pointed to a growing volume of evidence suggesting that the data acted upon by the United States was, quite simply, false. Saddam had disseminated the information, hoping to draw out the men who had betrayed him and heighten his standing in the Arab world (by showing that he was still considered such an important target that the Americans would flatten a city block in an attempt to kill him).

By now, Baghdad was rife with rumors about conspiracies and betrayals, implicating virtually the entire regime. The common denominator of these rumors was that the turning point in the war took place when senior officers and officials decided to give up the battle for Baghdad and betray Saddam. "Some of our senior officers have turned traitors and deliberately transferred our troops away so U.S. troops could enter Baghdad," the Republican Guard NCO explained. "We have subsequently caught many of these senior officers ourselves. We caught as many as seventy-five traitors. Our traitors used every possible means, including metallic communications equipment. They could just throw a small metal ball at our hiding place to let U.S. troops know where we were, and U.S. troops would come to bomb us. . . . We later learned that a senior official had betrayed the nation. As far as I know, the minister of defense had turned traitor and was later executed by the minister of the interior."

An Iraqi intelligence officer recounted vivid details. "According to a personal source of mine, Defense Minister Sultan Hashim [Ahmad] sold himself to the Americans a week before the final battle. He and all his men agreed on surrendering with the Americans. Sultan Hashim did not give any orders to his men, so Baghdad was left with no leadership and fell immediately, while Umm-Qasr and Basra resisted for fourteen days, astonishing the entire world. I also know that Saddam discovered his betrayal and personally killed the minister."

According to other prevailing rumors, Iraqi pilots were pleading for permission to use suicide strikes against the advancing coalition forces but were held back by traitorous senior officials. One account holds that a pilot was publicly executed when he insisted on flying and fighting.

On April 8, America's hold over Baghdad remained precarious at best. Actually, the United States was only capable of running heavily armored patrols through the undefended sectors of Baghdad. There was a revitalization of Iraqi resistance, as fedayeen, Baath militia, mujahedin forces, and commando units took to the streets throughout greater Baghdad. Forces loyal to Saddam held sectors of the city, mainly neighborhoods populated by Baghdad's elite. A U.S. Air Force A-10 was shot down by a shoulder-fired SAM during one of these engagements.

Iranian-controlled Shiite "militias" started popping up in the Shiite slums of Baghdad, all of them well armed, well organized, and well funded. These forces quickly took control over their neighborhoods with immense popular support. Significantly, they were capable of providing emergency food and medical services to the population. The Shiite political line was as much anti-Saddam as anti-American. In an act of defiance, the Shiite authorities in the large sprawl formerly known as "Saddam City" renamed the area "Sadr City," after Imam Baqir al-Sadr, whom Saddam had killed in the early nineties.

Meanwhile, intense fighting continued on and around two major bridges in Baghdad—the Jumhuriyah and the Sinak. Marine forces had to withdraw and reorganize before hitting the bridges, calling in massive support from aircraft and attack helicopters before they finally seized the damaged structures. Arab mujahedin showed impressive resolve throughout the battle, staying on to fight even when Iraqi regulars withdrew. The marines also launched an attack on Rashadiya Airport, south of Baghdad. In the afternoon, U.S. aircraft resumed bombing the city's key government buildings, while 3rd Infantry Division forces limited their presence to previously held positions at the edges of the city.

In the northwest of the country, Iraqi forces held on to the Haditha Dam region as well as the greater al-Qaim zone, and commandos actively prevented coalition Special Forces from getting anywhere near these regions. The Iraqis could still launch ballistic missiles into Israel from these sites; General Zeevi-Farkash, Israel's chief of military intelligence, warned the Knesset that 80 percent of the known and suspected sites of WMD and ballistic missiles were located in northwestern Iraq and were yet to be checked, let alone seized, by the coalition forces. Moreover, there were growing signs of intense Iraqi military activities at some of these sites.

On April 8, Sufian and his colleagues delivered what they had promised, ordering their troops to lay down their weapons. Sufian gave the order because he believed Saddam had been killed by the American bombing the day before, and all further resistance was therefore futile. Sufian issued a verbal order, confirmed by both Taher Jalil and Hussein Rashid, Sufian's two closest allies. Gen. Mahdi Abdallah al-Dulaymi, one of Baghdad's military chiefs, identified another member of the Sufian conspiracy—fedayeen Chief Abdul Rashid al-Tikriti, Hussein Rashid's brother. According to Dulaymi, Abdul Rashid "is believed to have passed information to the United States" in order to ensure that "Saddam's 100,000-strong Praetorian Guard would not intervene."

Later that day, Sufian, along with some twenty family members, was seen at the Baghdad International Airport boarding an American C-130 Hercules that took them to an undisclosed location. In order to protect Sufian, American officials announced his death five days before he left the country: "At one point [on April 2], an Iraqi major general, Sufian Tikiriti [sic], trying to flee Baghdad, ran right into a Marine checkpoint and died in a hail of machine-gun fire when he tried to drive past it," the Washington Post reported on April 13—the day the Israeli Internet news service DEBKAfile broke the story of Sufian's betrayal and escape. In addition, Al-Dulaymi observed that Sufian's name did not appear on the U.S. military's list of the most wanted. Instead, the list named Barzan al-Ghafur Sulayman Majid as the commander of the Special Republican Guard.

Starting in the predawn hours of April 9, American patrols and heavy units pushed deeper into Baghdad; the objective of the operation was to expand American control over key segments of the capital. The units involved advanced slowly for fear of urban warfare and its nasty surprises. The 3rd Infantry Division dispatched two patrols—one into the recently bombed Mansur neighborhood and the second into the Special Republican Guards' defensive line, all the way to the Tigris River and into the key presidential compounds and palaces. Arriving from the north, patrols from the 101st AAD pushed toward the Muthenna military air base and Baghdad's main railway junctions. The 1st MEF launched two major pushes: the first began at the Rasheed air base in the southeast and advanced toward the National Air Defense headquarters, Baghdad's main power station, and on along the Tigris, emerging right in front of the 3rd Infantry Division; the second array of patrols started from the northeast and attempted to penetrate the edges of Saddam (now Sadr) City. Throughout, the units continued their efforts to locate concealed openings to the underground system of routes, bunkers, and hiding places used by the elite, but to no avail.

In the afternoon, just as the patrols seemed to have been successful, widespread chaos, looting, and rioting erupted throughout Baghdad, making the city ungovernable. That much of the chaos was incited and organized by Baath operatives and activists did not color the impression of powerless American troops watching as Baghdad fell apart all around them. That evening saw the toppling of Saddam's statue at Shahid Square under the watchful eye of large U.S. forces. It was a symbolic gesture, as was the restoration of the landmark's old name, Firdos Square. Despite the rioting, American patrols resumed moving through most parts of Baghdad. However, they were unable or unwilling to restore order, stop looting, or do anything other than drive and shoot. But as Sufian had promised, the main elements of the Republican and Special Republican Guards—totaling anywhere between 70,000 and 100,000 troops, along with their heavy weapons (tanks, fighting vehicles, artillery, rocket launchers) and WMD shells and warheads—were nowhere to be seen. The Americans made no effort to locate the Iraqi formations.

Saddam Hussein and his entourage were still active in Baghdad. Saddam's bodyguard Muhammad Hamis, who was very close to the top (his sister is married to Abid Hamid Humud), told Yoichiro Kawai about Saddam's last days in Baghdad. Back on the afternoon of April 8, Saddam, Qusay, and Abid Hamid resurfaced from their hiding place. They linked up with a group of bodyguards, including Hamis, for a walk on Adhamiya street in the al-Bamiya district. From there, they rushed to a safe house in the al-Jamra neighborhood of Saddam City. They stayed there for about a couple of hours. Saddam felt sufficiently confident to walk out of the house and talk to the people. Subsequently, Saddam and his entourage returned to al-Bamiya. He ordered his guards to drop him, Qusay, and Abid Hamid near a house they've never seen before—a place the bodyguards did not recognize as a preplanned safe house. Saddam would stay in this safe house for the next ten hours.

On the morning of April 9, around 4 A.M., Saddam, Qusay, Abid Hamid, and a few bodyguards left the safe house for the Sahat Antar neighborhood. They were traveling in six nondescript cars. As they got into the neighborhood they discovered that several U.S. military patrols—most likely marines—were roaming the area. They turned around and quickly made their way back to the al-Bamiya district. Saddam then led the group to the Abu-Hanifa Mosque because he believed U.S. forces would not enter and search a mosque. After staying in the mosque for about half an hour, the group moved again.

It was now around 6 A.M. Saddam, Qusay, and Abid Hamid were in the first car leading the little convoy. A car with a few bodyguards was following Saddam's very closely. The other four cars, led by General Rashid, the chief of bodyguards, was traveling a short distance behind them. Hamis was in one of these cars. Traveling fast toward the Kadhimiya district, Saddam led the six cars around a corner. They were stunned to see a U.S. military column very close and advancing straight toward them. Immediately, Saddam's car and the one behind it veered sharply to a side street right under the Americans' nose. It was a very close call for Saddam, Hamis told Kawai. The other four cars stopped and let the American column pass by. Afterward, Rashid assured the group that "the President got away safely. Now you guys go home." Hamis went back to his home in Baghdad and from there drove his own car to Tikrit where he stayed the night.

Later that day, April 9, Saddam Hussein once again walked the streets of Baghdad, interacting with the adoring public and promising victory. Saddam also recorded his last TV speech, but it was too late in the game for Iraqi TV to broadcast it. A raw tape surfaced on April 18/19 and was shown on al-Jazeerah. Saddam's was a fiercely Islamist speech, laced with numerous Shiite themes. He talked mainly about betrayal and revival—both his own and Iraq's. Significantly, Saddam repeated the term "ghafla," meaning divine disappearance, occultation, before reappearance.

The next morning, April 10, Saddam was seen entering a mosque in the al-Azamiyah sector of Baghdad with Qusay and Abid Hamid. A spontaneous crowd gathered and cheered them, but Saddam and his small group did not stop to address the crowd. This was the last confirmed public sighting of Saddam Hussein. By midday Hamis had returned to Baghdad and contacted another bodyguard who knew where Saddam was. Saddam, Qusay, and Abid Hamid were now hiding in a small house in the al-Dawdi area of Baghdad. They stayed there for the next few days without leaving the house.

Then, on the morning of April 13, the three men suddenly decided to leave the house by themselves. At the last moment, Saddam called his bodyguards and bid them good-bye. "My regime is over. I know where I should be going. You guys go home now," Hamis recalled Saddam as saying. He gave each bodyguard five million Iraqi Dinars. Saddam, Qusay, and Abid Hamid then got into a Mercedes Benz and drove away. Hamis told Yoichiro Kawai that was the last time he saw Saddam.

Nevertheless, as far as Washington was concerned, the regime officially collapsed on April 10. "The game is over," Mohammed Al-Durri, Iraq's envoy to the United Nations, said in New York. However, chaos still reigned in Baghdad as looting and fighting negated any semblance of American control.

Saddam's loyalists—having established militias in cooperation with the Arab mujahedin hiding in their midst—still controlled western Baghdad. In the great mosque of Adhamiya, U.S. forces conducted a fierce firefight with the local Special Republican Guard detachments. In nearby Aden Square, American troops clashed with an Iraqi armored force; Apache helicopters and heavy reinforcements destroyed two tanks and three APCs before the rest of the Iraqis melted away into the urban shelters. In the Mansur district, U.S. aircraft bombed concentrations of mujahedin forces.

Nevertheless, the pro-Saddam forces continued to run roadblocks. By the afternoon, U.S. ground forces had withdrawn from contentious areas and aircraft resumed bombing, causing many civilian casualties, particularly among mobs hit by bombing and caught in the crossfire. American units also participated in a few intense clashes over control of key buildings in central Baghdad. At least one suicide bomber—a Sunni mujahid—blew himself up near marines outside the Hotel Palestine in central Baghdad, killing an officer and wounding three men. In Sadr City, another bomber—this time a local Shiite—killed several marines on patrol. In the

Dawrah district of southern Baghdad, at least twenty-one Iraqi civilians were killed by crossfire and bombing during a clash between fedayeen and American troops.

Elsewhere in Iraq, the military situation was similarly far from resolved. Pro-Saddam forces held most of the Faw Peninsula and the al-Amarah compound. The Sammara-Tikrit-Ramadi triangle was also firmly in the hands of Saddam's loyalists. Mosul and Kirkuk, the two main northern cities, were not in coalition hands either. Significantly, the huge al-Qaim area, with its WMD facilities, was still beyond the reach of the United States. Many questions—questions the administration was trying to avoid—lingered unanswered: Why did so many Iraqi units stop fighting and suddenly vanish? Where were the troops and weapons of some twenty-five Iraqi divisions? They did not surrender, and did not abandon the vast majority of their weapons—including such heavy equipment as tanks, artillery, APCs, and WMD munitions. They just vanished. And where were Iraq's leaders and senior officers?

10
THE REAL WAR BEGINS

Iraq has never been a real country, and neither the American incursion into Baghdad nor the political declarations from the administration could change this reality. From its inception, Iraq has remained an amalgam of hostile ethnic, national, and religious entities glued together in the early 1920s to further Britain's colonial, strategic, and economic interests. Winston S. Churchill acknowledged this phenomenon on the eve of the war: "It was my grandfather, Winston Churchill, who invented Iraq and laid the foundation for much of the modern Middle East. In 1921, as British colonial secretary, Churchill was responsible for creating Jordan and Iraq and for placing the Hashemite rulers, Abdullah and Feisal, on their respective thrones in Amman and Baghdad." Now, the assault on Iraq and the removal of Saddam Hussein and the Baath regime discredited and effectively destroyed the only mechanism holding these mutually hostile entities together.

By spring, the various groups and their indigenous leaders were no longer afraid of Saddam's repressive regime, and they reasserted their long-suppressed ethnic identities with a vengeance. As a result, the American and British forces that had invaded Iraq to overthrow the regime and to establish and sustain a pluralistic democrary in a unified Iraq were perceived by most Iraqis to be as much an enemy as Saddam himself. At the same time, fully cognizant of the unchallengeable might of the American and British armed forces, the various indigenous forces resorted to deceit, false cooperation, backstabbing, terrorism, and betrayal in the best traditions of the Arab Middle East. Throughout, Washington remained completely oblivious to these dominant trends.

* * *

Although they have been recipients of American and Western economic and political assistance for more than a decade, the Kurds still put their interests ahead of their patrons'. However, the United States failed to realize this and take it into consideration when formulating policy, even running special and covert operations in order to help the Kurds. This kind of disconnect could have disastrous consequences, as the British SAS was to learn.

On March 26, sixteen SAS troopers and four "pinkies"—heavily armed Land Rovers—were parachuted into northern Iraq by a U.S. Air Force C-130 Hercules. The entire operation was conducted at the behest of the United States and solely on the basis of American intelligence. The team's objective was to probe Republican Guard defenses in the northwestern desert toward Mosul. According to the U.S. liaison, the team would parachute into the desert 100 miles southwest of Mosul, an area controlled by friendly, CIA-sponsored Kurds. Preparing the mission, U.S. Special Forces command stressed that intelligence from satellites and Predators, as well as human sources on the ground, indicated there were no troops in the drop zone. "We hated having to rely solely on U.S. intelligence," an SAS insider conceded later.

The area the SAS dropped into was on the border between Kurdish and Sunni tribes, and by the time the team reached the ground, there was a large Iraqi force waiting for them. The SAS force organized without interference and started on their way toward Mosul, but a few hours later they were ambushed by the Iraqis lying in wait. The Kurds had alerted the Iraqis and betrayed the mission in exchange for help defending against Turkish units advancing on Sinjar—an encroachment, the Kurds were convinced, endorsed by Turkey's NATO allies the United States and Britain.

In the melee that ensued, three of the Land Rovers were able to regroup, disengage from their Iraqi pursuers, and withdraw to a safe zone. They were safely extracted from there by Royal Air Force Chinook helicopters. The fourth, however, was separated from the rest of the SAS force and surrounded by more than fifty Iraqi soldiers. After an intense firefight, the four SAS troopers had to abandon the vehicle because there was no way they could fight their way to it. The "pinkie" would be shown on al-Jazeera TV with Iraqi troops dancing around it, jubilantly firing their AK-47s in the air.

The four operatives were now isolated from both their vehicle and the rest of the SAS force, and trying to evade the Iraqi forces, they got separated from each other. One pair—armed only with M-16 rifles, pistols, and knives—spent seventy-two hours "dodging Iraqi bullets" as they fled into the desert. Fighting numerous nighttime battles in an effort to break free from the Iraqi forces hot in pursuit, they traveled 60 miles in seventy-two hours, living off small emergency rations and little water. After finally breaking away from the Iraqis, the two activated their emergency radio beacon and were ultimately extracted by an RAF Chinook.

The other two SAS troopers were not as fortunate. Although they managed to disengage from the pursuing Iraqis rather quickly, they found themselves isolated from all possible extraction points. They decided to walk to the Syrian border—remembering that Syrians had helped another escaping SAS trooper back in 1991. This time the reception was different. Syrian intelligence arrested the two and subjected them to brutal interrogation in an effort to gain information the Iraqis could use. It took an April "surprise visit" to Damascus by British Foreign Office minister Mike O'Brien, who met with Bashar al-Assad and then publicly contradicted the stern warnings to Damascus just issued by Colin Powell, to free the two SAS operatives from a Syrian jail. "This is the kind of cockup you get when you work from U.S. intelligence," another SAS insider said, summing up the incident.

This case is extreme but by no means without precedent, and it reflects the endemic problem American intelligence and policy-makers have had with all segments of the Iraqi population. As a rule, U.S. intelligence officers trust their sources. Moreover, U.S. intelligence does not have a solid understanding of local dynamics and is largely incapable of accurately judging the relative quality of the information it receives.

In this case, given the bitter rivalry between Kurds and Turkman, and taking into account repeated surges into the Sinjar area by Turkish Special Forces and military intelligence, it stood to reason that the Kurds would be most concerned with blocking the Turkish maneuver. Toward that end, the Kurds needed to secure their rear, and to do so they had to make deals with the Sunni tribes and the Iraqi Republican Guards. Of course the Kurds declared their commitment to America's cause in order to get money, weapons, and occasional bombing of their nemeses by U.S. aircraft, but the intelligence community, unable to grasp the Kurds' real priorities, accepted their information and promises of support without reservation. No one raised the question of why the Kurds should be expected to cooperate with the United States or the United Kingdom when such cooperation would degrade their ability to fight the Turks.

This endemic problem did not start in late March. As the slide to war progressed, and Washington's commitment to a viable central government in Baghdad, as well as its interest in deal-making with Ankara, became clear, the Kurds sensed that they were being betrayed. The Kurdish leadership had always been interested in either complete independence, which meant the dismemberment of Iraq, or far-reaching autonomy, which required a weak central government in Baghdad. But neither description fit the country the United States advocated, and as a result the Kurds felt that they had been stabbed in the back by their perceived ally. And, as has always been the case in the history of the Kurdish people, they immediately acted to ensure their own survival even if at the expense of their benefactors. For *all* Kurds, fighting Turkey and sustaining a semblance of Kurdish self-rule have always been far more important than destroying the regime to the south.

And there was yet another mundane aspect to American plans for postwar Iraq that unnerved the Kurds. During the 1990s, the Kurds traded poverty and near starvation for affluence on the wings of an "economy" based on sanction-busting—smuggling Iraqi oil to Turkey and smuggling forbidden goods back into Iraq. As the postwar Iraq would be able to both legally export its oil and legally import goods—mostly via Jordan and the Persian Gulf—the Kurds would lose their sole revenue-generating enterprise. Neither the United States nor any of the opposition groups had offered them substitute sources of income. Thus, rhetoric notwithstanding, an American victory in the war meant that the Kurds would at the very least lose their autonomy and burgeoning economy to an overwhelmingly Sunni government in Baghdad. Additionally, a deal between the United States and Turkey stipulating Ankara's support for an American-engineered government always cast dark shadows over Kurdistan.

On the eve of the war, officials assured the Kurdish leadership that the United States had completed plans for a northern front against Iraq despite the absence of an effective staging ground in Turkey. The Kurds remained somewhat skeptical, since the original plans had called for well over 60,000 troops to operate out of Iraqi Kurdistan and additional forces operating out of Turkey and Jordan. Moreover, the United States urged the Kurds to contribute more troops for the confrontation with Saddam, dispensing huge sums of cash all over Kurdistan to smooth and expedite the process. The Kurds boasted that they had 70,000 soldiers, albeit in several distinct "armies" answering to mutually hostile political parties. The Kurds were not worried about Saddam's forces, though: "The war will be relatively short. The bulk of the Iraqi army and much of the guard will not fight," Kurdish leader Barhim Salih predicted.

What the Kurds were more apprehensive about was an agreement between Turkey and the United States regarding "the rules of engagement in northern Iraq," including "the zones of operation by Turkish military forces." Under the agreement, Ankara pledged to keep its troops inside northern Iraq to within 20 kilometers of the Turkish-Iraqi border. At the time, however, there were more than 20,000 Turkish troops operating in a 40-kilometer-wide security zone inside Iraq, and there was no indication that they would withdraw. Ankara also notified the United States that Turkey had plans to send up to 80,000 troops into northern Iraq, and that over 50,000 troops had already been deployed along the Iraqi-Turkish border, ready to augment the 20,000 policing the security zone. Significantly, the agreement failed to address the character of postwar northern Iraq, even though Ankara had repeatedly stressed that it would consider the emergence of a Kurdish entity unacceptable, and faced with the possibility would mobilize for war.

Meanwhile, Kurdish leaders warned the United States that the presence of Turkish forces in northern Iraq made it virtually impossible for the Kurds to support the war effort. They told American officials that "[Kurdish] forces have been deployed along the Turkish border to fight any invading Turkish troops," because Turkey, rather than Saddam's Iraq, was the greatest threat facing them. Kurdish leaders also warned that "Turkey's entry into northern Iraq will result in Iranian and Syrian intervention."

At first, things looked all right. On March 21, Kurdish detachments led by U.S. Special Forces captured the key Kirkuk oil fields without any damage to its infrastructure. It was quite an achievement given the deployment of Mujahedin ul-Khalq (Iranian opposition units controlled by Iraqi intelligence), MUK commandos, who had orders to destroy the oil fields the moment hostile movement was detected. Despite their instructions, neither the MUK nor nearby Iraqi military units offered any resistance when the Kurdish and American teams reached the oil fields. Apparently the Iraqi defenders realized that the regime was collapsing, that resistance was pointless, and elected to avoid casualties; the MUK leadership decided not to oppose the action in an effort to reach a deal with the United States that would enable the MUK to continue its fight against the mullahs' regime in Tehran.

However, Kurdish cooperation would not last for long. Citing the need to secure their lines of communications, and emboldened by the presence of U.S. Special Forces teams with them, the Kurds started deploying forces into the Turkish "security zone," building roadblocks and establishing firing positions. Ankara seized on these developments as the long-sought excuse to escalate activities inside Iraq. Several new Turkish units entered northern Iraq from Hakkari just after midnight, and by the morning of March 22 these forces had joined the more than 20,000 troops already deployed inside Iraq in a stretch along the border.

Ankara was clearly adamant about preserving Turkey's hegemony over northern Iraq regardless of any American deals made with the Kurds, and according to sources in Ankara, "In the days ahead, the number of Turkish soldiers in northern Iraq will reach 50,000 to 65,000." Their objective would be to remove the threat posed by the Kurds and to consolidate Turkish hegemony over the areas claimed for the Turkman. Only hours after Turky ordered more troops across the border, its 2nd Army put 25,000 to 30,000 soldiers inside Iraq, and over 130,000 were poised to join them.

The Kurdish leadership now capitalized on the Turkish insertion, which it had provoked, as the excuse for not launching any major operations against the Iraqis. Repeated attempts by American Special Forces to goad the Kurds into attacking Kirkuk proved futile. According to the March 25 GRU report, "The Americans counted on the support of the Kurds, but the latter refused to take a direct part in the attack and demanded guarantees from the U.S. command that it will prevent a Turkish invasion. The Turkish themselves are avoiding making any promises."

U.S. Marine Corps Brigadier General Osman, commander of the forces in northern Iraq, requested the speedy deployment of American units, having given up on deputizing the Kurds. The next day, the United States dropped 1,000 troops of the 173rd Airborne Brigade into Harir Airport, a small air base north of Ibril used by Kurds and American Special Forces. The 173rd's troops were deployed to help bolster the Special Forces, as well as to reduce and restrain the escalating clashes between Kurdish, Turkman, and Arab tribal forces. Despite American declarations about opening a northern front, the U.S. deployment had very little impact on the fighting against the Iraqis.

By late March, once it became clear that the United States could not deploy an overwhelming force into the area, northern Iraq became a free-for-all, with intelligence services from Iraq, Syria, Iran, and Turkey actively involved in destabilizing the Kurds and establishing spheres of influence. Apprehensive about these trends, Kurdish leaders chose not to participate in the war against Iraq, distrusting the United States. The region was awash with rumors about U.S.-Turkish conspiracies against the Kurds, as seen in the GRU's report of March 27: "Yesterday . . . sources obtained information about a secret agreement reached between the U.S. and the Turkish government. In the agreement the U.S., behind the backs of the Kurds, promised Turkey not to support in any way the formation of a Kurdish state in this region. The U.S. has also promised not to prevent Turkey from sending its troops [into the area] immediately following [the coalition's] capture of northern Iraq." Iranian emissaries informed the Kurds that Washington and Ankara had conspired to deploy Kurdish forces into central Iraq so that Turkish forces could enter Iraqi Kurdistan and destroy all the Kurdish forces. The Turkish deployment inside Iraq had by then reached about 40,000 troops, and the entire force, on both sides of the border, was put on a high alert, maintaining a four-hour readiness to begin combat operations.

Given this dire state of affairs in Iraqi Kurdistan, the United States shifted its attention to confronting the Islamist terrorists of Ansar al-Islam, located near the Iranian border. By April 2, after a thirty-six-hour campaign, about a hundred U.S. Special Forces and several thousand PUK fighters finally destroyed the group's key positions, which were defended by about five hundred terrorists—mostly Islamist Kurds, but also dozens of Arab and Afghan volunteers. The United States used heavy air bombing, cruise missile strikes, and infantry attacks by elements of the 173rd Airborne Brigade before the defenders collapsed. Altogether, three hundred terrorists were killed and the rest were driven across the Iranian border. "In a day and a half, a terrorist organization that gripped this area was rooted out," a U.S. officer declared. Hoping to capitalize on the momentum of this assault, B-52s also targeted Iraqi military positions near Kirkuk, particularly the Nebuchadnezzar Brigade. However, the PUK forces refused to engage in a major battle.

Meanwhile, an American Special Forces detachment blew up an Iraqi pipeline delivering more than 200,000 barrels of oil a day to Syria, at the northern railroad link between the two countries. The operation was carried out by troops arriving from Jordan, and *not* by units working with the Kurds. After the SAS debacle, and given the Kurds' overall cooperation, the United States was not taking any chances.

By April, American commanders in northern Iraq were exasperated with their Kurdish "allies." The Kurds would not take on heavy Iraqi resistance, instead demanding that the Americans clear the way for them by calling in air support, which the Kurds often directed not, as they claimed, at Iraqi units, but rather at their own rivals and enemies. The Kurdish commanders also conditioned their cooperation on access to booty and postwar powers. According to the April 4 GRU report, Brigadier General Osman complained to a Pentagon official in a phone conversation that "to get them [the Kurds] to move forward, we literally have to throw a stack of dollars in front of them!" Despite heroic efforts by American Special Forces to enthuse the Kurds, the northern front was all but nonexistent.

Iraq's two most meddlesome neighbors—Syria and Iran—accelerated their preparations to destabilize Iraq and render it ungovernable. Both countries had already decided to use proxy forces to kick the Americans out of Baghdad, using the same strategy they had used twenty years earlier when they conspired to evict the Americans from Beirut. Both Damascus and Tehran knew that the Islamist world was increasingly agitated and actively preparing to confront the United States, and they were eager to put that anger and resentment to good use. March 5 saw a major development in the Islamist challenge to the House of al-Saud and the war on Iraq, when the important Saudi Islamist scholar Sheikh Salman Bin-Fahd al-Awdah ruled that "it is prohibited to fight the Iraqis, destroy their country, or ruin any of Iraq's military or civilian installations under any pretext." Al-Awdah is very close to bin Laden, and his ruling could have served as a justification for an uprising against the House of al-Saud in the event it became publicly known that Riyadh had tacitly permitted the use of Saudi facilities during the war.

Compounding Al-Awdah's decree, on March 10, al-Azhar University issued a ruling ordering all Muslims to wage a jihad against the United States and all allied forces participating in the war. "The Jihad against the crusader forces is a commandment on all Muslims should the foreign forces begin hostilities," al-Azhar's Supreme Council decreed.

Iran and Syria's grand strategy was formulated and committed to during their Tehran summit on March 16, 2003. Bashar al-Assad was accompanied by Abd-al-Halim Khaddam and Faruq al-Shara, meeting in a lengthy session with Ayatollah Ali Khamenei, also attended by Iranian President Mohammad Khatami. Senior Iranian diplomatic sources described the key points of the Khamenei and Assad meeting. Khamenei opined that "changing the geopolitical situation in the region was far beyond America's capability and resources." He noted that while the United States should be expected to occupy Iraq, "the resistance put up by various nations will ultimately inflict the greatest blow to America and result in the disintegration of that country's status as a superpower." Khamenei saw the war in Iraq in the context of larger regional dynamics in which "the Palestinian and Lebanese resistance represented real power and constituted an important obstacle to the realization of America's aims." He stressed that "all Islamic countries are duty-bound to help the Palestinian nation."

In his response, Assad pointed out that "American officials had explicitly said that the long-term aims of their country [were] to oppose various nations and countries that want to be independent" and warned that "America intends to impose a military governor on the Iraqi people. However, the Iraqi masses will definitely oppose occupation. In the long run, their steadfastness will wear America out and defeat it."

Assad also noted that "the other objectives that America was pursuing by moving its military forces to the region were to strengthen the Zionist regime and defeat the Intifada." He anticipated that the aggregate impact of terrorism and a regional insurgency would be devastating for the United States: "The Palestinian and Lebanese resistance, as well as that of other nations and countries in the region, will create another Vietnam for that country," he concluded.

An Iranian expert who advised Khamenei before the summit said Khamenei "stressed that nations of the region shall resist America, and added that the hatred against America was increasing." Majlis Deputy Majid Ansari, who was briefed about the summit, was even more explicit regarding Tehran's position. "Even if they [the Americans] succeed in capturing Iraq, in view of the regional nations' alertness and strong response of the international community, they will still face difficulties," he said. "We [the Iranian leadership] are hoping that the Americans would be bogged down in Iraq and fail to realize their expansionist policies. However, as the esteemed leader has repeatedly pointed out, even if America were to become victorious in Iraq for a short time to set up a puppet regime, it would not mean a lasting victory to resolve the problem. On the contrary, such a victory will be the beginning of serious problems for America's warmongering and expansionist politicians."

The mood in Damascus was also combative. A March 17 editorial in the government's Al-Baath newspaper noted that Assad's visit "constituted an important step in Syria's intensive political and diplomatic efforts at the Arab, regional, and international levels." The editorial also highlighted the Palestinian aspect of the crisis: "Syria's efforts also aim to warn against the massacres, cruel aggressions, and all-out genocide against the Palestinian people that Israel is carrying out while the world, including the Arab countries, is busy with the expected war on Iraq. . . . On this basis, Syria and Iran are making joint efforts to help strengthen a clear, solid, and principled Arab-regional-Islamic position that does not stop at opposing war but also takes all necessary measures to prevent war and deprive it of any legitimate cover." Damascus also stressed the long-term regional ramifications of the war in Iraq. "The disaster will not be limited to brotherly Iraq but it will cause tragedies in all the countries of the region without exception and without mercy on anyone, regardless of his position, role, or relations."

Finally, a March 18 editorial in the *Tehran Times* framed Khamenei's view of the crisis—stemming, in his opinion, from the long-term cooperation between several Arab states and the United States, and not just the forthcoming attack on Iraq. "We are where we are today because most nations and many leaders let Bush and his coconspirators get away with their childish dreams of a 'Pax Americana' for too long; a global nightmare that begins with total control of Middle Eastern oil and total immunity for Israeli leaders' barbarism and their century-old and barely concealed plans to control 'all land from the Nile to the Euphrates.'"

In practical terms, Tehran and Damascus concluded that they didn't have the power to prevent the attack or inevitable occupation. Their main objective, therefore, would be to take action soon after the war in order to prevent the United States from effectively controlling Iraq, imposing a government in Baghdad, and capitalizing on the victory to enhance its influence throughout the rest of the Middle East. "The Syrian and Iranian sides regard Iranian influence within the Shiite opposition circles in Iraq, and Syrian influence over the Palestinian opposition, and the two countries' strategic relationship with HizbAllah in Lebanon as strong points. The two sides regard all these things as points of strength for confronting possible U.S. pressures once Washington completes its war against Iraq," explained senior Arab officials soon after the Tehran summit.

On March 17, the day after the Tehran summit, HizbAllah declared an alert along the Israeli-Lebanese border and brought reinforcements to the area. The forces started deploying a wide array of rockets to the Shebaa Plateau, close to Israel's northern border; most of these rockets were shipped from HizbAllah's central arsenals in Lebanon's Bekaa Valley. HizbAllah gunners repeatedly fired antiaircraft artillery at Israeli Air Force jets, as well as at Israeli villages and towns. HizbAllah reconnaissance teams, mostly dressed in civilian clothes and often disguised as shepherds, were also sent to the border to gather intelligence on Israeli units. But Israel was apprehensive about renewed fighting in Lebanon and northern Israel, which would have harmed the war effort in Iraq, and opted not to react to HizbAllah's provocations.

At the same time, Syria and Iran expedited the flow of Islamist volunteers through their territory. With the war imminent, thousands of militants—Arabs, Pakistanis, Afghans, and Chechens—answered Saddam's call to arms and began traveling toward Iraq. Iran and Syria allowed them to pass through their territory without any documentation.

Additional volunteers—mostly supporters of al-Qaeda and its war against the United States—were recruited by Iraqi intelligence agents in Jordan. The bulk of the volunteers, most of them from Saudi Arabia and Yemen, were trained in suicide bombing and kidnapping operations targeting American soldiers. One of the main training bases was located at the Saad military camp northeast of Baghdad, and the training was administered by Qusay's own Special Security unit, the Amn Khass. Some 130 Islamist volunteers were also being trained in Saad in "specialized urban warfare"—a euphemism for spectacular terrorism—during the defense of Baghdad. At least 2,500 Lebanese nationals attended training in other camps run by the Amn Khass.

By the time fighting erupted, additional terrorist organizations affiliated with al-Qaeda had already dispatched thousands of volunteers to Iraq. A special intense course was organized by Uday's Saddam's Fedayeen for these Islamists. The most important organized volunteer force comprised some 700 Algerian members of the Salafist Brigade for Combat and Call. Naaman bin Othman, an expert on Islamist movements, pointed out that since the Islamist volunteers refused to be placed under the supervision of any secular group, such as the Baath Party, the terrorist leadership must have reached an agreement with Saddam that gave their men freedom of action against American targets.

Massive bombing of Baghdad on the night of March 21 would have a direct, though unintended, impact on the Islamist currents pervading Iraq. On March 20, coalition aircraft encountered redeployed Iraqi air defense for the first time and the first instances of widespread burning of oil trenches to create heavy smoke screens. To avoid further entanglement, American and British bombers flew through Iranian airspace to hit Baghdad from its less protected rear. The Iranian forces fired sporadic air defense, as if they were more interested in reminding coalition pilots that they were in the wrong place than in shooting down the aircraft.

Politically, however, these sorties could not have been conducted at a worse time. On March 22, Tehran and Damascus were immersed in hectic deliberations about the implementation of their joint strategy concerning the war in Iraq; American violations of their airspace so early in the war infuriated Iran's leaders. At this point, Iraqi Foreign Minister Naji Sabri suddenly arrived in Damascus on an unannounced mission to discuss the next phase of the war. At first, Sabri was full of bluster about the forthcoming battle for Baghdad and other Iraqi military achievements. However, he soon inquired about the implementation of the planned evacuation of the Iraqi political elite to Syria should the need arise.

Both Tehran and Damascus sensed in Sabri a lack of resolve and evidence that Baghdad's commitment was waning. And while Syria reiterated its commitment to help the Iraqis, short of all-out involvement in the war, Damascus and Tehran started a series of consultations on their strategy to be implemented after Iraq's inevitable collapse.

Despite the grim prospects for the Saddam regime, the Syrians decided to provide Iraqi intelligence with active support by serving as the launching spot for squads of suicide bombers dispatched to attack British and American interests around the Middle East. Most members of these squads were Iraqis from Saddam's Fedayeen or Islamist volunteers trained by the fedayeen. According to Turkish and Arab intelligence sources, the first major group arrived in Damascus on March 29. It comprised eleven Iraqis and ten Egyptians, all of whom were provided with genuine passports from several Gulf States, where they were sent by Damascus, on separate flights. Over the next few days, at least one other group of more than fifteen terrorists passed through Damascus, this time on its way to Western Europe.

In April, the agitation in the Arab world was rising, and growing numbers of Islamist volunteers flocked to Iraq via Syria, Iran, and Jordan. By April 7, Jordanian security officials estimated that more than 5,600 volunteers had crossed into Iraq via Jordan alone since the start of the war. Leading scholars were also adding their voices to the call to arms. Sheikh Muhammad Tantawi, the most important cleric in Sunni Islam, approved the use of martyrdom operations against coalition forces in Iraq, saying, "Martyr operations against the invading forces are permitted under religious law. . . . Whoever attacks others, spilling blood, harming the other's honor and land is a terrorist." Within a few hours of Tantawi's exhortations, Egyptian security authorities reported that the flow of Egyptian volunteers to Iraq had multiplied severalfold.

* * *

However, the most important dynamic, crucial to the determination of Iraq's future, was being played out in the Shiite heartland, particularly the holy city of Najaf. Both Washington and London had long recognized the importance of gaining the Shiite population's support, if only because they constitute about two-thirds of the population of Iraq. Before the war, Washington was convinced that the Shiites would be largely grateful to the Americans and the British for liberating them from the oppressive regime of Saddam Hussein and, once provided with a legitimate leader, would closely cooperate with the coalition authorities. Thus Washington failed to recognize both the Shiites' uncompromising refusal to accept any non-Muslim rule, no matter how supportive, and the extent of Iran's influence over the Iraqi Shiite population.

Oblivious to the real posture in the Shiite heartland, the coalition attempted to win over the Shiites by sending in a promising leader—Abdul Majid al-Khoi. The scion of one of the most important Shiite religious families in Iraq and a direct descendant of Muhammad, Khoi, forty-two, was the youngest son of the late Ayatollah Sayyid Abul Qassim al-Khoi—the spiritual leader of the Iraqi Shiite community who was directly involved in the failed 1991 uprising against Saddam and was later abused by the regime. After the uprising, part of the Khoi clan, including Abdul Majid, escaped into exile in Britain, where they run the Khoi Foundation, one of the preeminent Islamic charities in the West. In London, Abdul Majid became involved in liberal-moderate Islamic activities, as well as interfaith and liberal politics, and in due course became a personal friend of Tony Blair's. It was at Blair's request that Abdul Majid involved himself in Iraqi exile politics in 2002, and in April 2003 agreed to return to Iraq in order to harness and stabilize the Iraqi Shiites.

Abdul Majid al-Khoi returned to a jubilant Najaf on April 4. His name and lineage attracted large, supportive crowds, and within a couple of days he made contact with the Grand Ayatollah Ali Sistani—the supreme religious authority at the al-Hawza al-Ilmiyya Theological School in Najaf who had been under house arrest on Saddam's orders—and convinced him to issue a fatwa that urged all Shiites not to fight the Americans or hinder the invading forces in any other way. It was a major achievement for the moderate leadership, an achievement that now flew in the face of Iran's determined effort to control the Iraqi Shiites.

Alarmed by Sistani's fatwa, Tehran moved swiftly to implement damage control. First, senior Iraqi clerics based in Qom, all of them devotees of the al-Hawza al-Ilmiyya school, issued a clarification of Sistani's fatwa that essentially contradicted it. Meanwhile, pro-Iranian clerics unleashed a mob in Najaf that demanded that Sistani leave Najaf within forty-eight hours but did not dare to harm the revered leader and therefore confined him to house arrest.

But that was not enough. Tehran resolved to get rid of Khoi in such a way that his fate would deter other would-be-reformers. On April 10, Abdul Majid al-Khoi and a companion were attacked by a small group just outside the ornate Grand Imam Ali mosque. Both were killed and then hacked to pieces by the assailants. At first, the assassination was presented as a grassroots reaction to Khoi's mediation between rival Shiite groups, including clerics who had cooperated with the Baathist regime. According to multiple sources, including Israeli, Arab, and European intelligence agencies, the assassination was really organized by a Tehran-controlled hit team operating under the patronage of Jimaat-i-Sadr Thani, a group commanded by Moqtada Sadr, a twenty-nine-year-old militant cleric and the son of the late Imam Baqir al-Sadr.

"There is no doubt that [Khoi] was targeted for assassination," a Western intelligence source told MENL's Steve Rodan. "Iran had provided several indications that he was a threat to its interests." Indeed, Khoi's assassination removed whatever challenges stood in the way of the Iranian surge. The overall impact was swift: on the next day a Shiite court in Najaf reversed Sistani's fatwa approving cooperation with the United States, and the confined imam blessed the changes.

The formal policy formulations for Iran's actions were articulated in April at a high-level conference on "The American Attack on Iraq and Analysis of the Future of the Region," a seminar convened in Tehran. The keynote speaker was Dr. Mohsen Rezai, the former commander of the IRGC and presently secretary of the Expediency Council. He stressed that Tehran should examine the situation in and around Iraq in the context of both Iran's own narrow local interests and the larger American war against Islam. At the long-term level, there was no doubt about America's ultimate defeat because "Islamic awakening in Southwest Asia had been among the important threats that Americans have faced." Rezai further commented that "the emergence of the al-Qaeda group and the attacks on Washington and New York represented the apogee of this trend. Other forms of Islamic awakening also pose a threat to America and there is a whole spectrum of such threats in the region." He argued that "America would not be able to contain the Islamic awakening," adding, "even in the areas where the Islamic awakening had been contained, the threat had not been eliminated."

But Rezai nevertheless knew that the near-term challenges posed by the war on terrorism remained troubling, particularly to terrorism-sponsoring states throughout the Muslim world. "America's main objective is regime change and it wants to stay until another regime comes to power. When a puppet regime that they have installed themselves comes to power, they will remain ensconced in an area to counter the threats. . . . Therefore the Americans are trying to bring about a fundamental political transformation throughout Southwest Asia and the Middle East." Such a strategy constituted a mortal threat to the mullahs' regime, particularly in the immediate future, because Iran lacked the sort of deterrence that would dissuade the United States from attacking. Iran's strategy in Iraq aimed to compensate for this shortfall by denying the United States the ability to use Iraq as a springboard against Iran. Rezai noted that the emerging turmoil in the Muslim world, and the widespread hostility toward America, "would present opportunities to the Islamic Republic of Iran and that by taking advantage of those opportunities, the Islamic Republic of Iran will not only be able to avert war, but it will also be able to further Iran's interests."

From Tehran's point of view, the most expedient, proactive strategy would be to ensnare the United States in debilitating and protracted irregular warfare and terrorism, believing that the "Lebanonization" would ultimately lead to an ignominious withdrawal. Moreover, such an approach would come at a relatively low risk for Iran because of its heavy reliance on local proxies, all of whom had their own indigenous reasons for fighting the American occupation forces. In an April 6 editorial, Hoseyn Shariat-madari, the editor in chief of Iran's most important newspaper, *Keyhan,* alluded to the new thinking in Tehran, saying, "If the war that is being waged by America and Britain against Iraq turns into a war of attrition, this will be to the benefit of the world of Islam. Moreover, the Americans have shown that despite their previous allegations, they are unable to occupy Iraq." To expedite and quickly escalate the irregular war-by-proxy, Iran would help any group and organization willing and able to kill Americans and destabilize Iraq.

Tehran also ensured that there would be no theological gap or uncertainty following Ayatollah Sistani's rebuke. On April 8, Ayatollah Kadhem al-Husseini al-Haeri, a Qom-based, Iraqi-born cleric, issued a fatwa instructing Shiite mullahs in Iraq "to seize the first possible opportunity to fill the power vacuum in the administration of Iraqi cities." Haeri's fatwa emphasized pragmatism, instructing Iraq's Shiite leaders to "seize as many positions as possible to impose a fait accompli for any coming government."

Haeri stressed also that all Shiite institutions and opinions must be fiercely anti-American. "People have to be taught not to collapse morally before the means used by the Great Satan if it stays in Iraq," Haeri's fatwa decreed. "It will try to spread moral decay, incite lust by allowing easy access to stimulating satellite channels, and spread debauchery to weaken people's faith." Haeri ordered the Shiite mullahs to organize the communities and "raise the people's awareness of the Great Satan's plans and of the means to abort them." Significantly, Haeri's subsequent correspondence identified Moqtada Sadr as his leading emissary and representative in Iraq.

On April 13, the first massive demonstration of Shiites in Najaf against Sistani and supporting the Iranian line took place. A massive show of Shiite presence followed in Baghdad, particularly in Sadr City. "We are in control of all of Iraq, especially central and southern Iraq, not only Baghdad," said a leading cleric in Sadr City. The Shiite leadership was vying for power and would not tolerate challenges from the returned exiles supported by the West, and in Damascus, Iraqi opposition leader Jawad Khalsy warned that they all risked Khoi's fate. He explained that Khoi's killers "were angry people who were frustrated from occupation forces." Khalsy reiterated that the opposition figures "are not going to be welcomed [by Iraq's Shiites] and will be associated with the invaders." He suggested that they leave Iraq immediately.

Intriguingly, one of the first reports on the attack and assassination of Khoi came from Saudi intelligence. This report claimed that General Khazraji, also in Najaf on April 10, was attacked and assassinated by pro-Iranian operatives. A few days later, Sheikh Abu-Iyad, the emir of the mujahedin in Baghdad, reported that "the Special Forces from the mujahedin were successful in assassinating Nizar-al-Khazraji when he was coming to Baghdad to attend a meeting." The report went unconfirmed by an independent source for some time, but on April 14, several reliable Iraqi opposition sources acknowledged that Khazraji had been assassinated "recently." According to these sources, he was killed while on his way from Najaf to meet opposition leaders in Nasiriyah. Khazraji had not been seen since the beginning of war and had not communicated with his family in Denmark. However, "friends" delivered reassuring messages to his family that he was fine and hiding in Kurdistan—a rather strange place for him to be, given his intense activities in southern Iraq.

*   *   *

By the middle of April, the situation in Iraq was spiraling out of control. Overwhelmed and outnumbered, American forces were increasingly reacting to major indigenous trends, desperately trying to remain relevant in the wave of cultural reawakening and chaos unleashed by the destruction of the regime. In Baghdad the widespread riots and looting were now escalating to street battles between rival gangs and groups, and American troops were caught in the middle, wanting to quell the rampant violence and hated by the sides doing the fighting.

The northern front came to life on April 11, once news of America's entry into Baghdad spread. On April 11, local Kurdish forces rose up in Kirkuk, while overall chaos spread in Mosul. As a consequence, the United States was dragged by its Kurdish allies into storming Kirkuk and Mosul against its better judgment, and in contravention of any number of agreements reached with the Turks, local Arabs, and even Iraqi forces that were ready to surrender in an orderly fashion. All these agreements aimed at preventing any specific ethnic community, particularly the Kurds, from dominating the oil resources of northern Iraq. However, the Kurds, who knew about these promises and arrangements, immediately started advancing toward the cities.

Kurdish commanders threatened the U.S. Special Forces teams in their midst with anything from expulsion to outright hostilities if they did not cooperate and arrange for air support—at times directed against the same Iraqi units that had already agreed to surrender. Not wanting to be completely banished from Kurdistan, the Special Forces units went along with Kurdish demands, and aircraft bombed as requested. Unsurprisingly, Arab tribes and small Iraqi units organized in northwestern Iraq, mainly to challenge the Kurdish presence in Kirkuk. Alarmed by the brewing tension, the United States promised that the Kurds would leave Kirkuk and Mosul within twelve hours. The Kurds showed no such intent, and the Americans did not have enough troops on hand to evict the Kurds by force. By the evening of April 12, American units had nominal control over Mosul and Kirkuk, after deputizing some of the Kurds, and the other forces encamped right at the cities' edges.

The United States had to pacify the Arab tribes because American units were still far from the heart of the Iraqi WMD program—an area at the center of the tribal lands. On April 11, they began advancing toward al-Qaim, while aircraft bombed several objectives inside the Tikrit-Ramadi-

Samarra triangle, preventing local forces from interfering with the advance. Most of the Iraqi units stationed in al-Qaim were impressive and largely untouched by the war; for example, none of the major hangars, all camouflaged and shielded, had been hit by bombing. The main reason for the lack of air strikes was Washington's reasonable assumption that since WMD munitions were most likely stored in these hangars and hidden in nearby foliage, any hit could contaminate wide areas. Once American forces started advancing toward al-Qaim, intense activities were observed in the thick foliage along the Euphrates. Under cover of darkness, numerous large objects, tanks, and containers were moved from their hiding places and taken across the nearby border with Syria.

As U.S. forces began closing in on al-Qaim, they encountered an intense and sophisticated Iraqi defense. One military official said that if the Iraqis had been fighting like this elsewhere in Iraq, the Americans would still have been stuck at the gates of Nasiriyah. The bulk of the fighting—aimed at delaying the U.S. advance and channeling it away from certain areas—was conducted by elite units. Significantly, the Iraqi activities in the al-Qaim area were conducted and controlled from a new Syrian and Iraqi forward command post established by the Syrian government in Abu-Kamal, just across the border from al-Qaim. The Abu-Kamal headquarters still oversees intelligence activities and special operations related to Iraq.

Tehran and Damascus were using local proxies to actively exploit the absence of U.S. forces to consolidate control over strategic parts of Iraq. Syrian intelligence provided the heavy weapons—from ATGMs to SF-SAMs (shoulder-fired surface-to-air missiles)—used by the mujahedin fighting the Americans in Baghdad. For example, a U.S. Air Force A-10 was shot down over Baghdad by a Syrian "volunteer" using a missile of Syrian origin. Damascus had great expectations from the nascent Iraqi resistance: "The Iraqis only pause to catch their breath," declared an editorial in the Damascus *al-Thawara*, "and soon they will inflict painful strikes on the invaders."

Throughout northern Iraq, the Syrians relied on the Shamar tribes, whose habitat overlaps both northeastern Syria and northwestern Iraq. There is widespread political support for the Shamar tribes throughout the Arab world because members of their leading families have married into most Arab royal families; significantly, Crown Prince Abdallah's favorite wife is from a Shamar tribe in Syria. The Syrian military provided the Shamars with large quantities of weapons and supplies, and numerous Syrian intelligence operatives and commandos—all hailing from the Syrian side of the Shamar—"volunteered" to help their brethren across the border. Using this network, the Syrians built a set of forward bases in the western and northwestern Iraqi desert as a springboard for anti-American terrorism and expanded their assistance to the Kurds.

The Shamar tribes supported two major force groupings (as well as a host of smaller ones) in Iraq: the bulk of the Syrian volunteers operated under Mishan Jabbiri, a leading member of a tribe that lives on both sides of the Syrian-Iraqi border and is supported by Syrian intelligence; and the remainder under former chief of Iraqi military intelligence Wafiq Samar-rai, operating in and near Mosul. Samarrai's force emerged as the primary contact point with other factions of the Iraqi resistance and as a conduit for weapons, money, and other supplies from Syrian intelligence to the Iraqi resistance. These activities quickly tilted the balance in Mosul, be-cause the majority of the city's population is made up of Shamar Arabs and Turkman. With the Americans actively preventing Turkish intelli-gence from helping the Turkman, the Syrian-supported Shamar had the upper hand.

At the same time, American units frequently engaged fedayeen, Baath militias, and an assortment of fundamentalists in both Tikrit and Bagh-dad. Clashes began to spread to other locations throughout Iraq, with many incidents erupting in conjunction with activities initiated by the United States. Events in Mosul on April 15 should have been considered a sign of things to come, when a mob stormed a marine patrol as the new pro-American governor was trying to deliver a speech; the marines opened fire into the crowd, killing ten and wounding dozens of civilians, most of them unarmed. Violent riots and armed clashes ensued through-out northern Iraq.

Tension continued to escalate in Iraqi Kurdistan during the second half of April. The Kurds were increasingly apprehensive that the United States was betraying them and would not work to secure their autonomy. Meanwhile, Turkish Special Forces—usually disguised as civilians—ran operations into Kirkuk, arming, training, and organizing the Turkman militias. The Kurdish leaders feared that their forced withdrawal from Mo-sul, Kirkuk, and other cities would prevent them from repatriating Kurdish "refugees" back to the cities—that is, would impede their ability to effect the "Kurdization" of all the oil cities and key strategic areas through reset-tlement and ethnic cleansing. As a result, mutual hostility, mistrust, and bitterness took hold between the Kurds and the Americans, whom most Kurds held responsible for their inability to realize their aspirations during the war. Hence, the forces of both the PUK and KDP determined to keep all their war booty to themselves. (Barazani kept thirty-four tanks, fourteen APCs, thirty-seven artillery pieces, and an assortment of missiles and small arms; Talabani amassed twenty-one tanks, eleven APCs, four trucks, 125 MBRLs, and his own collection of missiles and smaller weapons.) The United States was rightfully nervous about whom these weapons would be turned against, as in late April both the KDP and the PUK mobilized most of their units against each other and against the Turks, and the small American detachments in the area were unable or unwilling to prevent these movements.

Meanwhile, the establishment of the Abu-Kamal headquarters was but one manifestation of the growing involvement of Damascus in supporting the Iraqi leadership. Syria committed wholeheartedly not only to helping the Iraqi leaders evade the American forces in Baghdad, but to organizing a base in exile for remnants of the Baathist regime so that they could still contribute to the insurrection in Iraq. April 9 was the turning point in the Syrian commitment: the United States became aware that several Middle Eastern countries, most notably Libya and Syria, were assisting the evacuation of key people from Baghdad, prompting Rumsfeld to comment that the Pentagon had "scraps of intelligence saying that Syria has been cooperative in facilitating the move of the people out of Iraq and into Syria." Imad Shuaibi, a Syrian analyst close to the political elite, shrugged off the American allegations. "Syria is not worried. There is no chance that these allegations will turn into threats," he said. "I see no threat in this statement; it is even milder than previous ones."

Although Iraqi high officials had been streaming to Syria since the night of April 5, it was the arrival of Qusay Saddam Hussein and a host of senior leaders on April 10, and the ensuing activation of an organized evacuation system, that spurred Damascus into action. Earlier that day, Saddam, Qusay, and Abid Hamid were seen entering a mosque in the al-Azamiyah sector of Baghdad. A still unknown escape system—which may have included the use of disguises and secret transportation to, perhaps, an underground tunnel—was waiting for them. Soon afterward, Qusay arrived in Damascus while Saddam relocated to a hiding place inside Iraq—most likely in the northwestern desert. Thousands of Iraqi officials were crossing into Syria, welcomed by Syrian intelligence officers and Iraqi "advisers" from the embassy in Damascus. Teams of Syrian and Iraqi agents checked the names of the officials against lists, and the approved individuals were sent to several shelter communities—usually countryside resorts used by the Syrian government—which had been organized by the Iraqis well in advance.

Tripoli was advised by Damascus to launch the evacuation program on the morning of April 9, and the first round of VIP evacuations to Libya took place on a Libyan Air Force Il-76 transport aircraft. The Il-76 departed Okba bin Nafa air base, just outside of Tripoli, for Damascus, at 6:00 P.M. In Damascus, the Il-76 took on a group of seven cars, along with considerable baggage and security. The aircraft then returned to Okba bin Nafa at 6:30 P.M. on April 10. The passengers deboarded at the air base and were taken to an undisclosed destination. Subsequently, family members of the Iraqi elite arrived at a "family compound" just outside Benghazi, Libya. Qusay and a host of senior officials evacuated to Libya via Damascus on April 13. That day, lines of black limousines with Iraqi license plates were observed in al-Mazaa Airport in Damascus, their passengers following Qusay to Libya.

Another favorite destination among Iraqi VIPs was Paris. The first group sent there—made up of scientists and spies—was flown to France from Damascus on the night of April 14 and provided with French travel documents by the embassy in Damascus. Essentially, Paris determined to hide from Washington's view the Iraqis who knew anything about the extent of French cooperation with Saddam on any number of sensitive issues—from nuclear technology to Iraqi campaign contributions to prominent French politicians. (These arrangements have been described by several sources, and in the French book *Our Friend Saddam*.)

As Syrian support for the Iraqi leadership grew, so did American scrutiny of Assad's government, and Washington increased its public warnings to Damascus. Testifying in Congress on April 11, Wolfowitz said they were monitoring Damascus "closely" and added that, as far as the administration was concerned, Syria was "behaving badly," and unless Assad's policies quickly changed, the basic policies toward Syria would have to be reexamined. Wolfowitz assured Congress that the administration had no plans to send armed forces into Syria in pursuit of fleeing Iraqi officials and WMD. Powell also stepped into the fray, issuing a harsh warning to Syria against providing Iraqi officials safe haven.

The Syrians didn't pay much attention to Powell, but they were alarmed by comments made by former senior CIA operative Robert Baer.

Baer told the Beirut *Daily Star* that the Pentagon had "pretty much decided to go after Syria," using the forces already in Iraq. The Syrians were "easy to get, they're vulnerable. There's been this buildup of rhetoric and, of course, the Israelis would like us to do it," Baer added. Assad and his inner circle were convinced that Baer's comments, rather than official statements made in Washington, accurately reflected the thinking in Langley. Therefore, Assad pleaded with Crown Prince Abdallah of Saudi Arabia to help avert an American attack. On April 14 Riyadh launched a diplomatic effort to avert a war in Syria, promising the administration that it would convince Assad to find Iraqi leaders in Syria and deliver them to the United States.

Ultimately, the Syrians would send roughly six "big names" back across the Iraqi border, but they continued to shield and support thousands of second-tier officials, operatives, and military experts; well over a hundred Iraqi leaders were in the Damascus area alone. Still apprehensive about a possible American strike, Damascus asked Moscow to convey to Washington that a group of Iraqi leaders would not be surrendered—among them Vice President Izzat Ibrahim Al-Durri; Saddam's bureau chief, Abid Hamid; Baath Party boss Aziz Salah; Special Security Service Chief Hanni Tefalah; Republican Guard Secretary Kamal Mustafa; Republican Guard commander Seif A-Din Suleih; Iraqi intelligence commander Taher Jaloul; and Special Republican Guard commander Gen. Barzan Suleiman Tikriti—because of their long-standing relationships with Syria's top leadership. The Russians interpreted the Syrian message to suggest that all other Iraqis were available for extradition.

But the offer had the opposite effect in Washington, convincing the skeptics that Damascus was intentionally shielding deposed Iraqis. Arab diplomats in Washington reported to their capitals that the White House and the Pentagon had already decided that the initial strikes on Syria would be brief across-the-border forays conforming to the "hot pursuit" clause in the rules of engagement, and that if these attacks failed to deliver satisfactory results, the United States would broaden the war against Syria. Alarmed by these reports, Hosni Mubarak arrived in Damascus on April 20 on a sudden emergency visit to discuss the mounting crisis with Bashar and methods of defusing it. Mubarak stressed that the United States was extremely angry with Syria and that the ramifications could be horrific. After the meeting, both presidents agreed that Egypt would mediate between Damascus and Washington.

The next day, Egypt arranged for one of the eight leaders, Kamal al-

Tikriti, to be turned over to American soldiers. He was pushed back across the border and into the waiting hands of Special Forces units. The Egyptian message to the administration was clear—with patience, and Cairo's help, things could be made to move in Damascus. A couple of days later, the Syrians handed over Muhammad Hazma al-Zubaydi, who was wanted for the mass murder of Kurdish civilians. His extradition defused tension between the Syrian-sponsored Shamar tribal militias and the Kurds—an outstanding conflict that obstructed their efforts at organizing a unified front against the United States and Turkey. Back in Cairo, Mubarak urged the Americans and British to "end occupation and withdraw the invading forces as soon as possible," and called for the UN and the Arab world to assume control in Iraq, given "the need for a concerted international effort to speed up the formation of a legitimate government chosen by the Iraqi people that represents all trends."

Ultimately, the crisis surrounding the Iraqi senior officials hiding in Syria forced the United States to reassess its entire approach to the postwar Middle East. By the middle of April, senior officials at the White House had concluded that with no great achievements at hand or in sight, the continued escalation and expansion of the war on terrorism would harm President Bush's reelection chances. In the debate, National Security Adviser Condoleezza Rice, the president's chief domestic adviser, Karl Rove, and Secretary of State Colin Powell emerged as the strongest proponents of self-imposed restraint and a greater emphasis on "peacemaking." What started as a series of whispers and private deliberations came to a head at a high-level meeting at the White House in which Rice articulated the new policy. "Rice's message was quite succinct: there will be no further military adventures during the remainder of the president's first term," a senior administration official told UPI's Richard Sale.

Both the tension and resolve within the Bush administration surfaced at a high-level meeting between Sharon's national security adviser, Efraim Halevy, top National Security Council officials, and White House advisers. Halevy brought with him to Washington the latest Israeli intelligence on the region, and when he opined that the radicalization and militancy in Syria and Iran necessitated a stern response before they undermined America's achievements in Iraq, Rice curtly reiterated that there would be "no more military adventures." Rumsfeld objected, citing the Pentagon's latest assessments; when Rice would not budge, Rumsfeld turned to Rove and asked for his opinion. Rove stated that the president agreed with Rice's position, and the meeting ended. "The hawks didn't understand the emphasis had all changed: Everything was focused, not on the war . . . but on the president's reelection," a source with knowledge of the White House meeting told Richard Sale.

11
THE SHIITE FACTOR
AND THE LAUNCH OF JIHAD

Iran and Syria weren't the only countries interested in seeing the United States fail in Iraq. As American forces consolidated their presence in Baghdad, European nations, particularly France and Germany, noticed a transformation of the Bush administration. With every European capital, particularly Paris and Berlin, desperate to share in the anticipated Iraqi reconstruction boom, the French realized that the direct approach would not work. Washington was too furious at the Europeans for their noisy opposition to the war, and the American economy too weak for the United States to seriously contemplate handing Iraq's riches to the Europeans. Therefore, Paris resolved to compel Washington to let France participate by first making Iraq "ungovernable" and then offering to assist in return for a viable role in the rebuilding.

On April 14, Paris launched a "charm offensive" aimed at diverting Washington's attention. French senior officials promised to be "pragmatic" about postwar Iraq and urged reconciliation with the United States through the good auspices of the UN. Other European officials argued that the UN should be given a dominant role in deciding Iraq's future in concert with the United States. "Let us be pragmatic, let us start from the reality of the problems . . . and one will see that everybody will be able to find its place," French Foreign Minister Dominique de Villepin stated on April 14. "It is obvious that the U.S. administration has a role to play," said Villepin. "It is useless to go back to what divided us . . . let us turn to the future."

As Villepin was speaking in Luxembourg, an unmarked Airbus of the French government was making its way to Tehran. Over the next two days—April 15 and 16—a high-level delegation from French intelligence, the foreign ministry, and key industries conducted a series of meetings with both Iranian leaders and key leaders of the Iraqi opposition. The French first met with the Iranian leadership and assured them that Paris shared their trepidation about the disastrous ramifications of the American occupation. They assured the Iranians that Paris was eager and ready to mobilize the European Union to provide extensive assistance to both Iran and a friendly Iraq. Tehran, convinced of their good faith, arranged for the French to meet Ayatollah Baqir al-Hakim and other Iraqi Shiites controlled by Iran.

The French offered the Iraqis lavish French and EU assistance—including military, economic, and political aid—for a role in the reconstruction of a Shiite-dominated Iraq. Their contributions, the French stressed, would be made after the eviction of the Americans. Ayatollah Baqir al-Hakim readily embraced the French offer. Moreover, the PUK's Talabani rushed to Tehran on April 16 for unscheduled meetings with the French in order to ensure that the Kurds were not left out of the deal. Meanwhile, Tehran checked with its friends in Berlin to determine if the French were really committed to such an audacious policy and received a ringing endorsement and confirmation from the Germans. According to Israeli and Turkish intelligence, by the end of several cycles of meetings with French senior officials, Tehran was confident that with French and broader European backing, Iran could securely sponsor the Shiite ascent and quest for power in Iraq.

At the same time, Tehran committed to a confrontation with the United States over the Shiite role in post-Saddam Iraq. While Iraqi politicians were careful to publicly disassociate Tehran from the activities inside Iraq and even urge, in the words of the shrewd Hashemi-Rafsanjani, the reexamination of U.S.-Iranian relations, Iran's actions spoke volumes. Inside Iraq, Moqtada al-Sadr, Haeri's chief representative, started sending couriers with signed edicts and bundles of cash to clerics in several Iraqi cities. The edicts, based on Haeri's fatwa, authorized the clerics to assume power and seize various public institutions to advance the Shiites' cause. Meanwhile, Iran unleashed a barrage of propaganda and incitement through new radio and satellite TV stations. Most important were *Istiqama* ("Standing Tall") TV and the Voice of the Mujahedin radio station—both ostensibly run by Iraqi Shiites. The Iran-sponsored media called for evicting the invaders and establishing a Shiite regime (although not exactly an Islamic republic).

The Shiites also started to build a public presence, testing America's patience for their defiance and hostility. In April, 20,000 Shiites marched in Nasiriyah screaming, "America will not decide! Only the *Hawza!*" (*Hawzas* are religious academies.) In Baghdad, Shiite clerics led a demonstration of more than 3,000 men chanting, "Yes, yes, Islam; No America, No Saddam," a protest against America's declared commitment to establishing an Iraqi government. "It is unreasonable to ignore a majority of more than three quarters of Iraq," Shiite students declared.

Newly returned to Iraq, SCIRI's deputy leader, Abdulaziz al-Hakim, told Iranian TV that while the Shiites were willing to compromise on their initial demands, there was no question about the ultimate character of post-Saddam Iraq. "We will first opt for a national political system, but eventually the Iraqi people will seek an Islamic republic," he said. The same themes were echoed in a major speech by Ayatollah Mohammed Baqir al-Hakim who was still in Iran.

On April 20, the Shiite Sheikh Sayid Abbas seized the municipality building in Kut and declared himself mayor. The local population poured into the streets in support for the audacious move. Abbas relied on the power of a large Iran-sponsored militia that had established a presence in Kut and deployed roadblocks throughout the area. "Iraq will not be unified until it is ruled by its own people. We will sacrifice ourselves toward [attaining] this goal," he declared in his first Friday sermon to a cheering crowd. Several Iraqi Shiites and Iranian senior intelligence operatives, as well as Pasdaran Special Forces, came to Kut, organizing local cells of HizbAllah, Badr Corps, and al-Dawa operatives, in order to expand the Islamic revolution to other parts of the Shiite south and the slums of Baghdad. American forces were slow to react to developments in Kut, and by the time they did try to evict Sayid Abbas from the municipality building, his authority and legitimacy were indisputable regardless of where he was holding court.

Meanwhile, Iran inserted two major force groupings into Iraq; both were nominally part of the al-Badr Corps, but actually included quality units of the IRGC and Iranian intelligence. Around 3,000 troops traveled to Baqubah, in the Diyalah district, roughly 30 miles northeast of Baghdad, and from there, Iran sent teams into the Shiite districts of Baghdad, al-Azamiya, and Sadr City. These Iranian teams immediately took over neighborhood security—in effect becoming the local police force. At the same time, the units in Baqubah wore uniforms in the Iranian style and used many Iranian military and Bassej vehicles. An Iranian force of some 4,000 troops also entered Iraq near al-Amarah and established its forward headquarters in Kut, then ruled by Sayid Abbas. From there, the Iranians sent three units of about 1,000 men each to Nasiriyah, Najaf, and Qarbalah. To avoid unnecessary tension with America, these forces wore civilian clothes. They also had several military vehicles and vans in good working order (which held heavy weapons and other supplies), again disguised in civilian colors. At the same time, the Jimaat-i-Sadr Thani under the command of Moqtada al-Sadr—now clearly involved in risky provocations on behalf of Iran—boasted more than 5,000 men. Their cells—each comprising Pasdaran operatives and Special Forces as well as locally recruited fighters—were spread all over the Shiite heartland.

Tehran chose April 22, Ashura Day (the holiest day in Shiite Islam), to demonstrate the Shiites' strength. It was a poignant symbol, since Saddam had suppressed the Ashura processions for decades. Over the previous few days, millions of devotees carrying Shiite flags, chanting slogans, and bloodying themselves with chains and swords started marching toward Najaf and Qarbalah from all over Iraq. As fervor overtook them, the marchers became hysterical by the time they reached their destination. From a logistical point of view, it was a master stroke: Iran directly sponsored, through local Shiite networks, the organization of roughly two million people marching to Qarbalah to commemorate the Ashura. Millions of others joined in from nearby communities and villages. All these marchers were provided with guidance and security, food and water, as well as religious artifacts. Thus, the Iranians and their supporters in Iraq effectively used Ashura Day as an instrument to demonstrate the strength, dedication, and resolve of the Shiite community. "Yes, yes to Islam, no to America, no to Israel, no to colonialism, no to occupation," chanted the Shiite throngs in Qarbalah. "We are against colonization and occupation. We have just finished with one oppressive regime and we don't want another," explained a young Shiite covered in his own blood, in reference to the possibility of an imposed regime.

During the Ashura processions, Iranian-affiliated forces also demonstrated their preeminence in the Shiite heartland. These units provided security and traffic control for million of people, and the whole community saw Iran's dominance in the Shiite zones. Significantly, the Iran-sponsored forces even challenged the ability of the U.S. military to move around their roadblocks—ostensibly erected to ensure the religious sanctity of the

Ashura ceremonies. The Iranians and their local allies used the marches to and from Qarbalah to move emissaries, funds, explosives, and weapons throughout the country and also as a shield for transferring Iranian operatives, first to Najaf and Qarbalah and ultimately back to the villages and towns the marchers had come from. (For example, Abdulaziz al-Hakim popped up in Qarbalah along with members of the SCIRI high command.)

The Shiites began advocating swift elections—chanting "one man, one vote," the same rallying cry used by Gore supporters during the uproar surrounding the 2000 presidential elections—to determine the style of government and basic character of the new Iraq, knowing full well that an overwhelming majority would support a Shiite-style government. U.S. declarations that it would not permit the establishment of an Islamic republic in the Iranian mode made a mockery of the administration's oft-repeated commitment to bringing democracy and freedom to Iraq. It's not surprising that Tehran pointedly ignored a stern American message calling for the withdrawal of the Badr Corps and all other Iranians from Iraq. Instead, pro-Iranian Shiite clerics vied ardently to fill the power vacuum created by Saddam's fall, and the absence of any viable alternative.

In retrospect, the most important outcome of the Ashura experience was the emboldening effect it had on the Shiite population. After decades of suppression and discrimination, they suddenly burst into the open and realized their own might. As a result, by early May, the Shiite population was confident of its right and ability to run its own communal affairs, as well as a future Iraq. Behind the scenes, extensive Iranian assistance and expertise made it possible for the emerging local leadership and activist groups to sustain operations. Local Shiite clerics took over virtually every position of power and management they could, directing the local population to specific mosques for access to a comprehensive system of social services, emergency food supplies, medical care, and education. The Shiites began running hospitals, markets, schools, and community and cultural centers, as well as police stations, in virtually every city, town, and township in Iraq. "When the U.S. invaded, there was a power vacuum. We are providing security. Most of the patrols in the streets are being done by clerics because the people will obey the clerics more than they will obey foreigners," Sheikh Tahsin al-Ekabi, a Shiite cleric and the acting director of the Qadissiya Hospital in Sadr City, told the London *Guardian*.

By that point, the Shiite elite had resolved to establish an Islamic republic. In tune with Iranian recommendations, the Shiite leaders would be prudent in confronting U.S. forces, and instead determined to further empower the local authorities and build their political power on that solid foundation. The Hawza, the main Shiite seminary of Najaf, now became the unofficial seat of power in predominantly Shiite Iraq. "Ninety-eight per cent of the people are Muslims. The Iraqi constitution must not commit to anything that will go against *Sharia* [Islamic law]," Sheikh Muhammad al-Yacobi, one of the Hawza's activists, told the London *Guardian*.

The Najaf Hawza provided for religious, judicial, medical, educational, and social programs, in addition to local security services, for over three quarters of Iraq's population, and the grassroots support for these mosque-based local governments was actively used to build political power. The Hawza elite committed to methodical progress at the national level, having resolved to ultimately establish an Islamic state even if the Shiite community had to fight the United States. Quais al-Khazaaly, another cleric in the Hawza, told the London *Guardian* that "the right decision is to have an Islamist state. If the U.S. blocks such a state and people want it, this will lead to lots of trouble with the U.S." Numerous Shiite militant groups, sponsored by Iran, were already actively preparing for that possibility.

In late April, the American military finally began paying attention to the growing Iran-sponsored military activities, particularly in the Baghdad area. U.S. troops, particularly the recently arrived 4th Infantry Division, were "fighting shadows" near the Iraq-Iran border. Overnight, U.S. artillery launched flares to illuminate potential infiltration routes from Iran to Baqubah, and army positions and patrols were frequently subject to small-arms fire and sporadic mortar shelling. Because of the scarcity of American forces, the quick reaction force of mechanized infantry of the 4th Infantry would appear on the scene a few hours after an attack and futilely give chaser to the assailants. The population remained hostile, refusing any help to the American forces; frequently the patrols would be pelted with rocks as they were trying to locate the attackers. In the Baghdad area, U.S. forces confronted HizbAllah-sponsored terrorists and raiding parties that had stayed behind after the fall of Baghdad.

A series of Special Forces ambushes near the Syrian border helped reduce the flow of additional volunteers. By May, the U.S. forces had detained some 700 HizbAllah fighters and other Jihadists, including two dozen Chechen terrorists, who had attempted to infiltrate Iraq from Syria with weapons and explosives. Still, given the overall rate of infiltration into Iraq, these captures were insignificant. Ultimately, the American intelligence community's reading of Iran's influence and ability to obstruct operations was woefully wrong. "There is a growing danger that radical Shiite extremists are infiltrating post-Saddam Iraq from neighboring Iran," U.S. intelligence officials briefed reporters on April 28. The Iranian IRGC "[was] expected to send infiltrators into southern Iraq," the officials said. "Thus far, however, there are no signs the infiltration has begun." While these officials were conducting the briefing, Iran-sponsored Shiite forces inside Iraq numbered somewhere between 25,000 and 30,000 armed troops.

The Shiites' initial success was expedited by the fact that U.S. authorities were caught unprepared by the surge. On April 23, Bush administration officials acknowledged to the *Washington Post* that they had "underestimated the Shiites' organizational strength and [were] unprepared to prevent the rise of an anti-American, Islamic fundamentalist government in the country." The officials acknowledged further that Washington had "failed to fully appreciate the force of Shiite aspirations and [was] now concerned that those sentiments could coalesce into a fundamentalist government."

The problem could be attributed to two dominant factors: the United States lacked intelligence about the overall situation in Iraq, particularly a comprehensive social and political reading of the population (the near total dependence on the various opposition groups in exile, each with its own agenda, did not help either); and the Bush administration was so fixated on overthrowing Saddam Hussein that it did not pay proper attention to the challenges of "the day after." "It is a complex equation, and the U.S. government is ill-equipped to figure out how this is going to shake out," a State Department official told the *Washington Post*. "I don't think anyone took a step backward and asked, 'What are we looking for?' The focus was on the overthrow of Saddam Hussein."

By late April, it was not broadly appreciated that the Ashura pilgrimage, rather than the photo-op toppling of Saddam's statue in Firdos Square, was the real manifestation of the new Iraq. The anti-American message of this Iraq was unmistakable: "Thank you for freeing us from Saddam, but now please go home," many sophisticated, Westernized Iraqis told U.S. officials.

For its part, Tehran was becoming increasingly assertive in confronting both the issue of America's presence in Iraq and accusations of Iranian interference within the Iraqi Shiite community, and on April 24, Tehran capitalized on the official visit of the French foreign minister to raise the ante. Dominique de Villepin arrived in Tehran in order to consolidate the working agreements over Iraq reached only a few days before. Hence, the Iranians knew, he would not challenge their public rebuke of the United States. "It is very interesting that the Americans have occupied Iraq but they accuse Iraq's neighbor of interfering in its affairs," Iranian Foreign Minister Kamal Kharrazi said in a joint press conference with Villepin. "Instead of raising accusations, the United States should adopt cooperation with Iran. The United States should welcome Iran's positive role." In his statement, Villepin echoed Kharrazi's message, stressing France's conviction that France and Iran could "jointly contribute to the political, economic, and social reconstruction of Iraq."

Meanwhile, the experts in Tehran knew that for the Shiites to ultimately triumph, they would have to escalate the armed confrontation with the United States. Although the Shiites had a head start, as demonstrated in the aftermath of the Ashura, the Iranians knew that America was still a great power to be reckoned with. For Tehran, the decisive milestone came on April 24, when the United States reached a cease-fire accord with the Mujahedin ul-Khalq forces in Iraq—a cultlike Iranian opposition group controlled by Iraqi intelligence and officially considered a terrorist organization by the United States. The cease-fire permitted the 4,000-strong Mujahedin ul-Khalq to hold on to their weapons, including tanks and artillery, provided they remained confined to their main bases near the Iranian border. Not without reason, Tehran concluded that the United States was contemplating using the Mujahedin ul-Khalq against Iran—perhaps to counter the continued infiltration of Badr Corps fighters. It was time to unleash the fury of Islamist terrorism, Iranian leaders decided.

In Lebanon, HizbAllah was gearing up to support the protracted struggle of its Iranian brethren. Ayatollah Muhammad Hussein Fadlallah, HizbAllah's spiritual leader and a graduate of the key religious schools in Najaf and Qarbalah, articulated the movement's advice to the Shiites of Iraq in his Friday sermon on May 2, commemorating the anniversary of the death of the Prophet Muhammad: "In Iraq, the American killing of demonstrating civilians under the pretense of self-defense is the same method the Israelis resort to. The Iraqis should learn this object lesson and learn that the Americans have come to exploit Iraq, when the role of their agent 'Saddam' has been done with, and not to liberate them. We are not calling upon them to an adventurist [sic] undertaking, but to study how to confront the forces of occupation and arrogance. To understand their plans and to be aware of their objectives. Let us be united in demanding the American withdrawal from Iraq and leaving the Iraqis to rule themselves for they have all the resources and potential when the atmosphere of freedom is available."

Tehran's sentiments were also expressed on May 2 in a sermon given by Ayatollah Ahmad Jannati, the secretary general of the Guardians Council and a prominent supporter of Islamist campaigns. "The Iraqi people are finally coming to understand that the solution is an uprising, and they have no other choice but to rise up and stage martyrdom operations," Jannati said. "This is the only solution; they are learning from the experience of Palestine." Jannati continued, saying that Tehran would provide staunch and unfailing support to the Iraqis provided they cooperated with Iran: "What we want from them is unity, taking sanctuary in mosques, following the clerics' path and making continued efforts to drive the enemy out of Iraq." He also assailed the cease-fire deal with the Mujahedin ul-Khalq, claiming that it was indicative of the duplicity and hostility of the U.S. government. "American leaders are cheaters ... they talk about fighting against terrorism but they are making deals with this terrorist group due to suppress Iraqis." To Jannati's mind, there was no alternative to fighting the U.S. forces, and he reminded his audience of Iran's past struggles with the United States, observing that "if they [the Americans] fear from death, they will have to surrender." He urged all Iraqis to learn not only from the legacy of Islamist struggles against the United States, but also from the lessons of Lebanese and Palestinians fighting against Israel. Islamist struggle had defeated, and once again would defeat, superior forces, he argued, and the Iraqi experience would be no different. "Iraqis will eventually reach the conclusion that the only way to oust Americans is an Intifada." For Tehran, there would be no going back.

On May 1, President Bush flew to the U.S.S. *Abraham Lincoln* and declared victory in the war in Iraq, but cautioned that the war on terrorism was far from over. "The Battle of Iraq is one victory in a war on terror that began on September 11th, 2001, and still goes on," Bush told nearly 5,000 sailors on the flight deck. Bush stressed that the victory in Iraq was "a crucial advance" in the war against worldwide terrorism, saying, "We have removed an ally of al-Qaeda and cut off a source of terrorist funding." As a result of America's having toppled Saddam, "no terrorist network will gain weapons of mass destruction from the Iraqi regime, because that regime is no more."

Bush urged other terrorism-sponsoring states, as well as terrorist organizations, to learn from Iraq's fate. "Any person involved in committing or planning terrorist attacks against the American people becomes an enemy of this country, and a target of American justice. Any person, organization, or government that supports, protects, or harbors terrorists is complicit in the murder of the innocent, and equally guilty of terrorist crimes," Bush warned, stating again that the United States would not hesitate to use force against other terrorist threats. "The use of force has been and remains our last resort. Yet all can know, friend and foe alike, that our nation has a mission. We will answer threats to our security and we will defend the peace."

Although his emphasis was on the next phases in the war on terrorism, Bush did not suggest that the crisis in Iraq was over. "We have difficult work to do in Iraq. We are bringing order to parts of that country that remain dangerous. We are pursuing and finding leaders of the old regime, who will be held to account for their crimes." But even these operations would be taking place in the context of a victory in Iraq: "It is a great advance when the guilty have more to fear from war than the innocent," Bush declared.

On his sixty-sixth birthday, April 28, Saddam Hussein sent his first letter to the Iraqi people. Significantly, copies of the letter were brought to the West, including the London-based *Al-Quds al-Arabi,* via the same channels that deliver messages from Osama bin Laden. Saddam aimed to set the record straight about the fall of Baghdad and set the tone for the forthcoming struggle against the occupation forces. Iraq was not defeated, Saddam insisted, it was betrayed. "They did not triumph over you, you who reject the occupation and humiliation and you who have Arabism and Islam in your hearts, except with treachery," he told the Iraqis. Saddam urged all Iraqis to rise above religious and sectarian divides and unite in fighting the occupation forces. "Rise against the occupier and do not trust those who talk about the Sunnis and Shiites, for the only issue that the homeland, your great Iraq, is facing at present is that of occupation. There are no priorities other than the expulsion of the infidel, criminal, killer, and cowardly occupier whom not a single honorable person shook his hand but only the traitors and agents," Saddam wrote. Intriguingly, Saddam told the Iraqis that "all the countries around you are against your resistance, but God is with you because you are fighting the infidels and defending your rights." Saddam concluded with numerous rallying cries including, "Long live the great Iraq and its people," and "Long live Palestine, free and Arab from the river to the sea."

Paradoxically, just as people later missed the repressive regimes that held sway in Eastern Bloc countries, Saddam's rule was missed by some Islamists, and by late April an intense campaign was already under way in fundamentalist communities all over the world that aimed to rehabilitate Saddam and to define the theological guidelines for jihad, not only in Iraq but throughout the Middle East as well. The April 22 communiqué issued by the Jamaat-ud-Daawa of Pakistan, Afghanistan, and Kashmir—the group is a close ally of bin Laden's—was one of the most lucid, explaining the emerging trend. For the Islamists, the crisis point in the current war was America's removal of the inscription *Allah hu-Akbar* from the Iraqi flag, which Saddam added in 1991, at the height of the first Gulf War. "Anybody who says that it is not a war between Islam and infidelity must be a fool," the Jamaat-ud-Daawa asserted. Saddam had committed numerous infringements against his fellow Arabs and Muslims, the communiqué readily acknowledged. Furthermore, "Saddam Hussein belonged to the Baath Party, a secular and Arab nationalist outfit." But a close examination of Saddam's record convinced the Jamaat-ud-Daawa that "Saddam Hussein was a nationalist but he was also a Muslim and used to chant slogans against Jews. . . . Saddam Hussein was a common Muslim in his personal life like other rulers but wanted to unite Arabs on the basis of nationalism against Israel." And throughout, "he read verses from the Koran during the war and called his nation for Jihad."

However, Saddam's lust for power had contributed to America's invasion. "Saddam Hussein should have also understood the situation and sacrificed the seat of power . . . so it would have deprived the United States of the reason to launch the aggression using the pretext that Saddam Hussein was an aggressor and a threat to the world's peace as he attacked Iran and Kuwait, although the United States was also behind those attacks."

Therefore, Saddam's transgressions paled in comparison with America's designs. The Jamaat-ud-Daawa communiqué concluded that "the Arab and Muslim would have to keep this in mind to draw a future line of action; otherwise, the Great Satan, the United States, will target us one by one. It is time for the Muslim rulers to wake up and also to wake up the Muslim Nation." In other words, the grave threat the United States posed warranted cooperation between the Islamists and Baathists, not just in Iraq but throughout the Muslim world.

In April, al-Qaeda's Center for Islamic Studies published a study entitled "The Crusaders' War Against Iraq," which stressed the Islamist role in Iraq. The American war against Iraq was but one facet of the fateful confrontation between Islam and the United States, al-Qaeda argued, and regardless of the outcome of the battle for Baghdad, "the battle is going to take place in various stages, and the stage which we believe will exhaust the enemy has not come yet. Therefore, we need to think practically about the way we can join this battle and support the Iraqi resistance force, which has so far exhibited enormous resistance, causing shock, fear, and confusion among the enemy. The Nation's duty today is to maintain the state of shock and fear among the enemy that has invaded the Muslim countries." Thabit bin Qays, al-Qaeda's new media coordinator, elaborated on the subject in an e-mail he sent to the Saudi-owned, London-based magazine *al-Majallah*. Thabit bin Qays wrote that "al-Qaeda's command is watching closely the events in Iraq as they unfold." He acknowledged that al-Qaeda was already involved in the war. "Our activities are connected with the events in Iraq," but all further details were "a matter concerning the leader of al-Qaeda, Sheikh Osama bin Laden, [and] will be announced when the right time comes."

A short time later, a new audiotape from Osama bin Laden surfaced in Pakistan. Bin Laden defined the regional context of the anti-American jihad, urging believers to go beyond fighting the American occupation forces in Iraq and rise up against the Arab governments that were aiding the United States in its attack on Iraq because their actions revealed them as illegal and un-Islamic entities. "All of them have been imposed upon you and Jihad against them is your duty," bin Laden declared. He anticipated that the war in Iraq would be the precursor of an American onslaught on the rest of the region. "The United States has attacked Iraq, and soon it will also attack Iran, Saudi Arabia, Egypt, and Sudan." In response to that danger, bin Laden urged a total war against the United States. "I ask the Muslim women to join Jihad by providing food to mujahedin. Elders should pray for us. Those people who cannot join forces in Jihad should give financial help to those mujahedin who are fighting against U.S. aggression." Bin Laden reserved his most effusive praise for suicide attackers, saying, "I am proud of those martyrs who sacrificed their lives for the sake of Islam," and adding that their primary contribution was in setting an example for a new generation to emulate. Addressing the mujahedin in Iraq, bin Laden downplayed the threat posed by high-tech American weaponry. "Do not be afraid of their tanks and armored personnel carriers. These are artificial things," bin Laden said. "If you start suicide attacks you will see the fear of Americans all over the world."

Bin Laden also singled out Egypt and Saudi Arabia as targets for the Islamist movements, demonstrating that he knew in advance about operations in both countries. According to highly authoritative Islamist sources in the United Kingdom, on the morning of April 8, an Egyptian military unit rebelled against the Mubarak regime, persuaded to do so by Islamist officers and enlisted men. The unit started marching toward Cairo, and 20 kilometers from the presidential headquarters in New Cairo, they were surrounded by Republican Guard units, military police, artillery units, and helicopter gunships. At first, senior officers attempted to negotiate with the rebels, who promptly tried to persuade the surrounding troops to join their movement. When several soldiers opted to stand with the rebellion, the officers ordered artillery and helicopter strikes until the mutiny was annihilated. Cairo went to great efforts to suppress news of the coup attempt; later that evening, local officials in New Cairo attributed the explosions and billowing smoke to unannounced and highly sensitive live-fire military exercises.

From the very beginning of the conflict, there had been a flow of Islamist volunteers to join the fight against the Americans. They came from Algeria, Tunisia, Egypt, Syria, Morocco, Yemen, Jordan, Saudi Arabia, Afghanistan, Pakistan, and Chechnya. Some came as part of organized volunteer groups, others as individuals. While some of the volunteers were inexperienced religious fanatics, most of them were highly trained veterans of prior struggles, including the wars in Afghanistan and Chechnya. "These are not just zealots who grabbed a gun and went to the front line. They know how to employ guerrilla tactics so someone had to have trained them. They are certainly organized, and if it's not bin Laden's people, its al-Qaeda by another name. But they certainly came here to fight the West," British officials told the London *Times*.

"The 'foreign legion' stunned British troops with their skills and fanaticism," the *Times* reported. The actual number of Islamist volunteers is not clear, but according to Amir Hamza, a central leader of the Jamaat-ud-Daawa, "40,000 Arab mujahedin had reached Iraq." Other Islamist leaders were more realistic, estimating that somewhere between 10,000 and 12,000 Islamists had entered Iraq.

However, it was between March and April—once the Iraqis appeared to be losing the war—that the most important flow of jihadists began. Several groups, all somehow affiliated with al-Qaeda, left their hideouts in Pakistan and Afghanistan on their way to southern Iraq via Iran; many of their passports had Iraqi visas listing "jihadi" as the reason for visiting Iraq. Among these groups were highly trained, expert terrorists, including Muslims born and raised in Britain and other Western European countries earmarked for special operations. Their task was not to contribute to the last phases of the battle for Baghdad, but rather to lay the foundations for the terrorist struggle that would follow. On April 2, an Islamist commander in Iraq reported that several al-Qaeda mujahedin were already in the country and had even entered Baghdad despite intensive bombing, exploiting the fact that American forces were preoccupied with fighting the Iraqi Army. The commander stressed that "the al-Qaeda members did not take part in the earlier mujahedin operations in which several mujahedin were martyred because they did not trust the Republican Guards' command and feared betrayal." But with the battle of Baghdad nearly over, bin Laden's commanders were ready to assume a prominent role.

April 11 was the turning point: A secret meeting took place at a safe house in Baghdad involving the leading emissaries of the Islamist organizations, including bin Laden's representative, and the senior commanders of Saddam's Fedayeen. The report to the Islamist leadership identified the participants as "the world-renowned elite strategic planners and top commanders related to Fedayeen operations of al-Qaeda, HAMAS, Islamic Jihad, and HizbAllah," and "the Saddam's Fedayeen commander."

The meeting charted the next phase of the war in Iraq. "New plans for thousands of Fedayeen and strategies for mujahedin after the fall of Baghdad was the topic of discussion. After a long debate, giving due importance to al-Qaeda's and HAMAS's specialists, a strategy was finalized for a guerilla war." The report stressed that "even though the basic points of this meeting are kept secret, the presence of al-Qaeda and HAMAS mujahedin clearly shows that the invaders will have to face the bloody ambushes of a hit-and-run strategy."

The participants agreed that the "Fedayeen will be aided by the thousands of Arab Mujahedin currently [in countries] surrounding Iraq" but who hadn't yet crossed over the border. They also resolved that "Palestinian Mujahedin" with extensive combat experience against Israel would "find an opportunity to work their plans in Iraq to create many problems for the U.S. in coming days." The report noted that in several places "Iraqi military and Fedayeen" had already been fighting "under the leadership of

those al-Qaeda Arab Mujahedin," employing proven irregular warfare tactics against the Americans. It was on the basis of this shared experience, the
Islamist report stated, that the high command of Saddam's Fedayeen now
wanted closer cooperation with the Islamists.

In April, the Islamists established the "Mujahedin in Iraq" framework,
under the command of a council comprising Khalid Shaykh, Abu-Iyad al-
Falastini, and Nasrallah al-Afghani. Sheikh Abu-Iyad al-Falastini, the al-
Qaeda-affiliated "Amir of the Mujahedin in Baghdad," emerged as the
leading figure because of his presence in Baghdad. A lengthy report he
wrote to the Islamist leadership provided additional background on the
Baghdad Agreement and negotiated jihad for "Iraq-ul-Islam." By early
April, Sheikh Abu-Iyad reported, he was in command of 8,000 mujahedin
in Iraq "who have come voluntarily from Syria, Sudan, Yemen, Algeria, Pakistan, Bangladesh, Malaysia, Albania, Bosnia, etc." These were highly
trained and organized mujahedin, and they shed tears "because they saw
the people of the cross in the Muslim land in Dar-ul-Salaam, in Baghdad, in
the cradle of the Abbassi Khilafah," and this sight spurred them into action.

The final phases of the war were conducted "in accordance with our
consultation between the leadership of the Mujahedin and the leadership
of the Iraqi forces." The mujahedin argued that the continued presence of
Iraqi regular forces in the cities was subjecting the civilian population to
heavy aerial bombing, and, as was the case in Afghanistan, they argued that
the regular forces should withdraw from the cities and then embark on a
guerrilla war. "We decided to use the same technique, and the Iraqi leadership, thank Allah, accepted our *Shura* [Council] and that showed us a sign
of responsibility from them that they realized that they could not fight the
U.S. as a regular army. Especially when you are living among your own
people because the *kuffaar* [infidels] will destroy you and destroy your
own people; so retreat, but this will mean you have lost the war politically,"
Abu-Iyad explained. "The agreement was that all the forces of Iraq, artillery, army, intelligence, informers, Republican Guard, Saddam's
Feyadeen, and all other troops will retreat from their places, leaving behind
them all those weapons that Iraq manufacturers, and come to the bunkers
leaving the cities for the *kuffaar* to enter."

The Iraqi forces withdrew to a vast system of tunnels and bunkers in
three different areas in Iraq that, according to Abu-Iyad, are capable of
concealing "150,000 fighters who are extremely loyal to the regime," along
with 150 combat aircraft and 2,500 Iraqi tanks. Abu-Iyad went on to intimate that the evacuation of Baghdad had been completed just in time.

"Thank Allah there was no Iraqi forces, no Iraqi soldiers, no Iraqi police in the street, otherwise there would have been fighting and blood up to the knees."

The first task the Islamists embarked on was to make sure their troops had the right Islamist motives. Abu-Iyad explained that the Islamist mujahedin "kept with [them] the young Mujahedin, those who used to be called Saddam's Fedayeen. With the help of the brothers and the *Ulemah* [Islamic leadership] with us they converted them to become Fedayeen Islam; they have denounced the Baath Party regime, they have denounced their views on Arab nationalism and declared the *Shahadah* [martyrdom], accepting the *Tawheed* [Islamic oneness] and declared to die for the sake of Allah and all this especially when they have been trained to be martyrs."

Another timely achievement of the Islamists was to convince the Shiite and Kurdish leadership not to rebel against Saddam but instead join the anti-American jihad. "We were aware that there was going to be an [anti-Saddam] uprising from the Kurds, the Shia, and even the people, and that was what America was gambling on. We decided not to give them this opportunity because this could have resulted in the war between us and them," Abu-Iyad noted.

By April the Islamist high command already had a clear plan for the guerrilla war they would launch once they felt that they were in charge. Abu-Iyad pointed to an April incident in Kurdistan as indicative of the kind of warfare he was leading. "The group of Mujahedin sent a letter to the Americans informing them of a military storage dump. As usual the Americans went there to collect the arsenal; when they arrived the whole area had been bugged with mines and huge explosives were timed off killing eight of them, their artillery being destroyed and many were wounded. The air jets were sent in and they bombed indiscriminately causing many civilian casualties. Only one of the Mujahedin became *Shaheed* [martyr], two were wounded and all the rest returned back safely to their caves. All you could see was a huge fire."

And this was only the beginning. The mujahedin expected a major escalation of the jihad in the future. "The Jihad will continue with Bush and Blair," Abu-Iyad reported. "In the battlefield there is killing, there is fighting, and they know the coming days will make them forget yesterday. We are waiting for the summer and when the summer comes *Inshallah* we will be able to hurt them badly by the heat of the sun and the heat of our weapons and the strategy of fighting we have adopted. The Mujahedin have their own Special Forces from Allah and that is the weather. May Allah keep sending U.S. all his soldiers."

Moreover, the Islamist leadership had already decided on using Iraq as the springboard to incite a broader jihad in Saudi Arabia and the Gulf States. "We call upon all the Muslims, in particular the ones in the Arabian Peninsula, to be ready, the *Maama* [confrontation] is going to start in the Arabian Peninsula. By Allah we have discovered a very rich land and very cultivated land full of weapons, good for training, and an enemy we can see. So be prepared and be firm, the Jihad will be on your doorstep, and remember those days, they are coming, they are going to be long days, they are going to be very difficult days, it needs your *Duaa* [invocation to Allah]," Sheikh Abu-Iyad al-Falastini declared prophetically.

Similar ideological documents circulated among leading Islamist communities corroborating Abu-Iyad's themes. "Baghdad may have fallen, but the *Ummah* is now united," declared an April 11 analysis prepared for the Islamist leadership. "The Crusaders have marched into Baghdad after three weeks of merciless bombardment with bombs and missiles that have killed thousands." But according to the report's author, despite losses and great suffering, the occupation served as a long-overdue call to action for the entire Muslim world. "The Muslims have realized that they are being picked on one by one: Afghanistan, Iraq, perhaps Syria and Iran next. They cannot stand against the *Kafir* as divided nation states. The Muslims have resorted to calling for unity on the basis of Islam and the brotherhood among Muslims. They realize the *Khilafah* [caliphate] and political Islam is the only common basis of uniting them, and that nationalism only seeks to divide them," the analysis explained. "The Fatwa of the Shia and Kurdish Imams urging the Iraqi Muslims to rise up in Jihad against the Crusaders" confirmed this trend, and the rest of the Muslim world was prepared to embrace the same ideology. "The Muslim world is now utterly ready to throw away the Western system, the Western agents, and Western politics. There is consensus on this, from farmers and bakers to academics and opinion columnists. The Muslims now call openly to the armies and the people of power to move against their regimes before they too have to face the Crusaders, alone and incapable of resisting. The Muslim armies, as individual forces, may not be a match for the Crusaders, but this *Ummah* united, with all its wealth, people, and armies, would shake and destroy the Crusaders without doubt."

By mid-April decisions reached at the Baghdad meetings were being implemented. Bin Laden's followers announced on April 14 the formation of the National Front for the Liberation of Iraq, which aimed to unify and guide the terrorists who would constitute the lynchpin of the insurgence. "The leaderships of the patriotic forces from all regions of Iraq immediately undertook a series of intense communications that ended with the formation of the National Front for the Liberation of Iraq. Field representatives of various armed groups took part in its establishment. The Resistance Brigades, some of which until now were still holding their positions, joined it, as did the volunteers from the fraternal Arab nations. In addition, a regrouping has begun of a large number of officers and men of the army, the Republican Guard, and the Special Forces, who had split apart and were without leaders. Iraq has been defeated. But it is not dying or surrendering," the statement read.

The next day, a new operational group calling itself "The Islamic Arab Grouping for Liberation—Iraq Command" issued a very important statement about their forthcoming jihad through bin-Laden-affiliated organizations. The Grouping promised to confront "invaders of Iraq, the agents of Zionism among the agent and treacherous Kurdish leaderships, and the mercenaries of Bush and Blair," and vowed to bring about the liberation of both Iraq and Palestine. The great significance of this communiqué was the delicate blend of Shiite and Sunni Islamist terminologies; the authors went out of their way to demonstrate common Islamist standing against their common foe—the Great Satan. Theologically, their rhetoric helped codify the common jihad that Iraq's different factions had agreed on.

While the intricacies of the jihad were being articulated, terrorism and subversion became more prevalent. On April 13, a Syrian mujahid disguised as a groundskeeper shot and killed a marine guarding a hospital in Baghdad. There and in other cities, American patrols were frequently attacked by Islamist forces made up of local Iraqis and volunteers from Syria, Sudan, Egypt, and Jordan. Indications of additional terrorist campaigns became apparent as well; for example, American soldiers discovered about three hundred suicide vests lined with explosives hidden in a Baghdad school, discovering at the same time that eighty more vests were missing. Special Forces units also captured several HizbAllah fighters as they crossed over from Syria. "They were planning to carry out operations against coalition forces," said a U.S. official quoted in *al-Hayah*. From these and other captured terrorists, the United States learned that hundreds of al-Qaeda and HizbAllah terrorists remained in Iraq after the fall of Baghdad and that by April, they were training both Iraqis and foreign mujahedin in guerrilla and terrorism tactics—car and suicide bombings, ambushes, sniper attacks, hit-and-run shootings, and grenade strikes.

The Arab volunteers held a growing appeal because of their ideological diversity, which helped build mutual trust among all the anti-American factions. A commentator on al-Jazeera TV explained this phenomenon by saying, "The Arab volunteers in Iraq differ from their predecessors in Afghanistan in the fact they belong to varieties of ideologies beside Islamists, who are the majority. Some of these volunteers may belong to secular movements, such as the 'Nasserists' in Egypt, who adopt the socialist thoughts of the former Egyptian President Gamal Abdel-Nasser. Some of the Arab volunteers did not even belong to any ideology, but just came to Iraq in order to fight the Americans whom they hate because of their oppressive actions in Palestine, Afghanistan, Libya, Sudan, and Somalia." That brand of cooperation was visible, for example, in Mosul, where observers noted that "most of the former Baathists . . . have been seen among the Iraqi Islamic Party, which is a branch of the Muslim Brotherhood [movement]."

The April 25 report to the Islamist leadership from the Arab mujahedin inside Iraq noted that many "Al-Qaeda and Taliban fighters had successfully entered the Iraqi territories and joined the other Mujahedin in a surprise that boosted the morale of all the fighters." The report noted that working arrangements with the Baathist forces were improving. At the same time, however, it stressed that "the headquarters of the Mujahedin were separate from the Iraqi troops and will struggle for one goal: to pave the way for an Islamic state in Iraq." The report further stated that "since the beginning of Anglo-American aggression, the Mujahedin leaders organized the groups of guerrilla fighters for two reasons: first, to estimate the points of strength and weakness of the enemy and select the best places for potential operations; second, to exhaust the enemy's troops with significant losses. The Mujahedin promised that they will adopt new techniques in the coming operations that will inflict the aggressors with great losses."

In an effort to mitigate the rise of Islamic fundamentalism, American authorities tacitly allowed Ahmad el-Kebeisey, sixty-eight, a conservative Sunni cleric exiled by Saddam in the mid-1990s, who had since enjoyed the protection of the royal families in several Gulf States, to return to Baghdad. On April 18, Kebeisey delivered his first Friday sermon at the Abu Hanifa mosque in the al-Aazamia district of Baghdad—the traditional stronghold of Saddam's loyalists. He urged all Iraqis to unite and get rid of the "American and British occupiers" before they destroyed the country. Iraq's future leadership, Kebeisey stressed, must rise from inside Iraq if only because the exiled opposition parties were "traitors and stooges of America working to realize Jewish aims."

One week later, Sheikh Munther al-Adaami delivered a sermon that was equally inflammatory. "We say no to the occupation and no to the Americans," he declared. "We don't want a U.S.-imposed peace, we want a united Muslim society with Sunnis and Shiites living together in peace and justice. . . . Baghdad has not been silenced." The Abu Hanifa mosque was also the site of a 10,000-strong demonstration protesting America's presence. Banners on the mosque's walls read "Pull out tanks, don't provoke people" and "No to Shiism, no to Sunnism—Yes to Islamic unity." American authorities should have been alarmed by these sentiments, because if the population of one of Baghdad's most Westernized and urbane districts aspired to erect an Islamic republic, the slums and countryside were sure to be far more radicalized.

A correspondent for French news agency AFP who talked to worshippers just outside the Abu Hanifa mosque on April 25 found them frustrated and uncompromisingly hostile to the United States. "We are running out of patience with the Americans here," Ammar al-Azami told AFP. "The Americans won't leave because they are after our oil, water, and land. They also want to settle here to protect Israel. But they're wrong to believe they'll succeed and that we'll stay silent. We were waiting for a Fatwa from our *ulemas* [Islamic leaders] to fight back." Another worshipper, Ala Hussein, added that the Americans "don't respect anything, not our land, not our people. They even shelled this mosque." He also stressed that the Iraqis were "keeping quiet just because our *ulemas* have asked us to." Some of the complaints against the United States were very pragmatic: a worshipper identified only as Ibrahim said, "The Americans came here to liberate us from Saddam, it's fine, but now what? There is no security, no electricity and chaos has taken over. . . . Our silence won't last. The day our *ulemas* tell us to fight, the Iraqi people, Sunnis and Shiites united, will rise in arms."

Other worshippers, AFP reported, used rhetoric that was considerably more militant. "We have weapons, we will blow ourselves up like the Palestinians," one man shouted. "There will be 100 Osama bin Ladens here if the Americans don't pull out," another angry man threatened. Significantly, the crowd supported the hostility.

The mainstream Arab media—government owned and reflecting the opinions of the ruling elites—were predicting an eruption of Islamist ter-

rorism and grassroots hostility toward the United States and accusing the
authorities in Iraq of insensitivity to local sentiments that was aggravating
an already explosive situation. Writing in the April 20 issue of *Arab News,*
which is affiliated with Crown Prince Abdallah, Abdulrahman Al-Rashed
accused America of unleashing the angry specter of militant Islam. "It
looks as if one consequence of Saddam's overthrow has been the collapse
of a secular Arabic regime. Iraq was a country that outclassed others in the
region, even Turkey, in eradicating fundamentalist movements. The
United States, which went so far in fragmenting the Taliban and chasing
al-Qaeda all over the world, has now freed Iraqi fundamentalism, both
Shiite and Sunni. It is equally paradoxical that the same Islamic fundamentalism always supported Saddam's regime, which itself represented
concepts that fundamentalism itself denounced and hated. . . . However,
let us admit that there is a political gap in the region, a gap which normally
the fundamentalists try to fill instead of leaving it to others, nationalists for
example, or liberal democrats."

Similarly, Mahmud Abdul-Karim, writing in the May 4 issue of *Al-
Ahram al-Masai,* owned by the Egyptian government, concluded that "coexistence between Iraqis [and] U.S. forces [was] impossible" because of the
grassroots hostility. "All the foregoing illustrate the gravity of the situation.
It shows also that occupation forces' exposure to fierce resistance will most
probably increase in the near future when the Iraqis begin to grasp what is
going on around them and get out of the state of amazement that many of
them are still in." Statements by the United States about the future of Iraq
"are meant to justify both the presence of U.S. troops in Iraq as long as
possible and the Anglo-American war against the brave Iraqi resistance
which Mr. Bush calls terrorist."

Thousands shouting anti-American slogans celebrated Saddam's
sixty-sixth birthday on April 28 in a noisy demonstration in Tikrit. Within
days, the Iraqi Resistance and Liberation Command, a Baathist entity, announced the start of a "war of attrition" against the U.S. occupation forces.
The Command issued a statement that Saddam "will send two handwritten messages, the first to the Iraqi people and the second to the people of
the Arab and Islamic Nation." In early May, an audiotape of Saddam surfaced, which had been circulating among his loyalists as well as Islamist
communities. (Saddam's reference to the birthday riots in Tikrit suggests
the tape was made around May 1.) On the recording, Saddam attempted to
gloss over the fall of Baghdad and concentrate on the escalation of the
anti-American struggle. "I do not want to bother you with a detailed talk

about the aggression, invasion, and occupation and how and why [that happened]. I am going to focus on how to confront the invaders to drive them out of our country," Saddam said. "In any case, going back to the secret action methods, which we began our life with, is the [appropriate] way for the Iraqis. Based on this, I am addressing you, my brothers, from inside glorious Iraq. I say to you—Arabs, Kurds, Turkman, Shiites, and Sunni people, Muslims and Christians, and people of all religions—that your main task is to kick the enemy out of our country. He who gives precedence to division over unity and seeks to disrupt ranks instead of unifying them is not only a servant of the foreign occupier, but also an enemy of God and people."

Meanwhile, Arab circles in London—both radical nationalists and Islamists—received several additional messages from Saddam Hussein and his confidants. Most important was a report on the communications between Saddam and the secretary of the Baath Party in Yemen, Qassam Salam. Saddam and Salam studied together in Egypt in the 1950s and have been good friends ever since; indeed, Salam stayed with Saddam in Baghdad throughout the war, leaving for Amman on April 12. Therefore, Salam's reading of both Saddam's and Iraq's situation was deemed highly accurate. Salam stressed that Saddam had gone underground in preparation for the struggle against the invading forces. Saddam told Salam that the preparatory period—the transfer from the anticipated battle for Baghdad to the forthcoming guerrilla war—would be longer than anticipated because he had to cope with the disastrous outcome of "the betrayal by the cowardly Republican Guards." Saddam and the patriotic resistance forces were nevertheless on the verge of launching an armed resistance that would deliver "harsh, decisive, and historical" strikes against the Americans. "To my knowledge, the resistance has not started yet, and the battle Saddam planned has not yet been waged. The preparations for that battle are still unfolding, and the millions of soldiers who evaded [fighting with the United States] are still there [to fight another day]," Salam stressed.

The Islamist forces—both foreign and Iraqi—were continuing to accelerate their operations in Baghdad and other Sunni cities. Several strikes and ambushes were launched on a daily basis, with the United States suffering a growing number of casualties. Far more important, these attacks caused a growing mistrust between the American forces and the Iraqi population around them, as increasingly drastic security measures alienated Iraqis, driving them into the fold of the Islamists. The May 5 report of the Arab mujahedin inside Iraq stressed that the building attrition was a pre-

cursor to a major escalation. "Their headquarters have divided the Mujahedin into groups to prepare for major operations against the American
troops," the report explained. "In Baghdad: The American troops in the
Iraqi capital were exhausted by relentless Mujahedin guerrilla operations
that aimed at two purposes in this stage; the first is strategic, which is to
keep engaging the Americans in fighting with the Mujahedin that will
never allow them to settle in Baghdad because of the losses they incur. The
second purpose is technical, which is to carry out varieties of large-scale
operations in order to keep the balance of power in the Mujahedin's favor."

The continued flow of foreign mujahedin and their growing prominence in anti-American terrorism all over Iraq was also being manifested
in the appearance of communiqués and statements from numerous Islamist organs loosely affiliated with al-Qaeda. Most important among
these publications was the May 5 statement of Hizb ut-Tahrir in Iraq, because of the party's prominence in Central Asia and Western Europe. "The
acceptance of occupation and the absence of the work for removing and
eliminating it is a great crime in the view of Islam. The cooperation with
the American occupiers, and the English occupiers attached to them, is a
greater crime. . . . Indeed Allah has categorically prohibited the Muslims
from allowing the *Kuffaar* to have authority over the Muslims' lands," the
communiqué decreed. Furthermore, no Iraqi government established by
the United States could be considered acceptable by Muslims. "No man-
made system will ever salvage the country; it rather increases its misfortune and hardships. You have tried the monarchical and republican
systems, and their like. They only brought you disgrace, oppression, and
injustice, from which you still suffer. Furthermore, these systems led the
country into the influence of the various foreign, disbelieving, colonialist
states. The wise person does not repeat again the cause of his misfortune
and hardship. Indeed, the believer must not be bitten from the same hole
twice."

For Hizb ut-Tahrir, the only viable solution was to capitalize on the escalating jihad in Iraq as the starting point for the reestablishment of the
Khilafah. The communiqué implied past cooperation with segments of the
Iraqi Army and security services, calling upon them to respond to the call.
"Hizb ut-Tahrir is present in Iraq, and it strongly struggled against the
manmade systems in its work to reestablish the *Khilafah*, where it was subject in that process to severe harm, harassment, imprisonment, torture,
and martyrdom. It is still present and undertakes the *Dawah* [awakening].
Hizb ut-Tahrir warmly calls you to stand with it and work with it; it re-

minds the influential people from among the army and outside the army of the times when they used to respond to the call to support it in establishing the *Khilafah*. They would answer by saying they were afraid of the loss of their life if they worked for the *Khilafah* due to the repression of the tyrants." With Saddam's regime toppled, the communiqué concluded, there was no reason for closeted Islamists in the military not to "heed the lesson from what took place in the past [and rush] to the support of Hizb ut-Tahrir and reestablishing the *Khilafah*." This call to jihad in Iraq by the leadership of Hizb ut-Tahrir would encourage many of its followers, primarily from Western Europe, to join the war.

Meanwhile, the growing hostility between the public and the American military was being exploited by the Islamist leadership—both locally and at the international level—to win over larger segments of the population. The grassroots reaction in Fallujah, an Islamist stronghold where clashes between Iraqis and U.S. forces resulted in numerous casualties, is indicative of the trend. The sermon on May 2 at the Great Mosque in Fallujah by Sheikh Jamal Shakir al-Nazzal elucidated Islamist sentiments: "What happened to us was not caused by the force of America. . . . What happened to us was because we distanced ourselves from Islam. It was not due to the power of the American forces, but because we followed Marxism and Socialism and violated the principles of Islam. . . . We have been unjust and have acted with tyranny, by means of the previous rulers. . . . We must awaken and return to Islam before the great catastrophes occur," Shiekh Nazal declared. "Why does America violate the sanctity of Islam in these lands? America, Britain, and others made a fuss when the Taliban destroyed the idols of Buddha—everyone knew what happened. But aren't emotions raging in the Arab, Islamic, and European countries over the blow to the sanctity of man in Iraq, in Baghdad, in our city, Fallujah? I ask you, American forces, have you found shells, missiles, [or] bombs in Fallujah, and is that why you are killing our children? . . . We say, we must act rationally and with faith, and according to the way of the Koran, the way of Muhammad. We call on the American forces to leave our city. We will protect our [own] people, city, and children."

Rather than address the rise of Islamist fervor, the U.S. authorities stubbornly concentrated on formally discrediting the remnants of the Baath Party. On May 11, the United States decreed that the coalition authorities would no longer "tolerate any activity" by the party. "The Arab Baath Socialist Party is dissolved," Gen. Tommy Franks said in a radio broadcast. "The apparatus of Iraqi security, intelligence, and military intelligence belonging to Saddam Hussein are deprived of their authority and power." Franks was stating the obvious, and few, if any, Iraqis genuinely cared. Instead, Saddam's supporters remained fiercely loyal to the man, if not the party, and actively prepared for the struggle ahead.

According to Iraqi opposition sources, Saddam, Qusay, Saddam's secretary Abid Hamid Humud, and a dozen or so regime leaders were wandering around the outskirts of Tikrit, frequently moving to different shelters, although Saddam's new center of power was in the area of Rabfiya in northeastern Iraq. "He is with his sons though not the entire time. He is traveling with a special escort and his former aides have no idea where is or what he is doing," Ahmad Chalabi told the London *Al-Sharq al-Awsat* on May 12. Saddam was enjoying the protection of numerous tribes and clans, and repeated Special Forces raids had failed to locate him. As for the anti-Saddam forces, they were also busy preparing for the conflict to come—readying to fight against the Americans and then join a fratricidal quest for power.

Indeed, May saw another jump in terrorism and subversion in Baghdad and other cities in the Sunni heartland. U.S. forces were suffering daily casualties, averaging one fatality a day. Iraqi security experts were increasingly worried that the situation was getting out of control. Noteworthy is the analysis of Dr. Sadun al-Dulaymi (a former brigadier general who defected in 1991 and had since served as an adviser for the Department of Defense), because he was Washington's favorite choice for minister of the interior, and would be responsible for internal security. "The situation in Iraq may lead to a civil war," al-Dulaymi warned. He noted that the initial American rush to enable "freedom" only contributed to the prevailing anarchy. Unchecked political activities and the uncontrollable return of exiles—particularly in the absence of indigenous police and security forces—enabled fringe elements to assume prominence. Moreover, the sole common denominator among all parties was hatred of the United States, and as a result, all the parties were now preparing to first evict the American occupiers and then fight each other for the right to determine Iraq's religious and political identity.

Al-Dulaymi noted that "parties that have come from abroad and others that have militias in Iraq are stockpiling weapons" and observed that the only reason "why any party would stockpile light, medium, and heavy weapons in warehouses" was that "they are preparing to use them against internal parties." He also warned that American "encouragement given to primitive tribal elements," ostensibly in order to counterbalance the Shiites, was only going to "turn Iraq into another Afghanistan." That al-Dulaymi is a senior member of the prominent Al-Dulaymi tribes only adds to the significance of his warning.

Saddam capitalized on the growing tension in Iraq, sending inflammatory letters to his followers. He urged the escalation of the armed resistance and close cooperation with the various Islamist movements. Saddam's May 7 letter, as received by the *Al-Quds al-Arabi*, urged all Iraqis to join the jihad because it was the winning trend. "Your brothers' Jihad has started to inflict successive losses daily on the criminal American and British enemy. Be with them because Allah is with them." Saddam called for the national mobilization of a fundamentally Muslim jihad involving all Iraqis, regardless of religion and ethnicity. "I call on you, the sons of Iraq, to make the mosques the centers for resistance and for coming to the aid of religion, Islam, and the homeland and to make the enemy feel that you hate him by word and deed. This great Iraq belongs to you all and not to one individual. It is a support for the Nation and Muslims and an inseparable part of them," Saddam concluded. In his May 9 letter, also sent to *Al-Quds al-Arabi*, Saddam alluded to his own harsh conditions. "I send this letter to you in the difficult conditions through which the nation is going, and Iraq is part of this nation. I write you this evening just before nightfall and without electricity. Writing is not an easy task in darkness. But the struggle will not stop, the resistance will not end, and the night must be followed by day."

Saddam went on to urge young Iraqis to take the lead in the struggle by launching a rebellion reminiscent of the first intifada. "As I urged the young men and women to carry out an operation against the cowardly and murderous enemy, I remembered all the bright moments in Islamic and Arab history. Such people make the future, as the sons of the Mujahid and great Palestinian people will make it." Saddam pointed to the help several Arab governments gave the United States during the war, and, using Islamist terms, urged all Arabs to rebel against their own governments. "You are the hope, not the regimes. If the Iraqi leadership had suffered all this because of its national and pan-Arab stances against imperialism and Zionism, then the road of Jihad will continue for this leadership that has chosen its slogan to be martyrs in the cause of Allah," Saddam concluded.

The regional jihad was indeed about to erupt.

12
THE ASCENT OF IRAN AND
THE RETURN OF OSAMA BIN LADEN

In early May, Tehran was fairly satisfied with the situation inside Iraq. The United States had clearly failed to gain popular support and legitimacy for its occupation, and the former opposition in exile was completely discredited. The Shiites had emerged as the strongest, best-organized, and most vibrant element of society. Since "the million-strong turnout of Iraqi Shiites in the city of Qarbalah [took place] only several days after the occupation of the whole of Iraq and the fall of Baghdad," said Iranian commentator A. S. Hoseyni, "this religious spectrum showed itself off to the occupiers. . . . Therefore, the Iraqi Shiites are duty bound to make the best of this tremendous achievement rather than bring in peripheral issues and thereby stop this newly formed fruit from ripening."

With Tehran's encouragement, the Shiite population was increasingly involved in grassroots resistance, albeit largely nonviolent. For example, Iranian sources closely following events inside Iraq noted that the predominantly Shiite population of Baghdad, al-Fallujah, Nasiriyah, Al-Amarah, Qarbalah, and Basra climbed up on the rooftops of mosques and houses and chanted "God is Great" every time an American or British patrol was in sight.

Nevertheless, pragmatists in Tehran remained apprehensive that the United States would not permit the Shiites to rule Iraq by virtue of their undisputed majority. The Iranians were alarmed when the Shiite leaders of the INC—the most pro-U.S. former opposition movement—gave up on the possibility of assuming power, even as a puppet regime. "There is a serious intention [by the United States] not to enable any Shiite figure to rule Iraq and not to allow a government that has a Shiite majority," INC leadership member Nizar Haydar told *Al-Sharq al-Awsat*. He noted that the United States had gained the support of the opposition by committing to "the establishment of a democratic regime" in post-Saddam Iraq. "This means that the people will govern themselves and therefore the scale will tilt toward the majority. But the INC has received confirmed information that there is an agreement to exclude the Shiites from power," Haydar stated. Tehran needed no further proof of an American anti-Shiite bias.

Tehran decided to move prudently, inserting a viable Shiite leadership and avoiding as much direct confrontation with the American occupation authorities as possible. The Iranians then launched a "charm offensive" in order to assuage many regional powers. The conservative Gulf States were Iran's top priority because their Sunni ruling families are constantly afraid of popular uprisings by their predominantly Shiite populations. Moreover, since the Iranian Revolution of 1979, Tehran and Imam Baqir al-Hakim had organized and incited Shiites throughout the Arabian Peninsula, and Tehran could not ignore this background when trying to empower Baqir al-Hakim in Iraq. Hence, Muhammad Baqir al-Hakim gave an interview to the May 4 Jeddah *Ukaz* aimed at placating the Saudis. He explained that "the U.S. and British forces are unable to maintain security and stability in the aftermath of Saddam" and went on to say that "The United Nations should take part in this mission because several local and foreign parties are trying to sow dissent among the Iraqis." Al-Hakim hoped that Saudi Arabia and other neighbors of Iraq would work jointly to help establish a "people's government" in Baghdad.

Iraqi Shiites also maintained a generally conciliatory approach, promising to help the American authorities as long as their legitimate interests were secured—that is, that a Shiite-dominated government would be established quickly. To further defuse tension, Tehran announced on May 5 that Ayatollah Sayyid Muhammad Baqir al-Hakim would resign his political post as SCIRI chief once he returned to Iraq and instead would assume a leading theological and legal position with no formal power. Al-Hakim reiterated that "SCIRI is prepared for any kind of participation in a government chosen by the Iraqi nation."

At the same time, Tehran remained certain that the establishment of an Iraqi regime friendly to the United States would be extremely dangerous to the mullahs. Speaking in an internal forum of SCIRI and other Tehran-sponsored and controlled groups, Ayatollah Baqir al-Hakim stressed the importance of constructing an Iran-style regime in Baghdad. "The future of Iraq belongs to Islam and we shall not refrain from any efforts along the path of securing Iraq's independence," he declared. "Our objectives are independence, realizing the will of the Iraqi people, implementation of justice, endeavoring to rebuild and develop our country, and establishment of good relations with our neighbors and friendly states." To ensure the implementation of such plans, Tehran imposed strict discipline on the Iraqi opposition groups in order to ensure close cooperation and compliance with their strategic instructions.

Similarly, the Islamist authorities in Qom were apprehensive that the consolidation of a less rigid theological elite in Najaf—arguably the traditional heart of Shiite Islam—of the kind advocated by Ayatollah Sistani might reduce Iran's influence. Iran considered it imperative to ensure the presence of pro-Qom Shiite luminaries in the Iraqi heartland, and the return of Ayatollah Baqir al-Hakim would largely solve this problem.

In May, the clandestine deployment of Pasdaran and Pasdaran-controlled elements to such cities as Qarbalah Najaf, and Nasiriyah could only counterbalance, and not overwhelm, American influence. Iranian leaders were convinced that only terrorism could defeat the United States and consequently undermine its grand designs.

Tehran had no illusions about Washington's desire to keep the military in Iraq for several years to come and was convinced that a wave of terrorism could compel the United States to withdraw. A May 10 editorial by Heshmatollah Falahat-Pisheh in the Tehran *Resalat* closely reflected the opinions of Iran's national security elite, particularly Khamenei and Hashemi-Rafsanjani:

> The American military remaining in Iraq is horrible news for the people of the Persian Gulf and the Middle East. Of course, during the past 55 years, wherever the Americans have carried out military operations, they have remained there unless the operations ended with a defeat for America, such as the cases in Vietnam, Somalia, Lebanon, and Tabas in Iran. Based on these historical experiences, we can predict that any plan that will be presented by Washington for the future of the Middle East assumes the military forces of that country will remain in the region. This is unless the will of the opponents of an American military presence impose another defeat on that power and force them out. Therefore, the future of the relations between America and the Middle East will be formed based on at least two different paths—either this sensitive region must accept America's imposed plans or in the future a chain of protest wars will take place [against] the occupying army.

Falahat-Pisheh also wrote that there was no alternative to quickly launching a guerrilla war against the United States: "If the countries of the region do not act to oppose America's rapid military deployment and turning the Middle East into the largest gathering place of that power's military, in the future they will suffer from a large part of the crises and crisis-makings in the world."

If the initial resistance to the United States was successful, though, Falahat-Pisheh believed it could serve as the springboard for a region-wide rejection of the United States. "The accelerated . . . removal of foreigners in the Middle Eastern countries is also an undeniable reality that must be institutionalized and implemented. The slogan of the people of Iraq about the necessity to end American's military presence has become widespread in the Middle East. This reality sees fit to heighten the actions by those opposed to the military presence of foreigners."

Meanwhile, with Ayatollah Baqir al-Hakim returning to Iraq, the SCIRI leadership continued their charm offensive in the Arab media. On May 10, al-Jazeera interviewed Abdulaziz al-Hakim, deputy chairman of SCIRI, in Baghdad about the ayatollah's anticipated role in Iraq. "[Ayatollah Baqir] Al-Hakim will remain a religious and political authority. He will address political issues. He will lead the Iraqi people politically. He will offer them guidance, particularly since he enjoys a special standing among the Iraqi people. I am not saying that he enjoys this status only among the ranks of the followers of the household of Prophet Muhammad [the Shiites], but also among all Iraqis, be they Iraqi Sunnis, Kurds, or Turkman. We maintain strong ties with the latter groups, who hold us in high esteem," Abdulaziz al-Hakim stated. Furthermore, on May 10, Bayan Jabr, officially in charge of SCIRI's Arab relations, gave an interview to *Al-Sharq al-Awsat* on SCIRI's political objectives and plans, emphasizing the pragmatic and conciliatory nature of the council's policies: "We opposed the war and demanded the regime's removal. We stressed that the war would hurt our people and interests. But it happened and no country in the world, not even those that have a veto in the Security Council, could stop the United States from launching it. We are therefore dealing with the reality. There are foreign forces occupying the country and we must do everything that is in our power to form a national government and then start a direct dialogue with Washington to hold free elections and form a parliament. Then the U.S. forces must leave Iraq," Bayan Jabr declared. The sentiments expressed in his interview cannily prepared the way for Baqir al-Hakim's first public appearance in Iraq.

On May 11, Ayatollah Muhammad Baqir al-Hakim arrived in Basra, the first stop in an emotionally loaded return to Najaf, after twenty-three years of exile in Iran. His return had a major impact on the Shiite posture in Iraq. Baqir al-Hakim entered Iraq quietly. He avoided inflammatory gestures and speeches, only at times waving to the crowd. In all his public statements he remained moderate—identifying as his priorities the destruction of the legacy of the Baath Party and the restoration of safety and prosperity for the entire Iraqi people. He did mention the need to get the invading forces out of Iraq, but judiciously omitted any mention of the necessary means. He repeated his call for the empowerment of the Iraqi people in a democratic fashion (but did not address the transparent logic behind it, namely, the empowerment of Iraq's Shiite majority). Moreover, the discussion of ensuring "safety" and "security" for the population became Baqir al-Hakim's favorite euphemism for sustaining the Badr Corps and other Shiite forces. Ultimately, Baqir al-Hakim's triumphant return to the Shiite heartland was conducted so professionally there was nothing the occupation authorities could complain about. The Shiite population, though, had no doubt whatsoever about the essence of Baqir al-Hakim's message and objectives.

Instead of authorizing Shiite forces to rebel against American and British control, Iran prioritized active support for all forms of Sunni terrorism—from the Baathist fedayeen to al-Qaeda Islamists. The Iranians would give preferential assistance to the Islamists, particularly groups that were affiliated with al-Qaeda, because they trusted their uncompromising zeal and hatred of the United States. This allowed Iran some room for plausible deniability and provided extra justification for Shiite rule.

Iran continued to look the other way as the Islamists crossed its borders on their way to Iraq, and now permitted them to run forward headquarters and logistical support centers for operations throughout Iraq and the Arabian Peninsula. However, to further deflect attention from Tehran, the Iranians insisted that the Islamists would build on prewar Iraqi activities and would not receive direct orders on new missions from Iran. At the same time, Tehran helped Damascus establish a joint Syrian and Hizb-Allah support system that provided for both Sunni and Shiite terrorists. The Syrian infrastructure also oversaw the arrival of volunteer mujahedin from all over the Arab world, without definitively implicating Tehran.

Iran further resolved to play a major facilitating role in regional destabilization, expanding its efforts beyond Iraq. Tehran's objective was to prevent the United States from establishing pro-American regimes throughout the Persian Gulf and Arabian Peninsula, and its working assumption was that regardless of the extent of insurgency and terrorism in Iraq, the United States would still be able to hold on to a few key military bases from which it would be possible to project power into Iran. However, unstable monarchies and emirates would most likely demand that American forces leave, hoping to placate local fundamentalists. Moreover, the aggregate threat of sabotage to all facets of the energy infrastructure in Iraq, the Persian Gulf, and the Arabian Peninsula would untenably strain the West's economy, generating tremendous pressure on the United States to compromise and defuse the crisis. Tehran concluded that major threats to local regimes, under the guise of anti-American Islamist terrorism, would lead most rulers to disengage from the United States in order to preserve their own power.

To achieve this ambitious goal, Tehran embarked on a most audacious gambit, providing Osama bin Laden and several of his closest aides and senior commanders with safe haven from which to unleash terrorism against Iraq, Saudi Arabia, and the Gulf sheikhdoms. This was considerably different from Iran's ongoing passive assistance, such as transferring mujahedin from Afghanistan and Pakistan to the Iraqi border, or providing shelter to the members of Ansar al-Islam after they clashed with American units in Iraqi Kurdistan. As of May, Iran would serve as the operational center for a major terrorist offensive with grand strategic objectives. Furthermore, once the forward headquarters were discovered by Western intelligence services, it would be very difficult for Tehran to deny that it hadn't provided, at the very least, tacit support for their construction.

Ultimately, the campaign was so crucial for the survival of the mullahs' regime in Tehran that Iran's leaders were determined to take all risks to facilitate the Islamist offensive. Reflecting its importance, execution of the conspiracy was put under the direct supervision of Intelligence Minister Ali Yunesi with close cooperation from the IRGC.

Tehran's decision was quite logical considering the long cooperation between the Pasdaran, Iranian intelligence, and Osama bin Laden—a relationship that had been institutionalized in 1996 with the establishment of HizbAllah International and vastly expanded since the summer of 2000. In the aftermath of September 11 and the attack on Afghanistan, the Iranians had helped al-Qaeda salvage numerous networks and facilities. "After the Afghanistan events and the Taliban's downfall, the Iranian Revolutionary

Guards decided to maintain a link with al-Qaeda and embraced many of its members after they had fled from Afghanistan. The Guards safeguarded many of the organization's leaders and even sheltered several prominent ones, provided them with the facilities to enter and leave the country, and turned a blind eye to many violations of Iran's border," said Libyan Islamist Numan bin-Uthman. The Iranian authorities permitted al-Qaeda to maintain several compounds in Tehran, Mashhad, and Zahedan. These compounds were under the protection of the IRGC.

By spring, al-Qaeda already had an operational group of about twenty commanders in Iran. The group shuttled between a Special Revolutionary Guard guesthouse in the Namak Abroud area north of Tehran, and a safe house in Torbat-e Heydariyeh in northeast Iran. Among the key members of this leadership group were Saad bin Osama bin Laden (Osama's son), Sayf-al-Adl (one of al-Qaeda's senior military chiefs), and Muhammad Shawqi al-Islambuli (aka Abu-Khalid, one of the leaders of Ayman al-Zawahiri's inner circle and the chief representative of al-Qaeda's intelligence in Iran, where he had been stationed for almost five years). Another long-term resident of Iran, Mustafa Hamzah (aka Abu-Hazim), replaced Abu-Khalid as the al-Qaeda "resident" in Iran in early summer.

As the war drew near, additional senior officials moved into Iran. Among the first to arrive was Abu-Musab al-Zarqawi—a Jordanian, and one of al-Qaeda's leading experts on weapons of mass destruction—who crossed the border from northern Iraq. In Tehran, Zarqawi was nominated chief of operations in and against Israel. Another key commander to arrive was Mahfuz Ould Waleed (aka Abu-Hafts), a Mauritanian. Once Tehran committed to the major escalation after the fall of Baghdad, the top leaders of al-Qaeda were invited to Iran in order to coordinate the escalation personally. A group of seven chiefs—including Osama bin Laden, Ayman al-Zawahiri, and Suleiman Abu-Ghayth, an al-Qaeda spokesman—arrived in Tehran in early May. Another commander who was in Tehran at the time is known only as Al-Qassimi, al-Qaeda's new chief of operations in the Persian Gulf and the Horn of Africa. Bin Laden and his aides were all housed in a special compound of Pasdaran safe houses, and were escorted to high-level meetings with the key leaders of Iran. According to eyewitnesses, bin Laden, Zawahiri, and their key aides were dressed like Pakistani Pashtuns. They had all trimmed their beards, nearly shaved their heads, and seemed to have added enough weight to alter their figures.

The Iranians went to such great lengths to host the most wanted man in the world and his entourage because they needed bin-Laden's authority to capitalize and even expand on the Iraqi intelligence operations that began in early 2003. The Iraqis were actively assisting al-Qaeda with strikes inside Saudi Arabia because, just like Tehran, Baghdad sought to exploit Islamist terrorism throughout the Arabian Peninsula in order to increase pressure on the United States, ultimately forcing the Americans to quit the region or, at the very least, make American hegemony illegitimate.

The original Iraqi program was very ambitious: In fall 2002, Unit 999 deployed (among other components) the Saudi Battalion, a group of some three hundred Saudi terrorists, to forward bases between Nasiriyah and the Saudi border, and the Naval Battalion, another three hundred terrorists from several Gulf sheikhdoms and emirates, to forward bases between Basra and the Kuwaiti border. Starting in early 2003, and increasingly as the war became imminent, Lt. Gen. Ali Hassan al-Majid, the Nasiriyah-based commander of southern Iraq, emptied the terrorist garrisons and training camps around Nasiriyah and, to a lesser extent, Fallujah. The terrorists, most of them from Saudi Arabia as well as elsewhere in the Gulf, were provided with numerous pickup trucks and SUVs full of weapons, explosives, and cash. They were then helped by Iraqi military intelligence to infiltrate Saudi Arabia—mainly through the northern Saudi province of Jawf, which borders southwestern Iraq.

To expedite the infiltration, Iraqi Intelligence helped the Islamists escalate a wave of terrorism, they had previously launched but could not sustain. In September 2002, an Islamist hit team assassinated Abdul Rahman Al-Suhaybani—a Saudi judge well known for his work combating subversion—in al-Jawf as he was leaving a mosque after Friday prayers. Although the Saudi security authorities did not capture any suspects at the time, the key members of the network had to escape by hiding in the desert, and their operations virtually ceased.

In early 2003, Iraqi intelligence helped the local networks sustain operations (through additional training for Saudi terrorists and the provision of weapons, equipment, and expertise in confronting security authorities). At the core of the new campaign was a series of assassination attempts against Saudi security officials, in order to preoccupy the authorities and divert their attention from the massive infiltrations from Iraq. The deputy governor of Jawf Province, Hamad al-Wardi, was assassinated in February on his way to his office. In March, a police officer was killed in Jawf Province, in the town of Sakaka. In April, Lt. Col. Hamoud Ali al-Rabie, the director of a police station in Sakaka, was shot dead as he returned from work. The Saudi security authorities concluded that "the killings appear to be the work of Islamic gunmen linked to al-Qaeda."

The emerging Islamist forces in Saudi Arabia were part of the reconstituted, post-9/11 al-Qaeda. New networks were rebuilt along local lines with greater emphasis put on domestic issues. The reason for this shift was the growing reliance on terrorist elements untainted by the Afghanistan and Pakistan-based training and global organizational system and therefore less likely to be identified by Western intelligence; if captured, they could not compromise networks or individuals in the West. Only top operational managers were still being drawn from a small, centralized cadre of highly trained terrorists.

In the case of Saudi Arabia, the local networks were organized in a new group called Al-Muwahhidun, commonly referred to as "al-Qaeda 2." The group's ideology is quite similar to bin Laden's, but operationally the Al-Muwahhidun networks focus on terrorism in the Arabian Peninsula and the Persian Gulf. Its spiritual guide was Sheikh Ali Bin-Khudayr al-Khudayr, forty-nine, a disciple of Saudi clerics rather than the pan-Islamist clerics who influenced bin Laden. However, both al-Khudayr and bin Laden considered themselves the disciples of the same Saudi luminaries—particularly the late Sheikh Humud al-Aqla al-Shuaybi (who died under mysterious circumstances in 2002, reportedly assassinated by the Saudi authorities).

Most of the expert cadres of Al-Muwahhidun were trained in Afghanistan, Pakistan, and Iraq, but by spring 2003, well over three hundred operatives had been recruited inside Saudi Arabia. The local character of the new group made it exceptionally dangerous to the House of al-Saud because of its grassroots support from segments of society that were reluctant to get involved in global jihad but that nonetheless hated the royal family because of its corruption and un-Islamic ways. By spring, the Saudi Islamists recently arrived from Iraq were natural reinforcements for the expanding networks and cells of Al-Muwahhidun.

By May, Tehran wanted to cooperate closely with and perhaps even harness Al-Muwahhidun and comparable networks all over the region. Prudently, the Iranians had no theological demands for these networks but offered tremendous assistance in return for operational cooperation. Nevertheless, the al-Qaeda-affiliated Islamists needed consent to enter into a partnership with the Shiite Iranians, and most of the Sunni commanders insisted that they needed bin Laden's approval. In Tehran, bin Laden provided exactly that assurance, and working together, Iranian intelligence and al-Qaeda were able to accomplish much more than just a dramatic escalation in terrorism in Saudi Arabia.

In early May, Iranian intelligence and al-Qaeda exploited the still innocuous nature of travel to Saudi Arabia, in order to brief Islamist leaders from both the Arab world and Western Europe on postwar strategy. The meeting took place in Jeddah, with participants arriving under a wide range of commercial and academic covers. An emissary delivered a special message from Osama bin Laden to the gathered commanders, which urged them to capitalize on the current turmoil, and promised extensive support.

"In the course of the meeting," according to senior European intelligence officials, "a decision was unanimously taken to carry out attacks not only against U.S., British, and Israeli interests, but also against groups of Western tourists, security officials, and military, political, and religious leaders in the Arab countries that are considered to be collaborators of the West." The nations topping the list were Saudi Arabia, the Gulf States, Jordan, Egypt, and Morocco.

Meanwhile, the Islamist teams that had come from Iraq linked up with the support networks and local cells inside Saudi Arabia and began to actively prepare their operations, On May 1, U.S. intelligence was sufficiently worried about the growing terrorist threat in Saudi Arabia to issue a formal warning regarding an imminent strike, particularly against Americans and other foreigners working in the kingdom. The next day an American contractor was shot four times in the abdomen while working at the King Abdul Aziz naval base near al-Jubail.

The Islamist terrorists launched their offensive against the House of al-Saud on May 6 with a bold attempt by two detachments to assassinate Defense Minister Prince Sultan Bin Abdul Aziz and Interior Minister Prince Nayef Bin Abdul Aziz. The plan called for small units of armed mujahedin to fight their way to the immediate vicinity of the princes so that suicide bombers could get close enough to kill them and their entourages in the process. The plan failed when the princes' security detachments held their ground in the initial phase of the assault. The shoot-out with the bodyguards quickly evolved into a series of intense firefights all over Riyadh as larger security forces chased the withdrawing terrorists to safe houses and hideaways. At least three major clashes continued for some thirty-six hours before the Islamist terrorists were able to evade the security forces and vanish. On May 8, Saudi Arabia announced it had forestalled a wave of Islamist terrorism in the kingdom. Yet nineteen would-be terrorists were still missing, and for the first time the Saudi authorities asked for public assistance in locating them.

Among the wanted was a senior supervisor from al-Qaeda with a Canadian passport. The leader of the cell, Khaled Muhammad al-Jahani, was a veteran of Afghanistan and Iraq (where he was trained by both Ansar al-Islam and Unit 999), who answered directly to Sayf al-Adl. In spring 2003, he shuttled between Riyadh, Jeddah, and Damascus to prepare for the major terrorist offensive. In the one safe house discovered by Saudi security organs, they found that the cell had accumulated a large amount of weapons, including the advanced RDX explosive, a standard supply in HizbAllah stockpiles in Syria, which could be used for major sabotage operations. The mere presence of RDX in this house proved cooperation between the Saudi Islamists, HizbAllah, and therefore HizbAllah's sponsoring states—Iran and Syria. The cell also had five computers and a number of telecommunications devices in the safe house. On May 9, Western intelligence experts interpreted the capture of the Saudi network as a proof that "al-Qaeda has revived operations in Saudi Arabia in an effort to overthrow the Saudi monarchy."

Bin Laden struck at the center of Riyadh in the predawn hours of May 13. Five car bombs exploded in key Western compounds in Riyadh, killing ninety-five people (ten of the dead were Americans) and wounding well over two hundred. Between nine and twelve suicide bombers and over sixty terrorists were involved in these attacks. The complex and multifaceted operation succeeded despite American warnings and Saudi sweeps in the aftermath of the previous week's street fights.

The first four car bombs exploded almost simultaneously around 1 A.M. The attacks were directed at the well-protected Garnata, Cordoba, and Ishbiliya compounds in eastern Riyadh, where key westerners live. Each of the strikes involved numerous suicide terrorists and hit teams equipped with small arms. The first three attacks were well coordinated and highly professional; with the exception of the martyr bombers, virtually all the attackers were able to escape into the night. In one case a suicide car bomb breached the gate and another followed, blowing up near an apartment building; in another, an attack team including suicide bombers took out the compound guards and opened the gate for the car bomb. The car bombs themselves contained powerful, highly sophisticated charges and fuel tanks, composite charges usually associated with Iranian operatives. The three bombing strikes evolved into protracted ten- to fifteen-minute shoot-outs with the security forces that failed to prevent the terrorists' escape.

The fifth car bomb exploded around 3 A.M. near the office building for Vinnell—an American company training Crown Prince Abdallah's National Guard. There, some of the terrorists that approached the gates wore National Guard uniforms, drove official cars, and carried standard-issue weapons. Significantly, they had the electronic access codes to the gates, all of which implies the active involvement of the guardsmen. Once the terrorists entered the gate, it took less than one minute for a bomber to drive a truck with a 440-pound bomb to the Vinnell complex and blow himself up. The selection of the Vinnell complex was a personal affront to Crown Prince Abdallah. He had been embarrassed—and just a few hours before Colin Powell arrived in Riyadh.

The May 13 operation was claimed by Abu-Muhammad al-Ablaj (aka Mullah Sayf-ad-Din) in the name of al-Qaeda. "The execution of this plan was not hampered by the recent announcement by the Saudi authorities of the seizure of large quantities of arms and explosives in the kingdom and the hunt for 19 people," al-Ablaj wrote in an e-mail. "Among the priorities of al-Qaeda's new strategy, besides strikes at the heart of the United States, are operations in the Gulf countries and countries allied to America, particularly Egypt and Jordan. These operations will target air bases, warships, [and] military camps everywhere on the Arabian Peninsula and in the Gulf."

Indeed, several Islamist networks in Saudi Arabia were known to be preparing for other strikes, including major attacks on oil fields and installations under the supervision of American and Canadian citizens. Bin Laden timed this attack to coincide with the formal ending of the war in Iraq and the beginning of America's effort to impose a new Middle East. Powell's visit was intended to highlight the announcement that the United States would start to transfer forces from Saudi Arabia to Qatar. As a result, the shock of the bombings overshadowed what could have been a day of grand achievement for Crown Prince Abdallah, long an advocate of an American withdrawal and Saudi Arabia assuming responsibility for regional defense.

The initial investigation of the incidents confirmed that members of the Saudi security forces, particularly the National Guard, were among the perpetrators, and U.S. intelligence officials warned Washington about the extent of al-Qaeda's penetration of the Saudi defense establishment.

"The only area where there is no evidence of a significant al-Qaeda presence is the Saudi Royal Air Force," an American intelligence official told MENL's Steve Rodan. "The police, army, navy, National Guard, and all the rest have been infiltrated by al-Qaeda." On May 20, George Tenet visited Riyadh secretly to assure Saudi-U.S. cooperation in the investigation and to assess the possibility of follow-up attacks, including ones that might include the use of WMD stolen or transferred from Iraq.

Meanwhile, Iran's knowledge of and involvement in the strikes in Riyadh was becoming apparent. Just before the bombings, there was a flurry of telephone communications between Riyadh and safe houses in Iran, indicating last-minute consultations with the al-Qaeda leadership. A few days before the bombing, the Pasdaran moved around twenty al-Qaeda commanders, including Muhammad al-Islambuli, Sayf-al-Adl, and Saad bin Osama bin Laden, from their safe house near the Caspian Sea to a facility in Zabol, in Iranian Baluchistan near the Afghan border, providing for the possibility that they might have to escape Iran. On the eve of the Riyadh attacks, Sulayman Abu-Ghayth was also moved to Zabol. Osama bin Laden, however, was seen in Tehran.

A few days after the Riyadh bombing, once the United States had accumulated evidence of Iranian complicity and warned Iran accordingly, Tehran decided to temper the confrontation. The Higher National Security Council convened in Tehran and decided to transfer some of the al-Qaeda commanders whose presence was known to the United States to a known haven for terrorists in Pakinsy Gore, on the Georgia-Chechnya border. These commanders were given new Iranian and Turkish documents and sent via Armenia to Georgia, where they were helped by local al-Qaeda cadres.

Meanwhile, the initial dragnet of the Saudi security forces failed to halt al-Qaeda's activities. Clashes and sporadic gunfights intensified throughout the kingdom, and major terrorist strikes were also attempted. On May 20, for example, three Moroccans were captured in the Jeddah airport trying to board a plane to Khartoum, carrying improvised knives and wills with them. (Other Saudi sources insist the three had suicide vests on or with them when apprehended.) After what the Saudis termed "intense interrogation," and "special treatment," two of the Moroccans claimed they were going to hijack the plane and crash it into a major objective near Jeddah. The third Moroccan insisted they were going to crash the airliner into Tel Aviv, or if blocked, into Eilat. Indeed, the Israeli Air Force scrambled fighters and conducted preventive patrols of the Gulf of Eilat for the next few days.

U.S. intelligence considered the Jeddah arrest a small victory in a larger campaign. On May 21, Washington formally warned Riyadh of an imminent terrorist attack by al-Qaeda or a local offshoot. The next day, U.S. intelligence refined its warning, stating that "al-Qaeda is believed to be targeting Saudi oil fields for attack." Islamist networks were detected at the Saudi oil facility at Ras Tanura, the largest oil complex in the world. Repeated raids by the Saudi security authorities forced the assailants away from the oil field, but none were apprehended.

By late May, the Islamist elite had decided to highlight its role in the rapidly escalating terrorism campaign all over the world. In addition to the strikes in Riyadh, the Islamists also struck in the space of a few days at Tel Aviv, Casablanca, and Grozny, using multiple suicide bombers in each strike. However, with Osama bin Laden still in Tehran, it would have been imprudent to embarrass their Iranian hosts, and therefore Ayman al-Zawahiri, whose presence in Iran was not advertised, delivered a public announcement. In a taped message that surfaced on May 21, Zawahiri articulated al-Qaeda's latest offensive in the context of the situation in Iraq. He warned that the entire Muslim world was being threatened by "the crusade campaign" motivated by "the U.S. president's thirst for blood" and charged that the United States was adamant about occupying and further dismembering all key Muslim powers in order to have Israel subjugate the Muslim world on its behalf. "After dividing Iraq, Saudi Arabia, Iran, Syria, and Pakistan will come next. They would leave around Israel only dismembered semistates that are subservient to the United States and Israel," Zawahiri declared. He added that the Arab rulers who provided direct and indirect help to the American war bore special responsibility for the plight of the entire Arab world and should therefore be dealt with by their own people.

Appealing to all Muslims, Ayman al-Zawahiri stressed that only a violent global eruption could reverse the American onslaught on the Muslim world. "Nothing will do you good but toting arms and taking revenge against your enemies, the Americans and the Jews." All forms of protest, he reiterated, "will not protect your jeopardized holy places or expel an occupying enemy, nor will they deter an arrogant aggressor. The Crusaders and the Jews do not understand but the language of killing and blood. They do not become convinced unless they see coffins returning to them, their interests being destroyed, their towers being torched, and their economy collapsing." Zawahiri urged all Muslims to attack Western "interests, companies, and employees" throughout the world and "Burn the ground under their feet, as they should not enjoy your protection, safety, or security. Expel those criminals out of your countries." Addressing the Iraqi people, Zawahiri implored them to study the various Islamist campaigns and use them as guides for a jihad against the United States. "We defeated those Crusaders several times before and expelled them out of our countries and holy shrines. You should know that you are not alone in this battle. Your mujahid brothers are tracking your enemies and lying in wait for them. The mujahedin in Palestine, Afghanistan, and Chechnya and even in the heart of America and the West are causing death to those Crusaders. The coming days will bring to you the news that will heal your breasts, God willing," Zawahiri concluded.

Meanwhile, the Saudi security forces were making progress in their investigation of the Riyadh bombing. The "intense interrogations" of suspects and family members led them, in the predawn hours of May 28, to an Internet Café in Medina. Storming the café, they killed three leaders of both al-Muwahhidun and al-Qaeda, among them one of al-Muwahhidun's military commanders. Abdul-Rahman al-Faqasi al-Ghamidi, widely considered to be the brains behind the Riyadh bombings, and the real target of the Medina raid, managed to escape along with another senior operative. Away from the security forces, al-Ghamidi used his cell phone to call an emergency access number that, via untraceable land relays, got him directly to Osama bin Laden. Al-Ghamidi broke the news that two of bin Laden's closest friends had just been martyred, and a shaken bin Laden said he would immediately convene the leadership council for an emergency session. Although it was impossible to electronically locate bin Laden's whereabouts, sources suggested he was near the Iran-Afghanistan-Pakistan border at the time, and this information, once intercepted, was passed immediately to the United States.

That day, al-Qaeda e-mailed an unprecedented communiqué to Arab newspapers announcing that the organization would soon avenge the assassination of its Saudi brethren by targeting the leading princes of the kingdom for assassination. "Sheikh Osama and the leaders of al-Qaeda in Afghanistan are closely following reports of the deaths of Sheikh Ali al-Khudayr and Ahmad al-Khaldi [both killed in the raid on the café]," the e-mail said. "If it was especially confirmed that Sheikh Ali al-Khudayr was martyred, then our response against the al-Saud family will be as great as the sheikh is to us." Throughout May 29, after the publication of the communiqué, there was intense, even unprecedented, traffic of encrypted messages throughout the Islamist community in the Middle East.

Against the background of the mounting crisis in Saudi Arabia, Tehran closely studied its next moves in relation to the continued American presence in Iraq. Before committing to any profound policy change, Tehran instructed a team of experts from the Center for Doctrinal Security without Borders—Iran's main doctrinal authority—led by the center's chief, Dr. Hassan Abbassi, to study the strategic posture in the region and recommend solutions.

On May 20, Abbassi presented the results at the center, stating that the war in Iraq should be viewed as an extremely threatening global dynamic. "The West, led by America, is seeking a special [world] order in which the Muslim nations carry out their commands," Abbassi declared. He presented an apocalyptic view of the overall ramifications of the war on terrorism, saying that "The difference between this war and previous wars is that this war began between Islamic civilization and the civilization of the West, while previous wars began within Western civilization."

Abbassi had no doubt that the West was bent on ultimately subjugating the entire Muslim world. However, in the first phase, priority would be given to confronting the regional powers in the Middle East capable of endangering Israel, "and Syria, Iran, and Saudi Arabia will be next." Dr. Abbassi went on to severely criticize the noninterventionist policies of the Iranian Ministry of Foreign Affairs regarding the war in Afghanistan and Iraq: "The fact that you are saying we should not give the enemy a pretext [to attack Iran] will put us to shame more each day, and the more we back down, the more they will still find pretexts," he warned the attending diplomats. Abbassi argued that continued restraint would soon prove detrimental to the very existence of Iran. Pointing to the heroic precedents set by HizbAllah and the Palestinian mujahedin, Abbassi stressed that millions of Iranians were eager to embrace martyrdom in defense of their country and Islam, concluding his address by declaring, "The world is looking for a hero, and you must now try to be those heroes."

Subsequent deliberations among Iran's national security team refined two tenets of their strategy. The first and most often repeated tenet was to make Iraq ungovernable, severely impeding America's ability to confront Iran. The other tenet was to capitalize on the Muslim world's increasingly negative reaction to an American presence in Iraq in order to consolidate Iran's own posture as the leading power preventing the United States from completely dominating the region.

This audacious strategy was articulated by Mohsen Rezai in an internal presentation in May. "The struggle against America should not be interpreted as an attempt to keep a group of people in power. On the contrary, it [this struggle] should be guided toward transforming Iran into a power in the region." Rezai emphasized that Tehran's response to the crisis in Iraq must be dominated by long-term strategic considerations at the same level as Washington's grander objectives. "The events in Afghanistan and Iraq are two links of the same chain. America's plan for the region consists of two parts. One is to change the region's regimes and the other is to replace some regimes so that they are under its control." At the same time, he noted, the United States had always been reluctant to abide pain in pursuit of its objectives. Addressing this point, Rezai argued that Saddam had played precisely into Washington's hands. "A combination of simplemindedness and deceit stopped Saddam from facing the Americans. A war wouldn't have occurred in that country if America had felt that the Iraqi people or army would resist. The Americans occupied Iraq very easily. However, America's main problems have started after Iraq's occupation. Insecurity in Iraq indicates that the Americans are faced with a difficult project." Rezai went on to say that the key to attaining Iran's long-term objective was to definitively convince Washington that "Iran is different from Iraq." For Tehran to realize this objective, he stressed, it must adopt an audacious and sophisticated national strategy: "We are not faced with the option of war and surrender. There is a third option. This option is to impose a rational, powerful Iran on America. It has to be proven that a war against Iran will be very damaging for America. The important thing is that the Americans should be made to believe that the Iranians are powerful. We have to use all our international potentials in that regard." The surge in Iran's nuclear program was only one facet of this strategy.

The other aspect of the Iranian strategy was to further expand and escalate anti-American irregular warfare in Iraq by assisting virtually any group or movement capable of killing Americans. The most profound change to Iran's existing policy of sponsoring terrorism in Iraq was the decision to actively assist the Baathist forces as well. The impetus for the decision came from bin Laden's cadres in Iran who assured Iranian intelligence of the quality of the attacks against U.S. troops conducted by the combined Baathist and Islamist forces. In late May, the Iranians invited senior Baathist political leaders hiding in Damascus to Tehran. They met with Hashemi-Rafsanjani and Khamenei and assured them that supporting the Sunni-nationalist Baathist forces would not compromise their broader plans. The Iranian leadership then instructed Ali Yunesi to personally lead the communications with the Baath military officials in order to form a new terrorist operation targeting American interests both in Iraq and all over the Arab world.

These decisions were reflected in Tehran's overt communications with the Shiite elite. For example, on May 24, Ayatollah Ali Khamenei sent a congratulatory note to Baqir al-Hakim in which he stressed the all-inclusive character of the confrontation with the United States. He expressed his hope that "all the classes of the people of Iraq would preserve their unity and unanimity" and that "they would witness the full liberation of their country from foreign hegemony and strive for the establishment of an independent system based on the rule of the people." Khamenei argued that post-Saddam Iraq had a unique opportunity to establish a new national unity. "With the downfall of that tyrannical regime, the Iraqi nation is now being tested by Almighty God and it is on the verge of a deep historical transformation. Now it will be able to establish the state it desires on the basis of Islamic laws and values." Such an Islamic state, according to Khamenei, must represent all Iraqis: "Religious scholars, Grand Ayatollahs, and political elites and representatives must rely upon the people and form the kind of government that the people desire to see. They must safeguard this great asset and prevent the advancement of aggressors who continue to occupy Iraq despite the explicit opposition of the Iraqi people, as well as that of the people of the world," Khamenei instructed Baqir al-Hakim.

Later that day, Baqir al-Hakim addressed a crowd in Qarbalah and repeated Khamenei's message. "The only solution to the Iraqi people's existing problems is to form a transition government and establish stability and security in Iraq." He stressed that "any future Iraqi government should not be dominated by just one group. . . . All the groups and parties that are active in Iraq must participate in the process of determining the political future of this country." Baqir al-Hakim also demanded that the United States withdraw from Iraq. "After the downfall of Saddam and the Baathist regime, the occupiers no longer have a pretext to remain in Iraq. They must leave Iraq," he declared.

On May 28, Saddam rejoined the fray, faxing a new letter to the London *Al-Quds al-Arabi*. He assured his readers that all Iraqis continued to "fight and hunt the cowardly American and British enemy" ceaselessly.

"Know, oh brothers in Jihad, that every American and British will continue to live on the land of the Arabs frightened, worried, and terrified if he does not withdraw from Iraq and change their position toward the criminal Zionist occupation of Arab Palestine," Saddam wrote. He also alluded to the joint Islamist and Baathist fighting ahead: "Oh mujahedin of the Muslims and Arabs and oh Baathists everywhere: This is your day that must show your role, which you cannot accept being confined to enthusiastic words that lack the right action."

In his May 30, Friday sermons in Tehran, Hashemi-Rafsanjani also alluded to the new understandings and doctrine. He stressed that "with reliance on the great strength that I see in the revolution's institutions, the armed forces, our revolutionary forces, and our capable managers, I think that Iran is one of those places that cannot be harmed very easily. And anyone who should want to stretch their hands toward Iran will have those hands cut off." He then elaborated on the American threat to Iran stemming from the building quagmire in Iraq, saying that the result of American "confusion and inability to resolve the [Iraqi] people's problems" imperiled the security of the mullahs' regime because "under such circumstances, instead of implementing their commitment based on international laws, the coalition forces are trying to find scapegoats for these problems and accusing others."

A weekend editorial in London's *Al-Quds al-Arabi* by Abdul Barri al-Atwan provided the most eloquent articulation of the convergence of the Islamist movement, Saddam's followers, and Iran. "The United States has stepped up accusations of Iran interfering in Iraq's affairs, sheltering members of al-Qaeda . . . and supporting certain groups hostile to U.S. occupation of Iraq," al-Atwan wrote. "This intensive campaign by the United States and Britain recalls similar ones that paved the way for the invasion of Iraq, overthrowing its regime, and placing the country under U.S.-British occupation." Al-Atwan concluded that Washington was increasingly alarmed by the overall situation in Iraq and sought to blame Tehran rather the American occupation itself, saying, "The deteriorating security situation in Iraq and the emergence of the Shiite role in political and religious life in Iraq have begun to cause concern to the Americans, prompting them to make muddled decisions, such as preventing the establishment in postwar Iraq of an Islamic regime similar to the Iranian model."

Al-Atwan went on to highlight what he considered the West's hypocrisy in dealing with Iran's influence in Iraq:

It is paradoxical that the United States and Britain should regard the demand by some Iraqi Shiite clergymen that movie theaters be closed and that the sale of alcohol be prevented as unacceptable behavior and intervention in Iraq's affairs, whereas they do not see their occupation of Iraq and the control of its oil wealth as something unusual. In other words, how does the U.S. administration allow itself to send 200,000 soldiers and travel 10,000 km to Iraq while it does not allow the Iranians . . . who are Muslims and who embrace the same faith and creed as the majority of the Iraqi people, to intervene in Iraqi affairs? The fault does not lie in Iran's intercession in Iraqi affairs, but in the U.S. occupation of Iraq and the humiliation of its population under the pretext of liberating them from the former regime and of destroying the weapons of mass destruction in the country.

Al-Atwan also explained that since the United States and the United Kingdom were incapable of solving the Iraqi predicament, the only way they could sustain their regional presence was by blaming Tehran for their own failures and then expanding the war to attack Iran. "The preludes indicate that the U.S. administration is now planning an aggression against Iran and is trying to find pretexts to justify it. The hawks in the U.S. administration, most of whom are ultraardent supporters of Zionism, are pushing in this direction because they want to eliminate any strategic danger that may threaten the Hebraic state or limit its military strategic superiority in the region. The goal of the accusations against Iran is crystal clear, and the target is Iran's nuclear program." To his mind, Iran had always been the real objective of a comprehensive American conspiracy: "The occupation of Iraq was a necessary step toward mounting a future offensive on Iran. Iran is now surrounded by U.S. troops on all sides: Afghanistan to the east, Azerbaijan, Tajikistan, and Georgia to the north, and Iraq to the west. The first stage of the offensive may take the form of embracing the Iranian opposition and finding an 'Iranian Chalabi' to serve as the spearhead in the forthcoming media and political campaigns to destabilize the Tehran regime. The important step will come next with the invasion and occupation of Iran if political pressure and domestic incitement fail to topple the conservative Islamist regime," al-Atwan warned.

The only way for Tehran to avert this doomsday scenario, he stressed, would be a drastic change in the policy toward the situation in Iraq. "Iran was mistaken to believe that it was not targeted, and thus cooperated with the United States in the war in Afghanistan, and took a neutral stand during the U.S. attack and occupation of Iraq," Abdul Barri al-Atwan admonished, hinting at things to come.

For its part, in early June Tehran accelerated its military preparations, readying for a possible attack. On June 2, in a statement commemorating the anniversary of Ayatollah Khomeini's death, the IRGC declared that "the brave Iranian people will dedicate their blood to the last drop to thwart any possible aggression against the country." The statement noted that "as every day passes, the world arrogance sees the Islamic Revolution is gaining strength so that it employs every conspiracy to undermine the Islamic Republic." These were not empty words. In June, in a maneuver timed to coincide with the gradual escalation of its direct involvement in Iraq, Iran also reinforced its naval presence in the northern Persian Gulf, explicitly in order to ensure that American naval vessels stayed out of its coastal waters. On June 1, in a show of resolve, the Iranian Coast Guard detained two boats carrying American soldiers and defense contractors for a few hours. The boats were heading from a Gulf oil terminal through the Shatt-al-Arab waterway to the Al-Faw Peninsula in Iraq. Although the U.S. Navy had habitually violated Iran's territorial waters, because navigating in its sector was easier, this was the first time that Iran had moved against American vessels. The Iranian maneuver was explicitly intended as a political signal to Washington. "For months, the Iranians didn't bother with our movements," an American official told MENL's Steve Rodan. "Now, amid tensions, it's become an issue."

On May 27, on his return from a visit to Baghdad, Secretary of Defense Donald Rumsfeld published an article in the *Wall Street Journal* in which he articulated the Bush administration's reading of the situation in Iraq. "There are still difficulties in Iraq, to be sure—crime, inflation, gas lines, unemployment," he acknowledged, but he then insisted that "no nation that has made the transition from tyranny to a free society has been immune to the difficulties and challenges of taking that path."

The possibility of Iraqi displeasure with the American "liberation" was not even considered. Instead, Rumsfeld stressed that Washington's primary interest in Iraq was the potential global and regional impact of America's success in molding a new democracy in the Middle East. "We have a stake in their success. For if Iraq—with its size, capabilities, and resources—is able to move to the path of representative democracy, the impact in the region and the world could be dramatic. Iraq could conceivably become a model—proof that a moderate Muslim state can succeed in the battle against extremism taking place in the Muslim world today." And while Washington was committed to establishing a "free society" in Iraq, Rumsfeld repeatedly indicated that the United States would not permit certain solutions—from dismemberment of Iraq into several independent states, to an Islamic Republic—irrespective of the wishes of the liberated Iraqis.

Moreover, Rumsfeld reminded readers that the coalition was committed to unilaterally staying in Iraq until a government acceptable to Washington was established and its authority secured. In the meantime, the authorities would promote Iraqis sharing Washington's views and objectives. Through the vaguely defined process of "de-Baathification," the American authorities would ruthlessly destroy any vestiges of the shattered regime.

Rumsfeld singled out Iran and its involvement in Iraqi affairs. He warned that "interference in Iraq by its neighbors or their proxies— including those whose objective is to remake Iraq in Iran's image—will not be accepted or permitted." Syria's active support for the anti-American forces was ignored, as was the challenge of grassroots opposition to the United States. The piece disregarded the overwhelming Shiite and Kurdish rejection of America's plans as well.

The question of how a people's government can be established against the explicit wishes of well over 80 percent of the population was not addressed. And, of course, the rapidly escalating armed resistance against American and British occupation forces was not mentioned at all. Instead, Rumsfeld concluded with a rosy depiction of Iraq's future as an instrument of Washington's global objectives and policies. "Iraqis have an historic opportunity to build a free and civil society. The road ahead will be difficult, but the coalition is committed to helping them succeed. As Iraqis take hold of their country, develop the institutions of self-government, and reclaim their place as responsible members of the international community, the world will have a new model for a successful transition from tyranny to self-reliance—and a new ally in the global war on terror and the struggle for freedom and moderation in the Muslim world." That only a precious few in Iraq would support such goals did not appear to matter to the Bush administration.

13
DISASTROUS DIVERSION

During the summer, the shock of the U.S. occupation gradually dissipated, emotions cooled down, and the Middle East started moving toward a calculated reaction to the new and unprecedented strategic posture. The reality of a long-term American occupation was sinking in, and its ever-changing conditions for leaving Iraq (or at least formally ending the occupation but keeping an elaborate presence) unnerved both political leaders and the "street." The commonly accepted conclusion was that an enduring American presence in, let alone occupation of, Iraq was unacceptable to the entire Arab and Muslim world.

Emboldened by the ability of the fledgling Iraqi resistance to draw American blood with relative impunity, officials and intellectuals began talking about a "new era in the resistance" in terms reminiscent of the myths surrounding HizbAllah's struggle against Israel and the international forces in Lebanon, as well as the Palestinian intifada. The message was clear—just as the Lebanese and Palestinian resistance ultimately defeated vastly superior forces after many years of "a war of attrition and guerrilla operations," so would the Iraqi resistance. Arab policy experts studied events in Iraq, seeing it as the latest development in a struggle that started with Israel's surprising withdrawal from Lebanon in May 2000. Writing in the July 12 issue of the Beirut *Al-Safir*, Nayif Kurayyim elucidated this new percept:

A few months after the humiliating Israeli withdrawal [from southern Lebanon] that opened the eyes of the Arab peoples to a new and uncustomary phase in the Arab-Israeli conflict, the Intifada erupted again in Palestine. It soon turned into a fierce military resistance that dealt painful blows to [Israel, compromising]

its security. And the same scenario seems to be repeating itself with
the United States in Iraq. The United States overran Iraq under the
pretext of overthrowing Saddam Hussein's regime and destroying
its alleged arsenal of weapons of mass destruction. After the
United States quickly accomplished its objective of overthrowing
the regime and after the White House hawks claimed a major victory, the Iraqi resistance erupted more quickly and more strongly
than was expected. In fact, the Americans never thought that a resistance movement would be formed against them after their victory along the lines of the Islamic resistance in Lebanon and the
resistance of Fatah, the Islamic Jihad, and HAMAS in Palestine.

Kurayyim argued that there was a direct correlation between the resistance movements throughout the Arab world, and as a result, even the initial achievements of the Iraqi resistance were bound to have a major
impact. "If the victory of the resistance movement in Lebanon triggered
the armed resistance in Palestine, and if the U.S. occupation of Iraq has led
to the encirclement of the resistance in Lebanon and Palestine, to what will
the strong eruption of the resistance in Iraq lead?" Kurayyim further observed that "in view of the deployment of a large number of U.S. troops in
the cities, the Iraqi resistance killed in two months as many Americans as
the Islamic resistance in Lebanon killed of Israelis in a whole year. This
shows the magnitude of the predicament in which the United States finds
itself." He anticipated the success of the Iraqi intifada in reversing the
shock suffered by the Arab resistance movements since the fall of Baghdad.
"The shrapnel of the Iraqi resistance will thus enable the resistance in
Palestine and Lebanon to regain the initiative that they lost after the U.S.
occupation of Iraq," Kurayyim stressed.

The Bush administration ignored these prevailing sentiments, however, and instead opted to capitalize on American preeminence in the region to once again attempt to dictate an end to the Israeli-Palestinian
conflict. In so doing, Washington also ignored the revival of Iraqi-
Palestinian cooperation to jointly ignite terrorism in the region, in an
arrangement that also involved HizbAllah, and thus Iran and Syria as well.
To a great extent, the administration exacerbated the regional crisis by devising the Road Map in April and, far more importantly, persevering with
it even as Palestinian terrorism tore at Israeli cities.

This rising profile of the Israeli-Palestinian conflict was the outcome of
a major decision by the White House to placate Arab opposition to Amer-

ica's occupation of Iraq by "helping" the Palestinians. The White House also perceived that addressing Palestinian concerns would win back support from Western Europe, which had always considered saving Arafat the greatest policy priority in the region. Tony Blair, faced with enormous hostility to the war, needed a major boost: "Bush had to choose between Arik [Sharon] and Tony [Blair], and he chose Tony," explained a White House insider in May. Bush's deference to Blair, and pursuit of the Road Map, however, left out of consideration the realities and perceptions in the Middle East itself, as Fouad Ajami explained in a May 26 article in *U.S. News & World Report*. "It may be the proper thing for America to take up the matter of Israel and the Palestinians; it may be a debt owed the stalwart British Prime Minister Tony Blair. But we should know the Arab world for what it is today and entertain no grand illusions about the gratitude the Road Map would deliver in Palestinian and Arab streets. We buy no friendship in Arab lands with pro-Palestinian diplomacy; we ward off no anti-American terrorism." The virulent anti-Americanism prevailing throughout the Arab world, Ajami warned, "can never be stilled with a diplomatic effort on behalf of the Palestinians."

Israel felt shocked and betrayed in view of its tremendous support for the United States during the war. From the very beginning of the conflict, Sharon had instructed the entire Israeli defense and intelligence establishments to give the Americans all possible assistance, and wanting not to unnecessarily complicate Washington's tenuous relations with the Arab world, Jerusalem agreed that their cooperation would go without public recognition or thanks. Several Israeli experts were in Iraq throughout the war, sharing their expertise and unique experience as well as risking their lives to help their American allies. Israeli intelligence played a major role in helping the CIA and other American intelligence agencies overcome some of their initial setbacks by providing access to unique sources and material. For example, as Sharon publicly acknowledged to American congressmen visiting Jerusalem, Israeli intelligence played a central role in locating Pvt. Jessica Lynch. Senior Israeli defense and intelligence officials described the Israeli assistance as going "significantly above and beyond the normal cooperation between two allied states."

Israel also provided the American military with specialized systems for urban warfare and special operations—many of which were taken from operational units of the Israel Defense Forces. No less than fourteen D-9 armored bulldozers were flown to Iraq in the middle of the war to help the 94th Engineer Combat Battalion, replacing the smaller and less protected

D-7 as the unit's main bulldozer. UAVs, unique smart munitions, and electronic protective systems were contributed by the Israeli Air Force, which also cleared room at bases and abandoned aerial routes to expedite arrival of American bombers, transports, and other special flights. Indications of this largely clandestine cooperation can be found in the GRU report of March 29.

> Radio communications intercepted during the last five days suggest that the coalition is using Israeli airfields for conducting night air strikes against Iraq. Combat aircraft taking off regularly from the [Israeli] Hatzerim and Navatim air bases do not return to the same bases but fly toward the border with Jordan while maintaining complete radio silence. Possibly these are just Israeli Air Force exercises. However, [Russian] radio intercept and radar units observe increased intensity of radio communications coming from the Jordanian Air Force and air defense communication centers during such overflights, as well as changes in the operating modes of the U.S. Army Patriot tracking radars deployed in Jordan. This indicates that the Israeli air bases are used as forward airfields or that some of the coalition air force units are based there.

As the major war was drawing to a close and the guerrilla warfare was taking shape, Israel was content to continue aiding Washington without any public recognition. However, Jerusalem did expect the Bush administration to take the Israeli contribution to the war effort into account when defining the postwar Middle East. Therefore, the formulation of a decidedly pro-Palestinian policy so soon after the war came as a total shock to the Knesset. The Road Map (a document including, for the first time, a defined set of chronological milestones leading to the establishment of a Palestinian state in 2005) was officially handed to Israel on April 30, after Abu-Mazen was sworn in as prime minister of the Palestinian Authority. The next day a British al-Qaeda martyr-bomber working on behalf of HAMAS bombed the Tel Aviv pub Mike's Place (a bar near the U.S. embassy), a fitting reaction to the new policy. Three civilians were killed and over twenty were wounded in the bombing.

Continuing to disregard realities in the region, the United States put extremely heavy pressure on Jerusalem to go along with the Road Map and ignore the Palestinians' ongoing terrorist activities, the daily casualties among Israeli civilians, and the firing of mortar shells and Qassam rockets at Israeli targets by HAMAS. Israeli analysis of the potential threat the Road Map constituted was elucidated by Uzi Landau—the cabinet minister responsible for strategic relations with the United States and oversight of the intelligence services—who considered the Road Map far more dangerous to Israel's future than the Oslo Process: "The Road Map is a huge prize for terror. In its wake the Palestinians will not only achieve their strategic goals, but will reach a clear conclusion: terror pays. They will get all the concessions we shower on them, organize themselves with money they get from the world and us, rebuild their terror units, and attack us at the moment convenient for them. Our experience from the Oslo agreement teaches us that for us, the map bodes a future in which terror is much, much worse."

On the Arab side, the key proponent of the Road Map was Egypt's Hosni Mubarak. Long implicated in numerous WMD and ballistic missile programs in cooperation with North Korea, Iraq, and Libya, he reinvented himself as the facilitator of Palestinian participation in the Road Map. In May, Mubarak dispatched Egyptian intelligence to negotiate a *Hudna* (truce)—see "Notes: The Historical Record," p. 517—between the Islamist terrorists, via the Palestinian Authority, and Israel in order to stifle Israel's objections to making unilateral concessions to the Palestinians as long as terrorism continued. Egypt's suggestions were readily accepted in Washington because the administration was reluctant to address, let alone immerse itself, in the real intricacies and complexities of the Arab-Israeli conflict. The administration cared only about the semblance of "progress" in resolving the Israeli-Palestinian war, which officials hoped would balance the killing of Iraqis with the rescuing of Palestinians.

The United States committed all its prestige and might to the Road Map—starting with Powell's arrival in Israel on May 10 with a list of demands requiring tangible Israeli concessions in return for vague assurances from the Palestinians. Israel was to cease "provocative" antiterrorist operations, freeze all settlement activities, release Palestinian terrorists, and permit Palestinian workers into Israel, including those in the age groups that provide cover for terrorists. Powell rudely ignored Jerusalem's reservations and insisted on sticking to the original Road Map. When the Palestinians adamantly refused to consider even the largely symbolic gestures the document requested, Powell announced that both sides would first concentrate on "confidence-building measures," with Israel expected to unilaterally undertake the same conciliatory measures originally demanded by the United States irrespective of Palestinian actions.

In May, Tehran launched a clear demonstration of its centrality to Middle Eastern dynamics. Iranian President Muhammad Khatami embarked on an unprecedented tour of both Syria and Lebanon, emphasizing the importance of the HizbAllah-affiliated Shiite community. Khatami met Sheikh Nasrallah to discuss strategy in the wake of Saddam's fall, and they concluded that more vehement active resistance to the United States and Israel was urgently required. "The [HizbAllah's] position is one of solidarity between the Islamic Republic [of Iran], Syria, Lebanon, the resistance, the Palestinian people, and all the honorable people of the Muslim community," Nasrallah explained. "The main point is that we will not bend and we will not give up our rights." In Damascus, Iran's ambassador to Syria, Hussein Sheikh-ol-Islam, pledged that Teheran would continue to support HizbAllah against America. "The United States has proved to be an unreliable party and Iran cannot trust it," he said. Nasrallah and Iranian officials also met with a HAMAS delegation comprising political chief Mussa Abu Marzouq, politburo member Muhammad Nazal, and the organization's representative in Lebanon, Osama Hamdan. According to HizbAllah sources, they discussed "developments in the region since the invasion of Iraq and its occupation" and agreed on a joint strategy to confront the "Zionist-American conspiracy," particularly efforts to disarm HAMAS and other insurgency groups in the context of political agreements with Israel. Khatami's entire visit was a flagrant challenge to the United States, which Washington chose to ignore to sustain the fallacy of the Road Map. Moreover, once Khatami returned to Tehran, HizbAllah ratcheted up its provocations, firing 57-mm air defense guns into northern Israel, causing damage to villages and cities. Israel, under pressure from Washington not to unnecessarily complicate the situation in the region, did not react or retaliate, once again projecting an incredibly dangerous image of weakness.

The Palestinian power structure continued to evolve in complete disregard of the Palestinian Authority's ostensible commitment to the Road Map. In Ramallah, Yasser Arafat and Tawfiq Tirawi remained in control of the bulk of the Palestinian security and terrorism infrastructure. Arafat was giving explicit instructions to the various terrorist organizations, from Fatah to HAMAS, on when and how to escalate and expand the strikes. The Palestinian Authority's intelligence arms—Security Chief Muhhamad Dahlan's great hope—were actively participating in terrorism without any attempt by Dahlan to disrupt their activities. Arafat also retained tight control of the Palestinian Authority's funds, channeling money to terrorist operations. Abu-Mazen and Salem Fiad—the minister of the treasury—abided by all Arafat's demands for funding. Most intriguing was the possible role of Security Chief Dahlan: that Dahlan's best friend was Muhammad Dief, the HAMAS operational chief in Gaza, and that Dr. Abdul Aziz Rantisi, the HAMAS political leader in the Gaza Strip, was Dahlan's children's pediatrician did not seem to the Bush administration to be impediments to Dahlan's ability to fight and suppress HAMAS terrorism in the Gaza Strip. Throughout, Israeli intelligence informed the cabinet about these developments in great detail, warning about their ramifications, but Jerusalem shared this information with a Washington increasingly reluctant to face reality.

When Israel launched preventive antiterrorist operations, Washington was reproachful. When Israeli officials presented intelligence data in Washington explaining the need to strike, they were met with more anger because the administration was forced to acknowledge the hypocrisy in its policy. Sanctimonious rhetoric notwithstanding, only the advancement of Bush's political interests mattered in Washington.

Israel agreed to political concessions, despite its reservations. On May 17, Sharon met Abu-Mazen, but the Palestinians refused to live up to Washington's promises that they would fight terrorism after significant Israeli withdrawals, and the meeting ended in impasse. The squabble was immediately followed by major terrorist attacks, such as the May 18 bombing of yet another bus in Jerusalem, killing seven and wounding twenty-four. The next day, a female suicide bomber hit a shopping mall in Afula, leaving three dead and more than seventy wounded. Both strikes were part of an offensive launched by the Islamist organizations and Fatah jointly, under the direct control of Arafat's *Muqataah,* and intended to flagrantly challenge the United States. Although exceptionally detailed intelligence left no doubt in Washington or Jerusalem that both bombings were directed from Arafat's headquarters in Ramallah, the Israel Defense Forces could not act because of intense U.S. pressure not to embarrass Bush by undermining the Road Map, even though the price would be paid with the lives and limbs of Israeli civilians.

In late May, the United States supported Dahlan's program to buy back weapons from the terrorist organizations at exorbitant prices and hold them as part of the Palestinian Authority's arsenal. The plan also called for the recruitment of terrorists into a new Palestinian Border Guards force, to be deployed at crossings into Israel. The Border Guards would be a 20,000 to 25,000 strong military force, funded by the United States and the European Union, to the tune of half a billion dollars a year. Dahlan assured Washington that that was the most he could presently do. "The problem is not that he cannot do anything," commented a senior Israeli official, "but that he does not want to."

On May 22, the Israel Defense Forces captured a boat bearing an Egyptian flag on its way to Gaza with highly sophisticated sabotage equipment, instructional material (including thirty-six CD-ROMs), fuses for 122-mm rockets, and instructions for extending the range of Qassam rockets. Also on the boat was Hamed Mussalem Mussa abu-Amarah, a senior HizbAllah instructor, organizer, and bomb-making expert, whose role was to prepare each of the local terrorist cadres to launch more audacious operations. In his personal luggage were equipment and instructions for the construction of extremely thin bomb vests so that suicide bombers would not have to wear heavy clothes that attracted suspicion during the hot Middle Eastern summers. The sponsors of the program in Gaza were senior officials in the Palestinian Authority security organizations operating under Arafat's direct authority.

That day, Abu-Mazen and Dahlan met with the Gaza-based leadership of HAMAS, Islamic Jihad, and other Islamists in an attempt to convince them to stop terrorist strikes in order to compel Israel to withdraw. The Islamists steadfastly refused to consider the idea. On the contrary, over the next few days the Islamists issued repeated warnings to Abu-Mazen not to sacrifice Palestinian destiny on the altar of pleasing the Americans, which the Muslim world would consider a betrayal. The United States capitalized on this tone in the internal Palestinian discussions to warn Israel that Abu-Mazen's life was in danger, that he could be assassinated at any moment, and that only greater concessions could placate the Palestinians and save his life. Foreign Minister Nabil Shaath and other Palestinian officials urged Washington to pressure Jerusalem, arguing that the *Hudna* was imminent and within reach if only Israel cooperated.

Dahlan launched his initial anti-terrorism operations in the West Bank by having his confidant, Bashir Nafa, invite leaders of terrorist cells for conversations about the expediency of lowering the level of violence. Nafa did not raise the possibility of stopping terrorism altogether. These were pleasant talks and no threats were made. Most important were the communications with four HAMAS leaders and one Islamic Jihad leader in the West Bank. Dahlan and Nafa knew all of them personally and came to their respective hideouts. Dahlan promised that in return for participation in the *Hudna,* Israel would not target them for capture or assassination, each would be well compensated in American dollars, their people would be recruited into Dahlan's security forces with large salaries, and Israel would release their people from jail. Moreover, the entire operational cadre of the Islamists was by now fully integrated into the al-Aqsa Martyrs Brigades, and Arafat forbade hurting their networks, regardless of American pressure.

In late May, once the White House began asking parties about the acceptability of summits with Arab and Israeli leaders, Arafat told the Executive Committee of the Palestine Liberation Organization to convene for a two-day session aimed at formulating the policies Abu-Mazen would have to implement in the forthcoming meetings with Sharon and Bush. Yassin reciprocated and announced the willingness of HAMAS to consider a short-term *Hudna* under the appropriate conditions. At Washington's request, Jerusalem released roughly two hundred million dollars in frozen Palestinian Authority funds; most went to Arafat rather than Abu-Mazen, despite American guarantees. Washington justified the transaction by claiming it was integral to enabling Abu-Mazen's attendance at the summits with Bush. Indeed, Sharon was very conciliatory in the meeting with Abu-Mazen, promising far-reaching concessions if the Palestinians brought terrorism to an end. Israel also continued to absorb terrorist attacks and launched only a few preemptive raids against terrorist leaders known to be organizing imminent operations. In discussions with the Americans, Dahlan and Abu-Mazen promised only to curtail small-scale terrorist operations and claimed they had no control over suicide bombings because these were run via Damascus and Tehran. They also argued that unduly heavy pressure on the Islamists would inevitably lead to a civil war that would only broaden the use of all forms of terrorism. Washington went along with the explanation, and Jerusalem succumbed to U.S. pressure.

On June 3, Bush met Mubarak, King Abdallah II, Crown Prince Abdallah, the Emir of Bahrain, and Abu-Mazen in Sharm al-Sheikh, a resort town at the southern tip of the Sinai Peninsula. Bush promised a Palestinian state with territorial continuity by 2005 in return for guarantees of Israel's security. He committed to refer to the Saudi plan—a tacit recognition of the need for an Israeli withdrawal to the 1967 borders—and promised to intercede with Sharon to lift the siege on Arafat, provided a viable effort was made to contain terrorism. The entire "summit" lasted half an hour instead of the planned three hours. The reason was the palpable tension between Bush and the Arab leaders, who did not try to hide their hostility toward the situation in Iraq. All Arab statements in the aftermath of the summit stressed the leaders' recognition of Arafat as the sole leader of the Palestinians and insisted on the unlimited and unconstrained right of return—a euphemism for the destruction of Israel.

The Palestinian Authority's position was elucidated in an *Al-Hayah al-Jadidah* article by Deputy Foreign Minister Adli Sadek: "The Arab-American summit is convening today with the presence of the snake-head of the American invasion of Iraq and the snake-head of the American oppression of the Palestinians and all Arabs as well." Sadek urged all participating Arab leaders to realize that "appeasing, and acquiescing to, the U.S. will not benefit them or their peoples." He ridiculed American achievements in Iraq, saying that Bush arrived at the summit "as if he accomplished a victory of the brave in Iraq," but the real winners were "the simple Iraqis [who] waged battles in remote villages, at the gates of their cities and deserts, to defend their country, not heeding the oppression, the tyranny, and occupation." Their resistance, rather than the Road Map, was the true indicator of U.S. might in the region. "These Iraqis could create a major crisis for Bush, his administration, and his military command," Sadek noted, and added that Bush must realize that the Arabs "still have resistance [forces] hidden in the heart of Iraqi society whose aim is to expel the defeated invaders." At the same time, fearing military strikes, the Arab leaders in Sharm el-Sheikh would smile at Bush rather than tell him the truth—that they had no intention of helping the United States "with its imperialistic goals disguised as the war on terrorism." Nor would they tell Bush that America's anti-Islamic policy was "the root cause of the vengeance leading young Arabs and Muslims to explode." Ultimately, Sadek concluded, the Arab leaders need not fear Bush, because America's "experience in Iraq is not bright" and because the United States was "sinking deeper and deeper into a putrid swamp from which it would only extricate itself as a defeated and stinking loser."

On June 4, Bush, Sharon, and Abu-Mazen met in Aqaba, Jordan, to bolster their commitment to the Road Map process. It was a nice and pleasant event; Abu-Mazen talked about his realization that there was no military solution to the Israeli-Palestinian dispute; Sharon promised to end Israel's rule over the Palestinians and reiterated his willingness to accept a viable Palestinian state; Bush guaranteed that Israel would remain after 2005 a Jewish state, implicitly confirming that any agreement would not implement a Palestinian right of return.

All of these statements and commitments were well received but irrelevant, as demonstrated in the continued assurances by emissaries of the Palestinian Authority to Islamist leaders in both Gaza and Cairo that the deal would not be accepted. To ensure that the ambience of the Aqaba summit was not spoiled, over the next few days Israel unilaterally refrained from retaliating against continued terrorist attacks despite mounting casualties. Nevertheless, Israeli intelligence warned the cabinet that the Palestinians were using the lull to prepare for a new wave of terrorism.

By June 10, accumulating intelligence about active preparations by HAMAS in the Gaza Strip, in concert with its headquarters in Damascus and Tehran, suggested an imminent terrorist offensive. Moreover, HAMAS activities were taking place without any interference from Palestinian security forces despite repeated Israeli requests. With no other recourse, Jerusalem launched a series of strikes against HAMAS leaders. First was an attempt on Rantisi's life that failed because he saw the helicopter-launched missile coming and bolted from the car at the last second. "HAMAS will take care of obliterating all the Jews so that not even a single one remains on the land of Palestine. If the Jews want security, they should return to where they came from," he declared from his hospital bed. Both Washington and Ramallah condemned the Israeli strikes.

On June 12, another suicide bomber, dressed as a religious Jew, blew himself up on a Jerusalem bus; the extremely powerful explosion killed sixteen and wounded over a hundred. The bomber was an al-Aqsa Martyrs Brigade member from Hebron, and the operation was preceded by long-term preparations and thus had nothing to do with the attempted assassination of Rantisi. However, HAMAS claimed responsibility in the name of Rantisi; Israel in turn resumed attacks on HAMAS commanders in Gaza, killing some of its targets. Meanwhile, Washington and Cairo did not consider the bombing a legitimate reason to revisit the viability of the *Hudna*. Washington requested that Egyptian intelligence intercede with HAMAS and promised to guarantee a cessation of Israeli attacks in return for a declared commitment to the *Hudna,* with no guarantees from the Egyptians or Palestinians that HAMAS would actually abide by its terms.

The American move came while Abu-Mazen was threatening to resign because he could no longer stand Arafat's incitement and his encouragement of HAMAS to strike out against Israel in order to derail the Road Map process.

The next day, the United States offered a compromise: The Israel Defense Forces would withdraw from the Gaza Strip in return for Dahlan's commitment that HAMAS would not attack Israel. According to the American suggestion, the Palestinian Authority was no longer required to fight and destroy HAMAS. Dahlan and Abu-Mazen acknowledged their limited control, given that Arafat was the driving force behind the new terrorism wave. To ensure that this message was clear, Arafat summoned Dahlan and his key commanders to Ramallah and instructed them on the Gaza deal with Israel. Arafat demanded a conciliatory attitude to the Islamists and ordered that Abu-Mazen's policies be ignored. Israel continued to hit terrorist commanders in Gaza and the West Bank and captured several would-be martyrs with their bombs. By June, Israeli security services were still receiving a flood of warnings regarding specific terrorist strikes already in the pipeline and the Palestinian Authority's inability or unwillingness to prevent them. All the while, small ambushes, primitive missile attacks, and mortar shelling continued unabated, with several strikes launched into the Israeli coastal plains.

The myth of the *Hudna* expanded as Abu-Mazen, Dahlan, Egyptian intelligence chief Omar Suleiman, and his deputy Mustafa al-Bukhairi were now striving to enact only "oral understandings" with the Islamists for limited periods of good behavior. They maintained negotiations with the HAMAS and Islamic Jihad leadership in Damascus Qatar, and de facto Tehran (via Qatar). The patterns in all of these negotiations left no doubt that the process was a sham aimed solely at soliciting American pressure on Israel to withdraw, without the Palestinians having to dismantle the terrorist infrastructure. Israeli efforts to convince the Bush administration that meaningful steps—rather than make-believe statements—were imperative were met with outright hostility and increased pressure on Israel to go along with the charade. The Americans pointed to recent attacks on Abu-Mazen and other "pro-American" Palestinian Authority officials as a viable reason for Israel to look the other way on Palestinian terrorist activities in the Gaza Strip and to bolster Abu-Mazen through unilateral concessions, primarily the suspension of preemptive strikes and the release of prisoners. High-level meetings between the two sides remained acrimonious and futile because the Palestinian Authority refused to cooperate in preventing specific terrorist attacks and only repeated American demands for Israeli concessions.

On June 19, a grocery store owner near Beit Shean, in northern Israel, prevented a bomber from entering his crowded shop and paid with his life. Because there were only a few casualties, Washington refused to recognize the incident as a major infringement of the *Hudna* talks, thus setting a dangerous precedent the Palestinians did not fail to notice. Previously the United States had ignored only prevented and failed operations that yielded no casualties. Mofaz warned John Wolfe, the American representative overseeing the Road Map process, that the Palestinians were not doing anything to stop terrorism and that accumulating intelligence caused him to suspect that the Palestinian leadership, and specifically Dahlan, was not really interested in fighting terrorism. Moreover, Arafat was still in complete control of 70 percent of the Palestinian security (read "terrorism") establishment, while Dahlan was still struggling to consolidate his control over the remaining 30 percent. Israel's warnings fell on deaf ears, and all the while terrorism continued unabated. Palestinian commentators emphasized that major strikes involving suicide bombers would be launched against Israel proper, not just the settlements in the territories.

On June 23, Colin Powell hailed the great progress in the Israeli-Palestinian talks but did not contradict Arafat's declaration that "Israel [was] torpedoing the Road Map." Nor did the United States repudiate the Palestinian demand that Israel withdraw unconditionally to the lines the Israel Defense Forces held on September 28, 2000—the day the Palestinians launched the intifada rather than accept Bill Clinton's peace initiative. Furthermore, in meetings with Israeli and American officials, Dahlan avoided presenting concrete plans for fighting terrorism in the areas to be vacated by the Israel Defense Forces. And on June 26, Dahlan did not address concrete evidence that Arafat had ordered the escalation in anti-Israel terrorism in order to scuttle the *Hudna* before it even began.

In June, Maj. Gen. Doron Almog, head of the Israel Defense Forces' Southern Command, talked to *Haaretz* while saying good-bye to units under his command. Almog was very blunt in articulating Israel's reading of Muhammad Dahlan and the overall situation in the Gaza Strip. Dahlan and Almog had worked together since 1994, and according to the general, "The last thing that interests Dahlan . . . is Israel's security." In that respect, Dahlan was not different from the bulk of the Palestinian leadership who, Almog asserted, were far more afraid of the Islamists in their midst than of

Israel and the United States. The Palestinian Authority security services would abide by the "temporary conditions" for a cease-fire for as long as it served their interests, but, said Almog, "They will never be 'arrest subcontractors' for us. No Palestinian wants to be seen as a collaborator. The [Palestinian Authority] will not fight HAMAS. Their model is calming things down without using force. The hard-core terrorists, the arms production, and the incitement will continue to exist, on top of the huge wells of hatred created by the preachers in the mosques every Friday. There they say explicitly: 'The fight will continue until Ashdod and Ashkelon are liberated.'" Because of the aggregate impact of HAMAS's hatred and determination and the Palestinian Authority's tacit support, a new round of Israeli-Palestinian fighting, in which the Islamists would be the dominant element, was virtually inevitable. "One must prepare for the next round, whether it erupts in five months or five years. HAMAS has [war] plans. The organization will attempt to seize political control over the [Palestinian] Authority while building its own military power." Given his position in the Gaza Strip, Almog concluded, Dahlan was playing a unique role in furthering these Palestinians designs.

Nevertheless, on June 27, Israel and the Palestinian Authority reached an agreement in principle on the transfer of security responsibility to the Palestinians in the Gaza Strip. Israel succumbed under immense American pressure to have the agreement in place by the time Condoleezza Rice arrived in the region in the next few days. To appease Washington, Jerusalem demonstrated flexibility and accepted virtually all the Palestinian demands in return for vague promises—most of them regarding the security posture after the expiration of the three-month *Hudna*. Essentially, Dahlan agreed to accept "security responsibility" over the areas vacated by Israel but stressed he would "not dismantle [the] terrorism infrastructure." In return, Israel agreed to stop most preemptive assassinations. That night, Arafat summoned Dahlan and all the security chiefs to his office in Ramallah. He demanded a detailed briefing from Dahlan and then dictated the "working arrangements" that in effect neutralized Dahlan's authority. The next day, two roadside bombs exploded near Beit Lahiyah in the Gaza Strip as two CIA SUVs drove by on their way to meetings with Palestinian security personnel to discuss an Israeli withdrawal. Israeli intelligence warned the cabinet that the Islamist groups did not have any intention to disarm; Palestinian officials concurred, admitting that "the *Hudna* is not worth the paper it is written on."

Fully aware that Jerusalem was in negotiations with Washington about the concessions made to the Palestinians, regardless of whether they moved to combat terrorism or not, Abu Mazen presented a visiting Condoleezza Rice with a new demand: The Palestinians would not disarm or fight terrorism unless there was a significant and viable international force—including American and European units covered by a UN mandate—deployed as a buffer between the Palestinian Authority and the Israel Defense Forces so that Israel could not harm the Palestinians once their "patriotic forces"—the terrorist forces—were disarmed. Abu Mazen also conditioned further cooperation on international guarantees that Israel would "unconditionally abide" by the agreement. With Rice pressuring Sharon, the Israel Defense Forces began to withdraw from the Gaza Strip despite the absence of a *Hudna* and other mechanisms for security coordination. Sharon ordered the unilateral withdrawal so that Jerusalem would not have to squabble with the administration.

Israel's national security adviser, Efraim Halevi, defined the Road Map process as an "experiment fraught with dangers to Israel," but the Americans would not listen. Instead, senior Israeli officials complained, Rice devoted her meetings with Sharon and key Israeli ministers to advocating a return to a national unity government in which the dovish Shimon Peres would serve as foreign minister. Rice's proposals were a flagrant intervention into Israel's internal affairs, motivated by the administration's belief that a unity government would be less inclined to protest Palestinian violations of the Road Map and other agreements and thus mean less trouble for the White House. Moreover, as Rice tried to remake Israel's political landscape, she ignored the continuing rash of terrorist strikes while she was in the Middle East.

On July 2, Israel withdrew from the greater Bethlehem area despite a lack of assurances and credible Palestinian Authority security activities. Moreover, a poll commissioned by the Palestinian Authority was published just as Rice was to meet Abu Mazen, and according to its results, 57 percent of Palestinians opposed an end to the armed intifada, with 41 percent in favor; 64 percent supported Arafat's line on negotiations; 53 percent considered Arafat the only leader with the right and ability to reach an agreement with Israel; and 65 percent were pessimistic about the likelihood of peace.

The day after the poll was published, Dahlan's people launched a missile attack on Kfar Darom, a settlement in the Gaza Strip. Immediately afterward, Dahlan demanded from Israel that one of his coterie, Colonel Abu-Mutalak, who was then in an Israeli jail for past involvement in terrorism, be immediately released because he was "the only one" capable of addressing the use of missiles with the Fatah and HAMAS squads. Not wanting to be accused of scuttling the *Hudna,* Israel agreed, and Abu-Mutalak was released along with thirty-three other members of Palestinian Authority security based in the Gaza Strip as a gesture of goodwill to Dahlan. By July 5, HAMAS had stopped firing the Qassams into Israeli settlements because Fatah, under Dahlan's assistant Rashid Abu-Shabak, had begun firing the vastly improved Nasser missiles. In the Bethlehem area, the Israel Defense Forces had to deploy elite units on all the approach roads into Jerusalem because of the intense preparatory activities of numerous terrorist cells, many of which traveled from Hebron and other cities without being intercepted by Dahlan's people. In Bethlehem, Fadi Shlat, a member of the al-Aqsa Martyrs Brigade, was captured wearing a bomb belt, while he was making his way to Jerusalem. Dahlan's security people arrested Shlat on the basis of a specific Israeli tip coupled with a threat that the Israel Defense Forces would reoccupy Bethlehem unless he was caught in time. It was only when the Palestinian Authority security personnel saw Israel Defense Forces tanks on the crest between the nearby Israeli suburb of Gilo and Bethlehem that they suddenly "discovered" Fadi Shlat.

HAMAS and Fatah resumed production of the Qassam and Nasser rockets at an accelerated pace without any hindrance from Dahlan's officers. Israeli intelligence learned that the Palestinians were planning to produce one thousand rockets quickly and that longer-range models were being test-launched into the sea. The Israel Defense Forces refrained from striking at the rebuilt workshops, fearing the total collapse of the *Hudna.* The Palestinians were also reconstituting their emergency storage sites—bringing additional ammunition, rockets, and shells from Egypt via tunnels into Gaza. Essentially the entire terrorist system in the Gaza Strip embarked on an intense effort to recover from losses caused by the Israel Defense Forces in the few months leading up to the *Hudna.* They were also trying to acquire new capabilities before the intifada resumed, in the negotiated three months or before. When terror groups began using the reopened trans–Gaza Strip road to transfer weapons and men to positions outside Jewish settlements, the Israel Defense Forces blocked the highway. The Palestinian Authority immediately complained to Washington, which promptly coerced Jerusalem into lifting the roadblocks. The terrorist buildup in the northern Gaza Strip continued unabated, albeit more discreetly.

Throughout this process, Arafat kept undermining Abu Mazen, who favored more constructive engagement with Israel, and on July 8, Abu Mazen resigned from the Central Committee of Fatah. It was a dramatic move that would lead to his resignation—*firing*, more accurately—from the office of prime minister as well, because Abu Mazen's mandate emanated from Fatah. Arafat convened an emergency meeting of Fatah's Central Committee members in Ramallah and demanded that Abu Mazen withdraw his resignation letter and honor Fatah's policy toward Israel. Meanwhile, Abu Mazen had already cancelled his meeting with Sharon scheduled for the next morning, and all other Israeli-Palestinian meetings were put on hold. In these maneuvers, Arafat demanded that Dahlan's powers be limited to ensure that he wouldn't be able to harm Arafat's terrorist infrastructure. Arafat therefore established a National Security Committee under his tight control; Arafat determined further that Dahlan must solicit the Committee's approval for every step his forces took. Similarly, Abu Mazen was obligated to ask the approval of Arafat's other committees, to the point where Abu Mazen was forced to send Arafat a formal letter requesting detailed instructions on how to proceed in the dealings with both Israel and the United States. Despite all the efforts at reconciliation, Arafat continued to undercut Abu Mazen, telling the UN special coordinator for the Middle East peace process on June 12 that the prime minister "betrays the interests of the Palestinian people." Arafat then appointed Dahlan's nemesis, Jibril Rajoub, coordinator and supervisor of all city governors and thus the real chief of the local defense committees and security forces. This new body in effect neutralized Dahlan in the West Bank.

The first confirmed operation run by Arafat's new terrorist system took place on July 8. A suicide bomber killed an elderly lady and wounded her three grandchildren in a village inside Israel's coastal plains. The terrorist misread his instructions and missed the crowded synagogue a block away. Although the bomber was identified as a Fatah member and thus a part of Arafat's new operational networks, U.S. officials pressured Israel to call the incident a "mysterious explosion" and allude to the possibility of a gas accident. Acting on recently acquired intelligence, the Israel Defense Forces located several new bomb storage sites in Jenin, Nablus, and Tulkarem and blew them up. The Palestinian Authority protested the Israel Defense Forces' incursion into the cities as a violation of the Road Map's understandings.

Arafat began organizing new terrorism networks in late June, once the *Hudna* and the Road Map had picked up enough momentum to seem cemented because of America's steamroller politics. Despite his apparent endorsement of Abu Mazen's ascent, Arafat was determined to remain the Palestinians' indisputable leader and neutralize both Abu Mazen and Dahlan even before they began to operate. Arafat's objective was to unleash another wave of terrorism against Israel in order to elicit a reaction that would bring about the collapse of the negotiated process. Tawfiq Tirawi was in command of the operation, and at the core of the new force were roughly two hundred terrorists hiding in the *Muqataah*. They included members of al-Fatah, Tanzim, al-Aqsa Martyrs Brigades, and a number of smaller organizations, as well as representatives of HizbAllah and Iraqi intelligence. As long as Arafat remained in the *Muqataah*, they were safe from Israeli assassination attempts, and since the Aqaba summit, their immunity exceeded the confines of the compound because Sharon was pressured to virtually cease all assassinations and arrests. Therefore, some of these terrorists began traveling during the day to other cities to coordinate operations with local cells and networks, but always returned to the *Muqataah*. Mahmud Abu-Diamra was nominated the coordinator of these efforts.

One of the first steps Arafat and Tirawi took was to reinstate the contingency and operational plans coordinated with Saddam before the war, for which resources and assets were already available at the *Muqataah*. Arafat's next step was the revival of the "popular committees" as the coordinating bodies with the Islamists—HAMAS, Islamic Jihad, HizbAllah, and al-Aqsa Martyrs Brigades—particularly in the Gaza Strip. One of the committee chiefs, Jamal Abu-Samadanah, also ran intensified smuggling of weapons and personnel via the sea and via tunnels from Egypt. Abu-Samadanah's control over the logistical effort gave him tremendous power over Dahlan. Indeed both Abu-Shabak and Abu-Mutalak—ostensibly Dahlan's deputies and key aides in the Gaza Strip—were working closely with Abu-Samadanah because he was the primary source of their weapons, ammunition, and missiles. Meanwhile, Arafat ordered the activation of new emergency networks in Nablus (including the Balata refugee camp), Jenin, Tulkarem, and Kalkiliya. These networks were made up of Fatah-affiliated cells and networks, mainly of the Tanzim and al-Aqsa Martyrs Brigades. The commander of this effort was Hussein al-Sheikh, who had been Arafat's financial chief since April, when the fear of American intervention led Arafat to establish a clandestine money-handling mechanism outside existing channels.

Hussein al-Sheikh, ostensibly Dahlan's confidant, was nominated to oversee implementation of the *Hudna* in the West Bank. However, by July, Dahlan did not dare to remove al-Sheikh, despite his association with terrorism, fearing Arafat's retribution. Tirawi and al-Sheikh tightly controlled the terrorist operations in the West Bank under a myriad of Islamist banners through three key headquarters—in Nablus, Jenin, and Tulkarem—that were manned by trusted commanders from Fatah's al-Aqsa Martyrs Brigades.

Although the Islamist leadership was enthusiastic about Arafat's work to undermine the Road Map process, they would not commit to following him blindly even against Israel. Indeed, both Tehran and Damascus were adamant about keeping independent options for exacerbating regional tensions through spectacular terrorist strikes even if Arafat decided not to participate. In July, senior intelligence officials in Damascus summoned the local chiefs of HizbAllah, HAMAS, Islamic Jihad, and several smaller Palestinian organizations for an urgent meeting, which included representatives of Iranian intelligence as well. The Syrian officials ordered the terrorist chieftains to prepare operational plans for a wave of major terrorist strikes against Israel aimed at derailing the Road Map process and weakening America's presence in the Middle East. The chieftains were promised huge sums of money by the Iranians to expedite preparations and were promised by both the Iranians and Syrians close cooperation with Arafat's cadres in the territories.

These assurances had an immediate impact on the Islamists in the Gaza Strip, and on July 13, Sheikh Yassin stressed that the *Hudna* was merely a tactical move deferring to prevailing issues but was not evidence of a strategic change. "Israeli occupation will be banished only through armed struggle, and the Palestinian people are ready to make sacrifices in the next one hundred years," Sheikh Yassin declared. In July, HAMAS and Islamic Jihad issued a joint communiqué in Gaza warning the Palestinian Authority that any attempt to collect their weapons and other equipment earmarked for armed struggle, including bombs and rockets, would result in the immediate cancellation of the *Hudna*. Dahlan's emissaries quickly placated the Islamists, assuring them that no such plans existed.

On the night of July 11, a sixty-three-year-old cabdriver, Eli Gurel, was kidnapped by Palestinian terrorists. Gurel picked up four Arab passengers—two men, a young woman, and a four-year-old girl—in Lod, just outside Tel Aviv, on a trip to Jerusalem. Once near their destination, the two young men grabbed Gurel, held a knife to his throat, and ordered him to drive to the north Jerusalem Arab neighborhood of Beit Hanina. From there, they walked through hillside fields into Ramallah and then west to the village of Bituniya. Gurel was then locked in a dry well. The kidnappers, from the nearby village of Beit Rima, were part of a family active in Fatah, the PFLP, and HAMAS. Indeed, the kidnappers demanded the release of two thousand Palestinian terrorists, with their own relatives topping the list: Marwan Bargouti, head of Fatah Tanzim in the West Bank, and a host of other HAMAS terrorists from Ramallah.

On July 14 the Israeli security services were able to identify and apprehend the woman who had gotten into Gorel's taxi with the kidnappers. Within less than twenty-four hours, Israel's key antiterrorist unit had raided several houses in nearby villages where the kidnappers and their assistants were hiding. On the night of July 15, the kidnappers led the Israeli security forces to Gorel, who was still tied up in the well but was otherwise fine.

The kidnapping raised hard questions in Jerusalem about the viability of the security understandings. Although Abu Mazen promised to assist the effort to find the driver, nothing was done. Tirawi even claimed he had established a special crisis team to handle the kidnapping, but he also had done no such thing. Israeli senior security officials complained that had Abu Mazen, Dahlan, and Tirawi really wanted to help, they would have had the culprits in their office in fifteen minutes and the whole issue would have been resolved there and then. In the process, Dahlan emerged as weaker than anticipated. His handling of the crisis demonstrated that he lacked real support in the security forces even in the Gaza Strip, let alone the West Bank, just as Israeli military intelligence had repeatedly warned the Sharon cabinet.

On July 15, the crisis between Abu Mazen and Arafat was formally "resolved," with Arafat further cementing his leadership; Abu Mazen announced that he and Arafat would "jointly conduct the negotiations with Israel"—a formal reversal of the policy set as a precondition for Israel's acceptance of the Road Map and a rebuke of the administration's position as well. To placate the Americans, who feared the implications of Arafat's participation, the real power was entrusted to the Higher Council for Security, a body dominated by Arafat. For reasons of political expediency, both Jerusalem and Washington simply ignored this development, and Arafat, not satisfied with the passive acceptance of his preeminence, resolved to stress the point further. The next day, Omar Suleiman and Abu Mazen visited Arafat at Suleiman's initiative. Arafat humiliated Abu Mazen, making sure he understood that Cairo accepted that Arafat was the omnipotent Palestinian leader and that the position of prime minister was a sham enacted to placate the Americans and the Israelis. According to a participant, the meeting was attended by a group of Abu Mazen's opponents whom Arafat used as a "jury in a revolutionary tribunal" aimed at convicting Abu Mazen, encouraged by the Egyptian chief of intelligence. By the time the meeting was over, Abu Mazen had no doubt about the extent of his power and influence.

Arafat also ordered a public demonstration to further clarify his singular leadership. On the night of July 14, Abu Mazen sent an emissary to Jenin to talk to the local leadership and beg for a cessation of terrorism before Israeli retaliation undermined the Road Map. Abu Mazen's emissary was rebuffed and sent back by Haydar a-Rashid, the governor of Jenin. On July 19, Arafat ordered his man in Jenin, the local commander of the al-Aqsa Martyrs Brigades, Zakariya Zubaydi, to kidnap and publicly humiliate a-Rashid. The formal accusations against him were corruption and cooperation with Israel; his real sin was that he dared to meet Abu Mazen's emissary without first getting permission from the *Muqataah*. Rashid was dragged from his home, beaten in the center of the city, and then taken to the Jenin refugee camp. Later that day, after one of Arafat's close confidants called Zubaydi, a-Rashid was promptly released. "For me, an instruction from Arafat is not open for negotiations, so I released him forthwith," Zubaydi told the Palestinian media. Arafat also sent another messenger with fifty thousand shekels (about twelve thousand dollars) in cash as a thank-you gift for Zubaydi.

Arafat capitalized on these incidents to smash Abu Mazen and Dahlan by demonstrating their inability to fight terrorism and deliver on issues of security. So as not to give Jerusalem and Washington any formal excuse to go after him, Arafat took an indirect approach, establishing three new institutions. One was the Palestinian Supreme Policy Committee for Negotiations with the United States and Israel; the committee chairman was Yasser Arafat, and most of the members were in his coterie. By presidential decree, Abu Mazen was obligated to clear any new policies, statements, and activities with the committee in advance. Secondly, Arafat formed the Palestinian Supreme Committee for Security and Military; Arafat again installed himself as the committee chairman and filled out the membership with intelligence, security, and terrorism chieftains. Arafat also decreed that Dahlan, like Abu Mazen, had to get authorization for his maneuvers from the committee. Dahlan was also obligated to share all pertinent intelligence information with the committee and get explicit approval for antiterrorist operations well in advance, in effect making it impossible for Israel, the United States, or any other foreign party to share intelligence with Dahlan.

Finally, Arafat formed the Supreme Secret Mediation Committee for the Prime Minister's Authority. The committee chairman was again Arafat, and the members were exclusively from his inner circle. Arafat was to convene the body whenever he thought Abu Mazen exceeded his authority, misspoke, or, more dramatically, committed the Palestinian Authority to taking a specific action that Arafat took issue with; the committee had final say in firing or otherwise penalizing Abu Mazen. Arafat made sure that all three committees were in place and functioning before Abu Mazen left for Washington, so that he had no illusions about his real power and authority.

At the same time, Washington kept pressuring Jerusalem, at the request of Abu Mazen and Mubarak, to lift the siege on Arafat. The real issue was not just Arafat's freedom of movement, but the Palestinians' insistence that the Israel Defense Forces not capitalize on Arafat's absence from the *Muqataah* to hunt down the two hundred terrorists hiding there and destroy Tirawi's elaborate command center. The meeting between Abu Mazen and Sharon before their respective trips to Washington ended with raised voices and sharp disagreements. Abu Mazen demanded more concessions, from withdrawals to prisoner releases, and insisted that the prevailing conditions in the territories prevented his forces from acting more aggressively against the terrorist infrastructure. The Bush administration pressured Israel for "goodwill" gestures, indicating that if Abu Mazen returned empty-handed it would be disastrous for the Road Map process. Washington's insistence continued even after Abu Mazen repudiated, on July 22, the key elements of the security understanding with the United States and Israel: "Cracking down on HAMAS, [Islamic] Jihad, and the Palestinian organizations is not an option at all," he declared. "We are applying the law, which we accepted under the leadership of the Palestinian Authority, and that is what we will do."

It is not surprising, therefore, that Jerusalem was having its doubts about the viability of the *Hudna* and the Road Map. Uzi Landau, the cabinet minister responsible for strategic relations with the United States and oversight of Israel's intelligence community, considered the prevailing situation to be "very temporary and dangerous" for Israel. "Everything we achieved against the terrorists and their infrastructures in the past two years is now down the drain," Landau said. "They are preparing one thousand Qassam rockets, and building up terror cells, and digging tunnels, and we can't do anything to stop them. . . . We have been sucked into this *Hudna,* and when we come to the Americans and tell them that the Palestinian Authority has not dismantled the terrorist infrastructure, they'll tell us to calm down. They'll say that we have to strengthen Abu Mazen, make more concessions, and keep on going toward the establishment of a Palestinian state."

The only chance for the Road Map process to succeed, Landau insisted, was for the Palestinian Authority to commit to specific actions, with Washington's guarantee that they would be implemented. "They must tell us exactly on what day they outlaw HAMAS, collect illegal weapons, and the like. We must know exactly when they plan to make the required changes in their educational system, such as including Israel on their maps. . . . In addition, there must be an absolute statement by the Palestinian Authority—without which Israel must make clear that it will not proceed another step in the Road Map—that it withdraws its demand for the 'right of return' of Arab refugees from 1948 and their descendants." Landau conceded that the Bush administration had shown no inclination to go along with such demands from the Palestinians.

But if Bush thought he was gaining Arab support for its Iraq policy by furthering the Palestinian cause, he was fundamentally wrong. Arab rulers have long used the Palestinian issue as a fig leaf to cover the brewing instability and discontent throughout the Arab world. Instead of acknowledging that riots and insurrection are aimed at their own regimes, Arab rulers insist that their populations are irate at the oppression of their Palestinian brethren. This has been a fundamental misconception that Washington has traditionally failed to grasp. Fouad Adjami elucidated this point, saying, "There are deeper furies that grip Arab society; we take up a false trail when we fall for the claim that our troubles in that world spring from our policy on Israel and Palestinians. This is the trail our interlocutors in those lands would have us follow. But they are shrewd men, the rulers who hold sway in those Arab lands. It is a cultural norm of the Arab world that strangers are never exposed to family demons. We are strangers in that world, and the Palestine story is all we shall be given, for it is the most convenient of tales."

At the same time, Arab rulers expect the United States to know the truth and read through their subterfuge. When the Bush administration failed to address Arab concerns regarding the Iraq war and instead concentrated on solving the Palestinian issue, the Arabs saw it as a betrayal. It is incomprehensible to Arab rulers that the United States does not comprehend their plight. For them, Washington's electing to deal with the Palestinians—rather than addressing their own concerns—meant that the administration did not care about its Arab allies and their demons. Most Arab leaders doubt that the Americans would come to their aid at a time of need, if only because the United States does not understand and does not care about their plight. To survive, these leaders feel compelled to make deals with their grassroots opponents—the militant Islamists.

While the Bush administration was embroiled in the Israeli-Palestinian crisis, an upsurge of Islamist insurgency in Iraq had a dramatic impact throughout the Middle East. The escalation in Iraq immediately emboldened the rejuvenated Palestinian intifada and other Islamist movements around the region. Nayif Kurayyim noted that "the high morale that will be triggered in the region by the Iraqi resistance operations against the U.S. occupation will show that the age of resistance is not over. . . . The Iraqi people, or at least a part of them, have joined the list of the Arab peoples that are resisting in Lebanon and Palestine, although it is likely that the geographic impact of the resistance may move from Lebanon and Palestine to Iraq." In this context, the quest for political solutions—particularly of the Israeli-Palestinian dispute—is perceived throughout the Arab world as an American conspiracy aimed at stifling the grassroots resistance. "That is why the Arab street was upset by the restrictions placed on HizbAllah in its attempts to support the resistance in Palestine and was even more upset by the restrictions placed on the resistance movement in Palestine and the imposition of the truce on the Palestinians. And that is why the Arab street today is pleased with the accelerating and escalating Iraqi resistance, which might offset the frustration that prevailed in the Arab street following the surprise fall of Baghdad," Kurayyim explained.

14
ONLY THE BEGINNING

By early June, the frequency of attacks on American forces was growing rapidly. On average, at least one attack a day resulted in casualties for the United States; the ambushes, firefights, and grenade assaults that failed to inflict American casualties were too numerous to count. Some of these ignored incidents were of strategic importance. For example, U.S. planes and helicopters regularly came under fire while attempting to land or take off all over Iraq—particularly in Baghdad, Mosul, and Tikrit. U.S. officials acknowledged that "Baghdad International Airport will remain closed to commercial flights as long as the shooting on the planes continues." American troops were beseiged on a daily basis with with pelted stones, waved fists, and shouted insults; the tires on their vehicles were burned regularly. Graffiti were beginning to pop up on walls in Baghdad and elsewhere, ranging from the broad—"Long live President Saddam Hussein!"—to the highly specific—"We swear to Allah that we will cut all the hands that waved to the Americans soldiers stained with the blood of our heroic martyrs." Such hostile activities reflected an increasingly despondent and hostile Iraqi population. Moreover, the professionalism of the armed resistance was improving, and more often than not they escaped safely in the aftermath of an ambush. Just as troubling, a growing number of innocent civilians were caught in the crossfire—especially when American soldiers returned enemy fire. For all intents and purposes Iraq was sliding into the initial phases of a full-scale armed resistance and guerrilla warfare campaign involving a large segment of the population. "We're all with the resistance against the occupation," declared a young prayer leader. "The Americans are occupiers. Occupiers cannot come and provide people with happiness and freedom." The initial communiqués announcing a new cycle of anti-American strikes suggested that a new phase in the liberation jihad had begun, involving the close cooperation of all key elements regardless of ideology or past rivalries.

In late May, for example, a statement from a group calling itself "The General Command for the Armed Forces, Resistance, and Liberation in Iraq" declared that "elite troops of the armed forces, the Fedayeen, Al-Faruq Brigades—'the military wing of the Islamic Resistance in Iraq'—Majami Al-Hussein, and members of the Arab Socialist Baath Party [had] succeeded in shooting down a U.S. helicopter in Al-Anbar Governorate, killing four military men who were on board." The collection of groups was significant: the message indicated that the Sunni Islamist al-Faruq Brigades, the pro-Iran Shiite al-Hussein Grouping, the Baathist forces, and the fedayeen were all cooperating. (The crash in question remains a murky episode: the UH-60 helicopter took off under a hail of small-arms fire, swerved sharply, and hit power lines before crashing; it's still unclear whether the crash was caused by hostile fire or pilot error in an attempt to avoid ground fire.) The statement proclaimed that "a new Vietnam or rather [a war] harsher than Vietnam has begun in Iraq. It will not end until the last occupier departs from Iraq's territory." The General Command also vowed to use all possible means to prevent the occupation forces from benefiting from Iraqi oil, "even if it costs us this oil to burn the invading forces."

The most ardent Islamist movements made similar statements. In the aftermath of the May 27 attack on U.S. forces in al-Fallujah, in which two American soldiers were killed and nine wounded, the most important claim came from "The Popular Resistance in Iraq," which identified itself as a bin Laden–style "Jihadist Islamic movement." The spiritual leader of this group was Sheikh Abdul Aziz al-Humayd, the imam of the Grand Mosque of al-Fallujah. Sheikh al-Humayd issued an imperative "to launch Jihad against the Americans in their capacity as an occupation force" and declared that "it is the duty of [all] Muslims to expel [the United States] from Iraq." Even though the Islamist movement was "composed of young men from [al-Fallujah] who [had] no connection with the Baath Party" but were "followers of the Sharia and seekers after Jihad," as well as "a large number of Arab volunteers," he declared that the Islamists must cooperate with all other anti-American forces in order to expedite the jihad and the ensuing eviction of the occupation forces.

Nevertheless, the United States continued to insist that the strikes were being conducted by the last remnants of the Saddam regime. "If you have 20,000 or 30,000 former members of the secret police—torturers, war criminals—those people are still around," Deputy Defense Secretary Paul

Wolfowitz told Congress. "They're making trouble. They attack armed American convoys every day. So you can imagine what they do to unarmed Iraqis who may support us." On June 1, American forces were ordered to prepare for "an insurgency war by the Sunni minority still loyal to Iraqi President Saddam Hussein." U.S. defense officials stressed that "all" resistance attacks were the work of "Saddam loyalists," and that the most lethal strikes were in western Iraq—particularly in Fallujah, Hit, and Ramadi. Lt. Gen. David McKiernan, the head of coalition ground forces, insisted that these attacks were part of "an insurrection fomented by Baath Party leaders who fled Baghdad during the war in April." Reflecting Washington's official position, McKiernan predicted that the attacks would die down once the perpetrators realized the futility of their actions. "I see it [the insurrection] being orchestrated by enemies whose future has gone," McKiernan said. "They were part of Saddam Hussein's regime, they were tied to him." From the start, this fixation with Saddam's connection to a Baathist-dominated guerrilla campaign prevented American authorities from realizing the gravity and complexity of the challenge they faced.

At the same time, however, the mounting casualties could not be ignored. The Pentagon was resigned to the need to keep a far larger force in Iraq than previously estimated. The original prewar plans had called for a force of about 100,000 U.S. troops and assumed a relatively quick force reduction, based on a number of assumptions: that "the Iraqis would hail the Americans as liberators[;] that Iraq had little history of ethnic strife"; that many countries would contribute peacekeeping forces in order to gain access to the postwar reconstruction boom.

By early June, however, the 145,000 U.S. and 15,000 U.K. troops already in Iraq were deemed insufficient. The 3rd Infantry Division, which expected to be rotated back to the United States, was deployed to the Fallujah area until at least August 2003, with some elements dispatched to Baghdad. Having missed the war, the 4th Infantry Division was now charged with policing the northern Sunni zone stretching between Tikrit, Kirkuk, and the Iranian border. The 4th Infantry Division also left a sizeable component in Baghdad. The 1st Armored Division, fresh from peacekeeping operations in the Balkans, assumed control of Baghdad with the aid of some 4,000 military police officers. U.S. Marines remained in predominantly Shiite southern Iraq, while British forces were still concentrated around Basra. Ultimately, this was a pitifully small force to police a country as huge as Iraq. The thinly stretched U.S. units could establish power in only a very small number of locations. In the rest of the country,

American forces asserted their presence by air and through sporadic patrols. The Iraqis recognized the shortfall and exploited it in conducting the next phase of their anti-American jihad.

The Iraqis were getting organized for war. With the initial shock of Baghdad's fall waning, the anti-American forces began preparing for protracted guerrilla warfare. Throughout most of June, the resistance forces strove to sustain, and even escalate, the pace of terrorist strikes against the allied forces. But their principal focus was on consolidating a comprehensive support system for the struggle ahead. Special attention was paid to recruiting and training additional mujahedin, establishing command and control grids throughout Iraq, and activating reliable communications networks. The leaders of the regional and nationwide organizations also made tremendous progress in shoring up cross-movement cooperation. At the same time, quality networks were gradually activated around Iraq, bringing with them both expertise and huge stockpiles of weapons.

Most important was Saddam Hussein's decision to activate the clandestine "rainy day," or "doomsday," irregular networks he had established in 1968. Soon after the Baath Party returned to power in Baghdad—with memories of the party's 1963 overthrow still painfully fresh—Saddam had created these networks, made up of fierce loyalists all over Baghdad. Intended to help sustain Baath influence in case of a new coup, the group was gradually transformed into an underground parallel party as Saddam assumed personal control; eventually it became his own personal safety net—a full-fledged paramilitary force. Its strike units were trained by Yugoslav and Soviet experts in partisan "people's war." By the early 1980s, they were a well-trained, well-funded, elite force with huge caches of weapons, funds, food, and means for conducting a Yugoslav-style protracted people's war. Once Saddam realized the extent of Washington's hostility and resolve in the 1990s, he brought in North Korean experts, with their own ideas for fighting and debilitating U.S.-type forces, to upgrade and expand the training of the cadres of his underground parallel party.

As tensions with the United States grew, Saddam poured huge resources into the underground parallel party, preparing it for the American occupation he knew would come sooner or later. Saddam's confidants were thoroughly prepared for the contingency, issuing written instructions to cadres all over Iraq. A January 23, 2003, "Emergency Secret Plan" issued to the fedayeen by the "Head of General Intelligence" instructed the operatives to "take the following measures in case of the fall of the Iraqi Leadership by the American-British-Zionist coalition, God forbid." The instructions ranged from making Iraqi cities ungovernable through sustained "looting and setting alight of all government offices," to strategies for "causing damage" to electrical power facilities and water plants, and cutting "internal and international communications." The operatives were instructed to penetrate Shiite religious institutions and "assassinate religious scholars and preachers from the mosques and places of prayer" in order to provoke anti-American insurrection. They were also to target returning exiles to prevent their cooperation with American authorities. The specific contingency plans outlined in this and similar documents had been carefully and thoroughly rehearsed since early 2003. Yet only in early June did Saddam decide that his forces could safely sustain a grassroots guerrilla war against the United States; he activated the parallel party's fighting units soon thereafter.

At the core of Saddam's decision to up the ante was his realization that the United States had no clue about his real escape, evasion, and sheltering system. Back in 1991, right after the conclusion of the first Gulf War, Saddam decided that his existing system of bunkers and escape routes was useless. Since these facilities had been built during the 1980s by German and Yugoslav experts, Saddam suspected—accurately—that their locations and secrets were now known to the United States. In the mid-1990s, after much internal debate, Saddam brought in North Korean and Chinese experts and construction teams to build a whole new system of underground facilities for himself, his inner circle, and the underground parallel party's fighting units. To ensure complete secrecy, the new system of underground facilities—bunkers, command centers, and communication storage sites—was built from scratch by North Korean workers. Since no Iraqi labor was involved, very few Iraqis knew about the existence, let alone the location, of these facilities. Furthermore, the North Koreans were able to render the facilities virtually impervious to detection by American surveillance. Their methods included digging a relatively small hole in a shaded mountainside, then expanding the underground spaces through laborious tunneling and carving from the inside. The dirt was evacuated through the hole during the night and dumped into nearby waterways, so that no visible traces of the excavation remained. Some of the key facilities were dug under nearby lakes, to further reduce the likelihood of detection by U.S. national technical means. The North Koreans' expertise in camouflage is superb, relying on exits and entrances placed close to waterways in areas covered with thick foliage. During the late 1990s, only Saddam and a small number of trusted loyalists visited the sites, using small boats and recreational vehicles to avoid detection.

Among the concealed bunkers built under Chinese supervision was a network of special long-term storage sites for strategic stockpiles of weapons and ammunition, including weapons of mass destruction, for times of extreme national emergency. A former Iraqi colonel with a Ph.D. in engineering, who escaped in 1999 and is now hiding in Australia, reported that he personally knows of five such secret storage bunkers that were built near Baghdad, Basra, and Tikrit. Other such bunkers were constructed in the deep desert of western Iraq. According to another Iraqi defector, Russian experts were brought to test the viability of the Chinese designs before more bunkers were constructed. The testing peaked when Chinese experts stayed inside a prototype bunker while it was subjected to a series of bombings and shelling by the Russians—only to emerge shaken but otherwise unharmed. The keys to the security of these bunkers were their depth and the special system of multiple-layered construction—a delicate task completed by the North Korean crews. A complex ventilation system was thoroughly camouflaged, making detection from the outside virtually impossible. The colonel reported that the three such bunkers he visited in the late 1990s were stocked with large quantities of conventional weapons and ammunition, artillery shells, and 122mm GRAD rockets armed with chemical warheads, as well as drums with chemical agents.

By the time this new system was finished in the late 1990s, there were only a few indistinct rumors about its existence. Most of the meager intelligence came from human sources within U.S.-allied intelligence services. Among the best of these sources was a bodyguard who had escorted Saddam to one of these facilities more than once over many years. But even he was able to provide only a general indication of the site's location and was unable to identify the exact place from overhead photographs. Jordanian intelligence had a similar experience with another knowledgeable source.

According to numerous sources, the North Korean–built underground infrastructure includes numerous small, long-term storage bunkers, mainly in the al-Jazeerah area in Iraq's northwestern desert, and three major complexes, each of which includes numerous underground facilities, some connected by underground tunnels and some autonomous and completely isolated. The first complex, and most likely the largest, is in the al-Qaim area, extending between al-Qaim and Lake Qadissiyah to the east. According to most reports, Saddam's main headquarters and hiding place in the early summer of 2003 were in this complex. The second complex extends from the Ramadi area and Lake Habbaniyah to the south. It is relatively easy to reach the center of Baghdad from this site via the capital's western slums. The third complex is spread in the triangle of Tikrit, Samarra, and the mountain lakes on the Jabal Hamarin range to the east of both cities. Moreover, all three complexes are in areas frequented by the Sunni Bedouin tribes that wander between Iraq, Syria, and Saudi Arabia; fiercely anti-American, these tribes are thus a reliable source of secure transportation.

During the first two weeks of June 2003, Saddam's underground parallel party was a relatively minor source of equipment for the majority of the anti-U.S. networks and cells in the Sunni heartland, parts of northern Iraq, and, to a lesser extent, the Shiite heartland (where Iranian intelligence was the dominant sponsor). Large caches of weapons, explosives, and other supplies from the al-Quds popular forces, the fedayeen, the Baath Party, and even the Iraqi Army remained available for use by the local resistance forces. Additional equipment could be easily smuggled from Syria as necessary. Hence there was no point in touching the safe, well-concealed caches of the underground parallel party.

But the expert cadres of the secret network did provide expertise to the resistance, explaining how to organize underground cells and ensure security and teaching ambush tactics and bomb-making techniques to rebels all over Iraq. Saddam's cadres assisted all elements that wanted such cooperation, including the most ardent anti-Baathist Islamist networks. In addition, they offered funds to any anti-American organizational initiative. Saddam's networks were also instrumental in facilitating the continued flow of Islamist volunteers—both Sunnis and Shiites—into Iraq via Syria. The intelligence officers of the underground parallel party realized that many of the Islamist and localized networks were fiercely anti-Saddam as well as anti-American; they recognized the limits of cooperation against a common enemy and drew the proper line between providing sufficient support to make these networks' operations more lethal, and the kind of attempts at intervention that might drive the networks to betray the Baathists to the Americans.

By mid-June, consequently, Iraq was filled with a myriad of loosely connected networks and cells driven and defined by a host of ideological frameworks—Islamist, ethnocentric, tribal Baathist, and even communist—all loosely interconnected in webs of self-interest and localized loyalties, and all virulently, uncompromisingly anti-American. And though Saddam's cadres were instrumental in running the command and control grids and communications networks, the Islamists were providing a growing number of fighters, including the most zealous mujahedin.

*   *   *

Much of this activity could not have taken place without Syria's position as both a sponsor and a safe haven. The Iraqi undertaking was personally supervised by Bashar al-Assad himself, while the sponsorship effort was managed by Bashar's brother-in-law, Assaf Shawkat, and Firas Tlass, the son of Syria's defense minister, who was responsible for Iraq's clandestine weapons acquisition networks and oil exports. The mere involvement of these three leaders indicates the importance Damascus accorded to sustaining, if not escalating, the anti-U.S. guerrilla war in Iraq. Indeed, by the summer of 2003, the forward headquarters in Abu-Kamal was expanded and assigned a large number of intelligence and commando officers. Most significant, the Syrians established direct secure communications from Abu-Kamal with both the Syrian General Staff's and Bashar's own "war room" at the presidential palace.

In Syria, Saddam's people maintained extensive organizational and safe-haven facilities. The Syrians facilitated cross-border movement for leaders and commanders. For example, Qusay returned from Libya (probably early in June) via Syria, and Abid Hamid Humud, Saddam's personal secretary, went to Damascus to collect material for Saddam just before his capture by U.S. forces in mid-June. The Syrians also permitted Iraqi officials and officers to cross into Syria as their operations required—some unconfirmed reports held that several wounded fighters were evacuated to Syria for better medical treatment. Saddam's people also maintained in Damascus a treasury of hundreds of millions of dollars—a few billion, according to some sources—in hard currency, gold, and jewels; the money was used to finance specialized weapons acquisition and other support for the Iraqi guerrilla warfare.

Syria also played a major role in recruiting and training Islamist volunteers for anti-U.S. measures inside Iraq. Many of these volunteers were recruited in Syria itself, several of them from the Sunni Madrassas of Damascus and northern Syria—all adherents of the teachings of bin Laden and the Muslim Brotherhood—others "volunteered" from Syrian commando and intelligence units. Syrian military intelligence also recruited Palestinian and Kurdish fighters from the terrorist camps and joined al-Qaeda senior commanders to launch recruitment drives in the refugee camps of southern Lebanon. Most of the recruits were Palestinian Islamist mujahedin; some were veterans of al-Qaeda fighting in Afghanistan and Chechnya.

Damascus assisted the flow of volunteers from all over the Muslim world via Damascus International Airport, and volunteers kept arriving from all over South Asia (mainly Pakistan and Afghanistan), the Far East (especially Indonesia and Malaysia), and the Arab world. Located near the border control, special Syrian military intelligence desks allowed would-be mujahedin to enter Syria without any papers. From the airport they were taken straight to training camps, mainly near Tadmur in the middle of the Syrian desert, where they were matched with Syrian and Palestinian Islamists. There they were trained together and organized into small cells ranging from roughly five to twelve mujahedin. They were equipped with small arms, high explosives, and antitank rockets for themselves as well as for the Iraqi mujahedin they were to assist. These cells were then sent across the border (using unmarked Bedouin desert roads) to join the Iraqi jihad in support of the Islamist networks. Upon leaving Syria they were provided with directions to prearranged meeting points, from which they were guided to the Islamist Iraqi forces they were to bolster. By late June this flow of volunteers had become a torrent, with hundreds of mujahedin crossing the border every night.

In addition to these activities, Damascus permitted Iranian intelligence to recruit, organize, and transfer Shiite HizbAllah fighters from Lebanon, along with weapons and other supplies, to bolster the Shiite forces in southern Iraq and the greater Baghdad area. The HizbAllah fighters reinforced the Iran-sponsored networks with highly experienced terrorists and organizers; they are uniquely important because all of them have extensive combat experience against Israel in southern Lebanon.

On June 18, the United States obtained firsthand, concrete intelligence of Syrian support for the Iraqi leadership. First, Saddam's personal secretary Abid Hamid Humud al-Tikriti—considered the closest nonfamily man to Saddam—was caught. While hiding in a simple house in Tikrit as an anonymous guest, he was betrayed by the Baathist who was supposed to pick him up for the next phase of his journey. In his initial interrogation, Humud insisted that Saddam and his two sons had left for Syria even before the end of the war. From Syria, he claimed, they continued to a third country, Libya.

According to Humud, Saddam's party had not traveled directly to Libya. Instead they flew from Minsk, Belarus, to Damascus, and from there to Chad, so that they could reach Libya over land. Indeed, Qadhafi had sent a message to Saddam—which was intercepted by the United States—instructing him to arrive by land in order to avoid detection by the Americans, who were monitoring all air traffic. However, a closer examination of Humud's belongings raised doubts about his story. According to Hoshayr Zabari, a senior Kurdish intelligence officer involved in the operation, Humud was captured while returning from Syria, en route to meet up with Saddam or other key figures. Significantly, Humud was carrying a set of Belarusian passports for key individuals, which he had just picked up in Damascus—contradicting his claim that key leaders had already left Iraq via Syria.

The United States knew that word of Humud's capture would spread quickly. At the very least, the major operation in the usually tranquil neighborhood of Tikrit was sufficient to attract attention and spread rumors. Not without reason, U.S. intelligence analysts assumed that once they learned about Humud's capture, Saddam or other "higher-level Iraqis" would try to flee Iraq for Syrian before their whereabouts were betrayed by either Humud or whoever had betrayed him.

In recent days, U.S. forces securing the border with Syria had already sustained attacks in the area. On June 9, for example, a car pulled up near an American roadblock near al-Qaim in the middle of the night. A couple of men jumped out and killed one American soldier with handguns and wounded others, throwing grenades as they escaped. With the U.S. forces preoccupied with finding the assailants—who vanished safely—the Iraqis and Syrians were able to run a few small convoys across the border. Hence, on June 18, U.S. forces led by Task Force 20 were closely watching the main roads into Syria. Shortly after Humud was captured, a Predator UAV noticed a small convoy racing into the Iraqi village of Dhib, about 70 miles south of al-Qaim. Armed helicopters attempted to hit the convoy, but instead struck a few buildings and caused several civilian casualties. Meanwhile, the convoy continued racing along the road toward the Syrian border. By then, the helicopter-borne Special Forces were joined by an AC-130 Spectre Gunship and A-10 attack fighters.

According to on-site Lebanese sources, the convoy was next engaged a few miles from the Syrian border, traveling on the al-Qaim-Abu-Kamal highway. Noticing the air activity, the convoy broke in two, with a few cars racing along the Iraqi side of the border and three cars speeding across to safety in the Syrian village of Dulaym. While the A-10s attacked and destroyed the convoy inside Iraq, the AC-130 escorted the helicopter-borne Special Forces in pursuit into Syrian territory. Syrian border guards opened fire in an attempt to prevent the American aircraft from crossing into Syria. Their positions were engaged by the AC-130 as the helicopters attacked and then closed in on the three cars. What followed was an intense shoot-out between members of Task Force 20 already on the ground and the Syrian forces. The AC-130 provided devastating air support; by the time the brief engagement was over, twenty-five to thirty Syrians had been killed and five captured, three of them wounded and one an army colonel. (The Syrians were released on June 30.) The three-car convoy was completely destroyed about a mile inside Syrian territory.

The most significant outcome of the June 18 clash was the indisputable exposure of the extent of Bashar al-Assad's involvement in the Iraq-related activities. Both Israeli and U.S. intelligence intercepted the flurry of communications between Damascus, Abu-Kamal, and the forward units near Dulaym. Soon after the Syrian forces in Abu-Kamal detected irregular U.S. military activities near the al-Qaim area, Bashar al-Assad and all key commanders were summoned to the war room in the General Staff building. After assessing the crisis, they quickly assumed direct control over the fighting near the Iraqi border.

At first, Bashar ordered the immediate grounding of all air activity inside Syria. This was done to prevent America from claiming that the Syrian Air Force had "threatened" U.S. aircraft and thus creating a pretext for deeper U.S. incursion and bombing. At the same time, Bashar ordered all ground forces in the area to engage the Americans. The Damascus war room insisted that the fighting continue, despite reports of heavy casualties from AC-130 strikes. In the aftermath, the Syrians kept quiet about the incident, even electing not to issue a diplomatic complaint about the clear violation of their border by U.S. forces. At the same time, the Syrian military reinforced its positions along the border with Iraq and increased its level of readiness. The active assistance to the Iraqi guerrilla war against the United States only grew.

Meanwhile, U.S. military activities continued to escalate and expand in reaction to the growing terrorist insurgency. In early June American forces began launching large-scale antiterrorism sweeps, but these were largely reactive and limited to areas of growing attacks. The extremely poor intelligence available to the U.S. forces, and the widespread hostility of the Iraqi population, ensured that the results of these sweeps were negligible. The Iraqi civilian population felt victimized and alienated by the heavy-handed approach of the U.S. forces, and more and more of them were driven into assisting the resistance.

The first major sweep was launched by several battalions of the 3rd Infantry Division on June 5. The objectives were guerrilla fighters in Fallujah and Habbaniyah; U.S. officials described the mission as "a search-and-destroy operation for Sunni insurgents." But despite such highly publicized "offensives," attacks on U.S. forces continued to escalate—and Fallujah, a region whose population merges Islamists and tribal Baathists, remained the key to region-wide insurgency. "I don't believe there is a single organized group," Lt. Col. Eric Schwartz, the commander of the Fallujah-based 1st Battalion, 64th Armored Brigade, told the *New York Times*. "The information that we have is that it may be a collection of folks. It may be Iraqis. It may be Syrians. It may be Palestinians. We believe that Al-Qaeda is possibly in there."

On the next day, June 6, a local mob gathered around the main police station in Fallujah and started demolishing the three-story building with hammers and axes. It was a well-organized operation, with the *shabab* arriving well equipped with tools and well led by "foremen" who gave precise instructions. "That attack was a warning to the Americans," a participant told the *Guardian*. "We have told them more than once that this is a residential area and we don't want them here. We have destroyed the walls, we took the windows and now we are going to destroy the whole building. . . . We are cleansing the place of Americans." By this point, the fighting in Baghdad and Fallujah already had all the characteristics of a fledgling urban guerrilla campaign. The attacking squads were highly professional and enjoyed widespread public support: new strikes were greeted by jubilant *shabab* cheering the attackers and pelting the burning vehicles and U.S. troops with stones.

The audacity of the insurgents grew around June 10, as rumors began spreading around Baghdad and the Sunni heartland that Saddam was in the area. According to these rumors, which were confirmed by Chalabi in Baghdad, Saddam was seen north of Baghdad handing large sums of money to the various fighters who had attacked or ambushed Americans and inflicted casualties. According to several Iraqi sources, Saddam was greeted with enthusiasm by the crowds. He exhorted them to kill all the Americans and create a "bloodbath for the invaders," and promised to pay a bounty for every American soldier killed or wounded. Saddam was said to be in a good mood and appeared self-confident—and despite the lack of direct eyewitnesses to the gatherings, the rumors electrified the population in Iraq's main Sunni cities, rejuvenating and emboldening people to participate in the anti-U.S. jihad.

On June 12, the Untied States launched Operation Peninsula Strike, described by American defense officials as "the largest U.S. operation in Iraq since the end of active hostilities in April." Central Command said the operation was part of "the continued effort to eradicate Baath Party loyalists, paramilitary groups, and other subversive elements." Some 4,000 troops of the 101st Airborne Division (Air Assault) and the 4th Infantry Division, aided by extensive helicopter and air support and river patrol boats, raided the Duluiyah-Ballad area—a strip stretching along the Tigris northwest of Baghdad, where U.S. intelligence had identified an Iraqi "terrorist training camp." By the end of the operation, U.S. forces had killed some seventy mujahedin and arrested roughly four hundred suspects— mostly Iraqis, but also volunteers from Saudi Arabia, Sudan, Yemen, and Afghanistan. Resistance during the operation was intense enough that F-16CG fighters were called in to provide air support. The mujahedin demonstrated that they were capable of mounting an effective air defense, shooting down both an AH-64 attack helicopter and one of the F-16CGs. The helicopter's crew was rescued under fire, with Iraqi forces closing in on them. The F-16CG's pilot ejected safely away from the fighting zone and was rescued soon afterward. The average U.S. soldier had a grim view of the operation's outcome. "It does not seem to have had much effect," a participating soldier said. "We are still being shot at every night."

But officials were still insistnig that the United States was not facing centrally organized resistance in Iraq, let alone a guerrilla war. "We are certainly seeing some organized resistance, particularly in the area west of Baghdad and the area north of Baghdad," L. Paul Bremer, the U.S. administrator for Iraq, said. "We do not see signs of central command and control direction in that resistance at this point. These are groups that are organized, but they're small. They may be five or six men conducting isolated attacks against our soldiers." Unfolding events, however, belied this rosy assessment. Before dawn on June 13, at least two major explosions ripped several holes in the newly activated Iraqi-Turkish oil pipeline designed to transfer Kirkuk's oil to Mediterranean ports in Turkey. The explosions ignited intense fires; during the morning, repeated terrorist ambushes and scattered mines on access roads to the pipeline hampered the firefighters' and recovery teams' efforts to stop the fire and repair the pipeline.

On June 15, U.S. forces launched yet another major sweep, this time in the Fallujah area. Operation Spartan Scorpion was defined by CENTCOM as "a crackdown to seize unauthorized weapons and insurgents" at "the center of Sunni unrest in western Iraq." Early in the morning, 1,400 troops of the 3rd Infantry's 2nd Brigade, with helicopter support, closed on Fallujah and started moving from house to house in search of fighters and weapons. "We wanted to focus on the people providing the resources and the command and control, and I think we did that," said Col. David Perkins, commander of the 2nd Brigade. But the results were abysmal: the search yielded no weapons, for the bulk of the mujahedin had already melted away, taking their weapons with them. As a show of defiance, the U.S. military headquarters in nearby Ramadi (from which Operation Spartan Scorpion was controlled) was attacked by mortar fire, and some buildings were damaged by fire.

The leadership of the Islamist resistance was encouraged by the building momentum of the insurgency. On June 16, in response to the recent offensive sweeps, they circulated a statement in the mosques and streets of Baghdad, urging Iraqis to break contact with the Americans lest they be injured in the forthcoming escalation of the jihad. "Iraqis should stay away from occupation soldiers, tanks, and armored vehicles, to allow our fighting cells to carry out their martyr operations without leaving civilian casualties," the statement read. "We will not feel guilty if any of those accompanying—or collaborating with—the Americans are killed."

The pace of clashes continued to rise, and American casualties increased on a daily basis. In numerous cities and townships, U.S. forces raided houses and neighborhoods in attempts to locate "Saddam's loyalists" and recover weapons. Scores were arrested, but most were released not long thereafter; a few weapons were recovered. But with the damage done to civilian property mounting, the Iraqi population became increasingly embittered and alienated and continued to gravitate toward the anti-American resistance. North of Baghdad, U.S. convoys were ambushed regularly, and several soldiers were injured. Isolated American guard posts and roadblocks were attacked by snipers, bursts of small-arms fire, and the occasional grenade. Several soldiers were killed and wounded in such attacks.

On June 18, American forces near the U.S. administrator's building opened fire on a demonstration of former soldiers demanding paychecks. Two former Iraqi soldiers were killed and many wounded; none were armed. By now the U.S. Army was expanding offensive operations against suspected terrorists and guerrilla fighters once again; in a few days, U.S. forces apprehended more than four hundred people. But only sixty of those apprehended were ultimately confirmed to be former members of the Iraqi intelligence service, Saddam's Fedayeen, or the Republican Guards, and the extent of their involvement in anti-U.S. terrorism was uncertain.

Senior U.S. commanders were beginning to sense the complexity of the problem. "I believe there are three groups out there right now," Maj. Gen. Raymond Odierno, commander of the 4th Infantry Division, told a June 18 briefing by video from Baghdad. "Basically, there is a group of ex-Saddam Baath Party loyalists, some Islamic fundamentalists, and then there are just some plain Iraqis who are poor and are being paid to attack U.S. forces." He confirmed that several detainees were combatants from Iran and Syria. Although acts of terrorism and insurgency were on the rise, he contended, what the United States was facing was not a guerrilla campaign, because the attacks were diffuse and seemingly disorganized. "This is not guerrilla warfare," Odierno stressed. "It is not close to guerrilla warfare because it's not coordinated, it's not organized, and it's not led." At the same time, representatives of Saddam's Fedayeen were launching a recruitment campaign for anti-U.S. fighters, announcing that additional forces were urgently needed for a major offensive against the United States. The recruiters promised high pay in American dollars; by late June, this recruitment drive was achieving great success in the Sunni heartland.

Throughout the summer of 2003, the United States remained incapable of sustaining oil production in the face of repeated sabotage—from the detonation of pipelines and facilities, to the simple theft and vandalism of equipment at key oil installations. On June 20, for example, two sophisticated bombs were activated by remote control, triggering several explosions that disrupted the flow of oil for some time. American forces were so thinly stretched they could not closely monitor the lengthy pipelines in the rugged mountains and desert—a reality that was exploited by the Iraqis. That night, in Fallujah, mujahedin fired RPGs into a power transformer under the nose of U.S. tanks on guard. The explosion sent a tower of flames into the night, and cut electricity to most of the city.

These attacks were the beginning of a broad new wave of terrorism targeting Iraq's civilian infrastructure—its power stations, gas stations, and water and sewage systems—to prevent American authorities from providing basic services to the Iraqi people. Along with the ongoing sabotage of oil pipelines and other installations, this intense campaign had a major impact on the already despairing Iraqi urban population. As the problems persisted, alienation and hostility in the Iraqi cities continued to rise. "Right now, U.S. soldiers inside Iraqi cities are like sitting ducks for terrorists," Iraqi National Congress spokesman Entifadh Qanbar told the June 24 *Globe and Mail.*

Activity on the Saudi front also continued escalating throughout the month of June. Saudi Islamist mujahedin—ideologically connected to Osama bin Laden—were active in the escalating insurgency in both Iraq and Saudi Arabia, and the flow of Islamists between the two nations was on the increase. A growing number of Saudi mujahedin were arriving in Iraq to fight the Americans, and many were returning home after a brief time on the Iraqi battlefield with combat experience, rejuvenated zeal, and new weapons. By mid-June several hundred Saudi mujahedin were fighting in Iraq, and several dozen had already been killed.

By now, the Islamist leadership—both international and Saudi—were convinced that the jihad in Iraq would be protracted and challenging and that "the Struggle for an Islamic Baghdad" could become a mobilizing factor for the entire Muslim world, much as the great jihad in Afghanistan had in the 1980s. The Saudi Islamists worked to consolidate their long-term presence and influence in Iraq. They started a web of outreach programs, beginning with the Islamist bastion in al-Fallujah. Several of the Saudi luminaries of bin Laden's radical Islam—most notably Sheikh Nasser al-Omar and Sheikh Safar al-Hawali—had already lent their guidance to the Iraqi Islamists; meanwhile, a group of Saudi-educated clerics, predominantly Iraqi but including Syrian, Egyptian, and Saudi-born members as well, began taking control of many of the city's mosques, with the Iraqis serving as imams and the foreigners providing educational and support services.

Operating out of these mosques, Islamist charities began dispensing funds, food, and other necessities to the civilian population. They also offered youth educational-vocational programs that included both food and a stipend—programs that served to incite anti-U.S. youth action while giving the Islamist supervisors an opportunity to spot new talent. Once they proved their commitment, the most promising young rebels were assured, they would be sent for higher learning in Saudi Arabia and other Arab states. The educational-vocational programs also consisted of terrorist training, including bomb-making techniques. Many of the clerics forcefully preached the merits and importance of martyrdom operations against the U.S. occupation forces.

Meanwhile, the Saudi Islamists were using safe havens in the Iraqi desert to reorganize, absorb new materiel from Iran, and resume the infiltration of new detachments back into western Saudi Arabia. On June 4, Saudi Arabia declared a state of national emergency in order to cope with mounting terrorist threats. All components of the security forces were put on high-readiness status, while counterintelligence groups launched a careful review of personnel to uncover al-Qaeda supporters and clandestine cells. Over the next couple of weeks, the security forces launched several searches, discovering safe houses in Riyadh, Medina, Assir, and Najran provinces near the Yemeni border. Drums full of chemicals and explosives were discovered and more than a thousand suspects arrested. These nighttime searches and raids in Riyadh, Jeddah, and Medina frequently evolved into intense clashes and firefights between terrorists and security forces. At least one commander was killed in early June; in his pocket the Saudis found a handwritten letter from Osama bin Laden, dated January 2003.

On June 14 and 15, the Saudi security forces engaged in some of their heaviest fighting ever in the Khaldiyah district of Mecca. Two Saudi officers were killed and five were wounded in the clashes. Five Islamists died, both in combat and as martyr bombers trying to blow up the security forces. The Saudi security forces ultimately managed to break into an apartment used as a safe house, where they discovered seventy-two bombs, machine guns, ammunition, communication devices, and chemical components for making explosives. However, more than thirty terrorists escaped.

After the fact, the Saudis discovered that the Mecca cell had been preparing to assassinate Prince Nayef. The cell had several operational plans for assassination attempts, first in Mecca and then, should the need arise, in Medina, Jeddah, and Mina as well—all places Prince Nayef was scheduled to visit on an upcoming inspection tour of local security arrangements. The al-Qaeda–affiliated force was divided into two cells, each fifteen to twenty members strong. Each cell maintained a separate safe house along with distinct weapons stockpiles and funding sources. The plan called for one cell to attempt the assassination and the other either to facilitate the assassins' getaway or implement a fallback plan in another city. In the Mecca assassination plan, the first cell was divided into three groups. The first group was to fire RPGs and LAW missiles on the prince's car. Once the convoy stalled, the second group would drive powerful car bombs into the prince's car in a suicide attack. The third group would protect the car bombs as well as engage security forces if they tried to intervene. (In the end, their plans were moot; the clashes in Mecca convinced the prince to cancel his trip at the last minute.)

The Saudis kept up their own efforts to bring the Islamist networks to heel, arresting about fifty suspects. The turnaround came on June 26, when Abdul-Rahman al-Faqasi al-Ghamidi surrendered to Saudi authorities. Al-Faqasi was hiding in the Buraida region, but after the leaders of Buraida were warned that the city would be subjected to a thorough dragnet operation to find him—and after the Saudis arrested and reportedly tortured al-Faqasi's wife—Sheikh Safar al-Hawali, who is also from the Ghamid tribe, approached al-Faqasi and mediated his surrender with Prince Muhammad Bin-Nayif. The surrender was conditioned on the release of al-Faqasi's wife and a promise that al-Faqasi himself was "not to be subjected to torture, to be allowed to have a fair trial, and to have a lawyer represent him," in the words of al-Hawali. Similar attempts, though, ended less successfully. On July 3, Saudi security authorities closed in on the safe house in Jawf where Saudi Arabia's most wanted man—Turki Nasser al-Dandani—was hiding. Five police officers were killed in the fierce battle that followed, but as Saudi security forces closed in, al-Dandani blew himself up along with two other terrorists, injuring several security personnel in the process.

The Saudi authorities expanded the purges throughout the security system. The number of officers and officials thought to have Islamist tendencies reached into the thousands. Apprehensive about growing public discontent, the Saudi security forces increased the number of patrols and roadblocks in all Saudi cities. Members of the Saudi elite noted a growing apprehension that the regime was increasingly unstable and vulnerable to Islamist subversion.

During the summer of 2003, many of the wanted Saudi terrorists escaped to Iraq and joined the Islamist insurgence. Given their high stature in the Islamist hierarchy, they had a profound influence on the zeal and motivation of the Iraq-based Islamist networks. They also brought with them additional funds for the jihad. It was no accident, then, that by late June there was a distinct increase in the number of Islamist attacks in Iraq. Notably, a growing number of Arab Afghans—mostly Saudis and Syrians, but also from countries all over the world, including Algeria and Chechnya—were emerging as leading fighters in some of the more audacious attacks on U.S. forces. Various al-Qaeda–affiliated groups began issuing their own theological flyers and communiqués, highlighting their growing role in the Iraqi jihad.

The first such communiqué was issued by "The Mujahedin Battalions of the Salafite Group in Iraq." The accompanying letter apologized for not issuing the communiqué earlier, noting that the "leaders are busy leading the resistance against the Americans in Iraq and it is difficult to convey their information." The communiqué provided an ideological statement of purpose for the group. "With Allah's support, we announce the establishment of the mujahid Salafite group, a unified Sunni group with a Salafite banner, doctrine, and orientation." The group "has an absolute and certain faith that Jihad for the sake of Allah is the only way and the proper route to restore the glory, pride, and dignity that have been taken away from this great Nation." The group promised that "the devil's soldiers, who are the enemies of Allah, will see from us what will discomfort them and disturb their sleep. Meanwhile, the sons of the Islamic Nation will see from us what will please them, make them feel vindicated, and clear anger from their hearts, with Allah's permission and support."

Significantly, the group disassociated itself from the former Baathists, identifying them as "the soldiers of tyranny and the devils of darkness. . . . Thousands of Baathists, Fedayeen, Special and Republican Guard have vanished, handing over this Muslim country to their American masters." Instead, the group was determined to rely on pure Islamist foundations. In the communiqué, the Mujahedin Battalions of the Salafite Group in Iraq declared itself "the beginning of a new project modeled after the Jihad groups that emerged in the 80s and 90s in some countries." The group went further in identifying with the legacy of the Afghan jihad by praising Abdallah Azzam, the preeminent spiritual leader of Osama bin Laden and virtually all Afghan Arabs.

Another Islamist communiqué of significance was released on June 20, in the form of a videotape of the "Iraqi National Front of Fedayeen." The texts and forms of the videotape pointed to a strong Palestinian-Islamist influence. Indeed, the video first surfaced through Palestinian-Islamist channels in Lebanon. Again, the communiqué stressed the pure Islamist character of the group, and its disassociation from the Baathists:

A message from the National Front of Fedayeen to Bush and his criminal henchmen: We have taken it upon ourselves that we will send back to them the bodies of their soldiers one after another in retaliation for the terrorist and provocative actions that their dirty, barbarous forces have carried out, including the arbitrary killings and various insults to all citizens. Before Allah, we are committed to deliver to them one strike after another, which will be even harder and more cruel than the previous strikes we dealt to them. This will be achieved with the help of Allah and the zeal of the good and noble members of this Fedayeen front, which has not had any contact, link, or relationship with the former regime. Therefore, we tell them [the Americans] that if they want their soldiers to be safe, they must leave our pure land. Otherwise, we will avenge every Iraqi they killed, humiliated, or had his house looted. You must know that the Iraqis have been disillusioned with your big lie about the liberation of Iraq.

By late June, the Saudi-Islamist influence was discernable in the sermons delivered by imams in many of Iraq's Sunni mosques. One of the most popular of these was Sheikh Abdul-Wahid al-Zoubaie; in his Friday, June 20, sermon he urged the escalation of the anti-American jihad in response to the anti-Iraqi posture of the United States. "The Americans are liars," al-Zoubaie declared. "They lied when they said they were coming here to re-build Iraq. If the high-handedness continues, the attacks will continue to rise."

Indeed, the mujahedin were growing increasingly confident in their ability to dominate the anti-American jihad. In early July, a mujahid going by the nom de guerre of Al-Irhabi reported on the situation in Iraq, stressing the growing role of the Islamists in the jihad and the decline in Saddam's influence: "Because I am in Iraq and see everything here, I want to tell you that Saddam is not really involved in the fighting. Only a few Baathists are taking part in the struggle, but the bulk of it is being carried out by some of the mujahedin who entered Iraq, and by the Iraqi heroes who refuse to accept Americans on Iraqi soil."

Al-Irhabi argued that the Iraqi people, despite their hatred of the United States, had already rejected Saddam. "Saddam's people have sold the country, and it is they who made it possible for the Americans to occupy it. How can Saddam call on the people now to fight and resist the occupation, having violated the people and the country for such a long time? The Baath era has ended and the people should no longer believe Saddam's lies. Everyone in Iraq knows that not one family in Iraq was left untouched or did not lose one of its members [because of Saddam and his regime]." Instead, it was "the Muslim Iraqi people" who were deriving inspiration and resilience from the Islamic revival and the spirit of Jihad. Al-Irhabi declared his confidence in "the Muslim Iraqi people," stressing his conviction that "they will not compromise with occupation; they will rid themselves of the American occupation."

Meanwhile, as all eyes were focused on the Sunni insurgency in Iraq and the Sunni-Islamist terrorism in Saudi Arabia, Iran was discreetly expanding and consolidating its hold over Iraq's Shiite heartland. Tehran took a comprehensive and pragmatic approach to Iraq; in the long term, Iran was committed to determining the character of post-Saddam Iraq through wars by proxy. The overall assessment within Iran was that the American occupation would not last long; the debilitating losses and spectacular terrorism, as well as the expansion of the war to Israel (using HizbAllah) and the Arabian Peninsula (using bin Laden), would make a lasting American presence in the region untenable. President Bush, Iranian experts believed, would have to withdraw from the region or else risk public discontent in an election year due to mounting losses in a futile war.

Guided by that analysis, the Iranians kept increasing their support for the anti-U.S. war. The Iranians, like the Syrians, were willing to help anybody who was ready to kill American and British troops, but they clearly favored the Shiite groups. Furthermore, as the Bush administration's anti-Iran rhetoric continued to rise, and Washington began openly discussing the overthrow of the mullahs' regime, Tehran's determination to stave off any potential U.S. move only strengthened. An outbreak of student demonstrations in Tehran in early June galvanized the mullahs into resolving to derail any U.S. initiative, using the readily incited Iraqi insurgency as their preferred instrument. "If anything, it [the Iraq insurgency] is just starting. There has been chaos in Iraq in the real sense of the word since early April. There are no signs that the chaos will come to an end anytime soon," Turkish political commentator Hasan Unal wrote in the June 23 issue of the Istanbul newspaper *Zaman*. "Under the circumstances, it might become impossible [for the United States] to deal with Iran."

Tehran took a twin-track approach to the confrontation. On one hand, the Iran-based SCIRI would urge a political solution to the occupation, while gradually raising the pressure on the Americans; its imperative was always to keep Ayatollah Baqir al-Hakim's hands completely clean. On the other, Iran would help the clandestine networks prepare to escalate the insurrection—both supporting anti-U.S. terrorism and helping disassociate the guerrilla war from the Baathists in a way that might lead to civil war and total chaos. The combination of both campaigns, Iranian experts argued, would make Iraq ungovernable by the United States while laying the groundwork for the Shiite majority to seize power, aided by their sheer numbers and Iranian support.

The first step in implementing this plan took place in early June, when SCIRI announced it was leaving its heavy weapons in Iran. As Abdulaziz al-Hakim told al-Jazeerah, "Badr Corps had been working against the criminal Baathist regime of Saddam Hussein. After the collapse of this regime, there is no justification for Badr Corps to keep its heavy weapons. Therefore, it left these weapons. Badr Corps intends to work in the fields of construction, keeping security, and supporting the Iraqi people in their political demands of establishing a national Iraqi government that is elected by the Iraqis. It also seeks to effectively participate in realizing security and stability in various Iraqi cities along with the other honorable Iraqis." The military arm of the Badr Corps was transformed into localized militias handling policing and security. SCIRI's community outreach campaign would extend to a wide network of social and economic services, employing large numbers of Iraqis in reconstruction and distribution of emergency food and medical aid. Iran provided extensive funding, and Iranian experts, arriving as pilgrims to the holy mosques in Najaf and Qarbalah, assisted in organizing and running these programs.

In early June, SCIRI began efforts to mobilize the Shiite community—either to put pressure on Washington to leave Iraq, or to launch a popular, predominantly Shiite intifada designed to expel the United States by force. The Shiite media even issued subtle threats to the U.S. authorities. On June 5, for example, Voice of the Mujahedin warned that the continuation of the current state of affairs might lead to violent eruption. "It is clear now that the U.S. administration has disavowed its promises to reconstruct Iraq and form a transitional Iraqi government that can shoulder its responsibilities toward its people and country. Such an attitude will cast dark shadows on the Iraqi situation. It will also raise many questions about the role that the White House administration wants to play in Iraq and the Middle East in general." While the swift empowerment of an Iraqi government and a U.S. withdrawal would defuse the crisis, an American decision to remain in Iraq as an occupying force would "push the Iraqis to a different stage of feeling and action that does not and will not satisfy the United States."

The primary audience for such agitation was the Iraqi Shiites; it was they who were being told to prepare for an armed insurrection. Ayatollah Baqir al-Hakim contributed indirectly to the campaign himself, stressing that the political and administrative solutions offered by the United States were un-Islamic. In a June 6 Friday sermon in Najaf, he declared that "the U.S. proposal to appoint an Iraqi council to draft a constitution and run the affairs of the country is a rejected proposal by Sharia and [Islamic Law]." Al-Hakim added that "the rule in Iraq should be democratic and federal and should be based on Islamic Sharia principles."

On June 7, Voice of the Mujahedin carried a highly explicit editorial, effectively declaring an official anti-American position on behalf of the Shiite people. In the aftermath of the war, "the Iraqis woke up from the nightmare of [the] despot Saddam and his repressive services to find the U.S. military machine in their country. They also woke up to realize that the Americans harbor grudges against Iraq, the Orient, Islam, and Arabs, although they do not explicitly vent these grudges because doing so now conflicts with the U.S. policy of deception and forgery." Moreover, in pursuit of America's own self-interest, "the U.S. plan moves in a completely opposite direction and conflicts with the will of the Iraqi people and their desire to build a free and independent country that enjoys an atmosphere of genuine freedom, dignity, pride, and full and real independence. This difference between the U.S. administration's goals in Iraq and the Iraqi people's wish will undoubtedly reach the point of collision, conflict, and confrontation sometime."

The editorial further warned the United States that the point of crisis was imminent: "To be candid with the Americans, if our people continue to make demands while the United States ignores them and does what it wants instead, then the next moment will be the moment of confrontation. It will be a step toward escalating the conflict and a moment of collision between our people, their leaders, and even politicians who talk with the U.S. administration on the one hand and this administration and those who represent it in Iraq on the other. This moment is the most dangerous on the security, military, and political levels." In order to understand what was at stake, the statement continued, the United States should learn from "the British experience in Iraq in the past, when the Iraqis torched the land under the feet of the invaders and did not let them enjoy Iraq's wealth. Therefore, Britain rushed to end its occupation and announce the independence of Iraq before other colonies. If it wants to avoid many of the problems arising from its occupation of Iraq, the United States must submit to the will of the Iraqi people and their desire to achieve their independence and freedom." On a positive note, the statement concluded by suggesting that once the United States left Iraq, Baghdad would not object to cooperation with the United States on the oil issue.

At the same time, Tehran's clandestine preparations for terrorism proceeded—under the guidance of Moqtada al-Sadr, Iran's other instrument of influence in Iraq. Working to prevent the Baathists from dominating the anti-U.S. guerrilla war (and thus postwar leadership in Baghdad), as well as supporting anti-U.S. terrorist efforts until the Shiite popular intifadah was launched, Moqtada arrived in Tehran on July 8 for a four-day "official" visit. There he met with Hashemi-Rafsanjani, Qasim Suleymani (the leader of the Qods Force), and senior officials in Khamenei's office. Ayatollah Seyyed Kadhem Haeri appointed Moqtada to be his deputy—a tremendous honor that offset his lack of formal religious learning.

In Tehran, Moqtada committed to a comprehensive action plan on behalf of the Iranians. The political objective of the Jimaat-i-Sadr Thani would be an Iraqi government based on the Iranian model, marrying politics and religion. The primary objective of this position was to make SCIRI's "moderate" version more appealing to the United States. At the same time, Moqtada was to further Khamenei's influence throughout the Iraqi Shiite elite. In that context, Moqtada was to organize *shabab* teams to disrupt any activities by Ayatollahs Sistani and al-Hakim that Tehran deemed contrary to the interests of the Islamic Revolution. Such actions might range from disruption of meetings to outright assassinations, as was the case with Imam Khoi in April.

Most important, Moqtada was to launch a grassroots campaign aimed at inciting popular resistance—both violent and nonviolent—to any form of U.S. or U.K. presence in Iraq. Here, the Iranian instructions were clear: Jimaat-i-Sadr Thani was to organize clandestine networks, tailored after the HizbAllah model, to conduct both anti-U.S. terrorism and other disruptions designed to push Iraq into chaos and civil war. Toward this end, the Jimaat-i-Sadr Thani would be provided with comprehensive support, expert assistance, and expert operatives from the ranks of HizbAllah and the Qods Forces.

Moqtada returned to Iraq on June 12. The day before he left, Ayatollah Seyyed Kadhem Haeri provided him with a crucial resource for the difficult task ahead: a fatwa sanctioning the killing of Baath figures and all others working for the return of Saddam. In his fatwa, Haeri gave what he believed to be the reasons for the war and his view of the posture emerging in postwar Iraq. The U.S. invasion, he declared was "the fire of dispute and war among the unjust ones themselves, and between the masters of arrogance [the United States] and their fiercest agent [Saddam], to whom the world has seen no match."

In this formulation, then, the United States had no issue with the form of government in Iraq, but merely with one of its own "agents," Saddam himself. Therefore, the real American interest was to restore the Baathist regime, but without Saddam himself, and under tighter U.S. control. "The arrogant Americans have left the Saddamist Baathists to despoil Iraq once again, undeterred and unhindered. Their objective behind the war was to bring Iraq under their direct authority, without the mediation of their agent, and this was what happened. Their goal was not to liberate the Iraqi people from the captivity of the Saddamist Baathists. Thus, Saddam's agents began to work to restore power to the Iraqi Baath Party so as to oppress us [the Shiites] once again."

Haeri went on to analyze the composition of the Baath Party membership, identifying five categories:

> The first consists of the majority, who have become party members to maintain their livelihoods or in quest for safety, despite the cheap life one would have under Saddam's rule. This group of people has not been involved in crimes against the Iraqi nation. The second consists of criminals who were involved in crime, whether through direct killing and torture, or through seeking to annihilate the believers by submitting reports that would lead to their death, imprisonment, torture, displacement, and the like. The third group consists of the Saddamists who began to reorganize themselves, even under different names, hoping for the return of Saddam if possible, or that they would be able to control us once again, even in the absence of Saddam if they cannot secure his return. The fourth group is made of Baath Party members who once again began to take leading positions in Iraq with a new face. The fifth group is those who have started working to despoil the people's lives with acts such as cutting power lines, demolishing houses, murders, inciting problems and infighting, and any such acts.

In other words, the members of the Baathist resistance, and the Iraqis cooperating with U.S. authorities, were both decreed to be enemies of the

Shiites as members of the Saddam regime. Haeri was very precise as to their prescribed punishment. "The last four categories are true examples of those who fight God and His messenger and strive for mischief on earth," Ayatollah Haeri decreed. "Based on this, the first category should not be touched and no harm should be done to it. The four other categories are condemned to death, so that the door of their corruption, mischief, and damage would be closed and so that their attempts to restore Saddam or bring the country under their control would be stopped." Ayatollah Haeri's fatwa became Moqtada's license to kill.

On June 21, increasingly apprehensive about the Shiite awakening, U.S. forces raided the SCIRI office building in the Al-Jabiriyah area of Baghdad. The formal excuse was concern that terrorists were hiding in the building—and indeed three guards were beaten and arrested and a single AK-47 found and confiscated. Thereafter, however, U.S. forces conducted a thorough search of the building, confiscating all the computers and photocopiers and a number of videotapes; both SCIRI and Tehran interpreted the raid as an American declaration of war on the Shiite political elite.

To the Shiite leadership, it was high time to demonstrate their escalatory potential to the Americans. For their targets they chose British servicemen, simply because it was much easier and quicker for the Iran-based operatives to get to the Basra area than to the Sunni heartland where U.S. forces were concentrated. The Iranians also had several networks in the area. Iran's activity did not go unnoticed, and for a few weeks tribal leaders had been warning British commanders that "bands of Islamic militants, trained and armed in Iran," had been working to establish an operational presence in southern Iraq, particularly in the remote villages around al-Majar al-Kabir, 90 miles north of Basra.

On June 24, two incidents took place in Majar al-Kabir; different in nature, each was aimed at delivering a particular message to the American and British authorities.

The first incident was the mob killing of six Royal Military Police troops at the center of Majar al-Kabir, where they had been dispatched to train the local police force. Pro-Iranian activists had been inciting the villagers to resist the British paratroopers conducting house-to-house weapons searches in the area, on the grounds that they were humiliating and un-Islamic and that the British must be taught a lesson. The moment the six police instructors arrived for their scheduled inspection, a well-armed mob of more than three hundred gathered around them. The Iraqi police trainees immediately abandoned the British. The crowd began shouting and pelting the British with stones, and when the British faced the crowd, the Iraqis opened fire and killed two on the spot. The other four fought their way to the nearby police station, where they held out for two hours as the Iraqi crowd grew rapidly outside. A third British soldier was killed in the ensuing firefight.

"Almost the whole city was outside," one of the police trainees who escaped told British interrogators. "It was not a small attack. It was like a war." Running low on ammunition, and having left their only radio in their abandoned Land Rover, the surviving three soldiers accepted a mediation offer from village notables: they would surrender their weapons in return for safe passage. The moment they handed over their weapons, however, they were immediately surrounded by the mob inside the police station and promptly executed. "This attack was unprovoked. It was murder," summed up Lt. Col. Ronnie McCourt, who investigated the incident.

The second incident took place just outside Majar al-Kabir. It began when a ten-man patrol of the British 1st Battalion of the Parachute Regiment was attacked by small-arms fire and a few rocket-propelled grenades. One of the British paratroopers was wounded in the attack, and the two vehicles were set on fire. Still, the ambush fire was sporadic and the attackers did not advance. The patrol called for emergency evacuation, and an RAF Chinook helicopter with a rapid response force of roughly twenty more paratroopers was dispatched, along with a medical team.

Just as the helicopter was about to land, though, a far larger ambushing force materialized and fired on the helicopter with small arms, machine guns, and rocket-propelled grenades. The Chinook was hit badly; seven on board were wounded, three of them seriously. At the same time, the Iraqis started closing in on the paratroopers on the ground. Despite the damage and continued heavy fire, the Chinook managed to land and pick up the ten paratroopers. But the lesson was clear: this was a carefully staged ambush, designed to lure in a helicopter and try to shoot it down after the British patrol called in reinforcements to tend to its initial casualties.

The two incidents of June 24 demonstrated to the British that they were facing a formidable foe in the Shiite zone. In a single day, the Shiite activists demonstrated their ability to incite a village to hysteria—culminating in a lynching—while carrying out a sophisticated, large-scale military attack nearby. The twin incidents left little doubt that professional soldiers were at work within the Shiite heartland.

On June 28, Ayatollah Ali al-Sistani issued a formal fatwa forbidding participation in the drafting of the Iraqi constitution or any other

American-sponsored political activity. "These [coalition] authorities do not have any power to appoint members of the constitution drafting committee," Sistani wrote. "Moreover, there is no guarantee that this council will draft a constitution that is in harmony with the higher interests of the Iraqi people and truly represents their national identity, the basic pillars of which are the true Islamic religion and the noble social values. The said draft is utterly unacceptable."

Then, in early July, the Shiite leadership increased the pressure on the United States, declaring that they would not wait forever for peaceful negotiations to succeed in ending the American occupation. "We call for using the legal and peaceful methods in order to put an end to this invasion and occupation, by using at first the peaceful methods and ways," Ayatollah Baqir al-Hakim told *The Times*. "If this will not give success, then we will think about other methods." Pressed about the possible use of force, he remained opaque. "When the peaceful methods are exhausted and when those who are now negotiating with the Americans discover there is no benefit or result of their negotiations, then we will think about it," Baqir al-Hakim said. "It is natural that we first start with negotiations and peaceful methods."

15
INTO THE CAULDRON

By late June of 2003, the United States was beginning to settle in Iraq for the duration, attempting to stabilize an Iraq that was effectively under direct U.S. control (the forthcoming Iraqi interim government notwithstanding), while trying to suppress the brewing guerrilla war. America's goal was to use Iraq's strategic infrastructure as a springboard for projecting American presence and influence throughout the region, and to make better use of the country's economic potential. With time, the United States hoped, Iraqi forces could be trained to suppress fellow countrymen who persisted in mounting resistance against American forces.

The U.S. authorities persisted in considering Baathist irregulars in the Sunni heartland as the main threat to American forces. On June 29, the 4th Infantry Division and Task Force Iron Horse launched Operation Sidewinder. "Our goal is to remove Baath Party officials, terrorists, and criminal elements who are preventing peace and security in Iraq and slowing rebuilding in the country," explained Maj. Sean Gibson, a military spokesman. The U.S. forces used newly arrived high-tech systems and fresh intelligence to detect and track Baathist insurgents over a large area of central Iraq, stretching from the Iranian border to Greater Baghdad and including Baghdad, Fallujah, Ramadi, and Tikrit. Within a few days, American forces had conducted more than twenty raids throughout the area, capturing some two hundred suspects, including an Iraqi colonel.

Yet long-term returns from the operation were disappointing, so in early July the U.S. Army shifted to smaller raids—some based on intelligence tips and others on proactive, at times random, operations. Despite the growing pace of U.S. operations, though, the intensity, sophistication, and frequency of the attacks on U.S. forces increased. The terrorists also introduced new weapons, including mines and mortars. The first mortar attack took place on July 3, and sixteen soldiers were injured in the shelling of a logistics post near Balad. In the week after that first strike, U.S. officials acknowledged, "mortar attacks have caused greater damage and casualties than automatic fire or rocket-propelled grenade strikes." Because of the growing use of tanks and armored vehicles in patrols, however, the overall level of U.S. casualties remained about the same.

Saddam Hussein then decided to reassert his own voice in the struggle by announcing the launch of an organized insurrection. On July 4, al-Jazeerah TV broadcast an audiotape of Saddam, recorded on June 14. On the tape, Saddam acknowledged that the difficulties of his underground life had forced him into silence and that "sending you [the Iraqis] an audio recording is not as easy as it used to be, despite our attempts to send it to you before now." He stressed that he and other members of his command council were still in Iraq, however, operating among the people. "Brothers and sons, brave women and men," he announced, "I bring you the good news that cells and brigades of Jihad [and] sacrifice, and their organizations, have indeed been formed on a large scale, comprising men and women mujahedin. They have started their honorable actions in fighting the enemy and the aggression. You must be hearing about them, although what you are hearing about them, especially the losses they are inflicting among the infidel invaders, is just a small part of the actual losses. Hardly a day or a week passes without the blood of the infidels being let on our chaste land thanks to the Jihad of the mujahedin." He assured all Iraqis that "the next days" would be "difficult for the infidel invaders and honorable for the believers." Saddam then urged all Iraqis to provide the resistance with as much help and shelter as possible, and reiterated his claim that the occupation authorities were adamant about enslaving and destroying Iraq.

On July 8, al-Jazeerah broadcast an undated follow-up tape from Saddam; its content suggested that it was recorded after June 14. On this tape, Saddam stressed the urgent imperative of the return to underground life and struggle to save Iraq. "Returning to the methods of secret action we had started at the very beginning is the appropriate method for the Iraqis to adopt. Based on this and through these methods I address you brothers from inside proud Iraq to say: Your main task now—as Arabs, Kurds, and Turkman; Shiites and Sunnis; Muslims and Christians; and under all titles and of all religions and denominations—is to expel the invaders from our country." He urged national unity and the emergence of a widespread popular resistance to the occupation forces. "Show your opposition to the occupation, each according to his ability and method, such as through graffiti and having the masses surround and obstruct the work of the forces of invasion and occupation. [You should also] boycott them by not selling or buying from them and carry out peaceful demonstrations and civil disobedience in addition to opening fire on the occupation forces from the rifles, artillery, and [rocket] launchers of the faithful youth. Do this so as not to give the occupation forces the chance to settle on your land without sustaining losses in terms of reputation, standing, and blood." Saddam concluded by promising that the struggle would continue until total victory.

The widespread attention paid to the broadcasts of Saddam's exhortations on al-Jazeerah and other Arab satellite TV stations, and the ensuing reappearance of pro-Saddam graffiti in Baghdad and other Sunni cities, reinforced America's resolve to find or kill Saddam and destroy the Baathist insurgency. Ultimately, however, neither America's pursuit of the Baathist forces nor Saddam's call to arms were the dominant factors in determining the overall situation in Iraq. It was the continued collapse of Iraqi society that led growing numbers to find solace in the fold of radical Islam—Sunni and Shiite alike—and from there the road to terrorism was very short.

By early July, the United States had still failed to restore electricity and basic services to the main cities; in Baghdad, electricity was available only four to six hours a day. U.S. authorities proved unable to halt the looting and rampant street crime, and most of the gasoline being sold came from emergency shipments imported from European reserves. Sabotage of Iraq's own oil infrastructure was rampant, from detonating pipes to theft of equipment by insiders and, increasingly, the theft of large quantities of oil by punching holes in pipelines.

In sharp contrast, the construction and refurbishment of buildings for the U.S. military and civilian authorities proceeded swiftly. American forces seized a whole sector in the Saadun district of Baghdad, including the Baghdad Hotel complex between Saadun and Abu-Nuwas Streets, as well as the city block between Firdos Square and Nasser Square (near the Grand Bus Station). This area is characterized by relatively modern highrises built by European companies, which could be repaired and refurbished rather quickly, and construction work soon began on what Iraqis refer to as the new U.S. governing compound. Soon there were rumors in Baghdad that the CIA had already signed a twenty-year lease with the owners of the Baghdad Hotel.

The continued construction of U.S. military, intelligence, and governing facilities all over Iraq created doubt among most Iraqis—including those most inclined to cooperate with the United States—about the sincerity of American promises to hand over power to the Iraqis as soon as possible. The much-touted interim government and council were widely perceived as little more than a powerless front for the U.S. authorities, as they are to this day. Attitudes toward working for the United States were much the same. In late June, for example, the United States announced the creation of a new Iraqi Army as a building block in the restoration of the Iraqi state. Iraqis, however, considered the army an American strategy designed to enlist Iraqis to take over fighting the guerrilla war—forcing them to kill their brethren and die for the Americans. American efforts to recruit Jordanian police and security service officers to oversee security in Iraq, especially via-à-vis local police, were also extremely unpopular.

Meanwhile, the various resistance forces began targeting Iraqis who were working to restore electricity, water, and other basic services—their attacks ranging from verbal abuse to beatings and, increasingly, public executions. Iraqi police and security personnel, including translators, were subjected to even harsher attacks. This campaign peaked with the July 5 bombing of a parade of Iraqi police cadets in Ramadi. It was a sophisticated bomb, made of military-grade TNT, concealed in a bag of rice and detonated by remote control. Seven cadets were killed and more than fifty were wounded in the bombing. That event alone persuaded hundreds of workers all over Iraq not to return to work. American authorities have so far failed to provide these workers with adequate protection; the dangers involved have become so great that untold numbers of workers have abandoned their jobs despite rampant unemployment and hyperinflation. The terrorists knew very well what they were doing; as the Shiite newspaper *al-Haqiqa* recently observed, "unemployment and the chaos of security are the root causes of Iraqis clashing with Americans."

A British study of the overall situation in Iraq in the first hundred days after the fall of Baghdad, published by the London *Telegraph*, pointed out the magnitude of the challenges ahead. In its analysis, the coalition occupation authorities had so far proved incapable of tackling most of Iraq's endemic problems: Electricity was still erratic at best, and even the implementation of signed contracts for repair was falling behind schedule. The 2003 repair budget was estimated by the British experts to constitute less than 20 percent of the expected actual cost. The water-supply situation was even worse: roughly half of Iraq's pumped water was classified as "unfit for human consumption." And fuel supply was in similarly poor condition—

in the Baghdad area, only 140 of the 260 pumping plants received diesel fuel from the UN. Baghdad's 250,000 telephone lines were still out of order, and the functioning lines could carry only local calls. In late July, a pirated extension of the Kuwaiti cell phone system suddenly came to life in Baghdad—even as occupation authorities were still awaiting bids on the restoration of a legal cell phone network.

The economy was in dire shape, with some 60 percent unemployment. Unrelenting street crime and looting, as well as a spree of resistance attacks on people working for the occupation authorities, prevented any real stabilization. The only service adequately administered was humanitarian aid, heavily subsidized by international organizations. Iraq's 240 hospitals were fully staffed, with employees earning four to six times their Saddam-era salaries but with acute shortages of equipment and medications—the aggregate impact of a decade of sanctions, American bombing, and the looting that followed the war. The country's 13,000 schools were being repaired, 1,000 new ones were being built, and some 324,000 Iraqi teachers and staff had their pay increased sevenfold.

In greater jeopardy was the standing Iraqi police force. Though the occupation authorities had some 31,000 police officers on payroll, only about 24,000 were actually serving, and each new round of attacks hurt recruitment and increased departure rates. The initial recruitment drive for the "new army" capitalized on the country's dire economic circumstances but failed to attract sufficient numbers of qualified recruits who could go into action within a short time. Moreover, the ultimate loyalty of both the Iraqi police and the future army were dubious at best. With the oil industry still being routinely sabotaged, no economic breakthrough or flow of indigenous revenue could be expected anytime soon. For the foreseeable future, then, the United States, its allies, and international organizations would be saddled with the fiscal burden of keeping Iraq afloat.

At the same time, there were initial signs that Iraqi society was beginning to recover from the shock of the occupation of Baghdad and the plight of instability. Wider segments of the urban middle class had grown resigned to the American presence and shifted their focus to exploiting the situation for their own gain. Western-educated Iraqis who were on the fringes of the Baathist elite—usually because they had family in the military, security, or defense industries—began opening businesses and attempted to win lucrative contracts from American authorities and Western businesses.

The dynamic in the slums, alas, was exactly the opposite. Still, Friday sermons in Iraq often encouraged listeners to participate in the stabilization and reconstruction of Iraq, even if it required cooperation with the occupation authorities. Urban Iraq accepted that the resumption of basic services and the rejuvenation of the economy would require cooperation between municipal and occupation authorities. All over Iraq, street markets and vendors—the best indicators of grassroots economic vitality—were returning to life. The population of Baghdad enjoyed unprecedented political and cultural freedoms, as manifested in the more than one hundred newspapers and weeklies being published. Although American soldiers still frequently raided editorial offices and detained editors and writers whose anti-American rhetoric was considered "incitement" by the occupation authorities, the crowds in the teahouses were large, and conversations on political and social issues free and noisy. The fear factor appeared to be on the wane.

Ultimately, however, the escalating guerrilla war continued to dominate the landscape in greater Iraq. Starting in mid-June of 2003, rumors spread throughout the Sunni heartland about the imminent unleashing of the Iraqi intifadah. Baathists openly talked about a formal declaration of a "liberation war" on Baath Day, July 17. As several prominent Baathist supporters asserted, this war would be characterized by spectacular terrorism, designed to inflict as many casualties on the Americans as possible and to prevent the consolidation of a post-Saddam Iraq. These were not empty warnings: the Baathists had already established a new central command designed to sustain a major escalation. Significantly, toward mid-July, senior Baathist commanders approached senior al-Qaeda–affiliated leaders to brief them about the new central command and invite the Islamists to join the new intifadah.

The Islamist senior commanders found the offer sufficiently intriguing to report to the supreme leadership that "Saddam Hussein has just completed the formation of a central command that will be supervising the resistance movement against the Anglo-American presence in all parts of Iraq." Although the Baathist leadership was eager to bring all Iraqis—regardless of their religious and tribal affiliation—into the intifadah, the top leadership would remain in the hands of Saddam's supporters. "The central command comprises a small, yet carefully selected group of qualified Baath Party members, Army and Republican Guards," the Islamist report read.

At the same time, the Islamist commanders reported, Saddam Hussein did not consider the central command and the intifadah to be instruments for his return to power. "Saddam does not intend to come back to power and will be content with the role of an honorary leader of the Baath Party, leaving the choice of leadership to the Iraqi people through democracy and the ballot system," the Islamist report continued. "Saddam's main goal is to free Iraqi soil, [but] his desire to take revenge against the Americans is there as well. He wants to transform U.S. military losses inside Iraq into an economic and political crisis inside the U.S., which should eventually cause George Bush and his administration to lose the coming elections."

The Baathist commanders assured their Islamist counterparts that a major escalation in the anti-U.S. insurrection was beginning. "Resistance is growing day after day and now extends from the north of Iraq all the way to the south," the Islamist commanders declared. "During the coming weeks, a number of political initiatives and treatises will be issued by the central command, most prominent of which will be a call to a general popular reconciliation in the face of the enemy and an effort to provide a true democratic and multiparty system after the liberation." The Islamist commanders recommended that the Islamist movement join this dynamic, without losing its distinction and independence.

Within the Baathist elite, however, Saddam's objectives were considered less benevolent. Saddam's master plan envisioned a major clash with American forces in which the Iraqis would inflict extremely heavy casualties—most likely through the use of WMD-tipped ballistic missiles and rockets—to the point where Washington would cut its losses and withdraw from Iraq and the Middle East. Adulated as a pan-Arab hero, Saddam would then be urged to return to power in Baghdad and a position of hegemonic influence over the Arab world. This scenario was espoused by numerous senior Baathists in Iraq, Syria, and other countries.

At the same time, there were indications in the Sunni heartland that something big was afoot. The center of activity was the underground enclave stretching from Samarra (70 miles northwest of Baghdad) to a point some 35 miles south of Tikrit. General Wafiq al-Samarrai, the former chief of Iraqi military intelligence, believed that Saddam Hussein and Ali Hassan al-Majid were hiding nearby, in an area of lush vegetation and small villages on the Tigris River between Baghdad and Samarra. The main Baathist forces were roaming in a desolate desert area in central Iraq, some 100 miles long and 60 to 70 miles wide, between Lake Tharthar and the Tigris River. U.S. military presence in this area was nonexistent, and Saddam's commanders were convinced that they had the upper hand there: the United States lacked the conventional forces required to attack this region, and Washington could not afford the high casualty ratio the U.S. forces would suffer in any such action.

Starting in early July, the Baathists launched a clandestine effort to recruit veterans of the Republican Guards, fedayeen, and other elite units throughout Iraq. Former members of these formations who had broken away from the pro-Saddam Baathists now made their way to Jordan and other neighboring Arab states, fearing that they would either be drawn back into Saddam's service or fall victim to a U.S. crackdown and dragnet. Some of these Iraqis attest to being told firsthand that Saddam was "rebuilding the Iraqi Army" and would "double the salaries they earned before the war." They were told to make their way to Samarra, where they would be taken care of.

Given the unemployment and the de-Baathification campaign, the result was no surprise: 12,000 to 15,000 veterans arrived in the area in the first half of July alone. After a few days in local guesthouses, most of them "vanished"—driving to the desert or remote villages in small groups and leaving no trace or forwarding addresses. Among them were several hundred staunch Baathists who had been involved in the operational use of WMD during the 1980s. Other Baathist forces already in the Samarra area by mid-July included roughly 5,000 fighters—mostly Saddam's Fedayeen, Iraqi commando, and Baathist militia—who were responsible for the anti-U.S. guerrilla warfare in the area. Another 6,000 volunteers from Syria (most of them highly trained tribesmen) and about 2,000 technical personnel responsible for maintaining and sustaining the underground facilities and stockpiles also responded to the Baathist recruitment. According to sources in the Baathist elite, Saddam's senior commanders were planning on organizing an army of more than 50,000 combat troops before confronting American forces. Given the accelerated pace of veterans flowing into the Sunni heartland, this was not an illogical goal.

This buildup was sustained by three main supply lines from Syria, all of them fully integrated into the traditional wandering routes of the Bedouin tribes and time-proven smugglers' routes. The first route runs from A-Sukkariya and Abu-Kamal in eastern Syria along the Upper Euphrates River to Dughaymah in western Iraq and then toward Ramadi and Fallujah. Because this route can be used by trucks and lighter vehicles, it is a major venue for delivering fighters, weapons, and medicine. The second route is concealed within the heavy Bedouin traffic between Adlah and

Fadgami on the Syrian border, via the Abu Hamdah *wadi* (river bed) to the Sinjar area and onward to Samarra. Because of the Bedouin traffic, many members of the Baathist elite use this route for travel in and out of Syria. The third route stretches from Al-Qamishli in Syria through the Shamar tribal lands and into Mosul and Tikrit. This route is also used mainly by Baathist notables.

Emboldened by the positive reaction to their call to arms, the Baathists then decided to raise their profile even further. On July 11 the Baath Party issued its first formal communiqué, bragging about the initial achievements of the anti-U.S. guerrilla campaign: "The heroic resistance led by the Arab Socialist Baath Party in the occupied country of Iraq is intensifying and resulting in qualitative operations of professional military combat applications that target the occupation forces' centers, convoys, and soldiers or in technical and interventionist actions to prevent the occupation administration from implementing or bolstering its occupation plans and measures in the security, administrative, economic, and other spheres," the communiqué read. Moreover, the increasing pace and intensity of the attacks "indicate the ability of the heroic resistance strugglers and mujahedin to carry out the operations entrusted to them and to intensify and deepen the resistance across noble Iraq." The Baath Party promised "a renewal of the threat [to the U.S. authorities] and an assertion of the combative determination to continue and intensify the resistance until the occupier is expelled and Iraq liberated." At the same time, the party urged the further consolidation of "the broad Iraqi national armed resistance environment."

Baathist underground commanders were made available for interviews to various Arab media as well as to Arab diplomats and intelligence officials operating in the greater Baghdad area. One of the most effective of these was "Khalid," a twenty-nine-year-old Saddam's Fedayeen commander who claimed to have planned recent attacks on U.S. forces. In a conversation with an Arab "diplomat," Khalid claimed that his objective was "expelling the U.S. troops from Iraq and returning Saddam Hussein to power." He emphasized that the fedayeen were "better organized than the Americans might think" because they had "prepared for such guerrilla war for a long time." Their manpower came from the ranks of Baath Party members, Iraqi soldiers, intelligence officers, and staunch supporters of Saddam.

Once the initial shock of occupation began to dissipate, Khalid explained, a growing number of "Saddam's Fedayeen, the intelligence services, and the Special Republican Guard began to reorganize in the various parts of Iraq and prepare to launch a protracted underground war." They were organized into cells of five or six members, each completely isolated from the others. To further confuse the Americans, they published their communiqués under several names, including Saddam's Fedayeen, the Iraqi Liberation Army, and Muhammad's Army. Consequently, Khalid stressed, "only few [senior commanders] know how widely spread this network is." In conclusion, Khalid stressed that "the Americans made a big mistake when they imagined that they [Saddam's supporters] had disappeared after the war."

The Arab media published two new audiotapes of Saddam Hussein later in July, further raising the public profile of his supporters. In the first tape, which surfaced on July 17 and seemed to have been recorded a couple of days earlier, Saddam argued that just as the period between July 17 and July 30, 1968, was a turning point in the Baath Revolution, so the same period in 2003 would see the resurrection of the anti-American revolutionary struggle. Saddam ridiculed the possibility of Iraqi coexistence with American authorities: "The right and duty to engage in Jihad is unmistakably obvious. Similarly, the falsehood of occupation and aggression is obvious. Any different talk or argument is not substantiated by religious principles or any principles pertaining to honor and patriotism," he declared.

The second tape, recorded on July 20, surfaced on July 23. In it, Saddam stressed that the Iraqi military defeat at the gates of Baghdad need not reflect the prospects of the resistance:

> We say to the men of the armed forces, the people, and the national security services that if America and other countries, their armies, and occupation armies that followed and cooperated with [America] have achieved superiority when the confrontation took place between the two sides, between the massive masses of their armies and the army of Iraq, then they have not and will not be able to eliminate the will to fight nor will they achieve superiority over the Iraqi people, their mujahedin, and the struggles of Iraq. . . . .Your rising all over again after the setback you suffered to lead the formations of Jihad and sacrifice, or to be a living and an effective part of them, is a new major rising and a new lesson that Allah has prepared for us in order to be in a different situation than before.

Saddam also acknowledged that the Baathist forces were cooperating with the Islamists and other resistance groups. He praised his people for "carrying out your honorable Jihad operations alongside your brother mujahedin, or when leading them in the battlefield" all over Iraq. Saddam concluded by personally reiterating the call to arms to all former personnel of the security forces. "I call upon our faithful, sincere men in the Special Guard, including the pensioners who served in this guard force and in the Republican Guard, to increase their actions according to their virtues and to abide by their recorded commitment."

Saddam's bluster notwithstanding, though, the Islamists were fast emerging as the most active and effective component of the anti-U.S. resistance. Furthermore, the bulk of the guerrilla warfare was anti-American rather than pro-Saddam. In his July 23 editorial, Saad al-Bazzaz, chief editor of the Baghdad newspaper *Al-Zaman,* stressed this point. Analyzing Saddam's latest tapes, Bazzaz observed that "Saddam is trying to suggest that all military operations against the U.S. forces are carried out by forces that support him or used to be affiliated with him. The reality is that anyone who reads the situation in Iraq now can see that a large number of these operations are carried out by forces that had not supported the previous regime and did not approve of Saddam's policy in the previous phase." That was also the prevailing sentiment in the Iraqi "street"—even among people who would not take part in armed insurrection. To many, it seemed that "tyranny has gone but infidels replaced it," and that given the disparity of power between the United States and the Iraqis, "the future of Iraq now looked horrible, even terrifying." The attendance at Friday prayers in Baghdad's main Sunni mosques kept increasing, and the sermons given there were virulently anti-American, with the imams stressing that "resisting foreign occupation is a sacred duty."

The Islamists, largely led by commanders affiliated with bin Laden's forces, were the up-and-coming group in the Sunni heartland, and increasingly in Kurdistan as well. Although many of the Islamist commanders vigorously denied any contact with Saddam or the Baathists, they readily accepted weapons, supplies, and funds from Saddam's stockpiles. One Islamist activist in Iraq noted that the Baath Party was "at least providing organizational and financial assistance to certain groups, in addition to providing them with weapons." The Islamists also launched an intense recruitment drive in Islamist communities worldwide, especially seeking veteran commanders with combat experience in Afghanistan, Bosnia, and Chechnya to fight in Iraq. By mid-July, the flow of mujahedin was intensifying. An Islamist commander in the Baghdad area reported on July 21 that "all acts of resistance and operations in Iraq" were being "carried out for the sake of Allah, nothing else." Although the perpetrators "have nothing to do with the former regime and have all suffered from the former regime," one could find in their ranks "officers, noncommissioned officers, members of the public, and ordinary citizens" who are "Sunnis, Shiites, Kurds, and Turkman." He expected new networks to go into action "all over Iraq."

Meanwhile, other Islamist leaders were keen to characterize the conflict in Iraq as an integral component of Osama bin Laden's global jihad movement. In mid-July, the al-Fallujah branch of the Armed Islamic Movement, an organization affiliated with al-Qaeda, circulated an audiotape claiming responsibility for a number of attacks on U.S. troops—while denying any link to Saddam or his supporters. "The cancer of the Islamic Nation is the Zionist entity, led by the United States. This cancer does not affect Iraq and Palestine only," the message read, defining the Iraqi jihad in the context of a global trend. The militants insisted that the Iraqi jihad operations were carried out "by the grace of Allah and through the patience of our mujahedin brothers. The end of the United States will be at the hands of Islam," they stressed. "The coming days will show you the blow that will break the back of America once and for all. We beseech God to grant us victory and to grant success to our brothers who are spread throughout the Iraqi governorates and the countries of the world, at the head of whom are His Eminence . . . Sheikh Osama bin Laden and Mullah Omar." With the audiotape came written reports about specific incidents in the greater Baghdad and Sunni triangle area strongly suggesting that these Islamist forces were indeed responsible for the attacks they claimed credit for.

Meanwhile, the Shiite forces were also becoming more autonomous and increasingly powerful, lowering their rhetoric while preparing for a major eruption if their political demands were not fully met by the Americans. On July 19, Moqtada al-Sadr announced the formation of a new Islamic army called the Mahdi Corps, with the mission of "fighting against conspiracies against Iraq" and "supporting the Holy Najaf Theological Seminary." The Mahdi Corps would act as a kind of Shiite fire brigade, called upon to protect the vital interests of the community. "The corps will be placed on alert as part of a general mobilization whenever it is necessary to do so," Sadr declared. He announced the formation of the corps before an audience of followers wearing shrouds, all of them apparently ready to declare their readiness for martyrdom. "Death to America!" the crowd chanted back. "Death to Israel!" "We will never accept the interim government council!"

The main reason for Sadr's confidence in the new organization was Iran's activation of the Iraqi HizbAllah networks throughout the Shiite heartland; each of these networks included an effective core of Iranian intelligence officials, Lebanese terrorist experts, and Iraqi-Shiite organizers. On July 24, the Iraqi HizbAllah issued an unprecedented ultimatum: "Our sole object is to kill the American invader and his collaborators. If American troops are not out of the Shiite cities of Iraq by August 2, HizbAllah will begin to attack them." With several hundred Iranian HizbAllah experts and a few thousand trained Iraqi terrorists at hand, including scores of would-be suicide bombers, the Iran-sponsored networks were well positioned to strike.

Another intriguing development was the sudden emergence of new nationalist forces rooted in the original anti-British jihad. On July 10, a statement labeled "Communiqué No. 1" announced the formation of the "Iraqi National Islamic Resistance" and its military wing, the "1920 Revolution Brigades." The communiqué claimed responsibility for several strikes in the Baghdad area (though without giving any specific detail). Though the organization had no "link or relationship" with Saddam, the statement declared, it was committed to "proceeding on the path of Jihad and martyrdom until the liberation of the land."

On July 14 the 1920 Revolution Brigades issued their own communiqué, stressing that they had inflicted "repeated blows against the occupation of Iraq in cooperation and coordination with other resistance factions." The statement warned that the brigades were about to escalate their operations, including the downing of "a large U.S. transport plane" south of Baghdad. Two days later, on July 16, a surface-to-air missile narrowly missed a U.S. C-130 Hercules as it was approaching Baghdad International Airport. As the only launch of a SAM in the Baghdad area since early April, this was no routine event; suddenly the claims of Iraqi National Islamic Resistance seemed credible indeed. (The next day, an organization called the "Iraqi Resistance Brigades" issued a similarly worded communiqué, announcing that "the Iraqi people's struggle to remove the occupation has nothing at all to do with the Saddam Hussein regime," because "the Iraqi people's revolution to drive out the occupation forces is a revolution for freedom and democracy" and not a return to tyranny.)

Meanwhile, the pace and lethality of attacks on U.S. forces rose to at least twenty-five per day. The insurgents were improving their tactics and making greater use of mortars, RPGs, and roadside bombs. By mid-July, American defense officials noted "a significant improvement in the capability of Sunni insurgents in Iraq." Compared with a few weeks before, the resistance was now "better organized, equipped, and coordinated," reflecting a better understanding of the U.S. Army's tactics and implementing well-planned countermeasures. The insurgency "is getting more organized, and it is learning," Gen. John Abizaid, the CENTCOM commander, told reporters in a Pentagon briefing. "It is adapting to our tactics, techniques, and procedures, and we've got to adapt to their tactics, techniques, and procedures. At the tactical level, they're better coordinated now. They're less amateurish, and [they have the] ability to use improvised explosive devices and combine the use of these explosive devices with some sort of tactical activity."

The U.S. Army was adjusting its own operations to meet the challenges. In mid-July, it began adopting Israeli-style counterterrorist techniques— from assertive small-unit tactics to better use of intelligence and heightened interaction with the civilian population. The 4th Infantry Division, operating throughout the Sunni heartland, proved especially effective at adopting the new tactics. Small teams now conducted an average of eighteen raids a day, concentrating on collecting intelligence that could lead to bigger operations. Special attention was paid to identifying and apprehending mid- and low-level Baath officials who would have extensive knowledge about Baathist activities in their immediate neighborhoods. Although the draconian security measures imposed by the Baath elite ensured that these officials knew little more than the immediate members of their own cells, they nevertheless provided useful insights into their networks, finances, and lines of communication—leads that proved useful, when compared against captured documents and electronic intercepts, in reconstructing larger networks. On the basis of such intelligence, U.S. Special Forces began a series of audacious raids against quality targets in Baghdad, Fallujah, Ramadi, and Balad, as well as targets in the al-Qaim region.

Although these U.S. operations were designed primarily to combat the Baath resistance, American forces were growing increasingly aware of the Islamist factor. By mid-July, the United States had launched Operation Ivy Serpent, the first counterinsurgency offensive specifically aimed at Islamist forces, particularly, in the words of CENTCOM officials, "the emerging pro-Saudi Wahabi insurgency movement." The main raids took place around the cities of Bayji, Huwayiah, and Samarra. In a second phase, forces of the 4th Infantry Division also launched raids in the towns of Balad and Baqouba along the Tigris. CENTCOM officials stressed the urgency of launching Ivy Serpent. "The alliance of the Wahabis and Saddam loyalists has resulted in an organized Sunni insurgency in northern Iraq," the officials said. "Sunni insurgents have formed a network of agents and scouts to track the movements of U.S. forces." It was imperative for the United States to contain the brewing insurgency before it became fully operational. From the Pentagon, Defense Department officials also warned against "the increased coordination between loyalists of the deposed regime of Iraqi President Saddam Hussein, Wahabi combatants supported by Saudi Arabia, and criminals who are paid to attack U.S. troops." As a result of this cooperation, they added, "the insurgents have improved their use of mortars, rocket-propelled grenades, and surface-to-air missiles, particularly against the [U.S.] Army's quick-reaction forces."

Indeed, American defense officials acknowledged in late July that American forces' recent successes had not managed to reverse the overall escalation of the guerrilla war. They expected resistance attacks to increase and foresaw that the overall security posture in Iraq would only grow worse in the foreseeable future. The growing desperation of the various resistance forces, particularly the Baathists, would push them into further acts of spectacular terrorism. U.S. officials began fearing the emergence in Iraq of Palestinian-style terrorism, including suicide and car bombing. A study conducted for the Defense Department concluded that the next three months—August, September, and October 2003—would be crucial for the stabilizing and revitalizing of Iraq. The study warned that "the U.S. military has until November to stem the Sunni insurgency and impose order on Iraq" or face an all-out eruption of irregular warfare and terrorism.

And there were major indications that a long-term guerrilla campaign was in the making. In mid-July, a Baathist command center was activated inside Syria; it would serve as a command post for the entire war against the United States. Western intelligence sources told MENL's Steve Rodan that "evidence suggests that Saddam and his younger son, Qusay, might have succeeded in escaping to Syria." They explained that "an examination of radio intercepts as well as other circumstantial evidence points to them relaying orders and funds from Syria to Sunni strongholds north of Baghdad." Given the extensive evidence of Saddam's presence in either the Sunni heartland or the western desert, the United States concluded that he and members of his inner circle were shuttling periodically between their Syrian safe haven and hideaways inside Iraq. Intelligence evidence acquired since mid-July bolstered the assessment that Saddam was increasingly operating from Syria; Saddam's latest audiotapes, for example, were distributed from the neighboring Baathist state. At the same time, Saddam, his sons, and other members of the leadership were still obliged to attend regular meetings with key members of the resistance in order to maintain their trust and support. But this regular passage between Syria and the Sunni heartland would soon lead to disaster for Saddam's family.

On the night of July 20, Uday, Qusay, Qusay's fourteen-year-old son, Mustafa, and a bodyguard were driving in a nondescript car not far from Tal Afar, on the western leg of the northern route from Syria to Sinjar, Mosul, and Tikrit. They were evidently on their way to Syria from the Sunni heartland after hiding for nearly a month in Mosul, at the house of their father's cousin, Marwan Zaydan of the Abu-Nasir tribe—one of Mosul's richest and most important leaders. His palace was in the Al-Falah northeastern district of Mosul, some 30 miles east of where they were driving. After apparently failing to link up with the escort, guides, and bodyguards who were supposed to lead them to their destination, they decided to return alone to their shelter.

Before dawn on July 21, the four knocked on Zaydan's front door to ask for shelter once again. These activities attracted the attention of a few Kurds loyal to Jalal Talabani, head of the Kurdish Patriotic Union (PUK). The Kurdish patrols first noted the loitering car, and Zaydan's Kurdish neighbors wondered who would have the audacity to knock on Zaydan's door so late at night and concluded that the visitors must be very important people. These reports reached Talabani himself, who immediately warned the United States about the suspicious development.

Later that day, Zaydan took notice—or was warned by a servant—of some Kurdish and American activity around his house. He immediately took his wife and son, escaped the house, surrendered to U.S. forces, and disclosed who his guests were. On the morning of July 22, U.S. Special Forces knocked on Zaydan's door and asked to enter. They were met by AK-47 fire from his guests, and three U.S. troops were wounded. About two hundred troops from the 101st Airborne Division and Task Force 20, supported by two OH-58D Kiowa Warrior helicopters, surrounded the house and urged the occupants to surrender. An intense firefight ensued, with the home's inhabitants throwing grenades and firing assault rifles at the U.S. forces. The Americans fired several TOW missiles from Humvees and the OH-58Ds before breaking into the house. Mustafa was the last to hold out—firing at the American troops until he was killed by a barrage of bullets. Close to a million dollars in American and Iraqi currency and an assortment of pills—including Viagra and painkillers—were found in their luggage. Four American soldiers were wounded in the operation.

*   *   *

The entire Arab world reacted with fury to the martyrdom of Uday and Qusay Saddam Hussein and Mustafa Qusay bin Saddam. As a rule, the Arab reaction turned on the impact the incident might have on Iraq and the region as a whole.

Among the very first to react were the Baathists, who promised revenge. The statement by the Saddam's Fedayeen organization in the Al-Anbar Governorate was the first of many like it:

> We are proud of what happened yesterday evening. For Uday and Qusay, the two sons of the mujahid leader President Saddam Hussein, were martyred in a ferocious battle staged by the occupation army. More than 200 American soldiers were used in the battle. Moreover, tanks and aircraft were used. The fighting continued for three full hours. They did not surrender. They preferred to face martyrdom, as the Americans themselves admitted. . . . .Yes, this is the martyrdom of the two sons of leader Saddam, the apples of his eye. We would like to tell leader President Saddam that his sons were killed. Nonetheless, the Iraqis and these youths were not killed. We are ready to sacrifice our blood for the sake of Iraq's soil. We pledge to our people's sons that we will continue with the Jihad against the infidels, and that the end of the two sons, their martyrdom, will strengthen our determination and support. The occupation troops said yesterday evening that the killing of Uday and Qusay will decrease the number of attacks. Nonetheless, we would like to tell them that their death will increase the number of attacks.

Wafiq al-Samarrai also contended that the execution of Hussein's sons would not bring about the collapse of the Iraqi resistance, crediting the growing predominance of the Islamist element for the movement's steadfast resolve. "The resistance operations are not linked to those individuals and not linked to Saddam Hussein," Samarrai said, stressing that he did "not mean the simple Islamic groups, but the other groups, such as Ansar al-Islam, Jund al-Islam, Jaysh Muhammad, and other extremist groups. These are the ones that are carrying out the operations." In addition to these, Samarrai noted, "some supporters of the former regime, who are very few, may have carried out operations. Therefore, we do not expect the operations to be affected much by the killing of Uday and Qusay." Several Iraqi and other Arab officials and security experts shared Samarrai's opinions and observations.

At the political level, the news of the martyrdom of Saddam's sons, coupled with the unconcealed gloating from both the White House and 10 Downing Street, sparked an outburst of hostility toward the United States. The news provided a moment of catharsis for the Arab media, which seized the opportunity to call for America's defeat in Iraq at the hands of the resistance. Among the most significant articles was a column by Nahid Hattar published on July 24 in the Amman newspaper *Al-Arab al-Yawm*—a mainstream, moderate newspaper for the intellectual, Westernized middle- and upper-class elite, the segment of Arab society the United States was hoping to make the foundation for any grassroots democratic movement. Hattar's commentary thus could be taken to reflect the attitudes of at least some of Washington's best friends in the Arab world.

Hattar stressed that both Uday and Qusay had led scandalous lives, and noted the bloody, repressive history of their father's regime. But their legacy, he argued, had changed in the aftermath of their death. "No matter what [they did in life]," Hattar asserted "the end of the two men was honorable. They died as martyrs while fighting the U.S. invaders and refusing to surrender. They valiantly confronted hundreds of soldiers, armored vehicles, and helicopters in an epic battle of glory. Uday and Qusay paid the blood tax to Iraq and to their father, who can now be proud of his two martyred sons. From the political point of view, following their heroic martyrdom Uday and Qusay have become an asset to the president, not a liability, as was the case in the past."

This act of defiance and courage should inspire all Iraqis to follow suit, Hattar argued, thus escalating the anti-American jihad. "The invaders' joy over this false 'victory,' which in the final analysis is a lowly crime that resulted in the death of four more Iraqis, will not last long in the face of a new spate of Iraqi resistance attacks. These attacks will not stop until the last invading soldier leaves Iraqi territory. The Iraqi resistance does not concern persons but concerns a political fact, namely, that Iraq is occupied. The role that Saddam Hussein will play in this resistance will be strengthened by the martyrdom of his two sons. He will now receive sympathy and support from the Iraqis in a way that will traumatize the invaders, who will not escape from the phantom of the president, a fighter, or a martyr."

Another July 24 editorial, this one by Ahmad al-Birri in Cairo's government-owned *Al-Ahram*, characterized the martyrdom of Saddam's sons as a turning point in the war in Iraq—the beginning of Iraq's march to victory over the occupying forces. To Birri, the American preoccupation with hunting down and killing Uday and Qusay confirmed that Washington neither comprehended nor cared about the real dynamics in Iraq. Under such conditions, it was only a matter of time before the indigenous resistance defeated the occupiers. "Saddam Hussein and his sons have nothing to do with the Iraqi resistance raging across the country against the Anglo-American occupation. The resistance has continued from the first moment the invading forces entered Baghdad. Not a single day has passed without their sustaining losses in life, so much so that the American troops are now scared to a hysterical degree that makes them open fire on anyone who draws near them in a replication of the horrendous crimes committed by the Israeli occupation forces against the Palestinians."

As a result, according to Birri, the occupation forces would be drawn into increasingly intense cycles of violence, irreversibly alienating the population of Iraq in the process. What Washington had failed to realize was that the killing of Saddam's sons demonstrated to all Arabs—not just Iraqis—that the whirlwind of violence was already sucking America in. "The biggest lesson," he concluded, "is that the invading forces will find themselves besieged by the valiant Iraqi resistance in a 'black' spot from which they cannot get out. The resistance springs from the people who reject the occupation of their country and resolutely struggle for its liberation. Qusay, Uday, and other icons of the Saddam Hussein regime no longer have any influence, and Iraq will return to the Iraqis in spite of Bush and Blair."

Other Arab observers and analysts considered the death of Saddam's sons and grandson a defining moment that forced the entire Middle East to recognize the condition it was in. The priorities of most Iraqis were gradually shifting—from ensuring that Saddam's dreaded regime did not return, to fighting the American attempt to occupy and remake their country. The killings in Mosul, and America's public display of the corpses—in a flagrant trampling upon Islamic sensitivities—convinced the Iraqi street that the first task was largely accomplished, and the second was an urgent imperative if Iraq were to survive as a Muslim country. Adnan Abu Odeh, a former adviser to Jordan's late King Hussein, articulated this point to *Newsweek*'s Christopher Dickey: "Ironically, if Saddam is killed as well as his two sons," he observed, "that will accelerate the process of seeing the Americans as the real enemy."

The Islamists—whether Osama bin Laden's Sunnis or Khamenei's Shiites—lost no time in exploiting this dynamic to emerge (after a long and painful jihad) as the region's dominant force. As Ghassan Sharbil wrote in a prescient article in the London *Al-Hayah* of July 19, even before Uday and Qusay's martyrdom, the overall shape of the American war in Iraq was increasingly playing into the hands of the Islamists. "It can be said here that George Bush has fulfilled Osama bin Laden's wish. The al-Qaeda leader's aim from the New York and Washington attack was to draw the U.S. [military] machine into a war on an Islamic land where it is difficult to win it by air forces alone. The current Iraqi situation provides it superbly: a confrontation on an Arab-Islamic land and in an inflammable region. The more the U.S. Army retaliates against the ambushes, the more profound its clashes with the population become."

The ultimate result of Baghdad's singular importance within the Muslim world—and of the electronic media's avid efforts to bring live images of Iraq to every member of the Muslim population—has been a globalization of the Iraqi jihad. "It is obvious that a continuation of the present situation portends an Iraqi fire that will attract non-Iraqis," Sharbil wrote; having contributed to the Iraqi jihad, many of these mujahedin would bring the flames of militant Islamism back to their own countries, as has been the case in previous jihads in Afghanistan, Bosnia, and Chechnya. The implications of all this were becoming painfully clear: unless Iraq's allure to all Islamists was swiftly reversed through the normalization and pacification of an Islamic Iraq, Sharbil warned, "the Iraqi fire will threaten to render the war on terrorism a failure and breed new generations of supporters for the September 11 attacks. Who knows, the countries of the region might later suffer from the 'returnees from Iraq' as they did with the 'returnees from Bosnia' and 'returnees from Afghanistan.' "

It is no surprise that Islamist activists are already gloating about the impact of the war on the Islamist movement. "George Bush may go down in the annals of history as the best thing that ever happened to the Muslim *Ummah*," said one Western Islamist activist. "With the invasion and rapid occupation of Iraq, it has become abundantly clear to the whole world that America intends to control all of the oil-rich Arab countries, and furthermore, it believes this can be easily accomplished." In other words, he continued, most Arab countries, no matter how pro-Western, had now realized that they surely were somewhere on the American list of targets for attack and occupation. They could not help fearing that whatever past friendship they may have had with the United States might pale, in the view of the United States, when compared with the lure of their large oil reserves.

This grim realization had already led both ruling elites and the Arab street to reexamine their world posture, the Islamist activist argued. "The biggest lesson of Iraq is surely that the amount of forces, the overwhelming airpower, and the indifference to noncombatants who are killed in the process means that no Arab country on its own can stop the American invasion of the Middle East. And that means the Arab world must drop its differences, rid itself of repressive regimes, and unite together or they themselves will soon be living under American occupation."

Furthermore, he asserted that the Islamists had a solution at the ready: "Osama bin Laden has called for Muslims across the world to set aside their differences in the 'blessed obligation of Jihad,' saying that 'there is a danger when a difference of opinion results in a loss of unity and then there is an obligation on the remaining groups to remain united and keep to the course.'" And all over the world, he concluded, thousands upon thousands of jihadists were eager and ready to rise up to meet bin Laden's challenge—not only to strike Americans wherever they might be, but also to topple any Arab and Muslim regimes that failed to heed bin Laden's call for Islamist unity in jihad.

The Islamists weren't the only ones who were bothered by the killing of Saddam's family members: senior Arab government and intelligence officials were equally concerned by America's interpretation of the event. Senior U.S. officials in both Baghdad and Washington declared that with the demise of Saddam's would-be heirs, along with the subsequent arrest of security personnel in Tikrit, Saddam's capture was "a matter of a few days if not hours" away. Although some of these officials later tried to argue that the assertion was largely an act of propaganda, American actions confirmed that Washington genuinely believed Saddam's capture was near. Indeed, in late July, elements of Task Force 20, the 4th Infantry Division, and the 101st AAD markedly intensified their raids throughout the Sunni heartland. These forces were aggressively capitalizing on "intelligence," including even frivolous rumors, about recent sightings of Saddam. In the process, U.S. units raided and destroyed many homes, shot at passing cars, and surrounded and imposed curfews on entire neighborhoods. U.S. forces swiftly opened fire in response to any suspicious activities or the slightest of provocations, killing and wounding dozens of innocent Iraqis in the process. None of these actions delivered any tangible results—other than profoundly alienating segments of the local population that had not already committed to the anti-U.S. jihad.

Senior Arab officials were mortified by America's depiction of the military activity throughout the Sunni heartland, because they knew that Saddam Hussein's chosen successor was Ali Hussein—the sixteen-year-old son of Saddam's second wife, Samira Shahbandar—and not Uday or Qusay. Samira hails from an Arab tribe that crosses over between Syria and Iraq; for many years she lived in Syria, secretly arriving at one of Saddam's northern palaces for brief periods. Samira's family roots and ties were of great importance to Bashar al-Assad, who in this period was acting as Saddam's main contact to the outside world. By summer 2003, Ali Hussein was constantly at the side of his doting father, being groomed as the future leader.

Unlike Uday and Qusay, who were violent playboys, Ali Hussein is commonly described as a serious and responsible young man; according to senior Arab officials who met him on the eve of the war, he is very knowledgeable and mature for his age. He has his father's charisma, and some of these Arab officials went so far as to call Ali a "genius." These officials were convinced that Saddam Hussein would continue fighting and struggling in order to empower Ali rather than to reclaim his own authority. The key to the Baathist nationalist guerrilla war was to sustain the Sunni power base—something endorsed and supported by all Arab governments—until Ali was ready to seize power and sustain a Sunni-dominated Baathist regime.

Arab officials were stunned to realize that Washington neither knew about Ali nor comprehended his unique importance to Saddam. Once these senior government and intelligence officials recognized that Washington actually believed Uday and Qusay were Saddam's intended heirs, their entire attitude toward the American activities in Iraq and the region as a whole changed drastically. For these key officials, America's misunderstanding of the Ali issue—including its relevance to Syria—was symptomatic of the shallowness and ignorance of the American approach to Iraq. This made them increasingly afraid that the explosive complexities of Iraq would blow up in everybody's face—"flaring the region with all-consuming Islamist flames nobody would be able to escape," in the words of a senior Saudi security official. Soon anxious Arab governments were reexamining their policies toward the United States and the new posture in the Middle East.

Finally Saddam himself, and the Baathist elite, issued their own reaction to the killing of Uday and Qusay. On July 29, a new Saddam audiotape was broadcast on al-Arabiyah TV. In an Islamist speech, he eulogized his "martyred" sons and grandson, and promised an escalation of the jihad. Saddam stressed his pride that they had "bestowed honor on the Iraqi nation" during their last stand against the American forces. Declaring that they had "died as martyrs in the Jihad," he reiterated his own desire to die the same way when his time came.

On the following day al-Arabiyah TV received a message from Izzat Ibrahim al-Durri, vowing to avenge the martyrdom of Uday and Qusay. "I swear that nobody will live in peace for as long as we do not avenge the death of Uday and Qusay, and for as long as Iraq is not liberated from the infidel occupiers and traitors who must be killed," Izzat Ibrahim declared. (The message would not be aired until August 18.) Other Baathist, pan-Arab, and nationalist groups issued communiqués along the same lines. None considered the martyrdom of Saddam's sons and grandson the end of the Saddam dynasty or regime.

At around the same time, Arab governments were informed by Iraqi emissaries that Saddam Hussein had resolved to commit suicide, using a powerful bomb vest, if American forces ever closed in on him. Saddam declared that he wanted to be blown to bits in order to ensure that his own corpse would not be made into a spectacle the way his sons' had. Saddam's defiance and resolve were met with respect by Arab officials, as they relayed in their responses to Saddam.

Moreover, these Arab governments interpreted Saddam's message as confirmation that he was committed to escalating the anti-American jihad until a final confrontation with the United States determined his own fate. The martyrdom of Uday and Qusay had graced the ugly legacy of Saddam's regime with an honorable end, and in doing so it breathed new life into the anti-American struggle. As this transformation gained widespread grassroots acceptance, it would soon bear fruit—in the form of vicious daily attacks on the American armed forces in Iraq.

16
THE IRAN FACTOR

In July, the pro-Western Arab governments were giving up on America's ability to pacify Iraq and establish a viable government in Baghdad. Most Arab experts and officials studying the situation in Iraq were convinced it was only a question of time before the Islamists—with or without Saddam—became the dominant power in the country. Of great significance to the Arab policy formulation process was the extent of Iranian influence, given the predominance of Shiites and Kurds—two communities Tehran had sponsored for decades. The key Arab governments resolved not to be left out of the emerging dynamics and set out to make deals with Tehran regarding Iraq.

The ensuing negotiations between Gen. Omar Suleiman, chief of Egyptian intelligence, and his Iranian counterpart, Ali Yunesi, were the groundbreaking event. Suleiman arrived in Tehran on July 22, ostensibly to discuss the extradition of Egyptian al-Qaeda terrorists held in Iran, especially Shawqi al-Islambuli, who had played a central role in the August 1995 assassination attempt aimed at both President Mubarak and Suleiman himself. However, in reality, Arab security officials explained, Suleiman arrived in Tehran to discuss cooperation in covert operations and insurgency against the American presence in Iraq. Suleiman wanted cross-border access into Iraq for Egyptian intelligence, and Cairo was willing to pay a lot for this privilege. He reassured Tehran that Cairo had no intention of requesting that Iran extradite the ostensibly incarcerated al-Qaeda terrorists and stressed that Cairo actually encouraged Tehran to send the fighters to Iraq to join the anti-American jihad. Cairo would also permit Egyptian Islamists to travel to Iraq, via Sudan and Syria, so that they could participate in the Iran-sponsored Islamist insurgency. In addition Suleiman offered Yunesi intelligence-sharing on American activities and vulnerabilities throughout the Middle East.

Suleiman stressed the increased Egyptian support for Tehran-sponsored Palestinian Islamists. He pointed out Egypt's assistance to the Palestinian Islamists and the back-stabbing of the Bush administration. The Egyptian reading of the situation in the Gaza Strip and the West Bank was strongly influenced by Cairo's assessment of the dominant trend in the entire Middle East—namely, the rise of the Islamists. Hence, Suleiman stressed, Cairo accepted that Hamas and the Islamists were the up-and-coming Palestinian forces. The Road Map only undermined the nationalist leaders, thus expediting the rise of the militant Islamists. He assured the Iranians that regardless of American pressure and Israeli threats, no Palestinian security official was going to attempt to disarm the Islamists. This trend was unfolding even though Egypt had repeatedly warned the U.S. against forwarding a "peace plan" that would embolden and strengthen the Palestinian radical Islamist forces, for—as Suleiman explained—they could constitute a threat to Mubarak's own stability. Cairo thus considered the "Road Map" an instance of American backstabbing, convincing them that it must seek and secure its own deals with the Islamists throughout the Middle East to prevent them from taking on the Mubarak regime. Therefore, it was imperative for Egypt to establish close cooperation with the Islamists—to help them with funds and weapons and assist in political confrontations against the United States and Israel and their Palestinian Quislings in return for an Islamist promise to refrain from helping their Egyptian brethren against Cairo. Suleiman stressed that the much-celebrated *Hudna* would serve as the foundation of improved relations between Egypt and the Palestinian Islamists. Toward that end, Egyptian intelligence was overseeing the expansion of a tunnel stretching from Egyptian military and border guard bases to the Gaza Strip, allowing for the smuggling of greater quantities of heavy weapons. Indeed, in August, Israeli security services discovered several such tunnels originating from Egyptian bases.

Meeting both friends and foes, senior Egyptian officials no longer tried to conceal that Cairo considered its vital interests endangered by American success in Iraq, and as a result, Mubarak reached out to Tehran to undermine the occupation. Indeed, the reports of Suleiman's negotiations for the extradition of Egyptian Islamists incarcerated in Iran were disinformation aimed at explaining the presence of Suleiman and other Egyptian senior intelligence officials in Tehran for such a long time. Having just persuaded and coerced the Egyptian Islamist leadership to re-nounce violence in return for either release from jail or easier terms of confinement, the last thing Cairo wanted was to bring bin-Laden–influenced firebrand Egyptian Islamists into the Egyptian prison system where they could challenge the theological foundations and veracity of the new nonviolent Islamism. It was in Cairo's self-interest to see these Egypt-ian Islamists ensnared in faraway jihads—such as Afghanistan, Chechnya, and now Iraq—rather than reach Egypt. Ultimately, Suleiman assured Yunesi, Cairo was eager to make reasonable deals with the Islamists—deals that would cement the Mubarak dynasty. Now, he was in Tehran to extend the deal to Iraq and the Persian Gulf States as well. After a few days of quiet deliberations, Yunesi informed Suleiman that Tehran had agreed to accept Cairo's proposal, clearing the way for a growing Egyptian role in Iraq, as well as an escalation in anti-American terrorism and sub-version.

As predicted by the Islamists, a major escalation in the guerrilla war started in July, and fighting further intensified in August. Although U.S. of-ficials kept blaming die-hard supporters of Saddam Hussein, the driving force behind the offensive was the Islamists. For them, the fighting consti-tuted the struggle for the future not only of Iraq but of the entire Arab Muslim world. On the ground, the escalation was the aggregate outcome of two major trends—the grassroots alienation of the population, and the growing professional expertise of mujahedin and Baathist fighting forces. Together, these factors facilitated the expansion of genuinely popular guer-rilla warfare, the quality of whose leadership and main fighting forces demonstrably improved through the flow of experts terrorists from all over the world.

The American authorities should have been most apprehensive about the long-term implications of this escalation because it was building on growing discontent within the population. Significantly, ethnic tensions were intensifying even within segments of the population long considered friendly to the United States—most notably the Kurds and Turkman—to the point of clashes between various communities and skirmishes with American units for attempting to sustain the status quo. Alluding to un-specified threats, Barazani ruled out disarming the Kurdish forces despite agreements with the United States and threatened to confront any force at-tempting to do so—a clear signal to the American authorities. "There is no power whatsoever that can force the Kurds to dissolve their militias so long as they remain in northern Iraq," Barazani said. In a demonstration of resolve, Kurdish forces prevented a Turkish military convoy from entering northern Iraq despite prior coordination with the United States. The Turkish convoy was carrying aid to the local Turkman forces. Ultimately, the growing ethnic and religious tension fueled recruitment drives, the flow of Iraqi volunteers, and most importantly the expansion and solidification of the grassroots support system that provided lodging, tactical intelligence, and other vital services to the fighting elements.

The intensification of the anti-American guerrilla warfare beginning in summer 2003 was the outcome of a coordinated effort between Osama bin Laden's Islamist forces, Saddam Hussein's Baathist forces, the key sponsoring states—Iran and Syria—and elements of the Saudi Arabian, Egyptian, and Pakistani governments and intelligence services. All shared a firm conviction of the crucial imperative of bringing about the complete and ignominious collapse of the American presence in Iraq. These governments and movements committed to imposing so decisive a strategic defeat upon the United States in Iraq that Washington would not dare take on any one of them in the future. The jihad in Iraq was deemed the most important objective of their respective national policies—a vital interest second to none, not even sustaining the Palestinian intifada. The jihad would be characterized by a concentrated effort to achieve more than just costly attrition or sporadic strikes at American installations and symbols of the occupation. Their objective was to demonstrate to the Arab world in deed and word that the Muslims of Iraq rejected their "liberation" and America's presence by making their country ungovernable. This was to be achieved through the impact of two approaches. One was headline-grabbing strikes—a series of spectacular strikes, mainly in Baghdad, that Arab and Western satellite TV would cover in real time. At the same time, the long-term populist jihad would erode America's authority and intensify popular alienation through the expansion of the guerrilla war against allied forces and vestiges of reconstruction. And while the initial operations in this jihad were conducted primarily by the Sunni-Islamist coalition of Islamic fundamentalists and Baathist forces, a major buildup of Shiite forces and tribal Kurdish militias was taking place in the background. By summer 2003, they were all ready to join a single common jihad.

The key to escalating the jihad was the emergence of a Baghdad-based, Iran-sponsored, all-Islamist "high command" cooperating with Baathist experts. The command was organized in the same fashion as HizbAllah International: established by Tehran in 1996, it was the first firm operational alliance between Osama bin Laden and assets of Iranian Intelligence, most notably Imad Moughniyah. By August, the high command was led by an elite team of al-Qaeda operatives under the command of Abu-Musab al-Zarqawi and two of Iran's most senior expert terrorists, Imad Moughniyah and Anis Naccache. Al-Zarqawi's authority stemmed from specific instructions and guidance he had received in Tehran from Osama bin Laden, Ayman al-Zawahiri, and Saad bin Osama bin Laden. Both Moughniyah and Naccache are protégés of the Iranian elite and are close personal friends of both Mohsen Rafiq-Dust and Ali Akbar Hashemi-Rafsanjani—effectively the source of their guidance and mandate. Moughniyah, who has known and cooperated with bin Laden since the mid-1990s, met with him in Tehran to formulate and coordinate their cooperation inside Iraq.

Under Al-Zarqawi were several operational commanders and experts, some of whom had arrived in Iraq around October 2002 to participate in the advanced training program conducted by Unit 999. Among the commanders were Othman Suleiman Daoud, an Afghan national who ran operations in the Sunni Triangle north of Baghdad, and Faraj Shaabi, a Libyan who arrived in Iraq in October 2002 after a decade in Sudan and now assumed command in northern Iraq. Also in Iraq were two leading operatives identified as Amin Hadad, also known as Baba Al Nada, and Muhammad Talahi, also known as Zakariya, both Algerians affiliated with the Salafist Brigade for Combat and Call, and both experts in recruiting and training martyr bombers. Their recruits would blow themselves up in Baghdad in the coming weeks. In August, these commanders assumed command over reconstituted cells and networks.

At the core of al-Qaeda's presence in Iraq were five insurgency squads—each comprising fifteen expert terrorist trainers, recruitment managers, and explosives experts. Most members of these squads were Saudis, Iraqis, and Syrians. They all worked closely with the Baathist cadres who provided the Islamists with new identities and genuine documents that linked them with leading Iraqi families. At that point, there were some 3,000 al-Qaeda expert terrorists in Iraq. "Al-Qaeda [operatives] are coming in from various places. Some are new but we have also found traces of sleeper cells. People have reported on their activities in several areas. We certainly know that top al-Qaeda bomb makers and organizers are in Iraq," Ayad Allawi, head of the Iraqi Governing Council's Security Committee, told the London *Telegraph* in August.

The Baathist commander affiliated with this high command was General Muhammad Khudair al-Dulaimi, former chief of special operations of Iraqi intelligence. An expert in bomb-making techniques, remote-control fuses, special operations, sabotage, and assassination, Khudair established a network of former Mukhabarat operatives to train and supply the growing Islamist networks in the Sunni heartland. Khudair's main base for trainers and organizers was in the lakeside area of Razaza, about 30 miles from Ramadi. Indeed, by mid-August, forensic analysis of the structure, chemical composition, and fusing of the bombs used against U.S. forces showed that these roadside bombs were local adaptations of the same basic design. This clearly demonstrated that specialists had recently traveled around the country and provided expert training in bomb-making and remote-control detonation. Insurgents in the Sunni heartland significantly improved their ability to activate remote-controlled bombs from 500 yards to between 1,000 and 2,000 yards depending on the terrain, thus leaving them better equipped to avoid detection by American patrols. There was a concurrent improvement in ambush tactics employed throughout the Sunni territory. A growing portion of these groups, irrespective of their ideologies and organizational affiliation, were relying on a centralized logistical and support infrastructure run by elements of Ansar al-Islam that had sought and received shelter in Iran during the war. These forces jointly claimed responsibility for the mounting attacks on American units under the banner of *Jaish Muhammad*—Muhammad's Army.

The significance of these developments was accentuated by even the slightest personal involvement of Saddam Hussein in their promotion, a point stressed by an Iraqi intelligence officer who escaped to Jordan in the first half of August. In order to ensure that the Baathist cells and networks actively supported the Islamist underground with weapons, expertise, and funds, the officer revealed, Saddam began moving around central and eastern Iraq to gain firsthand knowledge of the escalating guerrilla war. He also oversaw the implementation of his instructions to subsidize and support the expanded recruitment of Islamist cadres. Dressed as a shepherd, Saddam was reportedly moving in areas frequented by Bedouin tribes. After observing the activities of specific cells or groups from afar, Saddam dispatched comments and instructions through one of the two or three senior officers who still maintained direct contact with him.

According to the officer, Saddam concentrated on the expansion of two organizations—the Al-Awdah Party and the Baath Party—both of which nominally remained under his command. The power bases of both organizations consisted of officers from the al-Hillah, al-Ramadi, and al-

Diyali tribes. The Tikriti cadres were believed by Saddam to be penetrated by American spies and were therefore left under Ali Hassan al-Majid. The main Tikriti fighting units—predominantly made up of Saddam's former Fedayeen with a few local Islamists and Arab mujahedin—were concentrated in the area between Samarra, Tikrit, al-Duluiyah, and Balad. Saddam expected key elements of this organization to collapse within a short time, the officer explained, and therefore elected to stay out of its area of operations. Still, concurrent American raids, such as the 4th Infantry Division's Operation Ivy Lightning, were expressly launched in order "to capture loyalists of deposed Iraqi President Saddam Hussein," even though U.S. military officials acknowledged the capture or killing of Syrian, Saudi, and Yemeni mujahedin in those raids.

A comparable Baathist-supported Islamist force was also being organized in northern Iraq under the banner of Jund al-Islam. With a command center in the Bayarah area, Jund al-Islam consolidated several highly professional networks comprising veterans of Saddam's various intelligence and terrorist organizations as well as Iraqi Islamists and Arab mujahedin. Jund al-Islam was under the command of close confidants of Osama bin Laden's who had just arrived from Afghanistan via Iran. Another senior commander in the area was a Kurd known as Abu-Abdallah al-Shami (his real name is Nur-al-Din), who was dispatched to Kurdistan by bin Laden on September 1, 2001, to help organize the Islamist Kurdish group into what became Ansar al-Islam. By August, there was an alarming development when a large number of followers of Al-Wahdah—a local Islamist group led by the "moderate" Imam Ali Abd-al-Aziz—joined the Jund al-Islam cells. The militant cells were led by Abd-al-Aziz's son Tahsin—a staunch supporter of al-Qaeda's teachings. In August, Kurdish security forces had captured several members of Iraqi intelligence, including a former commander named Haydar Abbas al-Shammari. Al-Shammari confessed that he was designated by clandestine leaders of Saddam's intelligence services "to contact Jund al-Islam and build channels of coordination with it." To U.S. intelligence, these activities meant the return of the prewar Ansar al-Islam and not a new phenomenon. "Ansar al-Islam, which was in Iraq before the war, is in Iraq now, is a potential threat," Gen. Richard Myers said in a briefing on August 7.

Meanwhile, in the Shiite heartland, the expert terrorist cadres were being organized by training teams of Lebanese HizbAllah and Iranian Pasdaran experts. The organizational and logistical leadership of these cadres—now frequently referred to as the Iraqi HizbAllah—was assigned to Sheikh Moqtada al-Sadr. However, Moughniyah was a frequent visitor to their training and forward deployment sites, ensuring sophisticated preparations and the security integrity of the Shiite buildup. Indicative of things to come, more than 3,000 Shiite terrorist and intelligence operatives crossed from Iran in the second half of August, reinforcing and bolstering the special operations detachments of the Iraqi HizbAllah. In an August conversation with friends, Ahmad Chalabi identified the growing cooperation between Iran and Iraqi Sunni and Shiite groups as the key to Iraq's future. "Iran is winning this war, not America," he asserted.

Indeed, even a casual and superficial examination of the mounting violence in Iraq seemed to corroborate Chalabi's grim observation. Throughout the month of August, guerrilla warfare raged; on average, there were roughly twenty-five strikes a day, all aimed at inflicting attrition and fatigue on the American—killing for the sake of killing. Furthermore, the insurgents continued to sabotage oil pipelines and infrastructure, preventing the export of Iraqi oil. The terror campaign waged against Iraqis working with and for the U.S. occupation authorities and Western humanitarian organizations prevented the normalization and reconstruction of Iraq under Western auspices. Finally, there was a leap in the professionalism, audacity, and effectiveness of the Iraqi mujahedin.

Alarmingly, American military and intelligence services proved virtually powerless against this type of guerrilla warfare. The United States not only lacked the precise intelligence needed to prevent or forestall strikes, but American forces routinely aggravated the situation whenever attacked, by firing indiscriminately and killing innocent Iraqi civilians. On August 12, when a series of smaller raids by elements of the 4th Infantry Division failed to break the escalatory cycle, American commanders, frustrated, returned to the hitherto unsuccessful large-scale sweeps. Operation Ivy Lighting was launched in the Samarra area east of Tikrit in order to stifle the grassroots support system for Saddam Hussein and his loyalists. The CIA was convinced Saddam was hiding in the Tikrit area, and the U.S. Army command believed that growing pressure on the population would lead to a betrayal of Saddam's whereabouts. By then, the United States possessed intelligence from multiple sources about Saddam's presence in the tribal areas, but this intelligence was ignored in favor of clichés emphasizing the centrality of Tikrit.

Saddam himself dared the U.S. authorities when, on August 13, al-Jazeerah broadcast a handwritten letter from him reacting to questions from an al-Jazeerah correspondent regarding the president of the Iraqi

Governing Council, the proposed writing of a new Iraqi constitution, and his response to a call by Ayatollah Sistani for the peaceful eviction of all foreigners, considering it the highest priority facing all Iraqis. More than anything, Saddam's letter was a clear demonstration of his being up-to-date about all key political developments in Iraq and capable of delivering a timely reaction to them. In his letter, Saddam addressed all these issues succinctly. He then spoke harshly, urging the declaration of an armed, uncompromising jihad that would not only evict the foreigners but also unify the Iraqi people against factionalism. Significantly, Saddam stressed that this armed jihad would be the true manifestation of Sistani's decree on the liberation of Iraq. "The basic issue at this stage is to expel the foreign occupation and to ensure security and peace for Iraqis. Hence, the position of Al-Sistani and the entire Al-Hawzah in al-Najaf is important for the Jihad of Iraqis. As you know, Al-Hawzah has not called for pursuing Jihad to expel the occupation, thus far. This puts part of our people and of Al-Hawzah in a position that no sincere person wishes for it to continue, but rather hopes it would lead to declaring Jihad so that the entire people would be united in their position against the occupation. This unity would be manifest on all levels, occupations, trends, and leaderships," Saddam wrote.

The most drastic escalation of the jihad took shape with the emergence of strategic terrorism punctuated by spectacular strikes at the heart of Baghdad. These were not random strikes or capitalization on existing vulnerabilities, but rather expertly planned and well-prepared strikes carrying with them precise political messages for the Iraqi civilian population and its aspirant leaders. Although the perpetrators came from different backgrounds and affiliations, all the strikes reinforced each other in the context of a single coherent campaign of strategic terrorism. That effect proved the growing cooperation of all facets of the anti-American Iraqi insurgency.

The first attack took place on August 7 when a truck bomb exploded in front of the Jordanian embassy in Baghdad. It was a highly sophisticated bomb, expertly installed in a minivan. The van had been put in place the night before and then protected there by the Iraqis and Jordanian-Palestinian security personnel of the embassy. The bomb was activated by remote control the moment the consul general and key Jordanian officials were seen entering the building. The explosion was followed by an RPG and small-arms attack on the embassy's front area, which prevented local security and American military personnel from reaching the embassy. Under the cover of fire, an Iraqi mob stormed the embassy through the wreckage, brought out loot, and triumphantly burned pictures of King Abdallah II and the late King Hussein. The explosion and the ensuing attack killed at least fourteen Iraqis and Jordanians, including the Jordanian consul general. Echoing the official U.S. reaction and explanation, Jordanian officials linked the attack to Ansar al-Islam and al-Qaeda commander Abu Musab al-Zarqawi. "The style of the attack and the explosives used point towards Ansar al-Islam and in particular to Zarqawi, who is still on the run in Iraq," a senior Jordanian official told the London *Telegraph*. "Zarqawi blames Jordan for giving the United States information on his terror network and a secret Ansar al-Islam camp in northern Iraq, which makes him one of the chief suspects in this attack." However, neither Washington nor Amman would confront reality for political reasons. The real reason for the audacious attack, as articulated by several Iraqi leaders and imams, was to demonstrate to both capitals the irreconcilable grassroots opposition to restoring the Hashemite crown in Baghdad—a favorite solution among senior U.S. officials in both the White House and the Pentagon. These U.S. officials had long sought to reconcile their support for the empowerment of the Shiite Ahmad Chalabi with the adamant insistence of all the pro-U.S. Arab governments that the future ruler of Iraq must be Sunni (or their own regimes would be destabilized by their own radicalized Shiite minorities) by turning Iraq into a constitutional monarchy. In this model the Sunni Hashemite King would be the titular head of state, while the real power would rest with the Shiite prime minister. That the vast majority of Iraqis vehemently resented both the return of the hated Hashemites, and the empowerment of the despised westernized Shiites, did not seem to matter in official Washington.

The following days saw a mounting climate of fear in Baghdad, as another round of strikes demonstrated the mujahedin's uninterrupted ability to hit strategic objectives. First came a mortar attack on the al-Gharib prison in Baghdad, which caused six fatalities and wounded fifty-nine among the Iraqi prisoners. The objective of this strike was to demonstrate to the prisoners—all of them "political"—the growing strength and reach of the armed resistance. Then, on August 18, the insurgents blew up the main water pipeline of northern Baghdad, leaving some 300,000 people without water for days, and thus providing a clear example of the impotence of the occupation forces. Throughout, the mujahedin kept killing Iraqis working for the authorities, particularly the electric, oil, and civil works industries. Bombings of the oil pipelines and power grid also continued unabated.

Then, on August 19, around 4:40 P.M., the Islamists escalated their campaign by bombing the UN headquarters in Baghdad. The UN headquarters was located at the former Canal Hotel, in a well-protected compound. The explosive was a sophisticated truck bomb made of expertly organized and calibrated standard bombs and explosive charges—essentially 1,000 pounds of old munitions from the prewar arsenal including a single 500-pound aerial bomb—with a simple activation mechanism for a martyr bomber. Israeli intelligence confirmed that the truck bomb had been constructed by experts in the terrorism-support base near Abu-Kamal, in Syria, and then driven to Baghdad a few days before the strike. The martyr bomber was Fadhal Nassim, twenty-four, a Tunisian who had been trained and shielded for several years in a series of isolated safe houses in the vicinity of the Côte D'Azur, between Nice and Menton in southern France. He was run by a bin Laden–affiliated Islamist network called Black November that is based in Milan, Italy, and also arrived in Iraq via Syria. On August 19, Fadhal waited patiently for some three hundred Iraqi workers to be in the front of the building and for the UN emissary Sergio de-Mello and several high officials to convene a meeting in a room near the entrance, before surging into the building and detonating the bombs in a precise location. Iraqi security personnel provided the last-minute intelligence and then facilitated the truck's dash to the building's entrance. The explosion was devastatingly effective, collapsing the entire front section of the building. The human toll was horrific with several dozens dead, including de-Mello, and hundreds wounded. The next day, the UN and all international humanitarian nongovernmental organization evacuated their staffs to Jordan.

The bombing was designed to challenge an internationally sanctioned UN solution for the occupation. The anti-UN political message has long been an objective of Ayman al-Zawahiri. The Islamists fear that in presenting itself as a pro-Arab alternative to American hegemony, the UN gains support while it is actually an instrument of spreading foreign influence and values throughout the hub of Islam. In his December 2002 book, *Loyalty and Enmity—An Inherited Doctrine and a Lost Reality*, Zawahiri articulated his apprehension about the UN. "Islam views the United Nations as a hegemonic organization of world unbelief. . . . It exists to prevent the rule of Islamic law and to ensure submission to the rule of five of the greatest criminals on earth [the permanent members of the UN Security Council]." The day before the bombing, the Dubai-based Al-Arabiya TV broadcast a taped message by Abdul Rahman al-Najdi, a Saudi "spokesman" for al-Qaeda, in which he articulated the all-Islamic importance of the Iraqi jihad and urged all Muslims to fight the United States and its international allies in Iraq. The bombing was first claimed by the Vanguard of the Second Jaish Muhammad—a significant identification because Vanguard has been Zawahiri's signature name since the 1980s.

Another manifestation of Zawahiri's responsibility for the Baghdad operation was the spate of rumors and media reports from Tehran in the days surrounding the UN bombing about Zawahiri's disappearance from Iran. Zawahiri vanished, the rumors indicated, in the context of a power struggle in Tehran between the government, led by the ostensibly anti-al-Qaeda President Khatami, and "remnants" of the "extremist elements" in the security establishment. Starting in mid-August, Arab media, particularly London-based Saudi-owned newspapers and magazines, carried detailed stories about conflicts among Iran's top leaders regarding the extradition of al-Qaeda leaders to Saudi Arabia, Egypt, and other countries. There were detailed reports of face-offs at the Tehran and Merhabad airports, where intelligence operatives loyal to Intelligence Minister Ali Yunesi and the "hard-liners" prevented by force the takeoff of aircraft carrying al-Qaeda terrorists already earmarked for extradition on orders of Khatami and his "moderate" loyalists. This rumor mill stressed that although all al-Qaeda leaders in Iran—including bin Laden's son Saad, Seif al-Adel, and Zawahiri—ultimately received IRGC help in escaping arrest by the security forces loyal to Khatami, they still had no recourse but to leave Iran for neighboring countries. Thus, the message of all these rumors was identical—the bombing at the UN headquarters in Baghdad showed that Zawahiri and all other al-Qaeda leaders were no longer in Iran, and therefore Tehran should not be associated with the marked escalation in Islamist terrorism.

Reality was slightly different. Around August 17, a special team of senior intelligence operatives, at Yunesi's personal order, provided Zawahiri with the disguise and documents of an elderly Iranian Shiite cleric. They then helped him across the Turkish border, where an Iranian intelligence cell sheltered him in a safe house in eastern Turkey. There, Zawahiri was provided with the new identity—from documents to clothes—of a Sunni cleric. Then, capitalizing on the flow of Islamist volunteer mujahedin to Chechnya tacitly encouraged by Ankara and Baku, the Iranians escorted him all the way to al-Qaeda's bases in the Pakinsy Gore in northern Georgia on the Russian border. From there, Zawahiri made his way to the Fergana Valley in Kyrgyzstan and, via northern Afghanistan, onward to Pakistan. Zawahiri was asked to leave Iran because even the most anti-American mullahs did not want Tehran directly associated with the escalation in Islamist terrorism unleashed by Zawahiri. The timing of Zawahiri's hasty departure clearly indicates that Iranian intelligence had advance knowledge of the bombing of UN headquarters in Baghdad and did nothing to forewarn the UN or anybody else. Moreover, Saad bin Laden and Seif al-Adel were permitted to remain in Iran, mainly in Zabol. From there, they continued running terrorist operations in both Iraq and Saudi Arabia. After Zawahiri's expulsion, Tehran committed to not extraditing any of al-Qaeda's senior commanders still in Iran.

Tehran had good reason to fear the ramifications of the Baghdad bombing, given the implications of a series of concurrent events, starting with the sudden blackout of the northeastern United States and southeastern Canada. On Friday, August 15, Al-Qaeda made a very credible claim that it had caused the blackout in the New York area, and explained why they did it. Even though all evidence indicates that the blackout was the result of an accident, the communiqué offered a revealing insight into the mindset and objectives of the al-Qaeda top leadership at the time. The communiqué was issued in the name of the ostensibly U.S.-based Abu-Hafs al-Masri Brigades, named after a senior commander the United States killed in Kabul. The communiqué stated that the blackout was the first strike in a campaign aimed at significantly hurting the American economy, as instructed by Osama bin Laden, which he had indeed done on several occasions. However, even though al-Qaeda was only capitalizing on the dramatic effect of the blackout, the concluding paragraph of the communiqué was ominous. The Abu-Hafs al-Masri Brigades further stated that "sheikh mujahid Osama bin Laden's gift is on its way to the White House and then will come the Al-Aqsa gift. And what will make you realize what is the gift, when, and where? The answer is what you will see!!" The blunt warning claimed that bin Laden's people would soon strike at American interests to the point of attracting the attention of the White House, before attacking Israel, specifically Jerusalem.

Then, on August 18, al-Muhajiroun—bin Laden's front organ in the United Kingdom—issued a lengthy communiqué on how to prepare the Muslim communities in the West for the second anniversary of 9/11. The communiqué alluded to forthcoming dramatic challenges to the forces of Westernization in the Muslim world, and the rising of a global Islamic power that would supercede the current UN and, by extension, the West. It concluded by stating the Islamists' ultimate objective: "Two years on then, it seems that during their customary 1 minute's silence in New York and elsewhere on September the 11th 2003, Muslims worldwide will again be watching replays of the collapse of the Twin Towers, praying to Allah (SWT) to grant those magnificent 19 Paradise. They will also be praying for the reverberations to continue until the eradication of all man-made law and the implementation of divine law in the form of the *Khilafah*—carrying the message of Islam to the world and striving for Izhar ud-Deen . . . the total domination of the world by Islam."

Indeed, two dramatic events took place in quick succession on August 19. First, the bombing operation against the UN headquarters in Baghdad grabbed, as expected, the full attention of the Bush White House. Later that evening, a would-be bomber boarded a bus in Jerusalem near the Wailing Wall, close to the al-Aqsa Mosque. Some twenty minutes later he blew himself up, killing twenty and wounding over 130; most of the casualties were women and children. The operation was so horrific because the martyr bomber—himself the father of two small children—stood in the bus for up to twenty minutes, patiently waiting for the bus to fill with children before detonating his bombs. Israeli intelligence subsequently confirmed that the overall guidance and funding of the bombing came from Tehran.

The chain of command responsible for the bombing extended from Yasser Arafat to his chief of intelligence, Tawfiq Tirawi, and to the chief of terrorist operations in the West Bank, Hussein al-Sheikh, who coordinated the various participants in the operation. The direct commander of the Jerusalem bombing was Hamas operative Ahmad Bader, who is based in Bethlehem and protected by the Palestinian Authority's security forces. He runs the joint Islamist operations involving Hamas, Islamic Jihad, the al-Aqsa Martyrs Brigades, and bin Laden's people in the West Bank. For this operation, the Hamas cells in Hebron provided the would-be martyr, and the Islamic Jihad in Hebron provided the bomb and some support, including funds from Iran. Al-Aqsa Martyrs Brigades forces based in Bethlehem (safely, since the Israel Defense Forces withdrew in accordance with a deal brokered by the United States), arranged for scouting the target and getting the would-be martyr and his bomb to the Wailing Wall area.

Significantly, until his recent deployment to Baghdad, bin Laden's senior commander in Iraq—Abu Musab al-Zarqawi—had been responsible for coordination and cooperation with Hamas, Islamic Jihad, the al-Aqsa

Martyrs Brigades, and al Qaeda operatives in the West Bank and Jordan. Zawahiri was Zarqawi's direct commander in both assignments.

On August 19, the Abu-Hafs al-Masri Brigades issued a lengthy new communiqué claiming responsibility for the attack on the UN headquarters in Baghdad. The communiqué reached the West only on August 25 through venues closely associated with al-Qaeda. Echoing Zawahiri, the communiqué stated that "the United Nations is against Islam" and that it acts all over the world on behalf of the United States. The communiqué added that "the United Nations will remain in Iraq to bestow legitimacy on the United States and lighten its economic burden." The brigades reminded all Iraqis that the UN "is neither your aspired-for salvation nor your safety ring; it is a part of the conspiracy of the Crusaders and Jews against you. Do you not remember who was behind the killing of more than one million Iraqis in a siege that lasted more than twelve years?" Therefore, it was imperative to strike at the UN and all those assisting it in reinforcing the occupation of Iraq. "Whoever supports the United States or its lackeys, such as the United Nations that wants to justify the invasion of Iraq, is an unbeliever and apostate, even he if does that by word or signal," the brigades decreed—thus justifying the Iraqi casualties the bombing inflicted.

The bombing itself, the brigades' communiqué stated, "was a lesson to the United States and its State Department against Islam (the United Nations), which polishes the ugly U.S. image. The United States fights and the United Nations makes the excuses for it." The brigades stressed that they had planned to assassinate de Mello and other senior UN officials. "One of the mujahedin drove a truck full of explosives into the backyard of the UN center, near the office of Sergio Vieira de Mello," the communiqué stated. "The explosion occurred half an hour after the meeting the doomed de Mello held with the representative of the Civil Administration of the U.S. occupation, the criminal Paul Bremer, and some apostates. The mujahedin carried out the strike behind the building so that none of the innocent Iraqi passers-by would be hurt. The mujahedin had warned the Muslims not to come near the centers of infidels and apostates, especially in the coming days and weeks. God willing, this winter will be full of misfortunes for the enemies of Islam." The communiqué concluded by alluding to the brigades' promise of a simultaneous strike in Jerusalem. "Finally, greetings to the heroes of the holy land in Palestine, who pleased us with the damage they caused to the sons of the apes in Jerusalem. The Jerusalem gift, which we promised, comes, God willing."

On August 27, Al-Muhajiroun issued its own follow-up statement in which it also emphasized the connection between the "two tremendous operations by the mujahedin, one in Palestine and the other in Baghdad." The Baghdad bombing was commendable because the UN has always been "tool, tongue and hand of the U.S." in its relentless struggle against all Muslims. The al-Muhajiroun statement elaborated that "the UN is no more than a front to legitimize U.S. foreign policies. A rubber stamp to legalize the spilling of Muslim blood, a green light signaling the turning of a blind eye to any atrocities committed against Muslims." The statement stressed that in the aftermath of 9/11, the confrontation with the UN and the ideas it represents had become detrimental to the future of Islam. "One of the many benefits of 9/11 was that it clearly delineated the two camps of Islam and *kufr* [non-Islam], the camp of *haq* [truth] and that of *batil* [falsehood], the camp of sovereignty and supremacy for God as opposed to sovereignty and supremacy for man-made law. Verily Muslims have no choice but to reject all alliances apart from those with Muslims. This means rejecting the UN and any organization or body propagating man-made law," al-Muhajiroun decreed. However, he continued, the challenge ahead was not only rejecting what was un-Islamic but building an Islamic alternative—the Caliphate. "Let it be known therefore that all regimes, governments, and bodies (implementing man-made law) in the world today are rejected by Muslims and that the only legitimate authority, recognized in Islam on the state level, is that of the Islamic State, i.e., *Al-Khilafah*, which must be established by Muslims and which will carry the message of Islam to the world—striving for *Izhar ud-Deen*, i.e., the total domination of the world by Islam, through its divine foreign policy of Jihad."

In the second half of August, Osama bin Laden declared a general mobilization of the Islamist movement all over the world in order to defeat the United States in Iraq, confront Israel, and spark the historic upsurge of militant Islam. This effort, and specifically the jihad in Iraq, was to be waged even at the expense of other jihads, bin Laden's emissaries contended. In sermons and personal communications, believers were urged to concentrate on an all-out effort to confront the United States in Iraq because, the emissaries stressed, "victory over the United States will be far quicker than many think." The Iraqi jihad would be given precedence even over "the struggle in Palestine," bin Laden's emissaries stressed, because defeating the United States in Iraq would have a dramatic ripple effect on the entire jihadist movement all over the world. Bin Laden, his emissaries stressed, specifically ordered that the jihad encompass "the entire Iraqi nation"; that is, the entire ideological spectrum of the resistance. To accomplish this, bin Laden dispatched to Iraq a senior mujahedin commander and former chief of the training complexes in the Khowst area known as Abdul-Hadi al-Iraqi. Until his defection in the 1980s, Abdul-Hadi was a veteran member of the Iraqi Baathist security and intelligence apparatus. He was then drawn to radical Islam and ultimately escaped from Iraq to join the Afghan jihad, leaving behind many closet supporters among his colleagues. In August 2003, Osama bin Laden personally sent Abdul-Hadi to not only escalate the Islamist jihad but also reach out to and build cooperation with his former comrades now fighting the Americans. To expedite the anticipated escalation of the jihad, emphasis was also put on the activation of experienced cadres—veterans of Afghanistan, Chechnya, Bosnia, and other jihad theaters. They, along with new recruits under their supervision, were instructed to travel to "predetermined assembly points," from which they would be transported to "the decisive Jihad front"—Iraq. Another manifestation of the intensified al-Qaeda presence was the establishment, by Jordanian and Syrian nationals, of well over one hundred front companies and offices in Baghdad to finance Islamist activities—from humanitarian charities to terrorism.

One of the first commanders to react to bin Laden's call to arms was his senior commander in Chechnya, Abu al-Walid. Starting in mid-August, he dispatched several Chechen bomb-makers and snipers to Iraq via Syria in order to help the local cells improve capabilities without protracted training. Moreover, the Chechen expert terrorists are extremely knowledgeable about Soviet-origin weapons and munitions, which constitute the bulk of the arsenal available to the mujahedin in Iraq. Several hundred more experienced Saudi mujahedin had been diverted from traveling to Chechnya and Central Asia and were now sent to Iraq to bolster the ranks of the Islamists. In some of the Islamist detachments operating in the Mosul, al-Khaditah, Ramadi, and Fallujah areas, foreign mujahedin exceeded the number of Iraqi fighters. Zawahiri's brief presence in the Chechen camps in northern Georgia—on his way from Iran back to Pakistan—must have contributed to Abu al-Walid's decision to commit so many assets and resources to the Jihad in Iraq.

The other distinct source of assistance and volunteers for the Iraqi jihad that emerged in mid-August was the Palestinians. All the Syria-based and Iran-sponsored Palestinian organizations—most notably Hamas, Islamic Jihad, and the Popular Front for the Liberation of Palestine-General

Command (PFLP-GC)—rallied to the Islamist cause in Iraq even though ideologically they were committed fervently to the destruction of Israel. (Also, as in the case of the PFLP-GC and some of the smaller terrorist groups, they espouse radical nationalism and not radical Islam.) As was the case with the volunteers from Chechnya, the veteran Palestinian terrorists constituted a quality core around which new Islamist forces were organized in Syria before deployment to Iraq. Most of the Palestinian terrorists arrived in Iraq as part of predominantly Syrian Islamist detachments commonly referred to as al-Qaeda mujahedin. Not to be excluded, Arafat's people ran recruitment drives in the Palestinian refugee camps in Lebanon for volunteers to fight in Iraq. A few thousand Palestinians— ranging from eager teenagers to seasoned veterans of the terrorist campaigns of the 1970s and 1980s—rallied to the call within a couple of weeks.

Islamist reinforcements were being channeled into Iraq through three main routes. The first route was from Pakistan via Iran, with absorption and force organization centers in Zabol and Zahedan in eastern Iran. From there, volunteers were moved across Iran and into Iraq in operational groups, with instructions to meet up with Islamist cadres in central Iraq and the Baghdad area. Volunteers from Afghanistan and Central Asia, including locally based Arab mujahedin, flocked to Herat, Afghanistan, and on to Mashhad, Iran, where the first absorption took place. From Mashhad, the quality volunteers were moved to absorption centers in Mahabad and Oshnoviyeh, south of Tabriz, where they were organized into force groupings and assigned to commanders from Ansar al-Islam for crossing into Iraq. These mujahedin constituted the primary source of reinforcements for both Jund al-Islam and Jund-Allah for deployment mainly in the Baghdad area and the Sunni Triangle towns of Ramadi, Tikrit, Balad, and Fallujah. The second route served the myriad veteran mujahedin, commanders, and volunteers from Western Europe, Central Asia, Chechnya, the Balkans (mainly Kosovo and Bosnia), Saudi Arabia, the Gulf States, and even Iran. They were instructed to fly as individuals or in small groups to Damascus International Airport where they were met by bin Laden's representatives along with officers of Syrian military intelligence. The mujahedin commanders were organized and assigned to the new Islamist force operating in Iraq called *al-Ussad*—The Lions—in recognition of both Assad ["lion"] and Osama ["young lion"]. In camps in eastern Syria, the veterans were put in command of new fighters, recruited by al-Qaeda and other organizations, and organized into fighting detachments or forces of al-Ussad. They crossed in from Syria through the tribal routes as fighting units. The third route crossed Saudi Arabia, and was an expansion of a smuggling route first set up in mid-July. This route was divided into two main venues—the western venue snaking through the tribal lands along a number of routes between Syria and Saudi Arabia via Jordan; and the eastern route across the Persian Gulf by boat into Iran, and then into Iraq via the smuggler routes of the Basra–al-Amarah area. The Saudi route served thousands of Saudi, Yemeni, Sudanese, Egyptian, and other al-Qaeda mujahedin already affiliated with groups fighting inside Iraq. The Saudi route also allowed for infusions of cash into Iraq to support Islamist activities, from social and educational services to anti-American terrorism.

This flow of volunteers and resources contributed to the surging Islamist influence on the Baathist resistance. In the Baghdad area, for example, Baathist cells were integrated into Jaish Muhammad. Elsewhere, the Black Banner movement assumed responsibility for the repeated bombing of the oil pipelines in Islamist terms even though it was run by Iraqi commando and Unit 999 experts. In late August, the key Saddam-affiliated Islamist groups were Jaish Muhammad, the Black Banner movement, and the Iraqi Nasserite movement. Most of Jaish Muhammad's (well-equipped) fighters were locally recruited Islamists run by Baathist experts, mainly veteran Saddam's Fedayeen officers, and had operational centers in the Habaniyah, H-2, and H-3 areas.

The Black Banner movement—named after the Banner of the Abbasid rebellion against the Umayid Caliphate in the late seventh and early eighth centuries—was a highly professional underground run by Unit 999 and Engineering Corps sabotage experts, reinforced by Iran and HizbAllah-trained Iraqi Shiite experts in improvised bombing. The primary targets of the Black Banner were the Iraqi oil industry and pipelines. The Iraqi Nasserite movement, based mainly in Samarra and Baqubah, aimed to attract young leftist intellectuals, including Kurds and Turkman, to an essentially Baathist-Islamist guerrilla movement.

The Wahabi movement, based mainly in the Fallujah area, served as a clearinghouse for cooperation between the Islamists and the Baathists' grassroots reach. The *al-Adwah* (The Return) Brigades was a well-organized, highly trained, and well-funded urban guerrilla movement made up of expert terrorists and fighters of the Iraqi Special Forces and military intelligence who were openly advocating Saddam's return to power. Al-Adwah activities ranged from organizing, training, and equipping predominantly Islamist grassroots detachments that carried out most of the ambushes against American military traffic, to conducting highly professional clandestine operations against those cooperating with the authorities, assassination of Iraqi leaders, and so on.

Meanwhile, concurrent events in the Iraqi Shiite heartland were inducing a major crisis in Tehran, and especially in Qom. The Shiite awakening in Iraq instilled fears among the clerical elite in Iran about the revival of the Shiite religious center in Najaf as a competitor to Qom—a development with tremendous strategic-political ramifications for the world of Shiite Islam. "Najaf is a unique magnet," Ayatollah Mahmud Tabatabi told exiled Iranian journalist Amir Taheri. "It is here that major issues of Shiism have been decided for over twelve centuries." This was not an idle boast as, since the fall of Baghdad, some one thousand Shiite clerics and students of theology—not just Iraqis—had returned to Najaf, some after years of exile in Iran or Lebanon. One of the first Iranians to move from Qom to Najaf was Ayatollah Hassan Aminian. "We decided to move to Najaf because there we can debate and discuss all matters in full freedom," he told Taheri. "Shiism has always welcomed a plurality of views. Under the present Iranian regime, however, only the official view is allowed."

The political magnitude of the potential crisis in Shiite Islam burst into the open in August with the emergence in Najaf of Hossein Mussavi Khomeini—the grandson of the Grand Ayatollah Khomeini. Himself a theological scholar to be reckoned with, the young Khomeini criticized the regime in Tehran, calling it "the worst dictatorship in the world" and saying it abused the name of Islam. From the safety of Najaf, Khomeini called for democracy in Iran by "separating religion from the state and ending the despotic religious regime reminiscent of the rule of the church during the Dark Ages in Europe." He pointedly attacked the leadership in Tehran, stating that "all those who came to power after [the death in 1989 of his grandfather] exploited his name and that of Islam to continue their unfair rule." Khomeini called for the establishment of a religious center in Najaf advocating moderate Islam and democratic values under American protection. "I am transferring to Najaf because I know the Americans will not interfere in my work as a theologian," Khomeini explained. He did not conceal his hope that such theological work would ultimately encourage a popular uprising in Iran.

Trepidation grew in Tehran when Imam Muhammad Baqir al-Hakim, who had been Tehran's loyal protégé since the late 1970s, publicly ex-

pressed his support for the restoration of Najaf and Qarbalah to their historic roles as the leading centers of Shiite Islam at the expense of Qom.
Furthermore, Grand Ayatollah Ali-Muhammad Sistani, the most senior
Shiite cleric in Iraq, formally invited Grand Ayatollahs Hassan Qomi-
Tabatabai and Hussein Ali Montazeri—very senior Iranian clerics known
for their theological and political feuds with the mullahs' regime—to visit
him in Najaf to discuss the future of Shiite Islam. No such invitation was
sent to the grand ayatollahs associated with official Tehran. Moreover, both
Ayatollah Baqir al-Hakim and Imam Ibrahim Al-Jaafari, the leader of the
popular Al-Daawah Party, stressed their support for the gathering in Najaf
and promised that their militias would guarantee the safety of all those arriving from Iran. Both leaders suggested that they had coordinated their
position with and gained the tacit support of the occupation authorities in
Baghdad. Tehran of course concluded that such a gathering of grand ayatollahs in Najaf would surely constitute a flagrant and formidable challenge to its regime, and particularly its theological legitimacy. This was a
turn of events Khamenei and the mullahs of Tehran could not permit.

Iran had already consolidated a formidable intelligence and special
operations—in another word, terrorism—network throughout Iraq that
was not limited to the Shiite heartland. Tehran was adamant about securing and even furthering Iran's traditional interests in Iraq at all costs short
of a major war against the United States. At the core of the Iranian clandestine presence in Iraq were the four centers of Shiite power—al-Najaf,
Qarbalah, Samarra, and al-Kazimiyah—where Iran has maintained a presence through family, religious, and commercial contacts for centuries. This
comprehensive presence endured through the tumultuous Iraqi history,
including Saddam's reign of terror and suppression of the indigenous Shiite elite in the aftermath of the uprising in spring 1991. Iranian intelligence
had also established centers and stations in Basra, Amarah, and Mandali
and used them as its gateway into the rest of Iraq. From these centers, Iranian intelligence reached out to all opposition trends in Iraq, offering un-
conditional help and attempting to recruit their members. During the
1990s, Iran had trained and supplied a wide variety of political parties and
religious organizations of the Iraqi opposition in order to strike at security
forces and intelligence organs all over Iraq, instilling confusion, instability,
and fear. Although the Iraqi security services ruthlessly crushed many of
these cells, enough survived to willingly serve as the foundation for the re-
constitution of Iranian intelligence in Iraq. Simultaneously, Iranian intelligence had recruited large numbers of Iraqi refugees in Iran—Shiites,

Kurds, and even Sunnis—and trained them for sabotage operations, intelligence work, and network-building.

After the fall of Saddam Hussein, Iranian intelligence started a massive infiltration effort in order to expand its in-country networks before the Iraqi-Iranian border closed again. Most of the infiltrators were Iranians and Arab Shiites, and one of the main venues for these efforts was the large Iranian religious groups arriving at the Shiite holy sites. Most of the Iranian pilgrims were young males, and only a small fraction of them actually returned to Iran; many of them simply melted into the Iraqi countryside.

The entire Iranian intelligence system in Iraq was optimized for the conduct of anti-American subversion and terrorism. "Iran wants to embroil itself as a third party that has influence in order to spread confusion and disorder in the Iraqi street by using its supporters . . . to carry out operations against the U.S. forces with the collusion of many Iraqis that support such operations, thus exacerbating the already unstable political situation in Iraq. Iran wants to preoccupy the U.S. side and make it feel unsafe and insecure and thus decide to leave Iraq for good. Iran would thus accomplish two goals at the same time. It would avert the specter of the U.S. danger that is coming against it from Iraq and it would establish a pro-Iranian government in Iraq by continuing to put pressure and exploit the power of the religious parties and organizations that support it," warned Dr. Sabah Zankanah in the Baghdad paper *Al-Yawm al-Akhar*.

Iranian sponsorship also included a large-scale acquisition of weapons and ammunition for the Iraqi insurgency. Toward this end, Tehran used acquisition channels all over the former Soviet Union already in place for HizbAllah and Palestinian Islamists. In the summer of 2003, the Iranians acquired large quantities of night-vision goggles, shoulder-fired antiaircraft missiles, and sophisticated fuses for the IRGC-assisted Iraqi terrorists. These weapons were shipped to Iran and then smuggled by Iranian intelligence and the IRGC into Iraq for distribution among the most aggressive units. By summer 2003, the main smuggling route for these weapons was through northern Iraq—both the Shiite Kurdish areas and the erstwhile Ansar al-Islam zones of operations.

Starting in July, Tehran instructed its most loyal protégé—Sayyid Moqtada al-Sadr—to launch a campaign of provocations against other communities in the Shiite heartland. Sadr would start with the pro-Iranian Sunni community in Basra by seizing the local *Awqaf* [property held by Islamic endowments] and igniting violent clashes among Muslims and against the British forces. The Iranian objective was to create a climate of instability and fratricidal violence—a climate that would serve as a cover for a series of Iranian master strokes against the fledgling opposition in Najaf. Toward this end, in early August, a detachment of Iranian Special Forces called the Assadi Force was dispatched to the Shiite heartland to gauge the situation and be ready to conduct strikes—particularly assassinations. Another instrument of Iranian intelligence was called "God's Vengeance," highly professional hit teams led by Yassir Rafsanjani, deployed throughout the Shiite heartland. They were supported and assisted by Iraqi Shiite and other Arab teams from the Al-Quds Brigade, which is tightly controlled by Iranian intelligence and IRGC intelligence. By mid-August, forces answering to Moqtada al-Sadr were already fomenting Sunni-Shiite and inter-Shiite strife on behalf of Tehran throughout the Shiite heartland and in the Shiite suburbs of Baghdad. It was a suitable environment and proper time for both the Assadi Force and God's Vengeance to go into action.

First they made, and then aborted, an attempt on the life of Hossein Khomeini. Tehran activated a few hit squads linked to the Iranian Revolutionary Guard in Iraq; the squads were activated in Sadr City and Baghdad, as well as in Najaf and Qarbalah. Each squad included both Iranian experts and Iraqi Shiites. However, the Iraqi members of these squads could not locate Khomeini and or other Iranian dissident clergy. Iranian intelligence dispatched to Baghdad a few agents, two of whom, Said Abu-Talib and Suhayl Karimi, carried documents identifying them as journalists from Iranian TV. They began prodding the occupation authorities as well as Shiite opposition circles for details about Khomeini's whereabouts, ostensibly in order to interview him. When they pressed too much, ignoring other major stories in Baghdad and the Shiite heartland, the two were arrested by the U.S. authorities; the IRGC hit squads went underground immediately. Other Iraqi Shiite leaders of lesser stature were not so lucky. During late August, several died under mysterious circumstances. For example, on August 28, Hajj Sayyid Muhsin al-Husseini, the general-secretary of the Islamic Amal Organization of Iraq, died suddenly in Qarbalah. Al-Husseini's son claimed that his father "was either poisoned or died of a brain stroke."

Ultimately, Khomeini was not Iran's priority objective. The al-Hakim family of ayatollahs—fast evolving from instruments of Iranian influence to genuine leaders of the Iraqi Shiite community—was Tehran's first concern. In mid-August, Tehran sent two messengers to Baqir al-Hakim, warning him of the "potentially dire ramifications" of his policies. Then, on August 23, Iranian agents made the first attempt on the life of Grand Ayatollah Sayed al-Hakim, the elder half brother of Baqir al-Hakim. A cooking-gas tank was blown up in front of his house as he was coming out the door, killing three of his bodyguards and wounding nine, although he was only slightly hurt. In retrospect, it was a warning for Baqir al-Hakim to stop his assistance to Khomeini and others in establishing the Najaf center as a viable alternative to Qom. The bombing was carried out by Iraqis with the assistance of a few Saudis—all of them affiliated with the Al-Quds Brigade. According to Lebanese Shiite sources, the actual perpetrators were Sunni Iraqis and Saudis hailing from an offshoot of the Salafi movement committed to eradicating Shiite Islam. They had escaped from Pakistan (where they assisted the local *Sepah-ul-Islam* cells attack Shiite mosques) via Iran. In eastern Iran, they were arrested, tortured, and sentenced to death or, at the least, extradition to Saudi Arabia (where they would have been beheaded anyway). Then they were offered a deal—they would be released and permitted to cross into Iraq in return for carrying out terrorist attacks against Shiites. Since these Iraqis and Saudis were notorious as anti-Shiite militants, Tehran was convinced that even their capture would not implicate Tehran in an assassination attempt. Meanwhile, the mere botched attack resulted in the cancellation of trips to Najaf by many leading clergy in Qom.

The Iranians got their prime target a few days later. On August 29, two highly sophisticated car bombs were blown up simultaneously on both sides of the gate to the Imam Ali mosque in Najaf, killing Imam Baqir al-Hakim and close to two hundred worshippers and wounding close to a thousand more. According to Amir Farshad Ibrahimi, an Iranian exile and a former member of the IRGC's Al-Quds Force, who defected in October 2003 and who had firsthand knowledge of the attack, Tehran decided to assassinate Baqir al-Hakim because he was no longer loyal and controllable. The IRGC dispatched an eleven-man hit squad disguised as radio and television journalists to Najaf. They studied Baqir al-Hakim and in doing so decided the time, place, and method of the assassination. A senior Iranian intelligence official using the name Hajj Saidi, who was in charge of operations in Iraq, stated that the assassination of Baqir al-Hakim was "one of the most important achievements of the Quds Corps intelligence elements who succeeded in carrying out their mission and leaving Iraq without any difficulty." The actual perpetrators were not identified with certainty, although fingers were pointed at a small group of Iraqis, Saudis, Palestinians, and Syrians. A few were arrested by the U.S.-controlled Iraqi police but never indicted, let alone convicted. "We have learned of the arrest of a group of Saudis and others, including Sunni Salafist elements from the al-Qaeda network as well as a number of fedayeen of the leader of the ousted regime, who confessed to committing the crime," the Najaf Hawza said in a statement. In Lebanon, HizbAllah's Al-Manar TV cited a well-informed source in Najaf who stated that "those persons belong to the al-Qaeda organization. One of them was captured red-handed while he was communicating through the Internet in an area close to Al-Najaf. He was sending coded messages or e-mail giving some information. There are other details, but what is currently confirmed is that some individuals were apparently communicating with al-Qaeda members outside Iraq." No further evidence was provided by any Shiite source in Iraq, Iran, or Lebanon.

Meanwhile, the assassination pushed the Shiite community toward civil war with the Sunnis. Shiite preachers blamed the Americans for not providing the Shiites with adequate protection, and the Badr Corps was brought back to life as an armed force. Close to a million Shiites participated in the funeral, turning the event into yet another demonstration of Shiite power and anti-American defiance. In Najaf, the Grand Ayatollah Hussein al-Sistani issued a statement that carefully distinguished between the actual assassins and those responsible for the assassination. "Undoubtedly, behind such a horrific and barbaric crime, and also other crimes perpetrated earlier in Najaf and other areas of Iraq, there are those who do not want security and calm to return to this ravaged land. They are striving to sow the seeds of sedition, discord, and hate among the children of that land," the statement read. "While condemning such barbaric acts, we hold the occupying forces responsible for these operations, the insecurities and incendiary acts, which the people of Iraq are witnessing." The true impact of al-Hakim's assassination could be gauged on September 1, when Saddam sent a hasty audiotape stressing that his people were not behind the assassination. Al-Hakim's popularity was so extensive throughout the Shiite community that it was now imperative for the Baathists to disassociate themselves from the assassination, even though al-Hakim was notorious for his staunch anti-Saddam policies in the 1980s and 1990s. Indeed, most Shiites tended to accept Saddam's claim of innocence, blaming instead the Americans and the Zionists.

In Tehran, Spiritual Leader Khamenei led a choir of mourners accusing the United States of the assassination of Ayatollah Baqir al-Hakim. Iranian officials capitalized on the assassination to emphasize Tehran's political objectives. Mohammad Hassan Qadiri-Abyaneh, a political scientist and an analyst close to the Tehran elite, stressed the strategic ramifications of the assassination. "The assassination of Ayatollah Hakim was carried out with the approval of American President Bush and on his direct instructions," Qadiri-Abyaneh asserted. "The assassination of Iraqi religious leaders, particularly Shiite leaders, is part of the American strategy, which is aimed at ensuring the American presence in Iraq and the formation of a government of the people in that country. . . . The assassination of religious leaders and Iraqi political and religious figures that are popular among the people is a prerequisite to establishing American hegemony in Iraq." Tehran's own objectives, and methods, could not have been more succinctly defined. In Iraq, fearing fratricidal clashes and implosion of the community, Shiite leaders rushed to deny that any rival Shiite group or organization had anything to do with the assassination. They stressed the dire ramifications of the assassination for the Shiite political posture. The representative of the al-Daawah Party in Tehran warned that al-Hakim's martyrdom "will create a fundamental vacuum in the Iraqi scene," which "will have a negative impact on the Iraqi Shiite movement." That consequence ultimately served Tehran's purposes.

Of interest is the analysis of Iranian intellectuals away from the conformist political center. One such example is an August 30 editorial by Safaeddin Tabaraiyan in the Tehran *Nasim-e Saba*. Tabaraiyan is the son of an ayatollah, and both he and his father were students of Baqir al-Hakim's father. Tabaraiyan also studied in Najaf under Imam Sadr. The *Nasim-e Saba* is a reformist daily associated with the central council of the leftist Majmae Rowhaniyun-e Mobarez (Militant Clerics Society) that began publishing in February 2003 as part of President Khatami's effort to expand supportive media. Tabaraiyan attributed the assassination to Saddam's supporters, and observed that this tragic event would serve as a catalyst for the judicious expansion of the anti-American resistance movement. "Undoubtedly, the supporters of the martyred Ayatollah will take revenge for his blood from the perpetrators of this criminal act. This is a dangerous action, which was apparently perpetrated by the vestiges of Saddam who intend to spread the crisis from other parts of Iraq to the Shiite-inhabited areas in Mesopotamia and especially Najaf, which is operating as the center of the country, or to embark on a chimerical scenario to pave the way for a civil war in Iraq. Given these conditions, the need for alertness in establishing contacts with the various Iraqi groups that are active on the scene is felt more than ever before. Sometimes, by observing what colonialism and its minions aim at, one can realize the integrity of the actions by political leaders and groups. Ayatollah Hakim was not the first to be martyred at the altar of the Friday prayer and he may not be the last one in Iraq," Tabaraiyan concluded.

A September 1 editorial by Zahra Tohidi in the Tehran *Mardom Salari* compared the assassination of al-Hakim with that of Ahmad Shah Massud in Afghanistan, and stressed the role of al-Qaeda and its Arab supporters in both assassinations. The Tehran *Mardom Salari* is a pro-Khatami morning daily formally affiliated with the Party of Defenders of the Message of 2 Khordad. Tohidi attributed the assassination of both Massud and al-Hakim to the desperate determination by Saudi Arabia to prevent popular leaders in either Afghanistan or Iraq from realizing the aspirations of their respective peoples at the expense of pro-Wahabbi Sunni minorities. "The list of those accused of the terrorist incident in Najaf is a long list, and the remnants of the Baath regime of Iraq, especially the ex-bureaucratic intelligence service of this country and the Wahabbi radical members of al-Qaeda affiliated with Arab intelligence circles, are at the head of this list," Tohidi observed. "In the case of the organized assassination of Ayatollah Hakim also, the fingerprint of invisible hands of some Arab intelligence services can be traced. The interests of these circles are surely in deep contradiction with the realization of democracy and the first administration of justice with regard to the Iraqi Shiite majority. The reason for this contradiction of interests is the deep influence of intellectual radical groups of Saudi Arabia on the intelligence service of Iraq, which created a crisis in the relations between Saudi Arabia and America in Afghanistan and now in Iraq; the dormant crisis that came to the surface with the September 11th terrorist incident when the big role of Saudi nationals and even the radical circles in Saudi Arabia was proved," she concluded, hinting that the anti-Saudi interests of the United States and the Khatami circles in Iran actually coincide.

17
THE HISTORIC
TRANSFORMATION

As insurgency movements sprang up in Iraq, terrorism continued to roil Saudi Arabia. Although Saudi security authorities had intensified their own offensive against Islamist groups associated with al-Qaeda, they proved incapable of uncovering and destroying major cells and networks, although a few hundred suspects were arrested and dozens were killed in frequent clashes. Significantly, the Saudis failed to disrupt the large-scale traffic of Islamists between Saudi Arabia and Iraq.

By mid-August, the Islamists sought to regain the initiative by launching a centralized terrorist campaign, this time against British interests. A special team of roughly ten expert terrorists was entrusted with the task of devising and carrying out spectacular operations, while many localized cells were ordered to provide all possible support and protection. The Saudis learned about these plans early on and, resolving to destroy the networks, launched a series of raids.

The first such major clash took place in the al-Suwaidi suburb of southern Riyadh on the night of August 10, constituting the largest Saudi antiterror offensive in a long time. Altogether, the Saudis conducted more than fifteen major raids during August, uncovering a web of networks and sleeper cells all over Saudi Arabia, as well as arms caches and sophisticated equipment. Nevertheless, the Saudis failed to capture any terrorists at all.

The Saudis did, however, recover intelligence data, including a detailed document that demonstrated that the Islamists were contemplating attacks on British aircraft using shoulder-fired SAMs (either locally available SA-7s or more advanced SA-18s to be smuggled from Iraq); one of the cells had fairly detailed plans for downing a British Airways Boeing 777 near Riyadh airport. The Saudis acquired additional intelligence indicating that plans were made to hijack and destroy other British aircraft, although no further details were available. British Airways stopped flying to Saudi Arabia for several days despite Riyadh's protestations.

Both the magnitude of the terrorist infrastructure uncovered and the severity of the West's reaction shocked Riyadh. "The extremists had infiltrated and developed sleeper cells in Saudi Arabia to an extent that neither society nor the authorities were aware of. I believe they were still in the process of getting organized and setting themselves up when they were first raided by police in May," Mishari al-Thaidi acknowledged in the Saudi-owned *Al-Sharq al-Awsat*. This was the first indication of just how seriously the faction loyal to Crown Prince Abdallah, with whose policies *Al-Sharq al-Awsat* is identified, was taking the Islamist threat. Confronted by the potential for escalation, Crown Prince Abdallah issued on August 14 an unprecedented statement affirming the impossibility of compromise with Islamist terrorism. "In the decisive battle between powers of good and powers of evil, there is no room for neutrality or hesitancy," Crown Prince Abdallah declared in a statement that received massive coverage in the Saudi Arabian and Middle Eastern media. "He who protects or sympathizes with a terrorist is himself a terrorist and will receive his just punishment." Saudi officials echoed the statement, stressing that Riyadh had adopted "a zero-tolerance policy" toward the terrorists and their sponsors.

Still, despite all the declarations and continuing clashes, the Saudi security forces failed to stem the tide. During late August and early September, all the Islamist terrorist activities in Saudi Arabia and the Gulf states remained centrally controlled and run from headquarters in Iran. This command center was supervised by Saad bin Osama bin Laden and included leading cadres responsible for Iraq and the Arabian Peninsula. Despite the inability of the Saudi networks to launch a major operation due to the capture of documents, the buildup and preparations for an offensive surge continued. For example, on September 4, the Saudi authorities captured a truck full of SFSAMs and other weapons and ammunition not far from Jeddah. Interrogation of the driver and escort revealed that the shipment was one of a series of similar trucks—none of which had been found.

Meanwhile, despite great effort and occasional successes, the U.S. forces had still failed to crush the Iraqi resistance. Even in areas where the bulk of the population was docile or friendly—most notably in northern Iraq—the American authorities failed to build genuine trust and cooperation with the public at large. The alienation of the population was the result of mounting collateral damage and casualties caused during the sweeps and raids by American units; the number of Iraqi civilian casualties due to "jittery" U.S. soldiers jumped as troops unleashed barrages of fire in swift reaction to ambushes, roadside bombs, and violations of strict curfews. Quite simply, errors of judgment were made by young men under extreme pressure. The population's cooperation—particularly in the form of providing intelligence about terrorists in their midst—eroded steadily, primarily because of warranted apprehensions that any item of intelligence given to the Americans would immediately lead to a massive American raid, civilian casualties, and extensive damage, with the purveyors of the intelligence themselves frequently among the innocent victims. Grassroots support for the anti-American forces—particularly among Islamist and Bedouin elements—expanded rapidly.

By the second half of August, the American authorities found themselves relying increasingly on militias made up of minorities who were themselves at times mutually hostile, and the empowerment of these militias contributed to the further alienation of the general Arab population. With their forces thinly stretched and not suited to swift raids, the U.S. authorities in northern Iraq asked the Kurdish and Turkman parties to contribute militias and intelligence assets for the war against Sunni insurgents, particularly in the northern segments of the Sunni triangle. Although the relevant parties promised to commit a few thousand fighters each, they ended up concentrating on fighting each other for local turf. Severe clashes between Turkman and Kurdish fighters erupted in Kirkuk in late August, resulting in more than a dozen fatalities. Moreover, when U.S. forces attempted to intervene and impose disengagement, both Kurds and Turkman fired at their American allies. In response, the U.S. military fired indiscriminately in the general direction of the sources of hostile fire, inflicting several casualties among the already irate Kurdish and Turkman civilians.

Nevertheless, PUK intelligence assets did lead to some achievements. Hama Hussein, PUK's deputy chief of intelligence, cultivated a few key sources in the Mosul area, and on August 19 the Kurds apprehended Saddam Hussein's vice president, Taha Yassin Ramadan. "He was detained in Mosul as a result of cooperation between the political parties and residents," PUK official Adel Murad told Reuters in Baghdad. Ramadan's capture was the result of the earlier capture and "intense" interrogation of Col. Muhammad Rashid Dawdi, who was responsible for organizing Ramadan's safety by PUK intelligence. Two days later, on August 21, the

Kurds nabbed Ali Hassan al-Majid, aka Chemical Ali, whose death had been announced a few times during the war. Both leaders were immediately handed over to the U.S. authorities. PUK intelligence was convinced that it also had credible leads regarding the whereabouts of Saddam himself. Starting on August 28, large forces of the 101st AAD and Task Force 20 launched several searches and raids in a forest north of Mosul. U.S. authorities acknowledged that the forces were searching for a VIP—perhaps Saddam Hussein. Citing local Bedouin sources, Al-Arabiyah TV claimed that Saddam Hussein was indeed in the area and proceeded to broadcast interviews with eyewitnesses who claimed Saddam was "in good shape" and "looked good." The American raids, of course, proved futile.

Meanwhile, America's handling of the Kurdish achievements—from lax operational security in Mosul, particularly through the use of untrustworthy translators, to unnecessarily detailed background briefings to members of the media—resulted in the betrayal of the PUK operation before Dawdi's information could be fully exploited. PUK intelligence in Baghdad learned that several sources had warned the Baathist and fedayeen command about the American and PUK activities as things were happening. Significantly, a swift reaction to these developments came from the Islamist forces. On August 29, an Islamist hit team ostensibly affiliated with Ansar al-Islam penetrated the high security of a PUK intelligence compound in Sulaymaniyah and assassinated Hama Hussein and a host of intelligence officials. Most of the attackers were able to escape unharmed. The Islamist raids eliminated the PUK intelligence team that had been the driving force behind the discovery of Saddam's sons, Taha Yassin Ramadan, and Ali Hassan al-Majid. The conduct of the assassination raid was indicative of the close relations and cooperation between bin Laden's Islamists and the Baathist forces, as the Islamists avenged the capture and killing of people very close to Saddam by undertaking an operation that, successful or not, was virtually meaningless to their cause.

By early September, the number of major terrorist strikes had increased in the context of the expanding guerrilla war. The assailants repeatedly demonstrated that they had access to fairly good intelligence about the activities of the American leaders and their key Iraqi allies. For example, on September 2, Gen. Hassan Ali, the commander of the Baghdad police working on behalf of the occupation authorities, barely escaped a car bombing: An Iraqi resistance team was able to get the explosive into the well-protected police parking lot and evade American patrols, and they had an observer on-site who activated the car when Hassan Ali entered an office near the edge of the building. Had the car bomb been slightly more powerful he would not have survived. Two days later, on September 4, an Iraqi team almost hit an American transport approaching Baghdad International Airport with an SFSAM. This was not a routine flight—the transport was a test run checking conditions for the anticipated landing of Donald Rumsfeld's plane later that day. The ambush indicated the good and timely intelligence available to the Iraqi resistance, as well as the team's operational skills, since the assassination squad was able to penetrate the protected perimeter around the airport and withdraw safely after the launch. Indeed, by the time Rumsfeld's plane arrived, large U.S. military forces had established a huge defensive perimeter and exclusion zone around the Baghdad airport, with several helicopters providing air support and flare-launching protection for the plane. On September 7, several missiles were again fired at a U.S. transport plane as it was taking off from Baghdad. Only a massive use of countermeasures prevented a hit. Over the next few weeks, the frequency and audacity of comparable strikes grew, while U.S. forces failed to capture or eliminate any of the insurgent teams or their support elements. Even the contributions of American-run Iraqi troops from virtually all segments of the population trained to work as translators, intelligence gatherers, and operators of advanced equipment, tasks that required contact with the population, failed to reverse the growing mistrust between the Iraqi population and the American authorities, and the flow of quality intelligence continued to decline.

Most alarming was the increase in the recruitment of fighters to both Baathist and Islamist groups. These were indigenous volunteers coming from the local population—and were not former members of the fedayeen or elite Iraqi units. In other words, the population segment most crucial to the emergence of post-Saddam Iraq, the segment of society most sought after by the occupation authorities to rally and help rebuild the country, was joining the resistance in droves. The aggregate impact of several factors caused the growing alienation of the Iraqi youth and persuaded them to join the uprising: the collateral damage incurred during U.S. operations; the mounting hostility to the very existence of the American occupation; and finally the growing conviction that the United States would ultimately fail in Iraq, and those participating in the guerrilla war would be on the winning side. Alarmingly, despite the progressing reconstruction of Iraq's electrical system, the gradual return to normalcy in Baghdad, and the improving economic situation, the United States failed to reverse the widely held perception that the mujahedin would eventually force them out. Even the friendliest Iraqis grew disillusioned, restless, and hostile: "After this occupation, the American government became the enemy," Sheikh Annas Mahmud Aisawi, an imam from Fallujah who was leading prayers in Baghdad's Gilani mosque, told Tracy Wilkinson of the *Los Angeles Times*. "If the Americans do not keep their promises of allowing Iraqis to govern themselves and restoring security, then Iraqis must find a solution. They cannot be motionless and surrender. We tell our people they must be patient, but patience will not last." Iraq was a failed state, bordering on anarchy and quite close to the point of irreversible social collapse.

In mid-September, the fighting in Iraq seemed to have settled into a deadly routine. The attacks on the U.S. forces and their Iraqi allies, most notably the Iraqi police, averaged some twenty-five a day. Attacks were mostly ambushes with small arms, RPGs, and roadside bombs. In these attacks, the American units saw nearly two soldiers killed daily and close to a dozen wounded. Additionally, the Iraqi police and other workers for the United States, as well as their relatives, were being targeted for assassination, and several were killed on a daily basis. Emboldened, Iraqi guerrillas now targeted senior politicians, with Ms. Aquila Hashemi being the first member of the Governing Council to be assassinated. Also assassinated, by a roadside ambush, was the police chief of al-Khaldiya—one of the more important U.S.-nominated police chiefs.

Not only were the reconstruction programs progressing slowly, but the pace of sabotage of the oil pipelines and installations was increasing. However, the most disturbing development was the virtually identical themes employed in Islamist and Baathist propaganda and incitement. A grass-roots conviction was emerging that the resistance, regardless of the perpetrators of any specific attack, represented the entire nation. Moreover, under these circumstances, even the most ardently pro-American Iraqis were beginning to identify with the opposition. "In my heart, deep inside, we are with them against the occupation," police Lt. Ahmad Khalaf Hamed told Anthony Shadid of the *Washington Post*. "This is my country, and I encourage them." Iraq was crossing a historic threshold; its population was no longer afraid of American might and was not convinced that the omnipotent United States could impose its will on Iraq. That realization emboldened every Iraqi to join, or at the very least actively support, the anti-American warfare. Many responded to the call.

In Washington, experts in and out of government warned the White House that unless America swiftly and decisively quelled the escalating insurgency it might find itself fighting another major war in Iraq, this time against the Iraqi people the United States had purportedly just liberated from Saddam's clutches. Minority and dissident intelligence assessments circulating among U.S. officials warned that the discontent and hostility among ordinary Iraqis was fast becoming the primary threat to the U.S. A countrywide poll conducted by the State Department's intelligence branch identified growing hostility to America's mere presence in Iraq extending into the Shiite and Kurdish zones. "To a lot of Iraqis, we're no longer the guys who threw out Saddam, but the ones who are busting down doors and barging in on their wives and daughters," a defense official told the *New York Times*. This sentiment was echoed by Iraqi policemen in the aftermath of an American soldier shooting into a crowd of fellow officers. "I am full of hatred for the Americans and I am ready to kill them," an officer told the London *Times* after one such incident. "All Fallujah people are Mujahedin and they care only about killing Americans. We don't care about their powerful weapons, because we know that if we die we will become martyrs." Despite detailed briefing, the White House pointedly ignored these observations and recommendations, citing progress such as a concert tour by an Iraqi orchestra. Senior officials kept insisting that the overall situation was improving and that all criticism of American actions and the situation in Iraq was politically motivated.

On the eve of the second anniversary of the September 11 strikes, Osama bin Laden and Ayman al-Zawahiri resurfaced and ideologically charged the struggle for the future of Iraq. On September 10, Al-Jazeera TV broadcast a new video of bin Laden and Zawahiri. The video images were reportedly produced in late April or early May—the tape was certainly produced after the fall of Baghdad and the start of the insurrection. With the images, Al-Jazeera broadcast a brief voice-over message from bin Laden and a lengthy one from Zawahiri. Two days later, on September 12, Islamist sources distributed the full text of the messages, complementing the segments broadcast on Al-Jazeera TV, and emphasizing that the audiotapes were made on September 10.

In his message, bin Laden stressed the crucial importance of the legacy of the perpetrators of the original strikes on New York and Washington, particularly to the current jihad still unfolding in Iraq and Saudi Arabia. He alluded to the intent to have the 2001 strikes serve as inspiration to the current mujahedin by explaining that "this plan of aggression involving the [U.S.] occupation and partition of the region [Middle East] was

hatched more than six months before the two attacks [of September 11]."
Bin Laden articulated the political objectives of the September 11 strike—
executed to derail what he viewed as America's pre-9/11 ambition to impose Western-dominated peace and stability on the Middle East, and
undermine America's commitment to bolstering and sustaining the House
of al-Saud in Saudi Arabia. The September 11 strikes happened, bin Laden
declared, "when they [the attackers] opted for practical applications and
fundamental solutions to champion the cause of the faith and tossed aside
the unjust infidel solutions, the solutions offered by the United Nations,
and by the atheistic parliaments, the solutions offered by tyrannical rulers,
who have made themselves into gods who legislate in place of God. Moreover, they paid no attention to the futile solutions, the solutions of the pre-
varicators, the Arabs of the desert who sit down and hang back, who have
been preoccupied with their money and kindred and who have deceived
themselves to the effect that they have been busy [preparing for jihad] for
dozens of years."

More important was Zawahiri's message. "The second anniversary of
the attacks on New York and Washington comes as a challenge to America
and its Crusader campaign as it reels from the wounds it has sustained in
Afghanistan and Iraq. It exposes its deception as it conceals the extent of its
losses in those two lands," he said. Addressing the Americans, Zawahiri
warned that unless the U.S.-led aggression against the Muslim world ended
immediately, the jihad would erupt all over the world. "We wish to inform
you and to tell you that what you have seen so far is nothing but the first
skirmishes, just the beginning of the battle. The real epic has not yet begun.
So prepare yourselves for retaliation for your crimes." Zawahiri then addressed "our brothers the Mujahedin in Iraq" and urged them to persevere
and escalate their jihad. "We salute you and shake your hands and ask God
to bless your sacrifices and heroism in fighting the Crusaders. We say to the
Iraqis: God is with you and the whole Muslim world community supports
you. So rely on God and devour the Americans as lions devour their prey.
Bury them in the graveyard of Iraq, for victory is only a matter of one hour
of patient perseverance." Zawahiri further urged the people of Syria,
Turkey, and the Arabian Peninsula to join or otherwise support the Iraqi jihad. He stressed the help provided to the war by "the vanguards of the Jihad
in Afghanistan, Bosnia, and Chechnya" and appealed to the local mujahedin to launch their own attacks as part of a global campaign. "The Americans have come to you on their way to Iraq. So rise to teach them a lesson.
Give them a taste of the death from which they flee," Zawahiri declared.

Zawahiri then articulated the tenets of al-Qaeda's jihad, addressing "our Muslim world community in all the lands of Islam" as the mujahedin in the forthcoming global onslaught. He stressed that there could be no nonviolent solutions to Islam's plight. "The lesson that we have learned from the past two years is that victory comes with patient perseverance, and that our enemy is extremely weak. So be firm, Muslims, in the field of Jihad. Political solutions are good for nothing. Demonstrations will not defeat an enemy. Take up your weapons and defend your creed and your dignity. The interests of your enemies are spread out everywhere. So deny them security anywhere and in any place, even on their own ground." Zawahiri anticipated that the current jihad would serve as a catalyst for transformation of the Muslim world into a fundamentalist Islamic entity. "The Muslim world community today is uniting by the grace of God around the banner of Jihad against its Crusader and Jewish enemies. A new dawn of might and dignity is breaking over the lands of Islam. The Muslim community has learned the path of victory, martyrdom, and sacrifice in God's cause," Zawahiri concluded. "This age of Jihad has begun after governments and parties have crumbled. So have faith in the help of God. Storm the fields of Jihad."

Using his alias, Abu-Abdallah, Osama bin Laden issued on September 13 a dedicated "Call to the Mujahedin in Iraq." Copies were distributed all over Iraq within a week or so. It was both a very personal and a professional message "to the lionhearted Mujahedin (Arabs, Iraqis, Turks, etc.) in Iraq" from their leader. "Our Beloveds, We watch your great efforts while our hearts bleed that we could not be with you fighting all the polytheists and the Christians like they fight all of us. May Allah get us among you fighting them," bin Laden wrote. The jihad in Iraq was already having global results, he said. "*Inshallah,* there are good omens coming soon. We watched the Christians, the slaves of the cross, the Protestants, the Jews, both guards and slaves, Americans, British, and their followers cry out asking for help and relief from the UN organization to support their aggression and wrongful acts against the people of Iraq, a matter that made all the countries scoff at them, in particular France as it published in its press. The fire of sedition has started among their leaders! I want you to know that you're the ones who made them taste the bitters of distress and tribulation with the help of Allah. You placed in them fear and terror and their soldiers have begun to run away from Iraq." At the same time, bin Laden urged his mujahedin to be patient for it would take a long time and many sacrifices before the inevitable triumph was achieved. Jihad's victory in

Iraq would set the stage for an Islamist surge all over the world. With the Iraqi jihad escalating, "they will resist no more and we will watch with you and with the whole world their doom and after that their hometowns will fall down because they fight not for aims or belief. . . . Our Brothers, kill the Americans, the British, and who ever stands with them wherever you find them, with no mercy or pity."

On a practical note, bin Laden reminded his mujahedin of the merits of guerrilla warfare. "Keep in mind it was guerrilla warfare that defeated the Russians who were more powerful and stronger than them [the Americans and British]. And do tricks. Know that war is a trick." He urged all those who fought the occupation forces, irrespective of their ideological and organizational affiliation, to rally behind his chosen commanders. "Be one in unity and avoid disunity and be under one ensign of a man who leads you to victory in spite of your different positions. The man who is the best for being Mujahedin leader in Iraq is Sheikh Abu-Abdallah ash-Shafi (May Allah shield him), the deputy chief of the Ansar al-Islam organization." Bin Laden stressed that "he is recommended by many sheikhs such as Sheikh Mujahid Hamood bin Oklaa Al-Shiabi (May Allah's Mercy be upon him) and also from Sheikh Mujahid Ali Khodari (May Allah release him and all arrested Muslims). We urge you, our Brothers, to pay homage to him and be under his steerage, because unity is power, glory, and strength to you and a fast victory, *Inshallah*." Bin Laden stressed that there would be practical benefits from uniting behind the jihadist banner. "When you integrate together, it will be possible to coordinate and close the gaps; to supply money, food, supplies and share points of view, to receive good guidelines from Supreme Command, to conquer the strongholds to release our prisoners, and there are a lot of benefits and advantages of unity." These would come from a worldwide support system being put into action. "We have a lot of obligations coming to you, in particular *Duaa* to assist you, to supply you with money, warriors, weapons, war supplies, and other things," bin Laden assured his mujahedin in Iraq.

Concurrently, the Islamist Sharia Court of the United Kingdom issued a fatwa—symbolically dated September 11, 2003—forbidding Muslims in the West to cooperate in any way with U.S. or UK authorities. The fatwa was widely circulated throughout the West and the Middle East. "After the invasion of Iraq it has become clear for those, whether they are closer or further from the region, to discover the hidden agenda of the American government and its alliance: that is, the destruction of Islam, and to redraw the map of the region," the fatwa stated. "Therefore we are not sur-

prised that the disbelievers are planning to destroy Islam and Muslims, because that is one of their main tasks, even though it is impossible because
this plot will always be recorded until the Day of Judgment." The fatwa
warned Western Muslims, particularly those serving in the armed forces of
the United States and the United Kingdom, of the dire ramifications of
their betrayal of Islam and their brethren. The fatwa decreed that all Muslims, "particularly those Muslims in Iraq," who "fight side-by-side with the
UK and U.S. forces against Muslims will become apostate; he is at war with
Islam and Muslim, and his life and wealth will have no sanctity. He like the
disbelievers is a clear enemy of Islam and Muslims and consequently becomes a legitimate target for the Mujahedin, and if they die they will die
outside the fold of Islam, and they will never be dignified in their death nor
buried with the Muslims. . . . So fear Allah, O Muslims, bring an end to
working as spies, police, soldiers, ministers, and politicians for the *taghout*
[apostasy]," the fatwa concluded. Quite clearly, the court allowed for no
compromise on this issue.

Responding to the fatwas and invocations, a renewed flow of mujahedin crossed into Iraq. "Our entire group was trained in Syria," a Fallujah-
based commander named "Jamal" told Mark Franchetti of the London
Telegraph. Together with Iraqi Islamists, the foreign volunteers were
trained at the Martyrs of Islam camp near the village of Rouwayssat Naaman in eastern Syria and then organized into fighting cells. "Then we
crossed into Iraq. Other groups were trained there after us. We are here to
kill American soldiers and kick them out of Iraq forever. I have no plans to
go home. I will stay here until we have defeated them or I'll die here. All the
other fighters feel this way," Jamal explained. Once in Iraq, the mujahedin
were supplied with weapons and funds from local resources. All together,
there was an improvement in the cooperation between al-Qaeda and
Baathist cadres—largely the work of al-Zaraqawi. Increasingly alienated by
the lack of improvement of daily life and the increase of suffering from
U.S. "collateral damage," wider segments of the Iraqi population grew inclined to accept the Islamists' agitation about the Crusaders' threats, and
the impossibility of cooperation with the U.S. Grassroots cooperation
with, and support for, the foreign and local mujahedin only grew greater
and wider. "Our message to the Americans is clear," Jamal stated to
Franchetti. "You are our enemies. We do not want Saddam back but we
want you to go home. You are the enemies of Islam and you must leave Iraq
or be killed. Leave now, before it's too late."

By mid-September, not only mujahedin but improved weapons were crossing into Iraq from Syria. Most important were the SA-18 SFSAMs, originally purchased by Syria from Belarus in August 2003 and smuggled from Syria along with trained crews. New types of antitank weapons were also supplied via Syria.

By the end of the month, al-Qaeda had a large-scale recruitment system operating throughout the Muslim world—a system of organizing and financing travel to Iran, Lebanon, Syria, Saudi Arabia, and Yemen as gateways for travel over land to Iraq. By now the Islamists had also developed a system of payment for the mujahedin in Iraq, offering salaries and benefits amounting to hundreds of dollars per month. These salaries were almost ten times the average salary in Lebanon or Syria, and thus constituted an inducement for the multitude of unemployed and unemployable youth. Indeed, there emerged a stream of young Sunni recruits—mostly from Jordan, Syria, Lebanon, and Yemen—who joined in for the money. And there were other indications of impending Islamist upsurge in both Iraq and Saudi Arabia. On September 11, for example, Saudi sources reported that in the previous week Iranian intelligence had assisted Saad bin Laden and five senior operatives, including one referred to as "Abu Musafa the engineer," in leaving Iran without being detected. With Tehran apprehensive about the ramifications of potential upcoming anti-U.S. and anti-Saudi terrorism, they were anxious that no such figures remain within their borders.

Following bin-Laden and Zawahiri's lead, Saddam released another audiotape on September 17, which was promptly broadcast by Al-Arabiya TV. Urging all Iraqis to continue the jihad in terms similar to the Islamists', Saddam declared, "Oh Iraqi people, I am telling you the good news. . . . The fatigue is eating into the enemy's ranks. . . . You mujahedin, Iraqis and women, increase your attacks on your enemies." Unlike the Islamists, though, Saddam also urged political action, including demonstrations, imploring the Iraqis to protest against the occupation in the streets, to "beat the walls in protest," and to donate money to the resistance. The reaction to Saddam's speech was intriguing because, while there was no discernable escalation in the Baathists' guerrilla war (as opposed to the demonstrably more audacious attacks carried out by Islamist networks), there was a sudden surge in pro-Saddam graffiti, especially in Baghdad. "Saddam is coming back!" was painted on many walls; "Patience, Baghdad, we will exterminate the invasion army," read another, and "Saddam Hussein is the nation's conscience defying the American and Zionist evil." As a rule, Iraqis in the street expressed support for these messages.

However, by September there was growing apprehension by Saddam Hussein and his closest aides that they were becoming largely irrelevant to the Iraqi national liberation jihad. Therefore, around September, Saddam decided to abandon the safety of his bunkers in the western desert and return to the Sunni heartland in order to ensure contact with the fighters and the local leaders—that is, to regain relevance. To survive, Saddam established a new inner circle made up of fiercely loyal members of five extended families hailing from a few villages within a 12-mile radius of Tikrit, particularly a 12-mile-long corridor along the Tigris River with its center in Saddam's hometown of Aujah. Although some of these confidants were former members of the Special Security Organization and other intelligence and security organs, blood loyalty was the key reason for their place in the system. To function, Saddam relied on five key lieutenants, whom U.S. Army intelligence would dub "Saddam's enablers." All of them were members of the five families and had known Saddam for decades. Each one of these enablers had a specific task—logistics, planning, operations, financing, or security (namely, spying on all the others). The enablers relied on some forty loyalists who had periodic access to Saddam himself and who arranged his safe houses, food supplies, and transportation. Saddam was constantly moved by aging taxis, pickup trucks, and river boats between some thirty safe houses, mostly remote farmhouses surrounded by thick foliage. He rarely stayed more than a week in a single place. The Baathist activities—from resistance operations to distribution of funds and weapons to ideological propaganda—were run through the enablers, who personally activated lower tiers of loyalist cells. Since all communication was by word of mouth—mostly directly but at times through teenage messengers—Saddam's own guidance was only general in nature and was limited to setting strategic priorities and overall character for the guerrilla warfare. Ultimately Saddam's effort would prove ineffective and would not reverse the overall trend in the Iraqi popular resistance to the occupation.

Meanwhile, all the military and logistical preparations manifested themselves in attacks on U.S. forces that were more frequent, better aimed at quality targets, and discernibly more lethal. Ambushes against military convoys became better organized and thus more devastating. Incorporating Chechen know-how, the roadside bombs became increasingly powerful, reliable, and accurate. In Baghdad, barrages of rockets and mortar shells slammed into buildings used by the occupation authorities, including, early on September 26, the Al-Rashid Hotel, which housed senior U.S. military officers and civilian support staff. The assassination of Iraqi officials working with the authorities increased. Furthermore, wherever such attacks were taking place, Iraqi mobs would gather, dance around the wreckage of the American military vehicles, and fire Kalashnikovs in the air. They no longer feared indiscriminate retaliatory fire from American soldiers, although scores were injured. The Islamists encouraged these shows of defiance, as any Iraqi casualty would bring several relatives into the ranks of the jihad. At the same time, the growing pace of U.S. preventive raids and sweeps largely failed to deliver results—mainly due to the absence of accurate intelligence from human sources.

This trend continued into October. Car bombs driven by martyr bombers—a hallmark of the Islamist jihad—returned to Baghdad, albeit with low impact. On October 9, a martyr bomber blew his car up at a Sadr City police station, killing nine; on the 11th, another car blew up near the Baghdad Hotel, killing eight; on the 14th, a bomber tried to hit the Turkish embassy but blew up away from his target, killing one and wounding about a dozen. Overall, the guerrilla warfare continued despite several major offensive operations. American forces were now subjected to a daily average of some fifteen to twenty "discernable attacks" and many smaller incidents such as rock-pelting and fire from "stray bullets." Operational casualties now stood at a daily average of one fatality and six wounded. In Baghdad, the authorities could no longer ignore the trend. "The enemy has evolved— a little bit more lethal, a little more complex, a little more sophisticated, and in some cases, a little bit more tenacious," Lt. Gen. Ricardo Sanchez, an American commander in Iraq, said in an October 2 briefing. "The evolution is about what we expected to see over time." He expected the intensity of the fighting to grow. "As long as we are here, the coalition needs to be prepared to take casualties," Sanchez said. "We should not be surprised if one of these mornings we wake up and there has been a major firefight with some casualties or a significant terrorist attack that kills significant numbers of people." Still, Sanchez insisted that despite the qualitative improvement, the Iraqi guerrilla warfare remained local, although there were initial signs that a regional leadership was emerging. At the Pentagon, senior officials rushed to downplay Sanchez's message, stressing that the sweeps and offensive raids were having a tangible effect on the Iraqi guerrillas. Officials also insisted that American casualties would soon decrease, as recently trained Iraqi troops were taking over many of the security duties.

Developments in the field refuted Washington's optimism. There was a discernable increase in the Islamists' recruitment drives in both Western Europe and the Middle East. Special attention was paid to "clean" volunteers with West European passports or residency documents who could travel legally to Baghdad as volunteers of charity organizations and employees of European companies. Notably, many of these volunteers were veterans of the jihads in Bosnia, Kosovo, and Chechnya. Friendly security services determined, and so warned Washington, that a growing number of volunteers trained in Syria were departing for the Iraqi front. Jordanian intelligence confirmed that the local recruitment drive was conducted on Zarqawi's orders. A comparable recruitment drive was noted in Saudi Arabia.

In Washington, however, senior officials insisted that "the recruitment operation has been bolstered by aides of deposed President Saddam Hussein," and not al-Qaeda. They declared that "senior Baath members [had] fled Iraq for neighboring Jordan and Syria, where they have begun recruiting fighters for the Sunni war against the United States." The officials expected this pool of refugees to be exhausted soon. The White House remained unswervingly committed to its politically self-serving conviction that, with the exception of Saddam Hussein's loyalists, virtually all Iraqis were ready to support the U.S. occupation and remaking of Iraq. Since acknowledging the growing preeminence of the jihadists in the guerrilla war would have contradicted this belief, the Bush administration adamantly refused to face reality. The assessment did not change even as the Saudi Arabian security forces arrested several local mujahedin recruited by al-Qaeda specifically to fight in Iraq.

Meanwhile, sabotage of Iraq's national infrastructure, most notably oil pipelines, multiplied. Throughout, regular attacks on the U.S. forces continued unabated. In October, they peaked at thirty-five "discernable attacks" in one day, and leveled off to a daily average of twenty to twenty-five incidents. A series of proactive raids failed to change the pace and intensity of the guerrilla attacks.

Most alarming, however, was the gradual spread of active warfare into the Shiite zone, as Moqtada al-Sadr's al-Mahdi militia started to openly clash with both American units and Iraqi police. The turning point took place in Qarbalah on Friday, October 17. A patrol of the 101st AAD escorted several Iraqi policemen who tried to enter a building of the al-Mahdi militia to apprehend several fighters suspected of violating the night curfew. The militiamen opened fire on the Iraqi police. The U.S.

forces intervened and directed heavy fire toward the Shiite combatants. However, the Shiites were prepared and their positions fortified, and the American troops were unable to take the building. By the time the firing stopped a few hours later, three American and seven Iraqi soldiers had been killed, along with eight Shiite militiamen. The U.S. forces failed to break into the building. The mass funeral of the martyrs turned into a demonstration of virulent hatred for the United States—from fiery sermons at the gravesites to rioting by the mobs returning from the cemetery. Meanwhile, a standoff developed that lasted for a few days as the Shiite leaders refused to order the evacuation of their fighters from the contested building despite the amassing of American and Polish troops. Instead, a large mob of Shiite civilians, with women at the front, assembled around coalition forces, blocking their ability to act and move for fear of causing civilian casualties. At the same time, riots and disturbances spread throughout the Shiite heartland. The crisis "ended" suddenly when the Shiite militiamen clandestinely evacuated the building at night and melted into the crowd. When the U.S. forces discovered in the morning that they were laying siege to an abandoned building they withdrew. The al-Mahdi militia returned to the building triumphantly a few hours after the withdrawal of the U.S. and Polish forces. The lesson to the entire population of Iraq was clear—there was no reason to fear the United States and its armed forces.

In mid-October, with the holy month of Ramadan fast approaching, there were strong indications that unprecedented violence might soon erupt. Tehran summoned Osama bin Laden and Ayman al-Zawahiri back to Iran for consultations with the IRGC and Intelligence elites about the next phase of the jihad. Both stayed for over two weeks, using an IRGC guesthouse close to Najmabad, west of Tehran, as their base. From there, they were being driven by the official cars of the IRGC to meetings in Tehran and elsewhere. According to Iranian eyewitnesses, both looked like Pashtun officials—they were dressed in Pakistani-style clothes, had added quite a lot of weight, and had their heads nearly shaven and their beards stylishly trimmed. The IRGC and intelligence officers around them displayed tremendous respect. Bin Laden and Zawahiri were clearly involved with extremely high-level officials in Iran. A new audiotape from Osama bin Laden was broadcast by Al-Jazeera on October 19, and its message must have reflected the issues and policies agreed upon in Tehran. Although phrased as a message to the American people and the troops in Iraq, it was clearly aimed at the Arab world.

Bin Laden first warned the Americans that, having been "enslaved by your richest and the most influential among you, especially the Jews," they had become a murderous gang. He urged all Americans to notice the evil character of their leadership. "The blood of the children of Vietnam, Somalia, Afghanistan, and Iraq is still dripping from their teeth. They have fooled you and deceived you into invading Iraq a second time." The ramifications of an enduring occupation could be horrendous to all Americans, bin Laden cautioned. "Bush has sent your sons into the lion's den, to slaughter and be slaughtered, claiming that this act was in defense of international peace and America's security, thus concealing the facts." Ultimately, however, the invasion of Iraq would turn into a historic turning point—the beginning of the collapse of the United States and the ensuing triumphant upsurge of Islam. Bin Laden stressed the historic symbolism inherent in the fact that this fateful clash was being fought in and for Baghdad: "God sent [President Bush] to Baghdad, the seat of the Caliphate, the homeland of people who prefer death to honey. So they [the Iraqis] turned his profits into losses, his joy into sadness, and now he is merely looking for a way back home. Thanks be to God Almighty who has exposed the lies of George Bush and made his term as president a term of continual catastrophe."

All Americans and their allies would have to suffer the consequences of this policy, bin Laden stressed. He first addressed the actual participants in the war, particularly the allies of the United States. "We reserve the right to retaliate at the appropriate time and place against all countries involved," he stated. But bin Laden's main message was to the American people and defiantly stressed the uncompromising quintessence of the struggle ahead. Bin Laden's words were chilling and his threat precise. "In conclusion, I say to the American people we will continue to fight you and continue to conduct martyrdom operations inside and outside the United States until you depart from your oppressive course and abandon your follies and rein in your fools. You have to know that we are counting our dead, may God bless them, especially in Palestine, who are killed by your allies the Jews. We are going to take revenge for them from your blood, God willing, as we did on the day of New York. Remember what I said to you on that day about our security and your security. Baghdad, the seat of the Caliphate, will not fall to you, God willing, and we will fight you as long as we carry our guns. And if we fall, our sons will take our place."

The impact of bin Laden's message was electrifying and palpable. There was an immediate reaction from the main target audience—a visible awakening of both the sleeper cells and Islamist communities in the Arabian Peninsula and Western Europe. Some of these activities—virulent sermons, public displays of anti-Americanism—were clearly meant to deliver a message and attract the attention of both the local governments and Washington. The Muslim world was gearing up for the great Ramadan offensive.

However, it was Saddam Hussein who seemed to have taken the major step toward reorganizing the resistance forces for the forthcoming escalatory phase of the irregular war against the United States. He formulated an audacious plan designed to not only expedite an encompassing assault but improve his posture as a key leader in the anti-American struggle, even as the preeminent fighting forces consisted of Islamists and independent Baathists. According to senior Arab security officials, Saddam personally chaired a milestone strategy formulation meeting in early October in which the next phase of the war was determined. This meeting took place in the middle of the night in a nondescript house in Ramadi and involved some fifteen officers of the Republican Guard and the Special Republican Guard, as well as second-rank Baath security leaders not sought by the authorities. A representative of Syrian intelligence was also present, taking copious notes. An hour after all participants gathered, Saddam appeared suddenly, wearing a long beard and dressed as a lowly sheikh, escorted by two or three guards. The meeting lasted for a little over an hour.

Saddam was upbeat, insisting that the war was "moving according to the laid plan for the expulsion of the occupier," and that the Americans would soon confront "the actual beginning of the war for liberating Iraq." He assured the attendees that he was still "in command of thousands upon thousands of mujahedin and in command of weapons sufficient to confront them [the Americans] for decades to come." However, Saddam stressed, the time was ripe to decide the war and force an American withdrawal. He would describe "a new tactic to force them to leave and flee as quickly as possible." Saddam then outlined a complex operational plan involving several aspects. First, Iraq should be made ungovernable at the grassroots level by increasing riots and civil disobedience that, in turn, would create an environment of peer pressure on Iraqis working for the occupation authorities to desist. Simultaneously, the resistance would unleash an assassination campaign against Iraqis still cooperating with the occupation authorities, from low-level workers to the highest officials. The entire "patriotic" population should meanwhile actively prepare for a renewed, savage bout of guerrilla warfare extending into the Shiite and Kurdish areas. Saddam gave specific orders to local commanders regarding the use of concealed stockpiles in these areas.

Saddam announced that the resistance would profoundly change in the coming weeks from an irregular fight into an organized offensive that would wrest away control over villages and even towns. Initially, he cautioned, "the resistance heroes must choose districts in some cities to occupy during the night and control and defend them for the longest possible time, even if we lose martyrs." Saddam expected this escalation to deliver "another resounding psychological and military victory paving the way for the stage of decisiveness before the end of the year." Saddam insisted that his was not an abstract plan or a long-term dream. "We must get ready for launching this stage by unleashing the biggest and most massive wave of operations against the occupation forces during the Christmas and New Year's celebration period. Santa Claus will bring nothing but blood and death to all American homes, and there should be no single American left who does not live the catastrophe of Iraq's occupation. Iraq will not be Vietnam this time, but much more dangerous and much worse, and they will see how their festivities of the season will turn into daily funerals for their sons that will not stop anytime soon, Allah willing, until every last one of them leaves and until Bush Jr. pays the price of his conspiracy against the people of Iraq and the Arabs and Muslims," Saddam declared. Toward the end of the meeting, he announced that the participants would soon be informed about the specific "resistance leaders" of the next phase of warfare, and the "resistance zones" in which the war would be waged. The commanders would also get instructions to reorganize their forces into "Jihad cells" that would closely cooperate with "a special cell of intelligence operatives" responsible for guiding the war as well as securing the delivery of weapons and equipment from the more than of 2,500 clandestine depots spread all over Iraq.

Indeed, in mid-October, shortly after the Ramadi meeting, Saddam issued a decree activating emergency command elements for the sustenance of the postoccupation resistance. To emphasize his unique role, he actually signed the Presidential Decree, copies of which were then distributed all over Iraq, nominating himself as leader of the "Interim Command for Armed Activities against U.S. and Zionist Forces." Under the command he placed six senior officers, each of whom was both the commander-governor of a district and the coordinator of all "armed activities" executed by all anti-American forces. With the decree, Iraq was divided into six districts or theaters. Saddam's decree identified the six new districts and their commanders.

General Namiq Muhammad, the former deputy chief of security of the Special Republican Guard and a close friend of Saddam's late son Qusay, assumed control of the Ninveh District, which covered northern Iraq, including the crucial oil cities of Kirkuk and Mosul. General Ibrahim Abd-al-Sattar al-Tikriti took control of the Saladin District, which encompassed the Sunni Triangle, including Tikrit. Sattar, the former chief of staff of the Special Republican Guard, was regarded as one of Saddam's closest and most loyal aides.

Zuhair Rahim al-Tikriti, a central figure in Saddam's closest circle about whom little is known, commanded the Ramadi District, including the cities of Ramadi and Fallujah. Rumors held that Rahim was instrumental in Iraq's terrorism sponsorship, and, if true, it follows that Saddam would choose Rahim to administer the district boasting the most active guerrilla front and massive terrorist activity, seeing close cooperation between Baathist, Islamists, and other terrorist cells. Colonel Nufal Saad Muhammad al-Tikriti, once the commander of Saddam's Praetorian Guard, drew the Baghdad District, which included Greater Baghdad, the Habaniya air base, Baghdad International Airport, and the Salman Pak compound.

Muhammad Ali Abd-al-Jalil took Najaf, Qarbalah, and Babil, or the Babylon District. The area covered the bulk of the Shiite heartland, and Jalil was one of the few Shiites who had risen to the very top of the Baathist inner circle and accordingly was both respected and feared by the Shiite street. Finally, Daghir Muhammad Fadhil was given Basra, Qadissiyah, and the Wasit District, which covered the bulk of the British-held area, including the cities of Basra, Nasiriyah, al-Amra, and al-Kut. Fadhil was a strange choice for the position because he was the deputy director of the Iraqi military industries and as such in charge of Iraq's chemical and biological weapons development program, but his nomination to the post was perceived as an assurance to Saddam's other WMD officials that they had not been forgotten or abandoned.

The decree also included specific instructions to lower-level Baath officials of the national underground. They were ordered to widely advertise their existence in the context of the new governorships of Iraq. Local Iraqis were encouraged to approach these officials with any personal requests or needs, just as was the case during Saddam's reign. The officials were assured they would be provided with ample funds and other means to properly address the needs of the people. (By mid-November, the contrast between the Baathists' ability to provide for the population and America's failure to restore basic services coupled with continued intrusive sweeps was overwhelming.) Given the deepening alienation of the Iraqi civilian population and the building grassroots hostility toward the occupation forces, Saddam's decree came at a most opportune time and appealed directly to the genuine moods and aspirations of the public at large. The Baath officials were also ordered to collect intelligence on Iraqis cooperating with the occupation authorities, as well as to consolidate a support system to expedite the work of expert hit teams that would soon arrive to address the issue. (Indeed, in November the attacks on Iraqis cooperating with the United States and the United Kingdom would reach epidemic proportions, drastically degrading America's ability to restore normalization.)

A report about Saddam's decree was issued by the "Interim Regional Leadership of the Baath Arab Socialist Party of Iraq" and circulated in mid-October. The report announced the establishment of an "interim leadership to run armed operations against the American and Zionist forces." The report identified the six governors as being responsible for "escalating the resistance." Significantly, this report was shared with the Islamists' high command both in Iraq and overseas. The report arrived with an explanatory note stressing that the Islamists were invited to cooperate with, participate in, and benefit from the resources and capabilities of the Baathist forces loyal to Saddam without any preconditions. High-level Baathist sources also informed their Islamist counterparts that Hussein put Izzat Ibrahim al-Durri, the former vice chairman of the Revolutionary Command Council, in charge of cooperation and coordination between the Baathists and the various Islamist organizations. This nomination alone reflected just how important cooperation with the Islamists was for Saddam.

A few days later, another document was circulated among both Baathist and Islamist commanders, notifying them about the establishment of a "Special Forces unit" dedicated to the elimination of certain "agents" cooperating with the occupation authorities. The document ordered members of the Special Forces to "eliminate" the people on the attached list of names and requested that all units and agencies throughout Iraq immediately give information about the whereabouts of "these agents" to "station B3," instructing the Special Forces teams to "kill these agents whenever the opportunity arises without getting back to station M9."

In mid-October, Syria's role in anti-American warfare grew increasingly pronounced. Several senior American officials were convinced that Syria had no other option, because any tangible U.S. victory in Iraq would amount to the ideological defeat of Baathism, and not just Saddam's regime. A most significant manifestation of the Syrian determination to dominate the resistance in Iraq was the launching of a comprehensive ideological work aimed at transforming the remnants of the Iraqi Baath Party into a pro-Syrian party. A combination of veteran Iraqi exiles in Damascus and ambitious young Iraqi militants was drawn into the new Baath, giving Damascus yet another venue through which to influence the anti-American war. Arab officials were fully aware of the regional significance of Bashar's raising the ante, and a scathing attack on the new Syrian policy was published in the Kuwaiti newspaper *Al-Siyassa* in November. In a two-part article, the well-connected Ahmad al-Jarallah wrote, "Syrian President Dr. Bashar Al-Assad signaled a new era in the Syrian-led Iraqi struggle to drown the Americans in the Tigris and Euphrates, just as [Syria] threatened in the past to throw the Jews into the sea." Toward this end, Syria has committed to "inventing imaginary puppets [to be] used by Syria to defy the United States—the most recent puppet being the 'Iraqi opposition.'" By now, it was commonly accepted by Arab officials that Damascus had created—and was now sponsoring and controlling—major segments of the Iraqi opposition as an instrument of, or proxy for, fighting the U.S. in Iraq without being directly implicated.

With stronger strategic guarantees from Iran and emboldened by the growing Arab hostility to the United States, Bashar al-Assad felt increasingly confident in his ability to further expand Syrian sponsorship of the Iraqi resistance and facilitate its escalation. In the process, Syrian senior officials and fighters would assume a higher profile in the actual fighting inside Iraq. The intensified Syrian effort was personally in the hands of Maher al-Assad, Bashar's brother and the head of the Republican and Presidential Guards in Syria, who had close ties to Saddam's late sons, Uday and Qusay. Maher expanded the headquarters in Abu Kamel and invited several Iraqi senior officers and security officials to join his staff, thus creating a Syrian-controlled joint headquarters. One of the early manifestations of the tighter cooperation was the early November appearance in eastern Syria of VIP convoys comprising some fifteen vehicles and mixed security details made up of Syrian Presidential Guards' Special Forces and Iraqi Special Guards' Special Forces. These convoys were used by Iraqi and Syrian senior officers in their inspections of forward bases. Lebanese sources insist that Saddam Hussein used one of these convoys during a rare visit to Syria for consultations with Syrian and Iraqi senior officials.

In these high-level contacts, the former Iraqi senior officials grudgingly acknowledged that Saddam was not likely to return to power in Baghdad anytime soon. Therefore, Damascus decided to reduce the profile of its strategic cooperation with Saddam's Baghdad—particularly on issues pertaining to WMD. Toward this end, the Iraqi stockpiles then stored near Kamishli were now moved to permanent storage sites in central Syria and northeastern Lebanon. The moving and concealment of the Iraqi WMD were conducted under the command of General Zou al-Himma al-Shaleesh, a veteran of Syrian-Iraqi strategic cooperation and smuggling. Assaf Shawqat, Bashar's brother-in-law and deputy chief of Syrian military intelligence, personally supervised the undertaking. The first specific account of this action to transfer and hide of the Iraqi WMD was provided by Syrian opposition journalist Nizar Nayyouf, on the basis of detailed maps and notes he had received from "a Syrian senior officer who'd become a dissident." Several Lebanese, Syrian, and other Arab security and/or intelligence sources subsequently confirmed Nayyouf's reports, and provided additional details about the whereabouts of Iraq's WMD.

First to be moved were the large tanks containing chemical materials. They were put on flatbed trucks and moved to areas of northeastern Lebanon under Syrian military control where they were buried in deep pits near Hermel and in the northern Bekaa. The Iraqi operational weapons and other sensitive military components were transferred to three sites associated with comparable Syrian military activities. Most weapons and military equipment were moved in large wooden crates and barrels on flatbed trucks and by rail car; the most sensitive elements were transferred in ambulances. The Iraqi weapons and systems were concealed in three places at the heart of the Syrian military-industrial complex, where they could be used to improve Syria's own weapons and missile production.

Iraqi chemical warheads, ballistic missiles, and missile components (mainly engines and guidance kits) were concealed in North Korean–built tunnels in al-Baida, about 2 kilometers from Misyaf near Hama, the site of

Syria's main SCUD and warheads factories. The tunnel complex is controlled by Bureau 489 of the Cipher and Document Security Division of Syrian intelligence—the agency responsible for the security of Syria's most sensitive facilities. Vital parts of Iraq's WMD munitions were stored in a Syrian Air Force munitions factory near the village of Tal Sinan, between the towns of Hama and Salamiyyah. This factory produces aerial munitions and tanks for the Syrian Air Force.

Other unspecified sensitive equipment and systems were stored in tunnels near the village of Shinsar, some 40 kilometers south of Homs, 2 kilometers to the east of the Homs-Damascus highway, and not far from the Syrian-Lebanese border. These very deep tunnels are located in a large military complex that belongs to the 661st Battalion of the Syrian Air Force. Formally designated an aerial reconnaissance battalion, the 661st is responsible for Syria's electronic intelligence as well as the country's strategic and satellite communications. Hence, it is possible to assume that Iraqi electronic and intelligence systems are stored in Shinsar.

The Syrian contribution to the actual fighting in Iraq, meanwhile, ranged from dispatching members of the Syrian security forces and elite forces to fight with Baathist nationalist forces, to the recruitment and training of Syrian Islamists for suicide bombings and other terrorist strikes by al-Qaeda–affiliated forces. The most important upgrade as a consequence of Syrian involvement in the fighting in Iraq was the opening of a training base for mujahedin in the Jidayadit Shibani military base near Damascus, where the mujahedin participated in a forty-five-day-long training in advanced guerrilla warfare tactics. The graduates were flown by military helicopters to Kamishli and from there were smuggled into Iraq by Syrian intelligence. According to Jarallah, U.S. forces had already captured would-be "suicide bombers possessing Syrian identity cards with serial numbers of the [Syrian] secret service" who were about to strike in Iraq.

The growing forces were equipped through an expanded flow of improved weapons and other specialized systems; these supply lines were supervised by Firas Tlass. Damascus also permitted the Iraqis to establish a clandestine financial system in Syria for paying mercenaries recruited by both the Baathists and Islamists to provide unique skills and capabilities they could not get from the flow of volunteers or available Iraqis. Many mercenaries also received Syrian identification documents before crossing into Iraq in order to further protect them in case they were captured. All these activities were conducted under the close supervision of security of-

ficers under the command of Haitham al-Manaa, all of whom were answering directly to Maher al-Assad.

For the Islamists, the growing involvement of Damascus in the war in
Iraq, and particularly the Syrian facilitation of jihad, constituted the beginning of a strategic process aimed at throwing the entire region into
chaos. For the Islamists, the Iraqi jihad of fall 2003 constituted the historic
turning point in the fateful struggle between Islam and the West for control of the entire Middle East. In early November, well-informed Islamist
sources in Beirut explained that "the coming phase would witness an upsurge in resistance operations in Iraq to face the U.S.-Israeli plan to control the region and in retaliation for U.S. attempts to crack down on the
resistance forces." This escalation would be facilitated primarily through
Syria, as well as Iran, not only to buttress the escalation inside Iraq, but
also to compel the United States into a calamitous regional conflict. "U.S.
pressure on Syria and Iran to close their borders and crack down on the
resistance forces would not yield any result. Rather, a U.S. or a new Israeli
aggression on Syria would intensify the resistance operations and aggra-
vate hatred against the United States in Iraq and elsewhere. The influential
Islamic forces would not stand still in the event U.S. pressure on Syria de-
velops into a large-scale military action, and this would inflame the entire
region against the United States and Israel," the Islamist sources asserted.
The senior leaders in Damascus were cognizant of these grand designs and
actively supported them. Therefore, the Islamist sources concluded, "the
general situation in the region is not in favor of the United States, which is
sinking further into the Iraqi quagmire and sustaining more casualties
every day."

18

BEYOND THE RAMADAN OFFENSIVE

By late October, the anticipated guerrilla offensive was fast evolving, and it was the Islamists who immediately went into action in Iraq. Their first operations, attempted on October 23, were haphazard. First, a car bomb was discovered in Baghdad by Iraqi police, and its Syrian driver was arrested. He confessed that he was a recently trained bomb-maker determined to become a martyr bomber. Then American forces discovered another car in Baghdad's al-Doura district and arrested its Iraqi would-be bomber. The driver was in his early twenties, had been paid handsomely to deliver the car, and did not know he was to be martyred. Iraqi police officials stressed that the United States had found the second car bomb on the basis of a specific intelligence warning they had provided. In contrast, the discovery of the first car bomb was pure luck.

A few days later, however, the Islamists delivered a series of devastating strikes at the heart of Baghdad. The targets selected were a mixture of Islamist and Baathist nationalist objectives—a reflection of the growing strategic cooperation between the two main factions in the Iraqi resistance. Moreover, the operations themselves required comprehensive intelligence and a large support system, prerequisites neither the Islamist nor the Baathist networks were capable of mustering on their own.

On October 25, the insurgents downed an American UH-60 Black Hawk helicopter near Tikrit with an RPG round. Five soldiers were injured as the helicopter was consumed by flames. It was the first successful downing of a helicopter after numerous attempts in which helicopters had either been slightly damaged or survived near misses.

The first strategic strike, launched on the morning of October 26, targeted the al-Rashid Hotel in Baghdad precisely when Paul Wolfowitz, the deputy defense secretary most associated with the assault on Iraq, was preparing for his morning meetings. About ten rockets fired from a safe distance hit the floors occupied by the American VIPs. An American colonel was killed and a score of civilian and military officials were wounded in the attack. The attack was a sophisticated undertaking based on excellent intelligence and expert preparations. The rocket launchers were concealed in a large, portable, two-wheeled, blue-painted electricity generator, characteristic of the local electrical system. A nondescript truck towed the generator to the edge of a park some 500 yards from the hotel and parked it exactly in place. The rockets were activated by either remote control or a timer shortly afterward. Both al-Qaeda–affiliated Islamist sources and the military wing of the Islamic National Resistance claimed that the al-Rashid was hit by the indigenously developed "Ramadan-1" missiles, which were modified versions of rockets that had originated in France and the Soviet Union.

At first, officials put on a brave face, portraying the attack as a bump on America's road toward success. "With an audacious rocket attack Sunday [October 26] on the al-Rashid Hotel in Baghdad, Iraqi resistance fighters showed again how a strike against a high-profile target can overshadow weeks of slow progress and create the impression that the Bush administration lacks a plan for securing the country," military commanders and defense analysts in Baghdad told Vernon Loeb of the *Washington Post*. Actions, however, spoke volumes. Within hours of the rocket attack, the Coalition Provisional Authority withdrew its offices and headquarters from the eighteen-story al-Rashid Hotel to the heart of the "Green Zone" in Baghdad and military-held sites outside the city, such as the Salman Pak compound. Both actively and symbolically, the occupation authorities were increasing their isolation from Iraqi society, which the United States had just liberated and with whose elite it was now working closely to build a new Iraqi state.

The next morning, October 27, saw the nearly simultaneous launching of five martyr-driven car bombs—four of which succeeded in their mission. First, an ambulance full of explosives rammed a barrier and blew up just outside the Red Cross headquarters in Baghdad. At least ten Iraqis were killed and scores were wounded. Over the next hour, three other car bombs were detonated in front of Iraqi government offices and police stations; a fourth bombing team was, luckily, unable to complete its mission, as its Land Cruiser crashed into the cement barrier of the police compound but failed to explode. Once again, the driver had a Syrian passport. Altogether, some forty people were killed and over 230 wounded, most of them

Iraqis, in the Ramadan bombing offensive. These lethal attacks singled out Iraqis working for the United States, particularly with the police, and other international organizations. The terrorists achieved their objective, as the International Red Cross staff was evacuated from Baghdad, following the UN and other international organizations that had withdrawn their staffs after earlier bombings. Moreover, the occupation authorities had again failed to shield their Iraqi allies—the people who would eventually take over responsibility for the country.

Meanwhile, irregular warfare waged against U.S. forces and the Iraqis cooperating with them became even more vicious. On the afternoon of October 28, an M-1A1 tank was destroyed by a roadside bomb near Balad, some 40 miles north of Baghdad, killing two crew members and wounding a third. The attack took place in an area dominated by Baathist guerrilla forces, but the highly specialized antitank bomb had been constructed by the expert Chechen terrorists helping the Islamist networks. Similar bombs had been used successfully by Islamist terrorists against the Russian tanks in Chechnya and, following the arrival of Chechen experts in Gaza, against Israeli Merkaya tanks as well. Thus, this milestone attack reflected a new level of operational cooperation between the Baathists and the Islamists. Soon afterward, Faris Abdul Razzaq al-Assam, one of Baghdad's three deputy mayors and a close ally of the United States, was assassinated in the middle of Baghdad. Two hit men walked into an outdoor café where he was playing dominoes, shot him in the head at point-blank range, and then slipped into the night without anyone intervening. Later that night, an unusually intense mortar barrage hit Baghdad. The next morning, October 29, the resistance blew up a freight train carrying supplies for the U.S. military 4 miles west of Fallujah. The train was stopped by powerful bombs concealed under the tracks and activated by remote control from an observation post overlooking them. Four containers caught fire from the explosion, and local mobs shouting anti-American slogans looted the rest of the train with impunity. Later that day, a bomb exploded in Baghdad's Old City in a row of shops frequented by Iraqis working for the government, killing two and wounding a score. Another roadside bomb exploded north of Baghdad near a military police convoy, wounding two soldiers.

Active resistance also spread to areas considered relatively pacified and friendly to the United States. Most notable was the sudden eruption of violence in Mosul. Starting on Thursday, October 30, U.S. military patrols throughout the city were subjected to a series of harassing attacks, including a roadside bomb. Iraqi police stations and the city hall were also attacked by gunfire during the day. Overnight, the nearby American base was subjected to a mortar attack. The attacks continued throughout the next day, and during the noon prayers imams throughout Mosul read a fatwa from the city's Council of Imams forbidding any support for the United States. "Supporting them [the Americans] is apostasy [and] a betrayal of faith," the fatwa decreed. In Fallujah, a large bomb exploded in the office of the U.S.-installed mayor, causing heavy damage but no casualties. In the fiercely nationalist Abu-Ghraib western district of Baghdad, worshippers coming out of Friday prayers clashed with U.S. forces. When over a thousand people gathered near the mosque and began shouting pro-Saddam slogans, heavy American units—including Abrams tanks and Bradley combat vehicles escorted by helicopter gunships—closed in on the rioters. One of the American patrols was ambushed close to the riot site. A fierce firefight ensued, with American combat vehicles directing automatic fire indiscriminately into the crowd long after the attackers had fled, causing dozens of civilian casualties. Iraqi guerrillas retaliated by launching a barrage of mortar shells at nearby U.S. bases, inflicting damage but no casualties. Sporadic attacks on American units in Abu-Ghraib continued into the next day, as they did in Mosul, where a roadside bomb killed at least two soldiers. Additionally, the main oil pipeline was blown up and engulfed in flames in several spots some 10 miles north of Tikrit. It was a befitting reaction to the call for a "Day of Resistance" issued by the Baath Party.

If the Ramadan offensive caught the imagination of all Iraqis—and the entire Arab world—with its audacity and emphatic introduction of a new phase of the resistance, the fighting throughout the month of November constituted a distinctly new phase in the war, both in the intensity and sophistication of the strikes and in the hatred acutely felt by the Iraqis for American soldiers. "What is striking to a newcomer to Baghdad is the depth of hostility to the Americans, not just among the tiny minority who attack U.S. troops, but also among the millions of ordinary Iraqis who do not. It is astonishing how, in the space of six months, the image of the U.S. military has changed from that of welcome liberator to hated occupier," noted Martin Fletcher of the London *Times*. Ultimately, November would become the most lethal month in the guerrilla war of 2003.

The gravity of the situation did not escape the American authorities in Baghdad. On November 10, the CIA's Baghdad station chief sent a top secret report to the uppermost echelons of the Bush administration warning about the dire situation in Iraq. An intelligence source in Washington told Julian Borger of the *Guardian* that the report was a "bleak assessment that the resistance is broad, strong and getting stronger," despite all the efforts of the U.S. authorities. As reported by Douglas Jehl of the *New York Times*, the CIA had concluded that "the situation in Iraq is approaching a crucial turning point, with ordinary Iraqis losing faith in American-led occupation forces and in the United States–appointed Iraqi Governing Council." Jehl wrote that the CIA was increasingly apprehensive about "the danger that Iraqi Shiite Muslims, who represent a majority of the country's population, could soon join minority Sunni Muslims in carrying out armed attacks against American forces," and that there were "major obstacles to efforts by the United States and American-led Iraqi forces to halt a small but steady infiltration of foreign fighters from Syria and Iran." Julian Borger and Rory McCarthy of the *Guardian* added that the CIA report estimated the number of Iraqi insurgents to be 50,000 and growing. "There are thousands in the resistance—not just a core of Baathists. They are in the thousands, and growing every day. Not all those people are actually firing, but providing support, shelter and all that," Borger's intelligence source explained. The CIA report, Borger's source concluded, "Says we are going to lose the situation [in Iraq] unless there is a rapid and dramatic change of course."

Following the insurgency's successful downing of the Black Hawk on October 25, one of the most significant campaigns launched in November was the concentrated effort to shoot down helicopters and other transport aircraft. In this campaign, the insurgents used a variety of weapons ranging from SA-7 and SA-18 SFSAMs to modified RPG-7 rockets and heavy machine guns. The first such attack after October 25 took place a week later, on November 2. Near Hasi, about 65 kilometers southwest of Baghdad, insurgents fired two SA-7s at two CH-47 Chinooks on their way from Fallujah to Baghdad. One of the missiles struck an engine, bringing down the helicopter, killing sixteen and injuring twenty. Then, on November 7, terrorists fired modified RPG-7 rockets at UH-60 Black Hawks near Tikrit. One helicopter was hit and crashed, killing all six on board. On November 15, two UH-60 Black Hawks crashed near Mosul in northern Iraq after one helicopter was hit by an RPG rocket and small-arms fire and, maneuvering violently, collided with the other Black Hawk, bringing both down. Seventeen soldiers were killed and five wounded in the attack. The most tangible result of this antihelicopter campaign was that the U.S. Army was forced to drastically change its helicopters' flight paths and tactics in order to increase safety at the expense of combat effectiveness.

November also saw the geographic spread of major strikes—an expansion of the theater—which compounded the intensity of bombings and mortar shelling in the greater Baghdad area as well as persistent sabotage of the oil infrastructure. Violent attacks, including sporadic car bombings, aimed at Iraqis working for or cooperating with the occupation authorities and foreign companies, became more frequent; in early November both the deputy president of the Appeals Court in Mosul and a judge in Najaf were assassinated. These developments had a direct bearing on the overall security posture in Iraq, and as a result, American commanders reduced the frequency of patrols, and the Iraqi policemen who were supposed to take the Americans' place were now openly threatened and abused by word and weapon by a virulently hostile civilian population. Both American and Iraqi officials acknowledged that "the night belongs to the guerrillas."

By the middle of the month, the aggregate impact of the campaign of assassination and intimidation against Iraqis working for and with the United States had taken its toll. Population segments previously considered pacified—most notably the Kurdish and Turkman populations—began cooperating with the resistance. Similarly, the Bedouin wandering zones in western Iraq were now increasingly denied to U.S. forces, challenging again the viability of American arrangements and understandings with the main tribes. In the Shiite heartland, the widespread grassroots hostility was clearly demonstrated in attacks against not only the United States but also key NATO allies. On November 12, a truck bomb exploded in the Italian military headquarters in Nasiriyah, killing at least thirty-one people, including eighteen Italian carabinieri and security personnel. This was a dramatic escalation considering the Italians' proven ability to sustain neutrality in previous peacekeeping deployments in Beirut in the early 1980s and Somalia in the early 1990s.

The American military responded to the escalation in guerrilla warfare by modifying and expanding already initiated operations. The United States launched several major sweeps involving tanks and APCs and employing warlike tactics. American units now engaged their objectives from a greater distance, increasing the use of heavy firepower. The United States even resumed bombing raids by tactical aircraft such as F-15s and F-16s, destroying both inhabited and empty buildings at the heart of Baghdad and throughout the Iraqi countryside. In retrospect, the new tactics proved futile, if not counterproductive, because these raids failed to contain the insurgency while inflicting significant collateral damage, yet again sending a growing number of irate Iraqis into the fold of the anti-American forces. At the same time, U.S. casualties caused by the growing numbers of ambushes, roadside bombs, and shelling became, quite simply, routine.

Meanwhile, between mid-October and the first weeks of November, Saddam, hoping to boost his profile, began taking major risks. He traveled in a white Peugeot car escorted by only a couple of guards. He now arrived unannounced in villages throughout the Sunni heartland for meetings with the local sheikhs and other notables. Eyewitnesses stressed that Saddam's eyes were tired and sad. He encouraged the people to join the anti-American jihad under any flag. He was visibly relieved and happy when local sheikhs reiterated their devotion to him as their leader and their determination to sacrifice "their blood and sons" in the jihad. Saddam was willing to talk about the war, insisting that Baghdad had fallen because of betrayal by some of his closest confidants. He urged all Iraqis to intensify their "revenge strikes" against the Americans and hinted at a forthcoming escalation, instructing the sheikhs to organize their people "for the big battle" ahead. In these visits, Saddam ridiculed questions about his own personal security or concerns about capture by the United States. He stressed that, just like his two sons, he was determined to become a martyr in the jihad. Several sheikhs committed to wholeheartedly supporting Saddam and the anti-American jihad.

A tribal leader and resistance activist going by the name of Abu-Muhammad who met Saddam at that time described the war, and Saddam's role, to Rouba Kabbara of France's AFP news service. "Saddam Hussein is in good health and living in the west of Iraq," he said. "The Iraqi president is commanding the military operations against the American forces." However, the prevailing conditions in Iraq made it impossible for Saddam to have tight control over the war. "The operations are not centralized," Abu-Muhammad explained. "Saddam Hussein gives instructions and those who must carry them out find the means to do so." For the same reasons, the war was still being waged mainly with "no sophisticated weapons." Abu-Muhammad told Kabbara that Saddam had recently given orders to "fight against those who can bring comfort to the occupation," including Iraqis working for the occupation authorities for economic reasons only. As much as the Iraqi Baathist leadership sympathized with the plight of the impoverished, according to Abu-Muhammad, striking at the Americans and their local supporters "is a question of priority and there is no price on the liberation of the country."

In early November, Saddam was becoming audacious to the point of recklessness. On the evening of November 8, for example, he presided over a meeting of dozens of Baath security activists in Ramadi. Earlier that day, General Abizaid had visited Ramadi for a meeting with tribal leaders in which he pressed them to cooperate with the authorities. Nevertheless, Saddam decided to keep his appointment even though U.S. forces had established a tight security cordon around the entire area. Although Saddam had arrived in Ramadi a couple of days earlier and was moving between safe houses, he decided to remain in town once the strict security measures associated with Abizaid's visit were implemented. By now, however, Saddam's mood had begun to change. According to Iraqi sheikhs who met him, he was increasingly sullen and fatalistic. According to some, he became convinced that he was about to be killed or captured. Outwardly, however, he showed a brave face, urging his audiences to prepare for the forthcoming escalation in the fighting with the United States.

But Saddam's actions spoke volumes. He sent his beloved son Ali, who had stayed with him most of the time since the fall of Baghdad, to join his mother, Samira Shahbandar, then already in a shelter in Beirut. In Damascus both she and Ali received genuine Lebanese documents with false identities. Furthermore, Saddam maintained telephone contact with Samira and Ali despite the danger of intercepts, displaying both affection and a kind of fatalism he had never exercised before. Indeed, American and Israeli intelligence traced Saddam's calls to a transfer relay in the remote desert spot of Wadi al-Myrah, just inside Syria and very close to the border with Iraq. Saddam also sent letters to his family in Beirut. Talking in early December to Marie Colvin of the London *Sunday Times,* Samira anticipated Saddam's fall. Still, she insisted he would go down fighting rather than allow himself to be captured by the Americans. "If I know my husband, he will not be captured," she stressed.

Saddam's next audio message was delivered on November 16 and immediately broadcast by Al-Arabiyah TV. It was a defiant message loaded with Islamic themes and phrasing. He praised the Iraqi nation for withstanding the "the U.S.-Zionist-British aggression" and, through its resistance and defiance, demonstrating that "the evil ones will not be able to occupy and colonize Iraq." Saddam expected the war in Iraq to serve as a catalyst for a greater awakening throughout the Arab world. He explained that "Iraq is part of its [Arab] Nation, and when the circumstances are ripe, it plays a vanguard role or a vivid part of the vanguards of this Nation." He urged the United States to "resort to politics in order to correct the mistake, or even the heinous great crime" and restore Iraq's independence. Significantly, Saddam insisted on his own return to power in these negotiations. He demanded that "the sincere sons of Iraq should return by the free will of the people to manage the affairs of the country anew," and then clarified who these "sons" were. "The people have tested them [the "sons"] for tens of years, and the people know them. . . . The people know that they are loyal and dedicated even if they commit mistakes. All of this should happen when the soldiers of aggression and occupation are outside Iraq and when any illegitimate foreign presence is no longer there in Iraq, as was the situation in Iraq before." Saddam contrasted the devotion of his leadership with the treachery of the U.S.-appointed Governing Council. "Those who are brought by the armies of the foreigner and are decided by an unfree Iraqi will are like the foreigner. Therefore, resisting them and the foreigner, and even before the foreigner's armies, is a religious, national, and human duty."

By that point, however, Saddam and his loyalists were increasingly losing their grip over the anti-American resistance forces. This was the result of the continued transformation of the Sunni population at the grassroots level. Most important were the changes in the Baathist forces—particularly the distinctly pro-Saddam elements. Earlier in the fall, in the aftermath of Saddam's return to the Sunni heartland, a Baathist insurgency command was formed for these forces. In practice, this command oversaw, to varying degrees, only some one thousand insurgents in and around Baghdad and the Sunni Triangle, divided into twelve to fifteen groups, which ranged from as few as ten to as many as a hundred fighters. These cells followed Saddam's general directives, but operational decisions were left to the specific cells throughout the Sunni Triangle. In early November, these forces were visibly collapsing in the absence of guidance and inspiration from above. There was a concurrent shift of the operational center of the "Sunni Triangle" northward into the approaches of the Kurdish zones and the northeastern Shiite enclaves, and new, ostensibly pro-Saddam forces emerged in the process—specifically, two Saddam's Fedayeen suicide brigades under the command of Izzat Ibrahim al-Durri's thirty-eight-year-old son, Muhammad al-Durri. Each brigade was three to four hundred fighters strong, all of whom were highly trained veterans of the fedayeen and other Special Forces, and included specially trained teams for urban warfare, suicide bombings, and the clandestine use of WMD (though there's no clear evidence that they possessed any at the time). One brigade deployed to the new Sunni Triangle, and the second to the greater Mosul area.

Although these brigades emerged in the context of an underground ideological campaign stressing the dominance of Saddam's leadership, activities in the field contradicted these claims. During the fighting of late November in northern Iraq, the key Sunni detachments, under the direct command of Muhammad al-Durri, sought and made alliances with Kurdish and Shiite forces to expand the war in order to quickly expel occupation forces and consolidate ethnic ministates. There was apprehension among the younger Baathist elite—the group ostensibly closest to Saddam Hussein—that the United States would soon consolidate Shiite and Kurdish oil-rich areas, and would enable them to crush the Sunnis arrayed between them. Rather than follow the directives—both political and military—of the veteran elite loyal to Saddam and the Sunni insurgency command, the younger commanders opted to strike localized deals with the regionally dominant forces.

These dynamics were now reverberating to the very top of the Baathist elite still operating inside Iraq. To stay relevant, they had to adapt to the dominant trends of the Sunni population, and a new fracture emerged within the Baathist forces most connected with key members of Saddam's erstwhile loyal elite. These senior leaders consolidated existing force groupings into distinct "commands" with strong tribal characteristics as well as specific ideological taints. They not only took over key force formations and stockpiles, but overtly distanced themselves from Saddam Hussein's leadership in both practical and ideological terms. The Sunni population reacted to this ideological and operational transformation with a rejuvenated flocking of volunteers, both youngsters and veterans of the various intelligence and security services, into these forces. Most significant was the markedly expanded recruitment of fighters and intelligence agents from the modernized and educated urban population that had so far eluded the advances of both the Islamists and Saddam's Baathists. Essentially, the urban population now joining the resistance came from the same pool the U.S. considered its primary source of recruits for the American-controlled Iraqi police and security services, as well as the workforce for the oil industry and national infrastructure.

Ideologically and politically, most significant was the effort to rejuvenate the unified Baathist insurgency command in the "Sunni Triangle," which by mid-November was near collapse. At the core of this force was Saddam's own Tikriti clan. In the second half of November, not only did some of the key members of the clan dare to challenge Saddam's leadership, but the vast majority of the elite insurgents, all of them former members of the regime's key units, joined the new leadership. The shift was launched by two of Saddam's cousins, Hani Abdul-Latif al-Tilfah al-Tikriti, a former colonel in the Secret Services Organization, and his younger brother Rafi, also a former senior intelligence official. They were soon joined by Saddam's half brother Sabaawi Ibrahim al-Tikriti, who was then able to bring down the last vestiges of unwavering loyalty to Saddam Hussein among the leaders of the Tikriti clan. He achieved this by insisting in numerous meetings with sheikhs, elders, and other notables that in light of the emerging ethnic, religious, and political trends in Iraq—particularly the rise of the Islamists—remaining unswervingly loyal to Saddam would only harm the interests of their clan, and therefore it was imperative to adopt an independent policy designed exclusively to further the interests of the Tikritis. Another important member of this group was Lt. Gen. Tahir Dalil Harboush, a Soviet-trained intelligence expert, who brought with him control over and access to vast stockpiles of weapons, explosives, and cash. Of the thousand or so fighters under the Baathist centralized command, several hundred insurgents now followed the al-Tilfah brothers and their allies.

The ascent of Muhammad al-Durri was challenged by a new "Revolutionary Command Council" that declared its loyalty to his father, Izzat Ibrahim al-Durri. In reality, this new command had nothing to do with either Durri. It was established by Maj. Gen. Seyfallah Hassan Taha al-Rawi, the former chief of staff of the Presidential Guard; since the Rawi clan had repeated clashes with the Tikriti clan, Rawi relied on the Durri name and prestige in order to avoid needless alienation of the tribes and clans formally loyal to the Tikritis. Taha launched his command by recruiting former members of the Baath Party's secret military organization and Saddam's Fedayeen in the western parts of the northern "Sunni Triangle." Taha was soon joined by two former colleagues and prominent members of the Saadoun clan—the cousins Muhammad Zamam Abdul-Razzaq al-Saadoun and Abdul-Baqi Abdelkarim Abdallah al-Saadoun—who facilitated the flow of volunteers from the tribes in western Iraq and, through them, access to the Syrian border and Syrian military assistance. Another hallmark of this group was its close cooperation with the Islamist forces.

In the Baghdad area, Muhsin Khudhair al-Khafji, a former Baath Party apparatchik within Iraqi intelligence, used his international contacts to attempt to mobilize the Baathist cadres in western and northern Baghdad under the banner of the True Baath. Al-Khafji claimed to be "the president of the Iraqi branch of the Pan-Arab Socialist Baath Party," and pointed to his relations with Baath cells in Algeria, Yemen, Morocco, the United Arab Emirates, Jordan, Lebanon, Egypt, and various Palestinian terrorist organizations—all of which had been sponsored and funded by Iraqi intelligence until the collapse of Saddam's regime—as proof of his legitimacy. Al-Khafji also attempted to reach out to the Shiite population, relying on the good services of Khamis Sarhan al-Muhammad, the former head of the Baath Party in Qarbalah and a former member of the Iraqi intelligence service. Beyond his ideological audacity, al-Khafji controlled money and an urban underground made up of former intelligence officers. To enhance the popularity and legitimacy of his "True Baath," he put these resources at the disposal of the locally active resistance forces, Baathist or otherwise. This cooperation and sponsorship were instrumental in the surge of violence throughout the Baghdad area on November 21–22, notable for the close cooperation between nationalist and Islamist groups evident in the operation.

On November 21, the insurgents launched barrages of rockets against key buildings at the heart of Baghdad. The rocket launchers were concealed in commonly used donkey carts equipped with sophisticated timers and left parked in preselected areas. Most intense were the barrages aimed at the Palestine and Sheraton Hotels in the heavily guarded "Green Zone," which are used by foreign officials, industrialists, and journalists, and the barrage aimed at the Oil Ministry in central Baghdad. Two more rocket carts were found near the Italian embassy and defused in time. The rocket barrages caused few injuries and moderate damage. Unfortunately, the reaction of the security authorities and emergency services in Baghdad was complicated by a series of well-placed ambushes employing small arms and RPGs that necessitated the arrival of large military forces to clear the streets. Then, on November 22, the insurgents launched two martyrdom car bomb attacks, carried out by Islamists, on police stations north of Baghdad in which at least eighteen people, most of them Iraqi policemen, were killed and scores were wounded. The bombings of the police stations in the towns of Khan Bani Saad and Baquba were timed to coincide with the presence of large numbers of policemen; this kind of inside information came from guerrilla sympathizers in the ranks of the police, most of whom are Baathists.

Finally, a mixed group of Islamists and nationalists launched either an SA-7 or an SA-18 at a DHL Airbus that just had taken off from Baghdad airport. (In their first attempt to bring down a major aircraft, the insurgents chose a commercial airliner instead of a military transport because it was not equipped with antimissile systems, such as flares.) The wing caught fire, and the pilots barely succeeded in making an emergency landing. Altogether, this two-day offensive served to prove the enduring viability of the resistance in the greater Baghdad area despite the ideological and organizational upheavals of the previous weeks.

Thus, ultimately, and in sharp contrast to Saddam's brave words, the second half of November saw a decline in the intensity of fighting in the Sunni heartland. There was, however, continued sabotage of oil installations and other elements of the national infrastructure, as well as an intensified, multifaceted campaign against Iraqis cooperating with the occupation authorities. Nevertheless, the center of the Sunni insurgency had edged northward and farther away from Baghdad. The military authorities saw it as a noteworthy strategic development, perceiving that the organized insurgency had turned its attention away from American soldiers to Iraqis cooperating with them. "In the past two weeks, these attacks have gone down, attacks against coalition forces," Gen. John Abizaid told a November 28 briefing. "But unfortunately we find that attacks against Iraqis have increased." Lt. Gen. Ricardo Sanchez went on to provide specific details about the emerging trends in the Iraqi guerrilla operations during that period: "We had had some days where we went as high as fifty engagements, and over the last seven-day period we are down to an average twenty-two engagements per day," Sanchez said in this briefing. "And this decline is most significant in the areas where we have taken the fight to the enemy and where we have been the most aggressive in our offensive operations." But Sanchez went on to echo Abizaid's comments, saying, "These are attacks on key officials such as ministers, police chiefs, Iraqi security forces, and, more importantly, the innocent people of the country. . . . The stark reality that we all have to face is that these terrorists have no vision for the future of Iraq, except to create or recreate a repressive state."

American authorities, even as they analyzed the evolving threat, seemed still to be obsessed with the specter of the return of Saddam Hussein and his loyalists. This misreading of the character and motivation of the resistance was also prevalent among the U.S. field commanders. For example, Col. William Mayville, commander of the 173rd Airborne Brigade in Kirkuk, stated on November 21 that "I'm very uncomfortable about saying Islamists are involved [in the recent escalation]. It's 90 percent former regime loyalists and 10 percent is a margin of error. I have no evidence of links to Islamists." The United States would pay dearly for this misunderstanding of the enemy.

Meanwhile, and in sharp contrast to the waning of the Baathist resistance, a dramatic rejuvenation of the Islamist jihad began. This was the result of the efforts of Abdul-Hadi al-Iraqi and his team in the previous three months. By mid-November, it was the moment to emphasize the Islamic tenor of the jihad in Iraq, and the entire Middle East, for that matter. Both the achievements and the future potential of the Islamists in Iraq were recognized by Osama bin Laden and al-Qaeda's leadership; they now had high hopes for the Islamists' ability to seize and sustain the initiative in the jihad in Iraq and the region at large. As a result, bin Laden and Zawahiri decided to shift additional resources to assisting the jihad in the Middle East even at the expense of other fronts, including Afghanistan. Indeed, in mid-November, three senior representatives of bin Laden met with two senior Taliban commanders in Khowst and informed them that bin Laden had determined to cut al-Qaeda's monthly three-million-dollar contribution to the Taliban in half so that the remaining funds could be diverted to the Iraqi jihad, and that he had further ordered that as many veteran fighters as possible, especially instructors and organizers, be sent from Afghanistan and Pakistan to Iraq. These were not empty statements, as in some areas up to two thirds of the local Arab Afghans (that is, Arab volunteers fighting with al-Qaeda in Afghanistan), totaling a few thousand mujahedin, had left for Iraq via Iran before the end of November. Significantly, this all-out effort was complementing the general mobilization ordered in the second half of August.

The Islamists were convinced that Iraq was ripe for an expansion of the jihad, which could be effected by unleashing a fundamentalist popular war based on proven methods and tactics that had already succeeded against the United States and Israel, and which ended up with the eviction of vastly superior armies from Muslim lands. On November 25, for example, the Salafi Jihadist group in Iraq—an al-Qaeda affiliate—issued a communiqué about the current state of the jihad and its future prospects. They observed that "the enemy has been in Baghdad around six months, but members of the resistance have carried out qualitative strikes that have echoed so loudly that the enemy has been incapable of hiding them. These kinds of operations are important and are the basic aim of the Jihadist plan." The most important challenge, they concluded, was implementing the correct strategy for victory, and, the Islamists argued, such a strategy should be based on "adopting the Lebanese and Somali models to expel the Americans from Iraq."

To facilitate the expansion of the war from a series of strikes to a popular war, al-Qaeda issued instructions for running remote, ad hoc local training facilities in order to both ensure security and meet the demand for on-site training made necessary by a growing torrent of volunteer mujahedin. The actual training was not to take more than three days, during which the basics would be instilled. The objective of the program was for up to three instructors to quickly and quietly churn out small groups of five or six locally recruited mujahedin without the use of any facilities. Each of these groups would then constitute an isolated fighting cell, thus improving overall security. The commanders and trainers were also instructed to identify the religiously committed and operationally skillful mujahedin so that they could be sent for advanced training in spectacular operations to take place both in Iraq and worldwide.

Al-Qaeda assured the local cadres that there would be no shortage of weapons, military equipment, or operational funds. Although in the past al-Qaeda had bankrolled small, isolated facilities used specifically for training of future mujahedin, the flow of volunteers now vastly exceeded the capabilities of these facilities, and al-Qaeda had to devise novel methods to accommodate the young Iraqis yearning to join the Islamist jihad.

Perhaps the most important and telling aspect of the Islamist surge was the Baath efforts to integrate themselves into this trend. The Baathists now claimed to be leading an all-inclusive jihad of an increasingly Islamist character in the service of Islamist goals. Ideologically, this profound change was expressed in a series of new Baath communiqués promising support to all mujahedin, which highlighted Islamist themes. On November 17, the Political Media and Publication Department of the Arab Socialist Baath Party issued a lengthy memorandum arguing that the Baath-led "armed Iraqi resistance" had already succeeded in seizing the initiative from the occupation forces, claiming that the Americans were now "facing a dilemma in Iraq" regarding how to extricate themselves from the morass. The Baath hailed all the key components of the armed resistance, which included their own militant cadres, troops from the Republican Guard, Special Security and National Security services, Saddam's Fedayeen, Iraqi mujahedin, and "the noble Arab volunteers who operate within the mobilization framework and the formations operating in accordance with the requirements of the combat actions against the foreign occupation forces."

Another Baathist document, titled "Political and Strategic Course of the Iraqi Resistance," defined the Baath-led resistance as "a national liberation movement" and asserted that its "strategic goal" was "expelling the occupation forces, liberating Iraq, and maintaining it united and a homeland for all Iraqis." This constituted not just a broader definition of the jihad's goals, but pointedly omitted any reference to the reestablishment of a Baathist regime, let alone the return of Saddam Hussein. Furthermore, in concert with the Islamists' catch-all understanding of legitimate objectives, the document stressed that "anything that came and will come as a result of Iraq's occupation, whether the existence of allied forces from other nationalities, UN forces, or various administrations and bodies, will be regarded and dealt with as forces, administrations, and bodies of the occupation and therefore as legitimate targets for the resistance in its war of liberation."

Later, the Baathists distributed a notice through Islamist venues declaring December 1 "A Day for Commemorating the Martyrs." It was an Islamist document stressing jihadist themes—"This is the day when we hail the martyrs and remember the values of martyrdom that are deeply embedded in our hearts, inherited in our religion, secured in our creed, protected in our morals, and sought in our struggle and Jihad"—and omitting any reference to Baathism. The unfolding "heroic Iraqi national resistance" was deriving its inspiration from "the Jihad of [the Prophet's] companions and the bouts of the early conquest knights," it noted, favoring historical precedent over contemporary revolutionary ideology. Moreover, it defined the current war in Iraq as an integral component of "the free national, pan-Arab, and humanitarian choice to repel every aggression and liberate every occupied homeland." The Islamist leadership could not have asked for a clearer ideological alignment, and its distribution of this Baathist communiqué therefore spoke volumes.

The modalities of the uncompromising jihad were then articulated in a new series of fatwas distributed by the Islamists throughout the Middle East. The most complete sets of these fatwas, along with supporting theological writings, were discovered between late November and early December in Iraq, Saudi Arabia, and Morocco. Significantly, the new fatwas were derived from the classic "Shielding Fatwa" issued in the late 1990s by Sheikh Umar Mahmud Abu-Umar—better known by the pseudonym Abu-Qatadah al-Filistini—who is recognized as one of the most important ideologists of al-Qaeda. The "Shielding Fatwa" permitted the indiscriminate killing of the innocent, including Muslims, if they were shielding "the unbelievers" who constituted the ultimate objective of the strike. In Abu-Qatadah's view, the injunction to jihad is so uncompromising that "Even if an unbeliever is being shielded by a child, the killing of the child is permissible in this case."

The new fatwa justified the killing not only of Muslims cooperating with hostile authorities—either occupation forces or pro-Western regimes—but even innocent Muslims who just happened to be in the area. According to the fatwa, nobody is innocent when it comes to freeing Muslim lands from the presence of unbelievers and their local puppets. "The unbelievers may be killed if they are rulers or complacent peoples during night or day and without prior notice or advice, even if their women and children are killed in doing so," one of the fatwas decreed. Regarding the Muslim population, the fatwa specified that "all of those who have sought the refuge of an unbeliever may be killed, even if they are Muslims, if it is not possible to kill this unbeliever without killing them. In doing so, soldiers, the police, and the army may be killed if they try to defend the rulers and the unbelievers."

In Saudi Arabia, these fatwas provided the needed rationalizations for a new course of Islamist terrorism that began in late October. In early November the Saudi security forces raided a terrorist stronghold about 10 miles northeast of Mecca, killing a few terrorists and capturing large quantities of weapons and explosives. Notably, among the jihadist forces engaged were elite detachments of Nigerian and Indonesian mujahedin who intended to mingle among their countrymen in Mecca. Documents retrieved at the site included plans for an attack on the Grand Mosque of Mecca in which numerous pilgrims would have been killed. About one million Muslims were expected to pray at the mosque that Friday. Challenging the House of al-Saud's ability to control Islam's holy shrines has long been a major priority of the jihadists—beginning with the 1979 seizure of the same Grand Mosque of Mecca by a well-organized group of roughly 1,500 men under the leadership of Juhayman ibn-Muhammad ibn-Sayf al-Utaibi. The siege ended only after the Saudi authorities called in a group of French experts who used chemical weapons to subdue the attackers and their supporters. For the Islamists, the seizure of the Grand Mosque would demonstrate the inability of the House of al-Saud to live up to its role as custodian of Islam's holy shrines while empowering the Islamists in their place.

However, the achievements of the Saudi security forces could not prevent the Islamists from striking out elsewhere. On the night of November
9, the jihadists attempted a major strike in the Riyadh area, moving to assassinate a leading member of the House of al-Saud as his motorcade was
taking him to his palace near the Nahkil neighborhood. To enhance their
ability to elude the tightening dragnet of the Saudi security forces, the jihadists brought into Saudi Arabia an elite detachment of Lebanese and
Lebanese-Palestinian terrorists. The plan called for the two drivers of a
booby-trapped truck—a Saudi and a Lebanese-Palestinian—to ram the
prince's limousine as his security detail was engaged in a firefight with a
diversionary group. That night, thirteen mujahedin came down from the
mountains in two groups and laid an ambush near the Nakhil neighborhood. Meanwhile, the two bombers arrived in their truck—a converted
police jeep—and were able to park in full view of the road. At the prescribed time, the diversionary groups opened heavy fire on the Saudi security forces, creating mayhem. However, when the motorcade failed to show
up as planned, the overexcited suicide terrorists attacked their secondary
target, driving their jeep through the gates of the nearby al-Muhaya compound, getting as close to the princes' palaces as they could, and detonating
their bombs. The rest of the mujahedin withdrew safely after the explosion, using other vehicles.

At least thirty people were killed and several hundred were injured in
both the bombing and the shoot-out. The bulk of the casualties were families of senior financial advisers, technocrats, and experts serving the highest echelons of the Royal House of al-Saud, essentially facilitating their
reign. Many of the casualties were Christian Lebanese serving as the private bankers of the elite and orchestrating the transfer of billions of dollars
of undeclared funds. "The royal family is in a panic and now believes al-
Qaeda is playing for keeps," a senior Western intelligence source told
MENL's Steve Rodan. "Without its financial advisers, the family is completely exposed."

The Islamists had already consolidated a new generation of senior
commanders for the entire Arabian Peninsula. The al-Muhaya strike clarified the specific roles and responsibilities of the key jihadist commanders
in Saudi Arabia. Like all major terrorist operations in Saudi Arabia, the
Muhaya attack was ordered and directly supervised by Seif al-Adel using
satellite phone from his headquarters in Iran. He was operating at the time
from a forward headquarters in Iranian Baluchistan, in a remote camp
where some five hundred mujahedin were being trained by Iranian secu-

rity forces for future operations in Iraq, Saudi Arabia, and other Gulf States. The senior on-site commander, formally "Al-Qaeda's field commander in the Arabian Peninsula," was known only by the pseudonym Abu-al-Walid al-Najdi. In mid-November, he issued a communiqué urging "all mujahedin in the Arabian Peninsula" to "attack Crusader bases" and "punish those who betrayed the Nation." The senior commander in the Riyadh area, who planned and organized the Riyadh attacks, was Abdallah Muhammad al-Rushud, originally from the town of al-Aflaj. Al-Rushud continued to operate mainly in Saudi Arabia, although he was traveling frequently to Iraq to consult and coordinate with the senior jihadist commanders there. The operational commander of the Muhaya strike, who personally led the ambush groups, was Abdulaziz Issa Muhsin al-Muqrin, better known by as Abu-Hajar. He was a veteran of the jihads in Somalia, Bosnia-Herzegovina, and Afghanistan and received specialized training from IRGC intelligence in Croatia and Bosnia. Abu-Hajar was considered the most charismatic and inspiring jihadist commander in Saudi Arabia.

In mid-November, the Saudi security authorities intensified their hunt for Islamist networks in their midst. Several cells were destroyed in preemptive raids and lengthy firefights. On November 25, the Saudis were able to prevent at the last minute an enormous attack involving a car bomb at the heart of Riyadh. Acting on an intelligence tip, security forces identified the dark brown pickup truck painted with Saudi military insignias and packed with a ton of high explosives. When the security forces closed in on the truck, one of the martyr bombers—Musaid Muhammad al-Subaie—opened fire from the boot of the truck and then stormed the security forces, bewildering them for a moment. However, Subaie's partner and driver panicked, and instead of using the momentary confusion to complete their mission he blew himself up with a hand grenade. Documents found in the truck suggested that two more truck bombs were already in Riyadh. They are yet to be found.

On November 27, the Saudis discovered a major cache of weapons in the Riyadh area, including an SA-7 missile, ten RPG-22s, 200 hand grenades, 890 electronic fuses, six cellular telephones converted into remote-control detonators, about 84,500 pounds of RDX high explosives, 3,000 pounds of other types of high explosives, eighty Kalashnikov assault rifles, 168,000 bullets, 410 magazines, forty wireless devices, three computer sets with computer discs, 94,395 Saudi rials (in cash), documents, various identity cards, and Islamist pamphlets urging jihad and terrorism.

Riyadh knew this was only one of many such stockpiles already in the kingdom. At the same time, the Saudi security authorities failed to properly block the jihadist traffic across the northern border with Iraq and Jordan. Indeed, in late November and early December, numerous senior operatives who had escaped to Iraq during earlier cycles of security crackdowns returned to Saudi Arabia, bringing with them new mujahedin and large quantities of weapons and explosives. This inflow enabled the Islamists to sustain and even escalate the jihad in Saudi Arabia despite the frequent successes of the Saudi security forces.

With al-Qaeda's growing presence and grassroots mobilization seemingly unstoppable, the leadership of the Royal House of al-Saud was rethinking its strategy vis-à-vis Islamist terrorism. "This is a deliberate campaign that seeks to increase the pressure on the royal family by telling them they aren't safe anywhere, even within their own military," another Western intelligence analyst told MENL's Steve Rodan. "This has sparked a debate over how to reconcile with al-Qaeda and end this war." In December, U.S. intelligence learned, and so informed its Saudi counterparts, that "al-Qaeda has decided to target leading security officials in Saudi Arabia." American intelligence sources told Rodan that "the al-Qaeda effort is meant to intimidate the royal family from pursuing its offensive against the Islamic insurgency movement and divide the leadership." Riyadh was warned that the jihadists had already "obtained excellent intelligence on the identities and whereabouts of senior Saudi officials." For example, on December 5 the al-Qaeda–affiliated Al-Haramain Brigade narrowly missed Brig. Gen. Abdul Aziz al-Huwairini, the third highest official in the Interior Ministry.

At this point, U.S. intelligence determined that Saudi Arabia was "swamped by al-Qaeda." A CIA study warned that al-Qaeda could rely on a pool of some 10,000 Saudis for operations and support. Most significant was the marked increase in the number of leading jihadist commanders hailing from the key tribes of Saudi Arabia—hitherto the kernel of support for the House of al-Saud. Grassroots discontent was on the rise because of corruption and rising unemployment, and a dangerous status quo emerged: "The U.S. intelligence community does not believe al-Qaeda has the power to overthrow the Saudi regime, particularly in a frontal assault," intelligence analysts told Steve Rodan. However, "al-Qaeda has been effective in infiltrating Saudi security forces and military and obtaining key intelligence on vital regime installations," to the point of debilitating them, and, the analysts concluded, "the United States has determined that Saudi Arabia would require at least another year to achieve significant success in its war against al-Qaeda." And that was provided that the Saudis succeeded in sealing their borders with Iraq and Yemen, preventing the traffic of jihadists and their weapons.

The resumption of major fighting by the end of November was a manifestation of the latest major transformation of the Iraqi guerrilla movement, as it assumed a more popular character; as such, the fighting confirmed the trends delineated by recent ideological, political, and theological communiqués. Crucially, Sunni nationalists, and especially the tribes, had discovered the potency of Islamism and reached out to the jihadists in order to build anti-American coalitions. The tribal elites further resolved to tolerate, if not outright support, the Islamists as the superior force in Iraq. The leading sheikhs thus became the key to the accumulating pressure on the occupation forces by expediting the flow of jihadist mujahedin into the center of Iraq. Tribal chiefs on both sides of the Syrian-Iraqi border told an Arab interviewer that although they were capable of blocking the flow and activities of the various insurgents in the areas under their influence, they were not going to do so because it would look as if they were helping the hated Americans, and they and their tribes were not going to be identified as working against Iraqi and pan-Arab interests. America's distribution of large sums of money to the sheikhs, as well as the dispatching in November of former defense minister Sultan Hashem back to his Tai tribe in the Mosul area, did not change the overall attitude of the tribal elite. These sheikhs were convinced that the United States was irreversibly losing the war for Iraq.

By contrast, the overwhelmingly Sunni regions stayed relatively quiet. The only major clash there took place in Samarra on November 30, a desperate effort by the Baathist forces to replenish their financial resources by attacking two American military convoys transporting new money issued by the interim government in Baghdad to banks around the country. The convoys were traveling with heavy military escorts that sprang into action the moment the first shots were fired. The insurgents' forward forces were estimated at a hundred fighters—a far larger attack party than is seen in the average ambush. Ultimately, the U.S. Army's success in destroying the ambush was the result of its finally adopting Israeli tactics as well as unique weapon systems. The U.S. forces effectively used tank and helicopter fire to destroy the three buildings from which the ambush was launched. Ultimately the army estimated that between forty-six and fifty-four guerrilla fighters were killed in the clash and eight were captured, while the Americans suffered no casualties. Iraqi and Arab observers hotly disputed these figures, claiming that only a few fighters were killed and that civilian casualties were heavy, with perhaps as many as a hundred fatalities. However, alarming reporting from several Arab intelligence sources cited eyewitness reports that at least one fedayeen team was preparing to use identifiably WMD-tipped RPG-7 rockets against the Americans during the clashes. However, once they realized that the battle was lost, they, along with other fedayeen reinforcements, quickly vanished into the countryside.

On November 29, a highly professional Islamist insurgent force launched a lethal ambush in Sawariyah (near Najaf in the Shiite enclave) against eight Spanish intelligence officers, viciously killing seven and mutilating their bodies and leaving the eighth officer wounded so that he could "tell the story." Subsequently, other foreign workers and diplomats were killed in a spate of ambushes in the last weekend of November. Then, on December 3, al-Qaeda published a letter to "the Spanish people who were deceived by their politicians and leaders who led them into a war that has nothing to do with them." The letter presented the position of "the Iraqi resistance" from an all-Islamic, and not just Iraqi, perspective. The attack on the Spanish intelligence officers was driven more by events in Europe than in Iraq, al-Qaeda explained. "Although we acknowledge the courage of the Spanish people's stand during the war, we have not yet noticed any serious action to overthrow the government of war criminals. We in Iraq have vowed to liberate our territory and we would offer our blood and soul for this end." In the event that Spain didn't reverse course, al-Qaeda threatened to launch terror attacks against Spain proper, citing its torture of the murdered Spanish agents and promising to do worse. In case the Spanish people continued to support their government, al-Qaeda's letter warned, "you would incite us to escalate our resistance if the scene of the seven spies was not enough to move your feelings and prompt you to save your children. The resistance factions and the Ansar outside Iraq are able to increase the dose and make you forget the sight of the decomposed bodies."

Another major long-term development during this period was the early December arrival of Salah Omar al-Ali in Baghdad. Salah Omar al-Ali is a veteran Iraqi Baathist and one of the founders of the original and then unified Baath Party. In the 1960s, in the great ideological schism that tore the Baath Party apart, he sided with Salah Bittar against Michelle Aflaq—the favorite of the Iraqi branch of the Baath Party—and followed

Bittar into exile in Damascus. In December 2003, Omar al-Ali was made the head of the new Iraqi Baath Party, committed to the reunification and rejuvenation of a single Baath Party in Iraq, Syria, and the rest of the Mashriq (the Arab world east of the Mediterranean). He was surrounded by a mixture of veteran party operatives and young militants hailing from the ranks of the anti-American Baathist nationalist forces that have given the "New Baath" tremendous grassroots credibility. In early December, Bashar al-Assad saw al-Ali off with great fanfare. In Baghdad, al-Ali first discovered receptiveness among the intellectual elite—ideological Baathists and nationalists who wanted to use the "New Baath" to participate in the political dynamics. No less receptive were the underground Baath Party hacks yearning for a role in the anti-American struggle that would not require holding a gun or risking their lives and livelihoods. The popular acceptance of al-Ali and the Baathist ideological message coming from Damascus were indicative of the diminished influence of Saddam Hussein and his Aflaq-based Baathist ideology.

Meanwhile, the occupation authorities missed this crucial shift in inter-Iraqi policies. They were still obsessed with Saddam Hussein and his legacy, as demonstrated by their handling of the Izzat Ibrahim al-Durri saga. At some point near the end of 2003, rumors began to circulate alleging that al-Durri was suffering from a "terminal illness"—according to most reports, leukemia. Several Iraqi notables claimed to be emissaries on his behalf and launched a series of negotiations for his surrender and medical treatment. Since U.S. authorities still formally identified him as the commander of the pro-Saddam resistance, negotiations proceeded in earnest for some time. In late November, though, the negotiations faltered, ostensibly because the United States would not guarantee that al-Durri would not be extradited to Kuwait to be put on trial for his role in the 1990–91 occupation. This inference makes little sense, given al-Durri's own formal reconciliation with the crown princes of Saudi Arabia and Kuwait during the Arab Summit in Beirut in March 2002. Therefore, the negotiations were aborted because the Americans had never been serious about them to begin with, and in all likelihood, most of the "emissaries" were interested in the ten-million-dollar bounty on al-Durri's head, even though they could not deliver him. But the occupation authorities, unsatisfied, would not end their pursuit of al-Durri. And so a major offensive was launched against him, which included the bombing of his house by an F-16 and the arrest of his second wife and daughter, even though they had been estranged for quite some time. In the first days of December, rumors of al-Durri's capture or death spread throughout Baghdad, but in the end, only his former personal secretary was captured, and he had not been in touch with his former boss for a long time and thus knew little of relevance.

In sum, all the United States accomplished in its pursuit of Izzat Ibrahim al-Durri was to needlessly give prominence to the pro-Saddam Baathist forces at the same time that a growing number of members of the key Sunni clans, including the five extended families surrounding Saddam Hussein, were sliding toward the Baathist and even jihadist camps. The evolving situation in the Sunni heartland—as a coalition of fundamentalists and nationalists took precedence over Saddam's loyalists—constituted the predominant and growing threat to America's interests and presence in Iraq, rather than the increasingly irrelevant remnants of Saddam's regime.

Saddam himself was worried by the relative quiet in the Sunni Triangle and concluded that the Sunni population was exhausted by the intense pace of clashes with the United States. Therefore, he determined that the key to effecting an acceleration of the guerrilla war was to involve the Shiites in the fighting, and that only the infusion of specific instructions and military support from Iran would activate them. According to Lebanese sources, in early December an emissary of Saddam's made contact with senior Iranian and HizbAllah officials in both Syria and Lebanon to discuss the activation of the Shiite community. These officials expressed interest but would not commit, suggesting that Saddam dispatch a senior aide to deal directly with the Iranian leadership.

Therefore, a few days later, Saddam sent his son-in-law to Tehran to directly seek Iranian help in unleashing the Iraqi Shiites against the American forces. The senior Iranian intelligence and IRGC officials who met Saddam's son-in-law accorded him all honors and expressed great interest in Saddam's ideas about collaboration against the United States. As much as they would have liked to immediately mobilize and activate the Iraqi Shiites, they told the Iraqi emissary, such a move required a decision by Khamenei and the uppermost leadership. The Iranians promised to bring the issue to Khamenei's attention, hinting that collaboration would follow soon afterward. In reality, the Lebanese sources explained, the Iranians "fooled Saddam" by giving the impression they were ready to assist him, but Iranian intelligence and the IRGC leadership had concluded from the meeting that Saddam "was finished," and so informed Khamenei. Indeed, in December, Iranian intelligence augmented its support for the entire Islamist resistance—both Shiite and Sunni—although it channeled its assistance through pro-Iranian Shiites and Islamist venues, allowing Tehran influence over the insurrection without having to credit Saddam or the Baathists.

Meanwhile, high-quality terrorist operations continued, particularly in Baghdad. Most important, and audacious, was a December 6 assassination attempt aimed at L. Paul Bremer. Returning to Baghdad after seeing Donald Rumsfeld off at the Baghdad airport, Bremer's convoy came under small-arms attack and a large roadside bomb was detonated next to his armored car. The strong explosion blew out tires of a lead vehicle, and the windshield in Bremer's car was cracked by the blast. Most of the cars were hit by the small-arms fire, which failed to penetrate their armor. The correct counterambush tactics of Bremer's escorts enabled the convoy to speed away without further damage. American officials were quick to assert that the attempt on Bremer's life wasn't deliberate. Bremer's spokesman, Dan Senor, assured the media in Baghdad that "it was a random opportunistic attack not necessarily targeting him. The party was traveling from an impromptu meeting that was not scheduled." An American security official opined that Bremer was "a target of opportunity" on an airport road afflicted by frequent roadside bomb and small-arms attacks on U.S. convoys.

However, Iraqi sources insisted the attack was intentional and that insurgents had been tipped off about Bremer's movements, and British intelligence officials concurred. The U.S. authorities in Baghdad stressed the randomness of the attack because the assassination attempt reinforced a growing apprehension about the extent to which agents of the resistance had penetrated the Iraqi police and other groups working for the occupation authorities.

American investigation of the spate of car bomb attacks in Baghdad beginning in November concluded that American-trained Iraqi police officers coordinated at least some of the strikes. The evidence included policemen facilitating the access of car bombs, providing intelligence to the insurgents, and simply not showing up on the days that attacks took place. More disturbingly, specific intelligence about the connections of some policemen to insurgency cells came to light as well. Moreover, several attacks on Americans were coordinated by Iraqi civilians working for the U.S. military. Iraqis provided the resistance with timely intelligence on troop movements and the travels of high-ranking officers and officials. "Clearly those are concerns we have. We try to do the vetting [of Iraqi employees] as close as we can," Lt. Gen. Ricardo Sanchez explained in late November.

"There have been instances when police were coordinating attacks against the coalition and against the people." Outside Baghdad, Iraqi police frequently tipped off suspects throughout the Sunni heartland just before Americans were planning to raid their houses or hideaways. In December, the investigation concluded that agents of the resistance had penetrated the U.S. command in Iraq to the point of being able to undermine major activities and security operations. "We were badly infiltrated," an American official acknowledged to ABC News.

Nevertheless, the overall combat performance of the armed forces began to improve, through the absorption and integration of Israeli expertise. Israel's extensive experience with antiterrorism and urban warfare, acquired during the last three years of the intifada, proved invaluable to the American military. During the summer, with losses mounting and counterinsurgency operations failing to deliver results, Washington became less politically sensitive to the battlefield introduction of tactics and systems easily identified as Israeli. Senior military planners traveled to Israel for on-site lessons on Israel's tactics and training methods for the forces involved in antiterrorist operations. Select American combat commanders were even permitted to attend Israeli field headquarters and watch actual counterterrorism operations unfolding. In the fall, select American units were sent to undergo specialized training in Israeli facilities. Meanwhile, Israeli senior officers with extensive combat experience were sent to the United States to help their American counterparts. As the need for training deepened, Israeli instructors were sent to Fort Bragg and other installations to help train Special Forces and intelligence specialists prior to their deployment to Iraq.

In November, as American forces began to apply Israeli-style tactics and use specialized equipment, gains were made in the new cycle of operations in the Sunni heartland. Israeli input was noticeable primarily in urban battlefield tactics, especially the use of tanks, helicopters, and UAVs. For example, CENTCOM officials stressed that the Ivy Cyclone 2 offensive (a proactive operation intended to "permanently disrupt [the insurgent's] capability to plan attacks against coalition targets," according to CENTCOM), which was launched on November 16 "against Sunni insurgents," was an operation that combined "actionable intelligence" with "close-air support, army aviation, armor, artillery, mechanized infantry, and air-assault operations for rapid deployment of dismounted artillery," all hallmarks of Israeli-style urban warfare. The effectiveness of Israeli-style tactics and unique weapon systems clearly demonstrated in Ivy Cyclone 2 was also evident in the highly successful outcome of clashes in Samarra on November 30.

The Israeli contribution to the war effort in Iraq was most pronounced, and most important, in special operations and intelligence. While dealing with the intricacies of tribal, clannish, and jihadist societies was completely alien to the American defense establishment, Israel had confronted insurrection and terrorism fomented in this sort of social structure for fifty-five years. The Israelis, sharing some of their most closely held methods, taught the Americans how to identify sources, interrogate people, analyze family and clan structures, build operationally useable databases and organizational charts, and then capitalize on this data for special operations and proactive raids. There was a considerable amount of firsthand training, as Israeli Special Forces and intelligence specialists trained units in the United States, while Israeli "consultants" traveled to Iraq to secretly advise their counterparts in the field. By the fall, Special Forces were conducting aggressive counterinsurgency operations, which including hunting down and "neutralizing" key guerrilla commanders. American forces were now implementing such combat-proven methods as sealing off centers of resistance, at times entire villages, with razor wire, and razing buildings that sheltered terrorists. American platoons were also running Israeli-style random checkpoints and tracking militants with Israeli-made UAVs. The U.S. Army was now increasingly able to put militants on the defensive through frequent arrest raids and proactive searches as well as by enclosing villages and tightly supervising travel permits. The growing ability of the Israeli-trained Special Forces units to make use of intelligence information within minutes to seize or attack a moving target would soon prove crucial in key operations.

19
ENDGAME

On December 14, 2003, a gloating Paul Bremer addressed a hastily assembled press conference in Baghdad. "Ladies and gentlemen, we got him," he declared. "The tyrant is a prisoner." A few hours later, President Bush addressed the nation and the world on TV. Saddam's capture "marks the end of the road for him and all who killed and bullied in his name," Bush said. "You will not have to fear the rule of Saddam Hussein ever again," he assured the Iraqi people. At the same time, Bush conceded that Saddam's capture would not bring an end to the anti-American violence in Iraq. All over the world, televisions carried images of a bearded and disheveled Saddam Hussein being checked by American medical personnel. Saddam seemed dejected and resigned to his fate and humiliation. It was a symbolic achievement for the Bush administration, for few expected the capture to have a tangible impact on the spiraling violence. The capture of Saddam Hussein was the result of the confluence of two key factors—the dramatic shift in correlation of powers in the Sunni heartland and Iraq as a whole, and the marked improvement in the American military's tactical and analytical intelligence capabilities.

Great mystery still surrounds the precise activities of Saddam Hussein in the last few weeks prior to his capture. He was clearly under tremendous mental pressure. He was in a race against time and enemies—a desperate and increasingly futile effort to regain control, if only a semblance of control, over the rapidly escalating and expanding guerrilla warfare. Saddam seems to have realized the extent of his predicament. The personal ramifications of the predominance of the jihadists and Baathist nationalists, and the painful compromises his few remaining loyalists had to make with them, were finally dawning on Saddam. He was increasingly aware of his effective irrelevance in Iraq. Never a quitter, and the eternal survivor, he seems to have embarked on a desperate effort to reverse the trend. It was a daunting challenge, as Saddam activated and pushed into action veteran contacts and allies while escaping and evading a tightening noose of aspirant leaders in the Sunni heartland who now considered his very existence a threat to their rise to power. Furthermore, a growing number of brigands and hostile clans were increasingly interested in the twenty-five million-dollar price on Saddam's head. Kurdish Democratic Party (KDP) intelligence was also after Saddam for both political and financial reasons. These dire circumstances seem to have pushed Saddam further away from his normal circles of meetings and communications.

There were two sightings of Saddam in late November. On November 24, the first day of Eid al-Fitr, Saddam was seen praying and meditating at his stepfather's grave in al-Aujah. He was alone at the graveyard. It was very unusual for the secular Saddam to be praying, and this further confirms the mental strain he was under. However, encountered again a few days later, Saddam was his overconfident self again. He and a driver were spotted at a roadblock near Tikrit by an officer-turned-policeman in a battered orange and white taxicab. Saddam recognized the officer because he was a member of one of the region's key families, and admonished him for joining the police. When the officer responded that his family needed the money, Saddam gave him three hundred dollars in cash. The officer let Saddam continue and did not report the encounter. Neither sighting was reported until after Saddam's capture. According to most of Iraq and the Arab world, Saddam simply vanished. Then, in early December, Baghdad was swamped with rumors that Saddam was either dead or dying from a host of terminal illnesses. These rumors, originating with security officials of Talabani's Kurdish Patriotic Union (PUK) intelligence, sought to explain Saddam's sudden disappearance so soon after his burst of assertive activities in November. Some of Saddam's loyalists in the Arab world even speculated that he might have been assassinated by the PUK.

In Beirut, when communications died down, Samira was worried that Saddam might have been abducted, or even assassinated. She believed he might have fallen victim to Baathist nationalists seeking his endorsement for their power grabs in the Sunni heartland, or to bounty hunters. She concluded that Saddam was likely to be kept alive and in decent conditions in American hands, while his growing circle of enemies were likely to kill him at the first opportunity. As a result, Samira and her confidants resolved to assist the United States in capturing Saddam before he was killed. "Samira Shahbandar," stated well-informed Lebanese sources, "is believed

to have given the Americans and their allies some information about the
area where Saddam was hiding." However, by early December, Samira and
her confidants actually knew very few specific details about Saddam's precise whereabouts. Still, they leaked to the Americans a few names of people
they were convinced knew of Saddam's movements. These sources, thanks
to America's improved overall intelligence capabilities, enabled the analysts to better capitalize on existing information, identify key people, arrest
and interrogate them, and extract information leading to the capture of
Saddam Hussein.

In the second week of December, Saddam was desperately working on
revamping "his" Baathist Sunni insurgency. He was trying to rejuvenate
what was essentially a lost cause by facilitating what he hoped would be the
major escalation he had promised. According to Vitislav Oshakov, deputy
chairman of FSB (Russia's Foreign Intelligence Service), Russian intelligence learned that toward this end, "Saddam Hussein had distributed
more than seven million firearms among Iraqis days before his arrest." In
reality, Saddam was on the run from both real enemies and the realization
that he was no longer relevant to Iraq's unfolding present. He was increasingly stressed, drained, and disheveled. His last known meeting took place
on December 10 in an isolated farmhouse south of Tikrit. He had dinner
with Qais Hattam, one of his top lieutenants, who was responsible for
sponsoring and directing guerrilla operations north of Baghdad, particularly in the Samarra area. Hattam's main task was supplying the regional
fighting forces with funds and weapons. Saddam brought with him more
than a million dollars in cash earmarked to facilitate escalation of the ambushes and attacks along the "Highway of Death" between northern Baghdad and Tikrit. Saddam urged, if not demanded, an escalation, but Hattam
refused to commit. He promised to promptly raise the issue with the regional Saddam's Fedayeen commanders and together devise an operational plan that would take into account their own reading of the security
posture in their areas of operation. There was very little Saddam could do
once faced with such an argument, although Hattam did take Saddam's
money.

Saddam traveled from the meeting with Hattam to a prearranged
meeting spot near al-Dawr, 10 miles south of Tikrit. He was to be met by
two confidants—brothers Col. Muhammad Ibrahim al-Omar and Lt. Col.
Khalil Ibrahim al-Omar. They were to take Saddam to one of two nearby
farmhouses that had been secured as his next hideaway. Saddam must have
been seized at that point either by his would-be escorts—the Ibrahim

brothers—or by strangers with the brothers' cooperation. Since there was no sign of a struggle in the vicinity of al-Dawr, and no marks of violence were found on Saddam's body, it is safe to surmise that Saddam was captured by people he trusted. According to Kurdish intelligence officials, Saddam was drugged—most likely in the food and drink he was served at his meeting with Hattam—and therefore did not resist. Saddam was then taken to the "spider hole" where he would be held as prisoner until his eventual capture. The spider hole was a small, six-foot-deep shaft leading to a horizontal chamber where Saddam could barely lie down. Inside this cavern was a fan near the vertical shaft, where Saddam's head was located, and an air vent to the surface near Saddam's legs. There was no sanitation. The shaft was closed with a Styrofoam cover on top over which there was thick camouflage made of mud, bricks, and foliage. It was very difficult, if not impossible, to open the shaft's cover from the inside.

In all likelihood, Saddam's captors wanted to pressure him into recognizing a new leadership and command structure, and perhaps into handing over funds and stockpiles meant for the new forces. The detritus found in the small farmhouse near the spider hole indicates that Saddam's captors did not expect the confrontation to take a long time. The battered taxi that must have been used to transport Saddam was parked nearby. Near Saddam himself was roughly $750,000 in one-hundred-dollar banknotes and numerous documents related to the resistance in the Baghdad area, including a list of Iraqis working for the occupation authorities who were spying for the resistance. These funds and documents were intended for another lieutenant Saddam planned on meeting to further the escalation. Saddam's captors did not remove these items, believing that Saddam was likely to attend that meeting. There was very little food, a few items of clothing, and virtually no other supplies or communication equipment on the premises. There were only two guards at any given time, equipped with two AK-47s and a pistol—an indication of the self-confidence of the captors.

Meanwhile, U.S. intelligence, working with newly acquired intelligence data, were closing the net on Saddam. At the heart of the effort was an elaborate, multicolored organizational chart of Saddam's inner circle, dubbed the "Mongo Link" by its developers (a select team of military intelligence officers from the 4th Infantry Division). Originally started in June with four names, by December the Mongo Link boasted roughly two hundred and fifty, with more than nine thousand more spilling over into a supporting computerized database. The chart tracks and defines the interrelations among key members of the five major clans in the Tikrit area that constituted the core of Saddam's support system, and maps the intricate web of family and functional ties between Saddam's key loyalists.

The pace of the hunt for Saddam picked up in early December, as U.S. intelligence acquired sensitive new data. This happened about the same time that Samira Shahbandar arranged to have information leaked to the United States in order to save her husband by having him captured. According to PUK senior intelligence officials, they provided the United States with the crucial piece of information that led to Saddam's apprehension, after a high-ranking commander of their special intelligence unit named Qusrat Rasul Ali spoke by telephone with Samira. Ahmed Chalabi agreed that Qusrat and his team had provided "vital information and more" that led to Saddam's capture. Whatever the source, the new information clarified the members of, and the respective roles played by, members of the elaborate support system around Saddam.

On the basis of this data, in the ten days preceding Saddam's capture, American forces conducted a series of searches and preventive arrests, bringing in for interrogation between five and ten members of each of the key five clans. The primary objective of their interrogation was to ascertain the validity of recently acquired information regarding a specific individual—Muhammad Ibrahim Omar al-Musslit—and his relative importance to Saddam. Army intelligence had known of him for months, but did not ascribe to him the centrality and importance he really had in Saddam's inner circle. In December, though, they acquired very specific information indicating just how crucial Musslit really was—namely, that he was a key enabler of Saddam Hussein. The ensuing effort—the numerous raids, arrests, and interrogations—was aimed at confirming or disproving this key piece of information.

A couple of days before Saddam's capture, U.S. Army intelligence obtained a strong confirmation of Musslit's importance and began an intense search for him. Musslit was a senior officer in the Special Security Organization hailing from Abu-Ajeel, just north of Tikrit, who belonged to a very important family within one of the key five clans. On the next day, December 12, he was captured in the course of a series of raids in Baghdad. The next morning he was transferred to Tikrit and subjected to intense interrogation in which he was confronted with the wealth of knowledge already available to U.S. intelligence. Around 5 P.M., after about four hours of intense interrogation and confrontation with his captors, Musslit broke down and "blurted Saddam's location," in the words of Col. James Hickey of the 4th Infantry Division's 1st Combat Brigade team, telling his interrogators that Saddam should be hiding in one of two rural farmhouses in the vicinity of Al-Dawr.

The United States immediately launched Operation Red Dawn to capture Saddam. Just before 8 P.M., a convoy of more than thirty armored Humvees and other vehicles, carrying some six hundred assault troops from the 4th Infantry Division's 1st Combat Brigade team and Special Operations forces from Task Force 121, surrounded the Al-Dawr area and disconnected the electricity. A quarter of an hour later, the unit (assisted by, according to PUK intelligence officials, a special intelligence unit commanded by Qusrat Rasul Ali), secured the two farmhouses—now known by the code names Wolverine 1 and Wolverine 2. The Special Forces teams thoroughly searched the compounds of both farms but found nothing. Having been confronted with this information, Musslit kept insisting that Saddam Hussein should have been in this area, and a more thorough search was launched, with troops scouring every building, orchard, and field in the entire area. At 8:26 P.M., a soldier noticed a straight crack in the earth near a mud hut on a small sheep farm. A quick dig exposed the elaborate camouflage and the Styrofoam cover on top of the spider hole.

A Special Forces soldier was ready to toss a grenade into the hole in the ground when a disheveled head appeared. According to the official version, the figure raised both hands and declared in English, "I am Saddam Hussein, I am the president of Iraq, and I am willing to negotiate." A Special Forces soldier replied, "President Bush sends his regards." Saddam was then pulled out of the hole, bumping his head in the process. Not a shot was fired, the story went, even though Saddam had a pistol on him.

In reality, though, Saddam was too dazed and incoherent to make any statement, let alone to answer in English. He was unceremoniously pulled out of the spider hole, manhandled, and handcuffed. At this point he began struggling with his new captors, cursing in Arabic, and then spat in the face of one of the soldiers. The soldier promptly slugged him, with either his fist or a rifle butt. Saddam was stunned as his head was covered with a hood. He showed no resistance as he was put on a helicopter.

All agree that Saddam was mentally bedraggled, exhausted, and crushed when he was dragged out of the hole. Descriptions of Saddam by senior officers who saw him immediately after his capture lend credence to the report that he had been held prisoner in the spider hole and most likely drugged. Major General Odierno noted that Saddam climbed out of his hole "very much bewildered," and not in full control of himself. "Tired, he was a tired man, and also a man resigned to his fate," said Lieutenant General Sanchez. Another senior intelligence official concluded after his first encounter that "Saddam Hussein is a broken man." (By the next day, Saddam had regained his composure; in meetings with Paul Bremer and members of the Iraqi Governing Council, as well as in subsequent interrogations, he was reportedly assertive, hostile, and uncooperative.)

It's worth noting that Musslit, the enabler, had alerted his interrogators to two locations—the Wolverine farmhouses—where Saddam was supposed to be, but Saddam was in neither place. He was found in the nearby spider hole, which Musslit knew nothing about. Given the tight discipline of Saddam's inner circle, it is safe to surmise that Saddam was placed in the spider hole by people who broke ranks—that is, by hostile individuals who must have held Saddam against his will.

Meanwhile, as America celebrated Saddam's capture, another drama was unfolding as a consequence in the Tikrit area—a series of events that sheds light on the circumstances surrounding Saddam's last few days before capture. These developments appeared to be the work of Saddam's loyalists avenging those they held responsible for Saddam's capture.

First, a few hours after Saddam's arrest was announced on television, an Iraqi came to a U.S. Army base near Samarra and volunteered that Hattam would soon be meeting with several fedayeen commanders from the region. Two days later, the 3rd Brigade combat team of the 4th Infantry Division launched Operation Ivy Blizzard capturing Hattam and seventy-three fedayeen commanders and killing sixteen in a raid on a farmhouse between Tikrit and Samarra. They also recovered a huge cache of weapons and explosives, as well as documents accounting for the distribution of $1.9 million to finance the guerrilla war in the previous months. The more than one million dollars in cash Saddam had given Hattam was nowhere to be found.

Significantly, Hattam's name had been on the wanted list of the 4th Infantry Division's military intelligence for months, and an operation designed to apprehend him had been planned long before Saddam's capture but wasn't implemented until proper, timely intelligence could be gathered. It was only after Hattam's capture and interrogation that U.S. intelligence learned about his December 10 meeting with Saddam. Moreover, the overall circumstances of Operation Ivy Blizzard strongly suggest that Hattam had been intentionally betrayed because of Saddam's capture. The U.S. sweep was to include a whole series of raids on guerrilla commanders and operatives in the Samarra area known to be affiliated with Hattam. However, on the eve of Operation Ivy Blizzard, dozens of these suspects—

all of whom had long been under U.S. surveillance—fled Samarra. American military intelligence officials are convinced they had been warned of the forthcoming sweep. In all likelihood, those who decided to betray Hattam and his fedayeen commanders to the United States were also determined to ensure that loyal guerrilla commanders and operatives would not be harmed by the ensuing raid.

Then, on December 17, the bodies of Col. Muhammad Ibrahim al-Omar and Lt. Col. Khalil Ibrahim al-Omar were found in Tikrit, on the banks of the Tigris River not far from where Saddam had been captured. Both had been murdered, execution-style. Prevailing rumors stressed that the Ibrahim brothers were executed by Saddam loyalists because they had betrayed Saddam and their own clan's trust. Significantly, the brothers were not accused of disclosing Saddam's whereabouts to the Americans. The killing of both Ibrahim brothers suggests that Saddam's loyalists took revenge on those responsible for Saddam's predicament and capture.

Lastly, immediately after Saddam's capture was announced, Kurdish intelligence sources affiliated with the KDP insisted that they were responsible for his discovery and capture. The KDP's claim was extremely popular throughout the Sunni heartland and Baghdad, and was repeated by many notables. According to this version of events, at the beginning of the second week of December, KDP intelligence was alerted to Saddam's whereabouts by a member of the local al-Jabour tribe—a tribe considered loyal to the Baathists. However, the daughter of this specific tribesman had been viciously raped by Uday Saddam Hussein, and when the tribesman complained to the authorities, Uday Saddam's fedayeen attacked his family compound, and several members of his extended family were killed while others were arrested, tortured, and ultimately executed. Elders of the al-Jabour tribe then convinced the tribesman to forego further aggravation of the crisis, fearing for the lives of the entire tribe. Now, after so many years, the aggrieved father finally had the opportunity to avenge his humiliation and suffering. With the help of KDP intelligence operatives, the report went, the al-Jabour tribesman arranged for the capture of Saddam at a meeting place between two safe hideaways. Saddam was then drugged and placed in the spider hole, and the U.S. authorities were notified of his whereabouts. While this KDP version contradicts some of the key aspects of Saddam's capture—primarily the achievements of U.S. military intelligence and the Special Forces—the mere fact that it gained such popularity throughout the Sunni heartland and Baghdad is of great significance. This believability reflects the prevailing conviction among the majority of Sunnis that Saddam was indeed betrayed by his own trusted people before he was apprehended. And since the tribal and clannish code of honor makes it difficult to acknowledge, even internally, betrayal for the sake of a power struggle, the legend of an individual tribesman avenging dishonor and killing becomes appealing to many.

The reaction in the Iraqi street and the Arab world to the capture of Saddam Hussein was muted. Saddam had long been a diminishing factor in the Iraqi and Arab sociopolitical posture and power structure. Very few wanted him to return to power, and even fewer expected him to. However, in a society with a strong and obligatory code of honor, there was widespread shock and revulsion over the public humiliation Saddam endured at the hands of the Americans, shown to the whole world on TV. For example, the Muslim *Ulema* Council, the highest Sunni religious authority in Iraq, quickly issued a statement stressing that "former Iraqi President Saddam Hussein committed many mistakes that affected the Iraqi people. However, the way in which Saddam was arrested was a deliberate insult by the United States to Iraq and its people."

When the occupation authorities and the American-sponsored Iraqi leaders continued to publicly insult Saddam—for example, the United States had pictures published in an Iraqi newspaper of Saddam in pajamas sitting on the floor while meeting a properly dressed Ahmad Chalabi sitting on a chair—this revulsion quickly turned into anti-American rage over the flagrant disregard for Iraq's social norms; significantly, these sentiments were as strong among Iraqis and Arabs who considered themselves anti-Saddam and victims of his regime as among Baathists and Saddam's supporters. These public portrayals of Saddam's capture did not earn him any support—some 60 percent of Iraqis are still "happy" he is out of their lives—but elicited tremendous enmity toward the occupation authorities and their Iraqi allies.

American officials were startled by the absence of public gratitude for the removal of Saddam's presence from Iraqi society. This genuine bewilderment reflected the cardinal error of the occupation authorities: The vast majority of Iraqis considered the war a unique opportunity to regain and realize their traditional, religious, and social norms and codes of behavior. For them, the toppling of Saddam was a necessary evil on the path toward building the society of their own choosing—including the possible dismemberment of Iraq or the establishment of a Muslim theocratic state. Most Iraqis believe the United States toppled Saddam because he was an implacable enemy of the Bush administration who denied American hegemony over Iraq's vast oil resources, and not because the United States sought to liberate them. The relentless American effort to impose its own nation-building solution on Iraq is perceived as yet another method of suppressing the people of Iraq in order to control their oil resources and their land.

Thus, the American presentation of Saddam's capture as a key milestone toward the establishment of a U.S.-imposed social and political order has only reaffirmed the prevailing conviction of most Iraqis that there can be no reconciliation with the United States. Indeed, Washington's failure to comprehend the stark distinction between the aspirations of the Iraqi populace and the Bush administrations shoddy plans for a new and democratic Iraqi state has already sown the seeds of American defeat in Iraq. Having failed to see their own ethnocentric aspirations realized by the occupation authorities despite promises of liberation and self-determination for all Iraqis, the people of Iraq are rapidly returning to the fold of the power that, throughout their history, has steadfastly promised salvation and delivered stability and social order—namely, radical Islam. The Iraqi populace, the most socially progressive society in the Arab world, is willingly embracing traditionalist radical Islam as the sole power capable of shielding them against American encroachment, as well as facilitating the humiliation, defeat, and eviction of the hated Americans from their land and lives. The tangible long-term impact of Saddam's capture and public humiliation is not the removal of Saddam's Baathism from Iraqi society, but rather the irreversible perception of the Iraqi populace that they have no option but to embark on a fateful liberating jihad if they want to realize their manifest destiny.

The real milestone in the Iraqi war against the occupation took place in Baghdad on Friday, December 12, a day before the capture of Saddam Hussein. On that day, the Shiite imam of Baghdad, Sayed Ammar al-Husseini, joined the Sunni imam of Baghdad, Sheikh Ahmad Hassan al-Samharay, in conducting a joint Friday prayer at the Sunni Grand Mosque of Baghdad. It was an unprecedented event designed to highlight the singular importance the religious leadership gave to the expansion and deepening of the anti-American struggle. After the prayers, both imams delivered fiery sermons inciting their followers to unite in escalating the anti-American jihad. Imam al-Husseini, who spoke first, warned the believers of the wicked and corrupting influence of the U.S. forces and their culture of democracy. "O Muslims! Beware of what the infidels and the corrupt West are trying to inflict upon the Believers," al-Husseini declared. The audience responded by shouting "No, no to America! No, no to the Satan!" Sheikh al-Samharay, who spoke next, was both more subdued and more practical: He addressed the plight of a society in the midst of a major economic crisis that was being tempted by the lure of highly paying jobs with the occupation authorities. Since the United States, through the intelligence agencies that really constitute the occupation authorities, is working relentlessly to destroy Iraq and Islam, the sheikh continued, it is forbidden to work for the Americans, for it is sacrilegious to assist in any way the anti-Islamic evil forces. It is preferable to remain unemployed and suffering than become part of the grand conspiracy against Islam and Iraq. "Everybody who cooperates with the American spying entities," Sheikh al-Samharay declared, "is actually serving America, and America is serving the Jews!" The crowd chanted once again anti-American and anti-Jewish slogans.

The Islamists were quick to react to Saddam's arrest. On December 14, a couple of hours after it was announced that Saddam was in custody, the leadership of al-Qaeda issued a communiqué reacting to the arrest. In the West, the communiqué was distributed over the signature of "Daleel Almojahed"—the source of some of the more important terrorism warnings in late 2003. "Saddam is down and al-Qaeda is moving up," Daleel Almojahed wrote. With Saddam gone, al-Qaeda argued, the United States would be deprived of the excuse to ignore and conceal the extent of the Islamist jihad in Iraq. "After the capture of the dictator Saddam Hussein, al-Qaeda will now show the Americans who is behind all the attacks. Saddam was a Baath, killed a lot of his people and a lot of Muslims, and this is what God was planning for him and this is the end of every killer and dictator," the communiqué asserted. Daleel Almojahed concluded the communiqué with an explicit threat: "The message we send to the Americans and to Bush and Blair [is] don't be very happy, we promise you that both of you will cry tears very soon, and then, just then, you will know who al-Qaeda really is!"

Arab intellectuals and officials stressed that the impact of Saddam's arrest on the anti-American jihad had to be examined in this context. The Iraqi resistance has always been motivated by a mixture of religious, nationalist, and pragmatic factors as articulated in the sermons issued by Sheikh al-Samharay and Imam al-Husseini. Saddam's removal would serve as a catalyst for the expansion of the resistance, because Baathism could no longer compete with the ascent of the Islamist trend. Moreover, the various ethnic and nationalist groups and individuals who, because they had been victims of Saddam and his regime, stayed out of the anti-American jihad for fear of assisting Saddam's return to power could now feel free to join the conflict.

On December 15, this theme was elucidated by Abdul-Bari Atwan, chief editor of the London *Al-Quds al-Arabi,* in a front-page editorial. "The Iraqi resistance fighters are now free from this 'scarecrow' called Saddam Hussein and are rid of his dictatorial history. They have started to resist for the sake of Iraq, the noble Arab and Islamic Iraq that has the largest assets among the civilizations and in its creativity and defense of the causes of right and justice," Atwan declared. Atwan anticipated a marked escalation in anti-American guerrilla warfare. "President Saddam Hussein's capture . . . might definitely be a curse for the American invaders because the Iraqis, especially those conniving with the occupation, are deeply embarrassed." These Iraqis had justified their absence from the ranks of the resistance "by the fear of Saddam Hussein's return to power. But with what will they justify their position now?"

To that point, Atwan stressed, the Iraqi resistance had surged and expanded because it was motivated and driven by the traditional Islamic and historic values of Arab-Muslim Iraq. Even the shackles that Saddam's Baathism had put on the Iraqi resurgence could not stop its ascent. "The Iraqi resistance has become a culture as well as a creed and strategy. It has become contiguous with the Iraqis' dignity and honor and it definitely will not disappear with Saddam Hussein's capture, for Iraq has always remained larger than the leaders and a bloody bone in the throat of invaders and their allies," Atwan wrote. In the long term, the most important ramification of Saddam's capture was the removal of the last individual with a seemingly legitimate claim to leadership over Iraq. As a result, the guerrilla war would expand to include not only unwavering commitment to the complete eviction of the occupying forces, but also destruction of the vestiges of their presence, ensuring that the future leadership of Iraq would be home-grown and enjoy grassroots legitimacy and support. "The future Iraq will not be built by those who arrived aboard the American tanks but by those who have remained committed to their true Arab and Islamic identity and refused to be tools in the hands of the U.S.-Israeli occupation of their country. These will definitely appear soon to lead the new Iraq and bring to account all those who have conspired against it and collaborated with its enemies," Atwan concluded. And the

forthcoming marked escalation in the Iraqi jihad would deliver this outcome, he predicted.

The Iraqi resistance, particularly the Baathist nationalist trend, was
quick to react to Saddam's capture with vows to continue the war while es-
pousing all-Iraqi nationalist themes rather than a reiteration of Saddam's
Baathism. The first to react was the "Iraqi Resistance Movement." Only
hours after Saddam's capture was announced, the movement used Iranian
channels to put Saddam's arrest in the context of the overall struggle. Saddam's arrest and the ensuing TV spectacle were "a show in the service of
the American elections. . . . Everybody will now find out that the resistance
is not carried out for the benefit of the one on the throne, and it will therefore persevere, whatever the sacrifices, until the expulsion of the last
infidel-occupier from Iraq," the group's communiqué declared. "Those
who feared Saddam and justified their acceptance [of the presence] of the
American-British enemy in his [Saddam's] presence—must immediately
launch [armed] resistance or else they will be considered traitors." The
leadership of the Baath Party in Iraq quickly reacted with its own communiqué in which it urged all Iraqis to join the all-Iraqi struggle "to expel the
occupation forces, liberate Iraq, and keep it united and the homeland for
all Iraqis." It was a December 19 communiqué of the "Higher Command of
the Iraqi Resistance and Liberation Committee" that first suggested the
continuity of the resistance despite Saddam's capture. The communiqué
announced that "Izzat Ibrahim al-Durri was designated acting for former
Iraqi president Saddam Hussein," in accordance with prewar emergency
procedures. The communiqué also asserted that the capture of Saddam
would have little impact on the escalating guerrilla war. "President Saddam
Hussein had prepared extremely important plans that were to be implemented in case of his martyrdom or capture, and this means that he was
prepared for every emergency," the communiqué explained. The next day,
Izzat Ibrahim al-Durri issued his own first statement, warning the occupation authorities that they would be held accountable for Saddam's life and
well-being. Izzat reiterated that the command of the Baath Party designated him as Saddam's interim "vicar." Echoing the prevailing opinion
throughout the Arab world, Izzat also considered Saddam's capture "an incentive and a motivation for escalating the resistance until the occupation
forces are expelled out of Iraq."

However, at the end, it was the seemingly unstoppable collapse of the
Iraqi economy, the rampant unemployment, and the profound disappoint-
ment in the U.S.-dominated political process that drove most Iraqis into

the fold of radical Islam, militant nationalism, and armed jihad. And the overall situation in Iraq had been sharply deteriorating since November, fueling the bitterness, despair, and hostility of most Iraqis. Iraq's economy was stagnant and would have collapsed had it not been for an infusion of cash. Senior Iraqi officials warned that the absence of security prevented any hope of economic stabilization and recovery. Rather than address these mundane issues, the U.S. authorities decided to effect, in Paul Bremer's words, "a transition in the reconstruction effort, from a phase of emergency repairs to the longer-term development of new infrastructure and democratic institutions." But the overall situation continued to deteriorate, the sabotage of the Iraqi national infrastructure intensified, and public hostility grew.

Rather than acknowledge responsibility for the dire state of affairs, the occupation authorities blamed their hand-picked Governing Council for its failure to gain acceptance in a hostile Iraq. Washington was so alarmed by the failure of the council members to rise above the pursuit of their own personal political and economic interests that the administration began considering "possible alternatives" to the council. "We're unhappy with all of them. They're not acting as a legislative or governing body, and we need to get moving," a well-placed official told the *Washington Post*. "They just don't make decisions when they need to." American officials now acknowledged that the council had "less credibility today than it did when it was appointed, which has further undermined Iraq's stability."

In mid-November, Washington had announced that the United States would withdraw from Iraq by July 1, 2004, by which time there would be, in the words of President Bush, a "free and democratic society" in Iraq, serving as "a model for the rest of the Middle East." Officials hastened to clarify that the American commitment to a speedy withdrawal did not include the American military presence, which they expected to continue for several years. To divert attention from, and reduce the power of the Governing Council, the United States committed to "prompt elections," which would in turn increase the legitimacy of any interim authority in Baghdad.

But Iraq's demographic reality—the Shiite majority—had to be addressed. Hence, explained a senior British official in Baghdad, the United States decided on "the initial ballot [that] is not likely to meet the one-man-one-vote criterion in order to ensure that Iraq's Shia majority cannot dictate the new constitution." In response, the most conservative Shiite clerics, led by Ayatollah Ali Hussein al-Sistani, issued a series of fatwas demanding that the prospective constitution adhere to the principle of one-man-one-vote. "But the United States, along with more liberal members of the [Governing Council], fears that such an election so soon would produce a body dominated by the majority Shia, which would draw up a theocratic constitution," explained the British official. A tense political impasse emerged in response, in which the entire Shiite community—two thirds of Iraq's population—saw itself, not without reason, prevented from assuming political power.

However, the continued intensification of the guerrilla warfare and the growing alienation of the Iraqi population left the Bush administration with no alternative to hastening its political exit from Iraq before a full-fledged popular uprising erupted. There was no turning back from the announced decision "to return sovereignty to the Iraqis" by July 1, 2004. At the same time, the United States had to protect itself against any election-related complications, which would lead to a squabble with the Shiite elite. As a result, the administration rearranged its political priorities in Iraq to suit the exit schedule. Under the new American strategy, the occupation authority would first hand over power to an interim Iraqi government that would subsequently oversee the writing of a constitution and the holding of national elections—most likely in the form of town meetings or provincial elections—that would prevent the Shiites from coming to power. To ensure the legitimacy of the new future government and symbolize a clean break from the U.S.-sponsored authority, the U.S. authorities announced in November that the Iraqi Governing Council would dissolve itself before the establishment of the government. Within ten days, the key council members announced that they would stay on. The council now resolved to transform itself to an unelected upper body of parliament modeled after the British House of Lords. Although officials were quick to disassociate themselves from this idea, the Shiite elite was convinced that the occupation authorities were behind this initiative as yet another measure to stifle the Shiite ascent to power through democratic means.

During the first weeks of December, the Bush administration in Washington and the occupation authorities in Baghdad launched several initiatives to gain support and legitimacy from various segments of the Iraqi elite for complex mechanisms for the handing over of power to sovereign Iraqi authorities before July. While the U.S.-nominated Iraqi leaders would hear nothing about plans that would adversely affect their grip on power and wealth, the rest of the Iraqi elite would accept no solution that had Washington's stamp of approval and that involved the continued presence of the U.S. military in Iraq. The Bush administration asked various Arab governments to intercede with the Iraqi elite, only to be told that the Arab world was in full support of the Iraqis and adamantly opposed to America's enduring presence in Iraq.

With violence escalating despite the capture of Saddam Hussein, the administration decided to abandon some of its more ambitious initiatives—to privatize the Iraqi economy, democratize the political system, and establish security forces under civilian control—and instead concentrated on accelerating the process of handing over power from the occupation authority to an Iraqi government with a semblance of legitimacy. Washington also gave up on having an Iraqi constitution written and ratified before the transfer of sovereignty. "There's no question that many of the big-picture items have been pushed down the list or erased completely," a senior U.S. official told the *Washington Post*. "Right now, everyone's attention is focused [on] doing what we need to do to hand over sovereignty by next summer." The official further clarified that "ideology has become subordinate to the schedule."

By late December, the vast majority of the Iraqi public was increasingly hostile toward the occupation authorities because of the overall deterioration of the everyday situation in Iraq. A survey of the conditions in Iraq by Harry de Quetteville of the London *Telegraph* portrayed a very grim picture. Security remained "the most pressing issue for Iraqis," as the level of violent crimes reached a scale that all Iraqis insisted "would have been inconceivable under Saddam Hussein." With the majority of crimes going unreported, even the partial and incomplete statistics suggested that the serious crime level had more than tripled compared with prewar levels. The U.S.-organized Iraqi police were commonly mistrusted and considered a pathetic joke by most Iraqis. The production of electricity was still "hovering around two thirds of the pre-war level," and was not expected to satisfy the country's full needs before spring 2005, provided that sabotage of the national infrastructure ceased. Although Iraq had the world's second biggest oil reserves, virtually all the fuel and gas were imported. And still, the U.S. authorities had so far failed to establish a secure supply of fuel, imposing instead unrealistic 30-liter quotas and limiting drivers to buying fuel only every other day.

In the face of acute shortages, a black market selling fuel stolen by the resistance was flourishing, signaling dire security ramifications. Although doctors and nurses were better paid by the occupation authority, the public health sector was in disarray due to an acute shortage of modern equipment and supplies. The enduring legacy of the decade-long embargo was felt in the medical sector, and viable solutions were nowhere in sight. Mortality rates for children and the elderly remained high. Education could have been the American success story, as considerable funds and resources were earmarked for rebuilding the country's educational infrastructure, establishing computer labs and Internet networks, and markedly raising the pay of teachers in order to attract and retain the best. However, the heavy-handed "de-Baathification" and "de-Saddamization" campaigns were so similar in their basic character to the cultist campaigns of the previous regime that they tended to shatter the belief of both students and teachers in America's good intentions. Perhaps the most alarming statistic emanating from Iraq in December was the unabated climb of the unemployment rate, as it neared and passed 60 percent, and the percentage continues to grow. The undeclared unemployment rate—that is, the figure arrived at when taking into consideration the *shabab* loitering in the streets and the multitude of young men involved in the resistance—is estimated to be somewhere around 80 percent.

The bitterness and despair that follow as a consequence of rampant joblessness cultivate fertile ground for recruitment by all resistance and terrorist groups. And the occupation authorities have every reason to be alarmed by the brewing grassroots turmoil in Iraq. Several opinion polls conducted in December tallied disturbing, though not surprising, results; although these polls are not infallibly accurate, they do point to clear trends. Of the issues worrying the average Iraqi, the vast majority of them consider personal security the most unsettling; the acute shortages of oil and electricity are a close second; and the establishment of a post-Saddam Iraq a distant third. Asked to elaborate on the character of the future Iraq they would like to live in, the majority of Iraqis insist on a country governed by laws based on the Shariah and free of all vestiges of American occupation and influence.

It is these genuine grassroots aspirations that have long been the driving force behind the guerrilla war, and they remained the main reason for the surge in the war immediately before and after the arrest of Saddam Hussein. Initially, the various guerrilla organizations continued to carry out operations already in the pipeline—demonstrating in the process that the capture of Saddam had no impact on them. The first attack in this wave took place on December 14 in Khaldiyah a few hours before the United States announced Saddam's capture. A martyr bomber detonated a large car bomb near the local police station, killing at least twenty and wounding close to fifty—most of them Iraqi policemen. On the next day, December 15, two more car bombs exploded near Baghdad-area police stations. The first martyr bomber exploded his car bomb in the Husseiniya neighborhood, killing eight and wounding more than twenty—again, most of them policemen. Shortly afterward, another martyr bomber detonated a car bomb in the Amariyah suburb but only wounded twelve. A third car bomb was found and safely neutralized in central Baghdad after the would-be martyr failed to detonate it and escaped from the scene. On December 17, a major strike went awry. A would-be bomber was accelerating a huge truck bomb toward a police station in al-Bayaa, a poor neighborhood in southwest Baghdad, when a bus crossed his path. He could not avoid a collision. At least fifteen Iraqis were killed and over thirty were wounded in the huge fireball that the explosion ignited.

These bombings came on top of the continued expansion of the now "routine" guerrilla warfare. The numbers of the daily roadside bombs, ambushes, mortar and rocket barrages, derailings of cargo trains, and burnings of trucks and tankers, as well as the sabotage of oil and national infrastructure, continued to rise. More pipelines and storage tanks were burning on average than in previous months, causing further damage to the economy and unemployment. All of these actions also inflicted greater numbers of casualties upon U.S. forces. Ultimately, the ongoing violence prevented any chance of furthering normalization and pacification throughout Iraq. There was also an upsurge in assassinations of former Baathist activists, Shiite clerics refusing to toe the line, and leaders and activists of feuding clans and parties. By late 2003 there were dozens of such killings every day, on average. Given the honor code of Iraqi society, these killings also prompted cycles of blood revenge that further fed the slaughter.

And as 2003 ended, a terrorist offensive began, just as Saddam had promised. Significantly, however, the onslaught was perpetrated by the reinvigorated countrywide and all-Iraqi broad alliance of Islamists and Baathists, and not by remnants of Saddam's loyalists. The Christmas to New Years offensive started on December 24 with a spate of ambushes and roadside bombs against U.S. patrols and convoys. In Samarra, one of these bombs hit a vehicle, killing three soldiers. As well, several bombs were detonated against government-related buildings in the Kurdish and Shiite zones—including a major explosion in the Kurdish city of Irbil, which luckily caused few fatalities. Just before the dawn of Christmas Day, central

Baghdad was subjected to heavy attacks of grenade, rocket, and mortar fire. The targets included several hotels, two banks, several embassies, and an army base. During the night, there was a second round of mortar and rocket shelling—this time aimed at central Baghdad and the "Green Zone." The next day the resistance shelled a base northeast of Baghdad, killing two American soldiers.

The most significant attack took place on December 27 in Qarbalah. Martyr bombers detonated four car bombs throughout the city, heavily damaging the main Polish-Bulgarian garrison, the city hall building housing the U.S.-nominated governor, the main police station, and the university. The bombings caused more than twenty fatalities, including Bulgarian and Thai soldiers, and well over a hundred wounded, including American troops. Rescue and reaction forces were then attacked by machine-gun fire as they rushed to the scene of the explosions. At least five U.S. troops were wounded in this phase. Simultaneously, American and coalition military bases in the area were attacked by mortars, further complicating their ability to react to the bombings in Qarbalah. For the rest of the day, large crowds kept interfering with the rescue efforts and investigation while sheltering occasional snipers. "It was a coordinated, massive attack planned for a big scale and intended to do much harm," said Maj. Gen. Andrzej Tyszkiewicz, commander of the Polish-led multinational force responsible for the area around Qarbalah. It was a highly professional operation covering the entire city, involving hundreds of direct participants and thousands of supporters. Still, U.S. intelligence did not receive a single warning—a manifestation of the population's support for the escalation in the war. Thus, the strike succeeded in shattering the myth of cooperation in the region.

On New Year's Eve, a large martyr-driven car bomb exploded at the entrance of a restaurant in central Baghdad that was frequented by foreigners and Westernized Iraqis. The restaurant was destroyed in the middle of the New Year celebrations, with the attendees suffering eight fatalities and thirty wounded. Concurrently, regular guerrilla warfare continued at a higher pitch with ambushes and roadside bombs, including the shooting down of an OH-58D over Fallujah.

The overall significance of the war in Iraq to the jihadist movement and the emerging trends in the Islamist jihad were articulated in December by Osama bin Laden and his top leaders. Most significant was a new audiotape of Ayman al-Zawahiri, which was broadcast by Al-Jazeera TV on Friday, December 19. Zawahiri was upbeat about the unfolding jihad. Accumulating combat experience since September 2001, he stressed, had confirmed that American soldiers were cowards "with no faith in their leaders." Indeed, Zawahiri said, al-Qaeda was "pursuing the Americans and their allies everywhere, even in their own backyard." Most important were the jihad theaters "in Afghanistan, in Iraq, in Palestine, and in the Arab Peninsula." Discussing Iraq, Zawahiri declared that "America has been defeated [by] our fighters despite all its military might, its weaponry." Zawahiri considered the Islamist strikes since the fall of 2003 a turning point in the Islamist jihad in Iraq, asserting that "the American hemorrhage has started in Iraq; the American have become unable to defend themselves and not even their senior criminals, such as Wolfowitz, the arrogant Zionist." Zawahiri's message was followed a week later by an e-mail message from Abu-Muhammad al-Ablaj, a senior al-Qaeda leader, to the London-based Saudi weekly *Al-Majallah*. Ablaj devoted most of his communication to warning about forthcoming massive attacks on American territory, which bin Laden would use to announce the next phase of the fateful jihad. "Bin Laden will also reaffirm al-Qaeda's determination to continue its war against America, until its defeat," said Ablaj's message. He then stressed that the escalation of the jihad in the Middle East, particularly in Saudi Arabia and Iraq, would be a key facilitator of the forthcoming spectacular strikes at the heart of the United States. "We are benefiting from the situation that is prevailing in the region, and our calculations for the fatal strike deep inside U.S. territories are based on the continuity of this chaos and its intensification in the region," Ablaj stated.

However, while al-Qaeda was clearly the most prominent, articulate, and authoritative source of ideological guidance, the Islamist jihad in Iraq was being waged by a growing number of localized Islamist groups with distinct ideological characters but close operational cooperation when striking outside their immediate theaters of operation. These groups also provided localized support for the numerous expert terrorist cells—comprising both Iraqi and foreign mujahedin—inserted and controlled by bin Laden's senior on-site commanders. Some veteran Islamist groups continue their Islamist jihad in the framework of this web despite repeated clashes with American forces. Most notable among them are the Iraqi-Islamist Muhammad's Army and the National Islamic Resistance Movement, as well as the bin Laden–affiliated Brigades of Martyr Abdallah Azzam, which also has close relations with such Palestinian groups as HAMAS and Munir al-Maqdah's forces in southern Lebanon. Among the leading new groups making up this Islamist web are Ansar al-Sunnah, with its main following and theological guides hailing from Fallujah and Baquba in the Sunni heartland. Lajnat al-Iman originated in the Mosul area but in the fall expanded operations in and around Baghdad in close cooperation with Islamist operatives from Algeria and Saudi Arabia.

Originally a Kurdish affiliate of al-Qaeda, Ansar al-Islam morphed into an expert terrorist force operating mainly in the Baghdad area. Another growing Islamist force in the Baghdad area is the Ansar al-Iman; in December, Abu Al-Hassan Al-Byati, the alias of the group's strategist and ideologue, spoke for all jihadists when he stated that "the capture of Saddam will make no difference to the resistance" and that the jihad would escalate until the last American left. Ansar al-Iman is a conservative Islamist group with nationalist-leaning ideology that is not affiliated with al-Qaeda. According to Al-Byati, the group includes members of all Iraq's ethnic and religious groups united by their Islamic faith, Iraqi patriotism, and hatred of the United States.

The anti-American jihad is also sustained by small Islamist groups popping up locally throughout Iraq. Led by Islamist veterans of the Iraqi military and security services, these small groups have no formal affiliation with any larger party. Starting in the fall, a growing number of veteran Saddam's Fedayeen and Special Forces commanders who had been active in the ranks of the pro-Saddam Baathist insurgency forces have gravitated to the Islamist trend and joined these localized Islamist groups, bringing with them not only expertise but access to large stockpiles of weapons, explosives, and cash. At the same time, these groups see themselves as ideologically connected to the global network of Osama bin Laden. "Al-Qaeda is an Islamic group and we've learnt from them, and we learnt much from Osama bin Laden. He is our sheikh also," Muhammad, the commander of a small Islamist group in Rutba, told James Hider of the London *Times.* Muhammad and his people will closely and enthusiastically cooperate with any al-Qaeda group asking for their help. Echoing many other Islamist commanders, Muhammad noted that Saddam's capture only stiffened the mujahedin's resolve. "Saddam was our president. Even if he persecuted us, he represented Muslims and Iraq, so we don't accept him being humiliated like this," Muhammad told Hider. His jihad will continue until the establishment of a purely Islamist state in Iraq. "We don't accept that the U.S. should put any government in place, even one made up of Iraqis. They will be ruled by the devil Bush. We will fight until we are martyrs," Muhammad stated.

Such small groups constitute an intelligence nightmare. On the one hand, they are locally recruited, organized, and sustained, and thus unknown to the intelligence community worldwide. On the other hand, they are ideologically committed to the global message of Osama bin Laden and will therefore provide all available support to elite expert terrorists who might show up while preparing to launch a spectacular operation against the United States. And these are not abstract speculations, Iraqi security sources told MENL by December al-Qaeda already had fifteen fully rigged car bombs in Iraq. These vehicles—including trucks and ambulances—were obtained near the Iraqi-Turkish border and constructed in workshops near the Syrian border. Since then, at least eleven ambulances have been stolen from Baghdad, most likely to serve as car bombs. "The idea is for them to be disguised as service vehicles that would not normally be seen as suspicious," an Iraqi security source told MENL's Steve Rodan. "They could include ambulances or even garbage trucks." Moreover, both Baathists and jihadists now offer $25,000 plus a lifetime monthly salary for the family of any martyr bomber. In impoverished Iraq, that is a huge sum that can sustain an extended family.

However, the most important development still ahead is the activation of the elaborate Shiite terrorist infrastructure that has so far been largely dormant. In mid-December, Tehran dispatched Imad Moughniyah, along with a team of HizbAllah and Iranian intelligence experts, to southern Iraq in order to bolster the Shiite forces and organize a new anti-American terrorism campaign. Both Tehran and the Iraqi Shiite leadership expected a major crisis with the occupation authorities to erupt in the spring of 2004, anticipating that America would ignore Shiite demands for empowerment, as articulated in Sistani's "Democracy Fatwas." The Shiite forces were already well organized, trained, funded, and equipped. Several expert terrorists from all over the Shiite Middle East were hiding among them. Moughniyah's task was to prepare these forces for a strategic eruption and be in command of the ensuing guerrilla offensive. That the anticipated time for launching this offensive coincided with the first anniversary of the invasion of Iraq would only serve to heighten passion and anti-American sentiments throughout Iraq. The December 27 eruption in Qarbalah might have been Moughniyah's first test-strike.

Significantly, the Shiite forces, and especially the terrorist elite from Iran and HizbAllah, enjoyed close cooperation with the Kurds of northern Iraq, particularly the Shiite Kurds, who were desperate to get Iranian support against the growing Turkish encroachment. Increasingly frustrated with the American refusal to honor what the Kurdish elite considered its promises and guarantees for de facto Kurdish independence, the Kurds were now contemplating joining the Shiites in an all-out violent confrontation with the United States over the future of Iraq.

By the end of 2003, American tactical achievements against the Sunni Baathist forces, made possible through the successful adoption of Israeli-style tactics and combat experience, had seen the conflict evolve into a guerrilla war of attrition in the Sunni heartland and the Baghdad area. In this area, the U.S. forces were able to destroy several major Baathist force groupings and capture numerous generals and senior security officials of the Saddam Hussein regime. However, strategically, the United States was still fighting the past war in Iraq—chasing the ghosts of long-gone conflicts rather than proactively and preemptively confronting the next phase of the fateful jihad for the control of Iraq and the entire Arab Muslim world. The United States was fixated on destroying the 5,000 or so Baathist fighters while largely neglecting the far greater jihadist forces that, according to Arab and Islamist sources, were already anywhere from 20,000 to 50,000 soldiers strong and growing. The repeated failure of American intelligence to prevent the surprise launching of terrorist offensives in Iraq did not bode well for the future, as the new jihadist forces were far better trained and more disciplined than the proSaddam Baathists.

However, the cardinal error of the Bush administration—an error that might ultimately determine the fate of the American endeavor in Iraq—is Washington's abject failure to address and comprehend the profound transformation the Iraqi populace, in its entire ethnic and national tapestry, has undergone since American forces entered Baghdad. The enduring failure of the occupation authorities to normalize life in Iraq has bolstered the grassroots withdrawal into religious and ethnic social frameworks that are inherently and uncompromisingly anti-American. And this profound transformation of society breeds the growing popular support for and empowerment of the escalating guerrilla warfare. Fixated as it is with the struggle against the remnants of Saddam's regime, the Bush administration is missing this crucial development.

In early December, Washington continued to insist that the Iraqi resistance was small and dying. "Real insurgents need the support of the local population, and they don't have that," a senior civilian aide to Donald Rumsfeld told *Time* magazine. "They are going to wither and die. The question is how long it will take." While this observation might be true regarding some of the Baathist forces, it is patently wrong regarding the rapidly growing Baathist nationalist and myriad Islamist forces. Indeed, by the end of 2003, relying on a widening and deepening popular base, the jihadists were immersed in a large-scale recruitment and training program both in-country and throughout the Muslim world. The flow of volunteers into Iraq was growing—with numerous expert terrorists and veteran guerrilla leaders assuming command in Iraq. And while the Bush administration is closely watching the clock, desperate to finish the job by July 1, 2004, the Islamists' historic jihad has hardly even begun. And therein lie the roots of a grim future in Iraq.

CONCLUSION

In early 2004, at the time of this writing, the war in Iraq was only in its initial phase, with the indigenous resistance to the occupation, and American efforts to mold a future Iraq, only in their fledgling states. While attention was focused on the escalating war and terrorism in the Sunni heartland, Iraq's other four major population communities—Shiites, Sunni nomadic tribes, Kurds, and Turkman—were still relatively quiet while actively preparing for waging their own wars against the United States. These communities already had powerful, growing militias and were hastily reinforcing them. To date, their respective leaderships do not consider the vital interests of their communities sufficiently threatened to warrant hostilities with the United States, but that impression may change, as reflected in the mounting threats of Shiite-led violence from Ayatollah Sistani, or the Kurds' intense rearmament, including the acquisition of dozens of T-72 tanks and artillery pieces from Syria. This state of affairs is a far cry from—indeed a flagrant contradiction of—the situation the Bush administration anticipated in postwar Iraq when embarking on the war with Saddam Hussein. But this sorry state of affairs need not surprise, given the logic behind the American decision to go to war.

The United States embarked on Operation Iraqi Freedom not only to rid the world of one of its most dangerous dictators, but primarily to announce to the world the message of the new American Internationalism, or as it is more commonly known, the Bush Doctrine. Lawrence F. Kaplan and William Kristol articulated this principal case for the war in their 2002 book, *The War Over Iraq: Saddam's Tyranny and America's Mission*:

> The [American] mission begins in Baghdad, but it does not end there. Were the United States to retreat after victory into compla-

cency and self-absorption, as it did the last time it went to war in Iraq, new dangers would soon arise. Preventing this outcome will be a burden, of which war in Iraq represents but the first installment. But America cannot escape its responsibility for maintaining a decent world order. The answer to this challenge is the American idea itself, and behind it the unparalleled military and economic strength of its custodian. Duly armed, the United States can act to secure its safety and to advance the cause of liberty—in Baghdad and beyond.

Given the turbulence of the early twenty-first century and the prevailing uncertainties in the aftermath of both the Cold War and September 11, it is imperative for the United States to authoritatively state its role in the world; and to be taken seriously, Washington must substantiate such declarations with action. Washington had to demonstrate its resolve to act unilaterally, at times preemptively, in pursuit of policies the United States deemed crucial to its security. The war in Iraq served this purpose admirably.

Militarily, victory was never in doubt, given the disparity between American hyperpower and an emaciated Iraq; that the United States would conquer Iraq was only a question of time and price. Indeed, the unprecedented effectiveness and accuracy of its airpower left no doubt about American omnipotence. Moreover, the suspect military intelligence the United States acted upon did not upend the effort, despite its inaccuracies. As noted by several commanders, the quality of intelligence they received ranged from information enabling tactical excellence to poor analyses allowing for strategic failure.

The U.S. Army's first official history of the Iraq war concluded that there was virtually no reliable intelligence on Iraqi plans for the defense of Baghdad. "Intelligence officers at all echelons continued to have great difficulty accurately describing the threat in the city," the study concluded. But at the end, the sheer might of the military decided the engagement. This state of affairs is defined by John Keegan in his 2003 book, *Intelligence in War:* "Foreknowledge is no protection against disaster. Even real-time intelligence is never real enough. Only force finally counts." Thus, ultimately, the march on Baghdad, with all its imperfections, clearly delivered the message of Washington's resolve to friends and foes alike.

The goals of the first phase of the war accurately addressed America's security concerns, and, accordingly, what's good for America. But the framers of the new American Internationalism also sought to unilaterally determine what's good for the vanquished. Washington hoped that Iraq could become the first Arab democracy once "liberated" by U.S. forces. Noble as this objective is, it completely ignores the endemic problems of the Muslim world and Islam's millennia of bitter struggle against the encroachment of Westernization and modernity, and herein lie America's dangerous arrogance of power—the messianic belief that deep down everybody around the world wants to be like us, and that it is America's destiny and in its self-interest to make this happen. Moreover, the conviction of the devotees of the new American Internationalism was so strong that they failed to adequately prepare for the possibility that most Iraqis would consider themselves occupied and reject the lure of democratization. But this is exactly what happened, and the disparity between America's noble intentions and the grim reality in Iraq now threatens to reverse the great achievements of the American march on Baghdad, not only in Iraq but throughout the Muslim world.

This need not have happened. In Washington and among the allies there has been plenty of evidence to indicate that the administration had erred in its reading of the situation in Iraq and the Middle East at large, and many have tried to relay their concerns to the White House. But these warnings, as well as the threat assessments and intelligence analysis they were based on, were soundly ignored in Washington because their conclusions and ramifications fit neither the convictions of the Bush White House nor the conventional understanding of the American intelligence community. The war in Iraq is thus a story of interaction between a convinced, strong-willed administration and an emaciated, ignorant, but still arrogant intelligence community—both of whom were so self-confident that they would not stop to reexamine their basic assumptions, despite widespread indications that they had misread the strategic situation. The immense perils in such a relationship lie not in the mere existence of a strong commitment to a policy by an administration, but in the horrendous ramifications of an administration's unwillingness to consider adapting its objectives in accordance with the proclivities of other nations and regions, and the inability of the intelligence community to deliver pertinent, comprehensive, and relevant analysis regarding these regions and the world as a whole.

In the case of the crisis and war in Iraq, both trends reached extremes, to the detriment of the U.S. national interest. The Bush administration was adamant about not only toppling Saddam Hussein, but also using postwar Iraq to establish a precedent for the entire Arab and Muslim world to see and adopt. American intelligence agencies were, and still are, so ignorant of the intricacies of the Muslim world that they were incapable of making a convincing case for just how flawed, just how unrealistic the administration's perception of the situation and trends in Iraq really was. And in this kind of relationship the onus is on the intelligence community, because no matter how skewed the objectives of any administration might be, it is incumbent upon the intelligence community to provide the president with objective data and pertinent analysis to influence his decisions. The U.S. intelligence community, quite simply, did not warn the Bush administration about the pitfalls of Iraq. "It is very hard to see [the prewar analysis on Iraq] as anything but a failure in terms of the specifics that [the CIA] provided," Richard J. Kerr, former deputy director of the CIA, who investigated the agency's prewar analysis of Iraq, told the *Los Angeles Times*. The American debacle in Iraq is therefore not the result of conspiracies and bureaucratic manipulations hatched by the "neo-cons," or any other cabal, within the Bush administration, but first and foremost the result of a generation of crippling emaciation of the intelligence agencies—particularly as it regards human intelligence/open-source intelligence on-site presence, and open-minded analysis—coming home to roost. The massive funding and undeniable zeal committed to U.S. intelligence operations in the aftermath of September 11 and the ensuing declaration of the war on terrorism cannot, and indeed did not, counterbalance the decades of abuse and neglect of the U.S. intelligence community. The morass in Iraq is therefore an accurate manifestation of the systemic failure, if not outright collapse, of American intelligence.

Postwar Iraq—the commonly used euphemism for the Iraq aflame since the fall of Saddam's statue—is the true reflection of this intelligence failure. However, in early 2004, Washington and the media were fixated on another aspect of the colossal intelligence failure—the WMD saga—mainly because of the dire political ramifications for the Bush administration and the contentious elections of 2004. Although a minor issue by comparison, the issue of whether Saddam Hussein did in fact possess weapons of mass destruction cannot be ignored, and the issue has two distinct components—the quest for Saddam's WMD production facilities, and the verification of Iraq's unconventional operational capabilities.

The futile search for Iraq's WMD production facilities has already created a major and unnecessary political crisis, because had the Bush administration acknowledged its own failure to heed intelligence and expert advice, as well as the horrific failure of U.S. intelligence, it could also have provided a credible explanation for the inability to find these facilities and thus saved itself the lingering controversy. Leading into the war, the CIA and other agencies provided the Bush administration with profoundly wrong intelligence that, in turn, compelled the White House to create false expectations where there should not have been any. That the various search teams did not turn up any evidence of major WMD production facilities is not surprising because the United States had long known that Saddam moved virtually all production capabilities to Libya and Sudan somewhere between 1996 and 1998. Subsequently, in the summer of 2002, with Tehran's consent, the residual chemical weapons production capabilities were shipped to Iran, where they were first stored in two clusters of tunnels under the Zagros Mountains near Kermanshah, some 15 to 20 miles from the Iraqi border (near Baba-Abbas and Khorram-Abbad, and near Harour), and, on the eve of the war, transferred to Lavizan, near Tehran.

The evidence on all these transfers was overwhelming and timely. For example, on February 10, 1998, the Task Force on Terrorism and Unconventional Warfare of the U.S. House of Representatives issued a report titled "The Iraqi WMD Challenge—Myths and Reality." The report stressed the difference between Iraq's operational arsenal and production capacity, saying:

> Despite Baghdad's protestations, Iraq does have a small but very lethal operational arsenal of WMD and platforms capable of delivering them throughout the Middle East and even beyond. . . . Significantly, however, even if the U.S. and its allies will have managed to destroy the bulk of Saddam's WMD operational arsenal, this will provide only a short-term solution. No bombing campaign against Iraq, and even an occupation of that country for that matter, is capable of destroying the hard core of Saddam Hussein's primary WMD development and production programs. The reason is that under current conditions these programs are run outside of Iraq—mainly in Sudan and Libya, as well as Algeria (storage of some hot nuclear stuff).

Thus, the mere fact that a highly publicized search for major WMD production units was attempted after the war is indicative of the absence of corporate memory in the U.S. intelligence community. This is a colossal failure of intelligence that subjected the Bush administration to an unnecessary political embarrassment and humiliation.

The main reason for this debacle is that the American intelligence community refused to take into consideration other people's opinions and analysis, whether they be individual experts or foreign intelligence services. At times, the outcome of this penchant was embarrassing; the case of the Iraqi WMD-equipped UAV is a good example. In fall 2002, the intelligence community informed the White House of a major new discovery, namely, that Iraq was developing a WMD-equipped UAV capable of reaching America's coasts from ships at sea. The Bush administration immediately sought to capitalize on this hot new intelligence to generate additional support for the forthcoming war. Glenn Kessler and Walter Pincus of the *Washington Post* captured the melodramatic particulars of the administration's handling of the UAV issue in their February 1, 2004, story. "The information was so startling that CIA Director George J. Tenet, accompanied by Vice President Cheney, marched up to Capitol Hill to brief the four top Senate and House leaders the day after Labor Day, 2002. . . . In the briefing, Tenet and Cheney presented what one participant described as a 'smoking gun': New intelligence showed Iraq had developed unmanned airborne vehicles . . . that could deliver chemical or biological agents. In addition, Iraq had sought software that would allow it to produce sophisticated mapping of eastern U.S. cities." As expected, the briefing had a galvanizing effect on several senators and congressmen. In a January 2004 hearing, Sen. Bill Nelson (D-Florida) noted that it was the UAV data that persuaded him to vote for the war. "I was told not only that [Saddam had WMD] and that he had the means to deliver them through unmanned aerial vehicles, but that he had the capability of transporting those UAVs outside of Iraq and threatening the homeland here in America, specifically by putting them on ships off the eastern seaboard," Senator Nelson said. "I thought there was an imminent threat." The truthfulness of this warning has since been questioned by some of the administration's opponents on the basis of the absence of supporting evidence.

However, while the Tenet-Cheney briefing was largely factually correct, it contained very little new information. During the mid-1990s, the BND (German foreign intelligence) presented American and other allied intelligence services with extensive material about the Iraqi UAV development program. The February 10, 1998, Task Force Report noted that:

Iraq has even more effective and lethal platforms for the delivery of its weapons of mass destruction. In December 1996, German intelligence confirmed that Iraqi weapons technicians developed a drone described as "the little guy's cruise missile." This unmanned aircraft is made of plastics and plywood—simple and cheap to produce without any telltale equipment that can attract the UN inspectors. The drone has a range of about 700 kilometers and is equipped with a very accurate GPS navigation system illegally purchased in the West. Each drone can carry 30 to 40 kilograms of biological or chemical warfare agents to the intended target. It is almost impossible to detect this drone by radar because of its size, slow speed and lack of metal parts.

The BND's experts are most alarmed by Iraq's ability to field a version of this drone that can be also launched from ships. Consequently, one cannot rule out the possibility of an Iraqi-controlled commercial ship suddenly launching these drones outside the coasts of Europe—from where these missiles can reach and threaten London, Paris or Berlin—as well as the Atlantic coast of the US.

Nevertheless, in fall 2002, the Bush administration was genuinely startled when the CIA discovered the UAV's existence. Ultimately, the absence of corporate memory in the intelligence community, coupled with the disdain for "outside information," not only caused the Bush administration to skew—albeit unintentionally—its intelligence and threat presentation to the congressional leadership, but also deprived the administration of the supportive evidence it badly needed when the accuracy of the UAV claim was subsequently challenged.

The second aspect of the WMD imbroglio—the question of Saddam's operational capabilities—is far more serious. In February 2003, the United States committed to war with Iraq with very little knowledge of Iraqi intent to use WMD. In June 25, 2003, testimony to the Senate Armed Services Committee, Gen. John P. Abizaid stated that U.S. intelligence regarding Iraq's WMD was "perplexingly incomplete." American conclusions were based on information gathered through national technical means and, given the absence of comprehensive human intelligence capabilities, an overreliance on Iraqi opposition sources, whose information was dubious and who had a vested interest in skewing the data. On the eve of the war, Saddam Hussein did have a small but operational arsenal sufficient to meet the demands of Iraq's contingency plans, which could have been pressed into service in an offensive war with the United States and Israel, and especially in the event that Iraq was losing such a war.

Iraq's commitment to the use of WMD in the case of a defensive war was less strong, because some of Saddam's lieutenants warned that large-scale casualties among Iraqi Arabs (as distinct from Kurds) as a result of indiscriminate use of WMD munitions in urban environments might lead to a revolt against the regime. Once Saddam decided to adopt the defensive strategy, the majority of the weapons and incriminating evidence were either sent abroad or buried in the sand. U.S. intelligence failed to comprehend this dynamic and is therefore searching for evidence in the wrong places and interrogating the wrong people. Under these conditions, the key to finding the operational WMD still in Iraq lies with individuals who know the locations of the clandestine stockpiles, but they are afraid or unwilling to cooperate because of the prevalent assassination and intimidation campaigns against "traitors," as well as America's indiscriminate, hypocritical de-Baathification campaign. There is no incentive for confidence in or cooperation with the United States. By contrast, many inside the administration have long maintained the idle hope that Ahmed Chalabi's supporters in Iraq would stand in line and deliver all the weapons and evidence of their own volition as part of building a new democratic Iraq.

But although highlighted in the media and of immense political consequence for the administration as the president runs for reelection, the apparent absence of WMD munitions in Iraq demonstrates only one aspect of a comprehensive intelligence blunder, namely, the inability to account for the full extent of Saddam's arsenal, which was hidden both before and immediately after the war. The United States still does not know what happened to the bulk of Iraq's combat aircraft, tanks, and artillery pieces, let alone small arms and sabotage equipment.

There is an excellent and objective benchmark for the Iraqi operational arsenal—the massive parade of January 1, 2002. On that day, Saddam oversaw the two largest military parades since the first Gulf War. The first was a popular parade of battalions of mujahedin and volunteers to liberate Palestine, and the second was a show of conventional military might. Well over a thousand tanks and several hundred armored fighting vehicles and artillery pieces, along with an assortment of ballistic and antiaircraft missiles, rumbled through the Grand Festivities Square of Baghdad for more than four hours. Throughout, formations of jet fighters flew and helicopter gunships hovered over central Baghdad. Intelligence officials and journalists from several countries were on hand to record the quantities of weapons systems paraded; but by 2004, only a small fraction of these weapons had been accounted for, let alone recovered. Had the American intelligence agencies been functioning properly, the besieged Bush administration could have viewed this inexplicable situation as a blessing in disguise. There is no doubt the missing weapons systems existed, as they were seen on parade just a little over a year before the war. Still, they vanished as if—and actually because—the earth had swallowed them. It stands to reason that America's inability to discover WMD weaponry does not necessarily mean these weapons did not exist. Simply put, U.S. intelligence is woefully bad at extracting information from Saddam's loyalists, who know where the Iraqi arsenal—both conventional weapons and WMD munitions—has been hidden.

As of early 2004, the WMD saga was far from over and, in Washington, increasingly out of touch with reality. On the one hand, there is a bitter political war about what was really known on the eve of the war and whether the administration, as well as the Blair government, misled the public by juicing intelligence and threat analysis. Both governments presented the threat in the best way they could, but officials in the United Kingdom and the United States frequently made statements that were inaccurate, because their intelligence services knew very little and lacked corporate memory. Part of the problem was that in pursuit of their own political objectives, both intelligence communities told their respective national leaders what they thought both Bush and Blair wanted to hear.

Opposing politicians and the media have used the failure to discover WMD as a political weapon against the administration, but the real culprits are in the intelligence communities. There is no denying that on the eve of the war, American intelligence agencies provided inaccurate information and misleading analysis and created false expectations; in fact even before the agencies adapted their findings in accordance with the political climate, the intelligence community had gotten its facts and its analysis wrong.

There are many questions about the inner workings of the American intelligence community that still require satisfactory answers; no explanation has been given for the lack of corporate memory in the CIA, for why so many good and proven sources were ignored and why so many unreliable sources were embraced. Furthermore, how did the auditing and quality control mechanism that is supposed to prevent the skewing and tainting of intelligence fail so miserably?

And now, fear of another intelligence fiasco prevents Washington and London from addressing reports about Iraqi WMD stockpiles moved to other countries. There is ample evidence about the concealment of Iraqi WMD, particularly in Syria, and material recently provided by Muammar Qadhafi has confirmed data indicating the transfer of some of Iraq's development and production capabilities to Libya in the 1990s and also demonstrated the reliability of some of the key sources now pointing to Syria's possession of Iraq's WMD. But there is unwillingness in the Bush administration to do anything about these stockpiles, and given the huge political price of intelligence failures in Iraq, it is natural for the White House to be reluctant to embark on a new military adventure during a bitterly contested election. Ultimately, however, that the United States has not found Iraq's WMD is not the worst intelligence-related crisis looming for the administration.

Beyond America's bumbling attempts to find the whereabouts of Iraqi WMD, by far the most profound intelligence failures have been evident in the handling of the still escalating armed resistance, because the wellsprings of the grassroots violence in Iraq have been misperceived from the very beginning. The intelligence community went along with the politically motivated inclination of the Bush administration to blame everything on Saddam and his ilk. If the intelligence community had reservations about this assessment, it failed to articulate its case in Washington. The intelligence community did not challenge the White House's preconceived notion that most Iraqis would consider the occupiers a liberating force, in the same way Europeans free of the Nazis did at the close of World War II, and that the Iraqi resistance was akin to the Werewolves, insurgents who briefly made their presence felt in postwar Germany.

The ideological fixation with Saddam Hussein did not allow the Bush administration to admit that it had been profoundly wrong in reading the popular dynamics in postwar Iraq, in which Saddam was a marginal factor. Indications of this development were completely ignored; for example, soon after the fall of Baghdad, an Iraqi brigadier general stressed that Saddam Hussein "counts for nothing now. History has wiped him out. Only the legend lives on." Still, America focused myopically on Saddam and as a resultant misjudged the encompassing importance of Islam. As much as most Iraqis had suffered from Saddam, he was still an Arab Muslim leader and as such more legitimate than and preferable to the American occupiers no matter how benevolent or well-intentioned; most Iraqis hate the foreign occupation far more than they hated Saddam.

Conversely, the fact that an indigenous grassroots resistance would surge to counter the occupation was inconceivable in Washington because it stood in stark contrast to the underlying logic of the case for a war in Iraq. U.S. intelligence, the military, and the political establishment were found woefully unprepared to deal with the real-life postwar Iraq. "We did anticipate a level of violence," Gen. Tommy R. Franks testified before the Senate on June 10, 2003. "I can't tell you whether we anticipated that it would be . . . at the level that we see right now."

The Bush administration's profound misunderstanding of the realities in Iraq—particularly the country's convoluted ethnic and religious dynamics, which breed the armed resistance and terrorism—has only been aggravated by America's inexplicable refusal to literally see the writing on the wall—that is, the graffiti adorning walls throughout Baghdad and other Iraqi cities. In recent months the dominant theme of the anti-American slogans has become distinctly jihadist, with Saddam-related slogans virtually disappearing. Significantly, Baghdad's Sunni religious establishment, and not the fringe extremist groups, is the driving force behind this evolution.

In central Baghdad, the transformation of anti-Americanism was flagrantly there for the administration to see—if they only cared to look. Years prior, in the spring of 1991, one of the very first steps Saddam Hussein undertook to project Islamic legitimacy, along with adding the words *Allah Akbar* to the Iraqi flag, was to order the construction of a huge mosque in central Baghdad to be known as the Mother of All Battles Mosque. The mosque is a unique building, combining a classic main structure with minarets resembling SCUD missiles and the barrels of AK-47s. During the 1990s, the mosque was the bastion of pro-Saddam Sunni Islam, but in the summer of 2003, the mosque's council, led by its senior cleric, Imam Mahdi al-Sumaydai, formally changed the mosque's name to the Ibn Taimiya Mosque, and the fiery Friday sermons and other "cultural" activities conducted in the mosque are now in step with the teachings of its namesake. Among the "educational" activities conducted in the mosque were lessons in bomb-making and guerrilla tactics. Foreign mujahedin found refuge in the mosque and participated in these activities. The transformation of this mosque was a microcosm of the transformation of Iraq's Sunni population and, for that matter, the nation.

Acting on a tip, American soldiers first raided the mosque on

January 1, 2004, and arrested Imam Sumaydai and thirty-two others. The troops recovered explosives, a few Kalashnikov rifles, boxes of ammunition, grenades, a surface-to-air missile, two rocket-propelled grenade launchers, a 60-mm mortar tube, a 120-mm mortar base-plate, bomb-making equipment, and a couple of computers. Throughout Baghdad, the entire Islamic leadership—both Sunni and Shiite—mobilized to protest the raid as a manifestation of the anti-Islamic American war. At the Umm al-Tubul Mosque, Abd-al-Sattar al-Janabi devoted his Friday sermon to criticizing the Americans: "They claimed that there were explosives, weapons, and terrorists in the mosque. By Allah, who is the only God, they have not found anything like this," he declared. At the Ibn Taimiya Mosque, Sheik Ahmad Abdul Ghafour al-Samarrai stressed that the raid was "against Islam." After the Friday prayers, the mosque's council invited Arab and Western media to see a broken wooden door, ransacked offices, and several Korans lying on the floor. "A mess was all that was there, and I saw that some of the Koran books were scattered on the floor and the holiness of this mosque had been defiled by the allied forces," Dr. Adnan Muhammad Salman, head of the Council of the Sunni *Waqf* in Baghdad, told Arab satellite TV. All Iraqi clerics, as well as most Arab commentators, stressed the peaceful character of the defiled mosque. Yet all that the American officials attempting to stem the tide of virulent Islamist propaganda did was to repeat the list of weapons found in the mosque. Not one of them mentioned the mosque's current name as an indication of the ideological leaning of its council and, in all likelihood, community of worshippers. Instead, military officials included the raid in their list of operations against the remnants of Saddam's forces.

In early 2004, the misunderstanding of the ethnic and religious complications in Iraq was only aggravated by the CIA's attempt, begun in the fall of 2003, to remedy the endemic absence of intelligence sources by rebuilding the Iraqi intelligence and security services using veterans of Saddam's Mukhabarat. Senior Mukhabarat officers, including full colonels, all members of the Baath elite who have never hidden their past loyalty to and enduring admiration of Saddam Hussein, now joined the reconstituted U.S.-controlled Iraqi intelligence. The CIA even recruited veterans of the Fifth Section of the Mukhabarat who were involved in counterintelligence and security operations, including brutal torture of Saddam's suspected enemies. The CIA also attempted to convince Iraqi Mukhabarat veterans to continue running their sources and agents inside Iran. One colonel, a twenty-five-year veteran of the Fifth Section who freely admits to having been involved in torturing victims (employing electric shocks, attaching prisoners to a reinforced fan to be left to spin for hours from the ceiling, and severely beating both prisoners and their relatives), had a lengthy job interview with the CIA. His American interviewers did not flinch when the colonel described in detail his past practices, but instead offered him a huge salary if he agreed to continue running his double agents within the Shiite community. The CIA also demanded that he sign a declaration endorsing and supporting the invasion—a statement the colonel insists that as an Iraqi patriot he could not sign. Instead, he escaped to Jordan where he recounted his experience to a longtime friend and colleague from Jordanian intelligence. Indeed, in this recruiting drive the CIA offered blanket immunity from future prosecution for torture and murder, in addition to thousands of dollars, in return for lengthy interviews and serious consideration of working for the CIA. While this courting of Mukhabarat veterans might be a necessity given the escalating guerrilla warfare, it nevertheless makes a mockery of the heralded de-Baathification campaign of the occupation authorities.

One reason for adopting such drastic measures as courting and recruiting Mukhabarat veterans was the disastrous shape of American intelligence in Iraq. A lengthy study of the quality of military intelligence, conducted by the U.S. Army's Center for Army Lessons Learned, based in Fort Leavenworth, Kansas, and completed in late October, 2003, pointed to severe inadequacies of intelligence and warned that analysts had fallen far short of requirements for the military's mission in Iraq. The report sharply criticized the performance of the sixty-nine "tactical human intelligence teams" in Iraq. It found intelligence personnel to be poor in Arabic and to have "very little to no analytical skills." Most intelligence specialists demonstrated "weak intelligence briefing skills." The dependence on Iraqi interpreters was found to have a devastating impact on the military's ability to extract useful intelligence from detainees and sources because of the interpreters' low quality and reluctance to fully assist U.S. forces—a phenomenon leading to intentional mistranslation and otherwise misleading American intelligence personnel, who were too ignorant to notice the frequent omissions or deceptions. Nevertheless, and devoid of any other viable alternative, the Pentagon announced on November 2, 2003, new plans to increase the reliance on Iraqis for operational intelligence in response to the insurrection. Gen. Richard Myers, chairman of the Joint Chiefs of Staff, told a Pentagon briefing that "we are going to rely on Iraqis for intelligence."

Little wonder that the official threat analysis remained skewed. In November the military forces operating in the Sunni heartland still insisted that there was little cooperation between the Islamist forces and the Saddam loyalists in Iraq. American military intelligence officials believed that the Iraqis generally distrusted Arab and Islamist "foreign mercenaries," although they were employed in some operations. "We have not seen a large influx of foreign fighters thus far," Maj. Gen. Ray Odierno, commander of the 4th Infantry Division, told a November 11 briefing. "We have not seen the [predominantly Saudi] Wahabists and the former regime loyalists join together. We see them operating independently, [in] very small Wahabist cells." He attributed the undeniable indications of operational cooperation between the jihadist and Baathist forces to the growing desperation of the latter—desperation wrought by American military successes. "But I think when they get desperate, the former regime loyalists then might go to some use of foreign fighters," Odierno said. "And I think we're starting to see a little bit of that now because they're starting to get a little bit desperate." In truth, the jihadist forces were the most active and dominant element in the Iraqi insurgency, and the nationalist forces were striving to join them.

In November the U.S. Army claimed growing success in the use of intelligence extracted from and volunteered by Iraqis. Military intelligence insisted they now benefited from increasing and more accurate information on insurgency activities in Iraq. "We are getting more and more tips every day," Odierno told a Pentagon briefing. "In fact, it is probably ten or twenty-fold more than when we first started here—the number of people we have coming in to provide us human information. Even more importantly, it's more accurate human information." He claimed that the information provided by Iraqi informants was about 90 percent accurate—a dramatic improvement over the 40 percent accuracy in May. "Some of that has to do with our ability to understand what our good informants are and who gives us good information and who doesn't, because there are those who try to give us false information," Odierno said. "And we've sorted through most of that." Still, Odierno acknowledged that military intelligence must focus more on human intelligence, and particularly on the ability to quickly analyze and act on such information in operations. "We need to work toward developing a better HUMINT structure than is already embedded into our units," Odierno said, "because we believe that is what will work best against the threat that's out there, and then combining that with the national intelligence that's available and also . . . SIGINT and other intelligence assets that we have available to us."

But technical collection, long the hallmark of American intelligence capabilities, also failed in Iraq. In November, most disturbing was the failure of U.S. signal intelligence and electronic intelligence in the quest for Saddam Hussein. This was a total failure of the multifaceted electronic intelligence—from intercepts of communications to deciphering of encrypted communication to the locating of sources of transmission, either from radios or cell phones. Essentially, the United States failed to penetrate Saddam's communication system. Seeking a viable starting point, intelligence agencies even monitored the communication of key Arab satellite TV stations and Western correspondents known to have good contacts with the Iraqi resistance in the hope of intercepting messages from Saddam or his confidants. U.S. intelligence hoped that intercepting the delivery of one of Saddam's frequent audio messages might lead to him, but to no avail; instead, they soon realized that Saddam had loyalists—mostly, but not exclusively, Iraqi contract translators and service personnel—among the U.S. forces conducting the electronic surveillance and that they must have warned him to change venues of communications. On November 16, for example, Saddam's people overcame U.S. monitoring and delivered a new audio message to the Al-Arabiyah TV station in Dubai through a messenger who brought a cassette to the station's offices. Simultaneously, American use of UAVs and other technical systems, including a sensitive Israeli system for locating snipers, failed to provide real-time intelligence mainly through mismanagement of the raw material that the devices collected.

In December, the United States launched a major effort to improve intelligence in Iraq. In part this drive aimed to address the findings of the October report of the Center for Army Lessons Learned. Still, U.S. defense officials acknowledged, "The military remains short of intelligence analysts and sources required to detect and foil Sunni attacks." They stressed that "a key problem is the language barrier." The key to this new and improved intelligence capability was further reliance on the new "Iraqi intelligence," staffed by veteran Mukhabarat officers. Iraqi opposition officials were told in late 2003 that the CIA now had a dedicated budget of three billion dollars to be spent between 2004 and 2006 in an effort "to root out the Baathist regime loyalists behind the continuing insurgency in parts of Iraq." Most of these funds, the Iraqi officials were told, would be spent on expanding the CIA-controlled Iraqi intelligence by recruiting additional Mukhabarat officers as well as Shiite and Kurdish security officials.

A former U.S. intelligence officer familiar with the plan told Julian Coman of the *Sunday Telegraph* about its objectives. "If successfully set up, the group would work in tandem with American forces but would have its own structure and relative independence. It could be expected to be fairly ruthless in dealing with the remnants of [Saddam's regime]." The CIA officers in Baghdad would play a leading role in directing the Iraqis' operations from the background without getting directly involved. Officials in Washington told Coman that some 275 CIA officers already in Iraq were expected to control an Iraqi force that could eventually boast 10,000 operatives, "with the local knowledge, the motivation and the authority to hunt down pro-Saddam resistance fighters." According to the CIA's plan, Coman wrote, "small units of U.S. Special Forces would work with their Iraqi counterparts, including former senior Iraqi intelligence agents, on covert operations. . . . The Pentagon and CIA have told the White House that the organization will allow America to maintain control over the direction of the country as sovereignty is handed over to the Iraqi people during the course of this year." Indeed, the organization of the new CIA-dominated Iraqi Intelligence Service continued unabated. With some 500 officers, mostly Mukhabarat veterans, already employed, the master plan called for a force of some 2,000 officers to be operational by the time control of the country reverts back to the Iraqis on June 30, 2004. Former CIA officials considered the new venture the reincarnation of the Vietnam-era Phoenix Program.

The first official acknowledgment of nationalist and jihadist cooperation against American forces, and the perils of the guerrilla war, came only in January 2004. In a January 29 briefing, Gen. John Abizaid, head of the U.S. Central Command, warned that the guerrilla war in Iraq was about to escalate as a result of local al-Qaeda networks joining forces with Saddam Hussein's loyalists. He attributed this development to the realization by the remaining loyalists of the Baathist regime that they would not return to power. Therefore, these Baathists were shifting their strategy to preventing the United States from succeeding in building a new Iraq—an objective they shared with other insurgent groups, which therefore could cooperate in pursuing their common goals. In another briefing, Lt. Gen. Ricardo Sanchez, head of the coalition ground forces in Iraq, also stressed that the influence of al-Qaeda in Iraq had been growing in the last three months. "For months I've been saying that al-Qaeda fingerprints have been here in Iraq," Sanchez acknowledged. "Their tactics, techniques, and procedures have been here for a while," and, he added, "their operations are evolving." Sanchez further noted that al-Qaeda cells were adapting to the Iraqi environment and joining forces with elements still loyal to Saddam.

U.S. intelligence, however, was still woefully unprepared to meet the challenges of the escalating insurgency and terrorism in Iraq. If anything, the growing reliance on Mukhabarat veterans would only further hamper and degrade whatever limited capabilities it now possesses. As was the case in past decades, U.S. intelligence was once again falling into the trap of the Gehlen syndrome—namely, acceding to the relative ease of adopting local intelligence resources, including former enemies, as keys to capabilities in the absence of well-cultivated indigenous resources (see "Notes: The Historical Record," p. 517).

The United States was now repeating the errors of the late 1940s by establishing the new "Iraqi intelligence" at great cost, by hiring Baathists who not only have a track record of false reporting to Saddam but for decades have hated and despised Americans. Hence, the issue at hand is far more significant than the moral issue—the flagrant contradiction of the much heralded de-Baathification policy. Under Saddam Hussein's reign, these ex-Mukhabarat officers were entrusted with protecting the ranks of the Baath Party from penetration without stifling opposition, simply because Saddam only cared about the sanctity of his own power base. These officers know only how to penetrate Baath Party cells made up of former supporters of Saddam Hussein. They know nothing about the real threats facing the American presence in Iraq—the vast networks of the Baathists, the various Islamist trends, and of course the Shiites, Kurds, and Turkman, all angling to best position themselves as the U.S. prepares to transfer sovereignty. A vicious cycle will emerge where these Mukhabarat officers have the incentive to exaggerate the threat posed by the remnants of Saddam's forces in order to claim achievements and in so doing reinforce the preconceived and politically motivated threat perceptions of both American intelligence and the Bush administration. Furthermore, the U.S. intelligence agencies are so blind and ignorant they cannot even notice the rampant swindling and cheating by their own Mukhabarat protégés—just as was the case with Gehlen and his colleagues some sixty years ago.

Ultimately, while the removal of Saddam Hussein was urgent and long overdue, the war could have been avoided. The Russians could and should have been encouraged to topple Saddam through a military coup. Several

Arab allies—ranging from senior intelligence and security officials to exiled leaders (not only Iraqis), all with lengthy experience and unblemished track records—offered to bring down the Baathist regime and establish governments friendly to the United States. Several of these plans were practical and had a good chance of success. However, in most cases, these would have been region-wide undertakings affecting other Arab countries as well. Washington not only adamantly refused to consider any of these offers, but whenever possible sought to harm those who offered help, efforts that included putting at risk the lives of those who came forward to offer the United States their assistance. This attitude already has a profound impact on America's posture not only in Iraq but throughout the Muslim world.

Additionally, in the months leading to the war, several Arab allies raised the possibility of formal and informal meetings involving Saddam Hussein or members of his coterie and Americans perceived to be knowledgeable about the Middle East in order to further explore the possibility of a negotiated settlement. In most of these cases, the Arab interlocutors stressed that the mere occurrence of such a meeting would ameliorate regional instability and reduce the threat to their own countries or regimes. However, once committed to war, the Bush administration adamantly refused to permit any such meeting. While it is highly unlikely that any such meeting would have resulted in a viable solution to the Iraqi problem, most of these meetings should have taken place because of wider regional considerations. The aggregate impact of the Bush administration's refusal to sanction Russian and Arab attempts to topple Saddam, or meetings with him designed to at least speak to the concerns of Arab allies, has been the development of a wide gap of mistrust between the administration and the pro-U.S. Arab elite. These Arab officials correctly interpret Washington's fixation on ousting Saddam at the expense of their own interests as a manifestation of American disinterest in their allies' well-being or the long-term posture in the Middle East. As a result, there is a shift in Arab polity away from cooperating with the United States against common enemies—such as jihadist terrorism—to a quest for self-survival through shady deals between threatened regimes and their nemeses.

There were two reasons—not mutually exclusive—for Washington's behavior: the Bush administration was unwilling to cede the opportunity (and the credit) for destroying its enemy's regime; and both U.S. intelligence and the White House were so ignorant of the intricacies of Iraq and the region that they were incapable of grasping and comprehending the sophistication involved in manipulating subsegments of the population, discreet undercurrents, and Islamist factionalism. Similarly, both the intelligence community and the White House could not decipher the regional impact of their blanket refusal to permit meetings with Saddam, no matter how futile they really were. But the deed was done, and by the time the United States went to war, the bulk of the Arab world was implacably hostile to invasion.

America's march on Baghdad and the still intensely fought guerrilla war cloud the situation as well. Indeed, the lingering outcome of the quagmire in Iraq is that the United States forfeited deterrence in the Arab Muslim world. The Arabs—and particularly the leaders themselves—who dreaded American military might, outreach, and ability to punish them on the eve of the invasion of Iraq fear the United States no more. The inability to cope with the insurrection has been eye-opening for Islamists and pro-American rulers alike. The former are now encouraged and emboldened to take on the United States and its allies, and the latter are fearful that the U.S. would not be able to save them in their hour of need. Therefore, erstwhile U.S. allies now seek compromises with the Islamists and Jihadist threatening them, thus assisting the anti-American forces.

This regional turmoil would have been warranted had the United States achieved its primary objective—the establishment of a democratic pro-Western government in Baghdad. Instead, as a direct result of American mismanagement of the occupation, instability and anarchy have become epidemic and the prospect of near-term pacification and stabilization of the country is all but nonexistent. This could have been avoided had the Bush administration thoroughly studied the sociopolitical history and ethnic religious tapestry of Iraq before firing the first shot. After toppling Saddam's regime with a blunt instrument, the United States went on to repeat the British mistakes of the 1920s by inventing and building a unified Iraq where none exists and where the population is irreconcilably hostile to such a posture.

The predictable pitfalls of the strategy in Iraq are examined by Toby Dodge in his 2003 book, *Inventing Iraq: The Failure of Nation-Building and a History Denied*. Dodge warns that "the removal of Saddam Hussein was the beginning, not the culmination, of a long and very uncertain process of reform. It was also the continuation of a failed effort to create a modern liberal state on the part of the world's leading hegemony as part of a new world order." And just as the Iraqi state invented by Churchill in the 1920s degenerated into an extremely violent dictatorship as the sole viable alternative to fracturing under the pressure of its diverse population groupings, so will the new Iraq invented by Bush succumb to these indigenous and indestructible ethnic and religious forces—the "shadow state" in Dodge's terms.

Indeed, in early 2004, Washington's original plans for Iraq were unraveling. In late January, the CIA station in Baghdad warned of an impending civil war. Behind the CIA's bleak assessment was the realization that both the Shiite and Kurdish communities were increasingly afraid that any U.S.-imposed political solution would deprive them of what they considered to be their vital interests. Having failed to convince the occupation authorities in Baghdad of their demands, these communities were increasingly inclined to fight for them. "Both the Shiites and the Kurds think that now's their time," one intelligence officer told Warren P. Strobel and Jonathan S. Landay of the Knight Ridder Newspapers. "They think that if they don't get what they want now, they'll probably never get it. Both of them feel they've been betrayed by the United States before."

Foreign experts also warned of the deteriorating situation in Iraq. Marco Calamai, an Italian expert and the former special counselor to the Coalition Provisional Authority in the southern province of Dhi Qar, was convinced the occupation authorities had already mismanaged Iraq's reconstruction because they were "out of touch with Iraqis." As a consequence, the situation in Iraq was "frighteningly difficult," to the point of threatening the viability of any "formula for democracy and unity in Iraq." Public discontent was rising throughout Iraq, Calamai warns. "The weapons of mass destruction weren't there. The ferocious dictatorship was there, but it's gone. So it's natural the Iraqis are asking, 'Why are they [the Americans] still there?'"

Meanwhile, even the most optimistic supporters of the Bush administration's Iraq policies now acknowledged that the rebuilding of Iraq was simply not working. The White House was inclined to entertain "drastic refinements" to its policies, including the United States remaining in control of Iraq for at least another year instead of handing over sovereignty on June 30, 2004, as senior officials in Baghdad doubted their ability to establish a viable Iraqi government by the deadline. This grim assessment was the result of the demand for direct elections, and consequent Shiite empowerment, by Grand Ayatollah Ali Sistani, and the bitter and seemingly irreconcilable squabbling between the members of the U.S.-nominated Interim Governing Council. Any such drastic change would be a huge embarrassment for the Bush administration. Having studied the British failed and futile effort at nation-building in Iraq, Dodge's longer-term forecasts for the U.S.-installed Iraqi state are equally grim:

> As U.S. troops are withdrawn and U.S. public opinion loses interest in Iraq, the shadow state with new masters will once again come to dominate. A new governing structure will not have been built [by the United States]. Instead, a veneer of legal-rational bureaucracy will have been placed on top of the shadow state with its tried and tested use of violence, patronage, and favoritism. The shadow state will slowly come to dominate as international oversight diminishes. In the medium-term, Iraq will be prone to insecurity mitigated only by the degree of ruthlessness and efficiency exhibited by the new rulers in Baghdad. The long-term result can be expected, at best, to resemble Egypt, with a population demobilized and resentful. The state will dominate society through the use of high levels of organized violence. The governing elite will colonize all aspects of the economy and corruption will be the major source of the regime's longevity.

And while Washington was preoccupied with salvaging the political situation in Baghdad, the entire region, where so many vital interests of the United States are located, is going up in flames. Calamai believed the Americans "underestimated the anti-Western sentiment that is very prevalent in the Arab world, and therefore committed many mistakes in and around Iraq." Although immersed in fighting in both Iraq and Afghanistan, the American military is increasingly apprehensive about the long-term ramifications of the regional strategic challenge to U.S. interests. In a January briefing, General Abizaid identified the Islamist threat to Pakistan and Saudi Arabia as the "two broadest strategic problems" confronting the United States, rather than the "immediate problems" of ongoing fighting. The entire Muslim world is engulfed in a fateful struggle "between moderation and extremism" in which fighting al-Qaeda and other terrorist organizations has become as much a "battle of ideas" as a military confrontation, in Abizaid's view. Saudi Arabia and Pakistan being at the forefront of this struggle, the United States must provide them with "diplomatic, political, and social" support so that they can endure the forthcoming crises. "They're going to be tough fights in both places," Abizaid said. "And it's not the kind of fight that will be won tomorrow." Essentially, the fighting in Iraq and Afghanistan are sideshows to these dynamics. Although the military has been making "good progress" in both countries, combat operations are not likely to end anytime soon. Rather, Abizaid expects a major escalation, especially in Iraq. Because al-Qaeda and other terrorist organizations operating in Iraq "have professional capability to do a lot of damage," Abizaid predicted "increased levels of violence" in the foreseeable future. Not even the Bush administration can present this state of affairs as a success, or even a sign of progress and a reason for optimism.

Ultimately, however, the key to the future of Iraq and the region as a whole lies in Tehran. As the mullahs see the world, they are at a singularly important fork in the road, and Iraq is the signpost that will indicate whether Iran is moving toward a historic victory or total demise. Specifically, if the United States succeeds and establishes a pro-Western Iraq, the regime in Tehran will be stifled and soon collapse. If America fails in Iraq and is forced to withdraw ignominiously, Shiites will take over Baghdad and, for the first time since the days of Emperor Cyrus the Great in the sixth century B.C., the Persians will control the Mediterranean coast (by building a Shiite corridor through Iraq, Syria, and Lebanon) and the bulk of the Persian Gulf (relying on Shiite areas in Iraq, Saudi Arabia, and the Gulf States). In modern terms, Iran would also dominate virtually all the oil and gas resources of the Middle East. And there is an even more important aspect to this intersection for the mullahs of Tehran: the fate and future of Shiite Islam. Historically, the Shiite religious and political center was in Najaf, but in the late twentieth century, as a result of the Khomeini revolution and Saddam Hussein's anti-Shiite regime in Iraq, the seat of Shiism shifted to Qom, in Iran. After the fall of Saddam's regime, a Shiite reawakening began in Najaf, and Tehran's mullahs fear that their influence over Shiite Islam will soon wither, as Najaf resumes its role at Qom's expense.

Taking stock of all these issues, Tehran is adamant about securing victory for its regime and its brand of Shiite Islam and considers any means used to achieve its goals—including terrorism and fratricidal violence—legitimate under the circumstances. The escalation of anti-Shiite terrorism in Iraq is an integral part of this drive because Ayatollah Sistani leads the pro-Najaf—and anti-Qom—branch of Shiite Islam and is a threat to Tehran's vital interests. Meanwhile, Osama bin Laden and the Sunni jihadist camp are adamant about destroying the House of al-Saud and the traditional Sunni institutions that challenge the legitimacy of Shiite Islam. Bin Laden's success thus serves Tehran's interests. These steps, which have already achieved some measure of success, are aimed at pushing Iraqi Shiites into joining the Islamist jihad against the occupation forces and the U.S.-installed regime in Baghdad. Furthermore, ever since 1980, when the fledgling Khomeini regime manipulated the hostage crisis into toppling the Carter administration, Tehran has been obsessed with exploiting the traditional inaction that accompanies an American election year in order to dramatically further Iran's anti-American strategies. Indeed, Tehran is convinced it can exploit the 2004 election in a way that will ensure that its achievements are irreversible.

The mullahs are determined to make the right turn at the T—to save their regime, achieve a historic victory for Shiite Iran, and secure their own interests, and to do both they must upend America's plans for Iraq. Hence, the potential for a marked escalation—particularly of Iran-sponsored violence—was still ahead. Given Iran's track record, there should be no doubt about Tehran's next moves. Hajj Saidi elucidated the perception in Tehran.

> In the 1980's and on the orders of Imam Khomeini, we [Iranian intelligence] took our battle with the United States to Lebanon where we hit the U.S. marines base and the U.S. Embassy in Beirut and kidnaped William Buckley, head of the Central Intelligence Agency in the Middle East, and several American citizens. The United States was forced to recognize our [dominant] role in Lebanon. We are today moving our battle with the United States to Iraq on the orders of the Revolution Guide [Khamenei] so that it will recognize our [dominant] role there too.

And because American intelligence agencies have proved blind, the United States is not faring well in this war.

There is one dominant reason for the American debacle in Iraq—the desperately poor state of the nation's intelligence services. On the eve of the Iraq war, U.S. intelligence organizations failed to warn the Bush administration of the challenges ahead and the peculiarities of the country and its people. Since the occupation of Baghdad, U.S. intelligence has repeatedly failed to articulate to the decision-makers in Washington the nature and duration of the Iraqi jihad. At the core of these failures is the intelligence community's profound ignorance of the situation in the Muslim world, aggravated by the absence of human sources and overall presence on the ground. Catching up on the fly is a major challenge, but there seems to be no alternative given the still unfolding war on terrorism. Opening both the intelligence community and the White House to outside expertise, even if the opinions are dissenting, can also help expedite the rehabilitation of America's intelligence agencies and, as a consequence, bolster the president's ability to make crucial decisions. The Bush administration might be loath to acknowledge the extent of its shortcomings, especially in advance of what's certain to be a bitterly partisan election, but Washington has no alternative. Simply put, the United States cannot afford to repeat the Iraq experience.

There is a long and challenging World War IV still ahead of the United States and the rest of the civilized world. America's finest youth in uniform deserve that their leaders be better prepared for the next phases.

POSTSCRIPT

By the first of May 2004—exactly a year after President Bush declared an end to "major combat operations" from the deck of the USS *Abraham Lincoln*—Iraq was sliding into irreversible chaos, engendered by a genuinely grassroots jihadist intifada. Far more than a security challenge for the occupying authorities, the Iraqi intifada is first and foremost a crucial political development, which threatens America's ability to hold onto even the small victories it won during the invasion of Iraq. The simultaneous eruption of popular violence in both the Shiite and Sunni heartlands has sparked a rejuvenated Iraqi "spirit" across Iraq's numerous ethno-religious lines—based on the common denominator of virulent hatred of the United States.

The Iraqi intifada is also an integral component of a greater political dynamic, whose goal is to thoroughly and irreversibly delegitimize—at least in the Arab Muslim world—the Iraqi political entity to which Washington was planning on ceding power on June 30, 2004. Furthermore, al-Qaeda's terrorist offensive in Jordan, Israel, Saudi Arabia, and against the UN in Damascus, was another reminder of this regional push to humiliate the U.S. and banish it from the Arab Middle East. Al-Qaeda's campaign was expedited, if not facilitated, by the existence of jihadist safe havens in Iraq. The ongoing presence of al-Qaeda brought the stark ramifications of an enduring Iraqi intifada home to all Arab governments—solidifying their resolve to actively resist U.S. presence and interests in the region. At this writing, the Arab governments were actively seeking their own permanent political solution for the crisis in Iraq—a virulently anti-American solution, the only kind they believed could save them from the wrath of their increasingly Islamist peoples.

And herein lies the specter of an American defeat in Iraq.

The Iraqi intifada will have a far greater impact on the ultimate outcome of America's involvement with Iraq than even the fall of Saddam.
Most of the current crisis and its aftermath could have been avoided by
capitalizing on existing intelligence data. After all, back in late 2003,
Tehran's initial decision to provoke an Iraqi flare-up around the first anniversary of the U.S. invasion became known to Western intelligence services almost immediately. Yet U.S. intelligence failed to take notice and
apprise Washington of Iran's decision. Indeed, the U.S. was surprised by
the eruption of violence and the intensity of the fighting. Furthermore,
Washington profoundly misread the motives behind the intifada—and
thus its responses to date, both military and political, have only aggravated
the overall situation. Once again, poor intelligence and a profound misunderstanding of the situation on the ground were at the root of Washington's failures in Iraq.

Starting in early March 2004, there were several signs that Iran was preparing to provoke a major crisis. Tehran's first authoritative directive to the
Shiites of Iraq was first delivered on the Voice of the Mujahedin radio network on March 7. In a sermon broadcast from Qom, Ayatollah Haeri, the
spiritual leader of Moqtada al-Sadr, urged the entire Iraqi people to "confront injustice and demand freedom" in the aftermath of the Ashura mas-
sacre. Linking the lessons of the recent events with the Shiite interpretation
of the historic epic of the Ashura, he told the people of Iraq that there was
no substitute for "freedom and the defense of the homeland" from its foreign occupiers. Haeri reiterated his confidence that "the Iraqi people will
not give in to the United States' objection to considering Islam as the main
pillar for the [new Iraqi] constitution," and lamented "the feeling of humiliation [now] prevailing under the shadow of occupation." "The only solution [must be] based on complete independence for Iraq," he said, urging
all Iraqis to confront the occupation and struggle for their independence.
The following day Ayatollah Haeri issued a fatwa and condemned the State
Administration Law as an "illegitimate" code that "does not fulfill the Iraqi
people's minimum demands"; since the law regarded the American presence in Iraq as legitimate, he said, Muslims must neither recognize it nor
abide by it. Among Arab intelligence officials, Haeri's fatwa was greeted as
the first legal step toward ordering the Shiites into actively joining the anti-
American jihad.

Grassroots reaction in Iraq was immediate. On March 9, a leading Shiite preacher and civic leader in Nasiriyah named Sheikh Assad al-Nasiri accused the U.S. of launching anti-Shiite terrorism in order to cow the Shiites into accepting the occupation. Al-Nasiri charged that the U.S. had "created" the al-Qaeda organization, and was now using it "as a peg on which it hangs the bombing incidents . . . in order to keep the Iraqis from thinking of restoring the sovereignty of Iraq." He warned the U.S. to quickly end "its occupation of Iraq and arrogant dealings with its people" or else face the inevitable eruption of the Iraqi people. The sermons of March 12 were virulently anti-American; most of the Imams pointed to the proposed law as proof of America's implacable anti-Shiism. The rhetoric of Moqtada al-Sadr was particularly harsh, denouncing the law as "similar to the Balfour's Declaration which sold Palestine."

By this time, the finishing touches were being put on a formal Shiite intifada against the United States. The operational decision to launch the intifada was reached on March 13–14, 2004, in consultations under the cover of a conference in London on the "Islamic Movement and Iraq." The conference was attended by senior intelligence officials from Iran and Syria, senior emissaries of Moqtada's Mahdi Army, the HizbAllah, al-Qaeda, Sunni jihadist commanders from Iraq, Syria, Saudi Arabia, and the Gulf States, as well as Islamist leaders from all over Europe, whose followers were already fighting in Iraq.

The London branch of the Iraqi Islamic Party, which had already dispatched numerous British mujahedin to Iraq, invited the participants to "come together to stand up to the occupation and its agents" by escalating the armed resistance. One of the European participants explained that "the secret debate and decision to move the Shiite front against the American occupation in Iraq marked the most prominent among the recommendations finalized at the conference. . . . [Convinced] that Sunni resistance alone was not enough [to] turn the balance of power with the occupying forces . . . they agreed to find the necessary means and move the Shiite resistance from peaceful protests to a much more effective role" by giving Shiites a more active role in the resistance operations. The European leaders and the emissaries of the international terrorism organizations promised to provide expertise and push large-scale reinforcements into Iraq. Iranian intelligence would supervise and lead the entire undertaking, with al-Qaeda and HizbAllah providing on-site senior commanders.

Mindful of the strategic significance of the coming intifada, Tehran ordered the evacuation of key terrorist leaders from Iranian territory just days after the London conference. Four of the most senior Islamist terrorist chiefs—Ayman al-Zawahiri, Imad Moughniyah, Saad bin Osama bin Laden, and Seif al-Adl—were seen at the IRGC-controlled sector of the Mehrabad airport, near Tehran, boarding an unmarked official airplane. They were escorted to the plane by friendly IRGC and intelligence officials who saw them off. (According to an earlier report, Saad bin Osama bin Laden and Sayf al-Adl only saw Zawahiri and Moughniyah to the plane, but stayed with the IRGC officials in Iran.) In the past, these commanders (and others of similar stature) had been evacuated from Tehran and other Iranian centers before major terrorist strikes in order to prevent Tehran from being blamed as a sponsor. This time, however, U.S. intelligence failed to apprise the Bush administration of the significance of this evacuation; indeed, it continued to endorse the claim that Zawahiri was in Wana, on the Pakistani-Afghan border—a work of pure Pakistani disinformation.

The main reason Tehran was apprehensive about the presence of the al-Qaeda elite was that one Dr. Abu Hafiza—the Moroccan senior commander who had recently supervised the March 11, 2004, train bombing in Madrid in accordance with the early December 2003 al-Qaeda letter to the Spanish people—had played a critical role in planning the Iraqi intifada. Back in the spring and summer of 2003, Hafiza had spent four to six months in Fallujah, studying the situation on behalf of bin Laden and Zawahiri. Returning to Pakistan via Saudi Arabia in the fall, he wrote the strategy for what would become the Iraqi intifada. Abu Hafiza stressed the importance of enticing American forces into the cities in order to entangle them in costly urban warfare and make them easier targets for terrorism, and recommended that the jihadists expand their war to include the systematic destruction of Iraq's oil infrastructure. Abu Hafiza also raised the political context of the war, suggesting that American forces could be isolated politically and militarily in Iraq by forcing its allies to withdraw in reaction to spectacular acts of terrorism in their home countries and the taking of hostages in Iraq. He also urged the Sunni jihadists to cooperate closely with the Shiite elite through "responsible circles"—namely, the Iran-controlled terrorist elite led by Moughniyah—in order to build a comprehensive network in the Shiite heartland and mobilize local commanders such as Moqtada al-Sadr. On March 17, immediately after leaders left Tehran, a powerful car bomb exploded at the center of Baghdad, destroying the Mount Lebanon Hotel and a whole block of apartments, which burned for several hours.

Osama bin Laden personally articulated the framework of the forthcoming jihad in a message he recorded on March 23 (parts of which were aired by Al-Jazeera TV on April 15). Bin Laden described the fighting in Iraq in the context of the jihadists' reaction to the American-led war on terrorism. "Our acts are reaction to your own acts, which are represented by the destruction and killing of our people in Afghanistan, Iraq and Palestine. . . . Reciprocal treatment is fair. And the one who starts injustice bears greater blame." Warning the international community—especially the Europeans—against continued support for the occupation, he offered the Europeans "a reconciliation initiative . . . whose essence is our commitment to stopping operations against every country that commits itself to not attacking Muslims or interfering in their affairs—including the U.S. conspiracy on the greater Muslim world." Otherwise, he promised, Islamist terrorism within their countries would escalate. "For those who reject reconciliation and want war, we are ready. Stop spilling our blood so we can stop spilling your blood. It is in your hands to apply this easy, yet difficult, equation. You know that the situation will expand and increase if you delay things. If this happens, do not blame us. Blame yourselves. A rational person does not relinquish his security, money and children to please the liar of the White House." Bin Laden pointed to the recent terrorist strikes in Spain, as well as a forthcoming wave of jihadist strikes in the Muslim world, as signs of the fate awaiting the Europeans if they failed to heed his advice to abandon Iraq. "It is said that prevention is better than cure. A happy person is he who learns a lesson from the experience of others," bin Laden concluded.

A few days later, the nationalist-Baathist resistance in Iraq signaled its readiness to join the intifada by announcing the formation of the Patriotic Front for the Liberation of Iraq (PFLI). The PFLI would be instrumental to the long-term struggle against the occupation forces, and the Iraqi authorities they will empower in Baghdad. The PFLI communique stressed that the member organizations represent a myriad of "armed organizations" and "resistance trends" of diverse ideological character from all over Iraq, "Mujahid detachments" that "have come together in one organization now on the march towards one goal—the liberation of Iraq from Anglo-American colonialism" by force of arms. The PFLI stressed that its armed struggle would not end with the transfer of formal power from the U.S. occupation to Iraqi authorities. The PFLI is committed to continue its struggle until any regime in Baghdad established and sustained by the U.S. and its allies is finally destroyed. The PFLI warned that those supporting the occupation would face a "reckoning [that] will be severe and harsh because they have betrayed and deserted the homeland, delivering it up to foreigners on contemptible pretexts."

Indeed, it was a joint effort between Sunni Islamist and Baathist-nationalist forces that eventually sparked the dramatic emergence of the intifada in Fallujah. On March 31, four former U.S. special forces now providing security for humanitarian projects and food convoys were enticed to come to a meeting with local notables. Their vehicle was ambushed en route; the troops were brutally murdered, their bodies burned, mutilated, and hung from a Euphrates bridge by a jubilant mob. The plans for the ambush had been widely known: The streets were deserted as the American vehicles drove to the meeting, but large mobs assembled immediately after the vehicles were set on fire. At another location nearby, five newly arrived marines were killed and several were wounded when a roadside bomb destroyed their M113.

Meanwhile, oblivious to the mounting tensions and threats, the occupation authorities in Baghdad gave the Islamists another pretext for violence when they shut down the offices of the Shiite paper *Al-Hawza*. By Friday, Sunni and Shiite imams all over Iraq were inciting believers to rebel against the Americans, providing catharsis to their building frustration and rage. On the third of April, Moqtada's Mahdi Army marched into Baghdad; on the fourth it attacked Iraqi police stations in that city. Shiite forces spearheaded by the Mahdi Army of about 10,000 trained fighters also attacked several targets in Basra, Kufa, near Najaf, Amara, and Nasiriyah. The Iraqi intifada was spreading rapidly.

The widespread eruption of Shiite revolt all over southern Iraq was clearly well-prepared for the new campaign. Well-organized Shiite units moved quickly to attack garrisons of U.S. and coalition forces, and forced most to withdraw. Within a couple of days the Shiites managed to seize Iraq's key cities; before long Sunni and Shiite rebels were in effective control of Baghdad slums, Fallujah, Qarbalah, Nasiriyah, Ramadi, Amara, Kut, Najaf, and Basra. "From now on we are the striking arm of the HizbAllah and HAMAS in Iraq," Sadr declared in Kufa.

On April 5, the United States launched the Vigilant Resolve offensive against the Sunni strongholds in Fallujah and Ramadi, quickly blocking highways to Baghdad and the Jordanian border. But the U.S. effort was insufficient to reverse the surge of the intifada. In response, Shiite units joined Sunni forces in Ramadi and Fallujah—forcing the U.S. forces to withdraw from both cities. Meanwhile, Sadr and an elite force of about 3,000 Iraqis and a few hundred Iranians established headquarters between

Najaf and Kufa. The new Iraqi military and security forces were in a state of virtual collapse. Complete units were refusing to fight their "brethren" in the service of "the American occupiers"—a major blow to America's plans to rely on indigenous forces for routine security. On the night of April 8–9, the U.S. launched Operation Resolute Sword in order to recapture the Shiite heartland and southern Iraq. But the offensive was faced with widespread grassroots resistance, and stalled and faded away shortly thereafter.

In the early morning of April 9, U.S. Special Forces ambushed Sadr's convoy as he was leaving Najaf for the Friday prayers at the Kufa mosque. Sadr's bodyguards and nearby forces of the al-Mahdi army fought a pitched battle with the U.S. forces—enabling the convoy to turn back and return safely to Najaf. Senior aides of Sadr's claimed they were forewarned about the Special Forces' attempt to assassinate him. "We have received confirmed reports that the occupation troops are determined to assassinate His Eminence Hojjat-ol-Eslam val Muslemin Al-Sayyid Moqtada al-Sadr," said Sheikh Qays al-Khazali, "and that they are planning to put pressure on Grand Ayatollah Al-Sayyid Al-Sistani to make him calm down the situation following the assassination in the name of stopping the shedding of Muslim blood." Shortly afterward, Sadr delivered his Friday sermon from Najaf. "I say to my enemy Bush that if your pretext to wage war on Iraq was Saddam and the weapons of mass destruction, this has become part of the past. You are now fighting the Iraqi people," Sadr declared.

The American action was badly timed, pitting American troops against throngs of incited believers streaming out of the inflammatory Friday sermons. Although heavily armored American columns penetrated the centers of several cities, they were forced to withdraw under pressure from excited mobs fronted by stone-wielding women and children; some troops were ambushed in narrow streets and allies. Throughout the Shiite heartland, organized units of the Badr Army and other militias joined the battle against the coalition in an organized fashion, reflecting advance coordination with Sadr and the Iranian-sponsored command. U.S. intelligence was most surprised by the extent of the operational cooperation between Sunni (both jihadist and Baathist-nationalist) units and Shiite forces, who joined forces in battling the American-led forces. Once again, the resistance reflected a level of advance planning and coordination U.S. intelligence had been refusing to acknowledge for months. Emboldened, Moqtada sent forces to reinforce the defenders of such Sunni bastions as Fallujah and Ramadi. A tenuous standoff developed in Fallujah, as U.S.

forces proved incapable of retaking the city without suffering heavy casualties or inflicting heavy civilian casualties.

On April 9, Bremer announced a twenty-four-hour unilateral cease-fire in order to enable mediation by the Islamic Party—a unilateral concession that reflected a desperate effort to slow down the collapse of the U.S. posture in Iraq. By this point the Iraqi security forces—the key to sustaining U.S. influence after June 30—had crumbled entirely. The U.S.-trained and financed New Iraqi Army, police, border guard, protective units for oil installations, and intelligence forces were breaking down, with defections reaching fifty percent; several units changed sides altogether, bringing their weapons with them. Throughout the Iraqi and U.S. bureaucracies, senior and mid-rank officials were resigning or simply not showing up. Meanwhile, civilian mobs were intentionally blocking the U.S. forces from moving around. Afraid of inflicting heavy civilian casualties live on Al-Jazeerah and al-Arabiyah TV, American forces lost their ability to operate in the contested cities. Bremer's call for cease-fire was actually an attempt to put a brave face on disaster.

The overall situation in the Shiite heartland further deteriorated during the weekend of April 10–11, during the Shiite Arbain holiday. Between two and three million pilgrims, at least a third of them Iranian young men, made their way to Qarbalah and then the shrines of Najaf. The coalition forces were compelled to keep their distance from the agitated mob—leaving a clear field for Sadr. Moreover, this flow of humanity served as a cover for the rushing of significant reinforcements with weapons and funds from Iran to the Sadr and other Shiite forces. All the while, militant Imams were increasing their call to arms through massive rallies.

Battle lines were stabilized, and localized clashes intensified, as the jihadist and Baathist-nationalist forces kept the upper hand throughout the week that followed. The rebels expanded the war—blocking strategic axes of transportation, keeping American forces outside the cities and on the defensive. The insurgents inflicted heavy casualties, shooting down a few U.S. helicopters along the way. Insurgent forces intensified their attacks on U.S. bases and installations, including the center of Baghdad, with rockets and mortars. A spate of roadside bombs and ambushes further hampered the allies' ability to move forces and supplies between flashpoints.

In the Sunni heartland, and particularly Fallujah, the uneasy standoff was passed off by the Americans as a period of cease-fire negotiations. In truth, it reflected the allies' reluctance to get involved in costly battles to retake Fallujah—a hesitation the local jihadist and Baathist-nationalist forces understood and exploited fully. Repeated U.S. demands for the insurgents to surrender heavy weapons were ignored, only to elicit new deadlines and threats from the Americans around the city. The U.S. built a berm to besiege Fallujah, but it proved of little use against smugglers. The rebel forces in Fallujah exploited the hiatus to rebuild and expand; in a series of sporadic clashes, the rebels were able to actively prevent marine patrols from entering the city. At the same time, the U.S. attempted to break the deadlock by sending raiding forces toward the Syrian border near Al-Qaim and Qusaybah to stem the growing flow of fighters and heavy weapons from Syria to Ramadi and Fallujah, and ultimately Baghdad. On April 18, a clash erupted between the Marines and some 150 insurgents in Husaybah, near the Syrian border. In the lengthy battle that ensued, several marines and dozens of mujahedin were killed and scores more wounded. Syrian border guards opened fire on the U.S. forces to assist the mujahedin; the flow of reinforcements from Syria continued to grow.

By the end of April, after ten days of intense violence, the uneasy cease-fire was punctuated by a series of bloody terrorist strikes and brief intense clashes. The price was heavy. The U.S. armed forces suffered at least 136 fatalities, and ten to fifteen times as many Iraqis were killed—the vast majority of them innocent civilians. Several allied troops and Western contractors were also killed. And even though a myriad of formal and informal negotiations were taking place all over Iraq on new localized security arrangements, the die was cast.

For many, the success of the first month of the intifada was measured not in terms of pure casualties, but in the political status quo the occupation authorities accepted. The standoff between the American-led occupation and anti-occupation forces was seen by the vast majority of Iraqis as a great victory over the United States. For most Iraqis, America's failure to retaliate with ferocity after each new act of spectacular terrorism, after every new guerrilla attack on U.S. forces, is a sign of American weakness. The U.S. had been compelled to negotiate with the worst—Islamist-jihadists in Fallujah and Sadr's pro-Iranians in the Shiite heartland—in effect conferring political legitimacy on the anti-occupation forces and their extremist ideologies.

Furthermore, by bringing back former Maj. Gen. Jassim Muhammad Saleh of the Republican Guards and his Baathist forces to patrol Fallujah, as well as acknowledging the pragmatic need to reverse the much-celebrated de-Baathification, occupation authorities were sending the signal that Washington had nothing new to offer Iraq—only a return to the faces of Saddam's regime, now that Bush's personal revenge against Saddam Hussein himself had been exorcised. The growing cooperation among Sunni and Shiite forces added to the grassroots confidence that they would fare even better once hostilities resumed. From the point of view of most Iraqis, the forces behind the intifada had already won the war. The only remaining challenge would be to consolidate the Islamist-Jihadist victory.

The Islamist-jihadist movement in Iraq spent this period consolidating its ideological-theological posture in preparation for the next phase of the intifada. Among the most important developments was the formal recognition of Moqtada al-Sadr's preeminence within the Shiite community. In late April, Ayatollah Haeri formally declared that al-Sadr's intifada was a "great cause" in defense of the Muslim community. "There are times when it is necessary to rise up if we come under occupation by heretics," he decreed. Soon afterward, emissaries of Ayatollah Sistani conveyed his "direct support for Sayyid Moqtada al-Sadr's attitudes and acts," and promised all-out support for his intifada.

Starting in mid-April, the Islamist-Jihadists had escalated their jihad in and around Iraq. As well, the jihadists launched a region-wide terrorist offensive, with Iraqis (including Baathist-nationalist experts), Saudis, and local Islamists among the key perpetrators. Syria provided crucial sponsorship for these Islamist operations. The campaign addressed the Islamists' regional political objectives, targeting the governments and institutions considered the bulwark of the American effort to impose a political solution in Iraq; the Islamists launched spectacular strikes against security objectives in Jordan and Israel (which were narrowly averted at the last minute), as well as security and oil objectives in Saudi Arabia (which largely succeeded, despite efforts by the Saudi security forces). The Islamists also issued a warning to the United Nations, striking at an abandoned UN building in Damascus. All of these strikes were designed to remind the occupying forces that the situation in Iraq was merely a part of the larger regional puzzle. Putting this wave of jihadist terrorism in perspective, Abu Musab al-Zarqawi explained the attempted strike in Jordan in light of Amman's assistance to American forces in the Iraq war. "Indeed, the plan was that the building of the [Jordanian] Intelligence apparatus would have been completely destroyed," Zarqawi explained in an audio message broadcast by Al Arabiya TV on April 30. "The operation was aimed at the black source of evil in our land [Iraq]."

The ire of the Islamists and jihadists was especially provoked by UN support for the return of the Hashemites, which Washington is now endorsing. This push is being run by Lakhdar al-Ibrahimi (or Brahimi), the former Algerian foreign minister and now UN trouble-shooter for Iraq, and Amr Mussa, the Egyptian secretary general of the Arab League; it has gained new urgency and importance in the aftermath of the Iraqi intifada. At the core of the solution proposed by Ibrahimi and Mussa is a Hashemite constitutional monarchy, with a government acceptable to the Arab League. Though he is a progressive pan-Arabist, Ibrahimi is very close to the Hashemites; his daughter is engaged to Prince Ali, the son of Jordan's late King Hussein, and a half brother of King Abdullah II of Jordan. Mussa and Ibrahimi are calling for the establishment of an interim Iraqi government comprised of "honest, technically qualified and respected people," in Ibrahimi's words—in other words, the old elite.

Indeed, for months the Arab League and the UN had been reaching out to Iraqi alternative political forces not associated with the U.S.-nominated IGC, which have made themselves known through political communiques. They first reached out to the recently formed Liberation Front–Provisional General Command, which in mid-February announced the establishment of a clandestine Free Iraqi Government and openly challenged the legitimacy of any political arrangement for post-occupation Iraq. The Liberation Front positioned itself as a viable and legitimate alternative to the U.S.-sponsored IGC. "We categorically reject the so-called Interim Governing Council," the communique explained, because it is "the worst example of open and concealed lackeyism and treachery in this already bad period in the life of the Arabs and Muslims." The communique assured the Iraqi people that supporting the Liberation Front would allow them to "attain all their hopes," rather than reinforcing the U.S. occupation and rule through internationally supported elections. The communique concluded with a special address to the United Nations, heads of states, and the Arab League, informing them that they would soon be receiving a "special document/communique" regarding the legal leadership of Iraq by way of "special representatives for this purpose."

In late March 2004, roughly six weeks after the Liberation Front–Provisional General Command announced its formation and declared its political agenda—to the positive reaction of both the UN and the Arab League—the Iraqi resistance published a comprehensive and sophisticated political program. The program was issued as a communique of the Unified National Council of the Iraqi Resistance. Like the Liberation Front's original communique, the Council's political program was warmly endorsed by both the Westernized urban elite and the Islamist-jihadist leaders—supporting the Council's claim to represent a wide ideological spectrum and all segments of the Iraqi population. The release of a comprehensive political program in such a manner is extremely important, for this political process speaks directly to the Iraqi educated elite—particularly the Westernized elite of Baghdad and other urban centers. These Iraqis hold the key to any political posture in postwar Iraq—whether the future of Iraq promises to be pro-American or, as now seems more likely, implacably hostile to the United States. That both the UN and the Arab League have effectively committed to working with the political arm of the resistance only adds to its popularity and legitimacy in both Iraq and throughout the Arab world.

The mere existence of a viable alternative to America's vision of postwar Iraq, even one that comes in the form of underground communiques and messages, can only induce the Iraqi elite to distance itself from the American occupation—and even to assist the armed resistance, in hopes of hastening the emergence of a genuinely free and independent Iraq. Yet the Iraq Mussa and Ibrahimi vision amounts to restoring the old pan-Arab Baghdad, at the expense of the Islamists, the Shiites, and the Kurds—and, having tasted the scent of power during the intifada, it is naive to believe that those groups will abandon the power they have. Despite its passionately anti-U.S. philosophy, Mussa and Ibrahimi are convinced that Washington will ultimately accept their constitutional monarchy as the only way to avoid having a Shiite-dominated Islamist-jihadist Iraq rise from the flames of the intifada.

The Arab world is aware of the anti-American developments in Iraq, and supports them. As Abd-al-Bari Atwan has noted in a recent front page editorial in London's *Al-Quds al-Arabi*, however, it may be too late to reverse the gains of the Iraqi intifada. "The chaos in Iraq is increasing," he noted, and the popular reaction to the intifada constitutes "the start of the countdown for the American defeat in Iraq." Atwan stressed that "an Iraqi 'awakening' is becoming evident and national unity is crystallizing, based on rejecting the occupation." This rejuvenated Iraqi nation has now risen up in arms against the U.S. and the postwar Iraq it is attempting to create. "The Iraqi intifadah is backed by 50 million pieces of weapons, five million tons of ammunition, open borders with the neighboring countries, deteriorating internal conditions, and a 'Karzai-like group' representing the occupation authority, involved in corruption and favoritism and in disagreements about the division of positions and wealth."

This combative Iraqi nation could not be expected to walk away from the gains and sacrifices of its intifada. And America has very little to offer the Iraqi nation, Atwan noted. His editorial mocked the outcome of the year-long American effort to pacify Iraq: "Baghdad became Mogadishu, Basra became Kabul, and Mosul became Kandahar—no security, no water, and no electricity. Unemployment reached 80 percent. The soccer fields turned into new mass graveyards, but with American fingerprints." Atwan emphasized that he "cannot see an exit from this Iraqi crisis for the United States and its allies," for neither the Arab League nor the UN are willing to tolerate a pro-U.S. regime in Baghdad. Meanwhile, the Islamist-jihadists will increase their pressure through the escalation of both the intifada and worldwide terrorism. Atwan sees only grim prospects ahead. "The region is boiling, and this boiling is reinforcing extremism and increasing the caravans of human bombs and martyrdom operations. Is this what President Bush meant when he said that the world would become more secure after the invasion of Iraq?"

And so, in early May, the Bush administration found itself ensnared in a treacherous predicament—a whirlwind of its own making. A growing fear of negative political reaction to extremely heavy casualties among U.S. forces and Iraqi civilians rendered the administration unwilling to take steps to solve the crisis through military means; a shortage of fighting forces, lack of actionable intelligence, and absence of clear strategy placed such a solution out of reach even if Washington had felt able to pursue it. The Bush administration would have no choice but to go along with the UN and Arab League in order to ensure a semblance of victory—a transfer of sovereignty to an Iraqi entity by July 1. But this development is unacceptable to the leaders of neighboring Iran—and the Iraqi intifada's triumph to date has convinced Tehran that it can secure a strategic victory over the U.S. without an actual war. The Iranian government appears determined to avoid being encircled by hostile nations; instead it has set its sights on a strategic breakout and victory. Tehran's resolve was articulated by both Hashemi-Rafsanjani and Khamenei in fiery sermons on April 30, 2004; Tehran and its Iraqi allies were gearing up for a long and arduous struggle. Indeed, as of this writing a growing flow of intelligence reports is warning that the Iraqi Islamist-jihadist forces and their Iranian sponsors are already preparing for a major summer offensive designed to scuttle any chance of a successful transfer of power on the Americans' timetable.

The tragedy of America's predicament in Iraq is that most, if not all, of what has occurred could have been avoided, if only Washington had faced the realities of Iraq and the Arab Muslim world and acted accordingly. But the American intelligence community has consistently failed the Bush administration, providing a skewed analysis of the situation in Iraq, and encouraging false expectations. Under such circumstances, Washington's slide to the quagmire in Iraq was inevitable. As a May 1 editorial in the Jedda *Arab News*, the most important English-language newspaper in Saudi Arabia, succinctly put it: "In truth, the American behavior in Iraq could not have been more inept or more disastrous if George Bush had handed the planning of the occupation to Saddam Hussein himself. . . . The Americans have done pretty well everything wrong."

NOTES:
THE HISTORICAL RECORD

T he possibility of an Iraqi strategic deception influencing U.S. support for the anti-Saddam resistance to the point of directly contributing to its destruction becomes a frighteningly real probability when one considers the Soviet Union's historic record in this kind of operation.

Between 1917 and the mid-1950s the USSR was confronted by internal armed resistance and popular opposition. To deal with this, the Soviets pursued a strategy of creating and subverting anti-Soviet movements by penetrating and deceiving the Western intelligence services supporting them. Under this strategy, Soviet intelligence, from the Cheka to the KGB, succeeded in shifting Western assistance and support away from legitimate anti-Communist freedom fighters to make-believe organizations and fronts that the Soviets created. In almost every case, the West's misguided operations gained momentum from a perception of success, which prevented any chance of seeing through the Soviet ruse.

Indeed, the Soviet record is impressive: Soon after the 1917 Revolution, the Cheka set out to neutralize the vast network of its opponents that had been constructed around Russian émigrés and was supported by European secret services, by diverting their attention to an artificial entity— "The Trust"—as the genuine opposition to the Bolshevik rule. By the time Moscow decided to call off the deception, the Cheka had completely destroyed all indigenous opposition. Key leaders and operatives, including General Savinkov and the British Secret Intelligence Service's Sidney Reilly, were lured into the USSR, betrayed, and ultimately faced death at the hands of the Cheka. Further, through New Economic Policy (NEP), the economic component of the Trust operation, the West even ended up financing the economic recovery of Russia and the Bolsheviks' consolidation of power.

No less significant was the use of deception in suppressing the Basmachi revolt in Central Asia and the Caucasus revolt led by the heirs of Shamil (a legendary rebel of the mid-nineteenth century). In this case, the Soviets established special detachments that masqueraded as Basmachi forces. Operating near border areas and attracting massive Red Army reaction, these detachments made contacts with British and Turkish intelligence services and eventually received the bulk of their support. Moving throughout Central Asia, the detachments maneuvered the main Basmachi forces into raiding units of the Red Army. This ultimately led to the assassination of Turkish General Enver Pasha on August 4, 1922, and the consequent collapse of the Basmachi movement. Between 1925 and 1930, the remaining fragments of the Basmachi forces were raided by Soviet soldiers operating in Afghan Army uniforms and were destroyed, ending all organized resistance inside the USSR.

Soon after World War II, a wave of nationalist sentiment spread throughout Eastern Europe. Various ethnic groups in the Baltic, the Ukraine, Poland, and even Albania rose up in arms to resist Communist occupation. A coalition of Western intelligence services, led by the CIA and the SIS, moved to provide extensive military and financial assistance to these peoples, with special attention paid to the training of émigrés as commanders and leaders of these forces and to their para-dropping into their home countries to lead the rapidly escalating national revolts. The NKVD (Soviet intelligence) moved quickly to suppress these movements.

An important component of this Soviet counteroffensive was an effort to divert Western assistance away from the real liberation movements. Several NKVD agents, as well as coopting and extorting nationalist leaders, were sent to join and penetrate the nationalist movements both in Western Europe and in their home countries. Many rebel forces were created by the NKVD and then permitted to attack local Soviet militia units and other government objectives in order to gain credibility, and have their commanders—that is senior NKVD agents—exfiltrated to the West for thorough debriefing of the situation in their native countries. Furthermore, Western military support and intelligence-gathering equipment were then delivered to these commanders. Thus there emerged a vicious cycle in which the NKVD supplied the SIS and the CIA with false data on imaginary liberation groups and received extensive military and financial support in return.

In due course, the West became committed to the NKVD's puppet forces and the genuine resistance forces were betrayed to the Soviets by

NKVD penetrating agents and by the CIA and SIS urging them to make contact with the NKVD-sponsored resistance forces. Local resistance forces that would not participate in the West's grand designs were denied all help. Thus their ultimate destruction by the Soviets was only a question of time. By the mid-1950s, the NKVD had thoroughly subverted all internal opposition and had destroyed all the effective armed groups throughout the Soviet Union. They then swiftly ended the operation, clearly demonstrating how shallow and artificial the forces the CIA and the SIS had been supporting were. Indeed, in *The Red Web,* his milestone study of the KGB's compromising and controlling of SIS support for the Baltic resistance between 1944 and 1955, Tom Bower identifies the primary source for the disastrous failure of both the SIS and the Baltic patriots it supported: "SIS fed its own deception by its willingness to believe in its own success."

Soviet intelligence resorted to the same methods during the war in Afghanistan, the moment it realized that the United States was spearheading an international effort to sustain and support the Afghan mujahedin. Hence, although the prime protégé of the ISI (Pakistani intelligence) and the main recipient of CIA and Saudi help, Gulbaddin Hekmatiyar and his key commanders worked for the USSR to a certain degree during the 1980s. Upper echelons of Hezb-i-Islami, knowingly led by Gulbaddin Hekmatiyar, constituted a crucial component in a Soviet master deception operation against the United States aimed at neutralizing the Afghan resistance. For example, since the escalation of the fighting inside Afghanistan in 1979, the main fighting carried out by Hezb-i-Islami was against other resistance groups. The late commander Abdul-Haq observed that "Gulbaddin's problem is that he kills more mujahedin than Soviets." By 1989, some 80 percent of the resistance infighting inside Afghanistan involved Gulbaddin's men. This infighting was not only for local domination and access to resources, but also to contain developing resistance forces that could have caused trouble to local DRA (Democratic Republic of Afghanistan) forces later on.

One of the KGB's most successful agent-commanders was Shirgol. Known as Dervish, in 1984–1987 he was a senior Hezb-i-Islami commander in Parvan Province. In the early 1980s, Shirgol volunteered his services to the KhAD (Afghan intelligence), and once he began rising in the ranks, his case was taken over by the KGB. Initially Dervish fought other resistance forces in his area on orders from KhAD, and justified this to the ISI as a campaign to consolidate Gulbaddin's control over the province. In order to expedite this campaign, he received extra weapons, including surface-to-surface rockets and surface-to-air missiles. Over the next two years Dervish built a core force of some fifty mujahedin commanders loyal to him personally. They eventually followed him to Kabul in early 1987 in what became one of the most devastating propaganda coups for the Communist regime.

Shirgol's greatest achievement was the major strategic deception he ran, with active support from Gulbaddin, against the CIA and the ISI. During the mid-1980s, the CIA and the ISI were contemplating an audacious strategic gambit—to use Afghanistan as a springboard for the penetration, and perhaps even subversion, of Soviet Central Asia. Claiming to have refugees from Central Asia in Parvan, Gulbaddin convinced the ISI, and then the CIA, to make Shirgol the commander of the "Islamic Army" preparing for the liberation of Bokhara and the whole of Soviet Central Asia. Provided with lavish aid, Gulbaddin's representatives in Afghanistan's northernmost provinces convinced local inhabitants, many of whom came from Basmachi families that had escaped from the USSR in the 1920s and 1930s, to join Hezb-i-Islami in order to organize an Islamic Liberation Army. Gulbaddin even nominated a cousin of the last Emir of Bokhara, who had been dethroned by the Soviets in 1922, as the new Emir of Bokhara. Several Arab governments and foundations donated huge sums of money and weapons for this initiative. The training of the Bokhara Islamic Liberation Army started in late 1984 in the Parvan Province directly under Commander Dervish. Many Muslim defectors and refugees from Soviet Central Asia who had reached Pakistan were duly sent to join the Bokhara forces. The KGB and KhAD were kept fully informed on the progress of the training. In early 1987, less than a week after Shirgol's return to Kabul, the Soviet Air Force bombed the Bokhara Army's facilities, destroying its forces beyond recovery.

Hudna [truce] is a specific and loaded term in Muslim jurisprudence and international relations. From the very beginning of the Oslo Process, Arafat justified his involvement in the peace process by comparing it with Prophet Muhammad's Treaty of Hudaybiya signed with the Jewish tribe of Quraysh in 628 A.D. In the Treaty of Hudaybiya, Prophet Muhammad promised his enemies, under duress, peace for ten years, but violated it two years later, ostensibly in reaction to a provocation, but also, it's argued, because his armies were ready, and then conquered Mecca, which had been ruled by the Quraysh, and slaughtered all the members of the Jewish tribe.

Numerous Palestinian scholars elaborated on and clarified the relevance of the *Hudna* principle to the Israeli-Palestinian peace process. In these studies, the Palestinian elite never concealed its ultimate objectives. Even in early 2000, Kamal al-Astal, a senior "foreign ministry" official, analyzed the still active negotiations with Israel in an article in *Al-Siyasah al-Filastiniyah:* The "political agreement" negotiated with Israel was "a manifestation of a temporary *Hudna*" and not a permanent solution. There could be no termination of the conflict because "the Arab-Zionist conflict is a civilizational conflict that will prevail even if a peace agreement is signed," al-Astal explained. Even in the event of a negotiated solution, "the region [would] continue to live in the shadow of the axiom—imperfect peace and interminable war." Al-Astal stressed that "the [current] reconciliation [was] not historic" and that "the struggle [would] continue in all the trenches," irrespective of the negotiated process.

In summer 2003, as Hamas, Islamic Jihad, and the al-Aqsa Martyrs Brigades were engaged by the Palestinian Authority in negotiations about accepting a *Hudna,* the Palestinian Islamist leadership sought expert opinion about the validity and conditionality of accepting such a truce under contemporary conditions. One of the most important and authoritative responses was the July 13, 2003, study by Pakistani scholar Asif Khan, titled "Treaties in Islam." He stressed the inadmissibility of Western-type agreements and arrangements, particularly on issues pertaining to an Israeli-Palestinian agreement. Asif Khan stressed that in principle, since all of Palestine is Muslim land that belongs to the entire *Ummah* (Muslim Nation), the Palestinian Authority had no legal authority to negotiate over it. "Arafat and his Palestinian Authority were not authorized to represent the *Ummah* or enter a treaty with Israel, so whatever they agreed upon is null and void," Assif Khan decreed. He then argued that the sole legal precedent governing engagement in a contemporary *Hudna* (truce) was the Treaty of Hudaybiya. "The truce treaty between Muslims and disbelievers is permitted due to the truce of the Prophet . . . with the Quraysh at Hudaybiyah. However, the permissibility of a truce is restricted to the existence of an advantage for the foreign policy [of the Muslim side] or spreading of the *Dawah* (Islamic awakening)." Furthermore, the mere existence of a *Hudna* cannot alter the existing enmity and state of war between the parties. The *Hudna* simply buys temporary nonbelligerence until conditions are ripe for the resumption of jihad. "If the benefit in a truce treaty is verified, it must be measured for a specified and known period. No truce is allowed without a time period, because if it did not have one, this would be the suspension of the *Dawah* to Islam indefinitely, and also the Hudaybiyah truce had a specific period measured for it, which we are thus obliged to follow." Assif Khan stressed that numerous actions of the non-Muslim side "invalidate a truce" in the interest of the Muslim side. "It is allowed under these circumstances to recommence the foreign policy of the [Muslim] State, and surprise action against the enemy state is permitted. This is because when the messenger . . . came to a truce with the Quraysh and they broke their truce, it became permissible for the Islamic State to ignore the conditions of the truce that they agreed upon and he [Prophet Muhammad] conquered Mecca."

In summer 2003, the representatives of the major terrorist groups stressed that their legal interpretation of the three-month *Hudna* they agreed to was identical to Assif Khan's.

The Gehlen syndrome is named after Reinhard Gehlen (1902–1979). During the Second World War, Gehlen was the head of Military Intelligence with Foreign Armies—Germany's forces in the USSR and Eastern Europe—and ended the war with the rank of lieutenant general. Despite the colossal failure of German intelligence in the war with the Soviet Union, Gehlen was embraced by the U.S. occupation forces soon after the end of the Second World War and encouraged to establish a new West German intelligence organization using his wartime colleagues. Devoid of any intelligence resources in the Eastern Bloc as the Cold War was fast escalating, the United States was mesmerized by Gehlen's false claims to having vast experience in fighting the Soviets and extensive networks of agents at the heart of the USSR. Ultimately, Gehlen remained West Germany's spymaster for about a quarter of a century, chalking up a few successes and numerous failures. The opening of the East German and Soviet intelligence archives in the aftermath of the Cold War provided chilling evidence of the widespread penetration and subversion of Gehlen's organization by Soviet and East German intelligence services. In retrospect, Gehlen's worldview—his profound disdain for the Soviet political and military authorities in Moscow—laid the foundations for U.S. intelligence's overall perception of the USSR throughout the Cold War. This approach led to nearly five decades of mammoth intelligence failures that would have been catastrophic had a hot war erupted. America's embrace of Gehlen's perception of the Soviet Union led to profound errors ranging from endemic underestimation of Soviet military might to overestimation of the Soviet economic posture. Throughout, the United States completely missed the reawakening of Third World radicalism and militancy, most significantly the ascent of radical Islam—an omission for which the United States is now paying heavily.

NOTE ON SOURCES
AND METHODS

In a May 2003 interview with the *Guardian,* former secretary of defense Robert McNamara raised the ghosts of Vietnam. He attributed America's failure there to the realization that in Vietnam the United States was fighting its own war—a front in a global Cold War—while being completely oblivious to the peculiarities of Vietnam. "We didn't know the Vietnamese enough to empathize with them; we did not study their history or culture. We didn't see that they saw us as just replacing the French as the colonial power. We were fighting the Cold War, but to them it was a civil war. That was our mistake." For the United States that mistake was disastrous, as the trauma of Vietnam both scarred the fiber of American society and significantly degraded America's strategic posture. Presently, the discrepancy between the wars being waged in Iraq by the United States and the opposing Arab and Muslim coalition is even greater. Yet, as was the case during the Vietnam War, Washington refuses to recognize this phenomenon.

For the Arab Middle East, the war in Iraq is being fought both in the present and in the traumatic, several-hundred-years-distant past. While it is impossible to grasp the war without a detailed knowledge of unfolding events, it also cannot be understood without comprehending the history of Muslim Mesopotamia, as seen through Arab eyes. For Baghdad's intellectual elite—by far the most sophisticated and Westernized elite in the Arab world both because of and despite Saddam Hussein's reign—current events encapsulate the return of both the thirteenth-century Mongol armies that occupied and destroyed the Caliphate, and the antiimperialist struggle and nationalist awakening of the 1920s. For the rest of Iraq's population, irrespective of their brand of Islam and national or ethnic affiliation, the current war solely revisits the Mongol invasion, the sacking of Baghdad, and the Mongols' ultimate defeat.

Therefore, the Baghdad elite—who were expected to have grasped the importance of British-mandated "nation building" and forced moderniza-tion of society eighty years ago, and are presently expected to endorse the American "liberation" and cooperate with the occupation authorities to establish a modern democratic Iraq—still constitute the key to the recov-ery of a unified Iraq. However, this educated and Westernized middle class has been the primary victim of more than a decade of international sanc-tions and is now the primary victim of the de-Baathization campaign. It is not surprising that among this group there is both virulent hatred of the United States and shame for having allowed themselves to be oppressed and humiliated. Among many of them there is a belief that theirs is a com-munal shame that can only be cleansed with blood, from both martyrs and defilers. One of the best examples of that perception is that one of the most popular poems of the 1920s—a political protest written by Muhammad al-Obeidi—is making a comeback. (An excellent English translation can be found in Tariq Ali's 2003 book, *Bush in Babylon: The Recolonisation of Iraq.*)

> *Set fire noble Iraqis*
> *wash our shame with blood*
> *We are not slaves*
> *to adorn our necks with collars*
> *We are not prisoners*
> *to submit ourselves to be manacled*
> *We are not women*
> *whose only weapon is the tear*
> *We are not orphans*
> *that seek a Mandate for Iraq*
> *And if we bow before oppression*
> *We shall forfeit the pleasures of the Tigris*

There cannot be any semblance of a unified Iraq without the help of Baghdad's urban elite. The key to Iraq's future lies in whether they will cre-ate the mechanism that will hold together the diverse and mutually hostile ethnic and religious groups of Iraq. And therefore, as Iraqi intellectuals now warn, the great unknown concerning the future of Iraq lies more in the attitude of the elite than in the actions of the American occupiers. On the eve of the war, the Iraqi poet Mudhaffar al-Nawab warned his people of the dangers of repeating, and succumbing to, Iraq's recent legacy of political abuse. (An excellent English translation by Sarah Maguire and Hafiz Kheiri can also be found in Tariq Ali's book.)

> *O my people in love with our homeland,*
> *I'm not scared of barbarians gathered at our gates.*
> *No, I'm afraid of the enemies within—*
> *Tyranny, Autocracy, Dictatorship.*

To comprehend the current historic drama in Iraq, and the Arab Middle East as a whole, one must analyze unfolding events while bearing in mind Arab history, and its myths. This is not the past that history books write about; this history is an evolving acount of events—the people's oral history of their heritage as expressed in political debates, teahouse conversations, folklore, poetry, popular songs, and the imam's interpretation of recent events during the Friday sermons. The Arab historic myth adapts to the events of the day in order to explain and justify the present and future rather than articulate the past. To grasp the contemporary importance and profound meaning of this oral tradition, one has to be exposed to these themes in countless lengthy conversations over many years. Having to grapple with this approach determined the types of sources I used for writing *The Secret History of the Iraq War.*

Writing a book on still-unfolding events is quite a challenge—all the more so when the pace of events accelerates throughout the process of writing. Furthermore, this is a book about both high politics and discrete violent undertakings, about the events they inspired and the activities they caused, the ramifications of actions both taken and not taken. The ultimate outcome of the dynamics addressed holds tremendous importance for all the leaders—political, military, and terrorist—involved in this project. This reality has direct bearing on the commonly available public record. Powerful figures manipulate the media to steer politics, influence the record of their actions, and ensure their legacy in history. Quite often, objectivity is sacrificed on the altar of both short-term political expediency and the desire of powerful figures to write themselves forever into history and myth. And of course there are still the relatively unknown dynamics—clandestine contacts, covert operations, political brawling and deal-making—all of which take place in the dark.

In writing this book I relied as much as possible on contemporary indigenous sources—material collected from and communication with senior officials and professional staff directly involved in the events described. However, since many are inclined to tilt versions of events in their own favor, I relied on written reports whenever possible, as well as on contemporary documents and "nonpapers" prepared by the officials and staff. I also made heavy use of the region's vibrant media (including television, radio, Internet, and print), as well as a huge number of personal contacts on all sides of the conflict.

In recent years, specialized electronic news services and online periodicals have become an indispensable source of timely reporting. Officials and experts alike use these outlets as primary sources and as vehicles for disseminating their own take on events. As such, these newsletters and periodicals present a contemporary record of events against which the more private communications can be checked. Of the many news services, two merit singling out for their outstanding reporting: The Middle East News Line (MENL) and its chief editor, Steve Rodan, are indispensable resources for news and analysis on regional security matters. Comprehensive news and insightful analysis of global security developments is provided by the Global Information System (GIS) and its chief editor, Gregory R. Copley. (Although I have written several stories for GIS, I can say objectively that it is an outstanding resource.)

Regarding the war itself, Dr. Anthony H. Cordesman of the Center for Strategic and International Studies (CSIS) posted several noteworthy, valuable papers on the CSIS Web site. His analysis and "instant lessons" as events were unfolding were particularly helpful. Yigal Carmon's Middle East Media Research Institute was a most valuable source of annotated translations and media analysis from the entire Middle East. Boaz Ganor's Institute for Counter-Terrorism publishes excellent studies and maintains one of the finest archives on international terrorism with an emphasis on the Middle East. Giora Shamis's DEBKAfile is also noteworthy because of the unique scoops and intriguing analysis of Middle Eastern affairs they consistently publish.

The Secret History of the Iraq War is largely based on extensive source material from the Middle East, including Iraq and the various relevant Arab states, as well as Israel, Iran, and Turkey. Additional original source material comes from numerous Western European countries, Russia, Southwest Asia, and other parts of the Muslim world. Moreover, I have had extensive interactions with numerous government officials, diplomats, spies of many shades, senior security and defense officials, as well as terrorists, militia commanders, émigrés, and other individuals from all sides of the Middle East's tangled web of loyalties and associations. These unique sources supplement the large quantities of open sources—primarily the regional media—that by themselves provide a wealth of data and documentation. This open source material includes wire service reports by local and international news agencies; numerous articles from local newspapers, periodicals, and newsletters; articles from newspapers, periodicals, and newsletters of the Arab émigré community in Western Europe; clippings from newspapers, periodicals, newsletters, and academic journals in the United States, Europe, Russia, and other countries; transcripts of broadcasts from the local electronic media (mostly translated by the U.S. government's excellent Foreign Broadcast Information Service); and huge quantities of original source material retrieved through the Internet.

For background information, I also consulted a unique collection of primary sources—including original publications, documents, and reports—developed over more than a quarter of a century of intensive research. This wide range of sources constitutes a unique base for expert analysis regarding the subjects in question.

Special note should be taken of the Iraqi sources used throughout this book. Before the war, the Baathist regime saw in the electronic media a pure instrument of propaganda, conveying in word and image the messages Saddam Hussein wanted transmitted to the masses. The printed media was more serious and attempted to chronicle events as well as editorialize about their significance. Of course, the printed media operated within the strict guidelines of Baathist supervision, and whenever there was the slightest transgression, the offending newspaper—including Uday's own *Babil*—was temporarily prevented from publishing new editions. Quite a few journalists and editors vanished in Saddam's torture system, while others defected. During the Baath days, Iraq had two types of written media: the Baghdad-based national papers and the regional papers. The national media reflected the thinking of both the Baathist leadership and the Baghdad elite, while the regional media was less politicized and therefore more accurately reported events and prevailing moods. A myriad of opposition media also emerged in the Kurdish zones, but these publications were thoroughly politicized and so skewed as to cast their accuracy into doubt.

The fall of Saddam Hussein thoroughly changed the face of the Iraqi media. New media—mainly publications—sprang up almost immediately. The Iraqi Communist Party was the first to start publishing an independent newspaper in Baghdad, with the first issues being distributed in early April while bullets were still flying. The new Iraqi media is opinionated and sensationalist but nevertheless a unique reflection of Iraq's pulsing, vibrant diversity. At the same time, these new newspapers and periodicals are still subjected to iron-fisted censorship, now by American occupation authorities, and are also influenced by under-the-table payments from the CIA as part of an operation to buy Iraqi favor. Nevertheless, the new Iraqi media effectively portray the views and convictions held by both intellectuals and the broader population. (Publications in operation both during Saddam's era and after the fall of Baghdad are listed below.)

Ultimately, the dry definition of human sources does not do justice to the actual people involved. Over a quarter of a century, numerous people have helped me understand and analyze this complex region in two major ways. First, many hundreds, if not thousands, of people from all over the world communicated with me, in person or otherwise, and sent materials from obscure places, at times at a risk to life and liberty. Special thanks to those who patiently explained issues and answered what must have been countless dumb and overly detailed questions. Thanks to those who sought, acquired, and delivered piles of documents and other material in "funny" languages and illegible scripts. Many of these individuals live and operate "on the other side." They have communicated and provided material at great risk to themselves and their families; they have done so because they really care about their own countries and peoples. Others, usually members of "the other camp," have communicated because they want to make sure we understand what they stand for and believe in. Theirs was not an easy task either.

Secondly, It is not enough to have a wide variety of periodicals, newspapers, bulletins, newsletters, communiqués, and other written material pour in from the region. Quality varies from the absurd to the excellent, and so do reliability and pertinence. They are all important, as in their variety they accurately reflect a colorful and vibrant civilization. But these nuances are not easy to detect and comprehend. Thus, thanks to those native speakers who patiently translated and explained the multiple layers of meaning and innuendo present in these flowery, rich, and fascinating Muslim languages of the Middle East. Thanks to all the translators and readers who worked with me over the years, teaching me how to read even when I thought I knew the language. (Well, I knew the alphabet.)

Despite the diversity and multitude of the sources used, and despite the frequent use of published material, precise notation of all sources is inadvisable in this kind of writing, specifically because doing so could endanger the safety and survival of the human sources. As a rule, the moment a critical work is published, hostile counterintelligence and security organs launch relentless efforts to discover and silence the human sources still in their midst. Whenever such an individual is exposed, that person, along with his or her family, is punished most severely—usually they are tortured and killed—in order to deter others. Using "anonymous sources," or "officials," as specific entries in a book employing an otherwise academic style of notation is not sufficient to protect most human sources, particularly those providing access to extremely sensitive information. Being too specific in noting what material was acquired from such human sources helps opposing intelligence agencies narrow the scope of their search, better identify the institutions the leaks came from, and ultimately hunt down the human sources themselves. It has been my professional experience—both as the director of the Congressional Task Force on Terrorism and Unconventional Warfare since 1988 and as a published author for over a quarter of a century—that when confronted with a monolithic text in which the specific sources have been blurred, hostile counterintelligence and security organs find it virtually impossible to narrow down their searches and thus stifle the human sources.

We owe thanks to these brave individuals who, at great risk to themselves and their loved ones, provide crucial and distinct information. Every conceivable effort must be made to shield and protect them. The omission of precise source notes is the least one can do.

NATIONAL PERIODICALS OF SADDAM HUSSEIN'S IRAQ

Al-Iraq, newspaper focusing on Kurdish affairs; *Al-Jumhuriyah*, government-owned political newspaper; *Al-Qadisiyah*, government-owned political and military newspaper; *Al-Thawrah*, the Baath Party's newspaper; *Babil*, Uday Saddam Hussein's newspaper; *Iraq Daily*, Government-owned political newspaper published in English; *Al-Ilam*, weekly newspaper published by the Media Department of the Faculty of Arts, Baghdad University; *Al-Iqtisadi*, weekly published by the Iraqi Economists Society; *Al-Ittihad*, weekly published by the Iraqi Industries Union that focuses on domestic affairs; *Al-Rafidayn*, Uday Saddam Hussein's own political weekly; *Al-Ray*, weekly newspaper focusing on domestic Iraqi news; *Al-Zawra*, the "independent" weekly of the Iraqi Journalists Union run by Uday Saddam Hussein (being uniquely critical of the performance of government departments on domestic issues important to the average Iraqi, it thus served as a vehicle for the release of social steam); *Alif Ba*, government-owned political and cultural weekly magazine; *Nabd al-Shabab*, Uday Saddam Hussein's own weekly devoted to youth and domestic affairs; *Sawt al-Talabah*, weekly newspaper of the National Union of Iraqi Students.

KURDISTAN-BASED OPPOSITION PUBLICATIONS

Al-Ittihad, PUK's weekly newspaper in Arabic; *Baghdad* and *Nida al-Mustaqba*, INA's Arabic-language newspapers; *Brayati*, KDP's daily newspaper in Sorani Kurdish; *Buzutnaway Islami*, the Islamic Unity Movement in Kurdistan's bimonthly newspaper in Sorani Kurdish (replaced *Regay*

Yekbun in January 2002); *Govari Gulan*, KDP's monthly magazine in Sorani Kurdish; *Hawlati*, independent weekly newspaper in Sorani Kurdish; *Kaldo-Ashur*, the Communist Party of Iraqi Kurdistan's Arabic supplement of *Regay Kurdistan*; *Khabat*, KDP's weekly newspaper in Arabic; *Komal*, the Islamic Group of Iraqi Kurdistan's bimonthly newspaper in Sorani Kurdish; *Kurdistani Nuwe*, PUK's daily newspaper in Sorani Kurdish; *Nida al-Rafidayn*, SCIRI's bimonthly newspaper in Arabic; *Qardashliq Yolu*, the Turkman Brotherhood Party's bimonthly newspaper in Arabic; *Regay Kurdistan*, the Communist Party of Iraqi Kurdistan's weekly newspaper in Sorani Kurdish; *Traiq al-Shaab*, the Iraqi Communist Party's monthly newspaper in Arabic; *Turkmeneli*, the Turkman Front's weekly newspaper in Arabic and Turkman; *Yekgirtu*, the Iraqi Kurdish Islamic League's weekly newspaper in Sorani Kurdish.

POSTWAR IRAQI NATIONAL MEDIA

Adwa, an "independent" weekly published by "a group of journalists"; *Al-Adalah*, SCIRI's "general, political" daily; *Al-Ahali*, an "independent, political, liberal" newspaper; *Al-Ahd al-Jadid*, a "democratic, liberal, independent" weekly; *Al-Ahrar*, "The [weekly] newspaper of all Arabs" and an "independent political daily [*sic*]"; *Al-Akhbar*, an "independent, general" biweekly newspaper; *Al-Alam Bayn Yadayk*, an independent weekly; *Al-Amal*, a "political, economic, social, scientific, medical, and artistic" weekly issued by "an independent company"; *Al-Amal al-Islami*, the Islamic Action Organization's "Islamic" and "political" paper; *Al-Aswaq*, the Iraqi Industries Union's daily focusing on industry, commerce, and capital affairs; *Al-Aswar*, an "independent" daily; *Al-Awqat*, a "comprehensive Arab daily" run by veterans of Uday's *Babil*; *Al-Ayyam*, an "independent" daily, which "does not represent the viewpoint of any party, movement, or direction"; *Baladi*, the Iraqi Folklore Poets Union's periodical paper; *Al-Balagh*, the National Independence Party's newspaper; *Al-Balat*, the Iraqi National Coalition's "general" weekly newspaper; *Al-Baqi*, political and religious weekly published by the Media Center of al-Hawzah al-Ilmiyah, the Shiite theological seminary in Najaf (controlled loosely by Ayatollah Sistani); *Al-Bayan*, the Islamic Dawah Party's "political daily"; *Al-Bayda*, the Iraqi National Bloc's "cultural, political weekly" based in Mosul; *Al-Burkan*, an "independent, general, political daily" that is "not linked to any political party, organization, or trend"; *Al-Bursah*, ostensibly an independent newspaper but connected with Islamist circles, especially in northern Iraq; *Dar al-Salam,* the Iraqi Islamic Party's "political" weekly; *Al-Dawah,* the Islamic Dawah Party's Islamic (Shiite) newspaper, which is one of the boldest anti-American publications; *Al-Dimuqrati,* the Iraqi Rally for Democracy's weekly newspaper; *Dijlah,* a "general" weekly; *Al-Diyar,* a "self-financed, independent general, cultural, political weekly newspaper," which provides news "freely and without any restrictions"; *Al-Dustur,* an "independent political daily"; *Fajr Baghdad,* "The first democratic, independent newspaper to be published in Iraq after the change"; *Al-Firdaws,* the Free Democratic People's Party's political weekly and "the newspaper of all Iraqis"; *Al-Ghadir,* a weekly that "speaks for the masses"; *Al-Hadaf,* the al-Hadaf Foundation for Publication and Advertisement's "cultural" weekly; *Al-Hadath,* an "independent, general" weekly; *Al-Haqiqah,* an "independent" weekly affiliated with loyalists of the original antimonarchist Baath Party; *Al-Hawadith,* an "independent" weekly; *Al-Hawzah,* a "cultural, religious" (Shiite) weekly newspaper; *Al-Hayah al-Iraqiyah,* the 15 Shaban Islamic Movement's weekly; *Hazbazbuz Fi Zaman al-Awlamah,* an independent satirical weekly that is "neither Eastern nor Western, self-financed, and published by authorization from the public"; *Al-Hilal,* a "comprehensive, independent" daily, temporarily published as a weekly; *Al-Hiwar,* the National Front for Iraqi Intellectuals' "political" weekly; *Al-Hurr,* the Free Islamic Grouping's newspaper; *Al-Hurriyah,* the Arab Democratic Nationalists Movement's paper, which calls for broad participation in decision-making and is considered the most pro-U.S. paper; *Al-Hurriyah al-Ula,* an "independent" weekly; *Al-Iqtisadi al-Jadid,* an "independent, economic" weekly; *Al-Iraqi,* the Islamic Cultural Forum's weekly; *Al-Iraq al-Jadid,* a paper "published with the empowerment of the Iraqi national conscience"; *Al-Iraq al-Yawm,* a newspaper published by "a group of Iraqi journalists"; *Al-Istiqlal,* a "political and cultural" weekly newspaper; *Al-Ittijah al-Akhar,* an "independent, political" weekly published in The Hague, Netherlands, by the al-Watan Party and flown to Iraq; *Al-Jamahir,* the Organization Bureau of the Iraqi National Congress's "political weekly;" *Al-Jaridah,* a "general, political" daily; *Al-Jazirah,* an "independent, cultural, and social" weekly; *Kul Jadid,* the New Iraq Renaissance Movement's weekly; *Al-Liwa,* a "general, independent weekly that speaks for the Iraqi people"; *Al-Madar,* an "independent, social, cultural, national weekly" published by al-Madar House for Publishing and Distribution; *Al-Majd,* an "independent" weekly; *Al-Manar,* a "comprehensive, political" daily newspaper; *Al-Masa,* an "independent" newspaper published by "a group of Iraqi journalists"; *Al-Mawsil,* the Iraqi National Congress's newspaper (also published in Mosul); *Mujtama al-Amal al-Iraqi,* the Iraqi Businessmen's Association's "professional, economic weekly magazine"; *Al-Multaqa,* an "independent" daily; *Al-Mustaqillah,* an "independent" weekly and a "free forum for the sincere national writers," "not linked to any political party"; *Al-Mutamar,* the Iraqi National Congress's "political" weekly; *Al-Muwajahah,* an "independent" newspaper in Arabic and English; *Al-Naba,* an "independent" weekly published by "a group of Iraqi journalists" that reports "without ambiguity or bias"; *Al-Nahar,* an "independent" weekly; *Al-Nahdah,* a "cultural" weekly edited by "free, independent writers"; *Al-Nahdah,* the Iraqi Independent Democrats Movement's "daily political newspaper issued temporarily twice a week"; *Nahrayn,* the Supreme Council for the Islamic Revolution in Iraq's weekly; *Al-Nas,* an "independent, general" newspaper; *Al-Natur,* an "independent satirical, critical, and comical" weekly; *Nida al-Mustaqbal,* the Iraqi National Accord Movement's daily newspaper; *9 Nisan* (9 April), the Independent Political Prisoners Organization's weekly, named after "the day on which the tyrant fell and the new Iraq was born"; *Al-Nur,* the Islamic Cultural Center in Baghdad's weekly (the paper supports Grand Ayatollah Sistani and urges a Shiite-dominated Islamic Republic in the Iranian mold); *Al-Nur,* the Islamic Cultural Center in Baghdad's "independent, general, political weekly" (actually bimonthly), distinct from the weekly above; *Al-Qabas,* the New Iraq Charitable Society newspaper; *Qanadil,* an "independent" weekly; *Al-Raqib,* an "independent" weekly; *Al-Rasid,* an "independent" daily; *Al-Ray al-Amm,* an "independent, general" daily; *Al-Rihab,* the Democratic Royal Coalition's "political, Arab newspaper"; *Al-Risalah,* an "independent, free" weekly that deals with political, cultural, and religious issues; *Al-Saah,* the biweekly "political" newspaper of the Iraqi Unified National Movement (an independent Sunni Islamist organization); *Al-Sada,* an "independent, political" weekly; *Sada al-Hal,* the Kurdistan Democratic Solution Party's "political" weekly; *Sada al-Ummah,* the Supreme Council for the Liberation of Iraq's weekly; *Sadr al-Iraq,* an "independent, comprehensive, political" weekly (that is loyal to Moqtadah al-Sadr); *Al-Salam,* the Fraternity and Peace Movement's weekly; *Sawt al-Talabah,* the New Iraq Youth and Students Organization's weekly newspaper; *Sawt al-Taliah,* the Islamic Vanguards Organization's Islamist political weekly; *Al-Shahid,* a "general, political" weekly; *Al-Shams,* an "independent" weekly; *Al-Shira,* an "independent, general, political" weekly; *Al-Shira al-Siyasi,* a biweekly "independent" newspaper; *Spotlight,* a daily newspaper; *Al-Siyasah al-*

Yawm, an "independent" weekly; *Sumar,* an "independent, political" daily published in Kuwait; *Al-Tadamun,* the Reconciliation and Peace Party's "general, comprehensive" weekly; *Al-Tajammu,* the Iraqi Popular Grouping's weekly; *Al-Tayyar,* a "political" publication originally founded in London and now transferred to Baghdad; *Al-Thiqalayn,* a "religious" weekly; *Umm al-Rabiayn,* an "independent" weekly; *Wadi al-Rafidayn,* an "independent, social, cultural" weekly; *Al-Wasat,* the Unified National Coalition's weekly; *Al-Watan,* the Iraqi National Movement's weekly; *Al-Watan al-Iraqiyah,* the Iraqi National Unity Coalition's "economic, social, cultural, and political" newspaper; *Al-Yaqazah,* an "independent" political daily; *Al-Yawm al-Akhar,* an "independent" weekly; *Al-Zaman,* an "Iraqi, Arab, independent" daily published in Baghdad, al-Basrah, the United Kingdom, and Bahrain; *Al-Zawra,* the Iraqi Journalists Union's "general" weekly newspaper.

POSTWAR IRAQI REGIONAL MEDIA

Al-Awdah, the Social Society of Faili Kurds' bimonthly newspaper; *Brayati,* the Iraqi Kurdistan Democratic Party's Kurdish-language daily newspaper; *Govari Gulan,* the Iraqi Kurdistan Democratic Party's Kurdish-language monthly magazine; *Hawal,* an independent Kurdish-language weekly newspaper; *Hawlati,* an independent Kurdish-language weekly newspaper; *Al-Ittihad,* the Patriotic Union of Kurdistan's Arabic-language paper; *Jammawar,* an independent Kurdish-language weekly newspaper; *Kaldo-Ashur,* the Kurdish-language supplement to *Regay Kurdistan; Khabat,* the Islamic Unity Movement's Kurdish-language weekly newspaper; *Komal,* the Islamic Group of Iraqi Kurdistan's Kurdish-language bimonthly newspaper; *Kurdistan Nuwe,* the Patriotic Union of Kurdistan's Kurdish-language daily newspaper; *Qardashliq Yedu,* the Turkoman Brotherhood's bimonthly newspaper published in Turkoman, Kurdish, and Arabic; *Regay Kurdistan,* the Communist Party of Iraqi Kurdistan's Kurdish-language weekly newspaper; *Al-Taakhi,* the Iraqi Kurdistan Democratic Party's Arabic-language daily newspaper; *Tariq al-Shab,* the Iraqi Communist Party's Arabic-language monthly newspaper; *Turkomaneli,* the Turkoman Brotherhood Party's bimonthly newspaper published in both Turkoman and Arabic.

THE MAIN NON-IRAQI PERIODICALS

News Agencies
AFP (France); ANATOLIA (Turkey); ANSA (Italy); AP (U.S.); EFE (Spain); FNS (Russia); HINA (Croatia); INA (Iraq); INTERFAX (Russia); IPS (France-based Iranian Opposition); IRNA (Iran); ITAR-TASS (Russia); KYODO (Japan); Lebanon News Wire (Lebanon); MENA (Egypt); PANA (Pan-African); Petra (Jordan); REUTERS (U.S./UK); RIA-Novosti (Russia); SANA (Syria); SDA (Switzerland); SPA (Saudi Arabia); SUNA (Sudan); TANJUG (Yugoslavia); TASS (USSR); UPI (U.S./UK); WAFA (Palestinian); XINHUA (China).

Periodicals and Newspapers (Both Paper and Electronic Editions)
26 September (Yemen); *Abd-Rabouh* (Jordan); *Addis Tribune* (Ethiopia); *Akhbar* (Pakistan); *Al-Ahd* (Lebanon); *Al-Ahram* (Egypt); *Al-Ahram al-Masai* (Egypt); *Al-Akhbar* (Egypt); *Al-Alam* (Arabic newspaper published in the UK); *Al-Anwar* (Lebanon); *Al-Ayam* (Bahrain); *Al-Ayyam* (Palestinian); *Al-Ayyam* (Yemen); *Al-Baath* (Syria); *Al-Bayan* (UAE); *Al-Dustour* (Jordan); *Al-Gumhuria* (Egypt); *Al-Hadath* (Jordan); *Al-Hayah* (Arabic newspaper published in the UK); *Al-Hayah Al-Jadidah* (Palestinian); *Al-Islah* (Arabic newspaper published in the UK); *Al-Istiqlal* (Palestinian); *Al-Itidal* (Saudi Arabia); *Al-Ittihad* (UAE); *Al-Jazirah* (Saudi Arabia); *Al-Khaleej* (UAE); *Al-Madinah* (Saudi Arabia); *Al-Majalla* (Arabic newspaper published in the UK); *Al-Massaiah* (Saudi Arabia); *Al-Messa* (Egypt); *Al-Mizan* (Arabic newspaper published in the UK); *Al-Mussawar* (Egypt); *Al-Nahar* (Lebanon); *Al-Qabas* (Kuwait); *Al-Quds* (Palestinian); *Al-Quds al-Arabi* (Arabic newspaper published in the UK); *Al-Rai* (Jordan); *Al-Raya* (Qatar); *Al-Sabeel* (Jordan); *Al-Safir* (Lebanon); *Al-Shaab* (Egypt); *Al-Sharq al-Awsat* (Arabic newspaper published in the UK); *Al-Shira* (Lebanon); *Al-Thawarah* (Syria); *Al-Vefagh* (Iran); *Al-Wafd* (Egypt); *Al-Wasat* (Arabic newspaper published in the UK); *Al-Watan* (Kuwait); *Al-Watan* (Oman); *Al-Watan* (Qatar); *Al-Watan al-Arabi* (Arabic newspaper published in Europe); *Arab News* (Saudi Arabia); *Asian Age* (India/UK); *Ausaf* (Pakistan); *Bahrain Tribune* (Bahrain); *Bild* (Germany); *Bulvar* (Turkey); *Corriere Della Sera* (Italy); *The Crescent International* (UK/Canada); *Daily Excelsior* (India); *Daily Hot News* (Pakistan); *Daily Jang* (Pakistan); *Daily Jasarat* (Pakistan); *Daily News* (Pakistan); *The Daily Star* (Lebanon); *Daily Telegraph* (UK); *Dawn* (Pakistan); *Deccan Herald* (India); *Defence Journal* (Pakistan); *Defense & Foreign Affairs:*

Strategic Policy (UK/U.S.); *Der Spiegel* (Germany); *Die Welt* (Germany); *The Economist* (UK); *Egyptian Gazette* (Egypt); *Ettela'at* (Iran); *European* (UK); *Far Eastern Economic Review* (Hong Kong); *Financial Times* (UK); *Focus* (Germany); *Foreign Affairs* (U.S.); *Foreign Policy* (U.S.); *Foreign Report* (UK); *Frankfurter Allgemeine Zeitung* (Germany); *Friday Times* (Pakistan); *The Frontier Post* (Pakistan); *Globe and Mail* (Canada); *Guardian* (UK); *Gulf Daily News* (Bahrain); *Gulf News* (UAE); *Gulf Times* (Qatar); *Ha'Aretz* (Israel); *Ham-Shahri* (Iran); *The Hindu* (India); *Hindustan Times* (India); *Home News* (Sudan); *Hong Kong Standard* (Hong Kong); *Hurmat* (Pakistan); *Hurriyet* (Turkey); *Independent* (UK); *India Defence Review* (India); *India Today* (India); *The Indian Express* (India); *Indus News* (Pakistan); *Intelligence Newsletter* (France); *Iran Daily* (Iran); *Iran News* (Iran); *Iran Shahr* (Iran); *Israeli & Global News* (U.S.); *Izvestiya* (Russia); *Jane's Defence Weekly* (UK); *Jane's Intelligence Review* (formerly *Jane's Soviet Intelligence Review*) (UK); *Jang* (Pakistan); *Jasarat* (Pakistan); *Jerusalem Post* (Israel); *Jerusalem Times* (Palestinian); *Jeune Afrique* (France); *Jomhuri-ye Islami* (Iran); *Jordan Times* (Jordan); *Keyhan* (UK-based newspaper published by the Iranian Opposition); *Keyhan* (Iran); Khabrain (Pakistan); *Khaleej Times* (UAE); *Krasnaya Zvezda* (Russia); *Kuwait Times* (Kuwait); *La Revue du Liban* (Lebanon); *L'Evenement du Jeudi* (France); *L'Express* (France); *Le Figaro* (France); *Le Monde* (France); *Le Nouvel Observateur* (France); *Le Point* (France); *L'Orient-Le Jour* (Lebanon); *Los Angeles Times* (U.S.); *Maariv* (Israel); *Mashriq* (Pakistan); *Middle East Times* (Egypt); *Milliyet* (Turkey); *Mirror* (UK); *Moscow Times* (Russia); *The Muslim* (Pakistan); *Muslim News* (UK); *The Nation* (Pakistan); *Nawa-i-Waqt* (Pakistan); *The New York Times* (U.S.); *The News* (Pakistan); *News India-Times* (India); *The News International* (Pakistan); *Newsweek* (U.S.); *Nezavisimaya Gazeta* (Russia); *Nida-e-Khilfat* (Pakistan); *Nida-ul-Islam* (Australia); *Nimrooz* (UK-based newspaper published by the Iranian Opposition); *Observer* (UK); *October* (Egypt); *Oman Daily* (Oman); *Oman Daily Observer* (Oman); *Pakistan* (Pakistan); *The Pakistan Observer* (Pakistan); *The Pakistan Times* (Pakistan); *Pravda* (Russia); *Rose al-Youssuf* (Egypt); *SAPRA Review* (India); *Segodnya* (Russia); *Shihan* (Jordan); *South China Morning Post* (Hong Kong); *The Star* (Jordan); *The Statesman* (India); *The Straits Times* (Singapore); *The Sunday Telegraph* (UK); *The Sunday Times* (UK); *The Sunday Times* (UK); *Syria Daily* (Syria); *Syria Times* (Syria); *Takbeer* (Pakistan); *The Times* (UK); *The Times of India* (India); *Tehran Times* (Iran); *The Telegraph* (India); *The Telegraph* (UK); *Time* (U.S. and European editions); *Tishrin* (Syria);

Turkish Daily News (Turkey); *Ukaz* (Saudi Arabia); *U.S. News & World Report* (U.S.); *Voyenno Istoricheskiy Zhurnal* (Russia); *Washington Post* (U.S.); *Washington Times* (U.S.); *Y-net* (Israel); *Yediot Aharonot* (Israel); *Yemen Times* (Yemen); *Zarubezhnoye Voyennye Obozreniye* (Russia); *Zindagi* (Pakistan).

ACKNOWLEDGMENTS

The *Secret History of the Iraq War* could not have been written without the help of numerous people over many years. Although the scope of the book covers the most recent but still crucial eighteen months in the tumultuous history of the Middle East, it was my longtime friendships throughout the region—most of which have lasted well over a decade—that provided the most crucial information included in this book. No less important for its success were those anonymous individuals who contributed their knowledge and who provided the unique source material upon which this book is based. The nature and extent of their contribution is elaborated on in my "Note on Sources and Methods," but suffice it to say that this book could not have been written without them. Special gratitude for the warm hospitality many of these individuals showed me.

Embarking on this undertaking, I discovered just how blessed I've been with good friends whose help made this book possible. Unfortunately, two of my most important friends, who inspired me and provided immeasurable help throughout, cannot be recognized by name.

My "best friend"—a worthy scion of his family—opened my eyes in our lengthy all night conversations about the complexities of his home country, Iraq, and the Arab world as a whole. Our lengthy walk around the "lake" on the eve of the Iraq war was a unique, intellectually stimulating experience that made me think a lot about the wider consequences of the war. My best friend's continued involvement in the affairs of his country remains a source of hope that with young, dedicated, and sophisticated leaders like him at the helm, the Arab world will be able to endure the current crisis and emerge to take its deserved place in a modern and more free world. Special thanks to my best friend's mother and family for their warm and generous hospitality.

No words can do justice to the enduring contribution of "the doctor" to my work. In lengthy and inspiring conversations, he gave me a whole new perspective on this complex, fascinating, and at times forbidden world. The doctor elucidated the intricacies of the Arab power structure, dynamics, decision-making process, and the importance of personal relationships among leaders and ruling elites. His analysis of the regional dynamics in the aftermath of the war, delivered during a sumptuous dinner in fall 2003, was both brilliant and prophetic. The doctor's depth of knowledge and breadth of vision are always awe-inspiring. I'm humbled and proud to be considered his friend. One wishes that the doctor would soon attain the leadership position he rightfully deserves—the Middle East will then be a better place.

Of those who can be recognized by name, special thanks go to the members of the U.S. House of Representatives—Eric Cantor, Jim Saxton, and Duncan Hunter, as well as retired representatives Helen Delich Bentley and Bill McCollum, for their unyielding help and support, and for their friendship.

Gregory R. Copley, president of the International Strategic Studies Association, editor of *Defense & Foreign Affairs: Strategic Policy,* and first and foremost a friend for some twenty years, shared his vast knowledge and understanding of world affairs. Always ready to lend an ear to my doubts, his sound judgment helped me a lot. Special thanks to Pamela von Gruber.

Baroness Caroline Cox of Queensbury, the deputy speaker of the House of Lords, and Dr. John Marks, OBE, soul mates and dear friends, were far more than gracious hosts who made me feel at home whenever I was in London. They were exceptional and most patient sounding boards for my observations and analysis. Their sound judgment and wide knowledge were invaluable to my writing.

Professor Murray Kahl was there with me and for me throughout the chaotic experience of writing a book on still unfolding events. He helped by reading and commenting on early drafts, locating data on the Internet, "holding my hand" as my computers kept crashing, and just being a good friend.

Nagi Najjar, executive director of the Lebanon Foundation for Peace, provided extensive and unyielding support in more than one way. Warm thanks for his friendship and companionship as we traveled while I was researching and writing this book.

Other friends rallied as well. Steve Rodan, director of the Middle East News Line, was most generous with his vast knowledge and deep understanding of Middle Eastern security affairs. Yoichiro Kawai was exceptionally generous with his impressions and interview material accumulated during numerous visits to Iraq before and after the war. Guido Olimpio also shared a lot of material from his unique sources. Dr. Marc Ellenbogen, president of the Prague Society, and I had stimulating and thought-provoking conversations that helped me see things in the right perspective. The indefatigable "Jacques" did what only he can. Dr. Assad Homayoun shared his unique insight and knowledge of Iran. And last but not least, Rosanne Klass kept my files bursting with clippings.

Daniel Bial, my agent, took care of business as I kept typing. Thanks to Judith Regan and Calvert Morgan—who committed to the book from the very beginning—for the masterful editing and publishing. Thanks to the great team at ReganBooks for their contribution to the book's success, including Jonathan Malki, Ian Lundy, Cassie Jones, Shannon Ceci, Michelle Ishay, Stephanie Goralnick, Kurt Andrews, Tom Wengelewski, and Paul Olsewski.

Last but not least, thanks to my mother, Siona, for helping with French sources and for the flow of clippings from Israel, and thanks to my wife, Lena, for translating and helping with the Russian sources. Hugs and kisses to Lena and Masha for enduring my hectic typing and the loud jazz playing into the wee small hours and for their love. Special pats for Max—for being there.

INDEX